Matti Moosa is Professor of History at Gannon University and the author of *The Origins of Modern Arabic Fiction* and *The Maronites in History* (Syracuse University Press).

Extremist Shiites

Contemporary Issues in the Middle East

Extremist Shiites

The Ghulat Sects

Matti Moosa

SYRACUSE UNIVERSITY PRESS

Syracuse, New York 13244-5160

First published 1987

First Edition
93 92 91 90 89 88 6 5 4 3 2 1

The paper used in this publication meets the minimum requirements of American National Standard for Information Sciences—Permanence of Paper for Printed Library Materials, ANSI Z39.48-1984. ∞™

Extremist Shiites is published with the support of the Office of the Vice-President for Academic Affairs, Gannon University, Erie, Pennsylvania.

Library of Congress Cataloging-in-Publication Data

Moosa, Matti.
Extremist Shiites.

(Contemporary issues in the Middle East)
Bibliography: p.
Includes index.
1. Shi'ah. 2. Sufism. 3. Islamic sects.
4. Nosairians. I. Title. II. Series.
BP193.5.M68 1987 297'.82 87-25487
ISBN 0-8156-2411-5 (alk. paper)

MANUFACTURED IN THE UNITED STATES OF AMERICA

To
Hans, Mark, Petra, and Jessica
With Love

MATTI MOOSA is Professor of History at Gannon University and the author of *The Origins of Modern Arabic Fiction* and *The Maronites in History* (Syracuse University Press).

Contents

Preface

LITTLE IS KNOWN in the West about the division of the Islamic world into Sunnites and Shiites, and much less is known about the stratification of these two groups. This book is a comprehensive study of the cultural aspects of the different ghulat (extremist Shiites) sects in the Middle East. The extremism of these sects is essentially religious, and should not be confused with the religio-political radicalism of the Shiite regime in Iran and its antagonism to the West. The extremist Shiites discussed in this book are peaceful people, and, except for the Nusayris of Syria, they do not seem to be political activists or to have assumed political power.

The Shiite community at present is divided into many sects who hold religious beliefs quite at variance with those of other Muslims and who are therefore considered heretics. In fact, some of the beliefs of the Ghulat have a greater affinity with ancient astral cults and Christianity than with Islam; some Western writers therefore consider these Shiites as nominal "Christians."

Members of these sects live in an area extending from western Iran to Iraq, Syria, and Turkey. They are known by different names but share common religious beliefs, the most fundamental being that the Imam Ali, the blood cousin and son-in-law of the Prophet of Islam, is God. In Iran, these sects are called Ahl-i Haqq (truth-worshippers), or Ali Ilahis (deifiers of Ali): in Iraq they are called Shabak, Bajwan, Sarliyya, Kakaiyya, and Ibrahimiyya. In Syria they are known as Nusayris (Alawis), and in Turkey, as Bektashis, Kizilbash (Alevis), Takhtajis, and Çepnis. They are of different ethnic origins and speak different languages, mainly Turkish, Persian, Kurdish, and Arabic.

Transcending this multi-denominationalism is their common belief in the apotheosis of Ali (d. A.D. 661) and in a trinity of God, Muhammad, and Ali (Or, as among the Nusayris, of Ali, Muhammad, and Salman al-Farisi). They also share the practices of holy communion and public and private confession, which distinguish them from Sunnites and Ithnaashari (Twelver) Shiite Muslims. One of these sects, the Nusayris, managed to assume political and military power in Syria; the present president of Syria, Hafiz al-Asad, is a Nusayri, and his regime represents a minority of extremist Shiites considered by the majority of Sunnites as heretics.

The main objective of this book is to study the religious, social, political, and cultural life and institutions of these extremist Shiite sects, scattered over several Islamic countries of the Middle East. It focuses on the varying pagan and Christian elements—especially the Armenian Christian elements—of the beliefs and practices of the Kizilbash Kurds of the upper Euphrates valley.

Primary sources in Arabic, Persian, and Turkish have been extensively used throughout. Also utilized are many not readily available secondary sources and articles written by travelers, missionaries, and others who have lived and worked among these extremist Shiites for periods of up to forty years. Some of their observations, including those of Saeed Khan, Mirza Karam, H. Adjarian, Ahmad Hamid al-Sarraf, and Abd al-Munim al-Ghulami, are invaluable. These and other men quoted in the book have gained firsthand knowledge of the religious systems, practices, and ceremonies, and the social customs, of extremist Shiites.

It should be pointed out that the translation of Arabic passages is mine unless otherwise indicated.

This book should be of benefit to statesmen, scholars, and students of the history and cultures of the Middle East who desire a better understanding of the true nature of the beliefs of the contemporary Ghulat. It should also benefit both government and private organizations in the West by providing them with inaccessible information about the extremist Shiites.

This book could not have been completed without the assistance of many relatives, friends, and colleagues. I should first thank the Faculty Senate of Gannon University for offering me a summer grant to do research in the Middle East. I am grateful to Professor George Welch, Jr., of Indiana State University, and to Mary Rosenfeld and Kay Wojciak for their editorial assistance. I am indebted to Dr. Kamil Mustafa al-Shaibi, Professor Emeritus of Islamic Studies at the University of Baghdad, an authority on Shiite studies, for making his private library available to me and for providing me with sources and information about different aspects of the subject. I am also grateful to Fawzi Tadros of the Near East Section of the Library of Congress, Salwa Ferahian of McGill University, Montreal, Canada, Fawzi Abd al-Razzaq and Ahmad al-Jibari of Harvard University's Widener Library, Abazar Sepehri of the University of Texas Library at Austin, and Bassam Salous of Washington, D.C., for locating and checking many sources; to my sister Adiba Moosa, for locating many sources, especially several articles on the subject; and to my friend Edward Isa, M.D., of Baghdad, who provided me with several sources from his private library. The staff of Gannon Library, especially Rita Ann Nies, Grace Davies, Jean Stevenson, Margaret Zgainer, Nancy Speer, and Gerard Laurito, proved most helpful in obtaining numerous source materials through interlibrary loan. I should also recognize the assistance of Dr. Talha Dinibutun of Istanbul Teknik University in obtaining several Turkish sources, some of which are still in manuscript form. My sincere thanks are due to my colleagues, Dr. Mehmet Cultu and Dr. Haldun Haznedar, for explaining many Turkish terms and concepts, and to Dr. Hamid Torab for his help with several Persian terms. I am indebted to Professor Charles F. Beckingham of London University for the information on De Barros and Samuel Purchas, and to my colleague Professor Richard Dekmejian of the University of Southern California for explaining some Armenian terms. I wish to thank Dr. Paul Peterson, the Reverend Lance Robins, the Reverend Robert Clements, Lance Strasser, and Jane Randal for their assistance.

My very special and sincere thanks to my brothers Hazim and Akram for their assistance, especially to Hazim, who has supported me morally and materially in accomplishing this and other projects.

Last but not least, the writing of this book would not have been accomplished without the love, patience, and dedication of my wife, Ingeborg Jensen Moosa. She alone can appreciate the difficulty of bringing this work to fruition.

Erie, Pennsylvania MM

Introduction

Ghulat, plural of *ghali,* is an Arabic term deriving from the verb *ghala,* meaning "to exaggerate or exceed the proper bounds." The verbal noun is *ghuluw,* meaning "exaggeration."[1] In an Islamic theological context, the Ghulat are those who have exceeded the proper bounds of religion, ascribing divine attributes to human beings. In a strict religious sense, Muslim heresiographers define the Ghulat as those Shiites who have exaggerated their veneration of the Imams, from Ali Ibn Abi Talib (d. A.D. 661) to Muhammad the Mahdi (believed to have miraculously disappeared in A.D 874), by attributing to them qualities belonging only to God.[2] The Ghulat are those Shiites who deify the Imam Ali and the rest of the Imams. Thus, the apotheosis of Ali becomes the cornerstone of the Ghulat's religious system. By this definition, the Druzes, although rooted in Ismaili Shiism, are excluded because they deify the Fatimi Caliph al-Hakim bi Amr Allah (d. A.D. 1021), instead of Ali.

Like Ghulat, the term *Shiite* is also associated with Ali. It derives from the Arabic verb *shayaa,* meaning "to adhere to; to support a common cause; to be a partisan of." In an Islamic historical context, the term encompasses those Muslims who support the right of the Imam Ali, as the only lawful heir and successor to the Prophet Muhammed, to rule the Muslim community after the death of Muhammad in A.D. 632. The Shiites are the partisans or party of Ali, believing that Ali was and still is the only Muslim worthy to succeed the Prophet as the ruler of the Muslim community.[3] To this day, such belief constitutes one of the most significant differences between the two major denominations of Islam, the Sunnites and the Shiites.

The history of the Shiites dates back to the very early period of Islam, when the Prophet Muhammad was the head of the Muslim community. Muhammad was not only the Prophet who had delivered God's divine message to the Arabs, but also the ruler and the judge of the Muslim community. As long as he lived, his position as prophet and head of the community was exclusive and uncontested. But immediately after his death in A.D. 632, the question of a successor to the Prophet became urgent creating an internal power struggle for the leadership of the Muslim community. Muhammad left no male issue, a fact that complicated the question of who was to succeed him. His companions were aware that no Muslim could take the place of Muhammad as a prophet; he was their prophet par excellence.

Among his companions, however, surely there was one qualified to take Muhammad's place, not as a prophet, but as the leader of the Muslim community. But who? In Muhammad's lifetime, a group of devout companions such as Abu Dharr al-Ghifari, Ammar Ibn Yasir, Salman al-Farisi, al-Miqdad Ibn al-Aswad, Hudhayfa Ibn al-Yaman, and others favored Ali as the most eligible Muslim to succeed the Prophet in leading the Muslim community.[4] Ali had a praiseworthy character and many outstanding qualities, including courage, and eloquence, and a considerable knowledge of religious sciences. He was the blood cousin of the Prophet, and also his son-in-law, having married the Prophet's favorite daughter, Fatima, and had three sons by her—al-Hasan, al-Husayn, and Muhsin—the last of whom died in infancy. Moreover, the Prophet had been raised by Ali's father, Abu Talib, and, although Muhammad was many years older than Ali, the cousins had lived in one house, where Ali was believed to have acquired divine knowledge from Muhammad. Ali was also the second person to embrace Islam (after Khadija, the first wife of the Prophet) and therefore had the honor of being the first male Muslim to believe in Muhammad's message. Finally, the Shiites maintain that in his lifetime the Prophet Muhammad appointed his cousin Ali as his successor and ruler over the Muslim community. They cite several traditions concerning the Prophet to support this belief. The most outstanding of these traditions is that of Ghadir Khumm (the Khumm Pond), where the Prophet declared to many of his companions, "To whom I am Master, Ali, too, is Master." Tradition holds that on another occasion the Prophet said, "Tomorrow I will entrust the banner to a man who loves God and His apostle, and whom God and His apostle love." The people asked "Who is this man?" and Muhammad answered, "He is Ali." According to a third tradition, he asked, "Are you not satisfied to be in relation to me as Aaron was in relation to Moses, except that there will be no prophet after me?"[5]

Those men who supported Ali and believed he was the most

eligible Muslim to succeed the Prophet as the ruler of the Muslim community came to be known as the Shia or Shiites (partisans) of Ali. Thus, Shiism, or the support of Ali, grew in the early period of Islam as a spiritual movement, based on the assumption that the leadership of the Muslim community was a spiritual office and that Ali had been singled out from among all the Muslims to fill it.[6]

However, the course of events immediately after the death of Muhammad in A.D. 632 proved that the companions were engaged in a power struggle for the highest office in the community. As a result of this power struggle, Ali was bypassed, perhaps because of his youth (he was only thirty-one), and the elderly Abu Bakr was chosen as the Prophet's successor, and came to be called the khalifa (caliph) of the Prophet. Realizing that he had been bypassed, Ali withheld support from the newly chosen khalifa until six months after the latter's election. Later, Ali was bypassed twice more, once at the death of Abu Bakr in 634, when the Muslims chose Umar Ibn al-Khattab as their leader, and again when Umar was murdered in 644 and the Muslims chose Uthman Ibn Affan as their Khalifa. It was in the time of Uthman that the term *Shiite,* which until then had had only a spiritual connotation, began to assume a political significance. Those supporting Ali became known as the Shiites (partisans) of Ali, while those supporting Uthman became known as the Shiites (partisans) of Uthman.[7] During Uthman's tenure, the Shiites of Ali began to agitate against Uthman for his nepotism. The agitation turned into sedition, resulting in 656 in the killing of Uthman and the election of Ali to the office of the Caliphate.

Ali did not hold his new office for long, however, for he had many enemies, including the governor of Syria, Muawiya Ibn Abi Sufyan, from the house of Umayya, who contested his authority. When Ali was murdered in 661, Muawiya proclaimed himself caliph, and with him began the Umayyad dynasty.

During the caliphate of Ali, two events took place that have a great bearing on our study. First, Ali moved the seat of government from Medina to al-Kufa in Iraq, making al-Kufa the center of Shiite power. The Iraqis were now supporters of Ali just as the Syrians were supporters of Muawiya. When Ali was murdered in 661, the Muslims chose his son al-Hasan as their caliph. But al-Hasan abdicated in favor of Muawiya, who became caliph in the same year. The Shiites of Ali in al-Kufa invited Ali's second son, al-Husayn, to come to Iraq as their caliph. Al-Husayn agreed and, leaving Medina with his entourage of seventy souls, arrived at Karbala in Iraq. Unfortunately, the Shiites of Iraq had given only lip service to al-Husayn; in October 680, al-Husayn and his entourage were attacked by an Umayyad force and murdered in cold blood. Al-Husayn's head was cut off and sent to Yazid, who had succeeded his father Muawiya as caliph in Damascus. Only al-Husayn's young son Ali was spared from the massacre because of his poor health, and from this Ali the line of the Imams was continued.

The tragedy of Karbala consolidated the Shiites around their Imams, the descendants of Ali, against the Umayyads, and Shiism emerged as a distinct sect of Islam, holding the belief that the Umayyad caliphs were usurpers of the caliphate, which the Shiites called imamate, and that this imamate was restricted to Ahl al-Bayt, or the family of the Prophet—that is, Muhammad, his daughter Fatima, her husband Ali, and their two sons, al-Hasan and al-Husayn. This meant that only Ali and his descendants, the Imams, were legitimate heirs and successors of the Prophet Muhammad in leading the community of Islam. Thus, to the Shiites, the imamate is not a temporal but a spiritual office, whose holder is ordained by God through Muhammad as His Messenger and the members of Muhammad's family (Ahl al-Bayt) to rule and guide the Muslim community.[8] This view of the office of the imamate constitutes one of the most fundamental differences between the Shiites and Sunnites even to this day.

The rise of the Umayyads to power divided the Muslim community into two hostile camps: the Shiites, who believed that their Imams were the only legitimate rulers of the community, and the Umayyads, who considered the Shiites to be rebels and enemies who should be destroyed. It is no surprise, then, to find that the Umayyad caliphs persecuted the Shiites, killing those leaders who had supported Ali and his right to the imamate.[9] The persecution sent a wave of fright among the followers of Ali, who became fatalistic about their destiny and about dying at the hands of the Umayyads. When the Umayyads lost power to the Abbasids in 750, the Abbasid caliphs also persecuted the Shiites and their Imams, for fear that the Imams would overthrow them and destroy their power. Thus, the Shiite Imams were persecuted throughout the Umayyad and Abbasid periods (661–1258). As a result of their persecution and their inability to match the might of the Umayyads and the Abbasids, the Shiites began to weave legends around their hero Ali to compensate for their frustration and failure to rise to power. Shiite sources are filled with the miraculous attributes of Ali (to which we have devoted a whole chapter). Ali became so mythologized that, in many of the anecdotes about him or attributed to him, it is difficult to separate the real Ali from the legendary one. This brings us to the second major event of Ali's caliphate, namely, his deification.

Muslim heresiographers all agree that Abd Allah Ibn Saba, a Jewish convert to Islam from Yaman, was the first to attribute deity to Ali. According to Abu al-Hasan Ali Ibn Ismail al-Ashari (d. 935), the Sabaiyya (followers of Ibn Saba) claim that Ali never died, and will return on the day of Resurrection to replace the iniquity found on earth with an equal measure of justice. Al-Ashari further states that Ibn Saba told Ali, "You are, You are," meaning that Ali was God.[10] Abd al-Qahir al-Baghdadi (d. 1037) says that the Sabaiyya were the ones who called Ali a god, and, when Ali burned some of them, they turned to him, saying, "Now we know that you are truly God, because only God tortures people by fire."[11] A slightly different episode is related by Ali Ibn Hazm (d. 1063). Ibn Hazm states that a group of followers of Abd Allah Ibn Saba came to Ali saying, "You are He." Ali asked, "And who is He?" They ansered, "You are God," which Ali thought was abominable. He ordered a fire lit and the men thrown into it. As they were cast into the fire, they kept saying, "Now we believe that you are God, because no one tortures by fire except God." Ibn Hazm adds that, in connection with this incident, Ali recited the following verse:

> When I saw the matter was abominable
> I lighted my fire and called Qanbar [his freedman].[12]

Ibn Hazm also states that when the news of the assassination of Ali reached Ibn Saba, he denied that Ali had died. He said to those who brought the news, "If you brought us his head seventy times, we would never believe he has died." Ibn Saba continued to say that Ali would never die, and would replace the iniquity of earth with an equal measure of justice.[13] These writers, it should be pointed out, are Sunnites. But two tenth-century Shiite writers, Saad Ibn Abd Allah al-Ashari and al-Hasan Ibn Musa al-Nawbakhti, related the same anecdotes about Abd Allah Ibn Saba and his denial of the death of Ali.[14] We have no idea of the source from which all these Sunnite and Shiite writers drew their information about Abd Allah Ibn Saba and his apotheosis of Ali.

The first Muslim writer to mention Ibn Saba in connection with Ali was Abu Jafar Muhammad Ibn Jarir al-Tabari (d. 923), but in an entirely different context. Al-Tabari states that Ibn Saba was a Jew from the city of Sana in Yaman, who, because his mother was black, was nicknamed Ibn al-Sawda (son of the black woman). Ibn Saba embraced Islam in the time of the Caliph Uthman (644–56). However, he preached that the Prophet Muhammad, like Jesus, shall return to this earth, a belief not held by Muslims. He also proclaimed that Ali was the *wasi,* or testamentary trustee, of Muhammad, implying that if Muhammad was the last prophet, Ali should be his last heir and successor. Ibn Saba thus championed Ali's right to the caliphate and held that Uthman was a usurper. He wandered through the Muslim countries, from al-Hijaz to Basra, al-Kufa, al-Sham (Syria), and finally Egypt, proclaiming these beliefs and instigating the Shiites of Ali to revolt against the Caliph Uthman. Finally, revolt erupted in Egypt, and in Medina, supporters of Ali murdered Uthamn and installed Ali as caliph.[15]

Al-Tabari's account tells us that Ibn Saba proclaimed Ali to be the heir to Muhammad, but mentions nothing about his attribution of deity to Ali. The significance of the anecdote of Abd Allah Ibn Saba as related by writers other than al-Tabari is that he was the first to ascribe divine attributes to Ali and consider him God. In other words, Ibn Saba was the source of the ghuluw (extremism) in Islam. It is for this reason, says al-Nawbakhti, that the Shiites' adversaries maintain that Shiism actually derives from Judaism.[16]

Western writers like Israel Friedländer, Julius Wellhausen, and, most particularly, Leone Caetani, have discredited al-Tabari's account of Ibn Saba (based on the authority of Sayf Ibn Umar al-Tamimi) as unreliable. The gist of their argument is that Sayf exaggerated Ibn Saba's role in the events leading to the murder of the Caliph Uthman. They maintain that Sayf fabricated the episode about the killing of Uthman to exonerate the people of Medina from participation in the caliph's murder. Moreover, they maintain that sources older than that of al-Tabari are silent on Ibn Saba and his role in the sedition against Uthman. They aver that the movement for supporting Ali as heir and testamentary trustee of the Prophet did not exist in the time of Uthman as Ibn Saba had alleged. Therefore, they refuse to accept the authenticity of Ibn Saba's claim that Ali was the heir of the Prophet.[17]

Modern Muslim writers have also tended to discredit al-Tabari's account of Abd Allah Ibn Saba as sheer fiction. One such writer, Murtada al-Askari, wrote two books attempting to prove that Abd Allah Ibn Saba was a fictitious person, and that many Eastern and Western writers have copied al-Tabari's account of Ibn Saba without investigation. The thrust of al-Askari's argument is that al-Tabri, the first to relate the anecdote of Ibn Saba, used as his authority a certain Sayf Ibn Umar al-Tamimi al-Usayyidi, who according to many Muslim writers, was a liar, a fabricator of traditions, and a totally untrustworthy writer. Al-Askari relates fourteen historical events that he affirms were invented by Sayf Ibn Umar, none of which is associated with Ibn Saba.[18] Al-Askari's argument is unconvincing, however; he fails to point out any weaknesses in al-Tabari's account except the use of Sayf as an authority. Al-Tabari cites several authorities in addition to Sayf, however; unless these authorities are proven untrustworthy, al-Tabari's account remains valid and historically reliable. Another modern writer, Ali al-Wardi, after affirming that Abd Allah Ibn Saba is a fictitious name, asserts that Ibn Saba is none other than Ammar Ibn Yasir, one of Ali's most zealous companions and champions.[19] Al-Wardi maintains that study of the career of Ammar Ibn Yasir surprisingly reveals that many traits and actions attributed to Ibn Saba are identical to those attributed to Ammar. Al-Wardi notes that both Ibn Saba and Ammar Ibn Yasir were known as Ibn al-Sawda (son of the black woman), and that both men came from Yaman. He points out that, like Ibn Saba, Ammar was a zealous champion of Ali's right to the caliphate; that, like Ibn Saba, Ammar went to Egypt to rouse the people against the Caliph Uthman, preaching that Uthman had usurped the caliphate from Ali; that, like Ibn Saba, Ammar obstructed the peace effort between Ali and Aisha, the wife of Muhammad; and finally that, like Ibn Saba, Ammar is said to have been influenced by Abu Dharr al-Ghifari, a zealot companion of Ali, in his call for an Islamic "socialist" way of life. From this evidence, al-Wardi concludes that Ibn Saba is in fact Ammar Ibn Yasir. Though he admits that this is only an opinion and that he could be wrong, al-Wardi says that he is forced to state this opinion because the evidence of similarities between Abd Allah Ibn Saba and Ammar Ibn Yasir is so strong.[20] The similarities between Ibn Saba and Ammar Ibn Yasir presented by al-Wardi do not disprove the existence of Ibn Saba, however, and for further evidence of Ibn's Saba's existence, we should resort once more to al-Tabari's account. Al-Tabari mentions Ibn Saba in the very specific context of his encounter with Abu Dharr al-Ghifari. He states that Ibn Saba met Abu Dharr in Syria and asked him why he was not surprised that Muawiya had said that the possessions of the Muslims belong to God, by which Ibn Saba meant that Muawiya wanted to keep them for himself. Enraged at Ibn Saba's implication, Abu Dharr retorted that the possessions of God and the Muslims are one, that is, that anything belonging to the Muslims belongs to God. Abu Dharr then added "Who are you? By God, you are a Jew,"[21] meaning that Ibn Saba was an intruder. No such encounter took place between Abu Dharr and Ammar Ibn Yasir; if it had, it is certain that al-Tabari, or another Muslim historian would have mentioned this incident. Whether or not Abd Allah Ibn Saba was real or fictitious, and whether or not he originated the ghuluw (extremism) which means in this context, the deification of Ali, the fact remains that the Sabaiyya as a Ghulat sect did exist, and has received serious consideration by both Muslim Shiite and Sunnite heresiographers. It should be pointed out, however, that the ghuluw, or deification of Ali and the Imams, is an Arab phenomenon originating in al-Kufa, Iraq, the headquarters of the Imam Ali. It was in this city that several Ghulat flourished and preached their ghuluw.[22] From Iraq it was spread into Turkestan, Khurasan, and Central Asia by Ismaili propagandists. Some of the Ghulat lived in Syria, and from there spread their teaching into Anatolia in eastern Turkey.

But why did the Shiite Ghulat ascribe divine attributes to Ali and the rest of the Imams? Kamil Mustafa al-Shaibi is of the opinion that the ghuluw is part of man's nature; since the beginning of mankind, people have deified their kings and heroes, and the Muslims were no exception. In fact, when the Prophet Muhammad died, his companion Umar Ibn al-Khattab could not believe that the Prophet had died, because he believed that Muhammad was above death.[23] William Montgomery Watt maintains that most of the Arab tribes who lived in al-Kufa after the Islamic conquest of Iraq were monophysite Christians from Yaman who emphasized the divinity rather than the humanity of Jesus. After the conversion of some of these tribes to Islam, they became Ali's Shiites and found in him a charismatic leader homologous to Christ.[24] This may be true, but there were also in Ali's army Nestorians who did not emphasize the divinity of Christ. Furthermore, the monophysites who were adherents of the Syrian Church of Antioch did not emphasize the divinity of Christ over his humanity. Other writers, including Taha Husayn (d. 1973), argue that the people of al-Kufa, having failed Ali in his struggle against the Umayyad Muawiya, governor of Syria, and later having failed his son, al-Husayn, who was brutally murdered by the Umayyads, deified Ali and his descendants in atonement.[25] Still other writers suggest that the persecution of the members of Ahl al-Bayt (the family of the Prophet), meaning Ali and his descendants the Imams, by the Umayyads and the Abbasids after them, generated great sympathy among the followers of the Imams, some of whom reacted excessively by deifying them.[26] Whatever the reasons for the apotheosis of Ali and the rest of the Imams, historical evidence indicates that it dates back to Ali's lifetime, and it has become central to the teaching of the Ghulat. Historical evidence further indicates that the deification of Ali has been perpetuated by present-day Ghulat, as has been shown throughout this book. Through their contact with non-Muslim peoples, however, the modern Ghulat have adopted several concepts from other religions including the trinity, the seven manifestations of the deity in seven cycles, and (by the Nusayris) the personification of Ali in the form of sacramental wine concepts which are today an integral part of their religious system. The concept of metempsychosis, held by some contemporary Ghulat, dates back to the ancient Ghulat sects.

For moderate and extremist Shiites alike, the position of the Imam (and his office, the imamate) is fundamental to their religious system. Shiites believe that the Imams are infallible and sinless because God has purified and cleansed them from sin, according to Quran 33:33. Thus the sanctified Ahl al-Bayt (family of the Prophet) are transcendent and superior to all Muslims, indeed to all mankind. For this reason Shiites believe the Imams alone should rule over the Muslim community. This is not a mere earthly privilege, but a divine right ordained by God Himself. Each one of the Imams is considered by Shiites to be the ruler of the Muslim community in his generation. But when the last Imam, Muhammad the Mahdi, disappeared in 874, A.D. the Shiites assert that he entrusted the *Marji'iyya al-Diniyya* (Religious authority) to govern the Shiite community to four of his deputies, whom he guided from his place of concealment. These four deputies were Uthman Ibn Said al-Umari; his son Muhammad Ibn Said, known as al-Khullani (d. 917); al-Husayn Ibn Rawh al-Nawbakhti (d. 937); and Ali Ibn Muhammad al-Samari (d. 940). When al-Samari was on his deathbed and was asked to appoint a deputy, he answered that "the matter is left to God."[27] Since then, the Shiite community has been ruled by a Marji, who is chosen as the religious leader of the community. This Marji rules on behalf of the vanished Imam, the Mahdi. At present, Ayatollah Khomeini is regarded by most Shiites as the Marji who represents the Mahdi and governs on his behalf. Thus, the Shiite theocratic government is dependent on the person of the Imam, without whom there could be no government in the religious sense. This government of the Imam is called the *Wilayat al-Faqih* (the governance of the jurist, or of the highest religious authority). In fact, according to the Shiites, the presence of the Imam in every generation is so vital that any Shiite who dies without acknowledging the Imam of his time dies an infidel. Perhaps the Ghulat (and even some Ithnaashari Shiites) do not consider Khomeini to be their religious leader, but the Ghulat's veneration of the twelve Imams who constitute the essence of their religious system is in conformity with the belief of the Twelver Shiites (also called Imamis), of whom Khomeini is one.

Most of the contemporary Ghulat live in an area stretching from Iran to Syria and Turkey. They are of varied ethnic and linguistic backgrounds. Because they share many religious beliefs and traditions, some writers confuse one group with another. It should be pointed out that these Ghulat sects form Sufi *tariqas* (mystical orders), with a mystical rather than a ritual emphasis. The Bektashis are just one example of these tariqas. In fact, since the early period of Islam, the Shiites (staunch supporters of Ali for the office of the caliphate) were strict Zahids (ascetics), who were the forerunners of later Sufis. Thus, Shiism was closely associated with Sufism. Indeed, many prominent Sufis, such as Ibn Arabi (d. 1240), were greatly influenced by Shiite teaching and theology. However, it was not until the thirteenth century that extremist Shiite sects such as the Bektashis began to appear in Anatolia, and not until the late fifteenth century that the Safawi order in Iran adopted the Ithnaashari (Twelver) form of Shiism.

The contemporary Ghulat are very secretive about their religious beliefs and the nature of their religious ceremonies. Because they are secretive and conduct some of their ceremonies and prayers at night, outsiders, especially Sunnite Muslims, accuse them of indulging in sexual orgies. But since no outsider has ever attended these nocturnal meetings, such accusations should be treated as sheer calumnies founded on hearsay.

Of all the contemporary Ghulat sects, the Nusayris of Syria have drawn the most attention because of their rise to power and their role in Arab and Middle Eastern politics. The present president of Syria, Hafiz al-Asad, is a Nusayri, and the Syrian regime is controlled by Nusayris. For this reason we have devoted several chapters to the history and the religious system of the Nusayris. In these chapters we demonstrate how a small and despised minority group, considered by the majority of the Syrian Sunnites as heterodox, has risen to power and controlled the Syrian government. The Nusayris form the zenith of extreme Shiism. To them Ali is the Almighty God who takes the place of the God of the Bible and the Quran. Ali is superior to the Prophet Muhammad, whom Ali created. To the Nusayris, God appeared seven times in seven cycles, manifesting Himself finally as Ali. But before God appeared in the person of Ali in the Arab period, He had appeared in the persons of Persian kings. There is ample evidence in this book that Nusayrism is of Persian origin, and that the Nusayris believe that the Persians are superior to the Arabs.

Other chapters of the book deal at length with the different Ghulat sects, including the Shabak, Ahl-i Haqq of Iran, Sarliyya-Kakaiyya, Bajwan, and Ibrahimiyya, providing the first thorough discussion of many of them.

Finally, we caution the reader about the different Christian elements in the beliefs of the Ghulat, to which we have devoted the final chapters. He should not be misled into believing that these Ghulat are Christians, despite the fact that some of them claim that they are closer to Christianity than to Islam and that they maintain several Christian beliefs and practices. These Ghulat sects are basically Shiites who uphold the divine authority of the twelve Imams, from Ali to the Mahdi. They share many beliefs with the Twelver Shiites, who form the majority of the Shiites today, but they exceed the bounds of Twelver Shiism by attributing deity to Ali and the Imams. As we shall see, the Twelver Shiites believe in the preexistence of the Imams, who were created from the light of God and whose names are inscribed on the throne of God. The quotation of Ayatollah Khomeini produced in chapter 5 is an expression of this belief. We also show that the Shiites of Iran maintain that although Ali was not God, he is not far from being one. Such hyperbolic beliefs are totally alien to orthodox Islam. In sum, the Ghulat are Shiites who originated in a Shiite ambiance and uphold many Shiite beliefs, although they have been denounced by Twelver Shiites as unbelievers and polytheists.[28] The presence of Christian elements in their beliefs and tradition seems to be accidental rather than intrinsic. If they ever modify their tenets, it is certain that they will convert not to Christianity, but to moderate Twelver Shiism.

Extremist Shiites

1

The Shabak

THE SHABAK LIVE in several villages in northern Iraq, east of the city of Mosul. Religiously and ethnically different from the rest of the inhabitants of Iraq, they speak a strange language, difficult for others to understand—basically Turkish mixed with Persian, Kurdish, and Arabic. Like other villagers in northern Iraq, most of these Shabak are farmers, herdsmen, and small businessmen trading with Mosul. They live in humble mud huts without sanitary systems or other amenities. The only visible evidence of modern life are the television antennae jutting from many of the rooftops.

Until recent years, information about the beliefs and culture of the Shabak was fragmentary and faulty, as the account of Rev. Anastase Marie al-Karmali (d. 1947) illustrates. According to al-Karmali, the Shabak are of Kurdish origin, believe in the unity of God and love the Caliph or Imam Ali so much that they call him "Ali Rush."[1] This is an obvious error. The epithet Ali Rush (black Ali) is a name the Shabak use not for the Imam Ali, but for his grandson and namesake, the Imam Ali Zayn al-Abidin (the ornament of worshippers,) (d. 94/713, these dates corresponding to the Islamic and Christian calandars respectively), because of his piety, humility, and asceticism, and because of his penchant for wearing black.

Al-Karmali adds that the Shabak do not pray or fast like other orthodox Muslims, but that they do hold festivals with and visit the shrines of the Yezidis, commonly known as Devil Worshippers. As for their social customs, al-Karmali mentions a yearly meeting on the night known as Laylat al-Kafsha. This meeting usually takes place at the entrance to a cave, where the people indulge in eating, drinking, and committing most "objectionable immoralities," by which al-Karmali means sexual orgies.[2] Later we shall see that Iraqi writers who know the Shabak intimately reject this account, charging that the "Laylat al-Kafsha" episode is an insidious calumny concocted by the enemies of the Shabak because of the strict secrecy surrounding Shabak religious beliefs and rituals.[3]

It should be pointed out that al-Karmali did not obtain his information about the Shabak through personal experience with them. He admitted that he had never visited the area where the Shabak live, and that all the information he recorded was supplied by an unnamed person who had had business relations with the Shabak for more than twenty years. Much of the information provided by this informant was erroneous. Al-Karmali hoped that someday someone with broader, more intimate knowledge of the Shabak would expand and correct his account.

A similar account of the Shabak was provided by the Orientalist, Vladimir Minorsky. In his article on the Shabak in the *Encyclopedia of Islam* (1934), Minorsky leans heavily on al-Karmali's account, repeating most of the latter's statements about the Shabak.[4]

Another discussion of the Shabak occurs in an article published in the Egyptian periodical *al-Muqtataf* in 1921. Using the pseudonym Amkah, the author considers the Shabak to be of Kurdish origin and provides information about them little different from that provided by al-Karmali, with one exception: the anonymous author absolves the Shabak of the so-called immoralities that they were accused of committing on Laylat al-Kafsha, as related by al-Karmali.[5] This fact convinced one member of the Iraqi Academy that the author of the article was none other than al-Karmali himself. The academy member maintains that, after realizing the falsehood of the anecdote of Laylat al-Kafsha al-Karmali changed his original belief and contributed the article to *al-Muqtataf*, under the pseudonym Amkah.[6] Al-Karmali's alleged use of a pseudonym may have been a ploy to escape embarrassment.

Still another early account of the Shabak was based on the account of an anonymous informant. The account, in a letter to the physician and scholar, Dawud al-Chalabi, was in turn relayed in a letter by al-Chalabi to Ahmad Hamid al-Sarraf (d. 1985). In this letter, reproduced by al-Sarraf in his book, *al-Shabak*, al-Chalabi states that he has found a person from the city of Mosul with a broad knowledge of the conditions, beliefs, and religious practices of the Shabak.[7] Al-Chalabi maintains that the informant was trusted by the Shabak because, like them, he was an *Alawi Sayyid,* that is, a Shiite who claimed descent from the Prophet Muhammad's daughter Fatima and her husband Ali, the Prophet's blood cousin.

The Sayyid told al-Chalabi that the Shabak claim to have originally come from southern Iran, where they still have relatives, but they do not know why and how they came to live in the neighborhood of Mosul, Iraq.

According to al-Chalabi's source, the Shabak language is a mixture of Persian and Kurdish, with a smattering of Arabic. Al-Chalabi, however, believes that the Shabak language is basically Persian, spoken in a dialect similar to the Baluchi language.[8] He goes on to discuss aspects of Shabak religious beliefs and practices, citing the names of their villages and providing etymological origins for them.

Another writer whose information about the Shabak is drawn from a letter by al-Chalabi is Abbas al-Azzawi. The information al-Chalabi provided to al-Azzawi is so similar to that which he provided to al-Sarraf that one is inclined to believe that the two letters were identical.[9]

While the authors mentioned above derived their information from anonymous informants, Abd al-Munim al-Ghulami provides first-hand information about the Shabak. Al-Ghulami considers the Shabak to be of Persian origin because of their physical features, because of what other people related about them, and because of their language, which is preponderantly Persian, mixed with Arabic, Turkoman, and Kurdish. He speculates that they could have moved to northern Iraq at the time of the Safawis (beginning in 1500 or even earlier), either through incursions or through immigration in quest of pastureland. Although brief, al-Ghulami's monograph provides invaluable information not recounted by earlier writers about the faith, religious practices, and social customs of the Shabak and cognate sects.[10]

The idea that the Shabak came to Iraq from Persia is not new. A. Layard, who excavated in Iraq in the middle of the nineteenth century, suspected that the Shabak were descendants of Kurds who came from the Persian mountain slopes and still profess Shiite doctrines. Layard also believed that they might have an affinity with the Ali Ilahis, who believe in successive incarnations of the deity, one of whom is Ali.[11] Likewise, Abdullah, attendant of Miss Gertrude L. Bell, told her that the Shabak had come to Iraq with the armies of the Ajam (Persians).[12]

By far the most comprehensive study of the Shabak is the book *al-Shabak,* (in Arabic), by Ahmad Hamid al-Sarraf, mentioned earlier. More than any other writer, al-Sarraf was in a position to study the Shabak and their religious beliefs thoroughly. In 1937 he held the position of general prosecutor in the courts of Mosul. Because of this position and the concomitant need to investigate crimes, he was able to visit villages both east and west of Mosul.

Among these were the villages of the Shabak and related sects such as the Sarliyya. Al-Sarraf provides vivid descriptions of some of the villagers:

> I saw tall men of fair complexion graced with a bronzy touch. They do not shave their beards and mustaches but allow them to grow so long that they cover their mouths. They speak a strange language which is a mixture of Persian, Kurdish, Arabic and Turkish, the latter predominating. They are mostly farmers and shepherds. Whenever I asked one of the Shabak or the Sarliyya about his religious beliefs, I saw nothing but anxiety and muttering of lips followed by dead silence.[13]

Al-Sarraf received his information about the Shabak, their religious beliefs, and sacred books from Shaykh Ibrahim, a respected and well-informed member of the Shabak community, known among his people as "the Pasha." In 1938 the Pasha came to see al-Sarraf to lodge a complaint against the marauding Bedouin Arabs who frequently raided and pillaged his village of al-Qadiyya, lying to the east of Mosul.

This was the beginning of a long friendship between the two men. Whenever they met, al-Sarraf recited to the Pasha Arabic and Persian poems in praise of the Imam Ali and his descendants, the Imams, held by Shiites in the utmost esteem and adoration. In turn, the Pasha recited poems composed by Shabak religious men in the Turkoman language in praise of the Imam Ali and the members of the household or family of the Prophet Muhammad. But when al-Sarraf asked his Shabak friend to write down these poems, the Pasha refused. This refusal led al-Sarraf to conclude that the Shabak were very secretive about their religious beliefs, and that they, like the rest of the Shiites, practiced the *taqiyya* (dissimulation), that is, an outward confession contrary to the belief really held. The Shiites use the taqiyya to avoid openly confessing their beliefs, particularly to orthodox Muslims to escape antagonism or persecution. However, by using a great deal of persistance and pressure, including threats to suspend his relations with the Pasha, al-Sarraf claims that he finally convinced the Pasha to open his heart and tell all he knew about the Shabak and their religious beliefs and rituals. The Pasha even gave al-Sarraf a copy of a book entitled *Kitab al-Manaqib* (The book of exemplary acts), or, as the Pasha called it, the *Buyruk* (The book of commandments), held sacred by the Shabak.[14]

Written in the Turkoman language, the book consists primarily of a dialogue between Shaykh Safi al-Din of Ardabil (d. 1334) and his son, Shaykh Sadr al-Din (d. 1391), leaders of the Safawi Sufi (mystical) order of dervishes. They were also ancestors of Shah Ismail (d. 1524), founder of the Safawi dynasty in Iran.[15]

The historical importance of the *Buyruk* is that it serves as testimony to the fact that the Shabak and other cognate sects of northern Iraq were associated with the Safawis of Iran. We shall see in following chapters that, like the Safawis, the Shabak are Shiites who believe in the religious authority and infallibility of the twelve Imams, beginning with the Imam Ali (d. 661) and ending with the twelfth and last Imam, Muhammad, known as the Mahdi (Guided One). Shiites believe the Mahdi miraculously disappeared in A.D. 874, in the city of Samarra, Iraq, when he was still in his teens, and that he will reappear at the end of time to restore order and justice to a world filled with iniquity. Here we find the genesis of the Messianic concept in Shiite Islam.

Belief in the authority and infallibility of the twelve Imams is a cardinal dogma of that group of Shiites called the Ithnaasharis, or Twelvers, who constitute the majority of Shiites in the Middle East and in India.

Al-Sarraf expends great effort to identify the Shabak, but is undecided about their origin.[16] He cites *al-Suluk fi Ma'rifat Duwal al-Muluk* (Book of entrance to the knowledge of the dynasties of kings), by al-Maqrizi (d. 1442), which enumerates the different Kurdish tribes, speculating that one such tribe, called the Shanbakiyya, could be the Shabak.

Al-Sarraf also mentions a work by Ibn Fadl Allah-al-Umari (d. 1384), entitled *Masalik al-Absar fi Mamalik al-Amsar* (directing the eyesight in knowing the lands and countries), who mentions a group of people called *Shok,* from the district of Shwankara or Shbankara in Iran, whose name al-Sarraf speculates may have an affinity with the term *Shabak.*[17] Al-Sharraf then offers several possible explanations for the origin of the Shabak, the most important of which is that the Shabak are Turkomans who came to Iraq in the time of the Safaris.[18] Al-Sarraf states that this explanation lacks historical evidence.[19] But he does assert that the Shabak have the same religious beliefs as the Bektashis and Kizilbash.

> The creed of the Shabak is that of the Bektashi-Kizilbash with slight variation and the book, the Buyruk, is written in the Turkoman language, very similar to the contemporary language of the Shabak. This is a phenomenon which cannot be denied or refuted. The similarities between the language of the Shabak and that of the Buyruk emboldens us to advance such a claim despite the tenuous proof to support it. The truth is that the origin of the Shabak is still unknown.[20]

It appears that al-Sarraf held in his hand the key to the origin of the Shabak, but failed to open the door. He makes two significant propositions: First, that the Shabak were Turkomans, and second, that they held the same beliefs as the Bektashis and Kizilbash, beliefs which, combined with Islamic Sufism (mysticism), characterize the creed of the majority of Shiites.

Most significant is al-Sarraf's statement that the Shabak's book, the *Buyruk,* is written in the Turkoman language, which is very similar to the contemporary language of the Shabak. This constitutes strong evidence tht the Shabak are Turkomans who speak a Turkoman lanaguage, even though it has become interspersed with Persian, Kurdish, and Arabic words. We have already seen that the Shabak leader, Shaykh Ibrahim the Pasha, communicated with al-Sarraf in Turkish and recited to him poems composed in the Turkoman language by Shabak religious men in praise of the family of the Prophet.

The modern Iraqi writer Kamil Mustafa al-Shaibi maintains that the Shabak are Turkoman tribes, perhaps originating as Bektashis, who became followers of the Safawi Sufi order under Haydar Ibn Junayd (d. 1488), father of Ismail, the first Safawi shah of Persia. Haydar instructed the members of his order to adopt the doctrine of the Twelver Shiites, who believed in the spiritual authority and infallibility of the twelve Imams. He also ordered his followers to wear a high conical turban wrapped with a red cloth divided into twelve folds, symbolizing twelve Imams. Hence, his followers were known as Kizilbash ("red heads" in Turkish).[21]

Thus, al-Shaibi maintains the Shabak became Kizilbash followers of the Safawis of Persia. Al-Shaibi goes on to say that when Shaykh Haydar's son, Shah Ismail, fought the battle of Chaldiran (1514) with the Ottoman Sultan Selim I ("the Grim"), the Turkoman followers of the Safawis in Turkey marched through northern Iraq to join the forces of Shah Ismail at Chaldiran. They arrived too late, however; Shah Ismail had already been defeated. These Turkomans could not return home to Turkey for fear of retaliation by Sultan Selim I. They were forced to stay in northern Iraq, maintaining their religious beliefs and way of life in a new place, and in time becoming known as Shabak.[22]

In light of this account, Frederick W. Hasluck correctly observes that the term "Kizilbash has been associated from the beginning with both Persian nationality and Persian Shia religion, but has no ethnological significance whatsoever."[23] What Hasluck means in this context is that the term Kizilbash originated with Shaykh Haydar, whose Safawi order symbolized both the Shiite faith that Haydar brought into full force and the national aspirations of Persia. When the teaching of Haydar's Safawi order spread westward into Asia Minor, many Bektashis and other Turkomans became followers and were known as Kizilbash.

Futhermore, many Kurdish tribes in Western Persia and in Anatolia in eastern Turkey, especially those in the region of Dersim (Tunceli) in the upper Euphrates valley, became followers of the Safawi order and were also known as Kizilbash. The difference between the Bektashis and the Kizilbash (both Turkomans) of Asia Minor and the followers of the same Safawi order in Persia was one of leadership, since their beliefs, rituals, and traditions were the same.[24] In Persia (Iran) Safawi Shaykhs were leaders of the order of which the Kizilbash were members. In Asia Minor (Turkey), those who joined the same order were known as Kizilbash. Some of them were entrusted to the supervision of Haji Bayram (d. 1429) and became members of the Bayrami order.[25]

It should be pointed out that the southern part of Turkey, including the provinces of Aleppo and Mosul, where many Turkomans lived, was the homeland of many Sufi orders, including the Babaiyya and the Bektashis. It is not improbable that the Shabak, themselves Turkomans, lived in the same area and were originally members of the Bektashi order. The Shabak must have become Kizilbash in Haydar's time because of their allegiance to the Safawi order and later to the Safawi state founded by Shah Ismail (d. 1524) in 1501.[26] Shah Ismail attempted to extend the Safawi hegemony to the eastern part of Turkey (Anatolia) and to subjugate that area to Shiite Islam. The Ottoman Sultan Selim I (reigned 1512–20), persecuted the Safawi followers in Turkey and even had forty thousand of them murdered. Consequently, many followers of the Safawis left Turkey, hoping to join the Safawi army in Iran, but were forced to remain in Iraq when Shah Ismail lost the battle of Chaldiran, near Tabriz, to the Ottoman sultan on 23 August 1514. Finding that they could neither return to Anatolia nor join the forces of Shah Ismail at Chaldiran, they remained in the area east of Mosul and became farmers and herdsmen, but were not assimilated into the society of the area.[27]

These, then, are the theories regarding the ethnic and religious origins of the Shabak. If we ponder the ideas of al-Sarraf on the subject, we discover that his explanation may not be far from the truth. His statement that the Shabak were Turks who came to Iraq in the time of the Safawis is apparently correct; the Shabak were Turks, meaning Turkomans, who adhered to the Safawi order in its Shiite form, paying allegiance to the Safawi religious leaders, and later to Shah Ismail when he founded the Safawi state in 1501. Al-Sarraf also appears to be correct when he states that the religious creed of the Shabak is that of the

Bektashi-Kizilbash sect. However, he fails to explain the reasons for the Shabak's move to northern Iraq in the time of the Safawis.[28]

Although he does not mention the Shabak by name, Laurence Lockhart indirectly sheds light on the reasons the Turkoman followers of the Safawis, including the Shabak, moved to Iraq. He states that Shah Ismail won to his cause many Shiite Turkomans from Turkey and Syria, notably the Turkoman clans of Takallu, Ustajlu, Dhu al-Qadr, Shamlu, Ramlu, Afshars, Qajar, and Varshaq, who enthroned Ismail as the shah of Azerbayjan at Tabriz in July 1501 and became the backbone of Safawi military power.[29] The new shah rewarded the leaders of these clans with land fiefs, and they and their followers who "came from the Ottoman dominion" were given a state in Persia. Lockhart also states that when Shah Ismail lost the battle of the Chaldiran to the Ottoman Sultan Selim I, "these Turkomans, being unable to return to their homes in Turkey, adopted Persia as their country.[30] Obviously, some of these Turkomans (co-religionists with the Safawis) must have been Shabak who, according to al-Sarraf, came to Iraq in the time of the Safawis and, according to al-Shaibi, remained in northern Iraq because they could not return to their homes in Turkey.[31] If we recognize that between 1508 and 1510, the greater part of Iraq was occupied by Shah Ismail and became a Persian domain, we realize the importance of Lockhart's statement that these "Turkomans . . . adopted Persia as their country;"[32] it becomes a key point in al-Shaibi's attempts to explain why the Turkoman Shabak remained in northern Iraq after Chaldiran.[33]

A fact giving additional credence to the argument that the Shabak are Turkomans originating in Anatolia is that Anatolia was the home of the frontier dwellers known as the Byzantine Akritoi, and of the Ghazis (warriors of faith), who had fought for the cause of Islam against the Christians of Asia Minor and Europe since the eleventh century. Among these Turkomans were the Bektashis and the Kizilbash; moreover, the whole area between the mountains of Anatolia and Persia formed a kind of bridge and melting pot for a variety of peoples including the Persians, Turkomans, Kurds, and Armenians.[34] From the thirteenth to the sixteenth centuries, this area was a hotbed of Shiite propaganda, and toward the close of the fifteenth century it became the focal point of a dispute between the Shiite Safawi shahs and the Sunnite Ottoman sultans.

A great number of Kurds in the province of Dersim in the upper Euphrates valley were exposed to this Shiite propaganda and were converted to an extreme form of Shiism. Various Turkomans, including the Shabak, must have wandered through this area in northern Iraq and finally settled there. A few generations later, the relations of these Turkomans with both Anatolia and Persia weakened, and, like other ethno-religious groups in the area (the Assyrians or Nestorians, for example) they led a marginal cultural and economic existence.

It is evident, then, that the Shabak have a strong relationship with the Bektashis, the Kizilbash, and the Safawis of Persia. To place this relationship in its proper historical and religious perspective, and in order to shed more light on the identity, ethnicity, religious beliefs, rituals, and social customs of the Ghulat or extremist Shiite sects in Turkey, Iraq, and Persia, an account of the Bektashis, the Kizilbash, and the Safawis will be provided in the following chapters.

2

The Bektashis

The Bektashis were one of the many dervish Sufi orders or fraternities active in thirteenth-century Turkey. They derive their name from a certain Haji Bektash, whose identity and career are still subjects of controversy. Haji Bektash may have been one of the rival saints of the Turks of Central Asia venerated by the Bektashi and Menteshe tribes.[1] He may also have been the historical figure Muhammad Ibn Musa, who in the twelfth century came from Khurasan in Iran to the land of the Rum (Byzantines), perhaps at the behest of his master, Ahmad Yasawi (d. 1166–67), the great religious leader of the Turkomans.[2] Or, according to Shams al-Din Ahmad al-Arifi al-Aflaki (d. 1359) in his *Manaqib al-Arifin* (Exemplary acts of the Gnostics), Haji Bektash may have been the disciple of the rebellious Turkoman Sufi leader and founder of the Babaiyya movement, Baba Ishaq of Kfarsud, near Aleppo, Syria.[3]

Evliya Efendi (d. 1679; known as Çelebi) relates that Haji Bektash was the son of Sayyid Ibrahim Mukarram, a descendant of the Shiite Imam Musa al-Kazim. Bektash's father left Khurasan for Nishapur when Bektash was born. In his youth, Bektash was entrusted to the care of Luqman Perende, one of the disciples of Ahmad Yasawi, who taught him the *dahir* (outward) and *batin* (inward) religious science. This places Haji Bektash in the twelfth century with Ahmad Yasawi. But Evliya Efendi also says that by order of Ahmad Yasawi, Haji Bektash accompanied a host of pious men and saints (including Muhammad Bukhara, Sari Saltuk, Shams al-Din Tabrizi, and Muhyi al-Din Ibn Arabi) into the land of the Rum (Asia Minor), when the Ottoman dynasty was rising, and that Haji Bektash instituted the *Yeni Çeri* (Janissaries).[4] This would place Haji Bektash in the thirteenth century. The Janissaries, to be sure, were instituted by Sultan Orhan (d. 1360), founder of the Ottoman Empire. According to the fifteenth-century Turkish historian, Aşikpaşazadeh, Haji Bektash had no personal relations with the family of Osman (Uthman or Ottoman), father of Orhan.[5]

Another fifteenth-century Turkish historian, Oruc Bey, states that the Janissaries date back to the period of 1361–64.[6] However, Aşikpaşazadeh and Oruc Bey agree that the Janissaries were founded in the time of Sultan Murad Khan (reigned 1359–89), son of Orhan. It is most probable that Haji Bektash had nothing to do with the founding of the Janissaries.

The most plausible explanation of Bektash's identity is that he was one of the many dervishes who escaped Turkestan, Bukhara, and Khwarizm and sought refuge with the Seljuk Truks in Asia Minor when Turkestan was invaded by the Mongol army under Genghis Khan in 1219–23. The majority of these dervishes who fled their country were *qalandars* (vagrant dervishes) committed to lives of asceticism, poverty, and wandering.

According to M. Fuad Köplrülü, the qalandari movement was one of the most notable events in the history of Islam.[7] These qalandars usually wandered in armed bands and were probably similar to the Ayyars of medieval Islam or the Ghazis (zealot Muslim religious warriors).

These Ghazis, through *Jihad* (holy war) against the Christian "infidels," were instrumental in establishing the many Turkish Ghazi states and spreading Islam into Asia Minor after the battle of Malazgirt (or Manzikert) in 1071. This battle, in which the Byzantine army was defeated by the Seljuks, was really the beginning of the end of the Byzantine Empire in the east and the rise of the Seljuk Turks, and later of the Ottomans, to supremacy.

The objectives of the Ghazis in waging war were not always pure. Discontented and unemployed, they resorted to plundering and ravaging peaceful "infidel" Christian territories.[8] There is evidence that the Ghazis plundered and pillaged central Anatolia long before Malazgirt. What is significant, however, is that the opening of the Anatolian frontier to the Turkish nomadic tribes was the achievement not of the Seljuks, but of the Ghazis. The Seljuk sultans founded their Rum Seljuk state in 1077 only to assert their *de facto* presence and authority over the various Turkish Ghazi principalities. However, they encountered strong opposition to their rule from the Ghazis, especially the *Danishmends* ("learned men" in Persian), whose culture and traditions were very different from those of the Seljuks. Long before Malazgirt, the Byzantine system of defense in

Anatolia had weakened, and the efforts of the Armenians to establish independent petty states had caused great political confusion; this weakness and confusion allowed the Turkish nomadic tribes in Khurasan and Transoxiana to move to Anatolia.[9]

These Turkish tribes must have mingled with the heterogeneous native population of Armenians, Kurds, Syrian Aramaeans, and Arabs. For this reason we find several Christian Armenian religious traditions and beliefs among the practices of the extremist Shiites of Dersim in the upper Euphrates valley. There is some evidence that the Ghazi leaders, the Danishmends, were of Christian Armenian origin.[10] This would explain why the Ghazis felt more at home with the rest of the population of Anatolia than with the Seljuk Turks. These Ghazis remained true to their name—Warriors of Faith—but, unlike the Seljuks, they did not create a unified state in all Anatolia, although some of them succeeded in establishing a state that included Kastamuni, Amasya, Sivas, Kayseri, and Malatya (Melitene).

In 1172, this Danishmend state was conquered by the Seljuk Prince Izz al-Din Kilij Arslan (reigned 1156–88) and absorbed into the Seljuk state of Rum, reducing the Danishmend chiefs to mere puppets. With the death of the last Danishmend ruler, Dhu al-Nun in 1174 the Danishmend state ceased to exist, and six years later (1180) the Danishmends were eliminated.[11]

The territory of the Ghazis served as a buffer zone between the Seljuks of Rum and the Byzantines. There were no fixed boundaries between the Byzantines and the Seljuks of Rum; instead they were separated by a fairly wide strip of no-man's-land inhabited by Turkish elements. These Turks, according to Paul Wittek, were commonly called Turks of the Uj (that is, the Turks of the frontier) or Turkomans. These Turks of the Uj had maintained the Ghazi traditions of Malatya and Cilicia in southern Turkey; thus when the power of the Danishmend was extinguished in 1180, they were joined by other Ghazis, who sought their protection. Following Paul Wittek, then, we may assume that the term *Turkoman* denotes the Turks of the borderline area lying between the Byzantine territories and the Muslim Turkish principalities of the eastern borders of Anatolia, northern Syria, and Mesopotamia. The Turkomans were nomadic but also herded sheep. They continued to be Ghazis, however, "warriors of faith" who took by force many Byzantine towns in the no-man's-land region.[12]

Many Ghazis were zealous Muslim dervishes determined to spread Islam into the heart of Christian countries, but their faith was not in conformity with orthodox Islam. They were instead Alawis (in Turkish,

Alevis), extremist Shiites, or propagators of other heterodox beliefs combined with Sufism; such dervishes exerted great influence on the Turkoman tribes.[13] These tribes probably first met Islam in its Shiite form in the ninth century.

Islam began to spread among the Turks in the eighth century, especially after the battle of Talas of July 751. In this battle, fought near the present-day Awliya-Ata (Zambul in the southern Kazakh S.S.R.) the army of Ziyad Ibn Salih crushed the army of Kao Hsein-Chih, imperial commissioner of Kucha, resulting in the establishment and consolidation of Arab hegemony over Transoxiana.[14] In the following century, Islam gained considerable strength when the Samanis, who had established their dominance in Central Asia, embraced Islam. The conversion of the Samanis to Islam determined the fate of Central Asia, which became an Islamic rather than a Chinese territory.[15] When, under Ismail Ibn Ahmad (reigned 892–907), the Samanis conquered Taraz/Talas, many Turks were converted to Islam. Toward the end of Ismail's reign, pagan Turks made continuous incursions into Samani territory, provoking many zealot warriors from the eastern Muslim world to fight against them. These Turks were subdued and finally converted to Islam.[16]

In the middle of the tenth century a mass conversion to Islam of the Karakhanid Turks of Kashgaria, Ili, and the Issyl Kul occurred, giving Central Asia a definite Islamic character.[17] Their conversion was due as much to missionary activity as to military conquest. One of these missionaries, Abu al-Hasan al-Kalamati, was particularly active among the Karakhanids. As the Turks converted to Islam, the activity of zealot Muslim warriors recruited from the eastern part of the Islamic world was directed against the Byzantines. Thus, in 966, a great number of fighting men from Khurasan, including many Turks, passed through Iraq (then a Buwayhi territory) to the land of the Byzantines, preceding the rush of Turks into Asia Minor after the battle of Malazgirt (1071) by more than a century.[18]

In the early part of the tenth century, Shiism in the Zaydi form began to appear in the regions of Tabaristan and al-Daylam (the mountain region of Gilan). After thirteen years of indefatigable effort, the Zaydi Imam al-Hasan Ibn Ali al-Utrush, nicknamed al-Nasir al-Kabir (d. 304/916), was able in 301/913 to convert the people of Tabaristan to Zaydi Shiism. Al-Masudi (d. 956) states that al-Utrush lived for many years in al-Daylam and al-Jibal (Media) in northwestern Iran, where the people were Jahiliyya (pagan) and Majus (adherents of Mazdaism). Al-Utrush converted many of them to Islam (Zaydi Shiism) (excluding those in inaccessible mountainous regions), and built *masjids* (places of worship) for the new converts. Al-Masudi further relates that a number of Daylamite kings and chiefs, notably Muhammad Ibn Zayd al-Husayni, who tried to win the people of Tabaristan to his cause against the Abbasids, embraced Islam and supported the descendants of the Imam Ali.[19] This is confirmed by the fact that the Buwayhis, who appeared on the political stage in al-Daylam in the tenth century, became converts to Zaydi Shiism. When the Buwayhis occupied Baghdad, the capital of the Abbasids, in 945, however, they relinquished Zaydi Shiism and adopted Twelver Shiism, based on the spiritual supremacy and infallibility of the twelve Imams.[20] The intention of the Buwayhis, as Abu al-Rayhan al-Biruni (d. 1048) explains, was to establish a Shiite Alawi state on the premise that the members of the Ahl al-Bayt (the family of the Prophet), rather than the Abbasid caliphs, had the exclusive right to rule the Muslim community.[21] They did not abolish the Abbasid caliphate, but instead established a Shiite imamate until they were overthrown by the Sunnite Seljuk Turks in 1055.

Al-Masudi makes a revealing statement about political and religious affairs in the regions of al-Daylam and al-Jibal after the conversion of their inhabitants to Zaydi Shiism. He states that at the time of his writing (947), their doctrines were corrupted—that is, they embraced Ismaili Shiism—their opinions changed, and many of them became apostates recanting Islam. Nowhere in his account does al-Masudi mention Ismailism or Shiism, but he does elaborate on the struggle between the Zaydi leader al-Hasan Ibn al-Qasim al-Hasani, who occupied the Rayy province, and Nasr Ibn Ahmad Ibn Ismail, the governor of Khurasan, and Asfar Ibn Shirawayh, whom Nasr chose to fight for him against the Zaydi leader.[22] Al-Masudi states that Asfar Ibn Shirawayh was not a Muslim, but, according to Abd al-Qahir al-Baghdadi (d. 1037), Asfar was a convert to the *batini* (Ismaili Shiite) sect. Al-Baghdadi states that Abu Hatim (al-Razi, d. 934), who belonged to the batini sect, entered al-Daylam and converted a number of Daylamites, including Asfar Ibn Shirawayh, to Ismailism.[23] This indicates that the Ismaili *da'is* (propagandists) were active in northern Iran and were in conflict with the Zaydi Shiites. Indeed, Ismaili Shiism was so firmly established in Khurasan that Imad al-Din al-Isfahani (d. 1200) wrote that "Khurasan has become the nest of the batiniyya [Shite Ismailism]."[24] Rashid al-Din Fadl Allah al-Hamadhani (d. 1319), in his *Jami a-Tawarikh,* and al-Maqrizi (d. 1442), in his *Itti'az al al-Hunafa,* provide a detailed account of the activity of the Ismaili da'is in Khurasan, Rayy, and Transoxiana.[25] From their accounts we learn that Ismaili Shiism, known to Muslim writers as *al-Batiniyya,* had spread since the ninth century throughout the countries from northern India to northern Africa and Egypt and that it found a response among the various ethnic groups of those countries, including the Turkomans. According to Abd al-Qahir al-Baghdadi, even a group of Kurds from the mountain called al-Badin, in northern Iran, had become Batiniyya, i.e., Ismaili Shiites.[26]

Ismailism also attracted the Samani ruler, Nasr II Ibn Ahmad (reigned 913–43), who converted to this form of Shiism even though the Samanis were Sunnites of the Hanafite School.[27] In the eleventh century (1028), Sultan Mahmud Ghaznawi (reigned 999–1030) wrested al-Jibal (Media) and its capital Rayy from the Shiite Buwayhis. To justify his sack of the city of Rayy, Sultan Mahmud wrote to his patron, the caliph in Baghdad, that his main objective in using violence against al-Jibal was to cleanse it from the "infidel Batiniyya and evildoing innovators."[28] Although at this time the Buwayhis were adherents of the Ithnaashari form of Shiism, the use of the term *batiniyya* by Sultan Mahmud Ghaznawi indicates that there were Ismail Shiites in the district of al-Jibal (Media) and its capital Rayy.

Moreover, a branch of the Ismailis known as the Qaramita or Carmatians, that emerged in the ninth century in lower Iraq and spread into Bahrayn, Yaman, and Khurasan, continued to spread their doctrines until the eleventh century. Their heirs were the neo-Ismailis, known in Western sources as Assassins, who in 1090 established themselves in the security of the fortress of Alamut in the Burz mountains, northwest of Qazvin. From this fortress, the chief propagandist, or *da'i al-du'at,* with his votaries, terrorized the local people and captured other fortresses.

These neo-Ismailis resorted to assassination to achieve ther ultimate objective, the destruction of the Abbasid caliphate, which in the eleventh century was under Seljuk domination. Their assassination of the noble and learned Vizir Nizam al-Mulk in 1092 was directed toward this objective. Their end came in 1256, when the Mongol Hulago destroyed the fortress of Alamut. Ironically, two years later, he also destroyed the Abbasid caliphate in Baghdad.[29]

Hulago's invasion of Iran, Iraq, and other parts of the Middle East was a continuation of the wave of conquest begun by his grandfather, Genghis Khan. The turmoil caused by the Mongolian invasion drove many dervishes from Khurasan into Asia Minor. One of these dervishes was Jalal al-Din Rumi, who founded the Mawlawi (Mevlevi) order. These dervishes already harbored extreme Shiism shrouded with Sufism. Indeed, since the eleventh century, several prominent Sufis had emerged, among whom were Arslan Baba, Yusuf al-Hamadhani, Abu Muhammad Husayn al-Andaqi (the predecessor of Ahmad Yasawi), and Atabin

Arslan Baba (Yasawi's successor).[30] According to some sources, Haji Bektash was a disciple of Ahmad Yasawi.

It should be pointed out that since the opening of Asia Minor to the various Turkish tribes after the battle of Malazgirt in 1071, many Turkoman tribes had rushed to settle in that country. Their settlement of the new conquered Byzantine territory was probably a slow process. The important thing is that some of these frontier tribes brought along with them Islam in its Sufic, as well as extreme Shiite forms. The dervishes, who after the Mongolian invasion fled to Asia Minor, found there a great response among their Turkoman co-religionists.

According to Vladimir Minorsky, an important colony of Ismailis was discovered by Count A. A. Bobrinskoi in the gorges of Oriental Bukhara around the turn of this century. Minorsky further notes that the Ismailis of Central Asia have influenced the extremist Shiite sect of Ahl-i Haqq of western Iran with respect to some of their doctrines,[31] corroborating a statement by Henri Lammens (d. 1937) that the Ghulat (extremist Shiites), including the Ali Ilahis (Ahl-i Haqq) sprang from Ismaili Shiism.[32]

By the 1270s, Shiism had infiltrated from the interior into Mazandaran, where it was adop'ed by the majority of the people. Only a hundred years earlier, one could hardly find more than several hundred Shiites in that region.[33] The spread of Shiism may be attributed to the fact that, although Sunnites, the Seljuks of Rum (Asia Minor) were greatly influenced by and tolerant of the Shiite faith of the Turkomans. This influence was manifested in their veneration of the Imam Ali and his descendants, the Imams, and in their building of many *tekkes* (lodges) for devout Shiite shaykhs.[34] Franz Babinger goes so far as to say that Seljuk rulers were heretical, professing the beliefs of the Alawis the followers of Ali, beliefs that in fact meant they were Shiites.[35]

Not until the thirteenth century, however, did an extreme form of Shiism begin to have a great impact on the Turkoman tribes.[36] Heterodox religious movements like the Babaiyya also had an immediate effect on the Turkoman tribes, culminating in a revolution against the Seljuks in 1241. The Babaiyya movement takes its name from a leader known as Baba, about whom historical sources are inconsistent. While the Syrian writer Bar Hebraeus (d. 1286) makes this Baba the leader of the movement, and "Old Man Ishaq" his disciple,[37] al-Qaramani (d. 1610) makes Baba Elias the leader of the movement.[38] Still another writer, Nasir al-Din al-Husayn Yahya Ibn Muhammad, known as Ibn Bibi (d. 1272), states that Baba Ishaq was the leader of the Babaiyya movement and that Baba Elias was his collaborator.[39] Modern writers maintain that the leader of the Babaiyya movement was Baba Ishaq, a Turkoman preacher from the Kfarsud region on the Syrian-Euphrates border.[40]

According to Bar Hebraeus, Baba proclaimed himself the only true *Rasul* (apostle) while preaching in the country of Amasya, and stated that Muhammad was a "liar and not the apostle of God."[41] Baba's followers called him Rasul Allah (apostle of God) and Amir al-Muminin (commander of the faithful), and changed the Muslim Profession of Faith to read, (There is no God but God, and the Baba is the vicegerent of God).[42] They killed anyone who did not confess that the Baba was the divine apostle of God.[43] Many Turkomans adhered to the Baba and found in him the leader who would save them from the Seljuk yoke. Gathering their forces, the Turkomans revolted openly against the Seljuk sultan, Ghiyath al-Din Kaykhosraw (reigned 1236–45), in 1241.

The insurrection of Baba Ishaq and the Babaiyya movement was finally subdued, and the chief instigators were captured and killed. What is significant about the Babaiyya is its association with extreme Shiism. Shiite teachings were carried by Baba Elias, a disciple of Baba Ishaq, from his native country of Khurasan in northern Persia to the land of the Rum (Asia Minor) when the Mongol army swept through Khurasan at the beginning of the thirteenth century.[44] It should be pointed out that Baba Ishaq began preaching in the region of Kfarsud on the Syrian-Euphrates border, not too far from Aleppo and neighboring areas teaming with Ismailis and other extreme and moderate Shiites. According to Imad al-Din Ibn Kathir (d. 1373), al-Malik al-Afdal, the son of the celebrated Salah al-Din (Saladin) al-Ayyubi and ruler of Baba Isaq's native town of Shamishat (Samosata or present-day Samsat), was himself a Shiite.[45] We may assume from all this that the Babaiyya were strongly influenced by extreme Shiism, clothed in Sufi garb.[46] According to one source Haji Bektash, the eponym and patron of the extreme Shiite sect of Bektashism, was also a disciple of Baba Ishaq.[47] This is unlikely, but the Babaiyya must have paved the way for extreme Shiite and other Sufi orders in Asia Minor.

The failure of the Babaiyya insurrection did not halt the growth of the influence of the Sufic orders in Asia Minor. The constant warfare, the continual mingling of peoples and ideas, and the uncertainties of life for the common people combined to make possible the growth of the religious movement that ultimately developed into two orders: the Mawlawis (in Turkish, Mevlevis), founded by Jalal al-Din Rumi (d. 1273), and the Bektashis. The great majority of the villages in the area belonged to these orders. Furthermore, because they used the Turkish language as their literary medium and because that was the language of the common people, these two orders of dervishes "were destined to extend their influence throughout the Ottoman period."[48]

It should be pointed out that the practices of most of these dervishes represented the ancient teachings of Islamic Sufism, emphasizing the inner enlightenment of the soul rather than the external rituals and religious duties of Islam as the path to attaining knowledge of the Ultimate Reality, that is, God. As an established movement, Islamic Sufism did not emerge with the rise of Islam, although there are many statements in the Quran which can be considered mystical or Sufic. Furthermore, *zuhd* (piety) was a foremost trait of many Muslim believers in the time of the Prophet of Islam. As Islam spread into foreign lands and a vast Islamic state was established, Sufism emerged as an inchoate and primitive movement. Its members were townspeople of the lower middle class and were usually devoted to the study of religious sciences of the Quran and the Hadith (traditions of the Prophet). Although some were legalists, well versed in religious sciences, who tried to expound and adapt Quranic teachings and traditions to the Muslim community, many were mystics, spiritualists, and outright escapists. As Islam penetrated every aspect of Muslim life and Islamic orthodoxy became strictly legalistic (that is, bound by ritualism and formalism supported by the state), a myriad of sects and non-conformist groups emerged that defied both the state and the state-sponsored orthodoxy. The Sufic (mystical) schools developed in this ambience as a challenge to Islamic dogmatism and ritualism. According to Ignaz Goldziher, most Sufis looked upon Islamic religious obligations as externals of little or no spiritual value in the quest for knowledge of God. With this attitude, says Goldziher, they rejected the rituals and dogmas of orthodox Islam, developing their own eclectic beliefs from Gnosticism, Yoga, Shamanism, and Christianity. One group who did this was the Sufic order of the Bektashis.[49]

We do not know exactly when Haji Bektash began to preach his doctrine to the Turkoman tribes in Asia Minor. The two sources entitled *Vilayatnama* and *Maqalat* (Discourses) attribute to him miracles worthy only of a divine person. Bektash's teacher, Luqman Perende, claims to have seen Haji Bektash at the age of four in the classroom with two apparitions, one of the Prophet Muhammad and the other of the Imam Ali; Ali was teaching him the batin (inward or esoteric) and dahir (outward or literal) sciences of the interpretation of the Quran.[50] Indeed, there is no evidence that the *Maqalat* placed particular emphasis on the doctrine and rite of the Bektashi order.[51]

Frederick W. Hasluck contends that Haji Bektash, as a mere figurehead of Bektashism, had nothing to do with the present Bektashi doctrines, and that the real founder of Bektashism was Fadl Allah al-Astrabadi (d. 1401), founder of the Hurufi sect. He states that after al-Astrabadi's death, his disciples introduced his doctrine to the Bektashi lodge near Kirşehir and, under the guise of Bektashism, disseminated their Islamic heterodox Hurufi doctrine, based on numbers symbolizing religious truths.[52] While the Hurufis do have strong connections with the Bektashis and their order, there is no evidence that Fadl Allah al-Astrabadi was the real founder of Bektashism.[53]

Haji Bektash probably taught simple rituals, including the use of a candle and the celebration of a ceremonial meal and a dance. These rituals are essentially those of the Shabak and cognate sects in northern Iraq. It is also probable that Haji Bektash, because of his ascetic life, was recognized by the Turkoman tribes as a *wali* (saint), and that later in his life he sent missionaries to different areas to spread his teachings.[54]

This missionary work must have been vigorous and continuous, for it is reported that in the fourteenth century, in the province of Tekke in Asia Minor, the Kizilbash, also known there as Takhtajis (woodcutters), were converted to Shiite Islam through the efforts of missionaries from Konya.[55] It is also reasonable to assume that the simple mystical teachings of Haji Bektash were not tainted by theological polemics or doctrines. They were characterized by tolerance, as seems to be demonstrated by the stories and references to Jesus in the *Maqalat*.[56] This tolerance may have been a factor in the spread of Bektashism among the Janissaries, recruited by Ottoman sultans from captive Christian boys.[57] Such, then, were the Bektashi teachings bequeathed by Haji Bektash to his disciples. They were essentially Shiite teachings overshadowed by mysticism.

Only toward the beginning of the sixteenth century did the Bektashi leader Balim Sultan (d. 1516), considered by the Bektashis as their second pir (patron saint), give the Bektashi order its final form. According to legend, Balim Sultan was born miraculously to a Christian Bulgarian princess of the region of Demotika. The legend holds that the princess made a prayer rug and hung it on the wall. She told her mother that she would marry the first man who prayed on this rug, and no other. It happened that two old men, Sayyid Ali Sultan and Mursal Baba, visited the princess' family. Without asking the princess about the rug, they pulled it down from the wall and prayed on it together. The princess, who was still a young virgin, hated both these men because of their age and refused to marry either. In order to get rid of them, she pulled the rug from under them while they prayed, with such force that Sayyid Ali did not believe that the princess could possess such extraordinary strength. He rather believed that her power came from Balim Sultan, who would be borne by her. Mursal Baba asked for a jar of honey, then dipped his finger in it and put it in the mouth of the virgin princess, whereupon she immediately became pregnant. Thus Balim, whose name derives from the Turkish word *bal* (honey), came to be born.[58]

This legend is important as an example of the attempts of the Bektashis to make their Sufi order and teachings more appealing to the Christian population of Asia Minor; they served as intermediaries between Islam and Christianity. By attributing a miraculous birth to Balim Sultan, their second patron saint, they rendered him homologous with Jesus Christ, who also was born of a virgin without a human medium. It should be remembered, however, that the belief of the Bektashis in a trinity consisting of God, Muhammad, and Ali, as well as the concept of the miraculous birth of Balim Sultan, is alien to orthodox Islam.[59]

What is most significant is that under Balim Sultan the Bektashi order was influenced by the teachings of other Sufistic orders: the Hurufis (founded by Fadl Allah al-Astarabadi in the fourteenth century), the Babais, the Akhis, and the Abdals, among others. Nevertheless, the Bektashis continued to preserve the main features of their teachings, especially the *Ishq* (passionate love or yearning for God); belief in a trinity combining God, Muhammad, and Ali; and belief in the sanctity of the family of the Prophet. Most basic of all, the Bektashis maintained their belief that Haji Bektash was indistinguishable from the Prophet Muhammad and from the Imam Ali; essentially, these three were one and the same person.[60] We shall see later that similar doctrines are maintained by the majority of the Ghulat or extremist Shiite sects.

3

The Safawis and Kizilbash

THE SAFAWIS derive their name from Shaykh Safi al-Din Ishaq, who died at the ripe old age of eighty-five at Gilan in A.D. 1334. His ancestors were leaders of a Sufi order in the city of Ardabil in northern Persia, and were known for their piety and religious influence. According to the anonymous *History of Shah Isma'il,* the founder of the Safawi family was a certain Firuz, son of Muhammad, son of Sharafshah.[1]

Firuz gained prominence because of his participation in a revolt which began at a village named Sanjan, near Merv, the capital city of Khurasan. The purpose of this revolt was to spread Islam in Azerbayjan. It was successful, and Firuz was rewarded by being made the governor of Ardabil and its environs, either by Prince Ibrahim Ibn Adham or by his son, said to have been the representative of the King of Persia. Firuz became wealthy, soon owning so many cattle that he found it necessary to move to Rangin in Gilan in search of more pasture land. Upon his death, his son Awad moved into the village of Isfaranjan near Ardabil, where he died.[2] There is nothing at this point in the history of Firuz and Awad to indicate that they claimed spiritual or Sufistic life. It may have been an experience of Awad's son, Muhammad Hafiz, that allowed the heads of this family to claim a spiritual distinction (genealogy).

The authors of both *Safwat al-Safa* and *Silsilat al-Nasab Safawiyya* relate that when young Muhammad was only seven years old, he disappeared and was gone so long that he was thought to be dead. After seven years, however, the boy reappeared, wearing a garment the color of the jujube fruit and a cap wrapped with a white turban, carrying a copy of the Quran. When asked where he had been, he said that the *jinn* (celestial beings who acted as intermediaries between God and men), had kidnapped him and taught him the laws of Islam and the Quran. It is said that he knew the Quran by heart, which earned him the title "Hafiz," that is, "Memorizer of the Quran." Fantastic as this incident may seem, it probably initiated the awareness of the heads of the family of Firuz of their spiritual and saintly role within their community. Such a view is supported by the fact that after the death of Muhammad Hafiz, his son, Salah al-Din Rashid, distributed his wealth among the poor of Isfaranjan, wore the dress of a dervish, and moved to Gilkhwaran, a village near Ardabil, where he made a living by farming. Thus he renounced his wealth and position to lead a simple, ascetic life.[3] Rashid, his son Qutb al-Din Abu Baqi Ahmad, and Qutb al-Din's son Salih seem to have lived peacefully at Gilkhwaran until the Georgians attacked their territory (probably between 1203 and 1205) and massacred many people.[4]

The anonymous author of the *History of Shah Isma'il* states that the reason for the Georgians' attack was to take revenge on Salih for his role in converting Christians to Islam.[5] This is most unlikely, however, since at the time of the Georgians' incursion, Salih was only a year old. Be that as it may, Salih died and was buried in Gilkhwaran, leaving behind his son, Amin al-Din Jabrail.[6]

Like his father, Amin al-Din Jabrail engaged in agriculture and the management of his landed estate. However, because of the incursions of the Georgians and the calamities of war befalling the whole district of Ardabil, Amin al-Din Jabrail moved to Shiraz, where for ten years he became the disciple of a famous spiritual Sufi, Khwaja Kamal al-Din Arabshah of Ardabil, and married Arabshah's daughter, Dawlati.[7] The anonymous author of the *History of Shah Isma'il* places great importance on this marriage, interpreting it as a union between the Persian element, represented by Dawlati, and the Turkish element, represented by Amin al-Din Jabrail.[8] Following his sojourn in Shiraz, Amin al-Din Jabrail returned to his native Gilkhwaran, where conditions had improved enough to allow him to pursue farming and the management of his land. It was there, in the year 650/1252, that Dawlati bore him a son, Safi al-Din, from whom the Safawis derive their name, and with whom, Edward G. Browne states, "the family suddenly emerges from comparative obscurity into great fame."[9]

The importance of the marriage of Amin al-Din Jabrail to Dawlati was over-emphasized, as was that of the birth of Safi al-Din. The author of *Silsilat al-Nasab Safawiyya* exaggerated the ascetic life and saintliness of Dawlati, equating her with the famous Sufi lady, Rabia al-Adawiyya of Basra (d. 801). In fact, this same author conferred upon Dawlati the *isma* (infallibility and sinlessness) in order to make the birth of Safi al-Din a divinely-ordained incident.[10]

Amin al-Din Jabrail died in 656/1258, leaving his son Safi al-Din great wealth and prestige. Sufism was fashionable in the area where Safi al-Din lived, and he chose the life of the Sufis. He left for Shiraz in southern Persia, despite the opposition of his mother, to follow the path of the Sufis under Shaykh Najib al-Din Buzghush of Shiraz, but Buzghush was no longer alive by the time he arrived in that city.[11] In Shiraz he made the acquaintance of many Sufis and dervishes; finally, he found Shaykh Ibrahim, known as the Zahid (ascetic) of Gilan (d. 700/1301), in the village of Hilya-Kiran, in the Khanbali district of Gilan. Safi al-Din became Ibrahim's disciple and married his daughter, Bibi Fatima. Safi al-Din's decision to follow the way of the Sufis is remarkable, for it was rare for a wealthy man, the scion of a prominent family, to choose an ascetic life.

Young Safi al-Din must have believed that he had a divine calling, and that the choice of a Sufic career was beyond his mortal will. It is reported that in a dream he saw himself sitting on the legendary Mount Qaf, wearing a cap of sable fur on his head and a sword at his side. Then he saw the sun rise and cover the earth. Shaykh Ibrahim interpreted the dream to mean that the sword was the *walaya* or *wilaya* (spiritual sovereign power or leadership), and that the sun was its splendor.[12] Shaykh Safi al-Din may have had no political ambition at the time of this dream, or guessed at his own future prominence. But the dream did presage the rise of the Safawis to political power; in 1501, Safi al-Din's great-grandson, Ismail, was proclaimed shah at Tabriz.

When Shaykh Zahid of Gilan died in A.D. 1301, Safi al-Din, now himself a shaykh, succeeded him in office. He moved to Ardabil, where he had a great number of followers, and, until his death in 1334, he was the head of the Safawi Sufi order, the name of which derives from his name, Safi.[13] His popularity as a saint of exemplary piety and asceticism spread far and wide, from Azerbayjan to Anatolia, winning him many *murids* (followers), especially among the peasants. It is said that in only three months, no less than thirteen thousand followers from Asia Minor came to visit the saint. In fact, he had a few followers even in India.[14] We also learn from Hamd Allah Mustawfi (d. 1349), a contemporary of Shaykh Safi al-Din, that the latter enjoyed an eminent position in his lifetime, not only among his own people but among Mongol rulers.[15] In many instances he served as an arbiter in quarrels between villages, and he saved many a village population from the tyranny of the sultan.[16] In recognition of the prominent religious position of Safi al-Din, Rashid al-Din, a chief minister of the Mongol ruler, supplied his *khanqah* (monastery) with provisions, money, and perfumes on the occasion of the festival of the Prophet's birthday.[17] Safi al-Din was also sought by the Jalayri rulers to instruct and guide their sons in the path of the Sufis, that they might learn the humility and obedience for which Shaykh Safi al-Din was called the Padishah Ukhrawi (divine king)[18] by the author of *Safwat al-Safa*.

There is nothing in the available sources to indicate that Shaykh Safi al-Din was a Shiite. The genealogy in *Safwat al-Safa* showing him to be a descendant of the seventh Imam, Musa al-Kazim, is most likely spurious.[19] Likewise, the claim made by the anonymous author of the unpublished copy of *Manaqib-al-Awliya,* or *Buyruk* (Exemplary acts of the saints, or the book of commandments, different from the Shabak copy mentioned earlier), that Shaykh Safi was a sayyid (a scion of the Imam Ali) is historically untenable.[20] The Iranian writer Ahmad Kasrawi (d. 1946), who discussed this subject thoroughly, reached the conclusion that the book *Safwat al-Safa* had been tampered with, and that the genealogy of Safi al-Din showing him to be a Shiite descendant of the Imam Musa al-Kazim was a later interpolation.[21] The modern Iraqi writer Kamil Mustafa al-Shaibi also concludes that Shaykh Safi al-Din was not a Shiite. While he does this independently of Kasrawi, he credits Kasrawi as his forerunner on this subject.[22] If the genealogy of Safi al-Din as given by the author of *Safwat al-Safa* is authentic, how is it possible that neither Safi al-Din's wife nor his son, Shaykh Sadr al-Din (d. 1391), knew anything about it?[23] The author of *Safwat-al Safa* himself relates that Sadr al-Din did not know whether he was descended from al-Hasan or al-Husayn (the sons of Ali) an ambiguity putting the relationship of the father to the Imam Musa al-Kazim, a descendant of al-Husayn, in even greater doubt. Perhaps the most convincing evidence that Shaykh Safi al-Din was not a Shiite is his commentary on Quran 5:67. This Quranic passage states, "Apostle! Proclaim the Message which has been sent to you from your Lord, and if you do not, you will not have fulfilled and proclaimed His Message. And God will protect you from men [who mean mischief]." Shaykh Safi did not interpret it, as do all traditional Shiite commentators, to mean that the Prophet had appointed Ali as his legitimate successor, or Imam, at Ghadir Khumm. Furthermore, Safi al-Din failed to mention a single Shiite source or author in his commentary, although he referred to al-Ghazzali, Shurawardi, Najm al-Din al-Razi and other non-Shiite writers.[24]

It is clear, then that Shaykh Safi al-Din was not a Shiite. On the contrary, he and his followers may have been adherents of the Shafii school, one of the four theological schools of orthodox Islam. He was a spiritual shaykh to whom the author of *Safwat al-Safa* ascribed many *karamat* (miraculous gifts), exalting his piety, asceticism, and spiritual eminence.[25] These qualities were praised by Fadl Allah Ibn Ruzbihan Khunji as "unique in the world."[26] However, only one rather flimsy piece of evidence indicates that Shaykh Safi al-Din held the Imam Ali in devotion; Edward (. Browne reproduces the following quatrain, allegedly composed by Safi al-Din:

> The great God who forgives a multitude of sins shall
> forgive you Safi
> When you realize that the love of Ali is within you,
> even if you commit sin God will forgive you.[27]

Browne comments that this quatrain was ascribed to Safi al-Din in the same manner as other poems were ascribed to his descendant, Shah Ismail.[28]

In 1334, Shaykh Safi al-Din died and was succeeded by his son, Shaykh Sadr al-Din. It is said that Sadr al-Din dictated most of the book *Safwat al-Safa* to the dervish Ismail Tawakkuli, known as Ibn Bazzaz (d. 1350).[29] There is nothing spectacular in the fifty-nine-year leadership of Sadr al-Din at Ardabil except his conflict with al-Malik al-Ashraf Chubani, the Mongol governor of Ardabil, over the political control of that city.[30] Sadr al-Din was banished to Tabriz, but pressure from his followers forced al-Ashraf to allow him to return to Ardabil. However, Sadr al-Din was forced to leave Ardabil again, fleeing to Gilan, when al-Ashraf tried to poison him. When another Mongol, Arghon Bey, occupied Gilan and killed al-Ashraf, Sadr al-Din returned to Ardabil, where he died in 1391.

As with his father, there is no evidence that Shaykh Sadr al-Din was a Shiite. Sadr al-Din was, however, associated with Turkish *Akhis* (brethren) and the Futuwwa, a kind of Sufi order of chivalry whose members extended help to the poor and the distressed.[31] In the words of the Persian writer Nur Allah al-Tustari (d. 1610), Sadr al-Din was "one of the pillars of the Fityan, the perfection of the Futuwwa, and was exemplary in feeding the poor."[32] The association of Sadr al-Din with the Akhis and the Futuwwa fraternities is, perhaps, an indication of the metamorphosis of the contemplative Sufism of the Safawis into an empirical and pragmatic form of Sufism like that of the Akhis and Futuwwa, whose noble purpose was to help the wretched and the poor.

Strong Shiite tendencies among the Safawis are first detected in the time of Khwaja Ala al-Din Ali (d. 1429), the son of Sadr al-Din and his successor as religious leader of the order. Known as Siyah Push (the blackened) because he always wore a black garment as a sign of piety, Khwaja Ali saw the ninth Imam, Muhammad al-Taqi, in a dream. Muhammad al-Taqi inspired him to convert the inhabitiants of Dizful, in Arabistan (Khuzistan) in southwestern Persia, to Shiism, by miraculously stopping the Dizful river from flowing, a sign of the true "belief in and recognition of the supreme holiness of Ali Ibn Abi Talib."[33] The people ridiculed Khwaja Ali, but, through divine providence, he caused two huge boulders to come together and block the river from flowing. Seeing this miracle, the cynical people of Dizful accepted the command of the Sharia (Islamic law) and confessed the walaya [sainthood], khilafa [caliphate] and wisaya [testamentary trust] of Ali Ibn Abi Talib.[34] In other words, they were converted to Shiism. Edward G. Browne states that "this is perhaps the earliest sign of strong and decisive Shi'a propaganda on the part of the Safawis."[35]

There is an indication that a Shiite and Sufi movement under Khwaja Ali began to develop into a theocratic, militaristic power, represented by the first appearance of *fidaiyyin* (religious self-sacrifices) among the followers of the order.[36] Perhaps, recalling the association of Sadr al-Din with the Akhis and Futuwwa, the Safawi leaders were increasingly aware of their role as both religious and secular leaders.

There is further evidence that Shiism became the persuasion of the Safawis under Khwaja Ali. To distinguish the new Shiite members of his order, Khwaja Ali ordered his men to wear a new cap, divided into twelve pleats, representing the Twelve Imams. In this regard, the Portuguese writer Joao de Barros (d. 1570) writes: "And as a mark and symbol of his sect and his new religion, in memory of the Twleve Sons of Hocen [Husayn], whom we have mentioned, he [Khwaja Ali] adopted a headgear shaped like a mushroom which the Moors [Muslims] often wear on their heads, but with a pointed peak resembling a pyramid and folded into twelve vertical pleats. His son, Iune [Junayd] followed his custom.[37]

Although De Barros errs both in calling the Twelve Imams the "sons of Husayn" and in calling Iune (Junayd) Khwaja Ali's son (he was in fact his grandson), this passage clearly indicates that the Safawis were Shiites in Khwaja Ali's time and continued to be so.

Samuel Purchas (d. 1626) states that "Barrius" (de Barros) begins his "pedigree" (genealogy) of the Safawis with Guine (Junayd); Purchas continues: "He [De Barros] addeth, that for the Ensigne, Character, or Cognisance of his Sect, he [Khwaja Ali] ordayned, that in the midst of their Turban (which they weare with many folds) there should arise a sharpe top, in manner of a pyramid, divided into twelve parts (in remembrance of Ali and his twleve sons) from the top to the bottom.[38]

De Barros, however, does not say whether the turbans of the Safawi followers were wrapped with the red fabric for which they became known as Kizilbash (red heads). It is believed that Khwaja Ali's great-grandson, Shaykh Haydar Ibn Junayd, added the red cloth.

Another indication that the followers of the Safawi order became Shiites in the time of Khwaja Ali is his encounter with the Mongol conqueror Timur Lang (Tamerlane) (d. 1405). There are two accounts of this encounter; they agree on many points but only one mentions that the Safawis had become Shiites. According to a Persian manuscript on the genealogy and history of the Safawis, Timur, after defeating the Ottoman sultan Bayazid I and conquering Asia Minor, returned to Azerbayjan, bringing with him a great number of captives. He stopped at Ardabil, where he met with Khwaja Ali and offered him a cup of poison, perhaps to test his miraculous powers. As dervishes performed an ecstatic dance and the *dhikr* (a constant praise of God), Ali took the cup and drank of it, saying, "Ma'im Sarpush, Ma'im Zahrnush." Then he joined the dancers and perspired so much that the poison was excreted from his body through his sweat glands. He was not harmed by the poison. This incident convinced Timur of Khwaja Ali's miraculous powers and he declared himself one of Khwaja Ali's devoted disciples. In deference to the latter's spiritual power and position, he asked what favor he could extend to him. Khwaja Ali requested that Timur release the Turkish prisoners he had taken after his victory over Bayazid I, at the battle of Angora (Ankara) on 2 July 1402. Timur agreed and released the captives, of whom there appear to have been many. It is reported that Khwaja Ali stationed many of these captives near the mausoleum of his ancestors in Ardabil, and they and their descendants became very loyal followers of the Safawi order, coming to be known as Sufiyan-i-Rumlu.[39] Even more important, Khwaja Ali repatriated others of the captives to their homeland, Turkey, sending with them some religious leaders of the Safawi order, with the injunction that the time for the fulfillment of the religious belief of the Shiite Twelvers had come and that they should be ready to sacrifice their very lives to spread this faith. Perhaps this repatriation was also meant to provide Timur with spies against the sultan in the Ottoman homeland.[40]

De Barros also describes Khwaja Ali's encounter with Timur. His version is significant, as it indicates the beginning of Shiism among the Safawis. De Barros states that upon his return to Persia, Timur wanted to see Iuni (Junayd [although actually he means Junayd's grandfather Khwaja Ali]), whom he describes as a holy man. Ali and Timur discussed many matters, including the release of captives. Khwaja Ali requested Timur, in the name of justice, to release the men he had captured in his war with Bayazid I, because Islamic law forbids a Muslim to hold another Muslim captive, even though he may be master of the world or as powerful a prince as Timur, himself. De Barros goes on to say that Iune (actually Khwaja Ali) asked Timur to release the captives to him in order "to convert them to the true path of salvation which he himself professed, and of which he had been the champion for many in the teaching of Ali, their prophet."[41] De Barros concludes that at last Khwaja Ali convinced Timur in this fashion to release to him all the captives who accepted his teachings, and that he settled them on the land, where they later proved very useful to his son, Shayk Aidor or Haydar (actually his grandson Junayd).[42]

De Barros' account leaves no room for doubt that Khwaja Ali was a Shiite, that his followers were Shiites, and that he was the one who commanded his followers to wear a new cap with twelve pleats representing the Twelve Imams, in order to distinguish themselves from non-Shiite Muslims. There is no evidence, however, that the Shiism of Khwaja Ali was extreme, or that he himself was an extremist Shiite deifying Ali or the Imams. Commenting on the encounter of Khwaja Ali with Timur, Samuel Purchas states that Barrius (de Barros) and others attribute this incident to Guine (Junayd) and say that these slaves became his disciples first, and afterwards, soldiers of Junayd's son Hidar (Haydar), whom he used against the Christian Georgians.[43]

Although Khwaja Ali was a Shiite and told the repatriated captives that the fulfillment of the Shiite beliefs of the Twelvers had come, some non-Shiite sources mention him not as a Shiite, but as a devout Sufi, who was greatly loved and honored by his followers and who had a very strong relationship with them. Al-Sakhawi (d. 902/1496) calls him Shaykh al-Sufiyya, (chief of the Sufis in Iraq), which indicates the prominent position Khwaja Ali enjoyed in Muslim spiritual circles in his time.[44] Although the term Sufi could be applied to both Shiites and Sunnites, it seems strange that Khwaja Ali is called a Sufi exclusively, and not a Shiite Sufi. His spiritual eminence and popularity are further demonstrated by the wide following he had in Asia Minor, land of the

Rum (Byzantines), many of whom received their Sufi training under his direction.[45]

Returning from a pilgrimage to Mecca in 1429, Khwaji Ali died in Jerusalem and was buried there. His son and successor, Ibrahim, was young, weak, and inexperienced. Ibrahim's tenure in office at Ardabil, until his death in 1447, was so uneventful that he is scarcely mentioned in sources on the Safawis. Indeed some sources, when discussing the career of Ibrahim's youngest son, the active and daring Junayd, bypass Ibrahim completely, calling Junayd the son of Khwaja-Ali.[46]

Ibrahim was succeeded by Junayd, and it was with Junayd that the militant character of the family first asserted itself.[47] By the middle of the fifteenth century, the introspective Sufism of the Safawis had been transformed into a predominantly political movement, thanks perhaps to the political ambition of Shaykh Junayd. His followers came from Asia Minor, Persia, and other countries to pay him homage.[48] One of his contemporaries, the Sunnite writer Fadl Allah Ibn Ruzbihan Khunji, relates that the descendants of Shaykh Safi al-Din forsook poverty and humility for the throne of a secular kingdom.[49] Obviously, Khunji had Junayd in mind. A sign of his political ambition is the fact that Junayd was the first Safawi to assume the secular title of "sultan," which is incongruous with the religius title "shaykh," a title more appropriate for the spiritual leader of a Sufi order.[50]

Junayd's ambition to combine spiritual and secular power was even more manifest in his intention to create an extremist Shiite sect. This ambition was perhaps influenced by the Shiite movement of Muhammad Ibn Falah (d. 1462), known as al-Mushasha. Ibn Falah, who began his career as a Sufi disciple of Ahmad Ibn Fahd al-Hilli (d. 1438) and led a rather austere, ascetic life, suddenly became a political activist, claiming to be the awaited Mahdi (Muslim Messiah), and pledging to conquer the world and divide the countries and villages among his companions and followers.[51]

In a short time, Ibn Falah's political power extended from the Lower Euphrates region in Iraq to Ahwaz, the Arab territory in southwestern Iran. The latter region was later called Arabistan, or country of the Arabs, after the rise of Shah Ismail to power in 1501, and was renamed Khuzistan in this century when Riza Khan, later the first Pahlevi shah of Iran, occupied Ahwaz in 1925, and captured and banished to Tehran its last Arab chief, Shaykh Khazal.[52]

Like Ibn Falah, Shaykh Junayd exploited the extremist Shiite zeal of his followers to further his political ambitions. In fact, there is strong evidence that Shaykh Muhammad Ibn Uways al-Ardabili of Aleppo, who was a follower of the Safawis and the father of Junayd's first wife, objected to Junayd's use of his spiritual position to achieve political goals.[53]

Junayd moved to Aleppo after the governor of Azerbayjan, Ali Mirza Jahanshah Ibn Kara Yusuf (d. 1468) of the Turkoman Kara Koyunlu dynasty, forced him to leave Ardabil, fearing his power. Junayd hesitated to leave, but the unrelenting Jahanshah threatened to destroy Ardabil if he stayed. Under pressure, Junayd went first to Arbil, Iraq, then to Aleppo, Syria, and then to Diyarbakr in Turkey, where he married Khadija Begum, sister of Uzun Hasan (d. 1468), who was the ruler of the Ak Koyunlu Turkoman dynasty and an enemy of Jahanshah.[54] Junayd's marriage, which was most likely politically motivated, strengthened his position, particularly since Uzun Hasan was the follower and disciple of Junayd's grandfather, Khwaja Ali.[55]

While in Aleppo, Junayd increased his extremist Shiite activities. Just as the Ghulat (extremist) Shiites had deified Ali, Junayd's followers openly deified Junayd. They ascribed to him divine attributes, saying that he was the Living One, God, and that there was no God but him. They even called his son the "Son of God."[56] In fact, even before Junayd was ousted from Ardabil, rumors were circulating that the appearance at the end of time of the Shiite Alawi state, as foretold by the Mahdi, was at hand, and that it would be commanded by Junayd, who would fight in company with the Mahdi to establish that state. Eschatological expectations of the founding of the Shiite state were further promoted by astrologers and magicians.[57] The activities of Junayd, and particularly the attribution of divine qualities to him by his followers were too much for the orthodox Muslims of Aleppo to bear, especially the learned ones: Junayd was accused of heresy.

A council convened in 1456–57 to examine his faith, but Junayd declined to appear. His attitude infuriated the populace of Aleppo, and he and his supporters were attacked, with both groups suffering casualties.[58] Having discovered that his presence in Aleppo had become too risky, Junayd left for Diyarbakr and stayed with Uzun Hasan, whose sister he married. His desire to return to Ardabil, the center of his authority, never diminished, though, and finally, with the help of Uzun Hasan, he left to go there. While passing through the territory of Shirwanshah Khalil Allah Ibn Ibrahim, however, he and his men were attacked, and the ambitious Shaykh Junayd lost his life in March of 1460.[59]

In adopting extreme Shiism, Junayd may have been influenced by the extremist Shiite movement of the Mushasha Muhammad Ibn Falah.

Whatever his motivation, Junayd may have used extreme Shiism as a pretext to achieve his political objectives.[60] One of these objectives was to carve out a state for himself in northern Iran and, most probably, to extend it to other lands. Devout Safawi disciples had already spread throughout the entire area from Persia to Asia Minor, and were always ready to die for the Safawi cause. Most of all, the political ambition of Shaykh Junayd was whetted by the distintegration of the empire of Timur Lang. This Mongol conqueror had brought all the countries from India to Asia Minor under his control, but, after his death in 1405, his vast empire crumbled, and several ambitious men were able to challenge his successors and carve out petty states and principalities for themselves. These men were of the Uzbek, the Kara Koyunlu, and the Ak Koyunlu Turkoman dynasties.[61]

In fact, Persia itself was divided among several suzerains who were later brought into submission by Junayd's grandson, the future Shah Ismail.[62] It is not improbable that the absence of a central government in Persia, and the ambitions of many potentates (and even of such religious propagandists as Ibn Falah, the Mushasha) to build their political authority and carve out states for themselves, encouraged Junayd's political ambitions.

In a fundamental sense and transcending the boundaries of speculation, Junayd was a potentate, the sultan of a religious community that was a state in everything but name. Shiism served his purpose because it contained a sublime cause for which he would fight. This cause centered on the Imams, the descendants of the Prophet of Islam, and their Providential governance of the Muslim community, especially represented in the Twelfth Imam, the Mahdi. It is not certain whether, like Muhammad Ibn Falah the Mushasha, Junayd claimed to be the Mahdi. What cannot be doubted is that his followeres considered him "divine" in his lifetime and believed he would live forever after his death.[63] The metamorphosis of the mystical Sufi order into a militant political movement began under Junayd, gained momentum under his son Haydar, and culminated with the establishment of the Safawi state under Haydar's son, Ismail.

The untimely death of their "divine Sultan," Junayd, must have pierced the hearts of his followers, for they rallied around his young son, Shaykh Haydar Ibn Junayd, and made him the focus of their devotion. For several years, Haydar led a peaceful life in Ardabil, awaiting the opportunity to strike against his opponents and push the political movement begun by his father to its logical conclusion. The opportunity presented itself when his uncle, Uzun Hasan, gained control of all Iraq and Azerbayjan and killed Abu Said (1469), the last of the descendants of

Timur. Attracted by the Safawi order, Uzun Hasan asked Haydar to provide him with the insignia of Haydar's order, so that Hasan and his sons might wear it.[64] Hasan also invited Haydar to his headquarters in Diyarbakr and gave him in marriage his daughter Baki Aqa, whom Munajjim Bashi calls Alam Shah Begum. Baki Aqa's mother was the Christian princess Despina Khatun, daughter of Kalo Ioanness, the last emperor of Trebizond.[65] Perhaps Uzun Hasan's intention was to assist his nephew in establishing political authority in Ardabil, but in 1468 Hasan died and was succeeded by his son and heir apparent, Khalil. Khalil was killed several months later by his young brother Yaqub, who crowned himself ruler of the Ak Koyunlu dynasty.[66]

It was Haydar's misfortune that Yaqub could not tolerate his religious views. In fact, Yaqub called Haydar the "Leader of the People of Error," perhaps referring to Haydar's ultra-Shiite beliefs and his deification by his followers.[67] Yaqub's antagonism could not stop Haydar's ambition, however; he remained determined to subjugate the "infidel" Christian Cherkes (Circassians). We are told by an anonymous Venetian merchant that Haydar "bore an intense hatred for the Christians."[68] He may also have sought to subdue the petty Shirwan state, which had remained beyond the control of Uzun Hasan. While crossing the Shirwan territory, the only path leading to Circassian country, Haydar was attacked by the joint forces of Farrukh Yasar (the ruler of Shirwan and the son of Khalil, the killer of Haydar's father, Junayd) and Yaqub, who found it opportune to ally himself with the ruler of Shirwan in order to eliminate Haydar. Outnumbered by his enemies, Haydar was captured near Tabasaran, southwest of Darband, on the slopes of Elburz Mountains near the Caspian Sea, in 1488. His head was cut off and carried to Tabriz, where it was thrown to the dogs in the city square.[69]

We have already stated that under Haydar and his father, Junayd, the peaceful Sufi order of the Safawis was transformed into a militant religious band of zealous Muslims, or Ghazis (literally, invaders), who, to fulfill the religious duty of *jihad* (holy war), fought for the cause and the expansion of Islam by subjugating the non-Muslim "infidels." Their objective was conquest of their neighbors, the Christians of Georgia. The periodic expeditions against the Circassians which had been conducted under Junayd reached full force and became a major preoccupation of the order and its followers under Haydar,[70] who lost his life in this cause. Under Haydar, the Safawi Sufi order became a political force whose rallying point was Ithanaashari Shiism, and whose most formidable tool was the devout Ghazi people. Later these Ghazis were to play a decisive role in the establishment of the future Safawi state under Haydar's son,

Shah Ismail. Similarly, the Ghazis laid the groundwork for the creation of the Ottoman state in Anatolia.[71]

The Ghazis, whether in Persia or Turkey, were Turkoman tribes from which emerged the various Sufi orders, including the Bektashis and Kizilbash and such different extremist Shiite groups in northern Iraq as the Shabak. There is some question as to when the followers of the Safawis were given the name Kizilbash (red heads). Was it in the time of Shaykh Haydar, or during the reign of his son, Shah Ismail? The tradition that the term Kizilbash originated at the battle of Siffin (37/657), when the Imam Ali ordered his men, "Tie red upon your heads, so that ye slay not your own comrades in the thick of battle," is most likely a recent interpolation intended to legitimize Kizilbashism, which is an extreme form of Shiism, by making the Imam Ali its patron.[72]

It should be remembered that under Khwaja Ali, the members of the Safawi order wore a new cap with twelve pleats representing the Twelve Imams, but without a red cloth wrapped around the cap. Some sources maintain that the followers of the Safawis came to be known as *Kizilbash* (red heads) under Shaykh Haydar; others say that they were known by this name under Ismail. Attempting to give his Shiite followers divine sanction and distinguish them from the rest of the Islamic sects, Shaykh Haydar ordered his men to wear the cap his great-grandfather, Khwaja Ali, had designed, wrapped with a red cloth. The anonymous author of the *History of Shah Isma'il* states that it was the Imam Ali himself who designed this cap when he appeared to Haydar in a dream, asking him to have his men wear it. This author states:

> One night the Prince of the Throne of Guidance and Sanctity, that is to say the Commander of the Faithful Ali, upon whom be the prayers of God, appeared in a vision to Sultan Haidar, and said to him, "O my son, the time is now at hand when my child from among your descendants should rise and sweep Infidelity from off the face of the earth. It now behooves you to fashion a cap for the Sufis and your disciples, and you must make it of scarlet cloth." On awakening, Sultan Haidar remembered the form and, having cut out a cap to that pattern, ordained that all the Sufis should make for themselves caps like it and wear them. They gave it the name of Taj-i-Haidari or Haidar's cap, and as in the Turkish language, Kizil means scarlet, this holy body became known as Kizilbash or "Red Heads."[73]

E. Denison Ross states that this tradition is pure fabrication and, as Theodor Nöldeke suggested to him, "an attempt to attribute an honorable origin to the somewhat disreputable name Kizilbash."[74] This may not be the case, however; whether or not the term Kizilbash originated in the time of Haydar or even in the time of his son, Shah Ismail, there is no evidence that it was considered dishonorable in Persia. On the contrary, it was a source of pride, a mark of the religious zeal of the followers of the Safawi Sufi order. In fact, the red caps were considered the greatest honor for Shiite nobles.[75] The Ottoman Turks, enemies of the Safawis, did despise the Kizilbash, though, calling them many derogatory names. This contempt for the Kizilbash exists to this day among the majority of the Turkish people.

The Italian writer Giovanni Tommaso Minadoi (1540–1615) associates the term *Kizilbash* with Shaykh Haydar, the Safawi. In his book, *Historia della guerra fra Turchi et Persiana* (History of the wars between the Turks and the Persians), Minadoi states: "Afterwards the Persians were called Cheselbas [Kizilbash], because of a certain red mark which they carried on their heads, by an ordinance that was instituted for them by Arduelle [Ardabil], who was esteemed a very holy man, which name was confirmed afterwards in the succession of Isma'il."[76]

By the term Arduelle, Minadoi means Shaykh Haydar, whom he calls Aidere, which quite likely he copied from Paulo Giovio (d. 1552).[77] Apparently, Minadoi was correcting Giovio, who claimed that "Arduelle who was also called Aidere, [Haydar of Ardabil] was the founder of the Persian faction," meaning the Safawi order. Minadoi states that it was not Aidere who was "the inventor of this order, but Giunet Siec [Shaykh Junayd]," by whom he means not Junayd, the father of Haydar, but Shaykh Safi al-Din. He writes: "This Persian superstition was first brought in by Siec Giunet, the Safi, afterwards maintained by Siec Sedudin, and after him by Siec Giunet the second, then by Siec Aider (called by Giovio, Arduelle) and at last so increased and enlarged by Ismahel the Saha and Safi."[78] Obviously, Minadoi knew the genealogy of the Safawis, except that he refers to Shaykh Safi al-Din as Siec Guinet (Shaykh Junayd).

Another source indicates that the term Kizilbash originated in the time of Haydar's son, Shah Ismail. In his article "Shah Isma'il," Sir Albert Houtum-Schindler explains that the term *tark,* which E. Denison Ross translates as "points," in fact means "triangular or wedge-shaped pieces of cloth, a gore." Houtum-Schindler goes on to say that:

> The Farhang-i-Anjuman Ara, after explaining these words relating to this cap, adds that Isma'il shah, in order to distinguish the members of the Shia sect, had dervish caps consisting of twelve pieces of

> cloth, and on each piece was sewn (stitched or embroidered, as done now) the name of one of the twelve Imams. These caps were considered the greatest honor that could be bestowed on Shia nobles; and as the caps were red, the families wearing them were called Kizilbash, i.e., Red-Heads.[79]

From this quotation we learn that the term Kizilbash originated in the time of Shah Ismail, and that it was the mark of the greatest honor for the members of the Shia families. Be that as it may, the Kizilbash became staunch supporters of Shah Ismail in Turkey, a fact that strained relations between Persia and Turkey and culminated in a war between them and the defeat of Shah Ismail at Chaldiran in 1514.

We need not elaborate here on the rise of Ismail's power as the founder of the Safawi state. Suffice it to say that from the time he was declared a shah in Azerbayjan (1501) until his defeat at Chaldiran, he subdued most of Persia, Iraq, and Transoxiana, and intended to extend his authority to the heart of the Ottoman domain. The devout Kizilbash, the backbone of his army, loved and revered him as a god.[80]

The Safawi Sufi order had by now become a state, and there was no longer a need for the Safawi leaders to live the austere and humble life of their ancestor, Shaykh Safi al-Din. Sufism had outgrown its purpose, and introspective spiritualism was giving way to external ritualism based on outward devotion to the Twelve Imams. It is not surprising to see, as a result of this metamorphosis, the rise of a group of Kizilbash who called themselves the "Princes of Sufism."[81] There is sufficient evidence in the correspondence of the Ottoman Sultan Bayazid II (reigned 1481–1512) to demonstrate that the Kizilbash followers of Shah Ismail had become strong, and a potent source of trouble for the Ottomans. According to an anonymous Venetian merchant, many people—even chiefs of Anatolia—became subjects of Shah Ismail and followed his Safawi order.[82]

4

The Bektashis, the Kizilbash, and the Shabak

As we have seen, the term Kizilbash originated when the Safawi Shaykh Haydar Ibn Junayd ordered his followers to wear a conical red cap (hence Kizilbash, or redheads) with twelve folds symbolizing the twelve Imams. He did this in conjunction with his establishment of the Twelvers, to distinguish his followers from other religious groups. We may reasonably assume, then, that the Kizilbash included both Bektashis and Safawis, that is, followers of the Safawi order in Persia. Frederick W. Hasluck seems correct when he states that the term Kizilbash "is associated from the first both with Persian nationality and Persian Shi'a religion, but has no ethnological significance whatever."[1]

Within a few generations the Kizilbash, also called Alawis (*Alevis*, in Turkish), spread all over Turkey, but were mainly concentrated in the northeastern part of the country, especially in the provinces of Sivas, Erzerum, Diyarbakr, and Harput.[2] A great number of the inhabitants of these provinces became converts to the Safawi order and were called Kizilbash. This is the same term which the Turks of Anatolia applied to the Persians (meaning the Safawis), to whom the Kizilbash of Turkey owed great allegiance.[3] In fact, the Armenians who lived in these provinces called the Kizilbash "Garmir Gelukh" (red heads), by which they also meant Persians.[4] Among these Kizilbash were Kurds, known as the "western Kurdish Kizilbash," who spoke a distinct Kurdish-Turkish dialect called Zaza, and who are thought to have a strong admixture of Armenian blood. Among these Kurds was a group called the Mamakanli, who are believed to be descendants of the Armenian Mamigonians.[5] If this apparent racial affinity between the western Kurds and the Armenians is real, one can reasonably assume that the Christian elements among the religious beliefs of the Kizilbash may have resulted from it.[6] We shall elaborate on this subject later.

Some writers regard the Kizilbash as a group distinct from the Bektashis, although they agree that they are linked by alliance with the Bektashis.[7] J. G. Taylor, the British consul for Kurdistan who traveled through Armenia, Kurdistan, and upper Mesopotamia (Iraq) in 1866, observed that in the town of Arabkir in eastern Turkey, the Bektashi sect was favorable to the Kizilbash. He states that his host at Arabkir, Sayyid Osman (Uthman) Nuri, a Bektashi dervish, was greatly respected by the Kizilbash.[8] Other writers maintain that Kizilbash and Bektashis are two different names for the same people. J. W. Crowfoot, who visited the ancient provinces of Lykoonia and Kappadokia in the summer of 1900 to conduct archaeological research, had the opportunity to inquire into the character of the Kizilbash settlements in these provinces. He observed that the orthodox Turks (i.e., the Sunnite Muslim Turks) despised the Kizilbash and referred to them derogatorily by this name because they drank wine and did not perform public prayer according to the tenets of Islam. But the Kizilbash he visited called themselves "Bektashis," and when they gave orders to each other, they called out "Hie! Bektash!"[9] In other places in Turkey, such as Erzerum, the Kizilbash call themselves Bektashis.[10] It should be pointed out, however, that these differences between the two groups are of no great significance, since in many aspects of their religious beliefs and practices, and most significantly in their religious hierarchy, they are strongly linked. We have already mentioned that the Kizilbash in the province of Tekke, in Lycia, were converted to Bektashism by missionaries dispatched from Konya in the fourteenth century.[11] Like the Bektashis, they were Alawis (Alevis, in Turkish), that is, followers of Ali, and were associated with the Bektashi order of dervishes. In speaking of themselves, the Kizilbash of Turkey use the name Alevi.[12] But according to M. F. Grenard they refused to acknowledge themselves as Bektashis or Alawis, and claimed that they were merely faithful followers of the Prophet Muhammad.[13] They consider themselves Sunnite Muslims, and, in front of Muslim witnesses, openly perform the prayer prescribed by the Quran. Such ambivalent behavior by the Kizilbash is permitted as a form of taqiyya (dissimulation), an approved practice meant to save Shiite adherents from religious persecution by orthodox Muslims.

Rev. Horatio Southgate (later to become a bishop), an American Episcopalian missionary who traveled through the eastern part of Turkey in 1837–38, reports that the inhabitants of the region between Angora and Delikli Taş professed to be Muslims, though the Turks contemptuously called them Kizilbash. Southgate believes that the Kizilbash were the descendants of the Persians brought into the region as war captives, but he was unable to elicit any information about their faith or customs from the neighbors, who must have had no social intercourse with them.[14] However, there is evidence that in Cilicia the Takhtajis (woodcutters) were called Kizilbash by the Turks.[15] Furthermore, although both the Kizilbash and the Bektashis belong, by faith, to the Shiite sect of Islam their Shiism contains substantial Christian elements that have caused some writers to consider them not as part of the community of Islam, but as a corrupt Christian sect.[16]

Other writers maintain that the rituals of the Kizilbash betray their Christian origin.[17] Many of these writers are Western missionaries, mostly Americans, who worked among the different Muslim sects of Turkey in the nineteenth century. One of them, Dunmore, states that, based on information he received about the Kizilbash Kurds in the vicinity of Arabkir, he is satisfied that these "peculiar people . . . are descendants from Christian stock, made nominal Moslems by the sword." He goes on to say that when they are in the presence of Turks (Sunnite Muslims), they call themselves Muslims, though they have no sympathy for these Sunnites, but rather harbor profound hostility toward them. Dunmore adds that they do not accept the Quran as a book of God or Muhammad as a prophet of God, but do accept the Bible as a holy book and Jesus Christ as the Son of God, usually under the name of Ali.[18]

Another missionary, Mr. Ball, writing in 1857 about his visit to the Kizilbash villages near Yozgat, Turkey, states that these Kizilbash, though the disciples of Ali, had a greater respect for Christians than for Muslims. Like Dunmore, he says that they professed to receive the Bible, and that the Quran had little binding force on them. He adds that because their religion was a mixture of Christianity, Islam, and heathenism, they cannot properly be considered Muslims.[19]

Ellsworth Huntington (d. 1947), who successfully surveyed the Euphrates River in the region of Dersim in the upper Euphrates valley in 1901, writes that the inhabitants of the Harput Mountain were originally Armenian Christians who became nominal Muhammadans in the face of persecution, intermarrying with the invaders. He states that the religion of the Kizilbash is a mixture of Shiite Islam and Christianity, with traces of paganism, and says that the Kizilbash identify themselves more with Christians than with Muslims, believing in Adam, Moses, David, and Jesus, and considering Jesus the greatest of them all. Huntington further states that when he tried to talk to a Kurdish Kizilbash *agha* (chief) about Muhammad, the agha avoided the subject.[20]

What made these sectaries different from Orthodox Sunnite Muslims was their extreme love and deification of the Imam Ali and the other eleven Imams. In fact, they have preserved to this day the religious traditions that separate them from the Sunnites. Nur Yalman, who in the 1960s visited the Alawis of eastern Turkey (especially those of the village of Çiplaklar in Elbistan near Muş), writes of the great devotion of these Alawis to Ahl al-Bayt (the family of the Prophet). He states that the expression *Ali'm Allah* (my Ali is God) is common among them,[21] an indication of their deification of Ali. *Ali'm Allah* also means, "God is all-knowing," but manipulating the assonance of this phrase and removing the *m* from *Ali'm* produces *Ali Allah,* changing the meaning to "Ali is God."

The Alawis were also distinguished by their total disregard of traditional religious obligations such as prayer, fasting during Ramadan, and abstention from drinking wine, and by their celebration of a communal meal crudely resembling the Christian Eucharist. Furthermore, they had no mosques and no muezzins to call the worshippers to prayer. Instead they conducted prayers in places called ibadathane, behind closed doors, or in their homes, where both sexes attended worship.[22]

Rev. Southgate states that the Kurdish villages between Bitlis and Van—Kizilbash villages—had no mosques, and that their imam conducted prayer in his own house. In spite of this, he says, they professed to be Musulmans (Muslims).[23] So did another extremist Shiite sect, the Takhtajis, who likewise had no mosques.[24]

Nur Yalman makes the same observation about the Alawis of the village of Çiplaklar. He writes that the visitor to this village will immediately notice that there are no mosques, no calls to prayer, and no minarets. The people conduct some of their rituals in private homes.[25] They meet once a week to offer a sacrifice, usually a lamb whose bones must not be broken (a rule bringing to mind the Paschal Lamb of Exodus 12:3–11) and whose blood must not be spilled. The dede, or religious head, blesses the sacrifice and then distributes portions of it to the worshippers.

According to the modern Turkish writer Mehmet Eröz, the Kizilbash drink raki, an alcoholic beverage which they call *dolu*. The Bektashis, however, always drink wine during the ceremony, and after eating and drinking, spend the night dancing, as part of their worship. Eröz exonerates the Kizilbash from such night orgies, stating that they were attributed to the Kizilbash by their neighbors, Orthodox Sunnites Muslims who considered them heretics.[26] What Eröz means here is that the Kizilbash's drinking of alcoholic beverages during their religious ceremony is an ancient custom dating back to the time when the Kizilbash were pagans, and that they did not receive it from Christianity. However, for the reasons previously mentioned, Grenard designates the Kizilbash as the "Protestants of Islam."[27] There is some truth in Grenard's statement that these extremist Shiites were as distinct from the main body of Islam as the Protestants are from Roman Catholics.

There is evidence that some Kizilbash of Turkey did convert to Protestantism in the nineteenth century, and called themselves "Protestants." How and by whom they were converted to Protestantism is not clear, but, according to Dunmore, one of the seven Kurdish Kizilbash chiefs in Çemişgezek (the largest town in Dersim) claimed that he and his people were "Protestants" who believed in the gospel and in Jesus Christ as their only Savior, and that they knew nothing of Muhammad. This chief also told Dunmore, "My people and I celebrated the Lord's Supper before we found the gospel, but now we do it according to the gospel as our Savior did."[28]

The missionary Jewett, writing in December 1857, states that several Kizilbash Kurds from villages near Sivas visited the American missionaries in that city to seek religious instruction. They confessed themselves to be Protestants and said that they had suffered persecution, perhaps by Sunnite Muslims, because of their faith. Jewett does not explain when and how these Kurds had become Protestants, but he states that the missionaries who heard them could hardly believe their confession and were perplexed as to what advice they should give.[29] Another missionary, Winchester, speaks of fifty families of Kizilbash Kurds near Sivas, called Protestants, who begged him and other missionaries to teach them the Bible, saying that they wished "to learn the way of salvation."[30] Still another missionary, Herrick, probably referring to the same Kizilbash, writes of "a visit to the Protestant Koords [Kurds]." He calls them nominal Muhammadans whose faith in the Quran and Muhammad is mere lip confession.[31] Some of these Kizilbash must have attended Bible classes and religious services conducted by missionaries; others were neophytes and proposed to be enrolled as Protestants.[32]

Another indication that the creed of the Kizilbash has Christian elements is their belief in a trinity. This trinity is composed of God, Muhammad, and Ali, although Grenard maintains that it consists of God, Jesus, and Ali.[33] Its nature is further attested to by Ishaq Efendi, author of *Kashif al-Asrar Wa Dafi al-Ashrar* (The revealer of secrets and the repeller of evildoers), who probably was the first to discuss the Hurufi sect in modern times. Ishaq Efendi reproduces the statement of a Bektashi Baba (leader) which is typical of the Bektashi concept of the trinity. The Baba says: "Son, whom they call Muhammad, was nothing but Ali, and whom they called Allah was nothing but Ali; there is no other God."[34]

According to one tradition, the Imam Ali maintained that he and Christ were one. The tradition is related by Jabir al-Jufi, the *rawi* (narrator) of the Fifth Imam, Muhammad al-Baqir. Al-Jufi reports that in a *khutba* (sermon) from the pulpit in al-Kufa, the Imam Ali proclaimed, "I am al-Masih (the Christ), who heals the blind and the leper, who created the birds and dispersed the stormclouds. I am he, and he is I . . . Isa Ibn Maryam (Jesus Son of Mary) is part of me, and I am part of him. He is the supreme Word of God. He is the witness testifying to the mysteries, and I am that to which he testifies."[35]

There is evidence that the Kizilbash believe that Jesus and Ali are one and the same person. As noted earlier, the nineteenth century American missionary Dunmore recorded that the Kizilbash, among whom he worked, accepted Jesus Christ as the Son of God under the name of Ali.[36] Another missionary, Parson, visited the village of Sanjan, which was inhabited by both Kizilbash Kurds and Armenians. He reported that some Kizilbash of this village told him that they believed Jesus Christ was the Son of God and the Savior of men, and that He was God under the name of Ali, but that they could not profess this faith openly, for fear of persecution by the Sunnite Muslims.

Parson comments that he could not decide how truthful this statement of faith by the Kizilbash was.[37] But another missionary gives additional confirmation. G. E. White, who worked among the Kurds and Turks towards the end of the nineteenth century, chiefly in the town of Marsovan, relates that the Kizilbash, whom he calls the Shia of Turkey, believed that Jesus Christ and Ali are one and the same person, or are principals who appeared in two incarnations.[38]

The same observation is made by Grenard about the Kizilbash of eastern Turkey. He writes that the Kizilbash maintain that God manifested Himself in a thousand and one forms, for if He had manifested Himself in only one form, everyone would have come to true belief. The greatest of these manifestations of God was in the person of Jesus Christ, who is the Son of God, the Word of God, and the Savior of men, interceding with the Father on behalf of sinful mankind. After Jesus, God manifested Himself in Ali; thus, God, Jesus, and Ali are one in three persons. Grenard concludes that to the Kizilbash, "Ali is the terrestrial representative of the Father, just as Jesus is that of the Son."[39] When Stephen V. R. Trowbridge asked a well-known Alawi (Kizilbash) teacher whether the Alawis believe in atonement, the teacher answered that they do in "the sense of intercession through Ali and not through Jesus, because Ali is essentially the same as Jesus."[40]

Captain L. Molyneux-Seel, who in 1911 visited the district of Dersim, inhabited predominantly by Kizilbash Kurds, wrote that all the sayyids (religious leaders descended from al-Hasan and al-Husayn, the grandchildren of the Prophet Muhammad) whom he questioned in that district, asserted that Christ and Ali were one and the same, but had appeared in this world in different forms under different names.[41] In one of his poems, the Bektashi poet Virani praises Ali as the incarnation of God and maintains that the term *al-Ali,* in the Quran 2:255—"For He is al-Ali, that is, the Most High, the Supreme in Glory,"—denotes a member of the trinity.[42] It should also be noted that a large number of the Kizilbash in Adiyaman, near the city of Urfa in southern Turkey, call Christ the "Lion of God," the same epithet the Shiites apply to Ali. Nutting, an American missionary, states that one of the hymns chanted by the Kizilbash of Adiyaman contains the line, "We have drunk the Lion's blood," which he believes denotes the atonement of Christ through His blood.[43] We shall see later that the Shabak share with the Kizilbash most of these beliefs and practices, especially the disregard of the religious duties of Islam; their holy book, the *Buyruk,* probably provides the strongest link between the two groups.

What is the relationship between the Kizilbash and the Bektashis? Hasluck reports that a son of the shaykh of the convent at Rumeli Hisar (at the time a student at the American Roberts College in Istanbul), explained to him that the difference between the Kizilbash and the Bektashis is like that between Catholics and Protestants, with the Kizilbash being "Catholics" while the true Bektashis were the "Protestants." Hasluck comments that what this student really meant was that the Bektashi practices represented a "reformation," in which they disregarded what they thought to be external rituals of their faith.[44]

An extraordinary religious practice of the Kizilbash is reported by T. Gilbert, who wrote that the Kizilbash worship a large black dog in which they see the image of the deity. To the best of our knowledge, this is the only reference to dog worship by this sect. Others who mention this type of worship apparently copied Gilbert.[45]

The common origin of the Bektashis and the Kizilbash is further demonstrated by the direct organizational connection between the Kizilbash and the Çelebis of Haji Bektash Tekke.[46] This connection probably dates back to the thirteenth century, when a kind of people's religion emerged, containing a mixture of Islamic beliefs and non-Islamic beliefs of predominantly Christian origin. As a spiritual leader, Haji Bektash played a significant role in shaping this religious movement. Slowly but surely, he was to be recognized as its pir, or spiritual head, not only by those in Kirşehir who took the name Bektashi, but also by a great number of villagers throughout Asia Minor.

By the beginning of the sixteenth century, another spiritual leader, Balim Sultan, regarded by the Bektashis as their second pir, had arisen, one who preserved the rituals and organization of the Bektashi order.[47] In time, two kinds of leaders emerged in the village of Kirşehir, the headquarters of the Bektashis: the Akhi Dedes and the Çelebis. The Çelebis claimed to be the actual descendants of Haji Bektash and the only legitimate heads of the Bektashi order. The office of the Çelebis is supposed to be hereditary, although this practice does not always prevail. The ruling Çelebis resided in a convent at Kirsehir and was recognized by the Kizilbash and the village people of Asia Minor as their spiritual head, empowered to ordain shaykhs to minister to them.[48]

In the same convent with him, however, resided his rival, the Akhi Dede, who disputed his authority. The Akhi Dede, also called the Dede Baba, claimed that Haji Bektash had no children other than his followers. For this reason the Akhi Dedes considered themselves the spiritual successors of Haji Bektash, and ruled in this capacity over the convent of Haji Bektash and over a number of the Bektashis. In light of these facts, we may deduce that the Kizilbash were those members of the village population of Asia Minor who revered Haji Bektash and recognized the authority of the Çelebis residing in the village of Kirşehir.[49] They were a nomadic, illiterate, common folk who, unlike the Bektashis, had no cohesive fraternal organization and were commonly known as Alawis. But relations between the village groups and those of the towns were not friendly. The Kizilbash and their flock were looked down upon by the Bektashis as an "inferior and somewhat degenerate group of believers."[50] The Bektashis contemptuously called them "Sufis" and accused them of lacking organization and accepting superstitious doctrines.[51]

The two groups did share common beliefs and traditions, however. They had the same religious books and hymns and were alike in venerating Ali and the Imams to the point of apotheosizing them.[52] It should be pointed out that these Bektashi village groups were the Kizilbash and followers of the Safawis of Persia. As Shiites, they had no strong allegiance to the Sunnite Ottoman sultan and government. There is strong evidence that the Ottoman Sultan Bayazid II (1481–1512), a contemporary of Shah Ismail the Safawi, was suspicious of the loyalty of the followers of the Safawis in the country. In an undated letter included in the state papers compiled by Feridun Ahmad Bey (d. 1582) in 1574, Shah Ismail wrote to Bayazid, asking him to allow the Safawi followers in Turkey to visit him at Ardabil, the headquarters of the Safawi order. The sultan, who must have been fully aware of Shah Ismail's ambition to extend both his hegemony, and the Shiite faith to the heart of the Ottoman homeland, wrote back that the intention of these pilgrims was not to perform a religious duty, but to escape Ottoman military service.[53] From this correspondence, we learn that the Safawi adherents in Turkey must have been so numerous that their absence could affect the Ottoman military service. They must also have been dedicated to the Safawis and their Shiite cause, for in the last year of the reign of Bayazid II (1512), they revolted against the sultan. This revolt was led by a certain Shah Kul (slave of the shah), whom the Turks contemptously called Shaytan Kul (slave of Satan).[54] What is significant about Shah Kul is that he was the son of Hasan Khalifa, a disciple of Shaykh Haydar Ibn Junayd, the Safawi father of Shah Ismail. In fact, the influence of the Safawis on their Kizilbash followers in Turkey was so great that Shah Kul ventured to proclaim himself the representative of Shah Ismail in Turkey.[55]

Perhaps the greatest danger presented by this devastating revolt was to Sunnite Islam, rather than to the Ottoman state. Richard Knolles blames the revolt on the craftiness of Hasan Khalifa and his son, Shah Kul, describing them as hypocritical Persians who pretended holiness to gain great prestige among the Shiite followers of the Safawis. Also, by raising the question of whether Ali was the true successor of the Prophet, they were able to challenge the authority of the Ottoman sultan and foment rebellion among the people.[56]

Although short-lived, the rebellion of Shah Kul was devastating. Starting from Tascia, the followers of Shah Kul stormed Adalia, taking it by surprise. Then they advanced to Konya, where they were reinforced by Persian cavalry and foot-soldiers, but they failed to capture the city because they did not have guns to destroy its walls. The army of Shah Kul then marched to the northeast, capturing Kutahya. Turning east, the army engaged in battle with the Ottoman army at Angora, where Shah Kul was killed and his followers were dispersed. Some of them crossed the Halys River and were pursued by the Ottoman army at Tekke. Others escaped to Persia via Sivas and Maraş, capital of the principality of Dhu al-Qadr, whose inhabitants were predominantly Shiite followers of the Safawis. Both Turks and Persians suffered heavy losses; in addition, the caravans of rich merchants were plundered.[57]

Although Shah Kul lost his life and his followers were scattered, the growing influence of the Shiite Safawis in Turkey troubled Sultan Selim I, who ascended the throne in 1512. The new sultan hated and despised the Kizilbash followers of Shah Ismail, calling them the Awbash-i Kizilbash (ruffian red heads).[58] He treated them savagely and attempted to eradicate Shiism in Turkey. An "Inquisition" was begun throughout Turkey by the sultan's grand vizir, Yunus Pasha (executed in 1517), to persecute those who professed Shiism, the religion of the Persians. Many of Shah Kul's followers were put to death after being horribly tortured. As a result, relations between the Ottomans and the Safawis worsened. The final showdown came in a battle at Chaldiran (1514), where Shah Ismail was badly defeated. It is even reported that Sultan Selim I had already killed forty-thousand followers of the Safawis during his march eastward to meet Shah Ismail at Chaldiran.[59]

In the light of these events, it is possible to speculate that the Shabak were those Turkoman Kizilbash who came to northern Iraq in the time of the Safawis, and who fled the persecution inflicted upon them by Sultan Selim I. It should be pointed out that despite the persecution inflicted by the sultan on the Shiite followers of the Safawis, a great number of them remained faithful to Shiism and the Safawi cause. This was especially true of the inhabitants of the provinces of Tekke and Dhu al-Qadr.

Founded in 1378 in the Antitaurus near Maraş and Elbistan, the province of Dhu al-Qadr covered a large territory between the Ottoman Empire and Persia, including at one time Caesarea, the center of Bektashism. Although it was conquered and annexed by Sultan Selim I in 1515, it remained a turbulent center of Shiite propaganda for more than a decade. In 1527, when the son of Selim ascended the throne as Sultan Sulayman the Magnificent, a certain Qalandaroglu (allegedly a descendant of Haji Bektash) roused a great number of dervishes to join him in revolt in the province of Dhu al-Qadr, but they were eventually defeated near Elbistan.[60] Despite the barbarous treatment of the Shiite, however, Shiism survived in Turkey throughout the sixteenth century.

In 1573, the Venetian agent in Constantinople, Marcantonio Barbaro, wrote that many people in the provinces of the Ottoman Empire professed the same faith as the Persians: that is, Shiism. Barbaro observes that the Turks did not persecute these Shiites because they feared further rebellion. He seems to be correct; even after the defeat of Dhu al-Qadr and the transportation of Shiite rebels from Turkey to the Peloponnesus (Morea) and to Macedonia and Epirus by Sultan Selim I, Shiism was still prevalent in Turkey.[61] It is probable that many other districts of the Ottoman Empire were still inhabited by extremist Shiites, the majority being Turkoman nomads. It is not unlikely that these Turkoman nomads then made their way into Iraq, where other Turkoman nomads who had served in the Safawi army had already settled, not daring to return to their homeland, Turkey, for fear of persecution by the Ottoman sultan. These Turkomans lived in northern Iraq in a closed society, without being assimilated into the rest of the population.[62] In their isolation they were able to retain many of their beliefs and rituals, leading a marginal life and avoiding further persecution by Sultan Sulayman the Magnificent, who occupied Iraq in 1538, through the use of taqiyya (dissimulation). Though this tactic enabled them to survive for centuries, the Ottoman Sultan Abd al-Hamid II in 1890 dispatched Lieutenant General Umar Wahbi Pasha to introduce reforms in Iraq and to restore the heretical Muslim groups, including the Shabak and the Yezidis (the so-called devil worshippers), to orthodox Islam, even though doing so required him to destroy the temples of the Shabak and the Yezidis.[63]

It is thus evident that the Shabak were Alawi Shiites most probably originating as Bektashi or Kizilbash village groups, recognizing the religious authority of the Çelebis in Turkey. This is confirmed by the fact that the informant of Dawud al-Chalabi told him that until about the turn of the twentieth century, the Shabak were Bektashis who contacted the Çelebi of Konya for religious instruction. Moreover, when a Shabak visited the Shiite holy shrines in Karbala, he contacted the representative of the Çelebi of Konya in that city.[64] These Shabak became Kizilbash followers of the Safawis of Persia, and, like the Bektashis', their faith was characterized by excessive veneration and ultimately deification of Ali and the Twelve Imams. The religious differences between the Shabak and the Kizilbash are so minimal that the Iraqi writer Abbas al-Azzawi states, "It is a mistake to consider the Shabak different from the Kizilbash." The chief reasons al-Azzawi gives are that the order of the Shabak is that of the ancestor of Shah Ismail, Shaykh Safi al-Din (d.1334), from whom the Safawis derive their name, and that the *Buyruk,* the sacred book of the Kizilbash, is also the sacred book of the Shabak.[65] Al-Azzawi seems correct, because the non-Shiite Muslims living among the Shabak call them Kizilbash.[66] As will be seen later, a careful study of the beliefs and religious practices of the Shabak shows that except for some minor details, they are identical with those of the Bektashis and Kizilbash. However, the most important link between them and the Kizilbash is the *Buyruk*.[67]

Although there are many striking resemblances among the beliefs and rituals of the Shabak, the Bektashis, and the Kizilbash, one who attempts to investigate the faith and rituals of these groups today is faced with many difficulties. One of these is that until very recently, illiteracy among these groups was rife, and it was almost impossible to find anyone among them who could read or write. Even now, most of their religious leaders are illiterate, receiving and transmitting tradition by word of mouth. To complicate matters, they have no religious books or writings except the *Buyruk,* and no catechism or literature to facilitate the study of their religious systems. In addition, these groups guard their beliefs with absolute secrecy and refuse to divulge them to strangers. In fact, every Iraqi writer who has attempted to study their faith and rituals expresses utter frustration at being unable to receive satisfactory information from the so-called learned men of these groups.[68] Perhaps because of the secrecy with which they protect their religious faith and rituals, the Shabak have become the target of calumny from people outside their group, who accuse them of immoral practices. Such accusations have been observed by almost every writer who has studied the Shabak or such other groups, as the Bektashis, the Alawis, the Ali Ilahis, the Nusayris, and the Mutawila, as well as the Yezidis.

Despite these difficulties, a number of religious rituals and practices among the Shabak appear to justify the belief that they have a strong connection with the Bektashis and Kizilbash, for the Shabak express the same love for the family of the Prophet, that is, Ali; his wife Fatima, the daughter of the Prophet; their two sons, al-Hasan and al-Husayn; and all the Imams. Although they deny that they deify Ali, their prayers and hymns are filled with statements of the apotheosis of Ali. Like the Bektashis and Kizilbash, they have a total disregard for the religious duties that are essential for Muslims to qualify as believers. The Shabak drink wine, which is prohibited by the Quran; they do not pray; and they neither fast during the month of Ramadan nor perform the pilgrimage to Mecca.[69]

Furthermore, like the Bektashis and Kizilbash, they celebrate a ceremonial supper during which they eat cheese, drink wine, and confess their sins privately to the *baba,* or pir (religious elder or leader), who, after receiving their confession, offers them absolution of sins. Once each year, they hold a night ceremony for public penance and confession of sins. Moreover, like the Bektashis and Kizilbash, the Shabak have a religious hierarchy in which the *talib* (seeker or neophyte) holds the lowest position and the baba or pir the highest position. They also follow an elaborate ceremony for initiation into their order.

Obviously some of these rituals have their counterparts in Christian ritual: for example, the ceremonial supper and the private and public confession of sins. These rituals show the eclectic nature of Bektashism, whose founder probably tried to win to his fold the unsophisticated Christian peasants of Asia Minor, who would naturally have been attracted to people who used and respected Christian rituals.[70]

There is evidence of contact between the Bektashis and Christianity. In Turkey, the Bektashis have taken over a number of Christian churches, saints' tombs, and sanctuaries. These usurped places of worship were made accessible to Christians in order to convince them that the saint worshipped by Muslims was a Muslim secretly converted to Christianity. Obviously, the Bektashis see nothing spiritually wrong with the sharing of a shrine or sanctuary by Muslims and Christians.[71] The magnanimity of this Bektashi tactic can only be appreciated if one realizes that for the illiterate masses of Turkey, whether Muslim or Christian, the worship of saints and the veneration of their relics and tombs has a tremendous effect on the psyche.[72] In Konya in the thirteenth century, this same tactic was used by the Mawlawi (Mevlevi) dervish order to entice Christians to join. In fact, the Bektashi practice was most effective in the cult of the saints.[73]

However, it should be pointed out in this context that, although the rituals of the Bektashis and the Shabak may seem different in form, one can detect striking resemblances in content, especially in the *gulbanks* (hymns). As we have seen earlier, this is because Bektashism is by its very nature an eclectic composite of faith and practices. Its literature is a conglomeration, taken from many Sufi orders, among them the Akhi, Abdal, Hurufis, and Kizilbash.[74] In other words, no uniform and original type of Bektashism or Kizilbashism exists against which we can measure the faith and practices of the Shabak. Nevertheless, there are sufficient resemblances among the rituals of these groups to justify the opinion that they share a common origin.

Of greatest significance is the constant repetition of the numbers three, five, seven, twelve, and forty in their rituals. These numbers symbolize the whole religious system of the Shabak and their belief in Ali and the other Imams, as well as the degrees of their religious hierarchy. Through these numbers, the Shabak offer the Imams praise and adoration and invoke their divine help. That these numbers are likewise fundamental to the beliefs of the Bektashis is manifested in the following verse by the Bektashi poet Yunus Emré:

> My shaykh is an exalted person
> He is the heart of the Three, the Seven,
> and the Forty.

With the Twelve Imams, he is a possessor
of the Divine Mystery.[75]

The Three, the Five, the Seven, and the Forty are also mentioned in the hymn which closes the ceremony of initiation into the Bektashi order.[76] The same numbers are cited by Bektashis in a prayer of grace before meals, "By the breath of the Three, the Five, the Seven, the Fourteen, and the Forty true Saints, we thank thee."[77] These numbers, which symbolize the trinity, the members of the family of the Prophet, the twelve Imams, the seven degrees of religious hierarchy, the Fourteen Infallibles, and the Forty Abdal, are continually mentioned by the Alawis of eastern Turkey in performing their rituals.[78]

5

The Ghulat's "Trinity"

Contemporary Ghulat, or extremist Shiites, especially the Bektashis, the Kizilbash or Alawis, and the Shabak, deify the Imam Ali. The Shabak and some others deny that they do so, but as shall be seen later, there is ample evidence in their prayers and rituals to demonstrate this deification of Ali. They believe in a trinity consisting of God, Muhammad, and Ali as a composite, which they claim to be one person. This trinity is symbolized by the letters of the Arabic alphabet which begin their names: *alif* for Allah (God), *mim* for Muhammad, and *ayn* for Ali. They ascribe to Ali divine attributes, such as the creation of the world and the dispensation of the livelihood of his creatures. In a word, they consider Ali to be coequal and coeternal with God. Ali is also coequal with Muhammad in this trinity. This is manifested in a Shabak hymn in which both Ali and Muhammad are addressed as God: "My heart tells me that Ali is God, and he is also Muhammad."[1] In this regard, these Ghulat differ from another Ghulat group, the Nusayris of Syria (to be discussed later), whose trinity is denoted by *ayn* for Ali, *mim* for Muhammad, and *sin* for Salman al-Farisi (one of the companions of Muhammad).[2] To the Nusayris these initial letters represent the secrets of the trinity.[3]

In Bektashi literature, Ali and Muhammad are considered to be two names of the same person. They are identified with God as the Divine Reality.

> God, Muhammad, Ali are all one God.
> The Divine Reality, Muhammad, Ali is true.
> If you ask what I have in this world,

My answer is that
Muhammad and Ali is the one God I have.
God forbid that anyone should see them
as separate from one another.
Muhammad is Ali, Ali is Muhammad, and
with God they are but one God.[4]

This trinity is associated by the Bektashis with the Christian concept that God is love (1 John 4:8), as the following poem by Kul Himmet demonstrates:

There is no God but God is love.
Muhammad the Prophet of God is love.
Ali, the Prince, Saint of God is love.
Three names, in meaning one, love—
Love is the light which Gabriel saw
In the midst of God Muhammad Ali.[5]

The sacred book of the Shabak, the *Buyruk,* contains the hadith (tradition) of Muhammad, "I am the city of knowledge, and Ali is its gate."[6] Birge cites this same tradition in his discussion of the Bektashi trinity. He states that this tradition seems to make Muhammad more important, but that the Bektashis feel that Ali is preeminent. Birge further explains that, according to the Bektashis, "the first radiance emanating from the undifferentiated Godhead is called the Light of Muhammad." This Light is manifested in Muhammad as well as in the Quran, which contains the divine revelation of this Light. This is the Light of divine religious knowledge, which can only be acquired through Ali, who is the doorway leading to it.[7] This concept harmonizes perfectly with other traditions of the Prophet Muhammad, who is reported to have said, "I and Ali are of one Light," a statement immediately following the tradition cited above in the *Buyruk.*[8]

So important is the tradition, "I am the city of knowledge and Ali is its gate," to both extremist and moderate Shiites, that it has become part of the lore woven around Muhammad and Ali to show that Ali is coequal with Muhammad in every aspect except the prophethood, which belongs exclusively to Muhammad.

Muhammad Baqir al-Majlisi (d. 1699) relates, on the authority of the eleventh Imam al-Hasan al-Askari (d. 873), that one day some Jews came to Muhammad to discuss religious matters with him. Before he answered their questions, a wandering Arab appeared and asked Muhammad a question. Muhammad told the Arab to wait until he had answered the questions of the Jews, because they had been there before him. Futhermore, he told the Arab that he suspected him of being a conniver who had planned with Jews to ask him questions in order to deceive him. The Arab became angry and told Muhammad that he did not believe that Muhammad was a prophet. If he really were a prophet, the Arab went on, then he should prove his claim with a miracle. At this point, Muhammad called Ali to him. When Ali appeared before Muhammad, the Arab asked why Muhammad had called Ali into his presence. Muhammad told the Arab that if he wanted an answer to his question, Ali would be the only one who could provide it, "I am the city of knowledge, and Ali is its gate. Whoever seeks wisdom must enter this gate." Muhammad added, "Let him who pleases to look up to Adam and other Biblical patriarchs like Seth, Enoch, Noah, Abraham, and Moses for their faith, nobleness, devotion, fidelity, and struggle against the enemies of God, and who looks to Jesus for his love, finally look to Ali."[9] This story clearly shows that Ali and Muhammad are coequal regarding divine knowledge, and that their strengths are complementary.

Al-Haqiqa al-Muhammadiyya: Muhammad, the Ultimate Reality

The concept of *al-Haqiqa al-Muhammadiyya,* or Muhammad as the Ultimate Reality and a member of the Ghulat's trinity, dates back to Muhammad's own lifetime. According to one tradition, the Prophet is reported to have said, "The first thing God created was my light."[10] This concept is also expressed in a poem composed by Muhammad's uncle, al-Abbas, praising Muhammad's feat of capturing Tabuk in northern Arabia on the Syrian Byzantine border in 630 A.D. The poem also contains a hyperbolic description of Muhammad as the "Light" which existed in the loins of Adam in Paradise and remained with him after Adam was expelled from Paradise to labor on earth. This Light was transmitted from Adam to the loins of succeeding patriarchs, from generation to generation, until it shone throughout the world in the person of Muhammad at his birth.[11] The hadith "I and Ali are of one Light" may well be based on the concept of the Light of Muhammad contained in this poem.

Al-Shahrastani (d. 1153) relates a similar tradition of Ali, who is reported to have said, "I and Ahmad [Muhammad] are of one Light. The only difference between my light and his is that one preceded the other in time."[12] Another version of this tradition of Ali is related by the Shiite Fatimi Dai (propagandist) Tahir Ibn Ibrahim al-Harithi al-Yamani (d. 1188), as follows: "I and Muhammad are of one light, which by God's command was split in two halves. To the one half God said, 'Be Muhammad,' and to the other, 'Be Ali.' "[13] It is evident from this tradition that the Prophet and Ali are coequal in this "divine Light," consequently, the office of prophethood, occupied by Muhammad, and the office of the walaya (vicegerency, mastership) occupied by Ali enjoy the same dignity and status.[14] This concept was expressed from the eighth century onward by Shiite writers, who considered the Imam Ali homologous to, if not above, the Prophet of Islam and believed him worthy of the office of the imamate (leadership) of the Muslim community, an office assigned exclusively to Muhammad, as Prophet-king, in his lifetime. The emanation of Ali and Muhammad from the same divine light is central to the Shiites' concept of the imamate, be they Ghulat (extremists) or moderate like the Ithnaasharis (Twelvers).

The divine Light passed from Ali to his descendants, the Imams, generation after generation. Behind this divine Light of the Shiites is their belief in the necessity of the existence of an Imam who will lead the community of Islam in every age. In fact, Shiites aver that he who dies without knowing the Imam of his time dies an unbeliever.[15] This Imam is not a mere khalifa (caliph), that is, a successor of the Prophet charged with leading the *umma* (community) of Islam and carrying out the principles of the Sharia (Islamic law). He is, as Shiites see him, a wali (master), a supreme Pontiff, the vicar of God on earth, and an incarnation of the Divine Light, possessing spiritual powers surpassing those of a mortal being. Unlike the caliph, the Imam combines both earthly and spiritual powers through the Divine Light, which he has received by succession from eternity. In this sense, Shiite commentators interpret Quran 24:35, "God is the light of the heavens and the earth . . . Light upon Light; God guides to His Light whom He wills," to mean that Imam after Imam (i.e., generation after generation), God will guide those whom He wills to the light of the Imams.[16] This spiritual status of the Imam is a fundamental Shiite dogma. In the words of the Imam Ayatollah Ruhallah Khomeini:

> The spiritual status of the Imam is the universal vicegerency that is sometimes mentioned by the Imams (peace be upon them). It is a vicegerency pertaining to the whole of creation, by virtue of which all the atoms in the universe humble themselves before the holder of authority. It is one of the essential beliefs of our Shi'i school, and no

> one can attain the spiritual status of the Imams, not even the Cherubim or the Prophets. In fact, according to the traditions that have been handed down to us, the Most Noble Messenger (Muhammad) and the Imams existed before the creation of the world in the form of lights situated beneath the divine throne; they were superior to other men even in the sperm from which they grew and their physical composition.[17]

Here, then, we have the concept of *al-Haqiqa al-Muhammadiyya,* Muhammad as the "ultimate reality," the "essential idea," the "Light," and the "divine spirit," which God breathed into Adam and which became the essence of the universe, the source of life for all things, and the only means of association between God and man.[18] Briefly, then, Muhammad holds the same position as the Logos in the Christian dogma. Thus, according to the Shiites and to many Sufis as well, Muhammad existed before Adam was created. A famous hadith cited in the Shabak's sacred book, the *Buyruk,* states that Muhammad existed when "Adam was still between the water and the clay," that is, before Adam was formed.[19]

It should be pointed out at this juncture that the concept of the preexistence of Muhammad or of his being "the ultimate reality," is not an orthodox Islamic dogma. There is nothing in the Quran to indicate that Muhammad was preexistent, or that he was more than mortal, subject to sin and constantly in need of God's forgiveness.[20] This concept was rather the outgrowth of the teachings of both Shiites and Sufis, who considered the prophethood of Muhammad as the culmination of the spiritual office of the prophethood, which began with Adam, was transmitted through the Hebrew prophets, and ended with Muhammad, who is considered by Muslims as the seal of the Prophets.[21] Hence came the tradition cited above, in which Muhammad said, "I was a Prophet while Adam was still between the water and the clay."

This tradition was rejected by such Muslim traditionalists as Ibn Taymiyya (d. 1328), as false and invalid.[22] Ibn Taymiyya even branded those who transmitted this tradition as "street preachers."[23] Moreover, this tradition has reached us in different versions, thus casting a shadow of suspicion on its authenticity. In one of these versions, related by Qatada of al-Basra, the Prophet Muhammad is reported to have said, "I was the first man in the creation and the last one in the Resurrection,"[24] which brings to mind the words of Christ in the Book of Revelation 22:13, "I am Alpha and Omega, the beginning and the end, the first and the last."

The concept of the preexistence of Muhammad is maintained by both Shiites and Sufis, but to the Shiites it is of special dogmatic and political importance. It is through this tradition, that they impute divine offices and preexistence to the members of the family of the Prophet (Ahl al-Bayt), that is, the Imam Ali; his wife Fatima (daughter of the Prophet); and their sons al-Hasan and al-Husayn; and all the other Imams. The Light of Muhammad, thought to be created before Adam, became incarnate in Adam and passed from Muhammad to Ali, and from Ali to his descendants, the Imams. The tenth century Shiite scholastic writer and jurist al-Kul'ayni (d. 939) cites a tradition on this subject transmitted by one of the Imams:

> The Almighty God said, "Muhammad, I have created you and Ali, a spirit without body, before I created the heavens, the earth and my Throne, and you never ceased to glorify me. Then I gathered the souls of both of you and made them one soul, and you continued to hallow and magnify me. I divided your one soul into two and the two into yet another two, and they became four souls: one became Muhammad, one became Ali, one became al-Husan, and the last became al-Husayn." Then God created Fatima from the Light and spirit without body. Then God rubbed the Imams with His right hand, and His Light shone through all of us [the Imams].[25]

This concept is further elaborated by the historian Abu al-Hasan al-Masudi who cites a tradition related by the Imam Jafar al-Sadiq (d. 765), who in turn ascribes it to Ali. The tradition corroborates many of the essential points in al-Kulayni's statements, but differs slightly from it in detail. According to this tradition, when God wished to bring the creation into being, He first formed it of tiny particles. Then God sent a ray from His splendor and scattered it in the midst of these particles, and from the union of His Light with the invisible particles, He created the Prophet Muhammad. God told Muhammad that he was the chosen one to whom He trusted His light and guidance. God also informed Muhammad that, for his sake, He would raise the heavens, cause water to flow, punish and reward, and assign men to Paradise or to the fire of Hell. God also assured Muhammad that He would designate the members of his family, that is, the Imams, as guides for the believers, and make known to them the mysteries of His divine knowledge, keeping no truth or secret from them. God further promised to make the Imams a sign to mankind, and gave them authority to admonish men of His power and remind them of His unity. Having done this, God caused mankind to recognize that He had chosen Muhammad and the members of his family, and decreed that guidance of the Muslim community should be through the divine Light of Muhammad. Thus, God established the office of the imamate (leadership of the Muslim community) through Muhammad and his family alone.

Afterwards God created Adam, a noble being, and asked the angels to prostrate themselves before him and to recognize him as their Imam. Adam was highly favored by God because he had been endowed with God's Light, but this Light was hidden under the veil of time until Muhammad was exalted in holiness. The Light descended upon and shone through the Imams, who became the Light of the heavens and earth. Because of their endowment with this divine Light, the Imams were entrusted with the salvation of mankind and became the repositories of secret sciences and the ultimate goal which people endeavored to attain. The Mahdi, the last and hidden Imam, was the final proof, the seal of the Imams, and the source of all goodness. Briefly, then, through this divine Light, the Imams became the noblest of mankind, the most exalted beings, and the manifestation of God's creation. Those who adhere to the Imam will receive blessings in this world and great support at the hour of death.[26] The Imam Jafar al-Sadiq is reported to have said that the first being God created was the Light of Muhammad; the first of His created beings was the posterity of Muhammad, and the first thing that the divine pen wrote down was, "There is no God but God, and Muhammad is His Apostle."[27]

Here, then, we have the "divine" source of the exaltation of the imamate (leadership of the Muslim community) cherished by the Shiites. This established the preexistence of Muhammad as the "divine light," and, through this Light the imamate became a divine office, to be held by the Imams, who were designated to rule through God and the divine authority God had given them. Thus, the Imams were designated to rule the Muslim community not through an earthly political process but through the divine Light of God. Here the divine right of the Imams stands supreme.

This concept of the "divine Light" was later emphasized by Shiite writers, who found in it great support for their belief that the members of the family of the Prophet were an integral part of a divine process in which Muhammad preexisted as divine Light and the Imams were the incarnation of that Light. It is no surprise that Muhammad's daughter, Fatima, was included in the divine process of the Imams. Since Muhammad left no male heir to succeed him as Imam, it was necessary that Fatima should become an integral part of his succession of emanations of

Muhammad as divine Light, an incarnation of this Light to establish divine legitimacy for the Imams. Since she could not become an Imam, she became a Light unto herself and is considered by Shiites as the only channel through which the Imams descended from the Prophet. Hence came the Shiite tradition, related by the Prophet, that God created Fatima of the same Light from which He created Muhammad and Ali.[28]

A later Shiite writer who emphasized this same concept was Baha al-Din al-Amuli (d. 1392). In discussing *al-Haqiqa al-Muhammadiyya* (Muhammad as the Ultimate Reality), al-Amuli not only considered Muhammad and the members of his family as "One Soul" and "One Reality," but also considered Ali and Muhammad as one and the same person.[29] To demonstrate the preexistence of Ali and his coeternal oneness with Muhammad, he cites the hadiths, "I and Ali are of one Light," and, in a slightly altered form, "I was a Wali [vicegerent of God] while Adam was yet between the water and the clay."

Al-Amuli associated the concept of Muhammad as the "ultimate reality" with the concept of *al-Insan al-Kamil* (the perfect man) and considered Ali the archetype of this perfect man. He did so on the basis of the speech called Khutbat al-Bayan (The manifestation speech), attributed to Ali, in which Ali said, "I am the Face and the Side of God, I am the Beginning and the End, I am the Dahir [outward] and the Batin [inward]," and claimed many other divine attributes, indicating that Ali was the perfect manifestation of God.[30] Al-Amuli preceded Abd al-Karim al-Jili (d. 1402), who devoted a whole book to the concept of the perfect man.

In his book, *Hayat al-Qulub* (Life of hearts), the Shiite writer Muhammad Baqir al-Majlisi (d. 1699) relates several hadiths that demonstrate the simultaneous eternal creation of Muhammad with Ali, Fatima, and their two sons, al-Hasan and al-Husayn. According to one of these traditions, the Prophet is reported to have said that God created him, Ali, Fatima, al-Hasan and al-Husayn before He created Adam and did so before there were heavens and earth, darkness and light, sun and moon, Paradise and Hell. Then God uttered a word from which He formed Light. With another word he created spirit. Then God tempered the spirit with the Light and created Muhammad, Ali, Fatima, al-Hasan, and al-Husayn. When God willed the universe into existence, He expanded Muhammad's Light, and from that Light He created the empyrean. Muhammad is more excellent than the empyrean, because the latter was formed from his Light. The hadith continues that God then expanded the Light of his "brother," Ali, and from it He formed the angels. Thus, Ali became more excellent than the angels. Then God expanded the Light of the Prophet's daughter, Fatima, and from it He created the heavens and the earth, and Fatima became more excellent than both the heavens and the earth. Afterwards, God expanded the Light of the Prophet's grandson, al-Hasan, and from it He fashioned the sun and the moon. From the Light of Muhammad's other grandson, al-Husayn, He formed Paradise and the black-eyed *huris* (nymphs), and al-Hasan and al-Husayn became more exalted than all that God had created from their Lights.[31]

Another tradition, related by al-Khasibi (d. 957), reveals even more clearly the transmission of the divine Light through Adam to Muhammad and Ali and the association of Muhammad and Ali as one eternal Light. According to this tradition, Muhammad is reported to have said that he and Ali were created of one Light, and that they began praising God while standing on the right side of the empyrean, two thousand years before Adam was created. When God created Adam, he fixed the Light in his loins, and both Muhammad and Ali were with him in Paradise. They were also with Noah in the Ark, and with Abraham when he was cast into the fire by Nimrud. From age to age God transmitted this Light from Adam's loins to undefiled wombs, until Muhammad and Ali reached the loins of Abd al-Muttalib, their grandfather. In Abd al-Muttalib, the Light was divided into two portions; one rested in the loins of his son, Abd Allah, who begat Muhammad, and the other rested with Abu Talib, who begat Ali.[32]

From what has been said so far, it is obvious that both Shiites and Sufis maintain that Muhammad is the divine Light and that his descendants, the Imams, are celestial lights emanating from him. According to al-Kulayni and later Shiites like al-Hafiz Rajab al-Bursi (d. 1411) and al-Majlisi, this Light was manifested in Ali and his family. In essence, Muhammad and the members of his family are inseparable. The divine origin bestowed on him was bestowed on them as well. It is only in this sense that we can understand the tradition, "I and Ali are of one Light."[33] To this tradition the Shiite writer al-Hajj Masum Ali al-Shirazi (d. 1926) adds another, in which Ali says, "I am Adam, Noah, Abraham, Moses and Jesus, assuming different forms, however I will. He who has seen me has seen them all."[34] This echoes the saying of Christ, "He that has seen me has seen the Father." It puts Ali in the place of the Logos, a position such as al-Husayn Ibn Mansur al-Hallaj (d. 922), Ibn Arabi (d. 1240), and Abd al-Karim al-Jili (d. 1402) later attributed to Muhammad, and it identifies him with the highest type of humanity, the perfect man.[35] Al-Hallaj is probably the first Sufi to speak of an Islamic Logos and to attribute divinity and preexistence to Muhammad. He maintains that Muhammad existed before the creation of the world, and that he was known before substance and accident, and that his name was eternal before the Pen, that is, before God recorded the Quran with His divine pen. In fact, to al-Hallaj, Muhammad was the "infinite Light," more brilliant and more eternal than the pen.[36]

Furthermore, both Shiites and Sufis utilized the Biblical passage, "God created man in His own image," (Genesis 1:27) which became fundamental to their philosophy. This concept was utilized by al-Hallaj, who said, "God, who in essence, is love, created man after His own image, to the end that His creature, loving Him alone, may suffer a spiritual transformation, may find the divine image in himself, and may thus attain to union with the divine will and nature."[37]

Such transformation keeps occurring until man's humanity vanishes and he becomes "incarnated through the spirit of God, of which Jesus was the Son of Mary."[38] What al-Hallaj means is that God manifested Himself in Adam as He did in Jesus. Like Jesus, Adam combined in himself both natures, the divine and the human. This obviously Christian concept was later elaborated by such theosophists as Ibn Arabi and al-Jili, who replaced Adam with Muhammad, the Prophet of Islam, maintaining (as has been said earlier) that Muhammad's existence preceded that of Adam. According to Ibn Arabi, when God wanted to create the spirits to operate the visible (physical) world, He created first the "dispensational spirit," Muhammad. Then He created the spirits which existed in the invisible world. Having done this, God proclaimed to Muhammad the good news that he was a Prophet before all the prophets, who were only his deputies and harbingers of his advent. In essence, according to Ibn Arabi, Muhammad was the "dispensational spirit" whom God created before time and who became the source of all spirits, that is, the spirit of the whole creation.[39] It is in this sense that Ibn Arabi considers Muhammad the seal of the Prophets, the perfect man, and "the Spirit of which all prophetic and apostolic missions are but a manifestation."[40]

As the seal of the Prophets, Muhammad is the source from whom all the prophets derive their divine message; although his is physically and temporally the last manifestation, yet it has always existed. Muhammad's mission is eternal, existing when "Adam was still between the water and the clay;" other prophets began their mission only when God in time chose them and sent them to carry out their mission. In essence, to Ibn Arabi, Muhammad becomes the universal Logos, whose activities and perfection are manifested in other prophets. He symbolizes the wholeness of divine reality. He is the *nous* (first intellect) and the *Barzakh* (intermediary between God and the phenomenal world). He is perfect in every respect, as his name Ahmad (the praised one) indicates. He is the wisdom of singularity because he is the perfect creation. He is the clearest evidence of God, and God has given him the totality of the divine word. Briefly, then, he is the intermediary between the eternal and the temporal, between God and the cosmos.[41] In light of these supernatural characteristics attributed to Muhammad, we may deduce that Ibn Arabi has supplanted Jesus Christ with Muhammad.

Another Sufi, Abd al-Karim al-Jili, considers Muhammad the First Intellect, from whose essence God created the angel Gabriel as well as the whole universe. To al-Jili, "the essence of Muhammad is the *dhat* [essence] of God." In this sense al-Jili portrays Muhammad as the absolutely perfect man and the archetype of all created beings.[42] This, of course, is a concept of the Islamic Logos, which brings Muhammad in some respects close to the Logos of the Fourth Gospel and of the Pauline Epistles.[43] We have already seen this concept with al-Hallaj and Ibn Arabi. Reynold Nicholson, however, sees a sharp difference between this Islamic concept of the Logos and that of the Fourth Gospel. He states:

> The Fatherhood of God, the Incarnation, and the Atonement suggest an infinitely rich and sympathetic personality, whereas the Muhammadan Logos tends to identify itself with the active principle of revelation in the Divine essence. Muhammad is loved and adored as the perfect image or copy of God: "He that has seen me has seen Allah," says the Tradition (borrowed from St. John 14:9). Except that he is not quite co-equal and co-eternal with his Maker, there can be no limit to glorification of the Perfect Man.[44]

We may add here that the concept of the Logos has no foundation in the Quran or tradition. It is totally alien to the letter and spirit of Islam.

There is no evidence that al-Jili had read the Nicene Creed or knew about the Homousion, or the controversy connected with it. But to all intents and purposes, al-Jili, like al-Hallaj and Ibn Arabi, attributes to Muhammad the function of the Logos, which, according to Christian dogma, is one being with the Father and His perfect image, through whom and for whom God created the whole world. At the very least, we can detect in the ideas of al-Hallaj, Ibn Arabi, and al-Jili traces of Gnostic and Neo-Platonic philosophies.[45]

Some traditions attributed to Muhammad show that he was aware of his preexistence as the "primal element." According to these traditions, Muhammad is reported to have said, "The first thing which God created was my soul," and, "My soul was the Primal Element."[46] This primal element, as E. H. Palmer has shown, combines both the saintly and prophetic offices held by Muhammad. Sufis maintain that Muhammad was a primal saint who existed before all saints and prophets. This view would be in harmony with the tradition, cited earlier, quoting Muhammad as saying, "I was a Prophet while Adam was still between the water and the clay."[47] Ibn Arabi particularly elaborates on the sainthood, or state of sanctity predicated on the concept of the Light of Muhammad, which he considers a manifestation of the prophethood of Muhammad. To him Muhammad is not only a prophet but also a saint, and his sainthood is all-inclusive, universal, and without end. This sainthood is directly associated with the divine Truth; that is, God. Ibn Arabi avers both that Muhammad is the seal of the Prophets, after whom no prophet or apostle will ever be commissioned by God to deliver divine law, and that no community will exist after that of the Muslims to receive such a law. Yet Ibn Arabi also adds that sainthood transcends prophecy and, by its very nature as a theophany of God, is continuous and extends to other members of the Muslim community as *awliya* (saints), while prophethood is the exclusive function of Muhammad. Ibn Arabi sees sainthood as one of the divine names of God. He maintains that God Himself is not called "prophet" or "apostle," but calls himself "friend," the literal meaning of *wali* (saint). Ibn Arabi quotes the passages from the Quran, "God is the friend of those who believe," and "He is the friend of the Praiseworthy," to support his view.[48]

In this sense, Ibn Arabi could claim that he himself was the seal of Muhammadan Sainthood.[49] But let us not forget that, although to Ibn Arabi sainthood is universal and continuous and the Muslim *abd* (servant) can become the "friend" or wali of God, that same servant could not equal Muhammad in his office as a "Prophet-Saint." For to Ibn Arabi, Muhammad is the eternal Light from which God created the saints. And although these saints are the theophany of the Light of Muhammad, yet they stand second to the majesty of him [Muhammad] "whom the Truth that is God has chosen and made the repository of His majesty and the executor of His command."[50] Thus, in a fundamental sense, Muhammad becomes the universal Logos, whose activities and perfection are manifested in other prophets. We have recourse here also to the concept of *al-Haqiqa al-Muhammadaiyya,* on which Ibn Arabi built the principle of the Light of Muhammad, which became the central point of his theosophic teaching. This concept, to be sure, was not original with Ibn Arabi, but was developed earlier by Shiite writers, who predicated it on the principle of the Light of Muhammad.[51]

In a fundamental sense, Ibn Arabi is no different from the Shiites who maintain that the sainthood is superior to the prophethood, because prophethood indicates only an external transmission of God's revelation, while the sainthood comprehends the very essence of this revelation.[52]

Shiite writers maintain that Muhammad was the first creation of God, but that at the same time God created the Imams, who are His descendants and heirs. Thus, the divine dispensation of God extends to these Imams, and through them to the whole Shiite community.[53] In this regard, one is tempted to observe that such a belief was fashioned after the Christian concept of the church, the community of believers, as the body of Christ.

Reynold Nicholson observes that, according to this belief, the eternal existence of Muhammad appeared in the person of Ali and other members of Muhammad's family, the Imams.[54] In essence, the Shiites maintain that Muhammad was the Prophet par excellence, and that his prophethood was the first component of the primal element, while the Imams, especially the last one, the Mahdi, who will reappear at the end of time, are the true exponents of the saintly office constituting the second component of the primal element.[55]

However, there is a significant difference between the Shiites' and the Sufis' understanding of the terms *walaya* (sainthood) and *wali* (saint), when applied to Ali and the Imams. The Shiites maintain that as one who holds the walaya Ali is more than a saint, or friend of God, which the term *wali* means in Arabic. As a member of Ahl al-Bayt (the family of the Prophet), whom God (according to Quran 33:33) has sanctified, Ali is not only infallible, a saint, and the friend of God, but also a vicar, deputy, vicegerent, and heir of the Prophet in ruling the Muslim community, which is God's community. This may be deduced from the Imam Ali himself, who, in one of his speeches, stated that the members of Al Muhammad (the family of Muhammad) are so preeminent that no one in the whole community of Islam can measure up to them. They are, he says, "the foundation and straight path of religion and the exemplaries of the believers. They possess the right of the Wilaya or Walaya and the Wasiyya [testamentary trust], and of being heirs [to the Prophet]."[56]

Furthermore, Ali is the "Master" of the Muslim community, whom the Prophet had designated to lead after him. It is in this sense that Ali is called *wali* or *mawla*. It is of great significance that, according to the Shiites, Muhammad appointed Ali as his successor not by his own command, but by divine command. This is made clear by the fifth Imam, al-Baqir, who is reported to have said that obedience to Ali is as essential a religious duty as obedience to the Prophet. Al-Baqir further states that, just as the Prophet is the only gate leading to God, so Ali, the

Commander of the Faithful, is the same gate leading to God.[57] Al-Bursi explains that *walaya* means possession, governance, mastery, and deputization. He says that the phrase "Malik Yawm al-Din" in Quran 1:4 means "the possessor or master of the Day of Judgment," who is no other than the Almighty God. But, al-Bursi continues, since Ali was appointed by God as the master of His Prophet Muhammad, Ali becomes the possessor and master of the Day of Judgment as God's deputy. Thus, Ali's mastery or vicegerency becomes indispensable, uncircumscribed, and eternal. Al-Bursi concludes that anyone who rejects the walaya of Ali—his specific authority to rule the Muslim community in this life and the life to come—is an infidel.[58] Indeed, the walaya of Ali was, and still is, the cornerstone of Shiite belief, affirmed by Shiite writers and *ulama* (learned religious men).

A modern Shiite writer, Muhammad Baqir al-Sadr (d. 1980), wrote a penetrating treatise on this subject entitled *Bahth Hawl al-Walaya* (A treatise on the walaya). After presenting several arguments showing that it was incredible and illogical that a religious and political leader like the Prophet Muhammad should leave the Muslim community without a successor to continue his guidance of that community, al-Sadr avers that the Prophet had trained and prepared Ali to be his wali. Al-Sadr maintains that the Prophet chose Ali for this task not by his own will, but by God's command, the very God who had sanctified and purified Ahl al-Bayt (the family of the prophet) and by His providence entrusted the members of this family to rule his community.[59] Al-Sadr is, in fact, reiterating and reaffirming an ancient belief of the Shiites, that the walaya did not originate on earth, but in heaven.[60] In other words, the walaya of Ali is ordained by God.

According to another contemporary Shiite, Murtaza Mutahhari (d. 1979), the walaya is the divine authority by which the wali or the Imam, who holds it, is entrusted with the ruling of the Muslim community. Mutahhari explains that from the Shiite point of view, the walaya has three natures: it is political, pertaining to the leadership of the Muslim community; it is religious, falling to the person who possesses the divine knowledge needed to govern that community according to the laws of the Quran; and finally, it is ideological, in the sense that the leadership of the Muslim community is essential to the well-being and operation of that community, and that it is imperative that in every age there should be a perfect man who possesses supernatural influence over the world and has control of the hearts and souls of all Muslims. In this sense, Mutahhari believes that the walaya and the imamate are inseparable, and that Ali and his descendants, the Imams, are the only Muslims who possess the qualities required to be the exclusive rulers of the Muslim community.[61]

As Ali is inseparable from the divine Light, held by Shiites and Sufis to be Muhammad, in accordance with the tradition, "I and Ali are of one Light," so too is he inseparable from Muhammad's "Divine Knowledge," as is clear from the tradition, "I am the city of knowledge, and Ali is its gate." Both Shiites and Sufis aver that this tradition means that Ali not only received divine knowledge from Muhammad, but also possessed a great knowledge of the religious sciences of Islam. In other words, Ali had the knowledge of every outward and inward aspect of these sciences, especially the science of expounding the Quran, which is the source of these sciences.[62] Shiites and Sufis, maintain, moreover, that of all the companions of Muhammad, Ali was the only one who possessed exclusively the two distinguished qualities of *iman* (faith) and *ilm* (knowledge). This is supported by the tradition related by al-Tabarsi, in which Ali is reported to have said, "Ask me before you lose me. For by Him who created mankind and the soul of man, if you ask about any verse [of the Quran], whether revealed at Mecca or Medina, and the reason for its revelation, I will tell you about it."[63] This is further affirmed by the Imam Jafar al-Sadiq, who is reported to have said, "Ali is the Sirat [Straight Path of God] whom God entrusted with the knowledge of everything in heaven and earth. He is God's Wali over the people and the Trustee of His Truth."[64]

Abu Nasr al-Sarraj al-Tusi (d. 988) relates a tradition ascribed to Ali, who said that the Prophet had taught him seventy disciplines of knowledge which He had taught no one else.[65] From this tradition we may deduce that, although al-Sarraj distinguished between the knowledge of Muhammad and that of Ali, he seems to accord Ali a position no other companion of the Prophet Muhammad ever attained. Another writer, Baha al-Din al-Amuli (d. 1392), states that of all the saints, Ali is the only one who possessed *al-Ulum al-Laduniyya* (divine sciences) and *al-Haqa'iq al-Ilahiyya* (divine truths).[66] Be that as it may, it is certain that the Sufis and Shiites agree that Ali's knowledge of the inward and outward aspects of the religious sciences derives from his spiritual compatiblity with the Prophet of Islam.

Some Sufis, including Abu al-Qasim al-Junayd (d. 910), emphasize the importance of Ali's knowledge and its effect on the Sufis' teaching, but assert that such knowledge would have profited them much more if it had not been for the fact that Ali was constantly engaged in warfare.[67] The reason for this emphasis is their belief that the source of Ali's knowledge was not any personal endeavor on his part, but "divine providence." In this sense, al-Junayd equates Ali with the Muslim mythological character, the Khidr (more correctly, al-Khadir), who is said to have received divine knowledge inspired directly by God through mystical intuition.

Al-Junayd interprets Quran 18:65, "One of our servants . . . whom We had endowed with knowledge of the Quran," to mean that God had bestowed His knowledge on his servant, Ali. In fact, al-Junayd is attempting to establish that Ali's engagement in warfare prevented him from providing a wealth of religious interpretation and various kinds of knowledge which otherwise would have profited the Sufis, because the essence of Ali's knowledge was identical with that of the Sufis. Thus, Ali is considered the "head of the Sufis," although his leadership over them was not total.[68] Later Sufis, like the mystical poet Ibn al-Farid (d. 1235) in the celebrated ode "al-Ta'iyya al-Kubra," attributed to Ali the ability, through inward or esoteric religious knowledge, to interpret passages of the Quran and other spiritual problems because of the testamentary trust that Muhammad had bequeathed to him.[69] Other Sufis, such as Jalal al-Din Rumi (d. 1273), consider Ali as the outward and inward mystery of the whole world.[70] According to Reynold Nicholson, the Sufis intend that "they are the legitimate heirs and true interpreters of the esoteric teaching of the Prophet."[71]

But why should the mystic Sufis utilize an exclusively Shiite concept (in this case that of the testamentary trust giving Ali the authority to interpret problematic passages in the Quran) to confirm the belief that Ali is the spiritual heir and executor of the testamentary trust of the Prophet of Islam? Goldziher answers that although the Sunnites, including their own Sufis, deny both that Ali was the Imam (head) of Islamic Sufism, par excellence, and that the Prophet neither concealed any secret from his community nor imparted the inward knowledge of the Quran to anyone, yet the Sunnite Sufis sought to give the interpretation of the inward knowledge of the Quran a "Sunnite touch" from their overall Islamic point of view.[72]

6

The Miraculous Attributes of Ali

THE GHULAT or extremist Shiites attribute to Ali miracles of which only the divine Being is capable. To them Ali was a miraculous person from childhood. In common with the mainstream Twelver Shiites, these sects ascribe to Ali miracles ranging from the superhuman to the divine. In fact, they consider the very birth of Ali a miracle.

A modern Shiite writer, Sayyid Muhammad Kazim al-Qazwini, describes the miracle of Ali's birth as follows. Ali's mother, Fatima bint Asad, wanted Ali to be born in the holy shrine of the Kaba. When the time came to deliver him, she went to the Kaba, but found the door locked. Fatima implored God to give her an easy delivery. Instantly, the wall of the Kaba split; Fatima entered, sat on a red slab, and delivered Ali without suffering any of the usual throes of labor. Fatima's husband, Abu Talib, and some of his friends rushed to the Kaba intending to open the door and let in some women to help Fatima deliver. The door would not open, however, and they realized that this was a sign from God that Fatima should deliver her child unaided by women. After three days the door opened. Fatima came out carrying a newborn child as beautiful as the moon: Ali.

Muhammad, who had not yet received God's revelation to preach Islam, went to see the newborn child. As he entered the house, the baby Ali smiled broadly and spoke, reciting from Quran 23:1–10, where God says, "Successful are those believers who humble themselves in their prayers . . . and they will be the heirs." Muhammad turned to Ali and said, "Surely the believers have become successful through you." This was Ali's first miracle: speaking in the cradle like Jesus and, through divine revelation, reciting a portion of the Quran, even though God had not yet chosen Muhammad as His Messenger. Ali had the knowledge that the Quran existed eternally with God.[1]

According to Shiite tradition, the miraculous birth of Ali was foretold by a Christian monk, al-Mutharram Ibn Ruayb Ibn al-Shayqanam. This monk, it is reported, had worshipped God for 190 years without asking a single favor of him. One day he asked God to show him one of his vicegerents, and, in answer to his prayer, God sent him to Abu Talib. When the monk saw Abu Talib, he kissed him and thanked God, who had finally answered his request to see one of God's vicegerents before his death. Surprised by the monk's behavior, Abu Talib asked him for an explanation. The monk answered that God had revealed to him that Abu Talib would have a child named Ali who would be the vicegerent of the Prophet Muhammad and the Imam of pious men. Abu Talib said he would not believe this unless he was given a sign supporting the monk's claim. Abu Talib asked for a basket full of the fruits of Paradise. The monk began to pray and, behold, a basket laden with the fruits of Paradise suddenly appeared! Overcome with joy, Abu Talib picked a pomegranate from the basket; it instantly changed to semen in his loins. That night his wife, Fatima bint Asad, conceived a child: Ali. No sooner was Ali conceived, however, than the whole earth began to shake. Frightened, the people of the tribe of Quraysh rushed to the top of Mount Qubays near Mecca, asking their gods to stop the earthquake. But the gods of Quraysh could not stop the earthquake, and one after another, they began to succumb to the glory and power of the fetus that had been formed in the womb of Fatima bint Asad.

Seeing this miracle, Abu Talib told the people of Quraysh that if they did not believe in the imamate of of one whose conception had caused the whole earth to shake, they would be lost. They listened and believed, and their belief made Abu Talib cry for joy. When Fatima bint Asad was ready to deliver Ali, four women dressed in white silk went to her to alleviate her throes in childbirth. When Ali was born, he shone like the bright sun. He stood up and then prostrated himself on the ground, saying, "I bear witness that there is no God but Allah, that Muhammad is His Prophet, and I am His vicegerent. I am the Commander of the Faithful and the Seal of the Vicegerents of God, as Muhammad is the Seal of His Prophets." The four women took the babe Ali, and each in turn placed him on her lap. One of the women was Eve, and another was Maryam bint Imran (the Virgin Mary), mother of Isa (Jesus). When Mary placed the babe Ali on her lap, he looked at her saying, "Truly, this is the Virgin Mary and Jesus is my uncle." The other two women were the mother of Moses, Ibn Imran, and Asiya bint Muzahim.

When the monk al-Mutharram saw and heard all these things, he wept and worshipped God. Then he stretched out on his bed and died. For three days, Abu Talib waited in vain to see whether he would return to life. While he waited, a *hitan* (big fish) emerged and told Abu Talib that the monk was dead, and that he should go to Mecca to take care of his newly born son.[2]

In his *Kitab al-Irshad* (Book of Guidance), al-Shaykh al-Mufid (d. 1022) devotes an entire chapter to the various miracles of the Commander of the Faithful, Ali. One of these miracles, when Ali was a child of seven, was the perfection of his intellect and of his ability to acknowledge God and His apostle Muhammad when the latter invited him to profess Islam. This, al-Mufid states, is an "illustrious sign from God which transcends normal human behavior."[3] It indicates that Ali was chosen by God as His proof to mankind and that he was nurtured by God to succeed Muhammad as the sole Imam of the Muslim community. In this context, al-Mufid likens Ali to Jesus Christ—who, according to Quran 19:21, became while yet a child a sign to the people of God's mercy—and to John the Baptist—who, according to Quran 19:12, was given wisdom while still a boy. Al-Mufid also discusses such other miraculous gifts of Ali as his military prowess, and his knowledge of the secrets of the heart, and of the future.[4] Al-Mufid describes not only Ali's gifts, but also his miraculous feats: how he pulled away the gate of the fortress of Khaybar, which many men together had been unable to move; how he moved the rock and found water under it; how he defeated a group of unbelieving jinn who had plotted to kill Muhammad and his men on their march against the Jewish tribe of the Banu al-Mustaliq; and how he spoke to the fish and caused the waters of the Euphrates to recede at his command, to save the people of al-Kufa from drowning. When on this last occasion, the waters of the Euphrates abated by his order and the fish of the bottom appeared, the people who had watched Ali were amazed that all the fish greeted him with the title, Commander of the Faithful—all, that is, except the eels and the scaleless fish, which kept silent. When the people asked why these fish did not greet him, Ali answered that God had given those fish that were ritually pure the ability to speak to him, but had kept the impure fish silent. Consequently, eels and scaleless fish are forbidden food to the Shiites. Finally, al-Mufid relates that on two occasions, Ali moved the sun from west to east.[5]

Birge relates a story about young Ali taken from the *Tariqatnama* (Book of the way), attributed to Eşrefoglu Rumi, a popular Bektashi poet. A giant once caught a man behind Mount Qaf, a mythological mountain believed by Muslims to surround the terrestrial globe. But before the giant could devour his victim, a boy in the form of a lion appeared and bound the giant's hands around his neck with palm leaves. The giant appealed to all the prophets, beginning with Adam, for his release, but they were unable to release him. Finally, he appealed to Muhammad, who asked the giant whether he could recognize the boy who had bound him. When the giant answered that he could, Muhammad had Ali and his companions file before the giant so that he could pick out his captor. The giant trembled when he saw Ali and, pointing to him, said that this was the one who had bound him. Ali confessed to the Prophet Muhammad that he had bound the giant, but refused to release him until the giant professed Islam. When the giant declared his conversion to Islam, Ali, with a gesture of his finger, untied the giant and set him free.[6]

An almost identical story was related in person by a member of the Shabak community to the Iraqi writer Abd al-Munim al-Ghulami. According to this story, the Imam Ali existed before Adam and, at one time, became incensed against an *ifrit* of the jinn (celestial beings who acted as intermediaries between angels and men) for his *kufr* (unbelief) and bound the ifrit in chains. When God created Adam, the ifrit appealed to Adam for his release, but Adam could not free him. The ifrit then appealed to Noah and to all the succeeding prophets to release him, but they could not do so either. Finally, the Prophet Muhammad took the ifrit to young Ali. The ifrit pointed to Ali and shouted that this was the one who had bound him in chains. Muhammad implored Ali to release the ifrit and Ali agreed, on the condition that the ifrit should confess Islam. When the ifrit became a Muslim, Ali instantly shattered the iron chains and set him free.[7]

One of the greatest miraculous gifts the Shabak attribute to Ali is his power to cause the clouds to move. They also believe that thunder is his voice, and lightning the radiance of his whip. Therefore, whenever thunder and lightning appear, the Shabak shout, "Jan, Ali Jan."[8] The belief that Ali voices his power through thunder is common. Such beliefs are not the invention of the shabak; they are common among the Shiites of Persia,[9] dating back to the early centuries of Islam, when the highly controversial Abd Allah Ibn Saba, a Jewish convert to Islam and a contemporary of Ali, first ascribed divinity to him. Ibn Saba preached that Ali would one day return in the clouds, with thunder as his voice, and lightning as the radiance of his whip. Ali resented the followers of Ibn Saba, who came to be known as Sabaiyya, and their belief in his deity; he had them cast into fire, banishing Ibn Saba to Ctesiphon (al-Madain) in Iraq. Ibn Saba and his followers never ceased to deify Ali, however. When Ali was assassinated in 661, they did not acknowledge his death, but preached that he would return one day in the clouds.[10]

Bayan Ibn Siman al-Nahdi (also called al-Tamimi), who was burned to death in 737 for his extreme beliefs, was the founder of an extremist Shiite sect called, after him, the Bayaniyya. He, like Ibn Saba, preached the apotheosis of Ali. To support this deification of Ali, he interpreted Quran 2:209, "Are they waiting for God, to come down to them in the shadow of a cloud?" to mean that God is Ali, and that thunder is his voice, and lightning his smile.

One ancient extremist Shiite sect, the Alyaiyya (named after Alya Ibn Dhira al-Dawsi), disparaged the Prophet Muhammad. This sect was therefore also called Dhamiyya (from the Arabic verb *dhamma,* "to disparage").[11] The Dhamiyya maintain that Ali is God and that he sent Muhammad to proclaim His divine message to mankind, but that Muhammad instead claimed the prophethood for himself.[12] The Shabak believe that God chose Ali to be His messenger, but that the angel Gabriel delivered the message to Muhammad instead of to Ali. For this reason that Shabak call Gabriel the "betrayer of the Faithful One," that is, Ali.[13] This belief is also held by other Shiite sects.[14]

Other extremist Shiites believe that God originally sent Muhammad, not the angel Gabriel, to deliver His divine message to Ali, but that Muhammad, seduced by pride and ambition, claimed the prophethood for himself. Even many Shiites who do not deify Ali, do not deny that he could have been divine. There is a common saying in Persia: "Though I do not believe Ali to be God, I believe that he is not far from being so."[15] Addressing Ali, a Persian poet said, "If I call you God, that would be a sacrilege, but if I give you another name, that would be an alteration of your nature."[16] Some Ali Ilahis of Persia deify Ali; others maintain that, although Ali is not God, yet he is not separate from God and not different from Him.[17] On the surface, this view may seem compatible with the faith of those Shiites who do not deify Ali, but in fact it indicates that the Ali Ilahis consider Ali to be as divine as God.

According to the Shabak, the miraculous attributes of Ali extend to his sword, known as *Dhu al-Faqar* (that which has miraculous piercing power). This Shiite belief is not new and may date back to a very early period of Islamic history. According to a tradition related by the tenth-century Shiite writer al-Kulayni, Ali's sword, sheathed in a silver scabbard, was brought down from heaven by the angel Gabriel and passed from one person to another until finally it came into the possession of the eighth Imam, Ali al-Rida (d. 818).[18] Earlier, in 624, this sword was captured by the followers of Muhammad from its owner, al-Asi Ibn

Munabbih, at the skirmish of Badr and was presented by the Prophet Muhammad to Ali in gratitude for his heroic fight for the cause of Islam against the tribe of the Quraysh, unbelievers. The Shabak also believe that Ali's sword descended from heaven, and that Ali was miraculously able to shorten or lengthen it according to need.[19] In 1911, Captain L. Molyneux-Seel traveled through the district of Dersim in the upper Euphrates valley, where the majority of the inhabitants are Shiite Kizilbash. He reports seeing a rock split in two, the upper portion bearing a striking resemblance to a head surmounted by a fez, which the Kizilbash believe was the head of a hated Turk split by the mighty sword of Ali.[20] In a splendid ode, the celebrated Sufi Jalal al-Din Rumi ascribed divine attributes to this sword of Ali and portrayed it as the incarnation of the *Haqq* (Truth): that is, God. Here is the ode, as translated by Reynold Nicholson:

> Every moment the robber Beauty rises in a different shape, ravishes the soul, and disappears.
> Every instant that Loved One assumes a new garment, now of eld, now of youth.
> Now He plunged into the heart of the substance of the potter's clay-the Spirit plunged, like a diver.
> Anon He rose from the depths of mud that is moulded and baked, then He appeared in the world.
> He became Abraham and appeared in the midst of the fire, which turned to roses for His sake.
> For a while He was roaming on the earth to pleasure Himself,
> Then He became Jesus and ascended to the dome of Heaven and began to glorify God.
> In brief, it was He that was coming and going in every generation thou hast seen,
> Until at last He appeared in the form of an Arab and gained the empire of the world.
> What is it that is transferred? What is transmigration in reality? The lovely winner of hearts
> Became a sword and appeared in the hand of Ali and became the Slayer of the time.
> No! no! for 'twas even He that was crying in human shape, "Ana 'l-Haqq.[21]

Thus, Ali's sword was transformed from the corporeal into the incorporeal, becoming the essence of divine truth, to corroborate the Shiite belief in the spiritual supremacy of Ali as the vicegerent of God.

The anonymous author of the enigmatic *Umm al-Kitab* (Mother of the book), an eighth-century proto-Ismaili source, attributes to the fifth Shiite Imam, Muhammad al-Baqir, the interpretation of many Shiite dogmas. The work is written in interlocutory form: three disciples question al-Baqir on different religious subjects, and al-Baqir answers. In one of the answers, al-Baqir explains the mystical meaning of the sword of Ali and the metamorphosis by which it has become not only a Shiite spiritual symbol, but the epitome of Islamic beliefs. Al-Baqir explains that Ali's sword is an incorporeal spirit and everlasting. It is as serene and luminous as the bodies of angels. It represents not only faithfulness, but also the Lord of the faithful. It has a sacred function among the faithful, standing as a compassionate guardian of the downtrodden, the needy, and the poor. It is the protector of solid justice. It is resolute; it is deep as the sea; and it is the supreme spirit. It is subtle and discreet, sublime and knowledgeable. Al-Baqir goes on to say that Islam is constituted of all these sublime principles. The sword of Ali epitomizes all that is worthy, including the spirit of Islam. This characterization of Ali's sword accords with what the Prophets have said: that all things are accomplished by order of God, and nothing can be done without His command.[22] Thus, the spiritual power of Ali's sword was established by God's command and became part of His power foretold by the Prophets of old. It epitomizes the spirit of "true" Islam, as does the mastership of Ali.

Some Shiite sources relate that in warfare Ali, while mounting his horse, could cut off heads with great ease and even slice the bodies of his opponents in two; one half remaining on the horse's back, the other rolling to the ground. Sometimes Ali waited for his enemies to attack and then extended his arm, decapitating with his sword as many as thirty-three attackers in one blow.[23] In the campaign against the Khaybar, a Jewish tribe, Ali pulled down the gate of the fortress of Khaybar, called al-Qamus. This gate was made of solid rock in the shape of a millstone with a handle in the middle, and was eighteen cubits in diameter. Ali held the gate in his hand and continued fighting until God offered him victory. Then he threw it to the ground. Forty strong men who were eyewitnesses to this incident tried to move the gate, but could not. Some say it took seventy men to return the gate to its original position. Others say that Ali used the gate of the fortress as a buckle for his belt.[24] Abu Jafar Muhammad al-Tabarsi, a thirteenth-century Shiite writer, relates in his book, *Bisharat al-Mustafa li Shi'at al-al-Murtada* (the annunciation of the Chosen One, Muhammad, to the partisans of the one with whom God is pleased—Ali), that Ali wrote to Sahl Ibn Hanif, "By Allah! I have pulled out the gate of the Khaybar fortress and hurled it forty feet away not through physical power, but through divine power and the Light of God, for I am in relation to Muhammad as the relation of Light to Light.[25]

When the Prophet defeated the Jewish tribe of Khaybar and captured their fortress, he saw among the captives a beautiful young woman, Safiyya, the daughter of Huyayy, a Jewish leader. Fascinated by her beauty, Muhammad wanted her for a wife and ordered that she be brought to him. When she appeared before him, he noticed a cut on her face. He asked her how her face had been cut, and she answered that when Ali pulled out the gate of the fortress of Khaybar, the fortress collapsed, and all those who were inside fell to the ground. Safiyya said that at that moment she was lying in bed, and when the fortress collapsed, she fell and hit her face against the bed and cut it. The Prophet said, "Safiyya! Ali is most favored with God. When he pulled out the gate of the fortress of Khaybar, the fortress shook, and with it the seven heavens and the seven earths shook; even the throne of the Merciful shook in support of Ali."[26] On that day Umar Ibn al-Khattab, who later became caliph, asked Ali how he could have pulled down the gate of Khaybar, inasmuch as he had been fasting for three days. Ali answered that he did so through the aid of divine power.[27]

During the attack against the Jews of Khaybar, Ali, with one blow of his sword, split into two halves the head of an enemy named Marhab, to the utmost surprise of the angel Gabriel. The Prophet asked the angel Gabriel why he was so surprised. Gabriel said that when he was ordered by God to destroy the people of Lot (the people of Sodom and Gomorrah), he carried the seven cities in which these people dwelt on one feather of his wing, from the seventh nether world to the seventh upper heaven.[28] Gabriel carried these cities until the morning, awaiting the verdict of God regarding their fate. Gabriel then said that when Ali began to strike with his sword, God ordered him to hold the tip of the sword lest it fall and split the earth, reaching the bull on whose horns the earth stood and dividing him in two. If this had happened, Gabriel said, the bull would have lost its balance, and the earth would have turned over with all its inhabitants. Gabriel admitted that, despite the support given his arm by the two angels Israfil and Mikhail, the tip of Ali's sword was heavier than the seven cities of the people of Lot that he carried on one feather of his wing.[29]

Another writer, Ibn Shadhan (d. 1361), relates the following miracle connected with the sword of Ali. He states that Mohammad's companion, Ammar Ibn Yasir (d. 657), said that one day, while he was in Ali's presence in the city of al-Kufa (in present-day Iraq), he and Ali heard a voice crying outside the house. Ali said, "Ammar, go and fetch me my sword, Dhu al-Faqar, which cuts lives short." Ammar continued, "I brought him the sword, and he told me, 'Go out and order the man to stop molesting the woman. If he obeys, leave him alone. If he does not, I will go out and stop him with my sword.' " Ammar went out and saw a man holding onto the reins of a camel, shouting that the beast belonged to him. Challenging him was a woman claiming that the camel was hers. Ammar told the man, "The Commander of the Faithful, Ali, orders you to stop molesting the woman." The man answered, "Let Ali mind his own business and wash his hands from the blood of the Muslims he killed in the city of al-Basra. Now he wants to take my camel and give it to this lying woman." Ammar said that he returned to Ali, who left the house with an angry face. Ali walked up the man and said, "Woe unto you, leave the camel of this woman alone." The man said, "It is my camel." Ali replied, "You lie, you accursed one." The man said, "Ali! Who would testify that the woman is telling the truth?" Ali said, "One whom no one in al-Kufa could accuse of falsehood." The man said, "If a witness will come forward to testify that the woman is telling the truth, I will hand the camel to this woman." Ali, turned to the camel and said, "Camel! Speak up. To whom do you belong?" The camel answered in an eloquent tongue, "O, Commander of the Faithful, I have belonged to this woman for nineteen years." Ali turned to the woman and said, "Woman, take your camel." Then he turned to the man and with one blow of his sword split him in two.[30]

In one of his miracles, Ali invoked the powers of heaven in the Syriac language to cause water to gush out of the ground. During the battle of Siffin, which Ali fought against the Syrian governor, Muawiya Ibn Abi Sufyan, Ali's army camped near a village called Sandudya. One of Ali's men told him that the ground where the army had camped was unsuitable because it had no water. Ali told his men to dig in the ground for water; they did so, and found a huge black stone, to which was attached a silver ring. One hundred men tried to move the stone, but failed. Ali asked them to step aside and, raising his eyes to heaven, spoke in the Syriac language, repeating his words in Arabic: "Thou art gracious, O Lord of the worlds, the Lord of Moses and Aaron." (As cited by Muhammad Ibn al-Fattal al-Nisaburi (d. 1114). The original words were, "Tab Tab Marya Alam Taybutha. Mabutha Shtmayya Kutha Hamutha Tawditha Barjuna." It should be noted that some of them are so distorted that they make no sense in Syriac.) Ali then pulled the stone toward himself and hurled it forty cubits away. Immediately a very sweet and cold spring gushed out of the ground.

The whole army drank from the spring. Then Ali returned the rock to its place and ordered his men to cover it with earth. When the army departed, Ali asked his men whether they would be able to detect the place of the spring if they returned to it. They said that they would, but when they returned to the spot, they could not find the spring; the place was hidden from their eyes. Meanwhile, a monk who had left his cell came walking toward Ali and his company. When Ali saw him, he greeted him and asked "Are not you Simon?" The monk said that Simon was his special name, which his mother had given him at birth. He added that no one knew that his name was Simon except God and Ali. Ali said to the monk, "And what do you want, Simon?" The monk answered, "I want this spring of water." Ali said, "This spring is of Paradise. Three hundred prophets and thirteen wasis [testators] of whom I am the last, draw from it." The monk said that this was true because he had found it in the gospel; a monastery was built up on that rock, and the water of the spring flowed under the monastery. He added that no other mortal knew the story of the monastery and the spring except himself. As a result of this miracle, the monk embraced Islam.[31]

This story may remind us of the time Moses struck the rock and twelve springs gushed forth from it. It is simple enough to tell us that the Shiites have gone beyond reasonable bounds in ascribing to Ali miracles rivalling those of the prophets of Israel. But the interesting part of this miracle is that Ali invoked God's help in the Syriac language, using the Eastern (Nestorian) dialect. This may be explained by the fact that the Nestorians were living in almost every part of Iraq, especially in al-Hira and al-Kufa. Also, there is no doubt that many Nestorians had supported Ali and enlisted in his army for his war against Muawiya.

Convincing evidence that the Ghulat are a batini sect lies in their interpretation of some passages of the Quran and their application of the inward (batin) meaning of those passages to Ali and his descendants. For example, they interpret Quran 78:1, "Al-Naba al-Azim" to mean "Great Ali," and Quran 95:1–2, "The Tin and Zaytun" to mean al-Hasan and al-Husayn, the sons of Ali. They also take Quran 52:44, "And if they see a fragment of heaven falling down upon them, they say it is but a thick cloud," to mean that the "fragment of heaven" is Ali, who has descended from heaven to earth. Of Quran 55:17–22, "He has let the two seas; they meet one another. Yet between them stands a Barzakh (barrier) which they cannot overrun . . . pearls and corals come from both," they say that the two seas are Muhammad and Ali, and the pearls and corals which come forth from them are the Imams, who are the descendants of Ali and Fatima, daughter of Muhammad. Furthermore, they interpret Quran 9:18, "He was also merciful to the three who had been left behind," to mean the first three caliphs, Abu Bakr, Umar, and Uthman, who were "rejected" by the Shiite Muslim community.[32] In fact, the majority of Shiites denounce the first three caliphs as usurpers of the office of the caliphate, which they believe Ali should have been the first to fill. These interpretations of the Quran have been used by Shiites to support their belief in the "transcendentalism" of the members of the family of the Prophet. Abu Ali al-Fadl al-Tabarsi (d. 1154), in his *Majma al-Bayan fi Tafsir al-Qur'an,* (the confluence of eloquence in interpreting the Quran), relates on the authority of the Prophet's companion Salman al-Farisi, that the two seas in the passage cited above mean Ali and Fatima, that the Barzakh between them signifies Muhammad, and that the pearls and corals represent al-Hasan and al-Husayn, the sons of Ali by Fatima.[33] The same interpretation of this passage of the Quran is also reported by the traditionalist and companion of the Prophet, Anas Ibn Malik (d. 709 or 711).[34]

Finally, in order to defend their belief in the divine mission of Ali, the Ghulat, like many other Shiites, accuse the two caliphs, Abu Bakr and Umar, of burning ten *ajza* (sections) of the Quran because they did not harmonize with their intentions and beliefs.[35] They claim the caliphs deliberately eliminated those portions of the Quran that favored Ali and his descendants as the legitimate successors of the Prophet and leaders of the Muslim community. The author of *Dabistan al-Madhahib* (School of manners), however, attributes the burning of portions of the Quran not to Abu Bakr and Umar, but to the third caliph, Uthman. Fani produces a whole *sura* (chapter) of the Quran that he maintains was eliminated by Uthman when he had the Quran codified in its present form. This sura, entitled The sura of the two lights, begins with an exhortation to those who believe in the "Two Lights," that is, Muhammad and Ali, whom God has sent as His messengers to all mankind.[36] The obvious implication is that Ali is coequal with Muhammad as the "divine Light" and shares with him the divine message: the Quran. Such a belief fits perfectly with the tradition cited earlier: "I and Ali are of one Light."[37]

7

The Family of the Prophet

All Shiites, whether extremist or moderate, hold in utmost veneration the five members of the family of the Prophet—the Prophet Muhammad, his daughter Fatima, her husband Ali, and their sons al-Hasan and al-Husayn. These five are commonly known as Ahl al-Aba or Ahl al-Kisa, both of which literally mean "the people of the mantle." The names Ahl al-Aba and Ahl al-Kisa derive from an incident that occurred at the house of Umm Salama, one of Muhammad's wives. The Prophet called Ali, Fatima, and their two sons to him there, covered them with his *Khaybarite Aba* (mantle), and began to recite Quran 33:33, "For God wishes to remove abomination from you, ye members of His Family, and make you spotless." Then Muhammad began to plead, "O God, these are the members of my household whom you have promised me. Remove from them uncleanness and purify them." Umm Salama asked, "Am I one of them, O Prophet of Allah?" Muhammad answered, "Be of good cheer, Umm Salama. You are well off, but these are Ahl Bayti [my family].[1] Hence came the tradition of the Mantle.

According to another tradition, known as Hadith al-Thaqalayn, the Prophet is reported to have said, "I am leaving you two important things, such that if you adhere to them, you will never go astray—the Book of God [the Quran] and Ahl Bayti [my family], and the twain shall not be separated."[2] It could be argued on the basis of his answer to Umm Salama that these statements include the wives of Muhammad as part of his family. It could also be argued that the Family of the Prophet does not necessarily mean the four members of his immediate family; that is Ali, Fatima, and their two sons, al-Hasan and al-Husayn, but all believing Muslims. Abu al-Qasim Abd al-Karim al-Qushayri (d. 1072), relates a tradition pertaining to the Prophet who when asked, "Who are the family of Muhammad," answered, "they are every pious [Muslim]."[3]

Some writers, like Abd al-Qadir al-Jili (d. 1164) and Muhyi al-Din Ibn Arabi (d.1240), maintain that the term Ahl al-Bayt includes the wives of the Prophet.[4] Al-Jili includes within Ahl al-Bayt not only the wives of the Prophet, but other relatives, such as the Prophet's uncles and their descendants. (The sons of Muhammad's uncle al-Abbas established the Abbasid dynasty in 750). Al-Jili divides the family of the Prophet into four categories: Ali, Fatima, and their sons, al-Hasan and al-Husayn, as the Prophet's relatives of the first degree; the Prophet's wives, as those of the second degree; the descendants of al-Hasan and al-Husayn as those of the third degree; and all other relatives of Muhammad as those of the fourth degree.[5] Certain traditions concerning the Prophet and Ali are relevant to any discussion of the scope of Ahl al-Bayt. Both the Prophet and Ali considered Salman al-Farisi, a Persian convert to Islam and a companion of the Prophet, to be a member of Ahl al-Bayt. The Prophet is reported to have said, "Salman is one of us, Ahl al-Bayt."[6] Another tradition indicates that the Prophet did not consider his wives to be members of Ahl al-Bayt.[7] But Shiites and some Sunnite writers maintain that the terms household or family of the Prophet refer exclusively to Ali, Fatima, and their two sons, because they are the Prophet's relatives in the first degree.[8] Shiites frequently support this view by citing Quran 3:61–62: "This revelation, and this wise admonition, we recite to you. Jesus is like Adam in the sight of God. He created Him of dust and said to Him, 'Be,' and He was. This is the truth from your Lord; therefore, do not doubt it. To those who dispute with you concerning Jesus after the knowledge ye have received, say, 'Come, let us gather our sons and your sons, our wives and your wives, our people and your people. We will pray together and call down the curse of God on the ones who lie.' "[9]

Muslim commentators on the Quran call this verse the Mubahala (the imprecation, or calling down of God's curse on the liar). The revelation of this portion of the Quran took place during a meeting between Muhammad and the Christians of Najran in the southern part of present-day Saudi Arabia. In the year 631, a Christian delegation from Najran, numbering seventy men, went to Medina to debate religious matters with Muhammad. Muhammad censured the Christians for believing that Jesus was divine and asked them to embrace Islam, on the grounds that Islam is the only "true" religion of God which considers Jesus a created being like Adam. The debate between the two parties became so heated that Muhammad, reciting the aforementioned verse of the Quran, challenged the Christian party to appear on the next day, 15

January 631, for a Mubahala, so that the disputing parties could ask God to determine the truth of their beliefs concerning the divinity of Jesus, and call down God's curse on the party not telling the truth.

The Christian party seriously considered Muhammad's challenge. When they went to meet Muhammad the next day, they found that he was already on his way to the appointed place of the Mubahala. He was wearing a garment made of black hair and was carrying his grandchild, al-Hasan, on his shoulder while leading his other grandchild, al-Husayn by the hand; Ali and Fatima were walking behind him. When the leader of the Christian party saw Muhammad with the members of his family, he turned to his men, saying that he saw faces whose prayers could move mountains. He implored them not to accept Muhammad's challenge, because, if they did, they would certainly perish and their children would not live long. Therefore, the Christians of Najran rejected Muhammad's challenge and instead agreed to a directive imposed on them by Muhammad, that they retain their religion, but that they be willing to pay Muhammad tribute, including expensive garments, pieces of silver, lances, shields, horses, and camels. They also agreed to place themselves under the *dhimma* (protection) of the Muslims, and to extend hospitality for one month to any delegation Muhammad might send to them in the future. The Christians had no choice but to accept Muhammad's conditions, knowing that they were but a powerless few pitted against the determination of Muhammad and his followers to subjugate them.[10]

Another version of the revelation of the Mubahala is related by Abu al-Faraj al-Isfahani (d. 966) in his *Kitab al-Aghani* (Book of songs). According to this version, forty Christian dignitaries from Najran, including a bishop, went to see Muhammad to debate with him on religious matters. Addressing Muhammad as Abu al-Qasim (father of al-Qasim, a son of Muhammad who died in infancy), the bishop asked him, "Who is the father of Moses?" Muhammad answered, "Imran." The bishop asked, "Who is the father of Joseph?" Muhammad answered, "Jacob." "Who is your father?" The bishop asked. Muhammad answered, "My father is Abd Allah, son of Abd al-Muttalib." Finally, the bishop asked, "Who is the father of Isa [Jesus]?" Muhammad did not reply. Instantly, the angel Gabriel appeared to Muhammad, saying, "Isa is like Adam, whom God created from dust." [Quran 3:59]. The apostle of Allah recited this verse, transmitted by the angel Gabriel, and at that, the bishop collapsed in a dead faint. When the bishop regained consciousness, he raised his head to look at the Prophet and said, "You do believe that God revealed to you that Isa was created of dust, don't you? But we find no evidence of what has been revealed to you in what has been revealed to us [the New Testament]. Nor do we find evidence in what has been revealed to the Jews [the Old Testament]." At this point, God said to Muhammad, "To those who dispute with you concerning Jesus after the knowledge ye have received, [i.e., that he was created of dust like Adam] say, 'Come, let us gather our sons and your sons, our wives and your wives, our people and your people. We will then pray and call down God's curse on the liars.' " The next day, Muhammad went to meet the Christians at the place of the Mubahala, taking with him Ali, Fatima, and their two sons, but none of his wives. The Christians decided not to take part in the Mubahala because, so al-Isfahani relates, they believed that Muhammad was a prophet and feared that if they challenged him, they might perish. When he saw that they declined to challenge him, Muhammad said, "I swear by Him [God] who sent me in truth, if you had performed the Mubahala with me, no Christian man or woman on this earth would have escaped death." This account does not specify any conditions imposed by Muhammad on the defeated Christian party.[11]

Al-Shaykh al-Mufid also relates the affair of the Mubahala and includes a statement concerning Ali not found in the preceding accounts. He states that when the Christian bishop, Abu al-Haritha, saw the Prophet, Ali, Fatima, and their children on their way to the place of the Mubahala, he asked who they were. He was told that the young man was Ali, Muhammad's son-in-law and cousin, that the lady was Fatima, Muhammad's daughter; that the two boys were the Prophet's grandchildren; and that all of them were to him the dearest, most beloved, and closest to his heart. When the bishop saw that the Prophet had brought his family especially to perform the Mubahala, he knew the Prophet was sure that truth was on his side. Muhammad would not have brought those dearest to him, the bishop told his men, were he not sure that the evidence would favor him. The bishop then advised his men to yield to Muhammad and conform to his view.[12]

As we shall see shortly, al-Mufid makes the best of the Mubahala episode to demonstrate the merits of Ali and his equality with the Prophet. It is important to note that Imad al-Din Ibn Kathir, who relates yet another version of the Mubahala, never mentions Ali's accompanying Muhammad to the site. He names only al-Hasan, al-Husayn, and Fatima, adding that Fatima was walking closely behind Muhammad.[13]

We find in more than one source specific mention of the family of the Prophet as including Muhammad's immediate blood relatives—Fatima, Ali, and their two sons—but not his wives. However, the theosophist Ibn Arabi is of the opinion that the terms household and family of the Prophet should extend to all his relatives and wives. He maintains that Ali's sons by Fatima, al-Hasan and al-Husayn, and their descendants, the Imams, are infallible because "God has purified them and removed from them uncleanness, not by their action or merit, but by a preordained Providence of God. This is an excellence which God confers upon those whom He will, and certainly God is the greatest source of excellence." In fact, Ibn Arabi asserts, the Prophet Muhammad and the members of his family are indivisible, and whoever betrays one of them betrays the Prophet himself.[14]

The majority of Shiites maintain that the terms Ahl al-Aba and Ahl al-Kisa refer exclusively to Fatima, Ali, and their two sons, al-Hasan and al-Husayn. These four, with Muhammad, are exalted above the whole community of Islam, and no one in that community is equal to them in position or stature. They are regarded by the Shiites as the pillars of religion and the stronghold of the Islamic faith. Most significantly, only they, of all Muslims, are by right heirs of the Prophet in leadership of the Islamic community.[15] In this sense, they form a religious hierarchy not found in Sunnite Islam.

But why should the Shiites consider Ali, who is only a cousin of Muhammad and his son-in-law, a member of the Prophet's family, and exclude, for example, al-Abbas, the Prophet's uncle, who was a closer blood relation than Ali? What is it that makes Ali so significant in the eyes of the Shiites, who place him on a par with Muhammad? It is that the Shiites look upon Ali as a person who has been favored by God—not as a prophet, for the prophethood is the exclusive office of Muhammad, but as God's saint or beloved, and more specifically, his deputy to whom God has entrusted the imamate (leadership) of the Muslim community after Muhammad. In other words, Ali enjoys the same spiritual favor and position that God conferred on Muhammad. Therefore, to the Shiites, there is no difference in the spiritual status of Ali and Muhammad, except that Muhammad was entrusted with the office of prophethood, while Ali was favored with the office of vicegerent or saint and also with the imamate, which is a spiritual office ordained by God. Indeed, the sainthood is superior to the prophethood, because prophethood indicates only a mechanical transmission of God's revelation, while sainthood encompasses the hidden meaning of this revelation. For this reason the Shiites regard Ali as the "brother" of Muhammad, who shares with him the divine favor of God.

Al-Abbas, the uncle of the Prophet, did not receive any favor or spiritual office from God and therefore cannot be considered a member of the Prophet's family.[16] Briefly, he was not ordained by God as part of the spiritual hierarchy; Ali was. In fact, one modern Shiite writer devoted an entire book, *The Brother of the Prophet Muhammad,* to show the equality of Ali with the Prophet of Islam.[17] To demonstrate the spiritual position Ali enjoyed, the Shiite jurist, al-Kulayni, cites a tradition in which Ali says, "I am God's division between heaven and hell. I am the Scepter and the Sign. All angels and the spirit [probably the Holy Spirit] have recognized my attributes as they did those of Muhammad."[18]

Commenting on the tradition of Ali, the fifth Imam, al-Baqir, states that Ali was endowed with the same excellent qualities as the Prophet, and that obedience to Ali is as imperative as obedience to the Prophet. Al-Baqir states further that as the Prophet is the gateway leading those who enter it to God, so too, are Ali and the Imams after him.[19]

Al-Shaykh al-Mufid sees in the Mubahala evidence of the supremacy of the family of the Prophet and the equality of Ali with the Prophet. He states that in the episode of the Mubahala, God made Ali, his wife Fatima, and his two children, al-Hasan and al-Husayn, a proof that Muhammad was His Prophet and a testimony for His religion, Islam. He goes on to say that God gave judgment in the Quranic verse of the Mubahala that Ali should enjoy outstanding merit and equality with the Prophet. Through the verse, that is, God has purified the members of the family of the Prophet, who became not only infallible, but also God's proof against the Christians of Najran. This, as al-Mufid sees it, is "a merit which no other member of the Muslim community can share with them, or even approach their position.[20]

The spiritual equality of Ali with Muhammad, except for the prophethood, is further demonstrated by the episode of Muhammad's night journey from Mecca to Jerusalem. According to one tradition concerning the episode, Muhammad says that on the night journey, the angel Gabriel asked him, "Where is your brother Ali?" The Prophet answered, "I left him behind." Gabriel said, "Ask God that He may bring him to you." Muhammad did so and immediately saw the likeness of Ali in his company.[21] When Muhammad reached the seventh heaven, which led to the Throne of God, God called him, saying, "O Muhammad, you are my servant, and I am your Lord. Obey me, worship me, and depend completely on me, for I am pleased to have you as my servant, beloved, and apostle, and I am also pleased to have designated Ali as your successor and a gateway. He is my proof and my pact with my creation. In him my religion [Islam] shall be upheld, my laws observed and executed, and my lovers distinguished from my enemies. Through his descendants [the Imams] I shall have compassion upon my creation. And through the Mahdi I shall fill the earth with my praise, worship, and glory; purify it from my enemies; give life to my servants [the Shiites]; expose my treasures, reveal my mysteries; support him by my saints and angels and lead him to his final triumph, for he is truly my Wali [vicegerent] and the true Mahdi [guide] of my creation."[22] Muhammad also says that during his ascent to heaven, the angel Gabriel inquired of him about Ali, which led him to believe that Ali was better known in heaven than Muhammad was. When Muhammad reached the fourth heaven, he saw the angel of death, who told him that he had been charged by the Almighty to take the souls of all creatures except Muhammad and Ali. Their souls would be taken by God alone. When Muhammad came under the empyrean, he saw Ali standing there. He said to him, "How did you get here before me?" The angel Gabriel was present and asked Muhammad whom he was addressing. Muhammad said, "I am addressing my brother Ali." Gabriel said to Muhammad that the person he was addressing was not Ali, but an angel whom God had created in the likeness of Ali, and that those Prophets who were favored by God and wished to draw near and behold Ali had to visit this angel first.[23]

From this tradition we may deduce that, according to the Shiites, Ali is truly the "brother" of Muhammad, because the Prophet said so, and is his only heir and successor. He is, as Abu Jafar al-Tusi, (d. 1067 and known as Shaykh al-Taifa) says, "the brother of Muhammad, the sword of God against the infidels, the confidant of the Prophet, and the source of the Prophet's knowledge."[24]

When Shiite pilgrims visit the tomb of Ali at al-Najaf in present day Iraq, they greet his remains, saying, "Peace be upon the exalted essence of God. Peace be upon the Manna and the Quails."[25] Here Ali is depicted as food and sustenance for the believers, just as manna and quails were sent by God as food and sustenance for the children of Israel in Sinai. Ali is also the "essence" of God formed of the same substance as God; divine. This, of course, is hyperbole which the Ithnaashari Shiites do not accept, but it must have been accepted and used by other Shiites since the early period of Islam. In fact, in the year 420/1029, during the Friday prayer, a Shiite preacher in Baghdad would say after praising the Prophet, "And peace be upon the brother of Muhammad, the Commander of the Faithful, Ali, the human yet divine, who spoke to the skull, raised the dead, and upon the divine tidings talked to the People of the Cave [the Seven Sleepers of Ephesus]."[26] Wether this hyperbole is accepted or rejected, Ali remains the center of Shiism, and without him the whole Shiite theological system would collapse; to the Shiites, the tradition of the Prophet is very clear: to love Ali is to love God, and to hate him is to hate God.[27] To die for the love of Ali is martyrdom. Ali then becomes the redeemer and the hope of salvation of Shiites.[28] For all intents and purposes, the relationship of Ali to God is similar to that of Jesus to God. In fact, some Shiites equate Ali with Jesus, while others exalt him above Jesus.

In his commentary on the Quran, Ali Ibn Ibrahim (al-Qummi, d. 920) relates the following anecdote, on the authority of Salman al-Farisi, a companion of the Prophet. One day, while the Prophet was sitting with some of his companions, he said to them that someone like Jesus, the son of Mary, would enter upon them immediately. Behold, Ali Ibn Abi Talib entered the room. Some of those present were not pleased with what the Prophet had said. One of them retorted, "Is not Muhammad well pleased with us, that he honored Ali more than us and likened him unto Jesus, the son of Mary? By God, the idols which we worshipped in the Jahiliyya [pre-Islamic] period are much better than he [Ali]."[29]

The exaltation of Ali above Jesus is demonstrated by the following verse:

> If it is said that Christ is God
> And Muhammad is the beginning and the end,
> It should also be said that our Lord Ali,
> Who is the spirit of Muhammad,
> Is more worthy of this attribute [divinity]
> Than Christ or anyone else.[30]

Shiite literature is replete with traditions showing the "oneness" of the Imams with the Prophet of Islam, and their participation in all the divine privileges God has conferred upon him. One of these traditions is related by Muhammad's companion, Abu Hurayra, who heard him say to Ali, "I, you, Fatima, al-Hasan, and al-Husayn were created of the same clay, and our partisans [the Shiites] were created from the remainder of that clay."[31] A different tradition is related by another companion of the Prophet, who heard him say, "I am a tree whose main branch is Fatima, whose pollen is Ali, whose fruit is al-Hasan and al-Husayn, and whose leaves are the partisans [Shiites] and lovers of my community."[32]

The members of Ahl al-Bayt (the family of the Prophet) occupy a unique position in Shiite dogma. They are believed to be preexistent and sinless, and to serve as intercessors on behalf of those Shiite believers who seek their divine help. They are also believed to be miracle workers, and, of all the community of Muslims, the only ones highly favored by God. According to a commentary on the Quran ascribed to the eleventh Imam, al-Hasan al-Askari, God, when He created Adam, established

Muhammad, Fatima, Ali, al-Hasan, and al-Husayn as celestial beings in Adam's loins. The Imam al-Askari goes on to say that God then ordered the angels to prostrate themselves before Adam, whom He had exalted above all His creation, because Adam was the dwelling of these celestial beings. The angels obeyed the order of God and prostrated themselves before Adam, all except Iblis (Satan), who refused to obey God's order. Afterwards, God told Adam to raise his eyes to the summit of His throne. Adam did so and saw the *ashbah* (images or likenesses) of the celestial beings who were established in his loins inscribed on the throne of God, as the face of a man appears on the surface of a clear and shining mirror. Adam exclaimed, "What are these beings?" God answered, "They are the images of Muhammad and his family—the best of my creation."[33]

According to Ignaz Goldziher, the inscription of images on the throne of God is a Jewish concept found in the Haggadah and based on the prophecy of Ezekiel. In Ezekiel 1:26, we find a vivid description of a heavenly chariot which Ezekiel saw in a dream while he was captive near the river Khabur in northern Mesopotamia [present-day Iraq]. Ezekiel states that he saw "the likeness of a throne, and upon it was the likeness as the appearance of a man." Although Ezekiel [1:28] clearly states that "this was the appearance of the likeness of the glory of the Lord," the Jewish Haggadah holds that this "appearance of man" was that of Jacob, the father of the Twelve Tribes of Israel.[34]

From this episode related by Goldziher, we can see how striking the analogy is between the Jewish and Shiite concepts of images. Both ascribe to their respective progenitors a divine preexistence proven by the inscription of their "images" on the very throne of God.[35] In Shiite belief it should be noted, however, that only the "images" of the five who constitute the immediate family of the Prophet were inscribed on the throne of God. Indeed, a sect of Ghulat Shiites called the Mukhammisa (Fivers) emphasized, as their name indicates, the concept of images. These Fivers believed that God Himself was Muhammad and that He appeared in five different images—as Muhammad, Ali, Fatima, al-Hasan, and al-Husayn.[36]

The Ghulat Shiites deify the members of the family of the Prophet and believe them to be equally incarnated. Of these Ghulat, the followers of al-Shurayi maintain that Muhammad, Ali, Fatima, al-Hasan, and al-Husayn are gods because God was incarnated in every one of them. In order to demonstrate the truth of the incarnation of these five and their excellence over mankind, the followers of al-Shurayi believe that these five have five *addad* (adversaries directly opposite to the five). These opposite adversaries are the caliphs Abu Bakr, Umar, Uthman, and Muawiya, and the army commander Amr Ibn al-As, a staunch supporter of Muawiya in his struggle for the caliphate with Ali and his son, al-Hasan.[37] The significance of posing these latter five as adversary opposites of the five members of the family of the Prophet is that they were willfully instrumental in usurping the right of the imamate (leadership of the Muslim community) from Ali and his sons, whom Shiites believe are the only legitimate khulafa (caliphs, or successors to the Prophet) because the Prophet appointed Ali as his successor in leading the Muslim community. Those Shiites believe that whoever held the office of the imamate before and after Ali were usurpers of that divine office. Thus the family of the Prophet has been apotheosized to show that although Ali's descendants lost their bid for the caliphate, they gained immortality, becoming the divine protagonists of the Muslim community.

Some Ghulat consider Fatima as equal with the male members of the family of the Prophet. In his *Kitab al-Zina,* Abu Hatim Ahmad Ibn Hamdan al-Razi [d. 934], an Ismaili (Fatimi) propagandist at Daylam; states that some Ghulat claimed that Fatima was not a woman, and that they abhorred addressing her by the feminine name Fatima. Instead they called her Fatim, as the translation of following verse shows:

> According to my doctrinal belief I have loved Five after God—
> A Prophet [Muhammad], his two grandsons, A Shaykh [Ali]
> And Fatim [Fatima].[38]

The implication in this verse is that, since all the other members of the family of the Prophet are male, Fatima must be considered "not female" in order to become homologous with the rest, and to be considered a celestial being and part of the economy of God's providence.

The devotion of Shiites to the members of the family of the Prophet is universal and dates back to an early period of the Islamic community. To show their devotion to Fatima, a group of Shiites who succeeded in establishing a state in Egypt in the tenth century called their state the Fatimi state. Another Shiite dynasty was established in the same century in Baghdad by the Buwayhis, who controlled the Abbasid state and Abbasid caliphs until the year 1055. It is reported that in 341/952, in the time of Muizz al-Dawla Ibn Buwayh (a Shiite), a young man and a woman in Baghdad were caught and beaten, the young man because he believed that the spirit of Ali dwelt in him, the woman because she believed that the spirit of Fatima dwelt in her. When they were taken to Muizz al-Dawla, however, he ordered their release because they appealed to Ahl al-Bayt (the family of the Prophet) for intercession on their behalf.[39] Some Shiites liken Fatima to the Virgin Mary and, in fact, call her the Virgin Fatima and Maryam al-Kubra (great Mary). They refer to a tradition in which the Prophet, when asked, "What is a virgin?" answered, "A virgin is one who is not subject to menstruation because menstruation cannot happen to the daughters of prophets."[40] What Muhammad meant in this context was that his daughter, Fatima, unlike other women, was free from menstrual periods because she was his daughter.

In Iran the Ghulat as well as Sufis believe that the five members of the family of the Prophet are the cause of the universe, the mystery of existence and the source of subsistence, help, and blessing. They consider an oath taken by "the truth of the Five members of Ahl al-Aba" to be very binding.[41] Several references to Ahl al-Aba or Ahl al-Kisa can be found in Bektashi hymns especially among those recited by religious pirs during the ceremony of the initiation of a novice into the Bektashi order. In these hymns, the religious leader invokes the divine help of the family of the Mantle and seeks their intercession. Birge, who has translated hymns containing supplication for the divine intercession of the family of the Prophet, does not seem to identify the family with the five. However, in a footnote to a hymn which refers to the five, he states that "the Five" may denote the family of the Prophet. It certainly does.[42]

Summing up, the devotion of the Shiites to the Ahl al-Aba, or Ahl al-Kisa (family of the Prophet or family of the Mantle), is not merely part of the Shiite belief, but is, in fact central to their theological system. It may also have been a part of the ritual of some dervish orders. The seventeenth century traveler Evliya Efendi relates that he saw in Elbasan, in Albania, a dervish lodge still following the order of Ahl al-Aba.[43]

8

Religious Hierarchy

Among the Bektashis, Kizilbash, and Shabak, the number seven appears to represent the seven degrees of their spiritual hierarchy, corresponding to the stages of the mystical order. According to al-Sarraf, the hierarchy consists of seven degrees; according to al-Ghulami, it has only five degrees. It is most likely that the Shabak hierarchy originally had seven degrees, but that through the years distinctions were blurred and the structure was altered.

The seven degrees of the Shabak's religious hierarchy, from the lowest to the highest are described below.

1. The *muntasib* or *talib* (seeker, or neophyte) is attracted by the sufistic or mystical aspect of the order, but has not taken a definite step to join it. In Bektashism, the talib is a person not committed to the order, usually called an *ashiq* (passionate lover) of Sufi life. He is in love with the order, fascinated by its rules and by the conduct of its members, but he is not ready to join the order;

2. The *murid* (willing one) has shown willingness to join the order, but is still a neophyte. He receives instruction from a *murshid* (spiritual guide), who trains him in the ascetic life of the order and its requirements of solitude, prayer, fasting, and control of both physical and mental desires. In Bektashism, a person at the second degree is called a *muhib,* which, like *ashiq,* means passionate lover. Technically, the muhib is one who has made up his mind to take the vows of the order and has been initiated into the order. The initiation is a ceremony open to both sexes in which the *muhib* makes an *iqrar* (statement or profession of his faith);

3. The *dervish* has completed the period of trial at the convent and has obtained a high degree of piety and spiritual knowledge. The third degree is the same in Bektashism;

4. The Pir, or Murshid (spiritual guide), is usually a shaykh (elder), whose duty is to administer the convent or lodge. He has the highest spiritual authority in religious matters. He heads and conducts circles or *dhikr* (constant praise of God and invocation of His name), usually held on Friday evenings. He organizes the mourning ceremony commemorating the martyred Imam al-Husayn and the other Imams, held during Ashura (the first ten days of the month of Muharram in the Islamic calendar). He also receives confessions from the dervishes and other members of the community and grants them absolution. The degree is the same in Bektashism, except that the person who holds it is called the *baba* (equivalent to papa). It is his duty to exercise religious authority over the community, as the pir does among the Shabak;

5. The *qalandar* is not bound by religious duties or the legal restrictions of the Sharia (Islamic law). Because of his profound piety, purity, selflessness, ascetic life, and avoidance of the defilement brought about by worldly pleasures, and most of all because of his unceasing search for truth, the qalandar is considered by the community an exemplar of sanctity and perfection, a man distinguished not by the performance of supererogatory religious duties and rituals, but by the attainment of heavenly favors, especially the state of spiritual ecstasy and illumination;

6. *Al-Rind* is characterized by utmost purity of heart and a higher attainment of the divine mysteries. Like the qalandar, he is not bound by religious rules and traditions;

7. The *qutb* (pole, axis), who the highest spiritual authority, and is also called pir piran (exalted). He is considered the Star of Wisdom and the embodiment of the divine mysteries and teachings of the order. From him the dervishes receive blessing and guidance. The Shabak believe that he has karamat (miraculous gifts), and that he alone has the power to unravel the divine mysteries. He is not only the way which leads to the truth, he is the truth.[1]

This belief that the qutb is the truth is manifested in the following verse:

> My shaykh, my way, my director and my guide,
> Through you I have attained to the Truth,
> O Truth who hast shown me the Truth.[2]

In Bektashism, the qutb is referred to as the murshid. He is the only member of the hierarchy who knows the mysteries of the order, and without his help no member of the order can attain the truth. In this capacity, the Murshid becomes the only way that leads to God, the ultimate reality:

> He who has not attained the Murshid cannot know God;
> The Heart, the Soul of the Murshid derive from the
> breath of the Ultimate Reality.[3]

Al-Ghulami lists only five degrees in the Shabak's hierarchy. At the top is the agha, who is usually a secular leader. The term *agha* is of Kurdish origin and shows the Kurdish influence on the Shabak, which came from the social contact between the two peoples. Below him are the pir (spiritual guide), the *rahbar* (guide), the murid (neophyte), and the *mulla,* who is in charge of teaching the Quran, but has no specific religious authority. Al-Ghulami states that the Shabak previously had the rank of qalandar, which carried great spiritual power, but that this rank no longer exists.[4]

The spiritual leader enjoys a prominent position among the Bektashis, the Kizilbash, and the Shabak, who treat him with the utmost respect and reverence and seek his blessing. They kiss his hand, in conformity with a Middle Eastern custom practiced by both Muslims and Christians toward their religious leaders. They also kiss him on the mouth after he has had a meal, a custom not known among other peoples, such as the Sunnite Muslims and Christians.[5] Because they believe that they are Alawi—the religious leaders of the Sayyids (descendants of the Imam Ali)—the religious leaders of the Shabak consider themselves a separate caste, and avoid intermarriage with the laity. Barnum writes that the "priesthood" among the Kizilbash follows a distinct line of succession, as in the Levitical office of old, and these religious teachers are highly respected by the Kizilbash Kurds.[6] G. E. White writes that the *dedes* who are the priests of the Alawi Turks (Bektashis and Kizilbash) are held in high esteem. They visit their parishes, holding meetings usually at night, and are guarded by utmost secrecy when the ceremony of a sacramental meal is celebrated. The dedes rule their congregations with an iron hand, and disobedient members are disciplined, sometimes by excommunication. In this extreme case, the offender becomes a social outcast, and no member of his community will have anything to do with him.[7]

Grenard writes that the Kizilbash "priests," called dede, are considered intermediaries between God and man, while the "bishops" or pirs are invested with powers of a divine nature. These pirs are believed to be descendants of Ali, and in this capacity, are the trustees of God.[8] We shall see in the following chapters that the Ahl-i Haqq, or Ali Ilahis, consider their sayyids to be divine, and that the Nusayris hold their sayyids in high esteem, believing that they have the power to foretell the future.

For their livelihood, the religious leaders of the sects depend mostly on donations and alms received from their parishioners during certain seasons of the year.[9] In order to facilitate the collection of donations, the religious leaders usually divide the village congregations among themselves; no religious leader has the right to collect alms or donations from the congregation of a village not assigned to him.[10] There is a similar practice among the Alawis of eastern Turkey, especially in the village of Çiplaklar, where the villagers collect donations for the pir from every household, and the donated amounts are usually kept secret.[11]

9

The Twelve Imams

THE NUMBER TWELVE, which occurs often in the prayers and rituals of the contemporary Ghulat (especially the Bektashis, the Kizilbash, and the Shabak), signifies the twelve Imams. They are (1) Amir al-Muminin (Commander of the Faithful) Ali Ibn Abi Talib, the blood cousin of Muhammad and his son-in-law, assassinated in 661; (2) Ali's son, al-Hasan, who abdicated his right to the caliphate to the Umayyad Muawiya Ibn Abi Sufyan. Shiites maintain that al-Hasan was cheated and coerced by Muawiya into relinquishing his right to the caliphate. He was poisoned in 670 by a member of his household at the instigation of Muawiya; (3) Ali's second son, al-Husayn, known as Sayyid al-Shuhada (the lord of martyrs), murdered at Karbala, Iraq, along with seventy-two of his followers on 10 October 680; (4) Ali Ibn al-Husayn, known as Zayn al-Abidin (the ornament of pious men) and al-Sajjad (the worshipful), poisoned in 713 by al-Walid Ibn Abd al-Malik Ibn Marwan; (5) Muhammad Ibn Ali, known as al-Baqir (the investigator) because of his profound knowledge of the religious sciences of his time, poisoned in 732 by Ibrahim Ibn al-Walid Ibn Abd al-Allah, the nephew of the Umayyad Caliph Hisham; (6) Jafar al-Sadiq, considered outstanding in his knowledge of Islamic jurisprudence, and said to have been poisoned by the Abbasid Caliph al-Mansur in 765; (7) Musa al-Kazim (the patient), who is reported to have been poisoned while imprisoned by the Abbasid Caliph Harun al-Rashid; (8) Ali al-Rida, the son-in-law of the Abbasid Caliph al-Mamun (d. 833), who had al-Rida poisoned in 818; (9) Muhammad Ibn Ali, known as al-Taqi (the pious one) and al-Jawad (the benevolent), poisoned by his wife, Umm al-Fadl (daughter of the Abbasid Caliph al-Mamun), at the instigation of the Abbasid Caliph al-

Mutasim in 835; (10) Ali Ibn Muhammad, known as al-Hadi (guide to the right path) and al-Naqi (the pure), poisoned in 868 by the Abbasid Caliph al-Mutazz; (11) al-Hasan Ibn Ali, known as al-Askari because he lived in the Askar district of Samarra, Iraq, poisoned in 873, at the age of twenty-seven or twenty-eight, at the instigation of the Abbasid Caliph al-Mutamid; and (12) Muhammad al-Hasan, commonly known as al-Mahdi (the guided one). Shiites believe that in 874, when al-Mahdi was five years old, he miraculously disappeared from the cellar of his home in the city of Samarra in what is now Iraq. Shiites believe al-Mahdi, like the Messiah, is still living and will continue to live, though in disguise, until the end of time. They believe he communicates with people incognito, walking among the multitudes of pilgrims who flock to Mecca every year. He shall appear at the end of time as the the Guided One and, together with Jesus Christ, shall fill the earth with the knowledge of God and justice, even as it has been filled with iniquity and idolatry. Therefore, Shiites call this twelfth Imam "Sahib al-Zaman" (master of the age and time); "al-Hujja" (the proof of God to mankind); "Sahib-al-Sayf" (lord of the sword); "al-Qaim bi al-Haqq" (upholder of the Truth); "al-Qaim bial-Amr" (upholder of the divine Authority, that is, the office of the imamate; and "al-Muntazar" (the awaited one).[1] How serious Shiites are about the advent of the Mahdi is shown by the fact that the Safawi shahs of Iran, who styled themselves the "Slaves of the Master of the Age," always kept two horses ready saddled and groomed in their royal stables, one for the Mahdi and the other for Jesus Christ, who it is believed will accompany him when he comes again.[2]

Shiite writers see a strong similarity between the Mahdi and Jesus Christ, especially since the mother of the Mahdi was a Christian bondswoman, called Narjis. Abu Jafar Muhammad Ibn al-Hasan al-Tusi, known as Shaykh al-Taifa, emphasizes the connection between the Mahdi and Jesus, noting that the Mahdi's mother was not only a Christian, but a descendant of kings and of the Hawaris (apostles of Jesus).[3] Al-Tusi does not name the kings and apostles to whom Narjis was related, but a Nusayri writer, Yusuf Ibn al-Ajuz al-Nashshabi, states that her father was a Byzantine emperor, and her mother a descendant of the Apostle Simon Cephas (St. Peter).[4]

According to Shiite tradition, the return of the Mahdi was foretold by the Prophet Muhammad. The Shiite writer al-Shaykh al-Mufid relates a tradition in which the Prophet is reported to have said, "The days and nights will never end until God sends a man from my House, whose name will be the same as mine. He will fill the earth with Justice, as it was filled with oppression and tyranny."[5]

Another Shiite writer, Muhammad Baqir al-Majlisi, relates another tradition, in which Muhammad says, "I am the Prophet and Ali is my heir, and from us will descend the Mahdi, the Shah of the Imams, who will vanquish all other religions and take vengeance on the wicked. He will be the Elect and Chosen One of God and the heir to all divine knowledge."[6]

The Shiites belief in the Imams and the imamate is central to their religious doctrine. It is the imamate, more than any other Islamic concept or institution, that separates them from the Sunnites. According to al-Shahrastani, swords have never been so viciously used over any religious matter as over the imamate.[7] It is a concept on which no Shiite will compromise. What, then, is this imamate, and why is it so important to the Shiites? Literally, the imamate means leadership of Muslim worshippers in prayer. Whoever leads a group of Muslims in prayer, regardless of his social status, is called Imam (leader). In this sense, all Muslims could become Imams. But in a more fundamental sense, the imamate means leadership of the Muslim umma (community). In his lifetime, the Prophet Muhammad was the Imam par excellence, or leader of the Muslim community, because he was the messenger of God and His Prophet. The Shiites look upon the leadership of the community by the Prophet as an integral part of his religious message. Thus, the imamate is not a temporal office, but a religious one. For this reason the Shiites consider the imamate as one of the *arkan* (pillars and religious duties of Islam).[8]

As a religious office, the imamate could be transmitted by the Prophet to only one person, the person he considered fit to lead the community of Islam after his death. But did the Prophet designate anyone as his successor, the Imam (leader) of the Muslim community? This is the vital question that has divided the body of Islam into Shiites and Sunnites (commonly called orthodox Muslims by Western scholars) to this day.

When the Prophet died in A.D. 632, a controversy arose among his followers over who should succeed him. After some debate, the Muslim community chose an old man, Abu Bakr, a companion of the Prophet and his father-in-law, to lead the community; he was called the khalifa, or successor, to the Prophet of Allah.[9] Thus began the office of the khilafa (caliphate) and the succession of temporal heads of the Muslim community.

Another group, not satisfied with the election of Abu Bakr, held the opinion that Ali, the Prophet's blood cousin and son-in-law, should have been chosen as his successor. This group came to be known as shia or

Shiites, that is, supporters of Ali as the worthiest person to succeed the Prophet as Imam of the Muslim community.[10] To Shiites, Shiism was not an accidental phenomenon brought about by the fact that the Prophet died without naming a successor, but a spiritual phenomenon first manifesting itself during the Prophet's lifetime, at the moment that Ali professed his belief in Islam.

Traditions do exist indicating that there were men during the Prophet's lifetime known as the companions and supporters (Shia) of Ali. According to one such tradition, Muhammad said, "Ali! you and your companions will be in paradise."[11] Another tradition has several variations: "By Allah, in whose hand is my soul, this [Ali] and his shia [supporters] are the victorious ones on the Day of Resurrection;" "You [Ali] and your shia will be most blessed on the Day of Resurrection," and "You [Ali] and your shia will approach God [on the Day of Resurrection] well pleased and delighted."[12]

A modern Shiite, Shaykh Muhammad Baqir al-Sadr (d. 1980), argues that it is incredible that the Prophet Muhammad, after leading the greatest movement in history, a movement altering the values and way of life of pre-Islamic society, and transforming the heathen Arabs into a community of God, and causing them to carry the torch of their new Islamic faith to other peoples throughout the world, would leave his community without a guide or a leader. Al-Sadr concludes that, of all Muslims, Ali was the only one groomed by the Prophet to assume the leadership of the new community of Islam after him. He reasons that Ali was the first Muslim and the first *mujahid* (combatant) for the cause of Islam, and that he was raised and nurtured by the Prophet, who spent so much time teaching Ali the mysteries of the divine message, that finally the career, knowledge, and personality of Ali could no longer be separated from those of the Prophet. Al-Sadr then relates many Islamic traditions showing Ali's lofty position in the Muslim community and the unique relationship with the Prophet that qualified him to be Muhammad's heir apparent.[13]

From the foregoing evidence we may conclude that Shiism (the support of Ali) existed in the lifetime of the Prophet as a nascent movement, whose proponents were honest Muslims convinced that Ali was the spiritual heir of the Prophet and the leader of the Muslim community: the only member of Ahl al-Bayt (the family of the Prophet) who possessed spiritual traits distinguishing him from all other Muslims.[14]

Shiites maintain that the Imams alone, as members of the family of the Prophet, are the Prophet's rightful heirs according to God's promise to Ishmael, Abraham's son by his bondswoman Hagar, considered to be the primogenitor of the Arabs. This promise, they hold, was given by God in Genesis 17:20: "And as for Ishmael I have heard thee: Behold, I have blessed him, and will make him fruitful, and will multiply him exceedingly; twelve princes shall he beget, and I will make him a great nation." The Shiites believe that the twelve princes of this verse are the twelve Imams, who alone compose the family of the Prophet, and the "great nation" is the body of Shiites who follow these Imams.[15] In this sense, the Imams are the only rightful caliphs.

In maintaining their central belief that Ali, was the only Muslim worthy to be the Prophet's successor and the Imam (leader) of the Muslim community, the Shiites do not cite Ali's remarkable traits, magnificent conduct, or even the high esteem in which the Prophet held him but instead upheld his right to the imamate solely on the grounds that the Prophet specifically designated Ali as his successor and vicegerent. Thus all Shiites reject the principle of election of the Imam by the people and, except for the Zaydis (a group of Shiites presently found in Yemen), accept as the Prophet's successor no other Imam or Caliph but Ali.[16]

The earliest Shiite writers, Ali Ibn Ibrahim (d. 920), Abu Hatim al-Razi (d. 934), and al-Kulayni, related many traditions concerning the Prophet's designation of Ali as vicegerent. One of the most common of these traditions is that of Ghadir Khumm (the Khumm Pond), near Medina. Muhammad, stopping there with his companions, gave a speech and then asked, "Who is the most worthy to be your Wali [Master]?" The companions answered, "Allah and his Prophet," The Prophet then called Ali to him and said three times, "Hence, he who recognizes me as his Master, for him, too, Ali is Master. May Allah love those who love him and be the enemy of those who hate him."[17]

Al-Shahrastani (d. 1153) states that the Shiites who believe in the twelve Imams interpret this tradition as an explicit designation by the Prophet of Ali as mawla (master). Moreover, these Shiites maintain that the companions of the Prophet interpreted this tradition in the same way. Umar Ibn al-Khattab (d. 644), for example, is held to have told Ali, "Blessed are you, Ali, because you have become the Mawla of every believing Muslim man and woman."[18]

According to another tradition, related by Yahya Ibn al-Husayn (d. 971) (a descendant of Ali), the Prophet called Ali his khalifa. In the year 630, the Prophet led an expedition against Tabuk, near the Syrian border. Before leaving Medina, he appointed Ali as governor of that city. Some people of Medina were displeased with Ali's appointment as their governor. When Ali saw their dissatisfaction, he followed Muhammad to Tabuk to explain the situation and to excuse himself from returning to

Medina. But the Prophet said to him, "Brother, return to your post, because Medina will never be ruled better than by you." The Prophet also said, "You are my khalifa among my own family in the city to which I emigrated and among my own people. Are not you satisfied that you are in the same position to me as Aaron was to Moses, except that there will be no prophet after me?"[19]

Another version of this tradition is set at the storming of the Jewish fortress of Khaybar, during which Ali, so it is said, lifted the gate of the fortress, which was like a millstone, with his left hand and used it as a shield before hurling it to the ground. When the Prophet saw Ali's heroic deed, he said to him, "Were it not for the fact that I fear some sects of my community will say of you what the Christians said of Jesus [that is, that Jesus was divine and the Son of God], I would say something about you, so that you would pass no company that would not gather the dust on which you trod and use the water left over from your ablutions for their healing. But it is sufficient for you to be to me as Aaron was to Moses, except that there will be no prophet after me. You will be my heir and the first of my followers to enter the garden [paradise]. Your warfares will be my warfares, and your sons are my sons. The truth is with your flesh and blood as it has mingled with my own flesh and blood." Upon hearing these words, Ali fell worshipfully to the ground and said, "Praise be to Allah, who has favored me with the faith of Islam, taught me the Quran, and endeared me to the most exalted being, the Seal of the Prophets." The Prophet turned to Ali and said, "If it were not for you, no one would know the believers after I have departed this life."[20]

There is also evidence that the Prophet called Ali his *wazir* (helper, supporter, or deputy). In one of his speeches, Ali relates his close association with the Prophet and tells how he and the Prophet's wife Khadija were the first Muslims to witness God's revelation to Muhammad and choice of him as Prophet to deliver His message, the Quran. Ali relates that when God revealed the Quran to Muhammad, he heard Satan emit a terrible cry. He asked the Prophet the reason for Satan's outcry, and Muhammad answered that it was because of Satan's despair over his fallen state. Muhammad went on to say to Ali, "You can hear what I hear and see what I see, but you are not a Prophet; you are a wazir and you are well off."[21] It is this and similar pronouncements by the Prophet, like the one made at Ghadir Khumm, that confirm the Shiites' belief that the Prophet appointed Ali as his vicegerent.

It is also in this sense that the Shiites recognize Ali and his descendants, the twelve Imams, as the only rightful successors and heirs of the Prophet and as the only Muslims possessing the spiritual authority to lead the Muslim community. To the Shiites, the Imams are not mere caliphs but, like the Prophet, are divinely inspired; to recognize them is to recognize God. As belief in God is considered one of the pillars of Islam, so is recognizing the Imam, submitting to his will, and obeying his commands. According to a tradition attributed to the fifth Imam, al-Baqir, the walaya (that is, love of and allegiance to the Imams as possessors of divine authority) is the greatest of the pillars of Islam and leads to the rest of the pillars.[22] Thus, to the Shiites, the imamate becomes the essence of Islam. Or, as al-Baqir's son, the Imam Jafar al-Sadiq, is reported to have said, "The obedience of Ali is the last religious duty of Islam, by which God completed His grace and perfected Islam."[23] The Shiite writer Ibn Shahr Ashub (d. 1192) asserts that Ali is not only al-Sirat al-Mastaqim (the straight path), al-Urwa al-Wuthqa (the insoluble bond), Nur Allah al-Hadi (the guiding light of God), but also al-Imam wa al-Islam wa al-Sunna wa al-Salam (the very faith of Islam, the tradition of the Prophet, and peace). Ashub also affirms the importance of the imamate as the divine office and prerogatives of Ali and his infallible descendants, the Imams.[24]

So central is the position of the Imam to the Shiite doctrinal system that any member of the Shiite community who does not know or recognize the Imam in his lifetime is regarded as having died in ignorance or unbelief; that is, he perishes. All Shiites, except the Zaydis, attribute *isma* (infallibility and sinlessness) to the Imams and consider them to be the embodiments of faith and religious precepts and the possessors of divine knowledge, attributes placing them above ordinary people.[25]

In short, the Shiites consider the Imams the rulers of the Muslim community par excellence, by God's providence and dispensation. They believe that the twelfth Imam, the Mahdi, has continued since his disappearance to rule the world in his hidden state through the Imams of the Shiite community in every age. These Imams are mujtahids, men well-versed in the knowledge of the Sharia (Islamic law), and have the spiritual prerogative to interpret this Sharia for the proper guidance of the Shiite community. These mujtahids are not mere legists, jurists, or religious pedants; they are the spokesmen of the hidden Imam, the Mahdi, and their interpretation of the Sharia is inspired by him. Because they are representatives of the Mahdi, and the embodiment of his divine authority, their interpretation of the Sharia becomes binding on the Shiite community. Thus, the Shiites of every generation have one Imam who holds the highest authority and rules the Shiite community on behalf of the Mahdi. This divine authority of the Imam is called Wilayat al-Faqih, and most Shiites accept the Ayatollah Khomeini as its present-day holder:

the Faqih (representative) who rules the Shiite community on behalf of the Mahdi. Recognizing him in this capacity is an acknowledgment of the divine authority of the Imams. Indeed, the concept of Wilayat al-Faqih is so essential to the present theocratic Shiite state in Iran that it has been incorporated into the first two articles of the constitution of the Islamic state of Iran.[26] The divine authority of Khomeini is also confirmed by the general prosecutor, Muhammad Gilani. Gilani, one of Iran's ayatollahs, hosts a television show; each time, he begins the show by praising God and his Prophet Muhammad, and then adds, "Peace be upon our leader and guide, the Mahdi and his representative and Wali al-Amr [ruler, or man in change], the Imam, Khomeini.[27] At one time Khomeini called himself Sahib al-Zaman (master of the time), an epithet exclusively used by Ithnaashari Shiites for the twelfth Imam, the Mahdi. Indeed, even the call to prayer which constitutes the Islamic profession of faith, "I testify that there is no God but God and Muhammad is the apostle of God," was changed to suit Khomeini's concept of Wilayat al-Faqih. When the muezzins in Iran call the people to prayer they cry out, "Allah Akbar, Allah Akbar! Khomeini is Rahbar, Khomeini is Rahbar" (God is most great; God is most great! Khomeini is the religious guide; Khomeini is the religious guide), thus placing Khomeini before the testimony of faith that "There is no God but God and Muhammad is the apostle of God." Many religious men in Iran rejected the new formula of the call to prayer and were forced to pray at home because the religious authorities prevented them from praying at the mosques.[28]

According to the Shiite writer Muhammad Baqir al-Majlisi, most Shiite scholars agree that the Imams are free from all sin, venial or mortal, intentional or accidental, from the beginning to the end of their lives. Only a few scholars, like Ibn Babawayh and Muhammad Ibn al-Walid, have reservations about the sinlessness of the Imams. They maintain that the Imam is sinless only when he is holding the office of the imamate. When the Imam interprets principles of faith, these scholars believe, he can make no error.[29]

Al-Kulayni states that the Imam is free from sin and faults; he is masum (infallible) and is immune from the commission of sin because God has chosen him as the progeny of the prophets: Adam, Noah, Abraham, Ishmael, and Muhammad.[30] To al-Shaykh al-Mufid, the infallibility of the Imams is the highest degree of *kamal* (perfection), since the Imams occupy the same spiritual position as the prophets in executing judgments and legal punishment, preserving laws, and disciplining the people. In performing their duties, the Imams, like the prophets, are not subject to forgetfulness or negligence in matters of religion or legal judgments. The Imams are not only infallible but omniscient. Al-Mufid says that the Imams know the secrets of all arts and languages because God has perfected their intellects.[31] We may then deduce that the Shiites' dogma of the sinlessness of the Imams derives from their belief in the sinlessness of the Prophets; since the Imams are the successors of the Prophets, they too are sinless. Dwight Donaldson, who has elaborated on the origin of the infallibility of the Imams, concluded that this "sinlessness of the Imams is a unique Shiite dogma, without a trace of Jewish or Christian influence."[32]

We have seen in chapter 5 that the Shiites believe that their Imams transcend God's creation of the heavens and the earth. They were created from the divine light of God, and their names are inscribed on the throne of God. The Shiites interpret many passages in the Quran as showing the transcendentality of the Imams.

In his commentary on the Quran, Ali Ibn Ibrahim relates that the fifth Imam, al-Baqir, interpreted Quran 14:24–25—"Seest thou not how God sets forth a parable? A goodly word like a goodly tree, whose roots are firmly fixed, and its branches reach to the heavens. It brings forth its fruit at all times by the leaves of its Lord"—to mean that the tree is the Prophet of Allah; its roots are firmly fixed in the Banu Hashim; its branches are Ali Ibn Abi Talib; its fruit is Fatima and the Imams (the descendants of Ali and Fatima); and its leaves are the Shiites, the partisans of Ali. Ibn Ibrahim interprets Quran 6:96—"It is He that has created for you the stars, so that they may guide you in darkness"—to mean that the stars are the members of the family of the Prophet. He further interprets Quran 95:1–3—"By the fig and the olive and the Mount of Sinai, and this City of Security"—to mean that the fig is the Prophet, the olive is Ali, Mount Sinai is al-Hasan and al-Husayn, and the City of Security represents the Imams.[33]

In a similar vein, an interpretation of Quran 28:5—"It is our will to favor those who were oppressed in this earth and to make them Imams and heirs"—related by Abu Jafar al-Tusi and attributed by him to the Imam Ali, says that the heirs in this verse are the members of the family of the Prophet (the Imams), from whom shall come the Mahdi.[34]

When Ali was asked about the meaning of Quran 33:23—"Among the believers are men who have been true to their covenant with God; of them some have died and some are still waiting, but they have not changed their determination in the least"—he answered, after asking God's forgiveness, that this revelation was intended for him, his uncle Hamza, and his cousins, Ubayda Ibn al-Harith and Abd al-Muttalib. He went on to say that he was still waiting, and that his beloved Abu al-

Qasim (an epithet of the Prophet Muhammad) had entrusted him with his covenant.[35]

Shiites consider the Imams to be the "straight path" [Quran 1:6], the "insoluble bond," and the "pillars of Islam."[36] Moreover, according to the Imam Jafar al-Sadiq, the Imams are the "nation justly balanced" and "God's witness against mankind," as mentioned in Quran 2:132. Al-Sadiq says that even the births and deaths of the Imams transcend those of ordinary human beings, being more allegorical than real.[37]

From this evidence we reach two significant conclusions. First, the Shiites believe that the transcendentalism of the Imams is ordained by God, as delineated in the Quran. This transcendentalism is manifested in the miraculous actions of the Imams, surpassing those of the Hebrew prophets. It is reported by the eleventh Imam, al-Hasan al-Askari, that Moses was unable to part the sea to allow the children of Israel to cross onto dry land until he shouted, "O Lord, for the sake of Muhammad and his exalted family, do Thou split the sea," and the sea was split.[38]

A nineteenth-century Iranian writer, Nur Allah Khan, relates the following episode as further affirmation of the transcendentalism of the Imams. He states that the eighth Imam, al-Rida (whose shrine is in the city of Mashhad in Iran), was still living in his time and could respond to people's questions and supplications. He relates that Nasir al-Din, shah of Iran (reigned 1848–96), installed a telegraph line between the capital and Mashhad and sent the first message to the Imam al-Rida, who "graciously vouchsafed a reply."[39]

The second conclusion we reach from the foregoing evidence is that the imamate is the core of the Shiites' religious doctrine, and that they regard it as more than a temporal political office. To the Shiites, it is a divine office ordained by God and ranking equally with the prophethood; its occupants, the Imams, although not prophets, are almost like prophets. They have the divine right to deliver the message of the Prophet Muhammad to mankind and to propagate his teachings because they are his rightful heirs. Briefly then, the imamate is a divine hereditary office which the Imams received from Muhammad, who, in turn, received it from the prophets of the Old Testament, who received it from God. This divine transmission of the imamate from God through His prophets to Muhammad, and from him to Ali, was not arbitrary, but was passed through a *wasiyya* (testamentary trust) from generation to generation until it reached Ali, the only Imam to whom Muhammad delivered this trust. Therefore, the Shiites accept Ali and his descendants as the legitimate Imams and consider such caliphs as Abu Bakr, Umar, and Uthman to be usurpers.[40]

Extremist Shiites

Extremist Shiites believe in the twelve Imams and attribute to them infallibility and divine authority.[41] They seek the Imams' intercession and divine help, which they believe ward off calamities. The Shabak and related sects in Iraq commemorate the Imams on certain days of the year by visiting shrines built in their names and offering sacrifices to them. They name their sons after the Imams, believing that a child named after a member of the family of the Prophet will bring wealth and blessings to their homes and protect them and their neighbors from misfortune. The names most frequently used are Ali, al-Hasan, al-Husayn, Jafar, Sadiq, Mahdi, Fatima, Zaynab, and Kulthum. Male children are never named after the first three caliphs, Abu Bakr, Umar, and Uthman, whom the Shiites loathe and curse. To show their disrespect, especially for the Caliph Umar, they distort his name to Amruk; they also distort the name of Aisha, one of the Prophet's wives, to Ashasha.[42]

In this respect, the Shabak are no different from the other Shiites, moderate and extremist, especially the Kizilbash of the district of Dersim in Turkey, with whom they share a common religious heritage.[43] The Bektashis and the Kizilbash, along with the Shabak attribute divine dispensation to Ali and the rest of the Imams through the Mahdi, the last Imam. Birge reproduces a Bektashi hymn set to music by Baba Gunci, which has a parallel in the Shabak's literature. The Bektashi hymn says:

> Muhammad Ali establishes this Way. This is the rite
> of the Divine Reality for him who knows Reality.
>
> Without saying yes, Deniers cannot enter it.
> The Faithful enter. It is the place of the hero.
>
> This is what Hasan and Husayn loved,
> This is what Zayn al-Abidin saw.
>
> This is what Imam Baqir showed,
> This is the faith of Jafar al-Sadiq.
>
> A King separated himself from Musa al-Kazim;
> His last fruit was my Patron Saint Bektash.
>
> It is he who guided Rum aright, that rose-faced moon.
> He is the King of the Ayin-i Cem [religious assembly].

Imam Ali handed it to al-Taqi and al-Naqi;
Ali al-Naqi made it known to al-Askari.

Muhammad al-Mahdi also attained this secret;
This is the rotation of Muhammad Ali.[44]

Here is a similar hymn chanted by the Shabak, praising and describing each of the Imams:

Muhammad is the remedy of the world's ailments;
Ali is the example of mankind.
Al-Hasan is the delight of the eye of the Prophet;
So is al-Husayn, who is the purity of souls.
He who does not love Zayn al-Abidin, may calamity never leave him.
The Baqir is the light of God manifested to Jafar.
As for the Imam Musa al-Kazim, he is the descendant of Haydar [a name for Ali]

Al-Rida is the Beloved Wali [saint] in his own right.
Al-Taqi and al-Naqi are rebels.
The soil trodden by the feet of Hasan al-Askari is kuhl [pulverized antimony] for my eyes.
As for the disappearing Imam al-Mahdi, he will reappear one day holding in his hand the chosen banner [of the Prophet Muhammad].[45]

The Portrayal of the Imams in the *Buyruk*

No source portrays the heavenly favor and the divine state of the Imams as vividly as the *Buyruk,* the holy book of the Shabak. According to the *Buyruk,* God created the whole universe for the sake of the Imams, and because of their transcendental origin, the manifestation of divine favor, they became the refuge of the weak and the oppressed. The *Buyruk* contains a tradition of the Prophet showing the sinlessness of the twelve Imams and their divine power of intercession for those who seek their help. This sinlessness, ordained by God, was transmitted by Him as a testamentary trust to Adam and the rest of the biblical patriarchs, and from them to Fatima, daughter of the Prophet, and from Fatima to the Imams.[46] It is significant that this line of divine transmission bypasses the

Prophet Muhammad and ends with his daughter Fatima, for she and her husband Ali are considered by Shiites to be the legitimate progenitors of the Imams. Indeed, this tradition is so important that we find it necessary to translate it in full:

> It is reported that when the Chosen One of God, Adam (peace be upon him), was wandering through the garden of Paradise, he saw an emerald dome glittering with green light. The Huris [nymphs whom Muslim men believers will marry in paradise] and Ghilman [cupbearer] walked about and received light from the dome. Adam stopped at the dome, perplexed. He began walking around it trying to find its entrance, but could not. He asked the Lord God, saying, "Lord, by the sanctity of your power and might, would you not tell me the secret of this dome?" God answered, "Adam, this dome consists of several compartments. Each has its own private door, and on each door is inscribed the following, 'Read this inscription and ask for intercession, and the door will open for you to enter and see the light.' " When Adam heard God's words, he said, "Lord, no sooner said than done." Instantly, Adam saw before him a door. Written on its lintel was "I am Hamid, Majid, Ahmad, Mahmud, and we have sent you a mercy to the world." Another door was opened, on the lintel of which was this inscription: "I am the most sublime Ali. There is no majesty and power but in God. This is Ali, the Wali [vicar] of Allah." The door opened and Adam entered, only to see another door with the inscription, "Creator of heaven and earth, this is Fatima al-Zahra [Fatima, the Fair One]. May God be pleased with her." The door opened, and behind it was another, inscribed, "I am the best of the benevolents. Blessed are they, and blessed is their happy end." The door opened, and Adam saw still another door, inscribed, "I am the Prophetess of the shepherds. I am the best of the benevolent ones at this time." When Adam read the inscription, the door opened and he entered the dome.
>
> Inside the dome Adam saw twelve corners and a lofty throne, on which sat a Sultana [queen], girded with a sash of light, and wearing a crown ornamented with gems, and earrings made of light. Adam drew near and greeted the queen, who rose and welcomed Adam with great reverence, saying, "Father, do you know me?" Adam remained silent because he was utterly bewildered. The queen spoke again, "Father, I am Fatima al-Zahra, daughter of your son the Prophet of the last days, Muhammad (peace be upon him), for whom God created the heavens, the earth, the celestial spheres, the throne, the pen and the tablets. The crown you see on my head belongs to the Seal of the Prophets, Muhammad, and the twelve windows in this dome overlooking the Garden of Eden and provid-

> ing its light are my sons, the twelve Imams. The whole universe, space and place, indeed, all beings were created for them. My posterity shall not cease to exist, and my descendants shall be the intercessors of sinners until the Day of Judgment. Did not the Prophet say that Fatima al-Zahra is from his family? Therefore, Father Adam, my son the Mahdi, the last of the Imams, shall appear at the end of time to fill the earth with justice. And my sons, the Imams, shall answer the call of help from the oppressed and the wronged among their followers."
>
> Adam was greatly astonished. To dispel his astonishment, the angel Gabriel instantly descended from heaven carrying a message of peace. He said, "Adam, if you want your body to be immaculate and pure white, fast on the thirteenth, fourteenth, and fifteenth days of every month, and your desire will be fulfilled.' When Adam fasted on the thirteenth day of the month as the angel advised, he noticed that his legs had become white. When he fasted on the fourteenth day, he saw that his body, up to his chest, had become white. And when he fasted on the fifteenth day, he noticed that his entire body was white, and thus he became free from sin and human error, through the blessing of the names of the Imams. For to the Lord of Lords, these names are like red sulphur and the greatest antidotes. When Adam saw this miracle, he delivered it as a testamentary trust to his son, Seth, saying, "Son, do not be lax or remiss in honoring the sanctity of these names, because they are the means of intercession and fulfillment of desires." Seth accepted his father's instructions and, in turn, transmitted the trust to Idris [Enoch], who transmitted it to Noah, who transmitted it to Shem, who transmitted it to Salih, whose miracles overwhelmed the people of Thamud. Salih transmitted it to Abraham, and thereafter it was transmitted from one prophet to another, until the testamentary trust reached Abd al-Muttalib, who transmitted it to his son, Abd Allah. Abd Allah transmitted it to the great apostle [Muhammad], who transmitted it to Fatima al-Zahra. Then the light of the Imams shone like the sun and filled the whole world and will remain so until the Imam al-Qaim Muhammad al-Mahdi reappears and establishes the Muhammadan state."[47]

Although the twelfth Imam, the Mahdi, had not yet reappeared or established a state, the implication of the foregoing tradition is unmistakable: the Imams are not mere religious leaders; through their descent from Ali, they occupy a prominent place in the divine scheme, which culminates in the belief that God created all things for their sake. In other words, the Imams were the reason for creation, and their transcendence was divinely transmitted through the prophets and patriarchs to Muhammad, and to his descendants through his daughter Fatima. This is the epitome of the religious doctrine of the Twelver Shiites, so called because of their belief in the twelve Imams.

Like the Twelvers, the Shabak believe in the spiritual transcendence of these Imams, who stand above the prophets and patriarchs of old. According to the *Buyruk,* Joseph was rescued from his brothers, who had cast him into a well, through the blessing of the Imams.[48] However, nothing portrays the divine power and position of the Imams as vividly as the story of the legendary figure of al-Khadir, called by Middle Easterners, both Christians and Muslims, the Khidr, or Khidr Elias, the Prophet Elijah, mentioned in Quran 6:85. In Muslim tradition, he appears as a Muslim named Abu al-Abbas. The Khidr occupies a prominent place in Islamic hagiography as a raptured saint who was taken up to heaven, where, it is believed, he was permitted to drink from the fountain of life, thereby becoming immortal. The name al-Khadir (ever verdant) signifies his immortality.[49]

The *Buyruk* tells us that when Elias was suffering the agony of death and the angel of death (called Azrail by Muslims) came to take his soul, Elias moaned and cried at the thought of departing life. God expostulated with him, saying, "Do you loathe so much departing this life and coming to me? I swear by my power and majesty that I will remove your name from the record of the Prophets." Elias answered, "Lord of the world! How can I, your servant, refuse to be with you when the names of the twelve Imams, the sons of your chosen Prophet, Muhammad, have become the means of intercession through which the Prophet Noah was saved from the great flood, Abraham was saved from fire, and even Jesus, whom you call your Spirit, was saved from crucifixion and was lifted up by you to heaven? I am your wretched servant, asking only for your charity and benevolence to extend my days."

God said, "Elias, I have offered you long life, long enough for you to witness the advent of my Messenger, Muhammad, and to behold with your own eyes the light of his twelve sons, the Imams. Also, I have allowed you to meet and serve them, and to proclaim the duty of loving them so that men may recognize their position and honor with me."[50]

Al-Kulayni reports a tradition intending to show that the Khidr had prophesied the eternal existence of the Imams.[51] From this tradition, we may deduce that the Shabak believe the twelve Imams to be the repositories of the spiritual authority that originated with Adam, the first created of mankind. In this regard they are no different from the Twelver Shiites, or indeed, from other extremist Shiite groups, such as the Bektashis. This belief is manifested in the Bektashis' tradition of the girdle.

According to this tradition, a girdle on which was inscribed the formula of the Shiites' profession of faith—"There is no God but Allah, Muhammad is the Apostle of Allah, and Ali is the Wali [vicar] of Allah"—was delivered by God to the Prophet Muhammad through the angel Gabriel. Adam was the first to wear this girdle, and after him it passed on in succession to sixteen of his descendants, including Seth, Noah Idris (Enoch), Shuayb (Jethro, the Priest of Median), Job, Joseph, Abraham, Hosha (Hosea), Yusha (Joshua), Jirjis (St. George), Jonah, Salih, Zechariah, Khidr Elias, Jesus, Muhammad, and Ali, and thence to the twelve Imams.[52]

In the tradition of the Shabak, the function of Elias was to be a harbinger of the Imams, proclaiming to mankind the religious duty of loving and recognizing them. Perhaps this tradition had its origin in the gospel, where John the Baptist is considered to be Elijah (Matthew 11:10–15), who came to proclaim the coming of the Messiah.[53]

The transmission of spiritual authority from God to the Imams through this process of succession, as described in the Shabak tradition, is affirmed by another extremist Shiite sect, the Ismailis. The Ismailis break down the process of succession into seven historical periods. The first period begins with Adam and ends with Noah at the time of the great flood. The second extends from the flood to Abraham, the third from Abraham to Moses, the fourth from Moses to Jesus, the fifth from Jesus to Muhammad, the sixth from the time of Muhammad to the appearance of the Mahdi and the end of time, and the seventh and final period, which will be ushered in by the appearance of the Mahdi, is yet to come.[54] One branch of the Ismailis, the followers of Aga Khan, divides the first six periods into sub-periods, including the present one, in which they believe the spiritual authority of the Imams is invested in their present Imam, Karim Ali Khan.[55]

The belief of the contemporary Ghulat, and indeed of all Shiites, in the transcendence of the Imams has its parallels in Christianity, although it has not been established that the Shiites received this belief directly from Christianity. The Shiites consider the Imams to be as divine as Christians consider the members of the Trinity. They maintain that the Imams are an indispensable part of God's economy, and that the existence of the whole universe depends on them. Because the Imams are transcendent, the Shiites believe in the efficacy of their intercession. For this reason they devote a certain hour of the day to each of the Imams. The first hour on Sunday is usually devoted to prayer for Ali and Fatima; the second hour of each of the following days is devoted to al-Hasan, the third hour to al-Husayn, the fourth to Ali Zayn al-Abidin, the fifth to Muhammad al-Baqir, the sixth to Jafar al-Sadiq, the seventh to Musa al-

Kazim, the eighth to Ali al-Rida, the ninth to Muhammad al-Jawad, the tenth to Ali Hadi (al-Naqi), the eleventh to al-Hasan al-Askari, and the twelfth to Muhammad al-Mahdi.[56]

It is interesting to note, in this context, that W. Ivanow detected a similarity between the theological ideas of the Adoptionists of early Christianity and the Ismaili concept of the imamate, which prompted him to state that "the Adoptionists' idea underlies this Imamate."[57] The Adoptionists were those early Christians who maintained that Jesus Christ was born a mere man, but received divinity at the time of his baptism and through his righteous life and deeds, which qualified him to become the Adopted Son of God.[58] Ivanow maintains that, according to Ismaili belief, each Imam is born an ordinary man, but the *nur* (light) of the imamate descends upon him (as the Holy Spirit descended upon Jesus during baptism) the moment his father dies.[59]

The Ismailis are, however, only a splinter group of the Shiites. To the majority of Shiites, both moderate and extremist, the Imams are divine figures who, together with the Prophet Muhammad, were affixed from eternity as shining substances in the loins of Adam when God created him. Therefore, this light was divinely inherent by the Imams, who became an incarnation of the divine Light of God before the creation of heaven and earth. It did not descend upon them individually.[60] Ivanow's analogy gains significance, however, when considered together with the similarity between the beliefs of the Kizilbash Kurds, who are related to the Shabak and live in the upper Euphrates Valley, and those of the Christian Armenians of that same region. This will be discussed later.

Before closing this chapter, we should mention the fact that the Shabak add the Prophet Muhammad and his daughter Fatima to the twelve Imams and call them Chaharda Masum (the infallible fourteen).[61] The Bektashis have their own fourteen whom they call Dort Masum Pak (the pure and innocent fourteen). In the Bektashi tradition, these fourteen are not the Imams, however, but children who either died in infancy or were martyred with al-Husayn at Karbala. Bektashi sources quoted by Birge give the names of the fourteen innocents, the names of their fathers, the circumstances under which they were killed, who killed them, and where they are buried. However, these sources are not in conformity regarding this information. Although they died or were martyred in their youth, these fourteen Innocents are inseparable, in the Bektashi belief, from their parents, the Imams, who are the family of the Prophet. Together with the Prophet, the Imams, Fatima and even Khadija, the first wife of the Prophet, they are believed by the Bektashis to be epiphanies of God. This belief is also shared by such cognate groups as the Hurufis, the Nimat Ilahis, the Shabak, and others.[62]

In modern times, the Shaykhis, an offshoot of the Twelver Shiites, maintain an extreme belief in the infallible fourteen. The Shaykhis derive their name from Shaykh Ahmad al-Ahsai (d. 1830), who taught that the infallible fourteen are the cause of the universe, in whose hands are life and death and the livelihood of men. Al-Ahsai seems to justify this belief by explaining that God is too transcendent to operate the universe personally, and therefore deputized the infallible fourteen to operate the universe on His behalf.[63] Al-Ahsai further maintains that when a believer has achieved a high degree of purity and righteousness, he will be able to receive from these fourteen divine knowledge through sufic trances or dreams. He claims that he personally received divine knowledge from the fourteen, especially from the Imam al-Hasan. Al-Ahsai relates that once he saw al-Hasan in a dream and asked him some esoteric questions. Al-Hasan placed his mouth on that of al-Ahsai and emitted into it saliva which tasted sweet, like honey. Thus, al-Ahsai received divine knowledge from the Imam al-Hasan.[64]

10

The Abdal

In the rituals of the Ghulat, and in fact of the majority of Shiites and Sufis, the number forty signifies the forty Abdal, or budala (substitutes), also known as wasilun (those who have attained divine knowledge).[1] The Bektashis call them Erenler, which in Turkish has the same meaning. The term *abdal* derives from the Arabic verb *badala* (to change or substitute), and in the language of the Sufis it means those who possess the power to change from physical to spiritual forms.[2] Ibn Arabi states that such a being is called a badal because when he departs his domicile, he leaves in his place a *badal* or, more correctly, *badil* (substitute) exactly like him. Ibn Arabi says that anyone having this power is a badal.[3] Another writer, al-Jurjani (d. 1414), maintains that a badal is anyone who can substitute a replica so exactly like himself in form and action that no one can distinguish the replica from the real person.[4]

The concept of the abdal is supported by the tradition of the Prophet, although some Muslim writers, such as Abdal-Aziz Ibn Abd al-Salam (d. 660/1261), deny that such beings exist.[5] The majority of Muslim writers, however, believe in the existence of the abdal and produce a host of sayings of the Prophet to show that such beings are part of Muslim tradition. Jalal al-Din al-Suyuti (d. 911/1505) wrote a treatise, based on the traditions of the Prophet, to prove that the abdal exist, along with other ranks of the Sufic hierarchy. The abdal are usually males; only one tradition produced by al-Suyuti mentions women as abdal.[6]

To the Sufis, the abdal are Rijal al-Ghayb (men of the unseen spiritual realm): "Men of God," and "Hosts of God."[7] They belong to the hosts that form the unseen spiritual kingdom and determine the dispensation of the physical world.[8]

At the top of this spiritual realm stands the qutb (pole), considered the embodiment of saintliness, who presides over the congregation of the awliya (saints). Because he is endowed with thaumaturgic gifts, the qutb is also called the ghawth (refuge of those who seek divine help).[9] The qutb, whose domicile is in Mecca, enjoys a favorable position with God. Al-Jurjani states that the qutb is the patron of God in every age, to whom God has given the great talisman. He traverses the universe with his visible and invisible hosts as the spirit runs through the body. In his hand he carries the balance of divine bounty, knowledge, truth, and mystery.[10] In this sense, Adam Mez (d. 1917) sees the qutb as the "heir of the gnostic Demiurges."[11] Ibn Arabi sees him as the Imam or the Logos.[12]

The qutb occupies the same position with the Sufis as the Imam does with the Shiites.[13] Therefore, we can safely deduce that in the Shiite system, the Imam—and in an exclusively Shiite sense, the Imam Ali—is the Logos. Such an observation becomes more significant when we realize that the concept of the qutb has its origin in a public speech by the Imam Ali, known as "al-Khutba al-Shiqshiqiyya. In this speech, Ali refers to himself as the qutb in relation to the office of the caliphate or the imamate, claiming that he, rather more than the first caliph, Abu Bakr, was the rightful occupant of that office. He states, "By God, he [Abu Bakr] has secured it [the caliphate] while knowing that my position regarding it is like the position of Qutb al-Raha [the pivot of the water-mill], which allows the water to gush through it."[14] Thus the Imam Ali becomes the exclusive head of the spiritual realm for both Shiites and Sufis. Except for the office of prophethood, which is exclusively Muhammad's, Ali's position is equivalent to, if not more exalted, than Muhammad's. He is the wali (vicar of God) par excellence, and head of the awliya, the congregation of saints.

Below the qutb in this spiritual realm or congregation of saints stand other dignitaries, of whom al-Hujwiri lists three hundred akhyar (good), forty abdal (subtitutes), seven abrar (righteous), four awtad (supports) and three nujaba (overseers).[15] This Sufi hierarchy also includes two Imams, one standing on the right hand and the other on the left hand of the qutb, acting as his lieutenants; twelve nuqaba, whose number corresponds to the twelve signs of the zodiac, each one having been assigned a sign of the zodiac with its mysteries; one hawari (disciple) who, in defending the religion of Islam, combines both the sword and religious authority; five hundred asib (troops); and forty rajabiyyun, whose name derives from the month of Rajab in the Islamic calendar and whose duty is to affirm the glory of God, which can be done only in the month of Rajab.[16]

In Shiite tradition, the forty abdal were Shiites, or supporters of Ali, in the time of the Caliph Umar Ibn al-Khattab. They stood with Ali as well as with the rest of the Imams after him. According to the Imam Jafar al-Sadiq, the forty abdal were the "messengers of the Imam;"[20] they constituted a significant part of the Shiite spiritual tradition. Jafar al-Sadiq describes them as those men who are near to God and through whose favor with God the prophets deliver their message; without them, the earth would overturn with its inhabitants. The abdal never leave the company of the Imam. They are the door leading to the Imam, through which God wards off calamities. Twenty-eight of these abdal are nujaba and twelve are nuqaba in every time and age. Their number does not increase or decrease, but stands always at forty. They possess divine knowledge, and, for their righteousness, God has relieved them of such human needs as eating and drinking. Al-Sadiq states further that "the Abdal are visible to me. I see them and dispatch them to the nations of the earth."[17]

These celestial beings roam the physical world each night in response to the prayers of people in distress. It is their duty to watch over every part of the earth to find those mortals needing help. Any region that they fail to visit becomes plagued with adversity. Each day, one of them, the awtad, reports to the qutb any region they failed to visit, and through the prayer of the qutb the adversities of that region are remedied.[18] God gave the abdal in particular power to heal the sick, and to rush to the aid of the wronged and the oppressed. God operates the world through them and will end it through them. Their death will signify the coming of the hour of Resurrection.[19]

Muslim sources differ on the exact number of the abdal. The tradition of the Prophet reproduced by al-Suyuti indicates that the number of the abdal is twenty, forty, or sixty. According to Ibn Arabi, there are seven Abdal, through whom God sustains the seven regions of the earth.[20] But most traditions fixes the number of the abdal at forty.[21] As we have just seen, the Imam Jafar al-Sadiq states that there are forty abdal, a number that neither increases nor decreases. "Neither the five hundred nor the forty shall decrease, for whenever one of the five hundred dies, God replaces him with one of the forty."[22] The primary home of the abdal is al-Sham (Syria), although some live in Iraq, some in Lebanon, some in Egypt, some in Antioch, some in al-Massisa, and others live throughout the rest of the world.[23]

It is interesting to note that the number forty occurs constantly in both Christian and Muslim religious lore. F. W. Hasluck has meticulously elaborated on this subject, and we need not repeat his work here, but of all the examples he provides that of the forty martyrs of Sebaste (Sivas) comes closest to the forty abdal.[24] Both groups have prominent positions in the lore of the Middle East. The martyrs of Sebaste are still honored by Middle Eastern churches, especially those of Syria and Armenia, for dying for their faith. As new converts to Christianity, they defied Roman authority, and were thrown in the dead of winter into a lake near Sebaste. The forty abdal also continue to be honored for their spiritual mission, especially their aid to people in distress. However, the martyrs of Sebaste, although they died for their faith, were simply man, playing no role in the lives of other men on earth. The abdal are considered to be spiritual beings more prominent than the angels, part of God's economy and providence.[25]

As for Syria being the home of the forty abdal, it is possible that a clandestine Shiite community existed in Syria not known to the Syrians. It is believed that despite the enmity of the Umayyad Caliph Muawiya Ibn Abi Sufyan toward the Imam Ali and his Shiite supporters in Syria (the center of his power), he was unable to prevent the abdal from giving providential assistance to these Shiites. The primary task of these abdal was to spread the Shiite message and encourage the oppressed Shiites in Syria to resist the tyranny of the Umayyad rule.[26] Supporting this Shiite opinion—that the purpose of the abdal presence in Syria was to fight the tyranny of the Umayyad caliphs—is the tradition related by Ibn Asakir (d. 1176), in which the Imam Ali says that the abdal will support the Mahdi of the Muhammadan community when he appears.[27]

Indeed, Ali refused to curse the people of Syria who supported Muawiya against him because the abdal lived in that country. It is said that Ali told his supporters not to curse the people of Syria, but rather to curse their oppressors.[28] These oppressors were the Umayyads, whose leader, the Caliph Muawiya, was Ali's arch enemy. Muawiya outmaneuvered Ali at Siffin and later succeeded in convincing Ali's son, al-Hasan, to abdicate the caliphate in his favor. Tradition says that the abdal were among those oppressed by the Umayyads because of their role as the Shiite supporters of Ali.

According to Ibn Arabi, the abdal form a spiritual realm more eminent than the angelic host. He states that the world is divided into seven territories, each supremely ruled by one of the abdal, and presented through their governance by God. The abdal understand the mysteries of the movement of the planets and their arrival at the individual positions determined for them by God. So eminent is their spiritual station that to Ibn Arabi, their names signify the attributes of God.[29] The abdal are part of the divine Reality; through their intercession, God sends rain, wards off plagues and floods, and gives the Muslims victory over their enemies.[30]

Their eminence does not mean that the abdal are celestial beings like the angels, inhabiting only the unseen spiritual realm. The body of tradition on the abdal indicates that they are *siddiqun* (righteous) and awliya (saints): men who have attained the highest degree of spirituality, not only by observing religious rituals and ordinances such as fasting, prayers, or charity, but by practicing purity of heart, kindness, humility, and innocence, and by offering sound advice to other Muslims. They are the elite of the Muslim community who, through their exemplary spiritual behavior, have gained most favor with God, thereby preserving the world from utter destruction by Him. Only those who attain these qualities can be counted among the abdal, and because this attainment is so difficult, the Prophet once told Ali that among his community, the abdal "are dearer than red sulphur."[31]

The abdal are God's friends; God Himself said, "Behold! Verily, on the friends of God there is no fear, nor shall they grieve (Quran 10:62). God has chosen them to rule his kingdom, granting them the gift of performing miracles. "God," says al-Hujwiri, "has purified them from human passion, corruption, and preoccupation with worldly concerns, so much so that God alone fills their minds and souls. This has been the case from generation to generation since the world began, because God has exalted the Muslim community above all others and promised to perserve the religion of Muhammad. The proof of God's promise is manifested in the saints, who are the elect of God."[32]

As the elite whom god has chosen through his foreknowledge, the abdal are the heirs of the prophets, from Adam to Muhammad. Some of them follow Noah, Moses, Abraham, or David, and others follow Jesus.[33] Such a concept is in perfect harmony with the Islamic belief that Muhammad is the seal of the Prophets and the perfector of Islam, which is the religion of Abraham [Quran 2:132, 4:124, 5:4, 6:161, 22:78, and 33:4]. Since the office of prophethood from Abraham to Muhammad forms one continuous chain, it follows that the only religion established by God is Islam [Quran 3:19, 5:4, 39:11, 48:29 and 84]. Likewise, the walaya (sainthood) forms a continuous chain, and the abdal, who are simply a group of saints, are necessarily Muslims. A tradition related by Ibn Abi al-Dunya (d. 281/894) states that when the prophets, who are also the supports of the world, ceased to exist after Muhammad, God chose forty men called the abdal from the community of Muhammad to succeed them.[34] Al-Hakim a-Tirmidhi (d. 898), who also relates the tradition, adds that the abdal, as the heirs of the prophets, are the party of God and the successful ones.[35]

To al-Hujwiri, the saints, by whom he means men of the unseen spiritual realm including the abdal, are evidence that the office of prophethood has remained to the present, in order that "the signs of the Truth and the proof of Muhammad's veracity may continue to be clearly seen."[36] They are God's lieutenants, who rule the universe and have complete authority over nature. Some of them are visible, but many are invisible to humankind. The abdal, however, who are among the host, who are the officers of the divine court, and who loose and bind, know one another and act in concert with the other hosts constituting the spiritual hierarchy.[37] Thus the abdal are Islamic saints who, through God's favor and bounty, were granted spiritual power and endowed with the gift of metamorphosis from a physical to a spiritual state in order to help God's community, the community of Islam.

Some Muslim authors maintain that the abdal possess the miraculous power of guiding people in their travels. When a Muslim believer sets out on a journey, he should first turn to the place of the abdal and ask their help, saying, "Peace be upon you, Oh Rijal al-Ghayb [men of the spiritual realm hidden from mortals], peace be upon you, Oh holy spirits. Give me your help and watch over me, Oh, Guardians, Excellent Ones, Overseers, Substitutes, Supports, Oh Qutb." The supplicant may recite this petition in any language, and his desire shall be fulfilled.[38]

The forty abdal occupy a prominent place in Shabak ritual. They are commemorated in a tradition called Hadith al-Arbain (tradition of the forty) as well as in a hymn, as shall be seen later in the ceremony of initiation. In both, the Imam Ali is exalted above the Prophet Muhammad.

According to the tradition of the forty, the abdal, headed by Ali, met every Monday and Friday evening in a cave near the town of Sinjar, north of the city of Mosul in northern Iraq. The only other of these abdal known by name is Salman al-Farisi, one of the Prophet's companions. One evening, when the abdal were assembling, the Prophet Muhammad went to the place of their assembly and knocked on the door. "Who is it?" asked a voice from inside. "I am Muhammad," the Prophet answered, but no one opened the door. The Prophet knocked again and again the voice asked, "Who are you?" Muhammad answered, "I am the Messenger of Allah," but the door remained closed. Yet a third time, Muhammad knocked and was challenged. This time, Muhammad answered that he was the poorest of the poor. Upon hearing this answer,

Ali ordered Salman al-Farisi to open the door. When the door opened, Muhammad saw thirty-nine Abdal headed by Ali, with Salman al-Farisi sitting next to him. Turning to al-Farisi, Ali asked him to bring him a cluster of grapes, which al-Farisi did. Ali squeezed the grapes into juice, drank some, and gave the rest to the Abdal to drink. When they drank the juice, blood gushed from their arms. Ali turned to the Prophet and said, "Are you satisfied now with our tariqa [religious order]?" The Prophet replied, "Yes, I am satisfied." From that moment, Muhammad was counted among the forty abdal.[39] The Kizilbash also venerate forty personages, including Salman al-Farisi.[40]

The Bektashis have an almost identical tradition regarding the Abdal, whom they call Kirklar (the forty). According to this tradition, the Kirklar met regularly in the house of Fatima to receive spiritual nourishment from Ali. Once, when the Kirklar were meeting, the Prophet knocked at the door. Someone inside asked, "Who is it?" The Prophet answered, "Muhammad." "There is no room for Muhammad," said the voice. The Prophet knocked again and this time, when asked his identity, answered, "I am the poor one." At this the door opened, and Muhammad was admitted into the religious assembly. Ali, who was distributing grape juice to the Kirklar, gave some also to Muhammad. When Muhammad drank the juice, his eyes opened wide and, looking at Ali, he realized that Ali was the manifestation of the divine reality and offered him homage. Before this meeting, in which Muhammad became one of the Kirklar, the prophethood was manifested in Muhammad alone, but after he was admitted and saw Ali as the "true manifestation of the Divine Reality," Ali became the posessor of the *sirr* (mystery of sainthood).[41]

A similar tradition about the abdal concerns the episode of the Miraj (the Prophet's night journey). This tradition states that on the night Muhammad ascended into heaven, he was commanded by God to take in his company a *rahbar* (spiritual guide). On the way to heaven the Prophet met a lion, which frightened him greatly. God told him not be frightened, because the lion merely wanted some object from him as a token; Muhammad gave the lion a ring. When Muhammad arrived in God's presence, God told him that behind a curtain were ninety thousand mysteries. Muhammad asked God to raise the curtain; God did so, Muhammad saw Ali sitting behind it. Before Muhammad departed heaven, God handed him a cluster of grapes and asked him to deliver it to his grandchildren, al-Hasan and al-Husayn. Salman al-Farisi, who was in Muhammad's company, asked Muhammad for grapes, and Muhammad gave him some of the grapes God had given him. On his way down to earth, Muhammad met a group of forty men, but when he counted them, he found to his surprise that there were only thirty-nine. At that moment, Salman al-Farisi arrived, making the group complete. While the forty talked, an invisible hand squeezed the grapes that al-Farisi held in his hand and then gave the forty the juice to drink. When they drank the grape juice, they became intoxicated and began to dance and shout, "Hu, Hu! [Sufi for He: God]." In the meantime, Ali, who was more overcome with ecstasy than the rest of the forty, took from his mouth the ring that Muhammad had given the lion in heaven as a token. When Muhammad saw the ring, he immediately recognized the sublime position of Ali and understood his true nature. He realized that he had attained knowledge of the divine reality.[42]

Another version of the episode appears in the religious literature of different group of extremist Shiites, the Ahl-i Haqq (truth-worshippers), also known as the Ali Ilahis (deiffiers of Ali), found primarily in western Iran. The episode is incorporated in an epistle written by a dervish from Nishapur named Nur Ali (d. 1920) and reproduced in the religious book of the Ahl-i Haqq, *Tadhkira-i A'la*. According to Nur Ali, the forty are called Chihiltan-i Nur (forty men of light) meaning the Light of our Lord Ali). The first of these forty was Sultan Mahmud Patili, and the last was Salman, probably Salman al-Farisi.[43]

The episode recounted by Nur Ali begins with the Prophet's night ascent to heaven. At the end of his journey, Muhammad reached a dome made of emerald. He knocked at the door, and was asked to identify himself. When he said that he was the Prophet Muhammad, however, no one opened the door. Muhammad was denied admission because he lacked knowledge about the dome, the nature of the persons meeting in it, and the conditions required to join the group. The Angel Gabriel appeared, however, and taught Muhammad the secrets of the dome and everything associated with it. Gabriel explained that each part of the dome signified a member of Ahl-i Haqq community, dervish who had attained knowledge of the Ultimate Reality. The dome itself signified Dede Rashwan Ali, the door signified Lal Shahbaz Qalandar, and the door's handle, Jani; the custodian was Nur-i Nihal, and the owner of the house was Mir Shir Shah Sayyid Jalal Bukharai. Upon receiving this information, the Prophet realized that he had to act humbly if he desired admission to this divine assembly. This time, when Muhammad knocked on the door and was asked to identify himself, he answered humbly, "I am the servant of the poor." The door immediately opened, and the Prophet was admitted. He looked around and saw that all those assembled were naked. When he asked why they were naked, he was told that they were *faqirs* (mendicants). Upon hearing this, the Prophet took his turban, tore it into pieces, and gave a piece to each faqir to wrap around his waist. The first piece went to Sultan Mahmud-i Patili, who headed the forty.[44]

A similar version of this legend was related to Vladmir Minorsky in 1912 by a member of the Ahl-i Haqq community. In this version, on the night of his ascension to heaven, the Prophet saw a building with a dome. He knocked on the door and someone inside asked who it was, to which Muhammad answered, "The Prophet." He was not admitted, so he knocked again, and was again asked his identity. This time he answered, "The Messenger of God." Still he was denied admission. Muhammad prayed to God to tell him what to do. God inspired him to say, "I am the Master of the people and the servant of the poor." Immediately the door opened, and Muhammad entered the dome. He saw forty people sitting down. All were God. One of them got up and asked Muhammad what present he had brought with him. Embarrassed, Muhammad searched his clothes and found a dry grape, which was the pure wine mentioned in the Quran. He was given water to add to the grape, which made enough juice for himself and all forty to drink.

A barber appeared from the world of the Invisible to reveal to Muhammad the essence of the forty, one of his assistants bled and soon blood gushed from everyone's arms. the unity of God was manifested through those who looked outwardly like the forty. A list was produced with the names of the forty, not including the name of Ali. The list contained the names of persons believed to be the incarnation of some of the twelve Imams, including al-Hasan, al-Husayn, Zayn al-Abidin, and Jafar al-Sadiq. The fifth Imam, Muhammad al-Baqir, appeared on the list as the legendary figure al-Khadir (Khidr). The last of the forty was Muhammad the Mahdi, described as Sahib-Karam (the master of generosity). Minorsky states that the member of the Ahl-i Haqq who produced this information was very proud to be the possessor of the list of the forty saints, which he had received from a dervish, Akhund Mulla Tasoutch, called the Demi-God.[45] It should be noted that the list of the forty given by Minorsky differs from that of Nur Ali.

The tradition of drinking grape juice, practiced among the Bektashis in association with the forty Abdal, is also a part of the circumcision ceremony of the Ahl-i Haqq. Samuel Graham Wilson, an American missionary who spent many years in Persia toward the end of the nineteenth century, relates that he once attended such a ceremony. A lamb was sacrificed to Ali for the occasion, cooked, blessed, and then distributed by the Pir to those present, who ate it with bread, with the utmost reverence. The meal also included nuts and raisins, as a thanks offering for the harvest. Sherbet made from grapejuice was also served, diluted when served as a drink. The people who attended the ceremony told Wilson that their sect had originated with forty persons, one of whom was Ali. They believed that God had sent them a grape from heaven which Ali pressed, giving the juice to the forty, who drank it. Hence came their custom of drinking the sherbet.[46] Some of the Ahl-i Haqq consider the forty to be deities.[47]

In modern times, the term abdal has become more a term of contempt than one of spiritual honor. It is applied to the poor and wretched Sufi wanderers whose lives, like those of the old mendicant holy men dedicated to a spiritual (Sufi order), have become an anachronism in our materialistic world. The name of the Alawi village of Çiplaklar (the naked ones) may be a description of the condition of the Sufis' wandering Abdal.[48]

11

Rituals and Ceremonies

In the early chapters of this book we have shown that the Bektashis and Kizilbash (Alawis) are one and the same sect, except that the village and peasant Bektashis are called Kizilbash. We have also shown that the Shabak are identical with the Bektashis and Kizilbash, holding common beliefs and sharing common rituals, ceremonies, and practices with them. A few practices may vary among these groups, but the differences are very slight, as will be demonstrated in this and the following chapters.

Prayer

The Bektashis, Kizilbash, and Shabak have a total disregard for such Islamic religious duties and obligations as prayer, fasting, zakat (alms tax), and pilgrimage to Mecca.[1] They believe that prayer is not a religious duty because the Imam Ali was assassinated while on his way to the mosque to pray.[2] However, they do perform a group prayer every Friday night, not in a mosque, for they have no mosques, but in the house of the Pir or of the twelve persons representing the twelve Imams.[3] Children are not allowed to attend this group prayer until they are seven years old.

According to Shabak custom, when a child (boy or girl) reaches the age of seven, the parents take the child to the pir, or baba. After the child kisses the pir's hand three times, the pir girds the child with a belt of seven folds and dismisses him. Three days later the parents take the child back to the pir, who unfastens the seven folds of the belt. The child then offers to the pir forty coins and forty eggs, symbolizing the forty abdal, including Ali, who are believed to worship in a cave in the town of Sinjar, near Mosul. The initiation to group prayer ends with a special hymn.[4] Those attending the prayer prostrate themselves in a circle while the Pir chants the following hymn:

> May the tawalli [love for those who love the holy family of the Prophet] and tajalli [theophany or a mystery revealed to the heart] be acceptable. May their attainment be made easier. May good prevail in the evening and evil vanish. Hu [He, God] is for the truthful, and may those who hold falsehood perish. Hu is for those who made mystery, the mystery of Haji Bektash Wali and the Shaykhs of the Kizil [Kizilbash] and the Erenler [those who have attained full understanding of the Divine Reality], who came from Ardabil [the Safawi Shaykhs], and who set for us this tariqa [order]. Let us say Hu for those Erenler, God, Muhammad, Ali. Truth is beloved, the Pir is beloved, and falsehood is rejected.[5]

The Bektashi-Kizilbash elements in this prayer are obvious. The "Truth" here is that taught by the Bektashis and the leaders of the Kizilbash from Ardabil, who are none other than the Safawis. The Bektashi trinity of Allah, Muhammad, and Ali is also unmistakable.

Birge reports various Bektashi prayers, including morning and evening prayers. The Shabak also have morning and evening prayers, and it is interesting to note that the Bektashi prayer contains passages similar to thc Shabak prayer cited above, as in this excerpt from the Bektashi prayer.

> May the morning be prosperous; may good be victorious; may evil be warded off; may unbelievers be defeated; may the believers attain their wishes; may hypocrites be ruined; may the believers be happy; may God, Muhammad, Ali be our intercessor; may our Lord the patron Saint [Haji Bektash Wali] shame the unbelievers; for the reign of the true Erenler.[6]

Fasting

Unlike Orthodox Muslims, the Bektashis, Kizilbash, and Shabak do not fast during the month of Ramadan. They fast during the first ten days of the Arab month of Muharram to express their passion for al-Husayn, son of the Imam Ali, who was killed in Karbala on the tenth of Muharram (10 October 680).[7] Some Bektashis abstain totally from food and water during these ten days, but the majority do so only from the evening of the ninth to the afternoon of the tenth day.

The reason for this is that water was cut off from al-Husayn and his camp at Karbala from the evening of the ninth till the tenth of Muharram, when he and his men were struck down.[8] Some Shabak break their fast by drinking water mixed with dust collected from a spot near the tomb of al-Husayn.

If a Bektashi desires to fast throughout the month of Ramadan, he may do so; such fasting is considered a commendable human practice rather than a religious duty, however.[9]

The Shabak excuse themselves from fasting during the month of Ramadan on unusual grounds. They claim that Ramadan was reincarnated in the form of a man who drove a donkey. One day, as they walked along the highway, the donkey sank into a muddy hole and the driver, Ramadan, tried to pull the beast out. Some passersby saw Ramadan struggling to rescue the donkey and helped him pull the animal free. Ramadan thanked them and revealed his true identity. As a reward for their help, he excused them from the religious duty of fasting in the month of Ramadan.[10] Another reason given by the Shabak for not fasting in Ramadan is the fact that Ali was killed during this month.[11]

Zakat: Islamic Religious Tithe

Unlike all other Muslims, the Shabak do not tithe. They do, however, give one-fifth of their crops to the Sayyids, whom they believe to be the descendants of the Prophet through his daughter Fatima.[12]

Pilgrimage

The Bektashis, Kizilbash, and Shabak do not perform the pilgrimage to Mecca, going instead to the Shiite holy shrines in Baghdad, al-Najaf, and Karbala. Not many Bektashis and Kizilbash can afford the pilgrimage to their shrines in Iraq, so they visit the tomb of Haji Bektash at Kirşehir or the shrines of their saints, such as the sanctuary of Shaykh Khubayr, northeast of Sivas. They believe that such a pilgrimage must be made seven times in order to be religiously valid.[13]

The Drinking of Wine

The Bektashis, Kizilbash, and Shabak do not consider the drinking of wine to be a religious taboo. Al-Ghulami reports that while he was in a crowd of Shabak, one of the elders told him that the Quran did not forbid wine as it did pork; it decreed only that wine be avoided. The elder maintained that there is a great difference between these strictures.[14] It is interesting that while the Shabak justify their drinking of wine by claiming that the Quran does not expressly forbid wine, the Bektashis instead invoke Quran 76:21, "And drink of pure beverage shall their Lord give them," for the same purpose.[15] Whatever their justification, the Bektashis, Kizilbash, and Shabak all use wine in their rituals; the Shabak close some of their religious ceremonies with dancing and the drinking of wine,[16] and some Bektashis drink wine to the health of the Virgin Mary.[17]

Celebration of the New Year

The Bektashis, Kizilbash, and Shabak celebrate the New Year on the evening of 1 December; the reason they do so on this particular day is not known. The celebration usually begins in the afternoon and continues until midnight. It is a sacred celebration that cannot be performed without the presence of twelve men representing the twelve Imams. In the Shabak ceremony, these men are (1) the pir, who holds the highest position in the Shabak religious hierarchy; (2) the rahbar (guide), who assists the pir in performing religious rituals; (3) the Çiraci (candle lighter), who lights and puts out the candle during the celebration; (4) the broom bearer, who sweeps and cleans the Pir's house, where the ceremony is usually performed; (5) the water carrier, who brings drinking water to those assembled (saying to each person, "May Yazid [the Umayyad caliph responsible for murdering al-Husayn and his men at Karbala] be accursed," and receiving the answer, "May he be accursed"); (6) the butcher, who slaughters the animals or fowl—usually roosters—for sacrifice; (7) the first attendant, who receives the food brought to the pir's house by the celebrants; (8) the second attendant, who unfolds the cloth in which the food is wrapped; (9) the third attendant, who breaks a piece from every loaf of bread, which he then ties to the cloth in which the food of every donor is wrapped; (10) the fourth attendant, who returns the empty dishes and cloths to their owners; (11) the first doorman, who guards the outer door of the house to prevent entry by strangers; and finally (12) the second doorman, who guards the door of the room where the celebration takes place and is always ready to answer the pir's commands.[18]

On the day they celebrate the New Year, villagers of both sexes assemble at the house of the pir. Those who attend bring with them a cock, a jug of wine, and three loaves of bread. They hand them to a member of the twelve, whose duty it is to prepare them for the ceremonial meal. Before entering the hall of the celebration, each of the faithful kneels reverently and kisses the threshold. (This kissing of the threshold is also customary among the Bektashis.[19]) Then the villagers are ushered into a room where the Pir sits, surrounded by groups of ten people. When all have assembled in the room, they turn their faces toward a candle placed in a corner of the room, and prostrate themselves in solemn adoration. After they worship the candle, the Rahbar asks the villagers to prostrate themselves before the pir. If space is limited, they may do so in a circle around the pir. When all are prostrated, the pir touches the back of each one with his hand and chants several prayers containing constant references to the twelve Imams. When he finishes the prayer, he rubs the backs of the worshippers and recites, "Alif, Allah, Mim, Muhammad, Ayn, Ali, the Yellow Path [Order] of Sayyid Qasim. Heaven and earth shall change and this Path [Order] shall not. O Ali al-Murtada [with whom God is pleased], O Husayn, the Martyr in Karbala, do not separate us from you. O God, sin generates from us, and forgiveness from you. Of the mystery of the religion of Ali is the saying, 'No chivalrous youth except Ali, and no sword but Dhu al-Faqar [Ali's sword].' "

This ceremony takes place in the afternoon. At nightfall, the butcher, who holds the "holy knife," slaughters the cocks. He alone may do so; otherwise the slaughter is unlawful, and the cocks are considered unclean and cannot be eaten. The cocks are roasted and served with wine to the worshippers. After the meal, the company dances and celebrates until midnight. Finally, each worshipper kisses the pir's hand and takes his leave. Only those who have participated in this New Year celebration are entitled to attend the Friday night prayer. Moreover, people who have not attended may be shunned by those who have.[20]

Ashura

Like all other Shiites, the Bektashis, Kizilbash, and Shabak commemorate the massacre of al-Husayn during the first ten days of the month of Muharram. This period is known as the Ashura (ten). Some wear black as an expression of grief over the death of al-Husayn. The majority, however, fast for three days and then abstain from meat for another thirty days. On the tenth day of Ashura, the rich among the Shabak usually prepare food for the poor of their community.

The lamentation over the death of al-Husayn culminates on the tenth day of Ashura, when Shabak men, women, and children assemble in the village square or in one of their holy shrines, weeping and beating their breasts. Al-Sarraf reports that he attended the commemoration of Ashura in 1938 at the Shabak village of Bir Hillan, north of Mosul, and heard the pir chanting in Turkish to the mourners, "I have renounced Yazid from the depth of my soul. My heart has also renounced the Kharijiites; thus it has become a shining mirror. I am Husayni, Husayni, Husayni [the follower of al-Husayn]."

The mourners then slap their faces in lamentation, chanting in return, "I am Husayni, Husaynı, and I do curse Yazid."

The Pir continued: "In Karbala, al-Husayn is my king. He is the Abdal who supports me. Ali is my God, my God, my God. I am Husayni, Husayni, Husayni.[21]

This ceremony illustrates the height of the Shabak doctrinal extremism by identifying Ali as God, as well as a member of a trinity along with God and Muhammad. It also demonstrates their passionate hatred of the Umayyads, particularly the Caliph Yazid, and their view of the Umayyads as enemies of the family of the Prophet. As shall be seen later, the cursing of Yazid is an integral part of Shabak rituals.

Confession of Sins and Communion

It is the religious duty [perhaps of only the male members] of the Shabak to individually confess their sins to the pir, who alone has the right to hear confessions. (There is also a public confession service, which will be discussed later.) Private confessions are usually made in the house of the pir during the Friday night prayer meeting or during the New Year's celebration. They may also occur on the Night of Forgiveness of Sin, when the public confession takes place. The ceremony is attended by both sexes. As in the New Year's celebration, the worshippers bring with them cocks, bread, and wine, which are prepared and served in exactly the same way, as a kind of communion.[22] After confessing their sins to the Pir and receiving absolution, the worshippers dine on the roasted cocks, bread, and wine, and spend the rest of the evening in singing and dancing.

Rev. G. E. White describes a similar but secret ceremony observed by the Kizilbash in Turkey, He states that once or twice a year the Kizilbash (whom he calls "Red Head") Dede (religious leader) makes a pastoral visit to his parish. The visit ends with a ceremony conducted at midnight in a common house, in great secrecy. Guards are posted around the house to prevent intruders from gaining entrance. A table is set with sacramental food and wine for the worshippers. After the communion, the Dede preaches a sermon; this is followed by a religious dance performed by both men and women. White remarks that such ceremonies, are viewed as scandalous, or at least suspicious, in the East. Although White calls this ceremony "a debased form of the Lord's Supper," he is not convinced that it has the same origin.[23]

According to Ziya Gökalp, this sacrificial ceremony is very old, being practiced by the Turks of Central Asia before they embraced Islam. These ancient Turks held a meeting, the Ayin-i Cem, at which they sacrificed animals, ate meat and bread, and drank alcoholic beverages, singing and dancing throughout. After accepting Islam, says Gökalp, they continued to hold this pagan ceremony, introducing it into the Islamic religion, where it became the high point of the Bektashi-Alawi or Kizilbash *cem* (religious assembly).[24]

Georg Jacob attempts to trace the Bektashi "ritual meal," which he considers a Semitic element, to such religions as Mithraism, predating Christianity.[25] However, Grenard maintains that this religious ceremony of the Kizilbash is "basically nothing other than the Christian Mass, slightly changed in form." Grenard was told by a Kizilbash Kurd that at this ceremony, after the congregation makes a public confession of sins, a sheep is sacrificed and pieces of it, called luqmas, are distributed by the "priest" with bread and wine to those who have been absolved of their sins.[26]

A similar ceremony is known to be performed by the Bektashis. According to Ishaq Efendi, in *Kashif al-Asrar wa Dafi al-Ashrar,* Bektashi men and women meet in a certain hall, always in the morning. When the pir enters the hall, he is received with cheers. In the meantime, bread, wine, and cheese have been made ready, and the pir hands them to an attendant, who distributes them to the worshippers. After eating and drinking, the worshippers engage in ceremonial dancing. Although men and women participate in this ceremony, Ishaq Efendi maintains that he has found no evidence of immorality or lewd behavior by the worshippers.[27] A recent witness to this ceremony is Nur Yalman, who visited the Alawi (Kizilbash) village of Çiplaklar in eastern Turkey in the 1960s. Yalman states that the Alevis are greatly annoyed by the allegations of sexual intercourse and incest in their night ceremony. In defense against such accusations, they tell the story of a Sunnite who attended one such night ceremony hoping to indulge in the alleged orgy and was struck dead by God.[28]

Captain L. Molyneux-Seel also reports a ceremony resembling the communion, which the Kizilbash celebrate on the night of January 1 at the house of their sayyid (religious leader). At this ceremony, bread is blessed by the sayyid and offered to the communicants, two at a time.[29]

The Shabak regard confession as a religious duty that no member of their community should neglect.[30] The significance they give this duty is evident from several of their hymns, which promise not only heavenly reward for those who confess, but also retribution against those who do not. The pir is the only member of the religious hierarchy to whom the Shabak confess their sins, and only he has the power to offer them absolution after confession, as this prayer, which is recited before confession, illustrates.

> The talib [neophyte] never says "no" to his Shaykh or tells
> his secret to any person other than him.
> The talib who does not tell his secret to this Shaykh is a
> hypocrite and is counted as one of the "Jews of Khaybar."[31]
> The talib who keeps his secret from his Shaykh will be deprived of
> the garden of Allah [paradise] and would be behaving badly. He is
> also ignorant of knowledge and truth,
> which is, "You who seek after the truth serve your Shaykh,
> for he is the balm for your heart's wounds."[32]

The following prayer, usually recited by the penitent during confession, is addressed to the pir.

> I have sinned, my Pir; forgive my sin by the truth of God and
> Muhammad.
> I confess that my sin has extended the limit, so forgive me my sin
> by the truth of Ali al-Murtada.

Al-Hasan has entered the arena of Ishq, so forgive my sin by the truth of al-Husayn.
Forgive my sins by the truth of Zayn al-Abidin, al-Baqir, Jafar al-Sadiq, Musa al-Kazim, and Ali al-Rida.
I have reached the path of al-Taqi and al-Naqi, so forgive me my sins by the truth of Hasan al-Askari.
The twelve Imams are of one light, so forgive
Khatai by the truth of the Mahdi Sahib al-Zaman [Master of the Age].[33]

The mention of Khatai in this prayer is important because it shows that the Shabak must have been Kizilbash followers of the Safawis. Khatai is the pen name of Shah Ismail al-Safawi, who was famous as a great poet composing not in Persian, but in Turkish.

A hymn in the form of an interlocution between a neophyte and his dede, or pir, demonstrates the devotion of the Shabak to their faith and their adoration of the twelve Imams, but most of all, their passionate hatred for the enemies of the family of the Prophet, particularly the Umayyad Caliph Yazid, son of Muawiya, who was responsible for the killing of al-Husayn. What is interesting in the following hymn is that the neophyte, the interlocutor, is none other than Yazid, implying that Yazid has become conscious of the crime he committed against al-Husayn and desires to atone for his sin by seeking initiation into the order. He wants to believe, as the Bektashis and Kizilbash do, that Ali and the rest of the Imams are the manifestations of the divine Reality, but he is completely rebuffed and denied admission to the order. Despite Yazid's pleas and his claim that he recognizes the names of the Imams and is willing to sacrifice his life for them, his supplication is considered by the pir as no more than the barking of a dog. Here is the hymn in its entirety:

Talib or Neophyte: In the early morning I passed by the Shaykh.
I asked, "Shaykh, would not you ordain me a talib?
Forgive my my iniquity, and look not upon my sin.
O Shaykh! Would not you ordain me a talib?"

Dede: Go away, Yazid, and do not come close to us.
We proclaim our renunciation of you.
Are you Ashiq [passionate lover] of a bride or a maiden?
Go away, Yazid, for you will never become a talib.

Neophyte: The Almighty God is powerful over us.
May the place in which Yazid stands be rekindled with fire.
May my eye become blind if I am in love with a bride or maiden.
Shaykh! Would not you ordain me a talib?

Dede: Yazid! Do you know the three and the five?
Don't you know that when a broiled meat shrinks, the spit becomes burned?
Barking is Yazid's custom.
Turn away, Yazid, for you will never become a talib.

Neophyte: I am content with the might of the truth.
I even know the names of the twelve and could even write them.
I give my life for the believers.
My Shaykh, would not you make me a talib?

Dede: Yazid! What is the reason for your running away from your Shaykh?
You have hurt your father and relinquished his path.
You have separated yourself from us and deserted us.
Away with you, Yazid, for you cannot become a talib.

Neophyte Say, my Shaykh, that this is also of my misfortune:
I swam through the sea, leaving my crown and my throne.
If I were passionately in love with a bride or a maiden, this is also my misfortune.
My Shaykh! Would not you make me a talib?

Dede: The Dervish Ali swears by God, yes, by God, that there is no disagreement in our tariqa [order].
God knows that Yazid will never become a talib.
Go away, Yazid, for you will never become a talib.[34]

Another hymn is characterized by symbolism common to the Sufi (mystical) orders. It is intricate in form and rhapsodic in content.

If it were not for the mighty lions who live in this transient world, darkness would have prevailed.

Even if the mourners smile, darkness would
prevail and light of the day disappear.
If the Ashiqun [passionate lovers] did not find
their beloved ones, they would become insane.
Rob me of my senses and swing with delight,
my love, for you alone know who is the beloved.
Even if the leaves of the roses which I plucked
by my own hands did not wither,
My path leads to the truth, and the Truth
shall not mislead anyone.
Separation and death:
If it were not for the command of the
Truth I would have rid myself of both
separation and death.[40]

The following hymn, replete with mystical symbolism, is most probably one of the poems of Shah Ismail. The penultimate line begins with his pen name, Khatai; unfortunately, the rest of the line is missing.

Erenler [those who have attained spiritual mystery] and
companions,
All of you behold and ask where I have been.
I was drowned in that great ocean
In which those who drown have done
what is true and corect.
From the depth to depth, I was hidden like a mystery;
I was a martyr with al-Husayn.
On the Mount of Qaf I fought with Hamza,
and with Musa Ibn Imran [the Prophet Moses] I
reached the Tur [Mount Sinai].
I was with Noah in the Ark and witnessed
the flood.
He [Abraham] pulled the knife and struck with it the neck [of
Isaac], but the knife did not harm it.
Truth has made him [Isaac] free; I was with
his ram which became his Qurban [sacrifice].
I was with the Khalil [friend of God] Abraham in
the fire, with Jacob in his sorrows, with Joseph in
the well, and with Mansur al-Hallaj in his crucifixion.
Khatai . . .
I was on earth and in heaven
the Truth.[36]

If this poem is indeed Shah Ismail's, we may assume that he attributed to himself spiritual preexistence. There is evidence that Shah Ismail believed himself to be infallible, with no dividing line between him and the Mahdi, and also believed that he was the same Ismail meant by the Quranic verse, "Remember also Isma'il in the Book [Quran], for he was true to his promise, and he was an apostle and a prophet. And he commanded his family to observe prayer and to give alms, and he was acceptable unto his Lord" [Quran 19:54–56]. For this reason he was described as al-Murshid al-Kamil (the perfect guide), whose authority derived from Khatm al-Nubuwwa (the seal of prophethood) and Kamal al-Walaya (the perfection of sainthood).[37] There is also evidence that the followers of Shah Ismail considered him to be divine and worshipped him in his presence.

A Venetian merchant who was in Persia during the time of the Safawi Shah Ismail, calls him a Sophy (Sufi Mystic) who was loved and revered by his people, and especially by his soldiers, as a god. The merchant remarks, in fact, that in Persia the name of God is forgotten, while the name of Ismail is remembered. Ismail's name was even included in the Muslim profession of faith: "There is no God but God. Muhammad is the Prophet of God and Ismail is the Vicar of God." However, this Venetian merchant states that he had heard that Ismail was not pleased at being called a god or a prophet.[38]

Another hymn abounding with mystical symbolism. It is apparently composed by Hilmi, a Bektashi poet; this again betrays the Bektashi origin of the Shabak:

Heart! How astonishing!
What has happened that made you set
a funeral ceremony and lamentation?
If you kept moaning day and night, where,
then, are your prayer and dhikr [constant mention of God's name]?
Recite your dhikr always, O heart, and drink
from the cup of your hal [state of religious ecstasy].
In your sides you have a garden of roses
whose thorns have pricked you.
The pretty ones whom you passionately love
have no faithfulness.
If you are satisfied with beholding the face [of your beloved],
why turn to another?
Many are the black hairs on the temples,
but they have no fidelity;

the winking of their eyes is like targeted arrows.
What, then, is the barrier you have set before them?
Who founded this world, and who heard
and beheld? Why, then, are there beams of light in your eye?
Look at the universe; it was all created for you.
What has emanated from the "Truth" is truth, so why
this behavior and mien?
If the Sufi achieved union [with God],
he is no more deceived by plenty of talk.
You are a slave to the Lord of Glory. Why, then,
this changing behavior, and why this pride?
Come, enter the quarter of Reality, in order to
be introduced to the Truth.
Place the rememberance of the Truth on your
tongue; what more do you want from the
Truth other than the Truth is . . .
Do not forsake the Truth for one breath.
God alone is all that is, the rest is foolishness;
so why this baser self [that is lured to evil]?
Seek support in God in all actions, and relinquish
hatred and deception.
The murshid [guide] will correct your error,
for the existence of the murshid is necessary
to lead you to this state [righteousness].
He who does not participate in Ayin-i Cem
or the ceremonies of cem no one will know
his confession of faith.
Hilmi! I am awaiting the Truth. I know
widom, listen to the Truth, and proclaim the
Truth. So ascetic, what is it that you deny?[39]

The Night of Forgiveness

Once a year, the Shabak conduct a service for the forgiveness of sins a kind of public service of repentance, during which those who have borne a grudge or hatred are to reconcile with one another and apologize for the sins they have committed against their neighbors.[40] The service of forgiveness of sin is usually conducted on a Friday night at the house of the Pir. The ceremony, which begins one hour after sunset, is not conducted unless the twelve persons representing the twelve Imams, previously described in the section on the celebration of the New Year, are present.[41]

On the appointed night, each Shabak believer attending the ceremony brings whatever food he can afford to the house of the pir. Upon entering the house, he greets those present, saying, "We have seen you in your gladness." Those present answer "Welcome." Still carrying his food, he stands before the pir, places the big toe of his right foot on the big toe of his left foot,[42] and says, "God, yes, by God." The pir responds, "May the love of the family of the Prophet and the mystery revealed to the heart be acceptable. May good prevail in the evening and evil be repulsed. Hu, [God] is for the truthful and the believer, O Ali."[43]

When the prayer is over, one of the twelve takes the food, and the worshipper joins the others sitting in a circle around the pir. Then the candle bearer gets up and, turning to the pir, greets him three times, after which the pir recites,

> The lit candle is the pride of the Dervişler.
> Seek spiritual ardor from the Erenler.
> Pray upon our Lord Muhammad and the family of Muhammad.
> He who lit the lamp is in Ishq [passionate love]
> with the chosen one, Muhammad, and the elect one, Ali.

When the pir finishes this prayer, the candle bearer puts the candle or lamp in its proper place kisses the pir's hand, and returns to his place. He is followed by the broom bearer, who places a broom (preferably new and long-handled) on the threshold of the room. He prostrates himself over the broom three times and before the pir three times, and says, "Ask."

The pir turns to those present and asks loudly, "Is there one among you who is angry or hurt?" If anyone is angry or has for some reason harbors hatred against another person, he stands and explains his feelings, naming the person toward whom he feels angry. The pir then tells him, "Reconcile," and the two people who have been at odds approach the pir and kiss each other. If the object of the complainant's ill will is not present, the pir asks the complainant to seek him out and reconcile with him. This person then leaves the ceremony, taking with him as a witness another believer, in search of the man with whom he has been angry. Wherever they find this person, whether in his house or in his field, the confessor of angry feelings asks forgiveness. If reconciliation between the two cannot be accomplished promptly, the broom bearer remains standing; he will not sit down until all are reconciled with one another. When reconciliation is achieved, the broom bearer begins sweeping the room where the ceremony is conducted. Whenever he comes near a neophyte who is seeking initiation into the Sufi order, he bows down to him, saying, "My brother Sufi," and the neophyte answers, "May the head which bows down for worship be free from pain."

When the sweeping is done, the broom bearer makes three lines with the broom on the floor, saying, "Alif, Allah, Mim, Muhammad, Ayn, Ali [an affirmation of the Shabak's trinity]." Then he stands before the pir while the pir recites, "May the service of good be acceptable; its attainment is ready." The broom bearer gathers what he has swept up, and hides it under a seat saying "God is for the home of the one who upholds the divine mystery. The pir shouts, "Get ready for prayer!" and the worshippers remove their headgear and kneel, then the pir begins "May the heads that bow down in worship never ache."

All the worshippers prostrate themselves, and the pir continues:

> Allah, Allah, O Muhammad, O Ali, May the Twelve Imams and the Fourteen Innocents be our beloved and help, and may they ward off from us fate [decreed by God] and calamity, in order that the Muslim believers shall not be separated from each other. Let him who casts a stone at us strike his head with one. May all the Twelve [Imams], the forty [Abdal] and the Seven [those who occupy the seven degrees of the spiritual hierarchy] intercede in our behalf.[44]

After the pir finishes this prayer, the worshippers lift their heads and kiss each other on both sides of the foreheads. Then the water carrier brings a bowl filled with pure water, assisted by another person who carries an earthenware jar. The water carrier faces the pir, who recites the following prayer:

> I have given up my head and earthly possessions for the Ishq [passionate divine love], for the sake of the Erenler of the Rum, and for the sake of those who always behold and love the truth. And for the sake of those who sacrificed their lives, in the mournful desert of Karbala, I shed my tears and cry, O Water Carrier of al-Husayn.[45]

Those sitting respond, "The peace of God be upon al-Hasan and al-Husayn, who are in paradise."

At this point the water carrier walks toward the Pir and hands him the bowl of water. Before taking a sip, the pir says, "More." The worshippers respond "May God's curse be upon Yazid." the water carrier then hands the bowl to those present, and each takes a sip. Following the offering of the water, plates are placed on carpets spread on the floor. The food brought by the worshippers, wrapped in the customary kerchief, is now unwrapped. A piece of bread is broken off and placed on each plate. The worshippers recite the blessing traditionally said before meals, "May it become a lawful food."

The pir continues, "May the morsel become a provision. May abomination perish. Light for those who partake of it, and may it become a guide for those who supplied the food. God is for the truthful, for the believer, O Ali."

Then the rest of the food is put out, and the worshippers eat. After the meal, they remain in place, and say, "Open the path for us." The Pir answers, "Let the eyes of those old and young, whether standing or sitting, be directed towards those who possess divine knowledge. [God] is for the truth. Blessed is the house whose owner coughs or sneezes three times at the front door [a sign of alerting the people inside that there is someone at the door, Turkoman houses having no knockers]. For him who wants to leave, the door is open and for him who wants to stay, this home is considered as his own."

After this prayer, the worshippers rise and kiss the hand of the Pir, ending the prayer session.[46]

It is reported that the Baktashis and Kizilbash also confess their sins publicly once a year, on a night called the night of the forgiveness of sins. Reconciliation is urged among antagonists, but if the offense is too serious for that, the religious leader, or Baba, may impose a penalty on the guilty party, such as pilgrimage to Mecca or to the Shiite holy shrines at al-Najaf and Karbala in Iraq. The Bektashi community takes these penalties so seriously that the guilty party is regarded as dead until he performs his assigned penance, thereby achieving absolution.[47]

Based on accounts by Kizilbash, Grenard relates that the Kizilbash celebrate a nocturnal ceremony very similar to a Christian mass. The pir, or dede, whom Grenard calls a priest officiates, chanting prayers in honor of Ali, Jesus, Moses, and David. (David is particularly venerated. Portions of his psalms have been translated into the Turkish language and are chanted at services.) The pir carries a willow branch, which he dips into a bowl of water while he is saying prayers, thereby consecrating the water in the bowl. The consecrated water is then distributed to all households.

During the ceremony, the assistants publicly confess their sins in a manner similar to that of Christians. All lights are then extinguished, and the congregation mourn their sins in darkness. After a prescribed time, the lights are turned on, and the pir offers the congregation absolution.

Then he takes a slice of bread and a cup of wine, solemnly blesses them, dips the bread into the wine, and distributes pieces of it to the assistants who have confessed their sins and received absolution.[48]

G. E. White, who gives a similar account of the ceremony, states that the congregation partakes in a kind of communion, generally consisting of a morsel of a sacrificed lamb, or bread and wine. In some cases, the pir, or dede, asks those who have committed grave sins to atone for them by giving a sum of money to the poor.[49] This ceremony does indeed appear similar to a Christian celebration, but Ivanow is of the opinion that the Kizilbash ceremony may have had its origins in Zoroastrianism and Mithraism, resembling particularly the Yasne (sacrifice) ceremony celebrated by the Zoroastrian priests. It is not unlikely that this ancient custom, connected with a religious sacrifice, passed into the Dervish orders of Asia Minor, whose members originally came from Turkestan and Persia, the base of Zoroastrianism.[50]

The Extinguishing of Light Ceremony

Associated with both the commemoration of the tenth day of the Muharram (Ashura), the day on which al-Husayn, son of the Imam Ali, was killed at Karbala, and the Night of Forgiveness of Sin, is the Extinguishing of Lights ceremony. During the night of the tenth of Muharram, the Shabak, and kindred sects such as the Bajwan and the Sarliyya or Kakaiyya, extinguish all lamps or candles, take off their shoes, and spend the entire night mourning the killing of al-Husayn at Karbala, just as they do during the Night of the Forgiveness of Sins. When the lamps or candles are relit, the penitents are absolved of their sins by the religious leaders.[51] This practice is also known among the Kizilbash.[52] This lamentation of the death of al-Husayn on the tenth night of Muharram is not peculiar to the Shabak or the Kizilbash, being practiced by the great majority of Shiites in the city of Karbala in Iraq, where the people adhere so strictly to the rule of extinguishing all lights that an eye-witness, al-Sarraf, states that not one dares even to light a match.[53]

The secrecy surrounding these ceremonies and the exclusion of non-communicants have raised calmunious rumors regarding the moral behavior of the congregation during these ceremonies. Communicants are accused of promiscuous behavior and even participation in sexual orgies because the ceremonies are conducted in complete darkness. Rev. Anastase al-Karmali accuses the Shabak of such sexual orgies. He states that the Shabak have an obnoxious religious custom whereby, on a certain night each year, men and women meet at the mouth of a large secret cave and spend the night in eating, drinking, and revelry. Al-Karmali calls this night Laylat al-Kafsha, a name also used by the Sarliyya. He claims that the Shabak conclude the night's activities by "committing the most heinous immoralities."[54] Al-Karmali also claims that the term *Kafsha* drives from *Kafasha,* a colloquial term meaning "to grab," used by many people in Iraq, especially in the north; he adds that the reason for this appellation is obvious.[55]

In fact, the word *Kafsh* is of Persian origin and means "slippers" or "shoes." Perhaps the night of the Kafsha is so called because the mourners of al-Husayn usually take off their Kafshs, or slippers, and should really be called "The Night of [Removing] The Slippers."[56] Be that as it may, most writers reporting on the alleged immoralities committed on the "Night of the Kafsha" maintain that the charges are the products of overactive imaginations and have no truth to them.[57] While it is difficult to ascertain the truth about such practices, a member of another esoteric sect, the Yezidis, who live in villages close to those of the Shabak, has stated that the Yezidis do practice night orgies. Behnam, a Yezidi convert to Catholicism who became a Syrian Catholic monk at the Sharfa Monastery in Lebanon, states that it is true that in observance of Laylat al-Kafsha, men and women engage in sexual acts. He attended a Laylat al-Kafsha ceremony in the village of Bashiqa, near Mosul, Iraq.[58]

Hasluck cites other writers to show that ignorant Sunnite partisans pin the names Zarati and Mümsöndürun (candle extinguishers) on the Kizilbash, but comments that this is generally thought to be done maliciously. He also reports that similar accusations of incest and promiscuity were made by Benjamin of Tudela against the Druzes in the twelfth century and by the Arabs against the Druzes in modern times, as well as by the Turks against the Crypto-Jews of Salonica.[59]

Van Lennep remarks that the Kizilbash of Asia Minor have "mysterious and obscene rites, in which the initiated alone take part." He says further that their worship consists of dances in which both sexes participate, and that the "Turkish authorities have succeeded in falling upon them and disbanding them in the midst of their Saturnalian nightly orgies."[60]

T. Gilbert gives a similar account of this Kizilbash practice. He writes that once a year, the Kizilbash meet in an isolated spot to celebrate a ceremony that leaves far behind in its shameless rites those of the Oriental Bona Dea at Rome. After prayer, Gilbert says, the lights are extinguished, and the sexes intermingle without regard to age or the ties of kinship.[61]

According to Felix von Luschan, a similar ceremony is performed by the Takhtajis (woodcutters) of Turkey, who have great religious affinity with the Bektashis. Felix von Luschan states that the Takhtajis conduct their religious meeting in the evening, but does not mention a celebration of communion. He says only that those present dance and sing until midnight, and then fall into a mood of depression. Some of the participants show signs of hallucinations or hypnotic trances. During the ceremony, the religious leader offers his opinion on a variety of questions, religious and secular, even predicting the next rainfall. He also performs healing and other miracles. Then the participants confess their sins while the leader wraps a stick with rags, in the belief that the sins of the congregation are transferred to the stick with the rags. The leader then burns the stick and casts the ashes onto a river or stream, signifying that the communicants have received absolution for their sins.[62] The same Takhtaji ceremony is reported by Sir W. M. Ramsay, who states that the Takhtajis hold secret meetings during which they commit immoral sexual acts and "scandals with regard to Oedipal union and harried orgies."[63]

A modern writer, Nur Yalman, reports similar accusations made against the Alawi inhabitants of the village of Çiplaklar, in eastern Turkey. Yalman says that the Alawis's have a rite called Müm Söndü (candle extinguishing), source of "the myth of communal sexual intercourse and incest" that causes great annoyance to them.[64]

It seems that many secretive groups have been accused of nocturnal orgies and sexual license. Since these ceremonies sparking the rumors are conducted at night and in the utmost secrecy, it is difficult to ascertain whether the accusations are myth or reality. However, this practice of night ceremonies does seem to be universal in Middle Eastern society. Professor Robert L. Canfield, who has done research in Afghanistan, contributed a paper on the subject to the Conference on Symbols of Social Differentiation (1978), in which the author was a participant.[65] And as far back as the tenth century, Abu al-Hasan al-Shabushti (d. 998), in his book *al-Diyarat* (Monasteries), related that on a night called the "Night of the Mashush," a feast in the Convent of Ukbara near Baghdad, Iraq, men and women mingled, and no one denied the other anything.[66]

The Ceremony of Initiation

Like the Bektashis, the Shabak have a rather elaborate initiation ceremony which is conducted in absolute secrecy. A person desiring admission to the Shabak community must be married. He must find and befriend another married couple who intend to enter the same order. (This is similar to the Kizilbash tradition requiring that admission be open only to married persons who each have a companion of the opposite sex.[67] The two couples must live together for forty to seventy days, in accordance with the injunction of Saykh Safi al-Din (from whom the Safawis take their name), who said, "The spirit is one, the body is one, the four are one, and the mystery is one."[68] In other words, one couple represents the spirit, and the other the body. During this probationary period the seeker of admission and his wife associate closely with the other person and his spouse. The four live, eat, and pray together. At the end of the probationary period, they go to the pir, taking with them a sheep that is three years old and free of physical blemishes. They also bring forty or more bottles of wine. The pir then orders forty Sufi couples to attend the ceremony of initiation. In the meantime, an ox has been selected; both the sheep and the ox will later be slaughtered. While the flesh of the ox may be eaten by all the villagers, the sheep may be consumed only by the Sufis. This is in accordance with the teaching of Saykh Safi, who stated, "He who eats of the flesh of this sheep is in fact eaten the flesh of al-Husayn."[69] It is interesting to note that the ceremony is not considered authentic unless a sacrificial sheep is available at the time the meeting takes place.

The pir then sits in the place of honor in the hall, and on a lower level sit the eighty Sufis. The four initiates, the couple representing the spirit and the couple representing the body, enter the hall carrying wine, yogurt, and honey, which they place in a large container. They also bring four small cups. The couples then stand in the prescribed order: the wife representing the spirit facing the husband representing the body, and the husband representing the spirit facing the wife representing the body. The pir fills the cups and hands them to the guide, who in turn hands them to the four initiates. The pir then recites three times the following confession, called Iqrar Tulusi (complete confession):

"Spring water. And their Lord caused them to drink pure water" (Quran 76:21). "May this drink become a light to the drinker and a direction to the cup bearer".[70] The pir concludes by saying: "He who renounces this confession may be counted as a hypocrite and become like Yazid, son of Muawiya."

The pir then asks the four initiates to prostrate themselves—the "spirit" husband next to the "body" wife and the "body" husband next to the "spirit" wife. The four are covered with a blanket and the guide holds the Staff of Arkan (rituals) over them. The pir recites three prayers, rubbing the backs of the four at the end of each, and the guide touches their backs with the ritual staff, saying, "Alif, Allah, Mim, Muhammad, Ayn, Ali." Then the "spirit" husband crawls behind the "body" wife and the "spirit" wife crawls behind the "body" husband, and the couples kiss all the Sufis in the room, probably as a kind of "kiss of peace." Everybody stands while the pir offers a supplicatory prayer, and genuflect three times when he is finished, kissing the ground and saying, "Alif, Allah, Mim, Muhammad, Ayn, Ali." They also rub their chests with their hands and say, "The truth is beloved, the pir is beloved. The truth is Sultan. Away with falsehood." The guide then holds the staff while the pir approaches and worships it, kissing it at both ends and in the middle. The pir embraces the guide, placing his head on the guide's chest, and the guide rubs the pir's back three times with the staff and then does the same for each of the worshippers. The "spirit," the "body," and their wives stand before the pir, who recites, "May this place become a Hajj [pilgrimage] to those who attend; may it become a Miraj, and may their vows and supplications attain to the truth."[71]

After this prayer, the sheep is slaughtered in a trench dug in the meeting hall and the ox is slaughtered too. The villagers eat the ox, and the Sufis eat the lamb and drink wine. In the meantime, the pir recites the following hymn:

> I have roamed the seven territories and the four corners [of the earth] and found no one as exalted as Ali. Ali is the one who created eighteen thousand worlds. He is rich and able to provide daily bread. One of his names is Ali, the other is God; praise and thanks be to God. I have not seen an exalted one except Ali. No man came to this world like Ali. Truth has been revealed by his pen, which wrote on the tablet and filled the whole world with its light. Would anyone, I wonder, who calls on Ali remain deprived? I have dived into the depth of the sea and counted the hair of the yellow bull and its company, and ascended to earth and into heaven, and found no exalted one except Ali. The high gate, wells and chambers of the Garden [paradise] are made of garnet and pearls, are under the feet of Ali. Pir! Sultan! Ali is the head of the forty and one of the Abdal. Thus, my heart tells me that Ali is God and is also Muhammad.[72]

This hymn is a clear testimony that the Shabak are Ghulat (extremists) who deify Ali. It also demonstrates their trinity of God, Ali, and Muhammad, and shows that the Shabak share with other Ghulat the belief that Ali is the provider of daily bread, and that he is the "face of God," the "hand of God" and the "Gate of God."[73]

After reciting this hymn, the pir orders the door of the meeting hall to be opened, allowing the villagers who have been waiting outside to come in. The villagers enter the hall and congratulate those who have become Sufis, or members of the order. They kiss the hand of the pir and then drink wine, as the pir sings a song and plays the tunbur (musical instrument).

The ceremony of initiation ends with the collection of offerings. A member of the congregation ties a black kerchief around his neck and asks for gifts. Everyone puts whatever he can afford into the kerchief.[74]

Another Ghulat sect, the Ahl-i Haqq (or Ali Ilahis) of western Iran, who shall be discussed later, have as part of their tradition a covenant of confraternity, according to which persons make covenants among themselves to live in complete harmony in this life and share sins and virtues on the Day of Resurrection.

Al-Ghulami describes another version of the ceremony of initiation among the Shabak and other related groups. According to his account, the pir visits the villages, preaching the way of the Sufis, and through the power of his preaching, convinces some people to become talibs (seekers) as a preliminary step toward joining the Sufi order. The chosen neophytes then meet with the pir at the home of one of them, always on a Friday night. Food and wine are provided for the meeting and the pir sits in the place of honor, surrounded by the worshippers. Then the talibs approach him one by one; placing their right big toe on the left one and bowing solemnly, they say, "By God, yes by God, Birim." Afterwards, the pir rises and girds each of them with a sash, placing his right hand on each seeker's back and pressing it tightly, while saying, "Alif, Allah, Mim, Muhammad, Ayn, Ali." Al-Ghulami states that the Shabak and related groups believe that the image of the pir's hand will appear on the backs of the initiates on the Day of Resurrection, being the only sign entitling the initiate to enter Paradise.[75] When these ceremonies are over, the villagers waiting outside enter the house, congratulate the new initiates and kiss the hand of the pir. Then they drink wine, doing so until some of them lose consciousness. In the meantime, the pir, accompanying himself on his tunbur, sings the song previously mentioned.[76]

Obviously, the Shabak ceremony of initiation differs in some particulars from those of the Bektashis and the Kizilbash. However, there are some similarities between the Bektashis' ceremony of initiation and the Shabak ceremony of the Night of Forgiveness, such as the lighting of the lamp or candle, the sweeping of the meeting hall, and the offering of water by a cupbearer to the worshippers.[77] There is also the sacrificial cock or lamb, as reported by Brown and Garnett.[78] The Shabak ceremony of initiation, when compared with that of the Bektashis, reveals a Bektashi origin.

Holy Shrines of the Shabak

We close this chapter with a discussion of the holy shrines that signify the Shabak's attachment to and honor for the Imams. It should be noted that these shrines are not mosques or places of worship in private homes; they are instead the monuments of Shabak faith, which the Shabak visit during the two major Muslim festivals. Their distinctive conical domes, with twelve triangular sections rising above the shrines, betray their Kizilbash origins, resembling the Kizilbash *taj* (cap), which has twelve folds representing the twelve Imams. No other religious group in northern Iraq (except for the Yezidis) has shrines with domes like those of the Shabak.[79]

The Shabak have several holy shrines that testify to their Kizilbash origin. One of these shrines, called Ali Rush, is in the village of the same name. The second, called al-Abbas, is in the village of al-Abbasiyya, situated on al-Khosar, a small tributary of the Tigris River, near the ruins of ancient Nineveh. Al-Ghulami states that the Shabak do not know who this Abbas was.[80] Ali Rush is Ali, son of al-Husayn, nicknamed Zayn al-Abidin and al-Sajjad (worshipper of God) because of his extreme piety.[81] It is perhaps because he always dressed in black that the Shabak call him Ali Rush, Kurdish for "black." The Shabak usually visit this shrine on the first and second days of the two Muslim feasts of al-Fitr and al-Adha.[82] But why do the Shabak have a shrine for this son of al-Husayn at Ali Rush, when he died and was buried at al-Baqi in al-Madina? Perhaps the reason is that it was difficult for them to visit al-Madina; perhaps (and this is more plausible) it was because Ali Zayn al-Abidin represents the peak of Sufism, which has become an integral part of Shiism.[83]

The other shrine of the Shabak is that of al-Abbas, whom (according to al-Ghulami) the Shabak fail to identify. In fact, al-Abbas is a son of the Imam Ali and brother of al-Husayn. He was the Banner Bearer of al-Husayn and, like al-Husayn and many other members of his family, was killed and mutilated at al-Taff in Karbala. (His palms were cut off.) Although the Shabak do not know the identity of al-Abbas, they perform some rituals that obviously pertain to him. Al-Ghulami reports that during certain religious festivals, Shabak leaders visit their villages, carrying a bronze palm and exhibiting it to the people, who kiss it with great reverence. They receive a blessing for this act.[84] The only explanation of this bronze palm is that it represents the palm of al-Abbas, which was cut off at Karbala.[85]

Allegedly connected with the episode of the massacre at Karbala is the grave site of Ubayd Allah Ibn Ziyad, whom the Umayyad Caliph Yazid I appointed a governor of al-Kufa in Iraq in order to eliminate al-Husayn and his entourage.[86] Every year the Shabak visit Ubayd Allah's grave, which is twenty kilometers east of Mosul, Iraq, and cast stones at it, all the while cursing Ubayd Allah, who was directly responsible for killing of al-Husayn and his men. As time has passed, these stones have grown into a huge mound that attracts the eye of any passerby.[87]

The Shabak have another shrine called Hasan Fardosh, near the village of al-Darawish, on the road between Mosul and Bashiqa. The Yezidis in the area also venerate this shrine, and they and the Shabak meet once a year on a Friday, known as Tawwafa Friday. Both men and women spend the day dancing to the sound of musical instruments.[88] The important thing about these shrines is their domes which are of uniform conical shape, resembling the Kizilbash taj (cap), which consists of twelve strips to commemorate the twelve Imams.

12

Social Customs

In Middle Eastern societies, religion and religious affiliation play a fundamental role in the lives of the people. Identification with a religious sect is generally permanent; in the rare instances when a switch is made from one denomination to another, it is usually either the result of oppression or is undertaken out of self-interest. The American practice of "shopping for a religion" is unknown in the Middle East. A person born into a certain religious denomination will almost certainly live out his life within it. This religious striation shapes almost every aspect of life and social custom in the Middle East. Although it has been argued that advances in knowledge and education have weakened this religious rigidity, such thinking, on the whole, is fantasy. Religious striation tends to be especially rigid among the minority sects, whose social ethos and identity are bound up with their religious beliefs. Members of these sects may be loyal to their country and would certainly defend it, but their first allegiance is to the sect with which they identify.

Extremist Shiite sects, including the closely related Bektashis, Kizilbash, and Shabak, are no exception. For generations they have preserved their characteristic beliefs, customs, and way of life. A rural people, they have retained such tribal characteristics as a close sense of community, a system of patriarchal authority, and a cohesive family structure. Some extremist Shiite sects in Turkey, such as the Çepnis and Takhtajis, are nomads who make a living by cutting and selling wood. But most of these sects are permanently settled, living in towns and villages and working as farmers, herdsmen, and small businessmen. A great number of the educated new generation, however, have left their villages to seek greater employment opportunities in the cities.

Like other religious and ethnic groups in the Middle East, these sects keep to themselves intermarrying with those of their own faith. It is easy to identify these sectaries by their villages. When the author began his law practice in Mosul in 1946, he had many clients from the outlying villages. Most of these villages were notably homogeneous in character. Some were inhabited almost entirely by the Shabak, others almost entirely by Sarliyya. A few comprised members of two sects: for example, the Shabak and the Yezidis, or so-called devil worshippers. But even in villages with more than one sect, each sect retained a distinctive culture and community.

The Shabak are generally peaceful and hospitable, having amicable relations with most other people, be they Arab or Turkoman. Their men pride themselves on their long beards and mustaches, although the new generation is forsaking this custom. Rev. Anastase al-Karmali reports, on the authority of a resident of Mosul with firsthand knowledge of Shabak customs, that when the Shabak man eats, he uses his left hand to hold his mustache out of the way so that it does not become soiled while he is eating with his right hand.[1] This custom, especially common among Shabak religious leaders, is also prevalent among the Turkomans and may indicate the Turkoman origin of the Shabak.

It is interesting that other extremist Shiite groups, such as the Sarliyya (or Kakaiyya) and the Ahl-i Haqq (truth-worshippers)—also called Ali Ilahis (deifers of Ali)—associate the growing of mustaches with the Imam Ali. The Sarliyya claim that when the Prophet Muhammad died, Ali washed his body before burial, following Muslim custom. During the course of the ablutions, Ali drank the water that filled the Prophet's navel. This caused Ali's mustache to remain long, growing out immediately even when he cut it. This is why the Sarliyya do not shave off their mustaches.[3]

The Ahl-i Haqq also wear long mustaches that are not trimmed or tampered with in any way. According to their religious book, *Tadhkira-i A'la,* the mustache is considered an emblem distinguishing the Ahl-i Haqq from other people. The practice of wearing a long mustache is said to date back to the time of the Imam Ali, who is believed to have stated that whoever loved the Ahl-i Haqq ought not to clip his mustache. Thus, any attempt to alter a mustach is taboo, and the fully grown mustache is the badge of membership in the Ahl-i Haqq community. More important, the mustache is associated with Ali, who is more than a mere man to the extremist Shiite sects.[4]

The growing of beards and mustaches is also a Kizilbash-Bektashi custom. M. F Grenard writes that the Kizilbash in Turkey are distinguished from Sunnite Muslims only by their beards and hairstyle. They do not shave their beards, but allow them to grow full and free.[5]

While the Sunnite Muslims clip their mustaches in imitation of the Prophet, who they believe clipped his, extremist Shiites refuse to clip their mustaches, in imitation of their spiritual leader Ali.[6] The point is clear. What is "true" of the Prophet is also "true" of Ali, who is considered at least equal with, if not higher than, the Prophet.

The Birth of a Child

Seven days after a male child is born to a Shabak family, the parents take him to the pir to be blessed. They take along with them a lamb, bread, and wine. After the pir recites the blessing prayers over the child, the lamb is slaughtered, cooked, and served to all those in the ceremony. The guests eat, drink, and dance. The dance is performed in a semicircle, and is known among the villagers as the *chopi*.[7]

Marriage and Divorce

The Shabak hold women who are descendants of the Imam Ali in high esteem. They insist that only men and women descendents of Ali should intermarry, believing that a marriage with an outsider is ill-fated.[8] Al-Ghulami states that in conversations with leaders of the Shabak, he tried to explain to them that Islam does not forbid marriages with outsiders, pointing out that the second caliph, Umar Ibn al-Khattab, married Umam Kulthum, the daughter of the Imam Ali, even though he was not of Ali's family. Al-Ghulami says that his efforts were in vain, however; the Shabak remained convinced that their prohibition was necessary. A similar custom exists among the Zaydis, a moderate Shiite group. They believe that only a Fatimi man may marry a Fatimi woman, since both are descendents of Fatima, daughter of the Prophet and wife of the Imam Ali.[9]

The Shabak hold marriage sacred. A Shabak husband seldom deserts or divorces his wife, even when she is unable to fulfill her wifely duties. To the Shabak, divorce is detestable. If a Shabak husband does divorce his wife, he must pay dearly, fulfilling certain requirements before the divorce is final. First, he must sell all his major belongings—his home, land, his cattle. Dividing the proceeds into twelve shares, he must donate eleven shares to the Pir, retaining one share for himself.[10] He must travel then to Karbala, accompanied by two witnesses. In Karbala, at the tomb of al-Husayn, he must proclaim that he has divorced his wife. Upon returning to his village, he must buy forty bottles of *arak,* a licorice-flavored alcoholic beverage known in the United States as ouzo, and, along with the two eyewitnesses and other members of the community, he must proceed to the house of the pir. There a fire is built, and when the flames die down to ashes, the pir orders the man to stand on the hot ashes, with two stones tied around his neck, as a punishment for divorcing his wife. Then the pir turns to those present and asks "Are you pleased with this slave?" The answer: "If the Erenler are pleased with him, we are pleased, too." The pir replies, "The Erenler are benevolent." At this point, the divorce becomes final.

Commenting on this procedure, al-Sarraf indicates that the husband alone must bear the enormous burden entailed in divorcing his wife.[11] This practice is completely different from the standard practice of Islam, whereby a man may divorce his wife simply by saying that he is doing so.

The Kizilbash are generally monogamous, although polygamy is permitted if a first wife is barren, has become insane, or is incapable of performing her wifely duties, or if the husband is financially capable of supporting more than one wife. Divorce is forbidden.[12]

The Kizilbash seem to hold women in great respect, maintaining that, in spirit and love, women are equal to men. They believe in educating their daughters and permitting women to go about with their faces uncovered. Women are also free to become acquainted with men, especially Christian men.[13] Like many village women in the Middle East, the Kizilbash women assist their men in the fields, in addition to performing household chores and caring for the children.

Although it may be understood from the above that the woman has a special position in society, there is another side to this position, owing to the concept of *Ird.* Literally, *Ird* means a special kind of honor, associated with the protection of the female's virtue, whether she is a virgin or not. Any woman who indulges in illicit sexual acts outside wedlock may be put to death, for such behavior is believed to destroy the family's Ird. Thus, when a man in Middle Eastern society swears by his Ird, this is a very serious oath; he is swearing that all the female members of his tribe or family are sexually pure and have committed no illicit acts. This concept of Ird is not peculiar to the Extremist Shiites. It is universal in Middle Eastern societies, regardless of their ethnic or religious composition, their social status or their degree of sophistication.

In Iraq, the killing of a woman for an illicit sexual act is called *Ghasl al-Ar,* literally, "the washing of dishonor." This practice is highly esteemed throughout the Middle East, but it is especially prevalent among the rural tribal inhabitants of Iraq, including the Shabak and other related groups.[14] In fact, Article 216 of the Iraqi Penal Code, which the author studied and practiced in the courts of Iraq, states that if a man finds his wife or any close female relative in bed with a man and kills her instantly, he will be sentenced to only three years imprisonment, not death. Usually such a killer reports the incident to the police himself, proudly presenting the weapon he used in killing his victim and saying that he did it as *ghaslan li al-Ar.* In most cases, he becomes a hero, respected and honored in his community.[15]

Al-Sarraf states that the Shabak are "very protective of their Ird, and abstain from vice, adultery and whoredom."[16] He notes, however, the very different treatment given erring men and erring women. A Shabak man who is immoral or profligate is punished with a kind of excommunication. He is totally ostracized, cast out from the social and religious circles of his community. Unless he mends his ways, no member of the Shabak community will ever give his daughter to him in marriage. But a Shabak woman, married or single, who is even suspected of indulging in illicit sex or of indecorous conduct, will be slain.[17]

A leader of the Sarliyya, Khattab Agha, told al-Ghulami that outsiders, speaking from ignorance, accuse his sect of committing immoral sexual acts at the Çirağí Söndürün (extinguishing of lights). To defend his people's honor against such accusations, Khattab Agha cited many instances in which women who had committed adultery were "drowned in either the Khazir or Zab rivers [tributaries of the Tigris], or strangled, or had sharp daggers plunged into their bodies." Khattab Agha concluded with great pride that if this is the manner in which his people defend their honor, "How could anyone accuse us of meeting privately to commit what is abominable?"[18] It should be remembered that the concepts of Ird and Ghasl al-Ar apply only to women: not to men, who are equally guilty of unlawful sexual acts. This one-sided moral code can be understood only if one realizes that, almost without exception, Middle Eastern societies are male oriented.

Death

When a member of the Shabak dies, the pir goes to the house of the deceased and reads certain hymns over the corpse. The body is then washed, according to universal Muslim custom. Members of the family grieve over the body, wailing loudly. After the burial, the family usually prepares a meal which is distributed to the poor people of their villages.[19]

Drinking of Wine

Both men and women among the Shabak drink wine, claiming that, unlike pork, it is not forbidden by the Quran. Wine is considered by the Shabak to be one of the niceties of this life, and they imbibe it in quantity at their religious meetings and festivities. It is even used to treat the common cold. The drinking of wine or arak is so firmly associated with their religious belief that to the Shabak, "He who does not drink arak has no faith or religion."[20] Sometimes, the Shabak even give it to their horses as the treatment for certain diseases.[21] The drinking of wine is also allowed by the Bektashis, the Kizilbash, and other extremist Shiite sects.[22]

The Eating of Meats

Like orthodox Muslims, the members of the extremist Shiite sects do not eat pork. The Bektashis and Kizilbash, however, have an additional prohibition whose origin is unknown: they avoid eating or even touching hare. One explanation offered for this rather peculiar custom attitude of the Bektashis is that a companion of the Prophet Muhammad had a cat that turned into a hare. Another is that the Bektashis believe that after a hare is cooked, all that remains is a little blood, and blood is associated with the Umayyad Caliph Yazid, who was responsible for the unjust killing of al-Husayn at Karbala. Yet another explanation concerns the wife of a certain dervish. This woman tried to wipe clean a soiled soft spot with her veil and then hid the veil in a tree. Some of her inquisitive neighbors, who wanted to know what she had hidden in the tree, went to look and, behold, a hare jumped out of the tree.[23] It is most likely that this custom is an ancient one, dating back to the pagan practices of Turkish tribes.[24]

It is also peculiar that the Takhtajis (woodcutters), another extremist Shiite sect related to the Bektashis, consider the bear to be taboo. They avoid looking at bears and even touching bearskins. In fact, they never even use the word "bear," calling this animal "big son."[25] This aversion to the bear also derives from a tribal custom of the ancient Turks, associated with the belief of "Oncun," which forbids the eating of certain animals.[26]

Folk Medicine

Like other villagers and even some town dwellers in Iraq, the Shabak hold many superstitions, and practice folk medicine and faith healing. This does not mean that they shun medical advice and treatment, but the majority of the Shabak are illiterate and ignorant, and most of their villages have no doctors or treatment facilities. Moreover, it is difficult for them to transport their sick to Mosul, and in many cases, they fear that the sick could not stand the trip. Also, because of their religious and ethnic idiosyncrasies, they have developed their own habits, of which folk medicine is a part.

One common treatment given the sick is a soup called *Tarshok* (sour), made by boiling grain with the juice of edible sumac and lemon.[27] When someone becomes seriously ill, he is taken to a holy shrine or the house of the pir, or the pir is asked to visit the patient at home to recite certain prayers for him.

For boils on the face, two flintstones are struck together, producing sparks which are directed at the offending boils, and which the Shabak believe will cure them. For a stomach ache, the belly is lightly struck with an arrow.[28] Another treatment for stomach ache is bleeding and cauterization.

Trachoma is treated by applying to the infected eye a sticky substance extracted from the backs of frogs. This treatment is very painful, with the pain lasting as long as twenty-four hours, but the Shabak claim that it is effective.[29]

When a person suffers from a crooked jaw, perhaps resulting from a seizure or stroke, he is to be taken to the shrine of a saint, where he remains for seven days, the period assigned for his recovery. If he does not recover by the end of seven days, the pir or someone else strikes his jaw with his shoe to straighten it.[30]

Even more peculiar is the treatment of intermittent fever, probably due to malaria. The right arm of the sufferer is wrapped with a piece of cloth, which is left on until the fever is gone. A thread blessed by the Pir and tied around the patient's wrist is also used to treat a fever. Still another method of treating fever is to have the sick person take with him an onion, a jug of water, and a loaf of bread, and go to a special place outside the village. With the provisions beside him, the patient lies on his back on the ground, awaiting the full assault of the fever. When the fever has left him, the patient returns home, leaving behind the onion, the jug of water, and the loaf of bread.[31]

These treatments all pertain to fevers that strike in the daytime. A fever that comes on at night requires different treatment. Before sunset, a person from a family known for its hereditary medical tradition stands on the top of the village dunghill, holding a loaf of bread in his hand and shouts in the Kurdish language:

> Bastards! the fever attacks him
> [the patient] at night and leaves
> him in the daytime.
> Alongside the village, the riders of
> the brown horses gallop, stirring up
> dust.
> One comes from the village of Shamsi, and
> the other from the village of Zengana.
> What is the treatment of this night fever?
> Hu, Hu, Hu [He, i.e., God].

After he finishes, a man from the village who has at least two wives answers the question in the chant by saying the treatment requires two, three, or four sheep. Then the villagers shout, "Hu, Hu, Hu."

As a sign of great jubilation, the two wives at this point utter a long, drawn-out trill. Then the person who initiated this treatment ceremony calls the village dogs, which run to him. He throws the loaf of bread to the first dog reaching him. The dog, usually starved, eats the loaf of bread, and according to Shabak belief, the patient's fever is transferred to the dog. After this, the patient is required to provide the number of sheep mentioned by the man initiating the treatment. The sheep are slaughtered and cooked in the patient's home and distributed to the villagers after the patient and his family have enjoyed their share of the meal.[32]

13

Religious Books

Extremist Shiites do not have a religious book exclusively their own with a divine message like the Bible or the Quran. Rather, their religious or sacred books are treatises primarily concerned with Sufi ethics and traditions. Some of these books, such as the *Saranjam* or *Tadhkira-i A'la* of the Ahl-i Haqq, do contain such theological concepts as cosmogony and the appearance of God in seven theophanies. But their cardinal beliefs—in the preexistence, divine powers, and infallibility of the Imam—at least in the case of the Bektashis, are based on Khutbat al-Bayan (the sermon of eloquence or explanation), attributed to Ali.

Another sect, the Sarliyya or Kakaiyya, who shall be discussed later, hold Khutbat al-Bayan in higher esteem than the Quran. Such beliefs are also based on the many *Nefeses* (literally, "breaths," but in fact poems "breathing" the doctrines and practices of the Bektashis), composed by many Bektashi poets). These poems survive in many collections; Sadettin Nuzhet Bey's *Bektaşi Şairleri* is reported by Birge to contain the most cherished Shiite doctrinal poems.[1] Among those most revered by the Bektashis and Kizilbash of Turkey are those composed by Shah Ismail Safawi of Persia. Shah Ismail was defeated by the Sunnite Ottoman Sultan Selim I at Chaldiran in 1514, in a battle fought because the Sultan feared the spread of ultra-Shiism among the Bektashis and Kizilbash of Turkey. But, in the words of Baha Sait Bey, the real victor was Shah Ismail, for his pen was mightier than the sword of Selim I.[2]

The poems of Shah Ismail, preserved in *Divan Khata'i* (The anthology of Khatai [the pen-name of Shah Isma'il]), are a source of inspiration and pleasure for the Bektashis, Kizilbash, and Takhtajis of Turkey. His poem "Duwazdeh Imams," which praises and exalts the twelve Imams, is especially popular in the Takhtaji villages around Smyrna.[3] The religious book of the Shabak, the *Buyruk,* also contains a poem by Khatai.

If there is any religious book common to the different extremist sects, especially to the Kizilbash, Shabak, Ibrahimiyya, and Sarliyya or Kakaiyya, it is the *Buyruk.* J. G. Taylor, writing in the 1860s, noted that the Kizilbash of Dersim (present day Tunceli), in the upper Euphrates valley, had a book called the *Booywick* [Buyruk], a copy of which fell into his hands. Unfortunately, he fails to describe this book, commenting only that he has examined it and found that the Kizilbash's respect for the Prophet Muhammad "is simply a blind to deceive the Muslims, for they have nothing in common with them; no obligatory fasts, formal prayers, ablutions, or belief in the Koran."[4] The *Buyruk* is also mentioned by the American missionary Dunmore, who visited a village of Kizilbash Kurds in 1857. Dunmore states that the Kizilbash there had a large book called the *Buyruk* [he spells it Bouyouruk], which, as nearly as he can learn, "is an eclecticism from the Old Testament Scriptures, interspersed with their own traditions." Dunmore also mentions another book of these Kizilbash, called *Yusuf Kitab* (The book of Joseph), which he was assured contained portions of the New Testament.[5] Finally, writing in 1901, M. F. Grenard states that the Kizilbash told him that they do have a special book, but he could not obtain a copy or even discover its title.[6] We may then assume that the *Buyruk* is the religious book common to the greatest number of extremist Shiite sects, and therefore deserves full attention.

The chief religious book among the Shabak is *Kitab al-Manaqib* (The book of exemplary acts, commonly known as *Burkh*), which is a distortion of the Turkish *Buyruk* (Commandments). In 1938, Al-Sarraf became the first to obtain a copy of this book; he was given it by the Shabak leader Ibrahim, nicknamed al-Pasha. Al-Sarraf translated whole sections of it into Arabic, summarized other parts, and published it in his book *al-Shabak.* Al-Sarraf states that the copy of the *Buyruk* given to him by Ibrahim al-Pasha was written in Azeri Turkish. The handwriting was poor, and many parts were illegible. He hoped to find another and better copy to shed some light on the one he had. Fortunately, one of his friends, Sadiq Kammuna, an attorney, had obtained a copy of the *Buyruk* used by another extremist Shiite group, the Ibrahimiyya, whose members live mainly in the town of Tallafar,, north of Mosul. When Al-Sarraf studied this copy, he determined that its language is the same as that of his own, but found that the Ibrahimiyya version contained a brief biography of Shaykh Safi al-Din and some hymns composed by Kizilbash poets and by the Safawi Shah Ismail, not found in his Shabak copy. Furthermore, in some parts the Ibrahimayya version was more detailed than the Shabak Buyruk. For example, it described several disciplinary measures that the religious guide can inflict on a neophyte seeking admission to the Sufi order. These included reprimand, imprisonment, whipping, and even attachment of a millstone around the seeker's neck for more stringent discipline.[7]

The full title of the copy belonging to Kammuna is *Manaqib al-Awliya aw al-Buyruk* (Exemplary acts of the saints, or commandments). It may now be found in the Iraqi Museum Library (Turkish MS. 14760/1) and bears Kammuna's private seal, dated 1975. It consists of two parts. The first part, 111 pages, contains the biography, divine acts, and Sufistic instructions of Shaykh Safi al-Din. The second part, 50 pages, contains a collection of Turkish poems in praise of the twelve Imams. We learn from a colophon at the end of the manuscript that "this is the book in which the Sufis of Tallafar believe." Written in blue ink, this transcription was completed on 28 December 1953, but the identity of the person who made the transcription is not given.[8]

The fact that both versions of the *Buyruk* are anonymous gives rise to speculation regarding its authorship. Consulting the book *Kashf al-Zunun* by Haji Khalifa (d. 1076/1656), al-Sarraf found that Khalifa mentions a work which he calls *al-Manaqib* or *Safwat al-Safa*. Written in Persian by the dervish Ismail Tawakkuli Ibn Bazzaz (d. 1350), it contains a biography of Shaykh Safi al-Din, presenting his religious acts and Sufistic principles. In light of this information, al-Sarraf concludes that the *Buyruk* given him by Ibrahim al-Pasha is not the one described by Haji Khalifa. He reasons thus because Khalifa's *al-Manaqib* is written in Persian, while Ibrahim al-Pasha's copy of the Shabak book is written in Azeri Turkish and does not contain the biography or acts of Shaykh Safi al-Din. In sum, al-Sarraf cannot determine who wrote the Shabak *Buyruk*. He is not sure whether the author was Shaykh Safi al-Din; his son, Shaykh Sadr al-Din; Shah Ismail, or one of the followers of the Safawi Sufi order. However, judging by the style of the book, which is written in the form of interlocution between Safi al-Din and his son, Sadr al-Din on different religious matters, and particularly on the life and principles of the Sufi order, al-Sarraf concludes that his Shabak *Buyruk* was written by a great Kizilbash religious guide, a contemporary of Shaykh Sadr al-Din and one of his disciples.[9]

This conclusion is faulty; the *Buyruk* could not have been written by a Kizilbash contemporary of Shaykh Sadr al-Din because the followers of the Safawis were first called Kizilbash in the time of Shaykh Haydar Ibn Junayd, who died in 1488, while Shaykh Sadr al-Din died in

1391, almost a century earlier. Furthermore, the copy of the *Buyruk* published by al-Sarraf contains poems composed by Shah Ismail under the pseudonym "Khatai," indicating that the *Buyruk* must have been compiled in the time of Shah Ismail (d. 1524) or shortly thereafter.[10]

A study of the book *Safwat al-Safa* may shed some light on the origin of the *Buyruk*. This book was written by the dervish Ismail Tawakkuli Ibn Bazzaz at the behest of Shaykh Sadr al-Din, who in 1334 succeeded his father as head of the Safawi order, holding that office until 1391. *Safwat al-Safa* contains a biography of Shaykh Safi al-Din, an account of his miraculous acts and spiritual instructions, and the principles of the Safawi Sufi order, together with Safi al-Din's interpretation of some Quranic verses. It does not contain (as the *Buyruk* does) a dialogue between Safi al-Din and his son Sadr al-Din, or Sufistic poems composed by Shah Ismail. However, from its general content we may deduce that *Safwat al-Safa* was probably the basis of at least parts of the *Buyruk,* especially those dealing with the life of Shaykh Safi al-Din (as included in the Ibrahimiyya version obtained by Sadiq Kammuna), and with the spiritual principles of the Safawi Sufi order, as included in the Shabak version obtained and published by al-Sarraf.[11]

Further light is shed on the origin of the *Buyruk* by Abbas al-Azzawi. Among the several religious books of the Kakaiyya, al-Azzawi cites two of great importance to our study. One of these is *al-Mawahib al-Saniyya fi al-Manaqib al-Safawiyya* (The splendid gifts of the Safawi exemplary acts), which he states is none other than the book *Safwat al-Safa,* by Ismail Tawakkuli Ibn Bazzaz, already mentioned.[12]

The other book is the *Buyruk* itself. Al-Azzawi maintains that this book is no different from *Safwat al-Safa* except that it is shorter—in other words, a compendium. This compendium contains the biography and Sufi teachings of Shaykh Safi al-Din, thus resembling the Ibrahimiyya version of the *Buyruk,* rather than al-Sarraf's Shabak version. Therefore, we may safely assume that whoever wrote Kammuna's copy of *al-Manaqib* must have used the book *Safwat al-Safa,* by Ibn Bazzaz, as his major source. When later copies were made, the compilers for some reason dropped the biography of Shaykh Safi al-Din contained in *Safwat al-Safa* and interpolated poems by Shah Ismail to further confirm the dignity and spirituality of the Safawi order. It is likely that the interpolator was a contemporary of Shah Ismail. The significance of the Shabak copy of the *Buyruk* is that it serves as a link between the Shabak and the Kizilbash, both of whom are adherents of the Safawi order.[13]

So far we have information about three versions of the book called *Buyruk*. All deal in one way or another with aspects of the Safawi order.

They are used by such different religious groups as the Shabak, the Ibrahimiyya Sufi order of Tallafar, and the Kakaiyya, in and around the city of Kirkuk. But other versions bearing the title of *Buyruk* exist, used by the Kizilbash of Turkey, including these obtained by the two nineteenth-century men mentioned earlier; the Protestant missionary Dunmore,[14] and J. G. Taylor, the British Consul for Kurdistan.[15] All these different copies must have had a common origin, most likely *Safwat al-Safa,* but in the course of time, interpolations were made by different compilers to suit the religious idiosyncrasies of their particular groups.

The Shabak copy of the *Buyruk,* the focus of this study, contains the commandments of Shaykh Safi al-Din—who is described as Qutb al-Arifin (the pole of the Gnostics, or he who has tasted the joy of the divine mystery)—addressed to his son, Sadr al-Din. The purpose of these commandments is to demonstrate the relation between the shaykh (head) of the Sufi order founded by Shaykh Safi al-Din and the seeker or neophyte who desires to join the order.[16]

We learn at the beginning of the *Buyruk* that these commandments are not Safi al-Din's own creation, but were approved by God and delivered through the medium of the angel Gabriel to the Prophet Muhammad. They are divinely inspired and therefore constitute an essential part of God's message to the Prophet Muhammad and of the Sharia (law) of Islam. We learn further that these divine commandments were handed down by the angel Gabriel to Muhammad, through him to Ali, and then to his descendants, the Imams. Finally, they were entrusted to Shaykh Safi al-Din, who honored them and taught them to his disciples and dervishes to guide them to the love of the saints of the order. Thus, the legitimacy of the spiritual authority of Shaykh Safi al-Din and his Sufi order, through the Prophet Muhammad, Ali, and the Imams, is established. This authority, we are told in the *Buyruk,* must be respected and obeyed by the neophyte without argument or question, for the simple reason that these commandments contain the power to protect the neophyte from fear in this world and the world to come. Likewise, the neophyte who shuns or violates these commandments will be rejected by God, His Prophet, the saints, and the angels.[17]

In essence, the *Buyruk* contains the necessary ethical principles for training the character of the disciples of the Sufi order, stressing the importance of patience, total obedience, abstinence, charity, and altruism. From the Shiite point of view, it emphasizes the *tawalli* (love of the family of the Prophet, and specifically of Ali, his wife Fatima, and their descendants, the Imams), the profession of their *isma* (infallibility), and *tabarri* (renunciation of those who dishonor or hate the Imams).[18]

The *Buyruk*'s presentation of the commandments of Shaykh Safi al-Din to his son, its affirmation of their legitimacy as part of the message of the Prophet of Islam, handed down through divine dispensation through Ali and the rest of the Imams, and its emphasis on the concepts of tawalli and tabarri, seem to indicate that Shaykh Safi al-Din was a Shiite and in fact, the originator of Shiism among his adherents and descendants, the Safawis. It is an established fact that Shaykh Safi al-Din was a Sufi (mystic) who had many Sufi followers; however, as we have shown in chapter three, evidence that he was a Shiite is lacking. It was in Ardabil that he began to claim descent from Ali and to call himself Alawi, but no member of his family, not even his wife, had any idea that he was a descendant of Ali. Even his son, Sadr al-Din, could not determine whether Safi al-Din was descended from al-Hasan or al-Husayn, and this cast doubt on his father's claim to descent from Ali. Furthermore, in his interpretation of many Quranic verses, Shaykh Safi al-Din cites the opinions of Sunnite writers and expositors, which one does not find in Shiite writings.[19]

Turning to the commandments of Shaykh Safi al-Din as contained in the Shabak *Buyruk,* we find no traces of either moderate or extremist Shiite doctrine. The interlocution between Shaykh Safi al-Din and his son is of a totally Sufistic nature. The *Buyruk* which al-Sarraf published is divided into fifty-two sections. Sections 1–6 consist of an introduction and a summary of the commandments, with an account of their divine inspiration and transmission by the angel Gabriel to Muhammad, Ali, and the rest of the Imams, and finally to Shaykh Safi al-Din. It should be noted that Safi Al-Din had nothing to do with this account of divine transmission and succession. In fact, it stands separate from the main body of the commandments, which are presented in sections 7–36.[20]

It must have been written by a much later Safawi adherent, perhaps toward the end of the fifteenth century, when the Safawis adopted Shiism. In fact, each section of the commandements except section 34, which contains a poem by a Kizilbash poet, and section 36, which contains a poem by Khatai (Shah Ismail), begins with the words, "Shaykh Safi al-Din says," or "Shaykh Safi al-Din explains." We may assume that these sections contain the "genuine" Sufistic teaching of Shaykh Safi al-Din. In sections 37–52, however, the name of Safi al-Din does not appear. We are tempted to conclude that the *Buyruk* was compiled by an extremist Shiite in the time of Shah Ismail.

In section 37, the compiler of the *Buyruk* examines the succession of the Khilafa (caliphate) from the Prophet of Islam. He also discusses briefly the attributes and the qualifications of the caliph. The true Shiite opinion of the caliphate does not appear until the following section, when Ali and his eleven descendants, comprising the twelve Imams, are said to be the "only successors to the Prophet Muhammad."[21] Sections 39 through 42, with the exception of section 41, which contains a poem by Shah Ismail, present in detail the qualifications and attributes of the Khalifa (caliph).[22] Sections 43 through 46 describe the qualifications of the Sufi guide, or instructor. Sections 47 and 48 are of great significance, because they relate the tradition of Ghadir Khumm (the Khumm Pond), in which Shiites maintain that the Prophet Muhammad designated Ali as his legatee and successor. These sections also contain the traditions, "I am the city of knowledge and Ali is its gate," and "I and Ali are of one light."[23] Section 50 contains a narrative about Najm al-Din Kubra (d. 1221), a Sufi who states that if one offers his prayer to God in the name of Muhammad, Ali, and the twelve Imams, asking God to take care of his needs, God will answer his prayer.[24] The last sections, 51 and 52, affirm the spiritual transcendence of the family of the Prophet—Fatima, Ali, and their descendants the Imams—and their power of intercession representing all the prophets and patriarchs from the time of Adam. Their transcendence and favor with God are demonstrated by the fact that God created everything for them. In short, the Imams take the place of the Logos. In these two sections, Shiite hyperbole reaches its highest point.[25]

A final observation on section 49 may shed some light on the composition of the *Buyruk*. Several lines are missing in this section, making it difficult to ascertain an intelligible overall meaning. However, it contains the following statement, which seems to have no connection with the preceding sections: "I, the weak and poor Firishta Ibn Abd al-Majid, have translated the Khutba [the public speech of the Prophet Muhammad designating Ali as his heir and successor] from Arabic into Turkish."[26] This Firishta, whose full name is Abd al-Majid Ibn Firishta Zadeh (d. 1459), is a Bektashi writer, whose book, *Akhiratnama,* written in Turkish, contains the Bektashi doctrine of eschatology. He is also the one who introduced the doctrine of Hurufism into Anatolia.[27] Ibn Firishta's statement in the *Buyruk* is strange indeed, because there is no evidence that he was its compiler. It is obvious that the compiler, whoever he was interpolated into the *Buyruk* poems written by Shah Ismail under the pen name of Khatai and by other Kizilbash poets, along with Ibn Firishta's translation of the Khutba, in order to substantiate his extremist Shiite views and to legitimize the association of the Safawis with the "infallible" Imams. In this way he confirms the spiritual power of the Safawis over their adherents by combining Sufism and Shiism in the tenets of their order. This is borne out by the fact that Ibn Firishta himself was a Bektashi, whose extremist Shiite doctrine is not very different from that of the Kizilbash and the Shabak.

In the summer of 1984, I was in Iraq, doing research on the Shabak and other Ghulat sects. I learned through a friend that the Iraqi writer Shakir Sabir al-Zabit had in his possession manuscripts on the religion of the Shabak hitherto unknown to scholars. I visited al-Zabit twice at his home, and he told me that he did have two manuscripts which he had translated into Arabic. Al-Zabit was kind enough to let me read his translations of the manuscripts, but he refused to show me the originals. He also handed me his commentary on these manuscripts and told me that he intends to write a book on some extremist Shiite sects in Iraq, and that his commentary was just the beginning of his project. The commentary, together with other information, mostly on the Shabak, constituted forty-one typed pages, double-spaced on foolscap.

I perused the translation and commentary, making many notes. Since al-Zabit is a Turkoman from Kirkuk, and well-versed in the Turkish language as well as in the religious and social practices of his own people, his translation and commentary should be of interest to scholars.

Toward the end of July, before my departure from Baghdad, I met with al-Zabit again at his home, accompanied by my brother Akram and Adnan Sabri Yusuf. This time, al-Zabit insisted that I take no notes at all but only read the translation of the manuscript and ask him questions if I needed something clarified. He would not even let me hold a pen in my hand. I spent two hours reading the manuscript, satisfying myself that there was no more significant information to add to the copious notes I had already taken at my first reading of the manuscript.

Both manuscripts are very brief and both are anonymous. The first one is entitled *Kitab Shah Safi, known as Buyruk aw Kitab al-Manaqib* (Book of Shah Safi, known as the book of commandments, or the book of the exemplary acts of saints). A subtitle reads, *The Book of Shah Safi on Perfect Knowledge, as He Described it to Shaykh Sadr al-Din.*

The manuscript contains the Sufi teaching of Shaykh Safi al-Din as imparted similar to that of al-Sarraf's copy of the *Buyruk,* suggesting that they have a common origin. The only difference is that while al-Sarraf's *Buyruk* is written in the form of an interlocution, al-Zabit's manuscript is written as a discourse. My conclusion is that both works belong to the early Safawi period, perhaps the 1500s. To show his Shiite belief, the anonymous author of al-Zabit's copy inserted in the discourse traditions of the Prophet usually cited by the Shiites, such as, "Ali and Muhammad are of one light," "I am the city of knowledge, and Ali is its gate," and "Ali is the Wali of God and God is the upholder of Ali."

Al-Zabit's second manuscript, entitled *Sunbula Nama* (The book of the ear of corn), is written in the Chaghatai Turkish used in Turkistan. Al-Zabit claims that the manuscript is unique and clearly dates back to the twelfth century, because it contains the Sufic teaching of Ahmad Yasawi (d. 1166). A careful study of the manuscript, however, shows that it cannot have been written before the first half of the fifteenth century, because it contains teachings of Hurufism, whose founder, Fadl Allah al-Astrabadi, died in 1401. It was probably compiled by a fifteenth-century Bektashi-Hurufi author, who drew a variety of elements suitable to his Shiite views from the teachings of the both Bektashis and the Hurufis and tied them together.

What is interesting about the *Sunbula Nama* is that its author associates it with Salman al-Farisi, a companion of the Prophet, and one of the first to rally behind the Imam Ali and support him as the one designated to succeed the Prophet.[28] The manuscript quotes Salman al-Farisi as saying that this *Sunbula Nama* is the genealogy of the family of the Prophet. Because the members of the family of the Prophet (Ali, his wife Fatima, his two sons, al-Hasan and al-Husayn, and the rest of the Imams) are fixed to the stem of the Prophet as grains of wheat are fixed to the stem, the compiler chose the term "Sunbula" (ear of corn) as the title of the manuscript. What is peculiar about the *Sunbula Nama* is that the Imam Ali supposedly foretold its creation and transmission from Khurasan to the land of the Rum (Asia Minor), the home of many extremist Shiite dervish orders, including the Bektashiyya, whose founder came from Khurasan to Asia Minor. This foreshadowing betrays the Bektashi origin of the *Sunbula*. We read in the *Sunbula* that the Imam Ali, speaking in Persian, said that when those who attained the spiritual mystery, (i.e., those initiated into the Bektashi order) came from Khurasan to the land of the Rum, they translated this *Sunbula Nama* from Persian into Turkish. Therefore, the *Sunbula* is the essence of this order (which most likely means the Bektashi dervish order).

Another indication of the Bektashi origin of the *Sunbula Nama* is the association of later Shiite writers like Nasir al-Din al-Tusi (1201–74) with the early companions of the Prophet and of the Imam Ali. The *Sunbula Nama* reports for example, a tradition about Ali related by Salman al-Farisi. This tradition says that the Commander of the Faithful and "Sultan of the Walaya," Ali, was in the company of seven devoted adherents of the Bektashi order, namely Ibn Siman, Ammar Ibn Yasir, Nasir al-Tusi, Suhayb al-Rumi, Baba Umar, Salman al-Farisi, and Qanbar Ali. These men loved and supported Ali passionately, enough to sacrifice themselves for him.

One of them, Ammar Ibn Yasir, asked the Imam Ali if those who believed in him should follow after him. The Imam Ali answered that they should follow his sons, the Imams. Ali then made a Hurufi statement in which he applied the *huruf* (numbers) seven, fourteen, thirty-two, and seventy-two to his descendants, the Imams, and to those who would follow him. Ali concluded that everything in existence is connected with these numbers.

Al-Zabit did not identify the men discussed in the manuscript. However, Ibn Siman must be Bayan Ibn Siman al-Nahdi, also called al-Tamimi (d. 737), who was an extremist Shiite; Umar Baba must be Amr Ibn Umayya al-Dumari, who, together with Salman al-Farisi, al-Miqdad, Ammar Ibn Yasir, and Abu Dharr al-Ghifari, is considered by the Ghulat one of the deputies entrusted by the "God Ali" to supervise the affairs of this world.[29] Among these deputies is also included Nasir al-Din al-Tusi, already mentioned, who spread the Shiite teaching in Persia. It is interesting that al-Tusi is mentioned in a poem entitled "Fadilat Nama," composed in 1519 by the Bektashi poet, Yemini Baba, in honor of Ali.[30]

Further evidence that the *Sunbula Nama* is of Bektashi origin is its discussion of the fourteen Pure Innocents. Moderate Shiites and some extremists like the Hurufis believe that the twelve Imams, the Prophet Muhammad, and his daughter, Fatima are infallible. But the Bektashis believe, in addition, in the infallibility of the fourteen children of the Imams who died in their infancy, beginning with Ali and ending with the Imam al-Hasan al-Askari. They maintain that the recognition of the infallibility of these fourteen infants is essential to the perfection of the Bektashi dervish. The *Sunbula Nama* produces the names of the fourteen Pure Innocents, as does Birge in his book, *The Bektashi Order of Dervishes.*[31]

Finally, the Sunbula Nama contains twelve Sufi principles, attributed to Salman al-Farisi, that man must follow. The principles are (1) penitence, (2) shunning of objectionable deeds, (3) overcoming whims, (4) shunning lusts, (5) subjugating the soul, (6) being friendly with companions, (7) removing doubts. (8) readiness to serve others, (9) spending money generously for the cause of belief, (10) not treating others with contempt, (11) showing humility and reconciliation, and (12) total reliance on God, for God loves those who rely on Him.

The compiler of the *Sunbula Nama* states that these principles are required conditions and duties of the Sufi order, and that they are the path leading to Ishq (passionate love for God) and peace. These requirements for Sufi living are attributed to Salman al-Farisi who according to tradition, was considered to be a member of the family of the Prophet and was honored as the first to recognize the qualities and right of Ali as a successor to Muhammad. He is also considered to be one of the earliest Zuhhad ascetics or Sufis in Islam and a bridge over which Sufism crossed from Zoroastrianism to Christianity, and then to Islam.[32] We shall have more to say on Salman al-Farisi in our discussion of the Nusayris' religion.

14

The Bajwan and Ibrahimiyya

ANOTHER EXTREMIST SHIITE sharing many religious beliefs and social customs with the Shabak are the Bajwan. Most of the Bajwan live in rural villages north of Mosul and in the basin of the Khosar, a tributary of the river Tigris. Some of them live in Zohab and northern Luristan. In the seventeenth century, the Ottoman Sultan Murad IV (reigned 1623–40) ousted the Kalhur tribes from Zohab and gave their land to these Bajwan, or Bajilan, whom he brought from Mosul.[1] Like the Shabak, they are mostly farmers and herdsmen.

Their name, like that of the Shabak, is a subject of controversy. According to Rev. Anastase al-Karmali, they are called Bajoran, which he writes in French as "les Badjoran." No other writer has identified them by this name, however; they call themselves Bajwan, and are so called by outsiders who live or deal with them. Their language, al-Karmali states, is a mixture of Kurdish, Turkish, Persian, and Arabic, although Persia was their place of origin.[2] Dawud al-Chalabi states that the name Bajwan derives from the word Bajilan, but does not explain the etymological link between them. He maintains that the Bajwan are Sunnites who display great love for Ali as a courtesy to the Shabak, among whom they live.[3] Al-Azzawi maintains that the word Bajwan is a Kurdish compound of *Baj*, a distortion of *Baz* (falcon) and *ilan* (place). So Bajilan, or more correctly Bazilan, means the "home of falcons."

Al-Azzawi goes on to state that this Kurdish name is of no significance in determining the origin of the Bajwan sect. He avers that the Bajwan are Turks (i.e., Turkomans), whose language is interspersed with Kurdish, Persian, and Arabic words because they have lived with people who speak these languages.[4]

Another writer, Abd al-Munim al-Ghulami presents an explanation of their origin given by some of the Bajwan themselves. They maintain that they are Arabs who belong to the tribes of al-Jubur and Tayy. Several clans of the Tayy tribe lived in the village of Bajwaniyya, near the town of Hammam al-Alil, south of Mosul, Iraq. Members of these clans claim that one day they were raided by other clans from the tribe of Tayy and were forced to move to the district of Diyala, where they became known as Bajilan, the name mentioned by al-Azzawi. In time, some of these Bajilan moved again, to the area north of Mosul, where they lived among the Shabak and other Turkoman groups. There they became known as Bajwan, and gradually absorbed aspects of the Shabak language, traditions, and beliefs until many of them became identified with the Shabak. Al-Ghulami does not seem convinced by this explanation, however, he tends to support al-Azzawi's belief that the Bajwan are of Turkish origin, stating that they emigrated from their village (which he calls Baljwan), east of the city of Bukhara in Turkestan, to northern Iraq. Al-Ghulami further states that Baljwan is the village near which Enver Pasha, minister of war in the government of the Young Turks, was killed in 1922 while attempting to establish an Islamic state.[5]

In addition to controversy over their name and their origin, dispute abounds over the nature of the Bajwan sect and its beliefs. It is clear that most Bajwan share a large body of religious beliefs, traditions, rituals, and festivals, as well as many social customs, with the Shabak and the Kizilbash.[6] But al-Ghulami, writing in the late 1940s, reported that the Bajwan inhabitants of the village Umar Kapçi had begun to observe Sunnite tradition, and that, unlike the Shabak, they had a mosque in which both prayers and the Friday Khutba (sermon) were conducted according to Sunnite beliefs. Al-Ghulami also wrote that, in conformity with Sunnite tradition, the late Mukhtar (village headman) of the same village, Abd Allah al Tayyar, made the pilgrimage to Mecca rather than to Karbala.[7]

According to al-Karmali the Bajwan [he writes it "Bajoran"] have a "private religion which they call Allahi."[8] In fact, he is referring here to the Ali Ilahis (those who deify Ali), also known as Ahl-i Haqq (worshippers of the truth), who live in western Iran.[9] Al-Karmali goes on to say that the essence of the Bajwan religion is upholding the unity of God and love of the Prophets, although they "glorify Ismail more than any other Prophet."[10] But he does not identify this Ismail. Al-Shaibi is of the opinion that Ismail mentioned by al-Karmali is not the Biblical figure whom the Arabs consider their progenitor, but Ismail al-Safawi (Shah Ismail), who claimed that his Sufi leadership emanated from the "Seal of

Prophethood and the Perfection of Walaya."[11] This means that Ismail considered himself to be the epitome of extreme Shiism and in this sense he was glorified by the Shabak and not the Bajwan as stated by al-Karmali.[12]

The religious and social practices and customs of the Bajwan are not too different from those of the related sects among whom they live. They do not pray or fast during Ramadan, like the rest of the Muslims, and they consider the drinking of wine religiously lawful. However, they are not as stringent about divorce as the Shabak.[13]

The Bajwan have religious and social practices that are peculiar to their community. One of these is their method of supporting leaders. Six or seven families are responsible for providing a living for each of the Bajwan religious leaders. On a given festival day, the religious leader pays a visit to these families to celebrate the festivities. The head of each family under the jurisdiction of the leader chooses a seven day-old egg and has it boiled. Then the head of each family brings his boiled egg to the house in which the leader is staying. The religious leader peels the eggs, slices each one into seven pieces, and places the pieces on a dish. He blesses the eggs, saying, "These eggs are the sacrifice of Ismail, which no one of you dares to receive until he openly confesses his sins." After he finishes this prayer each member of the congregation begins to confess his sins. Then the congregation sits to eat a meal and drink wine.

Like the Shabak, the Bajwan commemorate the killing of al-Husayn during the first ten days of the Arab month of Muharram. They observe a unique custom, associated with their lamentation over al-Husayn's death. They choose several boys, cut their arms above the elbow with a knife, and then take them from one house to another to remind the people of the sorrows of al-Husayn. The villagers usually offer to these boys and to the religious leader food or grain which they have gathered and kept in one of the homes. On the ninth day of Muharram, the food that has been gathered is cooked. This meal called Sash, is distributed to all the Bajwan homes in the village.[15]

The Ibrahimiyya

Another Ghulat group whose religious beliefs are the same as those of the Shabak is the Ibrahimiyya. Its members live mostly in and around the town of Tallafar, northwest of Mosul, Iraq. Ethnically they are Turkomans, and, like the Shabak, they speak the Turkoman language. Also like the Shabak, they have a sacred book called the *Buyruk;* their version is very different from the *Buyruk* used by the Shabak, however.[16] Like the Shabak and the Kakaiyya, the Ibrahimiyya cherish a tradition concerning Ali and the forty Abdal. According to this tradition, when the Prophet Muhammad made his Miraj (night journey) to heaven, guided by the angel Gabriel, he met and conversed with Adam, Abraham, Joseph, Moses, and Jesus. But when he drew close to the presence of God, he saw a great lion with its mouth open wide, as if intending to swallow him. To pacify the lion, Muhammad took the ring off his finger and threw it into the lion's mouth, and the lion retreated immediately. When the Prophet descended from heaven and met with the forty abdal, he saw his ring on Ali's finger. He recognized that the lion which had confronted him in heaven was Ali. This is why Ali is called "the Lion of God."[17]

In essence, this anecdote is of Bektashi-Kizilbash origin and demonstrates that, like the Shabak, the Ibrahimiyya have a strong affinity with those groups.[18] Further evidence linking the Ibrahimiyya with the Bektashis and Kizilbash is the book, *al-Manaqib* (the *Buyruk*), which, as previously mentioned, is different from the version used by the Shabak. The fact that the Ibrahimiyya version of the *Buyruk* contains the biography, teaching, and miraculous gifts of Shaykh Safi al-Din is sufficient proof that the Ibrahimiyya are a remnant of the Safawi Sufi order. In other words, they are Kizilbash. Furthermore, the Ibrahimiyya *Buyruk* treats Haji Bektash and other Bektashi shaykhs as awliya (saints) and pillars of Sufism.[19] Since members of the Ibrahimiyya community, like the Shabak, speak Turkish and are ethnically Turkomans, it is not far-fetched to assume that they settled in northern Iraq as a result of the wars between the Safawis and the Ottoman Turks. It would be difficult to explain, otherwise, the presence of these Ibrahimiyya as the only extremist Shiite sect in a territory northwest of Mosul predominantly inhabited by Sunnites. There is evidence that the Ibrahimiyya have ties with the extremist Ali Ilahis and Nusayris, both of which groups deify Ali. The Ibrahimiyya hold two legendary figures. Moses and Reuben, in high esteem. These same two are also venerated by the Ali Ilahis and the Nusayris, who have shrines for them at Kerind in Iran, the center of these two sects. In fact, they consider Moses and Reuben as the Ghilman (men most favored by the Imam Ali) and believe that they were killed by the Zoroastrians at the time of the Arab conquest of Persia.[20]

Along with the Shabak and the Bektashis-Kizilbash, the Ibrahimiyya believe in a trinity comprised of Allah, Muhammad, and Ali.[21] But their leader, Muhammad Yunus (who represented Tallafar in the Iraqi parliament under the monarchy), denied that his people were extremist Shiites when confronted by al-Sarraf.[22] Al-Sarraf reports that during a visit to Kerind, Kermanshah, Sahna, and Kengavar in Iran, where the inhabitants are mostly Ali Ilahis, some people there asked him about the affairs of Muhammad Yunus. But when he asked them about their connection with Yunus, they gave no answer. Upon returning to Iraq, al-Sarraf happened to meet with Yunus and told him that some people in Iran had inquired about him. Al-Sarraf says that Yunus smiled and said that he was not an extremist Shiite, but instead followed the moderate belief in the twelve Imams, as do the Ibrahimiyya Shiites. He even denied that the Ibrahimiyya have a sacred book. Evidence supporting a strong religious connection between the Ibrahimiyya and the Ali Ilahis of Iran, however, is that an Iranian writer, Abd al-Hujja a-Balaghi, classifies the Ali Ilahis into four groups, one of which is the Shah Ibrahimiyya, most likely the same Ibrahimiyya discussed above.[24] When told by al-Sarraf that, like the Shabak and the Kakaiyya, the Ibrahimiyya are Ghulat (extremist Shiites), Yunus told him, "Our tariqa [order] sanctifies the attributes of the Imam [Ali], while you consider this sanctification as ghuluw (extremism)."[25] However, Yunus did not explain what he meant by the "sanctification of Ali's attributes."

15

The Sarliyya-Kakaiyya

THE SARLIYYA Kakaiyya are two subgroups of a single Ghulat sect that, like other sects already discussed, deify Ali. Ethnically, some members of this sect are Kurdish and others Turkoman in origin, inhabiting many villages and urban centers, especially in the north and northeast sections of Iraq, in the provinces of Mosul, Arbil, and Kirkuk. Many of them are also found in Iran, especially in Tehran, Tabriz, Hamadan, Kermanshah, Sahna, and Kerind. Judging by their religious beliefs, they are more akin to the Ahl-i Haqq or Ali Ilahis of Iran than the other Ghulat sects. Members of this sect who live in the villages in the province of Mosul are known as Sarliyya, while others who live in and around the city of Kirkuk, to the southeast of Mosul, are known as Kakaiyya.

The Sarliyya, especially those living in villages on the banks of the Diyala and Zab, tributaries of the Tigris river, are farmers and fishermen. They once lived in mud huts, but when I passed through their area in the summer of 1984, I noticed that many of them are building new homes, using cement blocks finished with plaster. The Iraqi government has extended electricity and water to their villages, and it is not unusual to see television antennae sticking out of the rooftops of the new houses.

The Kakaiyya tend to be more urbanized than the Sarliyya, and more culturally advanced. This may be because they live in and around the city of Kirkuk, which, under the Ottomans, was the center of a lively Turkish literary movement and the main source of civil servants for the Ottoman state.[1] Though some of the Kakaiyya are farmers and herdsmen, like the Sarliyya, many are small-businessmen, merchants, and government employees. Others, those with higher education, have gone into the professions, becoming doctors, lawyers, and teachers. The relative advancement of the Kakaiyya over the Sarliyya may be changing, however especially since the present Baath Party government of Iraq has extended educational and social facilities to provinces of Sulaymaniyya, Kirkuk, and Mosul, where the Sarliyya and Kakaiyya live.

Kakaiyya is a Kurdish term meaning "brotherhood" and is derived from the word *kaka* (brother). The Kakaiyya are also known to the Arabic-speaking people of the region as Akhiyya (brotherhood), a name derived from the Arabic term *akh* (brother). While the derivation of the name Kakaiyya is clear, the name Sarliyya poses a problem, and various theories have been advanced to explain its etymological origin.

According to one such theory, Sarliyya is an Arabic term deriving from the verb *sara* (to become), and its use is based on a tradition associated with the selling of sections of paradise. According to this tradition, any member of the Sarliyya, while in this life, can buy a piece of ground in paradise and then claim "The Garden of Paradise has become [*sarat*] mine by purchase." Hence, they are called Sarliyya. Al-Karmali, who relates this anecdote, believes that this explanation of the name Sarliyya is erroneous since it assumes that the name is Arabic when the Sarliyya are not Arabs.[2]

Another theory refers to the same tradition in a different way. It states that when Abd al-Rahman Ibn Muljam assassinated the Imam Ali in A.D. 661, he asked the fallen Imam how he thought Ibn Muljam should escape. Ali answered, "Iltaff." This is an Arabic verb meaning "to wrap," which translates as *sar* in Turkish. By this Ali meant, "Wrap yourself [with a reed mat], and you will be safe." Hence, the argument runs, the name Sarliyya was derived from the Turkish word *sar* (to wrap).[3]

Still another account of the origin of the name Sarliyya is given by Khattab Agha, a former leader of the Sarliyya in Mosul. According to Khattab Agha, when the Prophet of Islam invited people, especially the Arabian tribes, to accept his message, many of them responded and embraced Islam. In order to corroborate their new faith, they began to attach themselves to the companions of the Prophet. Some of these Arabians were unable to do this, however, since there was no companion left who had not already accepted Arabians as his protégés. Ali called these people to come to him and said, first in Kurdish ("Banim Baymiz") and then in Arabic "Saru li," "They have become mine." Since then the Sarliyya have been called by this name.[4]

Though the Sarliyya continue to relate these theories about the origin of their name, they are more fiction than history. According to historical sources, the Sarliyya were originally a Turkoman tribe, known as Sarlu. They are mentioned by Abd Allah Ibn Fath Allah al-Baghdadi al-Ghiyathi (d. 833/1478) in his *al-Tarikh al-Ghiyathi* (History of al-Ghiyathi), in which he discusses the historical events of the late fourteenth century in connection with the conquests of the Mongol, Timur Lang (Tamerlane, d. 1405). He states that after occupying Isfahan and Hamadan in 795/1392, Timur Lang fell upon the Sarlu Turkomans, plundering and killing many of them, while others escaped.[5]

We have already mentioned that the word Kakaiyya is of Kurdish origin and means "brotherhood." Its use as the name of the sect is also explained by legend. It is said that one of the founders of the Kakaiyya, a sayyid from the village of Barzanja, near the city of Sulaymaniyya in northern Iraq, built a lodge for his people. He planned to use poles to support the roof of the building, but when the poles were installed, they were found to be too short. The sayyid founder then told his brother, who was helping him, "Kaka [brother], extend the poles," and behold! the wooden poles became longer because of the miraculous gifts of the founding sayyid; hence the name Kakaiyya.[6] Another theory suggests that the name Kakaiyya may show Christian influence. W. Ivanow speculates that it may have been borrowed from the Christian custom of calling monks "brother" or "friar." This is an interesting opinion, but because of lack of evidence it remains sheer speculation.[7]

Some writers consider the Kakaiyya to be a tribe under the jurisdiction of the Barzanja sayyids.[8] In fact, the Kakaiyya are a religious sect rather than a tribe. The sect appeared in the waning days of the Seljuk state in Anatolia. Originally, its members were Sufi dervishes preaching brotherhood and cooperation among themselves and with other people. They were a very cohesive and secretive group, always helping one another. Some groups of these Sufis, however, took advantage of the decline of the Seljuk state toward the end of the thirteenth century and established petty states of their own in the vicinity of Angora and Sivas. Finally, the Ottoman Sultan Murad I (d. 1389) conquered these Sufis and annexed their states to his growing empire.[9]

Some historical sources call the Kakaiyya by their Arabic name, Akhiyya, and associate them with the ancient Arab order of the Futuwwa.[10] This concept of Akhiyya (brotherhood) is inherent in Islam for all Muslim believers are considered brothers in accordance with the Quranic verse 49:10, "The believers are brothers." The concept of Akhiyya was from the beginning associated with the concept of Futuwwa (the chivalrous or noble qualities of man's nature). This quality of Futuwwa was attributed particularly to the Imam Ali, considered by many to be the "exemplary and perfect man" because of his sublime human qualities. Hence came the saying, "no chivalrous youth except

Ali."[11] Thus, to the Shiites, Ali became the fountainhead of the Futuwwa.[12] Through the passage of time, however, the noble traits of brotherhood—doing good, shunning evil, and helping one another—became the rules of an organized tariqa (order) whose members, like the Shriners of our time, wore special trousers called "Sarawil al-Futuwwa." The members of Sufi orders who advocated human brotherhood and the attainment of an exemplary life praised and perhaps adopted the qualities of the Futuwwa, with whom they became identified.[13] It is no surprise that these traits of the Futuwwa survived in some Shiite-Sufi orders, including the Kakaiyya, whose contemporary designation, although Kurdish, signifies the ancient traits of the Akhiyya and the Futuwwa. In time, the Futuwwa organization degenerated; its members lost the noble traits that their predecessors had adopted and cherished, becoming as a result, a menace to society. This chaotic condition of the Futuwwa came to an end when the Abbasid Caliph al-Nasir li Din Allah (d. 1225) reorganized the Futuwwa order and restored its original fundamental and noble principles. Al-Nasir's intention in rejuvenating the Futuwwa was, perhaps, to challenge the authority of the Seljuk sultans who controlled the Abbasid state.[14] Whatever his intention, from the time of the Caliph al-Nasir on, "there was a convergence of the popular Futuwwa and the Futuwwa of the Sufis."[15] The Sufi Abu Hafs Umar al-Suhrawardi (d. 1234), advisor of the Caliph al-Nasir, played a great role in this convergence. Thus the ideals of the Futuwwa were absorbed into the Sufi orders, a process which, to quote Claude Cahen, "from the Middle Ages to our time has characterized such large sectors of social evolution in Muslim countries."[16] This convergence of popular Futuwwa and Sufism in the first quarter of the thirteenth century may have been carried by many Turkoman Sufis into Anatolia when Hulago, the grandson of Genghis Khan, occupied Iran in 1256 and captured, among other sites, the Alamut Castle of the Ismaili Assassins.[17] Many of the dervishes who fled Khurasan and other countries adjacent to Anatolia were Shiite (Alawi) mystics absorbed by the ideals of the Futuwwa and Akhiyya.[18]

In the fourteenth century, when the traveler Ibn Battuta visited Asia Minor, the Ahkiyya must have been dispersed widely among the Turkomans of every district, city, and village of that country. Ibn Battuta speaks highly of the noble traits of the Akhiyya, of their hospitality and chivalry, of the hospices they built and their succor of strangers, and of their struggle against the tyranny of the authorities and their ruffian associates. Ibn Battuta states that the Akhiyya were also called Futuwwa, and that nowhere in the world were there people who could match their chivalry.[19] The Kakaiyya, or those who lived among the Shabak and were called Sarliyya, may have been Turkomans who had fled to Anatolia. They may have formed those village groups of the Bektashis who, as was noted at the beginning of this study, became followers of the Safawis in Iran. There is evidence that in the thirteenth and fourteenth centuries the Akhis, including the Kakaiyya, flourished in both Iran and Anatolia. Some of them, living in Iran, became followers of the Sufi order of Shaykh Safi al-Din, ancestor of the Safawi shahs.[20] The followers of the Safawis in Iran and Anatolia came to be known as Kizilbash (redheads), as noted earlier. The Sarliyya-Kakaiyya, especially those with Anatolia, may have been the groups that joined Shah Ismail in his struggle against the Ottomans. And when the shah met Sultan Selim I in battle at Chaldiran, many of these Sarliyya-Kakaiyya, fearing persecution by the Ottoman Sultan, did not return to their country, but remained in Iraq.[21]

Like the Shabak, the Sarliyya-Kakaiyya are extremist Shiites, but they do not consider the Shabak to belong to their sect, claiming that the Shabak have adulterated their religion with alien beliefs, although it is not certain what they mean by this charge. For this reason they do not give their women in marriage to Shabak men, although they do allow their men to marry Shabak women.[22] They are very secretive about their beliefs and decline to discuss them. They also refuse to discuss their religious books. However, study of the beliefs, hagiology, and religious books of the Sarliyya-Kakaiyya indicates that, except for minor variations, their sect is identical with the Ahl-i Haqq or Ali Ilahis of western Iran, whom we will discuss in the following chapters.[23]

Religious Dogmas

According to the Sarliyya-Karkaiyya, God is incomprehensible, unknowable, and indescribable. There is no way for man to communicate with or approach God. However, in His infinite mercy, God condescended to reveal Himself through *hulul* (incarnation, or indwelling) in men. This incarnation is done in successive manifestations or cycles (Adwar al-Duhur). Since God is an incomprehensible light, it is necessary that He use the bodies of men for His incarnations. The fundamental point in this dogma is that God manifested Himself not "only and specifically" in Ali, but in many persons before and after Ali.[24] This dogma is no different from that held by the Nusayris and Ahl-i Haqq, as shall be seen in later chapters. Perhaps because they share this dogma with the Nusayris, some unsympathetic writers accuse the Sarliyya-Kakaiyya of being "atheists." In his book *Jami al-Anwar,* Murtada Nazmi states:

> It should be known that a stray group of atheists [the Sarliyya and Nusayriyya] which sprang from the seventy-three sects say that Buhlul is God, and that Ali Ibn Ali Talib is God, too. They have reprehensible dogmas, one of which is that God must manifest Himself or dwell (yahull) in human form in a corporeal body. In every generation when this body dies or perishes, God sheds it and enters another one. In the time of Moses, God dwelt in Moses. What is even more repugnant in the decreeing of some of these atheists that God dwelt in Pharaoh and in Yazid Ibn Mu'awiya [the Umayyad Caliph]; in the time of Isa [Jesus], God dwelt in Isa, and in the time of Buhlul, he dwelt in Buhlul. May God rise above what the transgressors say. They also believe that Satan is the angel Gabriel, and that he and his host dwell in human bodies in every age; that they accompany God, who also dwells in a human body; and that every one of them has a name by which he is known. Some of them believe that our Prophet [Muhammad], in fact, every prophet, is one of the angels in the company of Satan, and that he has dwelt in a human body. Others, however, attribute misguidance and deception to the Prophets (May God forgive them.) They say that these prophets have come on their own [not sent by God]. They also believe that the Qur'an was composed by the Prophet for memorization.[26]

Although we cannot establish the validity of most of what this author says about the Sarliyya and the Nusayris, he is correct about the dogmas of incarnation held by these sects.

Pantheism

Like many Sufis and Batinis, the Sarliyya-Kakaiyya maintain that the universe and all that is in it is God, and that every being in existence shall return to him.[27]

Metempsychosis

Metempsychosis is one of the major dogmas of the Sarliyya-Kakaiyya. They maintain that the soul becomes purified by passing through 1,001 incarnations, and after that it becomes a manifestation of the deity. The soul may achieve purification before the final incarnation, and this is demonstrated by performing miracles. However, it will never achieve theophany unless it completes the 1,001 cycles of incarnation. In light of this dogma, a man who passes through all the 1,001 stages of incarnation then becomes God.[28] This is very similar to the dogma maintained by the Ahl-i Haqq, who will be discussed in the following chapter.

Metempsychosis is not an Islamic dogma, and was most likely borrowed from Buddhism. According to Ignaz Goldziher, metempsychosis is the chief doctrine of the Sumaniyeh and was espoused by some Muslim philosophers. But why would Muslim philosophers believe in a dogma alien to the Quran? Goldziher speculates that this dogma may have provided the answer to the painful question of how a just God could inflict severe punishment on pious men. The answer is that God does so because the soul of a pious man has previously dwelt in the body of a sinful man. Goldziher concludes that this dogma is equivalent to the "Buddhist Karma."[29]

The Quran and the Prophet

The Sarliyya-Kakaiyya maintain that the Quran is the work of Muhammad and was collected by the Caliph Uthman. Therefore, they recite or quote it only to substantiate their own beliefs. In fact, they hold some of their own religious literature, as well as the Khutbat al-Bayan attributed to Ali, in higher esteem than they do the Quran. They do, however, believe that the Prophet Muhammad was great because he acquired his learning from Ali. But they add that Muhammad emphasized the outward meaning of the Quran, while overlooking its more essential inward meaning, because he could not comprehend or fathom its mysteries or the intentions of the Imam Ali.[30]

Eschatology

Their eschatology is based on the belief that on the Last Day, God will manifest Himself in a person whom they call Sahib al-Duhur (the master of theophany). Perhaps this is Sahib al-Zaman (the master of the age and time, the Mahdi), whose advent is awaited by moderate and extremist Shiites. The significance of the theophany of God and His dwelling in a person is that knowing God is like experiencing another life. From this we may assume that the knowledge of this incarnated God is sufficient to lead one to Paradise. This is probably why the Sarliyya-Kakaiyya do not recite over the deceased the formula of the profession of faith, as orthodox Muslims do.[31] They do, however, address their dead before burial as follows: "If Munkar and Nakir [two angels believed to test the true faith of departed Muslims] approach you, tell them, 'I have such and such a quantity of wheat and barley stored in barns.' If they are not satisfied, give them a bowl of lentils and a cup of wine. If they refuse to accept, then tell them, 'I am a Kaka'i. Depart from me and go to someone else.' With this they will leave you, and you will go to paradise."[32]

The belief that a soul goes to paradise as a final abode appears contradictory to the dogma of metempsychosis. Be that as it may, the Sarliyya-Kakaiyya do not grieve or weep over their dead, although they do carry them to their graves to the beating of drums.

Religious Practices

The Sarliyya-Kakaiyya do not pray five times a day like orthodox Muslims, nor do they hold worship services. Instead, their leaders recite supplications and canticles at sunrise and sunset, at certain ceremonies, and on such occasions as praying for the sick or blessing food.[33] They call Muslims who perform prayer five times daily the people of Namaz. They, like Ahl-i Haqq, consider themselves to be the people of Niyaz (people of the offerings and sacrifices). This is manifested in their celebration of a ceremonial meal, to be described shortly.[33]

They do not make the pilgrimage to Mecca made by orthodox Muslims. Neither do they make the pilgrimage to the Shiite holy shrines in Karbala, as the Shabak do. Instead they visit the graves of some of their prominent leaders (the Sayyids, descendants of the Prophet through his daughter Fatima and her husband Ali), or of the men whom they believe to be the theophany of God.[34]

They do not fast during the Muslim month of Ramadan, although some are reported to fast on the twenty-seventh, twenty-eighth and the twenty-ninth days of that month, holding a festival on the next day. Others are said to observe the tenth and fifteenth days of January by the Eastern calendar as days of fasting.[35] It is also reported that they mark the "Fast of Acceptance" on the eleventh of January each year, but it is not clear whether this day falls within the period of fasting observed in the month of January by the Eastern calendar.[36]

Like the Yezidis, the Sarliyya-Kakaiyya are said to honor Satan. They never curse him. They do not spit on the ground, lest they be thought to have spat on the devil.[37] The reason they give for this restraint is that since God, the Creator, has cursed Satan, it would be presumptuous of them to do likewise. Because they do not curse Satan, the Shabak accuse them of venerating the devil. They answer this accusation by stating simply that it is ludicrous to think that they would venerate Satan, a creature the Yezidis respect. Perhaps the reason the Sarliyya-Kakaiyya do not curse Satan is that their faith enjoins them to respect all religious beliefs, even those honoring the devil. Their religious ethics forbid them to criticize or inveigh against other faiths or the people who embrace them.[38] Such a principle is perhaps inherent in their faith, with its advocacy of human brotherhood, from which comes their name, Kakais (brothers). They are a peaceful people who expect compassion and understanding from others in return for their own tolerance. This is manifested in their saying, "May the arm of him who casts a stone at us be paralyzed."[39] They also seem to emphasize the group rather than the individual, as demonstrated by their saying, "He who says 'I' is not from us."[40]

An uncorroborated report by Rev. al-Karmali states that the Sarliyya-Kakaiyya buy and sell places in paradise. Usually the sale of these places is conducted by a shaykh (leader), who has the exclusive hereditary right to handle such transactions. The place is measured in cubits, and the price varies according to the place desired by the buyer. The transactions are usually made during the harvest season, when the shaykh visits the members of the community and offers to sell them plots in paradise. Those interested may buy two or more cubits of property in paradise, depending on their financial resources. When a transaction is completed, the shaykh is paid in cash and draws up a deed stating that he has sold the buyer so many cubits in Paradise and has received payment in cash. Then he fixes his seal on the deed and gives it to the buyer. If the buyer wants to extend his property in Paradise, he may do so, provided that he enters into a new deal during an ensuing harvest season. Terms are always cash—no credit is accepted. On his part, the buyer must keep and protect the deed all his life. At the time of his death, the deed is placed in his shroud, to be presented to Ridwan, considered by the Muslims as the guardian angel of Paradise. Upon receiving the deed, Ridwan immediately admits the owner to Paradise and leads him to the property he purchased on earth."[41] Al-Karmali reports such an anecdote about the Sarliyya in the vicinity of Mosul; it may also be true of the Kakaiyya of the Kirkuk area.

The ceremonial meal of love

Reported among the religious practices of the Sarliyya-Kakaiyya is a ceremonial meal of love, an agape observed on the New Year's day of the lunar calendar. On this day the shaykh visits his congregation to celebrate the New Year. Every married man in the congregation whose wife is still living slaughters a white cock, cooks it with rice or wheat (not in a soup), and brings it to the shaykh. The shaykh places all the cocks he receives on a table. When all the married men have arrived with their offerings, the believers sit at the table, the men facing their wives. The shaykh preaches to the congregation and then prays over and blesses the food. When the meal is over, the shaykh tells the congregation that this is a great night for love, and that if any married couple has intercourse and conceives a child, that child will be honored and loved by God.[42] This anecdote is related by al-Karmali, who adds that after the ceremonies, all the lights are extinguished in the hall where the men and women have gathered, and then "abominable things happen between them, things which the pen disdains to record."[43] This night is the Laylat al-Kafsha previously mentioned.[44] Al-Karmali states that the Sarliyya claim that such accusations are false and calumny.[45]

We have already discussed the allegations regarding Laylat al-Kafsha, showing that many sensible writers believe them to be false and slanderous. Some writers, however, connect this night with the celebration of the ceremonial meal of love and accuse the Kakaiyya of sexual orgies. One such writer, Muin al-Din Ashraf Ibn Abd al-Baqi, known as Mirza Makhdum (d. approximately 1580), attacks the Shiites in his book *al-Nawaqid li Bunyan al-Rawafid.* He asserts that on a designated night, the Kakaiyya men and women in a certain place lock the doors and put out the lights. Then each man takes hold of whatever woman is nearest, be she his wife, sister, daughter, or neighbor, and proceeds to have sexual intercourse with her. This orgy is followed by a meal, in which semen collected from the men is put into the food for a blessing.[46] The foregoing account must be regarded with extreme caution, as there is no concrete evidence to support it.

Religious Hierarchy

At the top of the religious hierarchy of the Sarliyya-Kakaiyya are the sayyids, who come mostly from Kirkuk and Iran. They are the "princes" of the community, combining religious and secular leadership. Because of their noble descent from the Prophet Muhammad through his daughter Fatima and his cousin Ali, the sayyids are believed to have the spiritual power to heal the sick. The "princes" are held in such high esteem that the villagers kiss their hands. One of the sayyids is designated pir; this man is accorded even more respect and given even greater obedience than the others, who are considered secondary to him. The Kakais obey the pir blindly, executing his commands without questioning their validity or purpose. A Kakai is not permitted to disobey the pir.[47] Such reverence for the pir and the sayyids, reaching the point of worship, is also reported of the Ahl-i Haqq, whose beliefs are very similar to those of the Kakais. The sayyids of the Ahl-i Haqq, usually known as Ujaqs, are considered to be incarnations of the Deity.[48]

The pir and the sayyids do not accept gifts or donations, but they have the right to collect money from all the Kakais.[49] The money collected is used in the public interest and for the needs of the community, and not for the personal gain of the pir or the sayyids.[50]

The pawas or religious leaders (sources indicate that the pawas are unknown outside the Sarliyya community) are believed by the Sarliyya to possess the power to heal people suffering from the stings of scorpions and the bites of snakes and rabid dogs. The Sarliyya also believe that the pawas have the power to heal the insane; the patient is lodged in the house of a pawa, where he is cared for by the pawa's family until he is cured.

Among the Kakais of Kirkuk, the pawas are known as dedes and are considered to be the learned men of the Kakaiyya community. They perform religious ceremonies and recite hymns like those of the Bektashis. They are extremely secretive about their beliefs, refusing to reveal them to even their closest friends.[52]

The mams, according to the Sarliyya, have a monopoly on the curing of persons suffering from night fevers. Among the Kakaiyya, the mam is also known as the murshid (guide or instructor).

The klaynatis are known only among the Sarliyya in the vicinity of Mosul. The Sarliyya believe that the klaynatis are descendants of Solomon, the Hebrew king and prophet. Presently, the office of the klaynati is restricted to two families, one residing in the village of Safiyya in the district of Arbil, and the other in Mosul. The klaynatis specialize in healing impotent men, whom they call *mamsuks* (those who cannot perform the sexual act). The mamsuks are usually brought to the house of the klaynati, who recites certain prayers to release them from impotence. In return, the klaynati receives a fixed amount of money, paid in advance. It is interesting that the klaynatis believe that if they eat the meat of a hornless goat, they will die.[53] The Yezidis also believe in the healing power of the klaynatis and take their sick to them for healing.

The mullas also are known only among the Sarliyya near Mosul. The mullas teach the children of the community to read and write, but they have no spiritual authority.[54] Finally, at the base of the Sarliyya-Kakaiyya hierarchy, are the lay people, known as Sarliyya in the villages near Mosul, and as Kakaiyya in and around Kirkuk.

Religious Books

We have noted earlier that the Sarliyya-Kakaiyya do not recite or quote the Quran, as orthodox Muslims do.[55] We may thus assume that they do not consider the Quran to be their sacred book. Because of the eclectic nature of their faith, they, like the Bektashis, accept and cherish several works, including the anthologies of some extremist Shiite authors, as their religious books. Abbas al-Azzawi discusses several books held sacred by the Kakaiyya. They include:

Khutbat al-Bayan (the sermon of eloquence or explanation)

This Khutba, attributed to the Imam Ali Ibn Abi Talib, is cherished by the Shiites, although it is not recorded in their books of hadith (tradition). The Khutba is associated with the Khilafa [caliphate, or imamate, the succession from Muhammad and leadership of the Islamic community], over which much blood has been shed. One day Ali wanted to ask the Prophet Muhammad who would be his successor as leader of the community of Islam. But, hesitant to ask Muhammad personally, Ali instead asked Muawiya Ibn Abi Sufyan to inquire about the matter. Muawiya agreed and asked the Prophet who would be his successor. The Prophet answered that Abu Bakr would succeed him, followed by Umar, who would be followed by Uthman. At this point the Prophet stopped, leading Muawiya to believe that these would be the only men succeeding the Prophet. Muawiya continued, pressing the Prophet to tell him who would succeed these men. The Prophet answered that the man who would succeed them was the one who had asked the question. Muawiya thought that since he had asked the question, he was to be that successor, but Ali rejected this since it was Ali who had initiated the idea of questioning the Prophet. Ali also contended that God had bestowed more virtues and excellence upon him than upon other men, and that God would bestow the same excellence upon his eleven descendants, the Imams. Muawiya, dissatisfied with Ali's reasoning, asked for proof. Ali then began to elaborate on his virtues in a Khutba (sermon) which came to be known as Khutbat al-Bayan.[56]

Khutbat al-Bayan contains seventy phrases reportedly used by Ali to describe his excellence, describing attributes worthy only of the Deity. In his *Kashf al-Zunun* (1: 360), Haji Khalifa refers to these phrases as "seventy words of falsehood." In Khutbat al-Bayan, Ali claims to be the one who possesses the keys to the unknown; the master of the two worlds; the judge of all creatures; the heart of God; the sanctuary and refuge of God; the creator of the clouds; the upholder of heaven; the friend of Job, whom he tested and then healed; and the divine light which Moses received for right guidance.

Ali goes on to say that he is sinless; that he is the evidence of everything in the heavens and on earth; that he is the first and the last trumpet, which will sound before the resurrection; that he is the face of God, the side of God, the beginning and the end, the dahir (outward knowledge) and the batin (inward knowledge); and that he is the creator of beings; and that he is the source of divine commands.[57] Furthermore, this Khutba contains statements making Ali homologous with Muhammad, such as the tradition in which Muhammad says, "I am the city of knowledge, and Ali is its gate," often quoted by moderate and extremist Shiites to prove that Ali is not only the rightful successor to Muhammad, but, because of his spiritual qualities, the rightful expositor of the true faith of Islam.[58] Later, we shall see that Nusayris, another extremist Shiite sect, consider Khutbat al-Bayan part of their dogma and quote it in their books.[59]

The Jawidan

This is the principal book of the Hurufi sect founded by Jalal al-Din Fadl Allah al-Astrabadi (d. 1401). Its full title is *Jawidan Nama Kabir,* and it is contained in Persian MS. at Cambridge University.[60] Like the Hurufis, the Kakaiyya consider the Jawidan one of their major books and follow its teachings and ideas.[61]

The Furqan al-Akhbar and *Saranjam* *(The book of accomplishment and the final word)*

The *Furqan al-Akhbar* and *Saranjam* are two sacred books of the Ahl-i Haqq also considered sacred by the Kakaiyya. Both books have been described by Vladimir Minorsky in his article "Ahl-i Hakk" in *The Encyclopedia of Islam* (1: 260–63). Beliefs shared by the Kakaiyya and Ahl-i Haqq, notably that of the 1,001 theophanies, have already been discussed. We may add here that *Saranjam* contains a collection of ancecdotes following the order of the human manifestations of the Deity.[62] This collection gives the chief human manifestations of God, including that in the person of Ali al-Murtada [the Imam Ali].[63] More information about the *Saranjam* will be found in the chapters on the Ahl-i Haqq.

The Zabur (Psalms) of Dawud (David)

The Zabur of David is considered by the Kakaiyya to be the only true book of Psalms, other Zaburs (by which they perhaps mean the Biblical book of Psalms) being but distortions.[64]

Among the other books esteemed by the Kakaiyya are anthologies of Bektashi and Shiite Sufi poets, including the poems of the Iraqi Turkish poet, Fuduli al-Baghdadi (d. 1555).[65]

Holy Shrines

The Sarliyya have several shrines, the most famous being that of Shah (Sayyid) Hayyas, in the village of Wurdak, situated near the confluence of the Khazir and the Upper Zab, tributaries of the Tigris River. The Sarliyya greatly venerate this Hayyas, offering animal sacrifices to him, and burying their dead near his shrine. He is considered to be so holy that the Sarliyya never take an oath in his name.[66]

Another shrine is that of Shaykh Umar Mandan, in the village of Kanhash. It consists of three parts, and is situated on the right bank of the Upper Zab.[67] Two other shrines named after Umar Mandan are venerated by the Kakais; one is in the town of Kufri, near Kirkuk, and the other on the Kirkuk-Arbil highway. Other shrines considered sacred by the Kakaiyya include the following:

1. The shrines of Sultan Sahak (Isaac), commonly known as Sahak. The name Sahak is Armenian rather than Arabic or Turkoman, and this fact may shed some light on the influence of Armenian Christianity on Shiite extremist groups. There are two shrines named for Sahak. One is in the Hawraman Mountain near the town of Sahna, the other in the village of Shaykhan in western Iran. Like the Ahl-i Haqq, the Kakaiyya greatly venerate Sultan Sahak and visit his shrines every year in the spring. They consider him to be one of their most prominent holy men and the first manifestation of God after the Imam Ali.[68] We shall hear more about Sultan Sahak in chapters 16 to 21 on the Ahl-i Haqq.

2. The Sayyid Ibrahim shrine, in the city of Baghdad. Sayyid Ibrahim, like Sultan Sahak, was God's theophany but Sayyid Ibrahim had six metempsychosis manifestations. The Kakaiyya are still waiting for his seventh appearance. They venerate him greatly, believing him to be the Mahdi who will appear at the end of time to establish justice and destroy evil.[69]

3. Dukkan Dawud, literally, David's Shop, a shrine in a cave on a high mountain between Sarbil and Pai Haq in western Iran, near Hamadan. Dawud (David) is considered the successor to Sultan Ishaq, and to the Kakaiyya he is a murshid (religious guide). They tell stories about his legendary powers, among them his ability to twist iron objects. They venerate him more than they do the Prophet Muhammad because they believe he is one of the theophanies of God, while Muhammad is not. For this reason the Kakaiyya never take the name of this Dawud in vain, and once they take an oath in his name, they will never tell a falsehood.[70] Dawud is also greatly venerated by the Kizilbash Kurds of the district of Dersim, in the upper Euphrates valley who confuse him with the King David of the Bible. Ellsworth Huntington says that a Kizilbash chief told him that the Kizilbash believed in four prophets, Adam, Moses, Dawud (David), and Jesus, and hold Jesus to be the greatest of them. It is significant that this extremist Shiite chief did not include the Prophet Muhammad among the four. When Huntington tried to talk about the Prophet Muhammad, the chief avoided the subject.[71] Dawud shall be discussed further in the chapters on the Ahl-i Haqq.

4. The shrine of Zayn al-Abidin, named for the grandson of the Imam Ali. Originally a Nestorian church in the village of Daquq near Arbil, Iraq, it was converted into a Kakaiyya shrine. In the fifth century the Nestorian church began to spread into Persia, including Iraq, but its advance was halted by the Islamic conquest of Iraq and Persia at the beginning of the seventh century.

5. The shrine of the saint Hajj Ahmad Virani Sultan, of Bektashi origin, who was venerated by the Bektashis during the Ottoman era. This saint is worshipped by the villagers of Daquq, Tuz Khurmatu, and Tisin, in the province of Kirkuk. They believe that he was a resident of the Bektashi lodge in the Shiite city of al-Najaf, and that he ascended into heaven and was transformed into a lion. They also believe that before his ascension into heaven he left his cap, which is still in his room in the lodge in al-Najaf. When they visit this lodge, they reverently kiss the place where the saint worshipped and from which he ascended into heaven.[72]

6. The shrine of Imam Ismail, near the town of Kizlribat in the province of Kirkuk. The Kakaiyya revere Imam Ismail for his miraculous gifts. They believe that swearing falsely by Imam Ismail will cause a person's jaw to become twisted. Conversely, a person with a twisted jaw, swearing truthfully by this Imam, will have his jaw healed.[73]

Other shrines of the Kakaiyya include those of Imam Ahmad in Kirkuk; Pawa Yadegar in Maydasht in Iran; Pawa Haydar in Iran; Sultan Saqi, Imam Qasim, Hawash, Shah Hayyas, and finally Shib (Shihab) al-Din al-Suhrawardi, who, despite being in a sleeping state, is believed to control the rain, as a kind of rain god.[74]

Social Practices

Marriage among the Sarliyya and the Kakaiyya does not require complicated ceremonies. However, the two groups have somewhat different methods of finalizing the marriage contract. Among the Sarliyya, the woman has no right to choose her husband. Usually he is chosen by her legal guardian, who receives a predetermined sum of money from the new husband. Furthermore, the woman has no right to demand inheritance from her husband or from any other legal heir.[75]

Among the Kakaiyya, marriage depends on the personal consent of both the man and the woman intending to marry, regardless of the wishes of the guardian or relatives. Weddings are usually celebrated on Mondays or Fridays, for these two days are considered holy by the Kakaiyya.[76] It is understandable that Friday should be considered a holy day, since it is a holy day for all Muslims, but the writer has been unable to discover why the Kakaiyya regard Monday as a holy day.

According to their religious rules, polygamy is not allowed by the Kakaiyya, but many Kakais have violated this rule. A murid (neophyte) of the Kakaiyya may not marry the daughter of his shaykh because she is considered his spiritual sister. By the same token, the shaykh is not allowed to marry the daughter of his murid.[77]

Among the Kakaiyya, divorce must be mutually agreed to by husband and wife; since marriage is contracted with the consent of both parties, it cannot be dissolved without the consent of both.

Abduction of a woman for marriage is common among the Sarliyya-Kakaiyya, as it is among most of the villagers of northern Iraq, being considered a sign of strength and manliness.[78] It is believed that a woman with many good qualities, especially beauty, will be desired as a wife by many men; therefore the most valiant man must hurry to make her his own by abducting her before a rival succeeds in taking her away.

A curious social custom of the Sarliyya is the growing of long beards by their shaykhs, or religious leaders. In fact, the shaykhs grow their beards so long that when they travel, they must stow their beards in a bag, taking them out only when they have reached their destination.[79]

One of the most remarkable characteristics of these people is the bond of brotherhood among them. The Kakais consider each man of the community to be a brother, and each woman a sister. A man is careful not to covet his "brother's wife;" therefore, when his wife or any other immediate female relative is seen in the company of another Kakai man, he does not suspect her of infidelity. It is even said that a Kakai man may sleep in one room with any Kakai woman without being suspected of wrongdoing. Therefore, a Kakai guest may enjoy full freedom in the home of his Kakai host, because they are "brothers."[80]

The drinking of wine is forbidden among the Kakais, and those who do drink are considered "disobedient." However, many of them do not observe this rule.

It is also reported that the Kakais consider it taboo to swear by the kazard (yellow cow) or by Pir Khawa (shaykh of the east), but no explanation is offered for such practices.[81] The Kakais' most prominent characteristic is their secretiveness in matters relating to their faith. This secretiveness is considered a religious duty. They are so secretive that their neighbors call anyone who keeps a secret a Kakai.[82]

16

The Ahl-i Haqq (Ali Ilahis)

Origin and Identity

The major extremist Shiite sect in Iran is known by different names, the most popular of which are Ahl-i-Haqq (or Ahl-i Haqiqat) and Ali Ilahis (or Ali Allahis). The Ahl-i Haqq (people of the truth) and Ali Ilahis (deifiers of Ali) are also known as the Taifa (sect) and Ahl-i Allah (the people of God).[1] In addition to these appellations, various subgroups of Ahl-i Haqq are known either by the names of specific saints, or by the names of objects peculiar to those groups. In Urmia and Salmas, they are known as Abd al-Baqis. In the Marars and Miandoab districts, they are known as Laks; in Tabriz, as Guran; in Khomsa (the chief city of Zenjan), as Sayyid Talibis and Sirr Talibis (seekers of the mystery of the Talibis). In Hamadan they are called Karamarganlu; in Kermanshah, Dawudis; and in Qazvin, Zerrin Kamar (golden girdles).[2]

The first Western writer to use the true name of the sect, Ahl-i Haqq, was Joseph Authur, Comte de Gobineau (d. 1882), although he discussed this sect under the heading of Les Nossayrys (the Nusayris).[3] Gobineau may have been justified in calling the Ahl-i Haqq the Nusayris, because these sectaries refer to themselves as Nusayris and regard Nusayr as their patron saint. According to a legend popular among the Ahl-i Haqq, Nusayr was the only son of a widow. He was a member of the fighting troops of the Imam Ali Ibn Abi Talib dispatched by the Prophet of Islam against the Jewish fortress of Khaybar. Nusayr was killed in this campaign, and his mother beseeched Ali to raise up her son from the dead, which Ali did. Upon opening his eyes and seeing Ali, Nusayr cried out, "Verily I see that you are God." Ali became angry because the young man considered him God, and in his wrath he slew Nusayr with his sword, Dhu al-Faqar. It is said that seven times Ali slew the young man and brought him back to life, trying to make him repent and stop his blaspheming. But Ali's efforts were in vain. Finally, Ali heard a voice coming from heaven, the voice of God, telling him that He is the only God, the Creator of heaven and earth, in whose hands are life and death. But God went on to tell Ali, "Never mind this time; I will be the God of all the world, and you will be the God of Nusayr." In obedience to God, Ali sent Nusayr back to his mother, alive and well.[4] The legend and the name of Nusayr should not mislead us into confusing the Ahl-i Haqq with another extremist Shiite sect, the Nusayris of Syria, who will be discussed in the following chapter, although they share with the Ahl-i Haqq the apotheosis of Ali.

Vladimir Minorsky is of the opinion that the name Ahl-i Haqq lacks precision when specifically applied to this sect because other sects, such as the Hurufis, occasionally use it. Likewise, he is not satisfied with the name Ahl-i Haqiqat, because it is used by the Sufis. Minorsky argues that the name Ahl-i Haqq is too broad and vague, and could be applied to all extremist Shiite sects.[5] This may be true if the name Ahl-i Haqq is interpreted as "the people of God" who is the all-comprehensive, absolute, and divine truth. In this sense, all those who maintain that God is the Ultimate Truth, including the Ahl-i Haqq, could apply this name to themselves, each convinced that it should be exclusively applied to themselves. It should be pointed out here that Gobineau considers the Ali Ilahis distinct from the Ahl-i Haqq, on the grounds that the latter have a more complex dogma than the Ali Ilahis, who outwardly pretend to be Muslims but inwardly habor animosity and contempt for Islam.[6] This distinction is unwarranted, as our study will show.

To the Ahl-i Haqq, *Haqiqat,* as explained by Sultan Sahak (a fourteenth-century holy man considered one of the seven incarnations of the Diety), is the knowledge or mystical experience of the Truth or the Divine Reality—God, who is omnipresent and ever-existing. This Truth (God) issues commandments, and those who obey these commandments are called Ahl-i Haqq (people of truth). Since Sultan Sahak is considered to be a theophany of God, he becomes the source of the moral law to be obeyed by the Ahl-i Haqq.[7] They regard themselves as the people of the Truth and regard others, like Muslims, Jews, and Christians as Ahl-i Shariat (people of the law), or those who possess divine law. They call the Sufis Ahl-i Tariqat, or those who belong to a [Sufi] order.[8]

The religious tradition of Ahl-i Haqq, including the concept of Haqiqat, may have come down to them from reformed post-Nizari Ismailism. This reform began on 17 Ramadan 559/8 August 1164), when the Ismaili leader Hasan II delivered a sermon at the Alamut Castle. In this sermon Hasan proclaimed that he was the vicar of the hidden Imam [the Mahdi], the living *Hujja* (divine proof) and the *Qaim* (the living Imam, or master of the time). In this last capacity, Hasan declared, he had freed his followers from the rules of the Sharia (Islamic Law) and had brought to them the Qiyama Kubra (Great Resurrection).[9] By this sermon, Hasan meant that, as the divine epiphany of the Mahdi he was to realize the long-awaited hope of the Ismailis to establish a true Islamic (Shiite) government on earth. Also, as the master of the time and the culmination of the spiritual authority of the Imams who preceded him, he had ushered in a new religious order in which his followers were absolved following Islamic law and enjoined instead to emphasize the mystical experience of the inner life and moral perfection, by following the example of the Imam [Hasan himself] as the only Reality. Hasan further meant that he was the Divine Essence who had saved his people from death and led them into the ultimate spiritual bliss of paradise: the knowledge of the Haqiqat. Therefore, his followers should obey his commands, which were binding in both religious and secular matters.[10] This proclamation at Alamut is the most significant doctrinal metamorphosis in Nizari Ismailism. It constitutes a radical shift from adherence to both the dahir and batin (outward and inward) essence of religion to the worship in spirit alone. It meant that the Ismaili community was ushered into the world of Haqiqat (i.e., God, who is the ultimate divine authority), without the burden of following Islamic law. It also meant that God becomes the ultimate Truth, as revealed to the Prophet Muhammad and completed by the Imams. For this reason the Nizari Ismailis call themselves Ahl-i Haqq or Ahl-i Haqiqat (people of the truth).[11]

Because of their deification of Ali, the Ahl-i Haqq are also called the Ali Ilahis (deifiers of Ali) or Ali Allahis (partisans of God-Ali).[12] Minorsky objects to the name Ali Ilahis on the grounds that Ali is not the dominant figure in the religion of this sect, and that the name "is used in connection with sects whose relations with Ahl-i Haqq have not been established." Although Minorsky does not suggest a proper name for this sect he seems to maintaiin that the name Ahl-i Haqq, when used to designate this particular sect, "has all the advantages of the name Ghulat or Ali Ilahis and Nusayris, which Muslims and most European travelers use in speaking about it."[13] We need not qualify this or any of the other names used by these extremist Shiites themselves or by strangers in speaking about them. Contemporary extremist Shiites are known by different names, as this study has shown, but their common denominator is their veneration of Ali as God or as the incarnation of God. We have seen in the previous chapter that the Kakaiyya-Sarliyya of Iraq hold the same belief, yet they are not known as Ahl-i Haqq or Ali Ilahis. In his *Rihla* (Journey), the nineteenth century writer al-Munshi al-Baghdadi describes as Ali Ilahis all the different sects of extremist Shiites living along the highway from Kermanshah, in western Iran, to Khanaqin and Kirkuk in Iraq.[14] Furthermore, if we predicate our judgment about the Ahl-i Haqq solely on their religious books, especially *Kitab-i Saranjam* (the book of the end or fulfillment), also called *Tadhkira-i A'la* (Remembrance or memorial of the most high), the fact that Ali appears as one of the seven incarnations of the Diety is sufficient proof that the Ahl-i Haqq believe him to be divine.[15] On the surface, Ali plays a less prominent role in the beliefs of the Ahl-i Haqq than the divine Sultan Sahak, who appears in the *Saranjam* as the supreme religious guide and pundit. But the *Saranjam* also contains evidence of the eternal existence of Ali, his miraculous birth and his preeminence over the Prophet Muhammad, who occupies an inferior position. In essence, the *Saranjam* comprises a hagiology of seven incarnations of the Deity, etiological myths, and symbolic legends, together with various religious commands and ethics, ritual formulas and prayers. Its significance lies in its syncretic nature, combining the religious principles of antiquity with Shiite legends and beliefs. In it, we find traces of Mithraic worship of the supreme deity, symbolized by the adoration of the sun and of different animals associated with the solar cult, a cult which had profound influence on the ancient Persians and other peoples of the Middle East. But alongside these Mithraic traces, one can detect Christian, Sufic, and Islamic elements in the *Saranjam,* these last being most prominent among the Ghulat and the Twelver Shiites.

Strong Shiite proclivities are also found in another document of Ahl-i Haqq entitled *Furqan al-Akhbar* (The proof of historical chronicles), a summary of which is given by Minorsky in his article "Ahl-i Hakk," in *The Encyclopedia of Islam,* (1:260–63). The *Furqan al Akhbar* is partly written by Hajj [Shah] Nimat Allah (d. 1920), of Jayhunabad, in the district of Dinawar.[16] In 1948, W. Ivanow inquired about this document from some of the Ahl-i Haqq who were presumably well-versed in the religious literature of their sect, but found that they had no knowledge of it.[17] From the summary of *Furqan al-Akhbar* given by Minorsky, we may deduce that the doctrinal beliefs it contains are very different from those in the *Saranjam,* or *Tadhkira,* and that they are probably the invention of Nimat Allah himself.

According to *Furqan al-Akhbar,* mankind is divided into two distinct groups. The saved or luminous are the members of the Ahl-i Haqq community, represented by Benyamin and Sayyid Muhammad who are considered to be incarnations of the Deity. The second group, the damned, belong to fire and darkness; they include the first three Rashidun (rightly guided) caliphs, Abu Bakr, Umar, and Uthman, together with Muawiya Ibn Abi Sufyan and Aisha, a wife of the Prophet, all of whom are loathed and cursed by all Shiites except the Zaydis. Furthermore, according to *Furqan al-Akhbar,* the religion of Haqq (Truth) has reestablished the authentic copy of the Quran, which contains those portions where the Prophet designated Ali as his legitimate successor in leading the community of Islam after him. These portions are believed to have been maliciously removed from the text of the Quran by the Caliphs Umar and Uthman.[18] This belief is still held by the Shiites today.

The popular oral traditions of these sectaries give greater insights into what they say about themselves and their religious beliefs. Most of our information about these traditions comes from men who have lived and worked among the Ahl-i Haqq, or from travelers, missionaries, and businessmen who had close contact with them. But let us not forget that, like other extremist religious minorities, the Ahl-i Haqq are very sensitive to curious outsiders who, they believe, intend to violate the sanctity of their beliefs. For this reason they are very secretive, refusing to divulge religious information to outsiders until long acquaintance has built unwavering trust. The current oppression of the Ahl-i Haqq by the Twelvers, who constitute the majority of Shiites in Iran and their history as an oppressed sect, has driven them to practice the stratagem of taqiyya (dissimulation) for their protection.[19] These factors, and their division into many groups with different ethnic origins and languages, and separated by geographical and political boundaries, account for the marked diversity among the beliefs of various subgroups of Ahl-i Haqq.[20] However, all the Ahl-i Haqq are essentially Ghulat; excessive Shiism is at the foundation of their religious system.[21]

The Ahl-i Haqq are subdivided into many branches bearing different names which can easily mislead writers into classifying them as separate sects. We have already mentioned some subdivisions of this sect, but the list is far from complete. Minorsky produced two lists of the Ahl-i Haqq's divisions with some overlapping between the lists.[22] A third list, produced by Gobineau contains eight divisions.[23] A fourth list, the work of the American missionary S. G. Wilson, gives seven subdivisions of the Ahl-i Haqq.[24] Several names are common to all four lists, and if the names are coordinated to avoid overlapping, the result is a list containing twenty-two subdivisions of the Ahl-i Haqq:

1. Sayyid Muhammad
2. Sultan Babasi
3. Shaykh Shah Abdin
4. Baba Yadegari
5. Shah Eyasi
6. Zarrin
7. Aali
8. Khan Atishi
9. Shah Ibrahimi
10. Atish Begi
11. Haft-tavanis
12. Mir, or Miri
13. Mustafa
14. Khamushi
15. Sayyid Jalali
16. Haji Bektashi
17. Dawudis
18. Sultan Baburi
19. Yedilar
20. Abd al-Baqi
21. Alevi
22. Benyamini

Other writers who erroneously refer to the subdivisions of the Ahl-i Haqq as separate sects have their own taxonomy. G. S. F. Napier states that the Ali Ilahis are divided into two main sects: the Atish Begis of Tehran, Demavand, Qazvin, and Azerbayjan; and the Haft-tavana of Kermanshah, Luristan, and Mosul.[25] Saeed Khan, an educated Kurd and convert to Christianity who lived and worked among the Ahl-i Haqq for forty years, divides them into eight sects, the most numerous being the Shah Ibrahimis and the Atish Begis.[26] The missionary F. M. Stead divides the Ali Ilahis into three main groups: the Dawudis, the Tausis, and the Nusayris.[27] It should be noted that both Napier and Saeed Khan include in their lists the Atish Begis, the Shah Ibrahimis, and the Haft-travanis. Stead's list, however, includes the Nusayris, the same name used by Gobineau for the Ali Ilahis.

The names of the subdivisions in the list we have compiled devise from the names of pirs (elders, or religious leaders) of this sect. Many of these pirs are considered manifestations of one another or of the Deity. The Benyaminis, for example, derive their name from Benyamin, an "angel" who was also considered a lieutenant of one of the incarnations of the Deity.

The Haft-tavanis (seven companions, or seven mighty ones), who, together with the Atish Begis, form the two greatest divisions of the Ahl-i Haqq, are considered by some authorities to be identical with the Haft-tan (seven bodies) named after the seven sons of Sultan Sahak, one of the incarnations of the Deity.[28] Others see the Haft-tavanis and the Haft-tan as two distinct groups, which is more nearly correct. According to Major H. Rawlinson, the original Haft-tan are considered to be the foremost of the divine incarnations, being seven spiritual leaders who lived in the early period of Islam and are worshipped as deities. Rawlinson concludes that these seven incarnations are considered one and the same, except that the divine manifestations appeared in different bodies.[29] The Haft-tavanis are the progenitors of the Ujaqs, or sayyids, of the Ahl-i Haqq. These sayyids have tremendous authority and control over the community. Considered incarnations of the Deity, they are worshipped by their votaries as God.[30]

The Ahl-i Haqq are scattered all over the Middle East. They are found in Turkey, Caucasus, Syria, Iraq, Baluchistan, Afghanistan, and India. But they are mainly concentrated in western Iran, in an area stretching from Azerbayjan down to Luristan and Arabistan (Khuzistan) in southwest Iran. The Shah Ibrahimis and Atish Begis live in Azerbayjan, especially in Urmia, and are the most numerous of all the Ahl-i Haqq groups. The Haft-tavanis live mostly in Kerind, Sahna, Dinawar, and Hamadan, and in the villages around Qazvin. Some, however, live in the villages around Khamseh, Mazandaran, Luristan, and Tehran.[31] There is also a concentration of Ahl-i Haqq called the Kalhur in the province of Kermanshah.[32] While Rawlinson states that the Kalhur and the Guran Kurdish tribes in the district of Zohab, near Kermanshah, are Ali Ilahis,[33] Napier states that all the tribes near Kermanshah *except* the Kalhur "are Ali Ilahis." However, Napier classifies the Kalhur as Shiites by religion, which means that by the time he was writing (1919), they must have embraced a moderate form of Shiism.[34]

According to Minorsky, two Ali Ilahi groups live in Transcaucasia, one in Elizabethpol, in the district of Jabrail, on the right bank of the Araxes (Araks) River. Minorsky personally knew the inhabitants of this village. He has no doubt that these Ali Ilahis belong to the same sect as those in Iran, and that they acknowledge the authority of the Atish Begis' sayyids.[35]

F. Sultanov reports that a second group of Ali Ilahis live in Kars, in eastern Turkey; in Yerevan, the capital of Armenia; and in Baku, on the Caspian Sea. Sultanov states that the Ali Ilahis of Kars call themselves Turkomans, but in fact have very little in common with the Turkomans. He says that they immigrated from Sivas in 1840, but maintained relations with their relatives there, and their shaykhs visit them every year. But as a small minority, they complain of maltreatment and abuse by their Turkish Sunnite neighbors, who accuse them of practicing usury in business and charge that their frequent divorces destroy the integrity of marriage.[36] These accusations are most likely false, because the Ali Ilahis are basically monogamous and do not allow divorce except under very strict circumstances; and even this they do in imitation of their Muslim neighbors, and not as a religious practice.[37] However, divorce is allowed in cases of adultery, or when a member of the sect marries a Shiite women who refuses to convert to his religious view or to live with him.[38]

One Ahl-i Haqq group, the Thoumaris, deserve special attention because their beliefs are different from those held by the rest of Ahl-i Haqq. They were first discussed by Professor H. Adjarian of the University of Yerevan. Adjarian's study is based on his three years' intercourse with the Thoumaris, who live in and around Tabriz. Most of his information pertains to two religious leaders of this group: Rasul, the son of Sim, considered an incarnation of the Deity; and Ramazan, a coppersmith by vocation, who was Rasul's assistant. Although Adjarian is obviously discussing the Ahl-i Haqq or Ali Ilahis in his study, he never mentions these two names. Yet he associates the Thoumaris with the Guran, the majority of whom belong to the Ahl-i Haqq sect. Adjarian states that this group is called Thoumaris because one of their incarnations of the Deity, Sim, brought their sacred book, called the *Thoumar,* from heaven. He explains that the *Thoumar* is the Greek *tomarion* (*tomar* in Armenian), which means literally "volume" or "book," but which in this context designates a new religion, the Thoumarian religion. This sacred book, the *Thoumar,* is still in manuscript form, consisting of sixteen volumes and containing a collection of poems almost the size of the Psalms.[39] Adjarian does not adequately describe this book, but from by his discussion of the religion of the Thoumaris and the references to Sultan Sahak and his four "angels," which will be discussed shortly, it appears Adjarian is most likely talking about a version of the *Saranjam* or *Takhkira-i A'la.* This religion, described by Adjarian as "new," is none other than the religion of the Ahl-i Haqq. The sixteen volumes constituting the *Thoumar,* as Adjarian was told, are sheer exaggeration by the sectaries.[40]

Like the rest of the Ghulat, the Ahl-i Haqq believe in one eternal God. Unlike some of them, however, they hold that God appeared in seven *duns* (literally, "garments"), that is, incarnations. Moreover, in each of these manifestations, He was accompanied by four "angels," or close associates, each having specific duties to perform. These seven incarnations of God and his four "angels" will be discussed at length in the next chapter.

Information about the Ahl-i Haqq's doctrine of God is inconsistent and confusing, as is that about their cosmogony. This confusion is due to the fact that there are two main sources for their religious ideas—their so-called religious books, and the information developed about the Ahl-i Haqq by Eastern and Western writers—which are not always compatible, especially with regard to the Imam Ali. Though Ali appears in the

Saranjam as the second of the seven incarnations of God, very little information is given about him. Compared with Sultan Sahak, Ali plays no significant role in the religious literature of the Ahl-i Haqq. Yet there is much in the *Saranjam* to indicate the strong association of the Ahl-i Haqq with the main body of Shiism. The majority of those who have written about the Ahl-i Haqq agree that the members of this sect deify Ali and place him above the Prophet Muhammad; it is for this reason they are called Ali Ilahis, or deifiers of Ali.

Except for the *Saranjam* and the recent *Shah Nama-ye Haqiqat,* the Ahl-i Haqq have few works of literature; this makes the task of investigating their beliefs difficult. The *Saranjam* is perhaps the only compete work available to us whose contents abound with the sect's folklore, containing etiological mythology (of obvious antiquity), traces of animism and ancient solar religion, Quranic-Biblical anecdotes, Twelver Shiite traditions, and miracles of the different incarnations, who are in fact some of the sect's prominent celebrities.[41] Of course, we may consider the *Saranjam* worthless, as did Mirza Karam, who wrote, "the book is a well without water."[42] Such a negative attitude would leave us with very little on which to build a viable explanation of the beliefs of the Ahl-i Haqq, however. After all, the *Saranjam* is their "sacred book," and it reflects the cultural ethos of their community.

17

The Ahl-i Haqq
Cosmology and Cosmogony

THE COSMOLOGICAL SYSTEM of the Ahl-i-Haqq is a conglomerate of fluid, inconsistent, and confusing ideas whose origins are not easy to trace. It shows the imprint of some beliefs so ancient that their genesis has faded or become totally lost. It also reveals traces of the Sufi religious symbolism utilized by the Bektashis, with whom the Ahl-i Haqq share common doctrines.

In discussing the origin of their religious beliefs, the Ahl-i Haqq speak of time before time began.[1] They believe that God existed in an inert state before time began: a state of *sirr* (mystery), characterized by complete stillness, which was later interrupted by the creation of the world.[2] God, the only Creator, brought creation from nonexistence to fulfill a purpose—not to reveal Himself to His creation, but, by bringing mankind into existence, to allow man to know himself. According to the *Tadhkira-i A'la,* man cannot hope to acquire a knowledge of the Haqq (Truth, God), if he has no knowledge of the Truth, i.e., God. This knowledge has the sublime spiritual and ethical purpose of leading people to repentance. Through the knowledge of God, people are enabled to seek purity, righteousness, and the ultimate state of perfection. It is very hard for man to know himself unless he first knows God.[3]

The oneness of God seems to be a cardinal tenet of the Ahl-i Haqq although one can find traces of pantheism in their beliefs. Yar, a symbolic name for God, is First and Last. It is He who was, He who looked, He who spoke, and He who listened. He was the seeker and the sought, the lover and the beloved, because there was nothing to be seen except Himself and for Himself. He was all in all.

Thousands of years passed, and God remained in His solitary state, with no sky, no earth, no angels, and no human beings moving about. He was alone and talking to Himself. Finally, He desired to get out of His solitary existence and unravel His mystery by creating the world and everything therein.[5]

The first thing God created was a pearl, in which were manifested five images in His likeness. According to another tradition of the Ahl-i-Haqq, the first essence was Yah, or Jah, before the creation came into being. This Yah subsisted in a pearl.[6] The pearl symbolizes purity, and its soft shine makes it the most precious and unique of all gems. To the Ahl-i Haqq it represents the oneness of God, because each pearl is uniquely enclosed in its shell. (The Arabs are fond of describing anything unique and matchless as a *durra yatima* [unique pearl]. The author of *Qutb Nama* (The book of the pole) states that "The inimitable sovereign manifested Himself in a pearl," because of the pearl's uniqueness.[7] The association of a pearl with God and the creation is also found in the cults of the Parsis and the Yezidis (the so-called devil-worshippers). The Parsis maintain that the first creation of God was "the precious jewel of the intellectual principle called Azad Bahnam (the first intelligence.[8] To the Yezidis, God is the first cause. Before creating the universe, He was strolling along the seashore and playing with a pearl in His hand. He desired to create the universe and threw the pearl into the sea, and behold, the universe came into being.[9] The mention of a pearl in the context of the creation by three separate sects—Ahl-i Haqq, the Parsis, and the Yezidis—is more than coincidence and betrays a common origin for the beliefs of these sects. According to Theodor Nöldeke, the concept of the Divinity enclosed in a pearl is of Manichaean origin.[10]

The cosmogony of the Ahl-i Haqq also includes traces of Sufic and Bektashi religious symbolism, based on the doctrine of the Dort Kapi (the four gateways). In the Bektashi system, these four gateways are the Shariat (Islamic law), *tariqat* (teaching and rituals of the order), *marifat* (knowledge of God), and haqiqat (truth, or mystical experience of the essence of the Divine Reality). These gateways are believed to be of divine origin. They were first revealed to Adam by the angel Gabriel. They were also affirmed by the Prophet Muhammad, who is reported to have said, "The shariat is my words, the tariqat is my action, the marifat is the chief of all my things, and the haqiqat is my spiritual state."[11] All these gateways lead to God, who is the ultimate haqiqat (Truth, or Reality). But the sharp difference between the Shariat and tariqat has significant bearing on the whole concept of cosmogony. According to the Shariat, as instituted in the Quran and the traditions of the Prophet, God is the only creator; he is totally independent of His creation, which has its own reality. But to those who attain the knowledge of God through the mystical teaching of the tariqat, God is not the all-powerful creator, but Truth itself. He is the only reality that ever existed. Such a concept is in perfect harmony with the belief of the Ahl-i Haqq that God existed in a motionless state before time began.[12] This state cannot be described better than it is in a tradition in which the Prophet, is reported to have said that God told David, "I was the hidden treasure; therefore was I fain to be known, and so I created the creation, in order that I should be known." We may then speculate that this concept is in full agreement with the Ahl-i Haqq belief that God existed in a pearl before He created the world. This image of the "hidden pearl" is often used in Bektashi poetry and is considered a *sirr* (mystery) by the Bektashis. Like the Bektashis, the Ahl-i Haqq maintain that God is an Absolute One Being who was before time was, and that the only way He could be known was through the world of non-existence.[13] To Ahl-i Haqq, the tariqat—that is, the whole order of worship, beliefs, and rituals of the sect—becomes the haqiqat itself, and the foundation of this haqiqat is the knowledge of God and His existence as the ultimate Truth. It should be pointed out that the teachings of the Islamic Sharia have not been totally discarded by the Ahl i-Haqq, but have instead been drastically modified or reinterpreted to conform to the principle of haqiqat. Thus, Sultan Sahak explains that the religious assembly of the Ahl-i Haqq is the Kaba of haqiqat. Those who adhere to the spiritual and moral principles of the haqiqat are entitled to participate in the assembly which is the spiritual Kaba (house of God). The Ahl i-Haqq do not perform the pilgrimage to the Kaba, the holy shrine of Muslims in Mecca. Nor do they consider pilgrimage a religious duty. But pilgrimage to the Kaba is in part a fulfillment of the Islamic Sharia, which is not binding on the Ahl i-Haqq, whose religious assembly has become their Kaba, according to the teaching of their tariqat, having the same sanctity and veneration as the Islamic Kaba. Furthermore, while the Ahl-i Haqq observe to an extent the burial rules of the Islamic Sharia, they prescribe a blood money higher than that fixed by the Sharia.[14] In sum, it is the haqiqat, the mystical experience of the essence of the Truth [God], and not observance of the Sharia, that is the essence of the Ahl-i Haqq belief. In this disregard for the dictates of the Islamic religious obligation prescribed by the Sharia, the Ahl-i Haqq are similar to the rest of the contemporary Ghulat.

The Ahl-i Haqq legend of the creation is associated with the initial incarnation of the Deity in the *dun* (form) of Khavandagar, who became the creator himself. Like later incarnations, Khavandagar is referred to by the Ahl-i Haqq as the king of the world. He is the "Truth" whom the

Ahl-i Haqq should implore day and night for help and forgiveness of sins. They also implore him to protect them from Satan.[15] Little is known about this Khavandagar, except that he is the first of the seven incarnations of the Deity. Since the second incarnation is Ali Ibn Abi Talib and the rest are Ahl-i Haqq celebrities, it is likely that Khavandagar was one of the sect's celebrities, and that his memory has been lost to them except for the fact that he is the first incarnation of the Deity. However, from Ahl-i Haqq legend we learn that Khavandagar subsisted in a pearl, was himself a pearl or jawhar (substance).[16] As the creator, he uttered a loud cry and water appeared; the skies were formed from its vapor, and earth from its foam.[17] From his exalted light, the king of the world created the five members of Ahl al-Aba (the family of the Prophet), a concept which is in complete harmony with Shiite tradition.[18] Then the king of the world created seven regions of the earth. In the mythology of the Ahl-i Haqq, the earth rests on the back of a holy cow, whose legs stand on the back of a fish.[19] Then the king of the world brought into existence four angels; Benyamin, whom he pulled from his sleeves; Dawud, whom he pulled from his mouth; Pir Musi, whom he pulled from his breath; and Razbar, a female, whom he pulled from his light. According to a different version of the creation of these angels, Benyamin was created from sweat, symbolizing modesty and shame, Dawud from the breath of *ghadab* (anger), Razbar from the pulse of *ihsan* (benevolence), and Pir Musi from the *sharib* (mustache) of *rahma* (mercy).[20] The mustache in this context probably refers to the legend associated with Ali, whose mustache received divine honor and continued to grow when he sucked the water from the navel of the Prophet's body after it had been washed in preparation for burial according to Islamic custom. For this reason the Ahl-i Haqq men do not clip their mustaches.[21] The number of these angels is four, as mentioned above, but some sources add a fifth, either Padsham or Mustafa-i Dawudan.[22]

These angels act as the ministers of the Deity, each occupying a certain office and fulfilling a certain function. According to *The Book of the Pole,* Benyamin is the *wakil* (steward) of the Deity, and the pir and director of consciences; Dawud is *nazir* (overseer) and judge of the actions of the believers; Pir Musi is the *wazir* (minister) who records the good and bad deeds of the people; and Razbar, a woman, is the angel of death.[23] After their creation, these angels began to fulfill the moral and religious duties assigned to them. Benyamin instituted three days of fasting a year; Dawud emphasized faith and rigid morality; Pir Musi was put in charge of writing the first prayer and making sure that the remembrance of good things should not fade away; and Razbar instituted the ceremony of communion (similar to the Christian communion), called *Khidmat* (service). The first service of communion was celebrated by these angels after the world came into existence.[24]

An Ahl-i Haqq group mentioned earlier, the Thoumaris, maintains a somewhat different doctrine of God and the creation. The world, according to the Thoumaris, is 300 million years old. It was created by God in three days. After His creation of the world, God manifested Himself in many human forms; among them, the Thoumaris name Hashir, Vezaver, Sim, Vasim, Shapur, Hinou Sagangam, Firengimchan, and Rere, but, according to Adjarian, the Thoumaris are unable to explain to whom the names refer. It is probable that these ancient religious doctrinal elements have become distorted over the centuries. However, according to the information Adjarian received regarding Ramazan, the assistant of Rasul, Sim was God; his elder son, who died as a youth, was also God; and so was his other son, Rasul. These three are God which Ramazan says is a great mystery. Like the rest of the Ahl-i Haqq, the Thoumaris believe that before creating the world, God manifested Himself in the persons of four ministers to whom He assigned the governance of the world. These were Yadegar, who issued from His breath; Remzebar (Razbar), who issued from His right eye; Zulfaqar [Dhu al-Faqar], who issued from His left eye; and Sultan, who issued from the very being of God. We do not find Benyamin, Dawud, and Pir Musi among these four ministers because the Thoumaris obviously included them within the Chihiltan-i Nur (forty men of light), discussed in chapter 10 on the Abdal.[25] Of these four ministers of the Thoumaris, we are able to recognize Yadegar and Razbar. Dhu al-Faqar is the name of the miraculous sword of Ali, to which extremist Shiites attribute supernatural power. Jalal al-Din Rumi considered it the Haqq (Truth).[26] It is no surprise that the Thoumaris associated the sword of Ali with the Haqq and believed it to have issued from the eye of God. After all, Shiites maintain that the sword of Ali was brought down from heaven by the angel Gabriel and that it was divine.[27] Thus the belief that Dhu al-Faqar is part of the divinity is compatible with Shiite belief. As for Sultan, Frédéric Macler, who translated Adjarian's article into French, is of the opinion that he is Sultan Mahmud Ghaznawi, but this is far-fetched.[28] In all probability he was Sultan Mahmud, a chief of the Lur tribe who, as Rawlinson states, is considered by the Ali Ilahis to be one of the Haft-tan (seven bodies) already discussed, whose shrine is visited by the Ali Ilahis.[29]

It is noteworthy that the four angels, Benyamin, Dawud, Pir Musi, and Razbar, belong not to the cycle of Khavandagar, the first manifestation of the Deity, but to that of Sultan Sahak, who lived in the first half of the fourteenth century and is considered to be the fourth manifestation of the Deity. The angels of Khavandagar are Jabrail, Mikhail, Azrail, and Israfil, some of whom are Biblical angels, while others belong to Islamic tradition. The confusion is probably a mistake by the compiler of the list of the seven incarnations and their accompanying angels. Or perhaps, since the era of Khavandagar is obscured in antiquity and inadequately documented, the compiler found it more convenient to place these angels in the era of Sultan Sahak, a renowned Kurdish chief who is considered the real founder of the Ahl-i Haqq's religion. Thus, the four angels of Khavandagar, who are celestial beings, appeared in the era of Sultan Sahak in human form in the persons of Benyamin, Dawud, Pir Musi, and Razbar, who were chosen by Sultan Sahak from among his followers.[30] There is nothing mysterious about these angels, especially Benyamin and Dawud, as F. M. Stead had thought, for they were the vicars of Sultan Sahak and pirs (elders) of the Ahl-i Haqq community.[31] We have already seen that two subdivisions of the Ahl-i Haqq bear the names of Benyamin and Dawud. However, in the religious system of the Ahl-i Haqq, these men become the avatars of angels of earlier cycles.

The concept of "angels" who carry out functions assigned to them by the Deity is not found in Sunnite Islam. It probably dates back to the Ismaili doctrine of the imamate and reached the Ahl-i Haqq in a distorted form. According to the Ismailis, the Prophet Muhammad was the messenger of God, entrusted with delivering God's message to mankind. But because of his limited lifetime, Muhammad was unable to complete this mission. Therefore, it was imperative that he should appoint an Imam to deliver the divine message to the world. And since the life of the Imam was likewise limited, it was imperative that in every generation there should be an Imam to bring the divine message of truth and implement the Sharia of Islam.[32] To the Ismailis, the Imam must always be present in order to execute and supervise the dissemination of the Islamic truth. This dissemination was carried out by propagandists, who followed the Imam's instructions and in performing their duties, became an extension of the Imam himself. They were mortals accomplishing a divine mission. However, the Ismaili method of operation changed after the destruction of Alamut Castle, their headquarters by the Mongol Hulago in 1256. The Imam, fearing persecution, lived in disguise, and the Ismaili movement went underground, control being entrusted to agents who assumed the guise of Sufis to evade persecution. Among the Ahl-i Haqq of Kurdistan, these agents, who came to be known as pirs, most probably arrogated to themselves greater spiritual functions in order to enhance their prestige and attract more followers. In time these pirs came to believe that they were the spiritual extension of the Imam and the executors of his divine will. They became the Imam's intermediaries with mankind, the door leading to the Imam. Thus, the angels of the Ahl-i Haqq were only the intermediaries of the different incarnations of the Deity, who were in reality their Imams. In order to make the functions of these intermediaries perpetual and timeless it was necessary that they should become consubstantial with the incarnations. Hence these angels of the Ahl-i Haqq were believed to have issued from the very being of Khavandagar in different forms.[33] It is interesting to note that the concept of the four angels Jabrail, Mikhail, Israfil, and Azrail constitutes an integral part of the Bektashi doctrine of the four gates. This may establish a point of contact between the Ahl-i Haqq and the Bektashis. Usually the Bektashis explain the emanation of the visible universe in terms of Ptolemaic cosmography. According to the Bektashis, the cycle of existence goes through four stages of development, represented by four angels symbolizing the four gateways. Thus the first stage, Alami Jabarut (the world of might) is the shariat, represented by Jabrail; Alami Malakut (the world of the heavenly kingdom) is the tariqat, represented by Mikhail; Alami Lahut (the World of Divinity, or godhead) is the marifat, represented by Israfil; and Alami Nasut (the world of man) is haqiqat, represented by Azrail.[34]

In Bektashi teaching, these four gateways were first revealed to Adam by the angel Gabriel. Their revelation is supported by a tradition of the Prophet, who is reported to have said, "The Shari'at is my words, the tariqat my actions, the ma'rifat my chief of all things, and the haqiqat is my spiritual state." The significance of these four gateways, Haji Bektash maintains, is that they correspond to four groups of people: the *abids* (worshippers), the people of the Shariat; the zahids (ascetics), the people of the tariqat; the arifin (gnostics), the people of the marifat; and the muhibs (lovers), the people of the haqiqat.[35] According to Minorsky, the first four cycles of the incarnation of the Deity, as understood by the Ahl-i Haqq, correspond to the four stages of religious knowledge, that is, shariat, tariqat, marifat, and haqiqat.[36] It is not mere coincidence that the Ahl-i Haqq assign the various religious groups to these four categories, retaining for themselves the fourth category, haqiqat, signifying their worship of the Truth.[37]

Returning to the four angels, we find that one of them, Benyamin, plays a significant role in the cosmography of the Ahl-i- Haqq. According to one tradition, he was the essence of God. Offering a rather peculiar interpretation of the Hebrew name Benyamin (son of the right hand), the

Ahl-i Haqq aver that *Ben,* a son of Yah or Jah (God), and *amin,* meaning "faithful" in Arabic, yield Benyamin the faithful son of Yah.[38] As the son of God, he becomes the Logos through whom God created the world and on whom depends the whole creation of God. He is the supreme manifestation of God, to whom all other manifestations are secondary. He is what the gospel according to St. John calls the Word, coeternal and consubstantial with God. Like Melchizedek, he is without beginning or end.[39]

The pearl in which God exteriorized Himself before the world was the being of Benyamin, wherein the essence of God is hidden. Stead was told by a prominent leader of the Ahl-i Haqq in western Persia, that Benyamin, whom his people worship, is only another name for Christ. This leader stated further that at the time of the conquest of Persia by the Muslim hordes, his people were Christians who were forced to convert to Islam. He explained that Benyamin (son of the right hand) was substituted for Jesus Christ, the Son of God.[40] Others maintain, on the basis of the etymology of the name Benyamin, that the Benyamin of the Ahl-i Haqq is connected with Benjamin, the son of Jacob in the Old Testament.[41] It is doubtful whether any affinity exists between the two persons, however. Such speculation has as little foundation as the argument that, because of their marked "Jewish" features, the Ali-Ilahis of western Iran are of Jewish origin.[42] W. Ivanow believes that the name Benyamin is an Armenian form of Benjamin, which accords with his opinion that the Ahl-i Haqq were influenced by Armenian Christianity.[43]

After God created the universe, the four angels, and the five members of Ahl al-Aba (the family of the Prophet), the Ahl-i Haqq believe that 1,001 *surats* (images) suddenly manifested themselves and formed a religious assembly.[44] We are not told who these 1,001 images were or what they looked like. We are left to speculate that they may have prefigured the community of Ahl-i Haqq, who form the religious assembly. Or they may have prefigured those righteous people of Ahl-i Haqq who bear the sufferings of this physical life without losing their faith, and then are rewarded by God for their endurance by being made celestial manifestations.[45]

What is significant about these 1,001 images is that they celebrated a kind of crude Christian *qurban* (communion). Soon after their manifestation, a sacrificial animal and a tablecloth suddenly appeared from the heavenly world of light. Those of the 1,001 who were assigned to prepare the animal for sacrifice had it slaughtered, separated the meat from the bones, cooked it, and distributed it to the assembly.[46]

The appearance of the 1,001 images was followed by the creation of the Saj-i Nar (fiery plate), a rather strange phenomenon peculiar to the Ahl-i Haqq religion.[47] The Saj-i Nar is a plate or round pan, about fifteen inches in diameter, used by Middle Easterners for baking certain round, not very thick loaves of bread. This writer vividly recalls that the use of this Saj was prevalent in his native city of Mosul, Iraq, even by his own family.

In the primitive Ahl-i Haqq version of the creation, the Saj-i Nar was used in the formation of the clouds, wind, earth, and Hell. According to their cosmogony, nothing existed in the beginning but water, over which God moved. Then God created Saj-i Nar, the fiery plate, on which He placed a bowl full of water. As the water boiled, it turned to foam. God caused the water to cease foaming, but vapor continued to rise, forming clouds. He formed the vapor into wind, which began to move the clouds. The wind had the same functions as *ruh* (spirit) in the human body.[48] Then God created earth out of the foam, and from one spark produced by the Saj-i Nar God created immense fire and called it Hell.

This concept of the Saj-i Nar seems to be unique to the Ahl-i Haqq's cosmogony, and, according to Saeed Khan, it is a very important name to remember when dealing with the Ahl-i Haqq.[49]

After creating the clouds, wind, earth, and Hell with the Saj-i Nar, God created the heavens (the higher world) from the *Jawhar* (substance), and the sun, moon, and stars from *dharrat* (particles or atoms) of His pure light. Next, he brought into being hosts of higher and lower angels, together with *ghilman* and *huris* (nymphs).[50] According to the Quran and Islamic tradition, the *ghilman* will serve as cupbearers for the Muslim believers in Paradise.[51]

Then God desired to create man. Jabrail asked Him why He wanted to create man. God said that He wanted to create man so that Mikhail could guide him, Israfil could record his deeds, and Azrail could seize his soul. Jabrail was not satisfied with this explanation. When God asked Jabrail to gather dust from the earth with which He would create man, Jabrail refused to do it. So God sent Israfil to gather dust from the earth, but he too refused. Finally, God sent Azrail, who obeyed God and gathered dust from the earth. God handed the dust to Jabrail and ordered him to fashion the figure of Adam in the image of God, which is also the image of Ahl al-Aba (the five members of the family of the Prophet). The idea that Adam was created in the image of God and of the five members of the family of the Prophet is of utmost importance to the Shiite belief in the Imamate, or leadership of the Muslim community. By maintaining the divine origin of the family of the Prophet, the Shiites could legitimize their claim that the Imamate is a divine office, assigned by God to the members of the family of the Prophet and the Imams, to the exclusion of other Muslims. (See chapters 5 and 7 of this book.)

The story of the creation closes with Adam's transformation into a living being. Then, according to Quran 2:34, God ordered the angels to prostrate themselves before Adam. All obeyed except Iblis (Satan), who refused to do so. For this reason, God expelled Iblis from His presence, and he became the *Rajim* (the stoned, or condemned one). At this point, the story moves immediately to the second manifestation of God, which is that of Ali.[52]

The story of God's appointing Azrail as the Angel of Death may be found in a treatise entitled *Verification of Azra'il and the Manner of Taking Spirits,* discussed by Birge.[53] In the treatise, Azrail is created of the Light of Muhammad. In the *Tadhkira-i A'la,* Azrail and the other angels (Jabrail, Mikhail, and Israfil), are created from the Pure Light of God. In both sources, Azrail is sent by God to gather dust from the earth for the creation of Adam. For his obedience, Azrail is appointed the Angel of Death.[54] Whether the compiler of the *Tadhkira* had access to this treatise about Azrail is not known. What seems clear is that Ahl-i Haqq beliefs are drawn from a variety of Islamic sources.

A different version of the creation, accepted by some Ahl-i Haqq, was related to Minorsky by the Sayyid of Kalardasht, a well-informed member of the Ahl-i Haqq community. This version contains a statement about the nature of Adam not found in other sources on this sect. In this account, God was in a pearl, but He came out to see Benyamin swimming in the water which covered the earth. He asked Benyamin who he was, and Benyamin answered, "I am I, you are you." God burned the wings of Benyamin because of his attitude and then asked him the same question a second time. Again Benyamin gave Him the same answer. Then God appeared to Benyamin (who was also Jabrail) in a new form, and for the third time asked him who he was. This time Benyamin answered, "You are the Creator, and I am your servant." God, who had entered an air bubble, asked Benyamin to get into the bubble with Him. Benyamin obeyed, and found three other angels present, Dawud, Pir Musi, and Razbar, of the manifestation of Sultan Sahak. Then Razbar brought out a loaf of bread, which was divided into six pieces, of which God kept two. The angels ate the bread in the company of God, exclaiming, "Hu!" (He, or God), and suddenly the world appeared. At this point the Sayyid of Kalardasht states, "Adam, the first man, was also God." He goes on to say that history began and the prophets came to the world.[55]

The concept that Adam was also God is alien to the Biblical-Quranic tradition. It is not clear where the Sayyid of Kalardasht formulated this idea. He states that he relies on oral traditions, which accord with the books of other religions. At any rate, the concept of Adam-God seems to be a genuine Ahl-i Haqq belief. In the Shirazi fragment of the Ali Ilahis, published by Ivanow, Adam appears as the name given to an endless series of eternal beings. This same Shirazi fragment contains the statements, "The Creator made Himself remain in the form of Adam," and, "He is the first and the last Adam."[56] This means simply that Adam is the only God there is.

Curiously, the concept that Adam is God, meaning that God is a corporeal being, is a basic Mormon doctrine. "Adam," said Brigham Young, "is our father and our God, and the only God with whom we have to do."[57] A similar materialistic concept of God formed the basic philosophy of Thomas Hobbes (d. 1679), who maintained that nothing existed except matter and in this sense, God, if He existed, must have had a physical body. This materialistic concept of God was observed by Gobineau, who wrote that the Ahl-i Haqq, whom he calls "Nossayrys," claim that God and the universe are one and the same [pantheism], and that God is the required energy, which is represented as a pearl or a king. Later, a part of the divine nature (God) was transformed and gave birth to human beings. Gobineau says the Ahl-i Haqq also state that the five angels, Pir Padsham, Benyamin, Dawud, Musi, and Razbar, who are so indispensable that without them there would be no universe, emanated from the same divine nature.[58]

The other cosmic phenomenon associated by the Ahl-i Haqq with the myth of creation is Razbar (also Ramzbar or Remzebar) who is generally reported to be female, but may have been a hermaphrodite. She seems to be unique to the literature of the Ahl-i Haqq, having had no counterpart among other extremist Shiite sects discussed earlier.[59] For most Shiites, the only female who plays a part in God's economy is Fatima, the daughter of the Prophet, whose significance rests solely on her filial relation to Muhammad. The mysterious Razbar of the Ahl-i Haqq belief system, however, is associated directly with the Creator, being assigned by Him to act as the protector of man on the Day of Resurrection. When God assigned Mikhail to act as man's spiritual guide, Israfil to record his deeds, and Azrail to seize his soul, man was left without a protector. So God looked upon Azrail with a benevolent eye and split him in two, one part becoming Razbar. The splitting of Azrail into male and female calls to mind Zrvan (or Zurvan), the great deity in Mithraism, and the bisexual man/woman in Manichaeanism.[60]

Razbar is the Khatun-i Qiyamat (Lady of Resurrection), who will come to help human beings on the Day of Resurrection. She is not only an angel of mercy, but an intermediary between God and man through her celebration of the "first communion" with God and the four angels, Mikhail, Jabrail, Israfil, and Azrail. This "first communion" occurred while the angels were sitting on the surface of the water. Suddenly Razbar, the holy substance, rose out of the water bearing a loaf of bread, [Kulucha], which had been formed from a drop of the divine light when God split Azrail into two parts. God ordered the four angels to form an assembly and to partake of this bread while He offered prayers. God said that the Kulucha bread would be for the benefit of man. Immediately thereafter, the bread became the firmament.[61]

Thus, in the tradition of the Ahl-i Haqq, a communion between God and man is established, somewhat similar to the Christian communion. Like the Christian churches of the East, the Ahl-i Haqq call their communion *Khidmat* (service).[62] In fact, the Eastern churches call the office of the Mass or the celebration of the Holy Eucharist the Khidmat al-Quddas. Would it be far-fetched to assume that the *Khidmat* (communion) of the Ahl-i Haqq is borrowed from Eastern Christianity?

Ivanow maintains that Khidmat means "service," that is, "obligation" or "benefit," but that to the Ahl-i Haqq, it never meant anything like the Christian "divine service." Nevertheless, in this context, the term Khidmat does mean an "office" and signifies the offering of a sacrifice like that of the Christians, as Gobineau has maintained.[63]

It is interesting that Ivanow, who meticulously tries to show that the sacrifice of the Ahl-i Haqq, which was elevated to the level of a sacrament, had strong connections with the *agape* (communal meal) of the Armenian heretical sect, the Paulicians or Tondrakites, avers that it was never meant to be like the Christian Eucharist.[64] What Ivanow probably means is that the Ahl-i Haqq Khidmat, like the Paulicans' sacrament of Holy Communion is merely a memorial service, totally devoid of the concept of transubstantiation, (the total transformation of the bread and the wine into the real body and blood of Christ), basic to the Christian Eucharist. This concept of the Eucharist was upheld by Ulrich Zwingli (d. 1531) during the Reformation.

The writer, Frédéric Macler, claims that the name Razbar [which he spells Remzebar] is of Arabic origin and means "secret of the creator."[65] Ivanow sees a similarity between Razbar and the two female deities, Rtish (or Arti, Urti, Ashi) and Parandi, wives of Mithra. He attempts to show that the name Razbar evolved from Rtish-Parandi, which he claims went through such stages as Rati-Parandi and Radh-Par, finally becoming Razbar.[66] Ivanow also tries to show an affinity between the origins and values of Rtish and Razbar. Rtish, the first wife of Mithra, was, according to Mithraic tradition, the symbol of righteousness and closely associated with Ardvisura Anahita, the goddess of fertilizing waters. Razbar, too, was a *dhat-i pak* (holy substance) who emerged from the waters, bringing forth a loaf of bread.[67]

Ivanow also sees a Christian element in the episode of the bread taken out of the sea. He explains that in early Christianity, a fish was the symbol for Christ. The Adoptionists maintained that Christ became the adopted Son of God at His baptism. In other words, like a fish, Christ was "born" in the water. Thus the sacramental loaf of bread, coming out of the sea, is in harmony with this Adoptionist belief, which was perpetuated by the Paulicians or Tondrakites, an Armenian Adoptionist sect that survived until the nineteenth century. The Tondrakites maintained that the bread of the communion should be a single loaf, distributed among the communicants together with wine.[68]

As mentioned in chapter 16, the Ahl-i Haqq believe that God appeared in seven human manifestations, each accompanied by four "angels," or companions. These seven incarnations are as follows:

Incarnation	*Angels*
Khavandagar	Jabrail, Mikhail, Israfil, Azrail
Murtaza Ali	Qanbar, Salman al-Farisi, Hazrati Muhammad (the Prophet Muhammad), Malik Tayyar
Shah Kushin	Hasan Gavyar, Kaka Rida, Shakkak Ahmad, Baba Buzurg
Sultan Sahak	Dawud, Benyamin, Pir Musi, Razbar
Qirmizi	Kamir Jan, Kamal Jan, Kaka Rahman, Kaka Arab
Muhammad Beg	Qara Pust, Pireh, Qalandar, Dada Karbalai
Khan Atish	Khan Abdal, Khan Almas, Khan Jamshid, Khatun Pari Khan[69]

Each of these seven manifestations of the Deity is believed to be the incarnation of the preceding manifestation. The accompanying "angels" possess certain attributes and are charged with performing specific duties. The first serves as the vicar of the Deity and director of conscience, the second acts as the judge of the faithful, the third records the good and bad deeds of the faithful, and the fourth acts as the angel of death.[70]

It is difficult to determine whether all members of the Ahl-i Haqq community accept these seven manifestations as final. W. Ivanow, who investigated this subject extensively, was still unable to determine whether the Ahl-i Haqq consider the list complete. He states that the Atish Begis maintain that the list is incomplete because there have been many other manifestations of the Deity.[71] Two such manifestations are mentioned; one is Sayyid Shihab, a predecessor of Shah Kushin, and the other is Baus, who came between Shah Kushin and Sultan Sahak. Ivanow is of the opinion that Baus is an Armenian form of Bohos (Paul), which most probably indicates the influence of the Tondrakites, an Armenian heretical sect, on the Ahl-i Haqq.

Other members of the Ahl-i Haqq aver that there are many manifestations of the Deity, but that they cannot remember their names.[72] The idea of the multiplicity of the incarnations is confirmed by the *Tadhkira* (a version of the *Saranjam*), whose compiler explicitly states that incarnations of the Deity have already appeared and will continue to appear until the Mahdi [Shiite Messiah] shall manifest himself at the end of time to fulfill the wishes of mankind.[73] The Haft-tan, already mentioned, are considered incarnations of the Deity. Baba Yadegar (a late sixteenth century pir) is also considered an incarnation of God, and the Ahl-i Haqq make a pilgrimage to his shrine in the mountain fastness of Ban Zarda, near Zohab.[74] His real name is said to be Sayyid Muhammad Nurbakhsh, and the Ahl-i Haqq believe him to be the incarnation of the Shiite Imam al-Husayn.[75] But, according to the traveler Khurshid Efendi, the real name of Baba Yadegar was Sayyid Muhammad Ibn Sayyid Ali Shaykh Musa, and he was a black man. He is greatly venerated by the Kurdish Guran tribe, most of whom are Ahl-i Haqq. Because of his sanctity, the Guran make an oath by tracing a circle on the ground and placing within it three stones, a sword or a dagger, and a piece of wood, which respectively represent Dukkan Dawud, one of the four angels; Dhu al-Faqar, the hallowed sword of Ali; and the tree of Baba Yadegar.[76] Miracles are attributed to Baba Yadegar, like the saving of the life of a dervish who had cast himself into the chasm where the tomb of Baba Yadegar is located, shouting, "I have come, Baba Yadegar, keep me."[77] Some of the Ali Ilahis believe that the tomb of Baba Yadegar is the abode of Elias.[78]

The manifestations of the Deity among the Ahl-i Haqq seem to continue, and some of them believe that the nineteenth-century Sayyid Rustam is God.[79] Some of their sayyids believe themselves to be sinless. Rev. S. G. Wilson states that Pir Semmet Agha, an Ali Ilahi Sayyid who invited Wilson to a wedding at the village of Ilkachi, twenty miles south of Tabriz, considered himself sinless, and said that his sinlessness was a gift from God. When Wilson explained to him the true meaning of sinlessness, Semmet Agha admitted his sinfulness.[80]

At the beginning of this century, a prominent member of the Ahl-i Haqq, Hajj Nimat Allah (d. 1920), already mentioned, who lived at Jayhunabad near Sahna and considered himself a prophet, claimed that the manifestation of the Deity would appear in his time. Many people believed him and were anxiously awaiting the appearance of the Lord. When Nimat Allah announced the exact time of the divine manifestation, they, like the Seventh Day Adventists in the United States who awaited the advent of Jesus in 1843, sold their land and homes and sacrificed sheep and cattle in honor of the Lord. Nimat Allah instructed the people to repent their sins and, as an act of humility, crawl on their hands and knees and bark like dogs. Crowds gathered outside his house and kept a long vigil, lest they miss the blessed occasion. When the appointed hour passed and the theophany failed to occur, much to the bitter disappointment of the people, Nimat Allah told them it was because of their sins that the Deity had chosen not to appear. However, he assured them that he would appear a second time on a new date Nimat Allah would specify. When the theophany failed a second time, Nimat Allah locked himself in his house, fasting and praying to expiate the sins of his followers.

F. M. Stead, a missionary who was an eyewitness to these events, says that at the time Nimat Allah wrote him a letter saying that he was awaiting the descent of the Holy Spirit. Nimat Allah also sent him a piece of clay which he alleged had clung to the feet of Jesus and possessed a divine healing power. Stead reports that Nimat Allah died in 1920 and his son succeeded him as leader of the sect.[81] This son, Nur Ali Shah, continued the message of his father, claiming that the greatest manifestation would appear in his lifetime.

Saeed Khan relates that the Ahl-i Haqq believe that the hour of the advent of the theophany will come when Evat, one of the Ahl-i Haqq's holy men, will rise by divine order from his grave near Qazvin and blow the trumpet that will quicken the dead to rise from their graves. The immediate sign of the theophany will be the overturning of the stone of Evat's tomb. Somewhat sarcastically, Saeed Khan says that every now and then some wicked men spread the rumor that the stone over the grave has been overturned, and that the theophany is imminent, telling the people that it is useless to hoard money, and that it ought to be spent on the poor.[82] Minorsky relates that M. S. Wilson, in a letter sent in January 1904, told him that an Ahl-i Haqq Sayyid, Muhammad Hasan of Maku, pretended to be the actual "incarnation" of the Deity and said that by his manifestation he would show the world the true faith of Ahl-i Haqq.[83]

The Ahl-i Haqq seem to believe that the successive incarnations of the Deity are individuals who, at certain times, have become possessed by a divine being. Such possession, they believe, is not necessarily confined to members of their own Ahl-i Haqq community; there have been incarnations of the Deity, throughout history, such as Buddha, Confucius, the Hebrew prophets, Jesus, and Muhammad. Some of the Ahl-i Haqq even believe that Shah Ismail (d. 1524), Shah Hayyas, and Henry Martyn (d. 1812), a pioneer Western missionary to the Muslims, were incarnations of God.[84]

Even though many Ahl-i Haqq appear to believe that God has manifested himself in human incarnations many times thoughout history, and that this is a continuing process, the seven manifestations listed earlier in this chapter hold a central place in the belief system of the Ahl-i Haqq sect.

The *Saranjam,* or *Tadhkira-i A'la,* offers only meager information about the first two incarnations of the Deity, Khavandagar and Ali. It passes immediately to the third incarnation, Shah Kushin, and then to Khan Atish, the last of the seven incarnations. Since the second incarnation, the Imam Ali, lends his name to the Ahl-i Haqq, who are also called Ali Ilahis (deifiers of Ali), we shall defer our discussion of Ali and his position in the tradition of Ahl-i Haqq until later.

One noteworthy characteristic of some of the remaining incarnations is their supernatural birth, without a human medium. Shah Kushin was born from a particle of sunlight. His mother, Mama Jalala, was a virgin, the only daugher of Mirza Mana (most likely Muin al-Din), who had six sons. Tradition holds that one morning Mama Jalala was watching the sunrise when a particle of sunlight suddenly descended and entered her womb. She tried hard to get rid of this particle of light but she was unable to do so. As time passed, Mama Jalala discovered she was pregnant. People began to speak ill of her, and her father and brothers decided to kill her. When one of her brothers placed his sword on her neck to behead her, the maiden sighed and vomited a son like a ball of quicksilver—Kushin. The infant turned to the would-be executioner and said, "Jalala is a virgin, the son is king of kings." Kaka Rida, one of the four angels of Shah Kushin, saw the sun brought down three times, signifying the appearance of the incarnation. He rushed to the scene and saw the infant, Shah Kushin, playing with the sun.[85]

Sultan Sahak, the fourth manifestation of the Deity, reportedly was born in the form of a divine falcon. His father, Shaykh Isa, was a very old man, whose dervishes wanted him to marry despite his old age. He kept refusing, and they kept insisting, in the hope of witnessing a manifestation of the Deity. Finally, the dervishes found a young woman, Khatun Dayerah, the daughter of a certain Hasan Beg, for Shaykh Isa. In time the girl became pregnant, and the people began accusing her of adultery, as they felt that her husband was far too old to father a child. When the time for her delivery drew near, one of the dervishes went out into the garden to find a watermelon to present to friends. Suddenly he saw a falcon descend from the skies and perch on a dried-up mulberry tree. The dead tree sparkled with life. The promise had been fulfilled; the divine falcon was Sultan Sahak, the manifestation of God.[86]

Qirmizi was reportedly created from a piece of mutton. The four angels, Benyamin, Dawud, Pir Musi, and Razbar, in the guise of Qalandars (vagrant mendicants) went to see a certain pious man named Qanbar Shahui. They asked him whether he had a son, and he answered that he did not. Benyamin produced an apple from his pocket and gave it to Qanbar Shahui, saying, "The King of the World grants you a son. Do not name him. I will return and personally give him a name." A year later the angels returned, but Qanbar's wife had not became pregnant and of course had no son. To hide this failure, she wrapped a piece of mutton in a cloth and placed it in a cradle. Benyamin went to the cradle, picked up the piece of mutton, and unwrapped it. There, much to the surprise of Qanbar's wife, was a beautiful child with a healthy red color—*qirmizi*—in his face. Benyamin named the child Shah Vali (Wali) Quli.[87]

Khan Atish, the seventh incarnation, was likewise miraculously born. Four religious leaders from Luristan in southern Iran went to see Muhammad Beg, considered to be the fifth incarnation of the Diety. On their way, they found a strange bird which had fallen near the stream of Ajuri. The bird was unlike other birds; its feathers were of a thousand colors and its eyes were those of a human being. The four caught the bird and brought it to Muhammad Beg. He took the bird and placed it under his cloak. Then, to the astonishment of all, a beautiful eight-year old girl emerged from beneath the cloak. Upon seeing her, Muhammad Beg exclaimed three times, "My Suna, very welcome!" Later on, a platonic marriage took place, and Khan Atish Beg, the seventh incarnation, was born of her.[88]

The concept of the supernatural birth of pirs, or patrons, seems to be a part of the religious tradition of the contemporary Ghulat. As related in chapter 2, Balim Sultan, second patron of the Bektashis, was born miraculously of a Christian Bulgarian princess without a human medium. We shall also encounter it later among the Kizilbash of Anatolia, who believe that the fifth Shiite Imam, Muhammad al-Baqir, was born miraculously of the daughter of an Armenian priest (see chapter 38). Therefore, it is not surprising that the Ahl-i Haqq believe some of their pirs to have been born supernaturally.[89]

Historically, the most important event in the cycle of Shah Kushin was the formation of the Ahl-i Haqq community as a fraternity of dervishes, even though it was substantiated by claims of supernatural powers to confirm the position of Shah Kushin as the undisputed leader of the community. The *Saranjam* does not make clear the exact era of Shah Kushin, but we may assume that he lived in the latter part of the thirteenth century; Professor V. A. Joukovsky (d. 1918) places Baba Tahir and Jalal al-Din Tabrizi as thirteenth-century men.[90] During this period, the dervishes and qalandars (vagrant mendicants) became a powerful group within the community, to the point of challenging the authority of Shah Kushin himself, who was no more than a pir.

From the *Saranjam,* we learn that some of Kushin's subordinates contested his "divine" authority and rebelled against him. One of the rebels was Shakkak Kaka Ahmad. Shah Kushin marshaled an army of young men and went to meet Shakkak Ahmad. When the two men met, Shah Kushin ordered Ahmad to submit to him as the shah (king) of the world, or fight a war to settle the dispute. Shakkak Ahmad replied that he was greater than Shah Kushin and saw no reason to pay him homage. Kushin asked Ahmad how he was greater, and Shakkak Ahmad answered, "In weight." A scale was brought out, and Shah Kushin had Ahmad sit on one side of the scale. Kushin placed his shoes on the other side of the scale, and they alone outweighed Ahmad. Witnessing this miracle, the inner eye of Shakkak Ahmad was opened; he fell to the ground in obeisance, and offered homage to the shah of the world.[91]

Another pretender who disputed the authority of Shah Kushin was Baba Buzurg. The people of Luristan in southwest Iran worship him as a great saint, making pilgrimages to his tomb, which is near Burujud in the mountains of Bawalin.[92] He is known to them as Baba Vali Allah (Baba, the vicar of God).[93] He is venerated so greatly that they will not bear false witness or tell a falsehood after swearing by his name.[94] Shah Kushin marched against Baba Buzurg, but Buzurg attempted to outsmart Kushin by magically turning himself into a wild ass and disappearing in herd of asses. His trick failed; he was spotted and brought back to Kushin. As a sign of his obedience, he offered Shah Kushin two boys whom he had brought from China. These boys became progenitors of the Delfan tribe.

Later, Shah Kushin visited Baba Tahir in Hamadan (his grave is still shown in this city), where the latter offered Kushin a hidden treasure, perhaps as a sign of submission. Shah Kushin also reduced another of his associates. Hasan Gavyar, to submission.[95]

The whole period of Shah Kushin's leadership is characterized by his efforts to subdue the dervishes in revolt against his authority. His claim to be an incarnation of God and the miracles he performed were meant only to confirm his uncontested authority over the Ahl-i Haqq community. This is supported by Shah Kushin's statement that he was the first and last qalandar, and that he would not reveal the qalandars' path to anyone.[96] In a poem often quoted by Ahl-i Haqq, Shah Kushin is reported to have said that he had been in existence since the time of Adam and would remain in existence until the end of the world.[97] Through such claims, Shah Kushin asserted his authority over his followers and reduced his opponents to submission.

It should be noted that the four associates of Shah Kushin are not considered to have been incarnate "angels," as were the associates of Khavandagar, the first incarnation of the Deity. Kushin's associates were generally called "Babas" and were treated as rebels. One of them, however, Kaka Rida, is considered to be an incarnation of Salman al-Farisi. These associates, we shall see, played a very prominent role under Sultan Sahak. This significant change in their role and activity indicates that the foundation and development of the Ahl-i Haqq community was the work of dervishes, who appeared in great numbers in Kurdistan. This is reflected in a myth about Shah Kushin, in which he turns into a white falcon at the direction of Yafta-Kuh in Luristan, not far from the tomb of Baba Buzurg. Kushin appeared among his followers in this guise to test the strength of their faith, rewarding the dervishes who were loyal and ordering one of his lieutenants, Mustafa-i Dawudan, to punish those who remained accurate. In his attempt to regulate the affairs of the community of dervishes, Shah Kushin went to the Vamarz Pass and distributed land to his subordinates, in order that each might know his abode. Many of his followers had high hopes of receiving not only land, but money as well. Through these tactics, and through the ostensible use of magical power, Shah Kushin was able to reduce his rebellious associates to submission.[98]

The *Tadhkira* contains two interesting stories not found in the *Saranjam* that illustrate the influence of Christianity and Shiism on the beliefs of the Ahl-i Haqq. The first story concerns a white-bearded *dhimmi* (a Christian or Jew under Muslim protection) named Abu Nuy, and his two sons. One day Abu Nuy saw Jesus in the person of Shah

Kushin. He recognized Jesus by a distinct star on his forehead. Abu Nuy and his sons entreated Jesus to admit them to the haqiqat (truth), but Jesus ordered them to go to Shah Kushin for admittance to the haqiqat. Shah Kushin refused to admit them because they had eaten forbidden flesh. When they insisted, he decided to test their intention; he ordered a big fire to be built, and told the three men that in order to be admitted into the haqiqat, they had to step into the fire. They did so and were immediately consumed by it. The ashes were gathered and placed in a bedsheet. Turning to face the ashes, Shah Kushin king of the world, cried out, "Abu Nuy, get up." Lo and behold, the three men came back to life and joined the haqiqat. They were now members of the Ahl-i Haqq, worshippers of the Truth.[99]

Who are this Abu Nuy and his sons, and what might be their connection with the Ahl-i Haqq? If we assume, as did Ivanow, that Nuy is the Armenian form of the name Noah, then Abu Nuy and his two sons are Armenians, and the appearance of Jesus in person of Shah Kushin is meant to show the contact between Shah Kushin and the Armenian Christians in Persia.[100] Unfortunately, the compiler of the *Tadhkira* does not give us any clues about this legend or the purpose behind it. We are left to conjecture that, like the Bektashis of Anatolia, who showed great tolerance toward the indigenous Christians in order to win acceptance for themselves and their order, the author of this legend showed that Shah Kushin was an incarnation of Jesus in order that through him, Armenian Christians might be admitted to the community of the Ahl-i Haqq.

The second story shows the association of Shah Kushin with the Imam Ali, which explains the Ahl-i Haqq's connection with Shiism. The story goes that Shah Kushin went to Kufa, Ali's headquarters in Iraq, and entered the mosque there. He lifted one of the pillars of the mosque and took out a bowl of curd on which lay a *magu* (document or charter of mystery). He unfolded the charter and handed it to one of his associates. The charter bore the seals of the twelve Imams, with the signature and seal of the Imam Ali, the shah of dominion. Seeing the seals of the Imams, Shah Kushin exclaimed, "I am Shah Kushin, the Lord of heaven and earth."[101] This must mean that the leaders of the Ahl-i Haqq accepted the divine authority of Ali and the rest of the Imams, and that they became an extension of that authority.

18

Sultan Sahak

Founder of the Ahl-i Haqq

SULTAN SAHAK, believed by the Ahl-i Haqq to be the fourth of seven incarnations of the deity, is perhaps their most prominent leader. He appears to be founder of the sect in its present form, as well as the reformer who revived its ancient law. It was he who instituted the covenant of Benyamin, regulated the different offices of his "angels," or associates, and organized the rituals of initiation and sacrifice. Indeed, many Ahl-i Haqq sayyids (leaders) trace their genealogy to his sons, the Haft-tavana. The prominent leader of the Kurds in Iraq, Shaykh Mahmud Barzani, who after World War I claimed to be the king of Kurdistan, traced his ancestry to the brother of Sultan Sahak.[1]

Frédéric Macler maintains that the name Sahak is the current Armenian form of Isaac. It is in this Armenian form that the Kakaiyya of Iraq and the Ahl-i Haqq write the name. Macler also seems to identify Sultan Sahak with the ninth-century Sahak Mahout, nicknamed Apikourech, who caused much controversy because of his violence and is also remembered for his response to the letter of Photius, Patriarch of Constantinople (d. 892).[2] This identification is erroneous; as shall be seen later, Sultan Sahak appeared in the fourteenth century. Among other names which the Ahl-i Haqq use in their Armenian forms are Baus for Bohos (Paul), Benyamin for Benjamin, and Nuy for Noah.[3] The use of these names in their Armenian form, together with some Armenian religious practices of the Ahl-i Haqq (to be discussed in detail in a later chapter), perhaps indicates the influence of Armenian Christianity on the Ahl-i Haqq and their religious beliefs.

According to Ivanow, Christianity had reached the confines of Kurdistan and penetrated Armenia by the end of the second century, long before the conversion of that country to Christianity by St. Gregory the Illuminator. At this time, Christianity was infested with many heresies, especially that of Paul of Samosata, Patriarch of Antioch, who was condemned and deposed in A.D. 269 for teaching that Jesus was born a mere man, only later becoming God at His baptism, after the Holy Spirit descended upon Him. Paul taught, in other words, that Jesus was the Son of God by adoption. Ivanow maintains that the adherents of this and other similar heresies were persecuted in the ninth and tenth centuries by the Byzantine Church and state, which forced them to seek refuge in Muslim lands, where many of them converted to Islam. They mingled among the Muslims, carrying with them their heretical views, and thus influencing the beliefs of such sects as the Ahl-i Haqq. Many of the Paulicians (followers of Paul of Samosata) were Armenians whose heretical beliefs survive in an Armenian book called *The Key of Truth.* This book discovered in manuscript form, was translated into English with invaluable comments and an introduction by F. C. Conybeare, and published by Oxford in 1898. Ivanow attempts to show the influence on the dogma of the Ahl-i Haqq of the teachings embodied in *The Key of Truth,* particularly those regarding the incarnation of God in human form, a concept totally alien to Islam.[4] This idea applies directly to Sultan Sahak, believed by the Ahl-i Haqq to be an incarnation of the Diety, belief that, together with their use of the Armenian name Sahak, suggests the heretical Armenian influence on the Ahl-i Haqq. We shall elaborate this subject in chapter 38.

Sultan Sahak apparently appeared in the Armenian mountains in western Iran in the first half of the fourteenth century. Sahak was a Kurd, and a dervish pir—not one of the wandering mendicant dervishes, but rather a settled dervish who was also known as the pir of Perdivar and Shahu, two villages on the river Servan (Diyala), a tributary of the Tigris River. To the Ahl-i Haqq, Perdivar is a sacred shrine, as Mecca is to the Muslims. It is here that Shah Kushin probably appeared as a manifestation of the Deity, and that the *Saranjam,* believed to have been written by Benyamin, was revealed. It was also at Perdivar that the sultan was able to win the allegiance of the notorious Pir Mikhail by performing miracles. Sultan Sahak is buried near the village of Shaykhan on the river Servan (Diyala), not far from Perdivar. Minorsky, who visited the site in 1914, gives a vividly description of the location of the sanctuary and some of the rituals associated with it.[5]

An episode about Sultan Sahak which I have not found in any other source is related by Adjarian. He states that the Thoumaris, a subgroup of the Ahl-i Haqq, believe that Sultan Sahak is a prophet who was sent to announce the advent of the god Sim, but that Sim did not appear. Sahak was followed by Kuşcuöglu (son of a bird-seller), a Turkish poet who also announced the advent of Sim, who finally did appear in human form, being born in Tabriz in the first half of the nineteenth century.[6]

Sultan Sahak came from a well-known line of Barzanja Kurdish Shaykhs. His father was Shaykh Isa, and his mother was Khatun Dayerah, daughter of Hasan Beg of the famous Jaf Kurdish tribe.[7] According to Ahl-i Haqq mythology, his birth was miraculous, and he appeared in the form of a divine falcon.[8]

As a chief dervish, Sultan Sahak had many followers (twelve thousand in Hawraman alone), of whom he chose four as his close associates to carry out his religious instructions and authority. These were the four "angels," Benyamin, Pir Musi, Dawud, and Razbar. Although according to the Ahl-i Haqq creation myth these "angels" were created during the first manifestation of the Deity, Khavandagar, in a historical sense they belong to the era of Sultan Sahak, who chose them as his lieutenants from among his dervishes. Since the *Saranjam,* consisting mainly of poems by Sultan Sahak incorporating the doctrines of the Ahl-i Haqq, was "revealed" (that is, written down) by Benyamin at Perdivar, it is not unlikely that the compilor of the *Saranjam* concocted the myth of the seven theophanies of God and made the four associates of Sultan Sahak "divinely created beings" in order to offer the new pir of the Ahl-i Haqq unchallenged authority over the community.[9]

It was Sultan Sahak who appointed these functionaries to their offices. Benyamin became the Pir-i Shart (one who received the covenant, or the vicar of Sultan Sahak in religious matters). Dawud became an instructor, and Pir Musi an administrator and bookkeeper. Sultan Sahak instructed his followers to obey the orders of these associates and to follow the principles laid down by them.[10]

It was at Perdivar that the principles of haqiqat (Truth), which constitute the religious and moral order of the Ahl-i Haqq, were instituted. When Sultan Sahak told his four angels to lay down the principles of haqiqat (Truth), Benyamin asked on what foundation they should be based. Sultan Sahak said that one must know that the principle of haqiqat is the omniscient and omnipresent God, and that the rules of behavior are based on the fear of God.[11]

This haqiqat requires the highest ethical conduct by the Ahl-i Haqq. Every member of the community is expected to learn how to control his senses and check his lusts. Those who subjugate the senses to their will realize that the Truth is manifested in their actions. It is also imperative that the members of the community recognize the omnipresence of the lord of the world: that is, Sultan Sahak.[12] What this means (as shall be seen later) is that the recognition of the leader of the community is a religious requirement.

In Shiism, knowing the Imam is like knowing God Himself, and a Shiite who dies without knowing the Imam of his time dies an infidel.[13] Members of the Ahl-i Haqq community must, in addition, distinguish between what is lawful and what is unlawful. They should not wrong one another, and they should be content with what God has given them. They should not stretch out their hands to beg. They should be sober and patient, neither given to worrying, nor causing others to worry. Sultan Sahak said that anyone following these rules became his son and whoseover recognizes his own position has in fact recognized the Truth.

After Sahak uttered these principles of haqiqat (Truth), Benyamin suggested to him that a covenant be concluded that whosoever observes these principles in truthfulness and sincerity will triumph at the end, becoming a perfect follower of the order. Those who follow the principles blindly, however, obeying them not in spirit but as rigid rituals, will forever be rejected.

Responding to this suggestion, Sultan Sahak explained that these principles, like the Miraj (night journey) of the Prophet Muhammad, are an unfathomable mystery, not to be revealed to the ignorant. He also cited his poems, which were revealed to him as an unutterable mystery, as being beyond the comprehension of the ignorant. This is the first time we encounter Sultan Sahak's claim to prophecy and his equation of his own revealed words as a supernatural phenomenon comparable with the Miraj of the Prophet of Islam. Sultan Sahak is also called, in this context, the Qutb (pole, or center), the highest position in the Sufi hierarchy. This may indicate that in the time of Sultan Sahak, the Ahl-i Haqq community had developed into a Sufi order of dervishes in Iran, similar to the Safawi order.

A story in the *Tadhkira* sheds an interesting light on this development. The story asserts that Shaykh Safi al-Din (d. 1334), from whom the Safawi Dynasty in Iran derives its name, sought investiture by Sultan Sahak. Shaykh Ibrahim (d. 1301), known as the Zahid of Gilan, the religious guide of Safi al-Din, sent the latter to Perdivar to be invested by Sultan Sahak as a Sufi murshid. With Safi al-Din, the Zahid of Gilan sent a fried fish in a basket. Sultan Sahak received the fish and ordered a ring brought to him; he placed it in the mouth of the fish and then threw the fish into a water tank. Miraculously, the fish came back to life and reappeared in the water tank of Zahid of Gilan.[14] The compiler of the *Tadhkira* attempted to show by this miracle that Sultan Sahak was no ordinary dervish or shaykh, but a spiritual guide endowed with divine attributes. It was also probably meant to impress Zahid of Gilan, who was renowned for his ascetic life. As a gesture of respect, Safi al-Din was admitted to the religious assembly, greatly venerated by the Ahl-i Haqq as the center of their worship. But when Safi al-Din saw women mingling with men at the assembly, he condemned this practice as indecent.

When Sultan Sahak learned that Safi al-Din had condemned worship by men and women together at the religious assembly, he sent Safi al-Din back without investiture. With him, however, he sent gifts: a bottle of water, fire, and a piece of cotton, all in their natural state without being affected by each other. The water did not extinguish the flame, and the flame did not consume the piece of cotton. By this supernatural phenomenon, Sultan Sahak was trying to prove to Safi al-Din and his instructor, Zahid of Gilan, that the congregation of men and women at the assembly was not immoral. Zahid of Gilan seemed convinced by the demonstration, and he sent Safi al-Din back to Sultan Sahak, who, through the intercession of Benyamin, invested Safi al-Din with the office of an independent Sufi guide.[15]

Whether real or contrived, this episode indicates that at the beginning of the fourteenth century, the Ahl-i Haqq community was a Sufi order of dervishes, probably lacking extremist Shiite tendencies.[16] In fact, we do not know whether Sultan Sahak was a Shiite. Certainly there is no concrete evidence that Shaykh Safi al-Din was a Shiite; otherwise, he would have sought investiture from a Shiite mujtahid.[17]

Meanwhile, Shiism had advanced into the Caspian provinces of Iran, including Ardabil, the hometown of Shaykh Safi al-Din, and the Hawraman district of north-western Iran, the home of the Ahl-i Haqq.

By the beginning of the sixteenth century, Shiism under Shah Isma'il had triumphed in Iran, and many dervish orders, including the Qadiris, Rifais and Naqshbandis, had disappeared. It was then that those dervishes or qalandars associated with Shiism were called Haydaris, or Jalalis, or Khaksar. Although it is not certain whether the Haydaris formed a monastic order in Iran, as did the Bektashis in Asia Minor, Ivanow states that "their close connection with Ahl-i Haqq is undeniable."[18]

We may assume, then, based on the available religious literature and traditions of the Ahl-i Haqq, that they were a community of dervishes like the Bektashis, closely associated with Shiism. Indeed, one tradition of the Ahl-i Haqq makes Sultan Sahak the originator of the Bektashi order of dervishes. According to this tradition, related by Saeed Khan, after Sultan Sahak organized the affairs of his own community, laying down rules and doctrines, and confirming the believers in the faith, he vanished, reappearing under the name of Haji Bektash, in Asia Minor, where he founded the Bektashi order in Turkey.[19] Curiously, this same tradition is also related of Muhammad Beg, the sixth incarnation of the Deity and the son of the fifth incarnation, Qirmizi. Many years after his manifestation, Muhammad Beg instructed his community to remain steadfast in the faith and set off for the land of the Rum (i.e., Turkey "Ala Kapi" or the Sublime Porte, the nineteenth-century designation for the seat of the Ottoman sultan), a journey his father had wanted to make but did not. Muhammad Beg remarried in Turkey several years after assuming the name of Haji Bektash.[20] Although this tradition is unsubstantiated, it offers some latitude for speculation that there has been communication between the Ahl-i Haqq and the Bektashis. Like the rest of the Ghulat, both are associated with the cult of Ali.[21]

Perhaps the real reason for the inclusion in the *Tadhkira* of the episode of Shaykh Safi al-Din's investiture by Sultan Sahak was to establish a legitimate "ecclesiastical" authority for the Safawis, whose ancestor, Safi al-Din, had founded a Sufi order and had drawn a great following. This episode gains greater significance when we realize that Safi al-Din was considered by the Turkomans to be their spiritual leader, even serving as an arbiter of disputes among the Turkoman villagers.[22]

Another interesting episode showing the connections between the Safawis and the Ahl-i Haqq appears in an addition to the *Tadhkira*. This episode links the genealogy of the Safawis with the Imam Ali. It states that Sayyid Shihab al-Din, who was buried in Qaradagh in Ahar, a town on the Rum-Persian border in Azerbayjan, was the grandfather of Sayyid Jabrail, in turn the grandfather of Shaykh Safi al-Din, the ancestor of Shah Ismail, who was "the substance of Ali Qalandar," that is, the Imam Ali. This episode ends with the revealing statement that Ardabil (headquarters of the Safawi order), is the fountain of haqiqat. Although the genealogy of the Safawis does not mention a Sayyid Shihab al-Din, this statement indicates an intention to associate the Safawis with the Ahl-i Haqq.

A prominent feature of the religious system of the Ahl-i Haqq is the covenant of Benyamin. It is so firmly associated with the principle of the haqiqat, the religious assembly, and the position of the ujaqs (sayyids), that it is synonymous with the Ahl-i Haqq.[23] The genesis of this covenant is confusing. In the book of *Saranjam*, or *Tadhkira-i A'la*, it appears for the first time in association with the myth of the creation. It was then that God in the first manifestation created from His divine light the Ahl al-Aba (family of the Prophet) together with the four angels, including Benyamin, the founder of the covenant.[24]

After he created the four angels, God in his first incarnation instituted the covenant of the spiritual guide. (Benyamin also appears as the reincarnation of the angel Gabriel, with whom God entered into that covenant.) God warned Benyamin that if he became the pir or leader of the community, he would be unable to carry out God's orders because he would lack God's authority. However, if God in his human form, as the divine leader of the community, became the disciple and Benyamin became his pir (leader or chief), then Benyamin could implement the instructions of the pir.[25] This proposal to reverse the positions of the pir, who guides, and the disciple, who obeys, seems paradoxical. But the parodox is explained by the fact that when the pir becomes a disciple, he retains his divine power, and thus can still carry out the orders of his disciple, who has assumed the position of pir, but, being a creature without authority, cannot carry out the orders of the Deity.[26]

Minorsky attempts to rationalize this paradox by stating that the covenant of Benyamin probably symbolizes the rite of "delivery, or dedicating the head" of every member of the Ahl-i Haqq to his pir at the ceremony of initiation into the community. It is an act of submission to the pir, found in almost all the sects discussed so far. Minorsky also sees traces of Ismailism in the covenant of Benyamin. He states that among the Ahl-i Haqq, the Deity assumed the same position as the *natiq* (proclaimer or prophetic Imam) of the Ismailis. In Ismailism, God acted as the minister of the natiq, who represents the universal truth. It is possible, says Minorsky, that the covenant of Benyamin with the Deity is an echo of this Ismaili theory.[27]

Saeed Khan seems to share Minorsky's opinion on this point. He states that having a pir with whom the member of Ahl-i Haqq identifies himself is so momentous that even the Sultan Sahak set an example by choosing Benyamin as his pir, in imitation of Christ's request to be baptized by John the Baptist.[28]

This may be so, but in order to fully understand the significance of the covenant of Benyamin, we must turn to the *Saranjam,* or *Tadhkira,* which sheds great light on this covenant and the circumstances that necessitated its institution.

We have already seen that the covenant of Benyamin was instituted by Sultan Sahak in connection with the laying down of the principle of haqiqat (Truth). The belief that the covenant was formed at the time of the creation endows the religion of the Ahl-i Haqq with divine origin and timelessness. Its initiation by Sultan Sahak demonstrates his divine authority, gives him a legitimate spiritual descent as one of the seven incarnations of God, and establishes him as a perceptive teacher of the haqiqat, who could condescend to accept the position of murid, while retaining the spiritual authority of a pir.

It seems that the power struggle between Sultan Sahak and his dervishes became so heated that the sultan disappeared, refusing to reappear until he had instituted the covenant of Benyamin, which demanded the obedience of his followers. The compiler of the *Saranjam* or *Tadhkira* relates this whole affair as yet another incident in the Ahl-i Haqq mythology, giving the following account:

Sultan Sahak disappeared from the land and went to live at the bottom of the sea, in order to converse with the inhabitants of the sea under the Saj-i Nar (fiery pan). The dervishes, possibly fearing an insurrection by the people who were waiting for the return of their spiritual leader, sent emissaries to Sultan Sahak, asking him to return to his people. One of these emissaries, Pir Ali, was undoubtedly a prominent member of the Ahl-i Haqq community. The sultan refused to return. Finally, Benyamin cast himself into the sea and found the sultan conversing with the sea-dwellers. At first Benyamin could not get near the sultan, being kept back by the heat of the fiery pan. But after great effort, he managed to reach him and implored him to return to his followers.

Sultan Sahak told Benyamin that he felt great indignation toward his followers because they were disobedient, treacherous, and not confirmed in faithfulness. Benyamin kept imploring the sultan to forgive his followers their sins, and fulfill his promise to return. Finally, Sultan Sahak agreed to return to his people on the condition that Benyamin become his pir, while he became Benyamin's follower.

Benyamin thought that such a deception was a strange proposition. But the sultan explained that followers must accept the authority of the pir and obey his every command. If Sultan Sahak became the pir and Benyamin his follower, Benyamin would not be able to carry out the sultan's commands. But if Benyamin became the pir, and Sultan Sahak the follower, whatever the pir ordered, the follower would be obliged to do. Only if Benyamin agreed to this proposition, the sultan said, would he return to his people.[29]

This mythological account gives the impression that the covenant of Benyamin with its paradoxical reversal of the roles of the Pir and the murid, was a strategem devised by Sultan Sahak to pacify the recalcitrant dervishes, not by surrendering his authority, but by condescending to share it with them while keeping final decisions on morals and religious matters in the community as his prerogative. Ivanow believes, however, that it is possible that the dervishes, led by Pir Benyamin, took real control and managed the affairs of the community, while Sultan Sahak became a mere puppet in their hands.[30]

From this point on, the covenant became the golden rule for the Ahl-i Haqq community. It was invoked whenever the pir had trouble with his dervishes or members of his family, and whenever the religious and moral rules of the community were violated. Its efficacy was shown when Sultan Sahak had trouble with a half-brother over the inheritance left by his father.

To exact the inheritance from Sultan Sahak, the half-brother sought the assistance of a certain Chichak, who may have been the headman of a village by the same name, near Lake Urmia. Chichak marshaled his tribe against Sultan Sahak, who hid himself in a cave. To survive the ordeal, Sultan Sahak resorted to magic. He sent one of his lieutenants, Dawud, to throw a handful of dust on Chichak's men, causing them to panic and disperse in confusion. The magic used was the invocation of Benyamin's covenant, the golden pen of Pir Musi, and the pure service of Razbar.[31]

This use of magic against an enemy recalls similar stories told about modern Iranian soldiers, who are reported to have thrown dust at the tanks of their Iraqi enemies to make them disappear.[32] This story perhaps demonstrates the tribal opposition to the authority of Sultan Sahak and his struggle for survival.[33] Be that as it may, the covenant of Benyamin became the rule by which the community was expected to abide.

The covenant of Benyamin was also invoked during the time of Qirmizi, the fifth incarnation of the Deity, when the question arose as to whether the Ahl-i Haqq should fast or not. Qirmizi told them that they should fast and remain faithful to the covenant of Benyamin, that is, the rules of the religion of Ahl-i Haqq.[34]

During the time of the sixth incarnation of the Deity, Muhammad Beg, the covenant of Benyamin was cited as being synonymous with the religion of Ahl-i Haqq: "He who has no faith in this world of unutterable mystery is alien to the Shart of Benyamin," that is, the Ahl-i Haqq community.[35]

The seventh and last incarnation of the Deity was Khan Atish, who lived in the late seventeenth century. Khan Atish reportedly refused to pray during the celebration of the communal meal after some celebrants poured cooked food into a basin from a cauldron. Khan Atish rejected the food as unlawful because, he said, the cauldron had been stolen. He therefore refused to say the prayer from the covenant of Benyamin that is customarily recited over food.[36]

So important is Benyamin to the religion of Ahl-i Haqq that he is called Pir-i amin and Murshid-i amin (faithful pir or spiritual guide). He is, as Sultan Sahak said, "the king of my people," whom he has accepted as their pir.[37]

Ivanow sees a parallel between Benyamin and Srosho, the principal associate of Mithra. Srosho is identified as the chief of police, the head spy, and Mithra's ear. These functions may mean, in a religious context, that Srosho was the faithful and trusted confidant of Mithra who conveyed to his lord the prayers of suffering humanity. In this sense, Benyamin, who is also the incarnation of the angel Gabriel, is called the "faithful reporter."[38]

Ivanow presents another parallel between Srosho and Benyamin which he says is not entirely fortuitous. In Mithraism, Srosho is called *dena-dish,* or *daena dish,* meaning "instructor in religion," or spiritual guide. This, Ivanow asserts, is "strikingly reminiscent of Benyamin, after whom the Ahl-i Haqq religion is called Shart-i Benyamin, and who appears as Pir-i Shart, a spiritual master of the covenant."[39]

Benyamin is more than a faithful and trusted spiritual guide to the Ahl-i Haqq. He is the *Ben* (son) of Yah, and the *amin* (faithful). We have already seen in chapter 17 that Benyamin is considered to be the essence of God, the one for whom God created everything, and on whom everything depends. Briefly, then, he is to the religion of the Ahl-i Haqq what Christ is to Christianity. A prominent Ali Ilahi (Ahl-i Haqq) religious leader, greatly revered by his people as a prophet, told the missionary F. M. Stead that Benyamin, whom his people worship, is only another name for Christ.[40]

Saeed Khan has produced tristichs composed by Nur Ali Shah (the son of Shah [Haji] Nimat Allah, who partly wrote *Furqan al-Akhbar*), revealing his beliefs about Benyamin. To Nur Ali Shah, the Truth is homologous with Benyamin, who is no other than Christ and the Holy Spirit. This is very close to saying that Benyamin, Christ, and the Holy Spirit form a trinity, the first trinity encountered among the Ahl-i Haqq. More significantly, this Ahl-i Haqq poet associates the commandments of Christ with Benyamin and his covenant, and concludes by stating that only through the law of Christ can one know the truth. It is not certain how much Nur Ali Shah knew about the Gospel, but he must have either known or read of it, as his words, "Jesus, whose net is the Gospel," attest.[41]

19

The Ahl-i Haqq
The Cult of Dawud

THE INDIVIDUAL who occupies perhaps the most prominent position in the religion of the Ahl-i Haqq after Sultan Sahak is Dawud (David). In fact, a sizable division of the sect is known as the Dawudis or Dawudiyyun, after Dawud.[1] These Dawudis are mostly Kurds living in Dinawar, Sahna, Kerind, and Biwenij in western Iran.[2] Many of them also live in the Iraqi towns of Khanaqin and Mandali on the Iraqi-Iranian border, those living in Mandali being known as the Mir al-Hajj.[3] Other Dawudis are found around Qazvin and Rasht.

But who is this Dawud (David), who F. M. Stead says is less mysterious than Benyamin? Some of the Ahl-i Haqq identify him with the Hebrew King David of the Bible. Perhaps they hope to use the secular and spiritual prominence of the Biblical prophet-king to impress the Shiite and Sunnite Muslims who look down upon them with contempt.[4] Or perhaps, as some claim, they follow and venerate the Prophet David more than other prophets because God chose him to be a prophet-king, exalting him above all the kings of the world, and giving him extraordinary power over his enemies. If God has conferred upon David glory and honor of this great magnitude, they ask, how much more must man try to honor him?[5]

For this reason they hold the *Zabur* (the Psalms of David) to be one of their sacred books and read it with reverence.[6] According to al-Karmali, the Dawudiyyun regard the Book of Psalms as so sacred that they almost never show it to outsiders, although they did show it to some Christians, including a Roman Catholic colporteur who was selling copies of the Bible in the town of Mandali, Iraq. The colporteur met one of the Dawudis, who asked him if he was a Christian. When the colporteur answered that he was, the Dawudi then said that their two beliefs were similar, because, like the Christians, the Dawudis believe in the prophethood of King David. The Dawudi took the colporteur to his religious Shaykh, who bought a copy of the Bible. The shaykh told the colporteur that the Dawudis were not Muslims, and that they had their own independent religion dating back to the Prophet-King David. He also told this colporteur that the *Zabur* (Book of Psalms) is their sacred book, and that they follow its religious rules and principles.[7]

We have no information on where and how this group of Ahl-i Haqq obtained a copy of the *Zabur.* Al-Karmali's informant saw a few pages of the copy owned by the Ahl-i Haqq shaykh. Written in an archaic Turkish script, the pages consisted of part of a translation of the Psalms that had suffered a great deal of alteration.[8] It should be pointed out here that ancient manuscript copies of an apocryphal Muslim Psalter, *Zabur Dawud,* have been known among Muslims for a long time. One copy found in Berlin was discussed by Rev. Louis Cheikho.[9] Another copy, dated 1172/1758, was purchased in Cairo by the American missionary and Orientalist Samuel Zwemer (d. 1952).[10]

There is nothing in the religious literature and traditions of the Ahl-i Haqq to indicate that their Dawud and the King David of the Bible are connected by anything more than a semantic accident.[11] A prominent Ahl-i Haqq sayyid of Kalardasht (an informant of Vladimir Minorsky) avers that there is no relation between King David and Dawud of the Ahl-i Haqq.[12] However, some Ahl-i Haqq believe that Dawud was the servant of the Imam Ali and even confuse him with Nusayr, who reportedly was killed during the Muslim attack against the Jewish fortress of Khaybar and brought to life by Ali, whereupon Nusayr declared that Ali was God.[13]

Stripped of the mythological fantasies built around him and his "angels," Dawud was a prominent dervish chosen by Sultan Sahak as one of his lieutenants or "four angels." According to the *Tadhkira,* Dawud was appointed by Sultan Sahak as a religious instructor.[14] He was the guardian of the faith and an advocate of strict morality, because high standards of morality were greatly emphasized by the Ahl-i Haqq.[15]

As a dervish, he had to bow to the authority of his chief, Sultan Sahak, and recognize the limits of his own position. Once he asked Sultan Sahak a favor, and the sultan refused it on the grounds that it was not fitting to grant a favor to a sinner.[16]

We have no idea what the favor was, but what Sultan Sahak was trying to say was that he could not grant a favor to Dawud because Dawud was not a saint. However, in the Ahl-i Haqq mythology, Dawud, like Sultan Sahak and the rest of the "angels," was a celestial being. He "was created from the breath of God," when God pulled him out of His mouth. Then, together with the other "angels," he took part in the first religious assembly and offered the first sacrifice.[17] He and Benyamin are considered to be manifestations of God.[18] Sometimes he is referred to as the rider on a dark gray horse, but I found no explanation for this description.[19]

According to the *Tadhkira,* Dawud was appointed before time began to intercede on behalf of sinners and to help people in distress. This appointment was confirmed when Sultan Sahak appointed Benyamin as Pir-i amin (faithful pir) and chose Dawud as his witness. When Dawud asked what this position would entail, Sultan Sahak replied that his duty would be to guide and help people in distress, on land as well as on the sea.[20] Many ask him for help, and those in pain cry out to him, "Ya Dawud (O, David)." When a child tries to lift a heavy object, he invokes Dawud for help.[21] Dawud is very popular among the Guran and Kalhur tribes, who call on him frequently, and sacrifice a sheep for him when they go to war.[22] The Dawudis, who bear his name, never use his name in vain or tell a lie when they are asked to swear by Dawud to tell the truth.[23]

The *Tadhkira* contains anecdotes about Dawud's intercessions and divine help. He is held to have miraculously saved the child of a woman thrown into a river by a rogue.[24] He is also said to have interceded on behalf of the people of Hawraman [Awraman] when, during a religious assembly, Sultan Sahak discovered that one of them had committed an unlawful act. A man of Hawraman had picked up a piece of wood belonging to an outsider and used it as a yoke for his oxen. The wheat grown in the field of the culprit, and the bread made from that wheat, which he had brought to the assembly, became unlawful because he had plowed his field with oxen whose yoke was fashioned from a piece of wood not belonging to him.

Sultan Sahak ordered that the people of Hawraman be punished for this man's transgression. They became enraged, being unable to understand the nature of their crime. Sultan Sahak ordered Dawud to take pebbles from the women in the assembly and use them to destroy the houses of the Hawramanis; Dawud complied. Knowing the rules of the covenant of Benyamin, the Hawramanis collected a sum of money and gave it to Dawud, asking him to intercede with Sultan Sahak on their behalf. Dawud did so, and gave the money to Sultan Sahak. In compassion for the Hawramanis, Sultan Sahak sent Dawud back to them, and Dawud miraculously restored the ruined dwellings.[25] This story is probably apocryphal; it is unlikely that such a severe conflict between Sultan Sahak and the people of Hawraman could have arisen that he would order their homes destroyed, even if they were later restored.

Dawud's divine help is also illustrated in another story, which may have some seeds of truth in it. This story concerns passengers on a ship being tossed about by high winds. Among the passengers was a poor man, Galim-Kul, dressed in rags. As in the Biblical story of Jonah, the other passengers decided to throw Galim-Kul overboard as a sacrifice, to calm the waters and save the ship from disaster. The poor man began praying to Dawud to save him as well as the ship, and lo, his prayers were answered. To show their gratitude, the passengers showered the poor man with money, but he refused to take it. Though he kept refusing, a piece worth 100 dinars somehow became embedded in his turban.[26]

Ivanow sees these two stories as promoting a fund called Dawud's Collection [Mal-i Dawud], in contradistinction to another called the Jam Collection [Mal-i Jam]. Both funds are intended for the purchase of sacrificial sheep for the religious assembly.[27] The two funds are independent, and members of the Ahl-i Haqq may make separate donations to each of the funds. Every year, a certain Rasul donated one hundred tumans worth of the produce of his fields to the mal-i Dawud, in addition to his donation to the mal-i Jam.[28]

Finally, Dawud is considered an intercessor between the Ahl-i Haqq and the Deity at the end of the world. When the end comes and the world is ruined from the east to the west and Sahib al-Zaman (i.e., the Mahdi), appears, all the people that dwell on the earth will have become Ahl-i Haqq, and they will appeal to Dawud to intercede on their behalf with the Deity.[29]

In one of his poems, Kuşcuöglu, the Ahl-i Haqq divine poet, speaks through Dawud, saying that the Ahl-i Haqq should follow in the footsteps of Christ. He goes on to proclaim that "Christ is the Friend Who has the knowledge of the truth, Whose principles are perfect, and Whose inner thoughts are sacred," echoing Jesus's statement that He is the Way and the Truth. There is no doubt that Kuscuöglu believed that Jesus is God, for he says, "For in the realm of truth, Jesus, Son of Mary, is He—God."[30]

Those who venerate Dawud visit a tomb situated between Serpol and Pai Taq, built in a cavern upon a high mountain. The Ahl-i Haqq call this place Dukkan-i Dawud [Dawud's Shop], believing, according to Rawlinson, that the Hebrew King David (whom they believe was the same person as Dawud), followed the calling of a blacksmith, and this place was his smithy. Some also believe, Rawlinson adds, that this shop is David's dwelling. The broken shafts are called his anvils, and part of the tomb is supposed to be the reservoir where he kept the water he used to temper his metal. It is greatly venerated by the Ahl-i Haqq, who visit it on pilgrimages, prostrating themselves on the ground and offering sacrifices at the shrine.[31] In fact, however, the "smithy" is probably an ancient Persian sculpture representing a Zoroastrian religious ceremony.[32] Dukkan-i Dawud is also sacred to the Kakaiyya of Iraq, whose religious beliefs, as we have seen, are almost identical with those of the Ahl-i Haqq.[33]

Because it is subdivided into many branches of diverse ethnicity, the Ahl-i Haqq community lacks cohesion and central organization. The management of the affairs of each community, therefore, depends on the different ujaqs, or families of sayyids, who perform religious ceremonies and initiate new members into the community. *Ujaq* is a Turkish word meaning "fireplace," or "hearth," symbolizing the ujaq's duty to provide a safe and comfortable place for guests or strangers, who are asked to stay in his house.[34]

It is of the utmost importance to the Ahl-i Haqq to have a sayyid. In fact, different groups among them distinguish each other by the sayyids they follow.[35] Not having a sayyid or pir is considered almost a sign of infidelity to the faith, and a member of Ahl-i Haqq who has no sayyid becomes an object of reproach to others, who say contemptuously, "He is without a pir."[36] It is not surprising to see a member of the Ahl-i Haqq traveling from Iran to Iraq to find a sayyid to whom he can "deliver his head," that is, offer complete submission as a votary. Submission to a sayyid is tantamount to submitting one's will to God, because the Ahl-i Haqq believe their sayyids to be the theophanies of both God and Sahib-i Karam (The master of generosity): the Imam Ali.[37]

Writing in 1912, E. B. Soane states that the head of the Ali Ilahi (Ahl-i Haqq) sect, Sayyid Rustam, is considered the incarnation of God.[38] This is probably the same Sayyid Rustam mentioned by F. M. Stead in 1932. Stead, a missionary who lived among the Ali Ilahis, states that one of the tribal chiefs he visited told him, "May God forgive me for saying so, but Sayyid Rustam is my God."[39]

Stead also reports that people coming to pay homage to this Sayyid Rustam knelt down and kissed the ground as they approached his gate.[40] The same practice was observed by the American missionary, S. G. Wilson, who lived among the Ahl-i Haqq for fifteen years. Writing toward the end of the nineteenth century, Wilson states that Sayyid Semmet Agha of the Ilkachi village believed himself to be sinless. Those believers who came to visit him kissed his hand, offered him gifts, and sacrificed a sheep in his honor. The poor among them who could not afford a sheep brought offerings of bread, prostrated themselves, and kissed his feet.[41]

As representatives of the Deity, the sayyids form the only link between the members of Ahl-i Haqq and the Deity. Therefore, to see and touch a sayyid is to see and touch one of the manifestations of the Deity, chief among whom is Sultan Sahak. This idea dates back to Shiite Ismailism and its development of the Imamate. Ivanow relates that in one of his poems, Nasir-i Khosraw (d. 1060) voiced the desire to touch the same hand of the prophet that had been touched by early Shiite saints like Salman al-Farisi, Abu Dharr, and Miqdad. His desire was fulfilled when he went to Egypt and saw the Fatimi Caliph and Imam al-Mustansir bi Allah.[42]

The office of the pir or sayyid is hereditary, or at least confined to a priestly family.[43] Since the ujaq sayyids are considered to be manifestations of the Deity, the descendants of Sultan Sahak are the only people truly eligible to be sayyids. They are the sayyids par excellence.

The compiler of the *Tadhkira* records a myth showing that sayyids should be the descendants of Sultan Sahak, who himself was a manifestation of God. The four "angels" insisted that Sultan Sahak marry and beget children, laying the foundation of a dynasty. According to the *Tadhkira,* he therefore married the sister of Khosraw Khan Barzanja, chief of the Kurdish tribe of Jaf.[44] (According to Saeed Khan, he married Khosraw's daughter, Khatuneh Bashir.)[45] Sultan Sahak retired with his bride to a cave for seven days. His associates waited patiently for them to come out of the cave, but they did not emerge. Some of the men even tried to get them out, to no avail. Finally, Benyamin entered the cave to bring the bridegroom out. To his utter astonishment, he saw seven young men who looked exactly like Sultan Sahak emerging from behind the curtain in the bridal chamber. They were Sayyid Muhammad, Sayyid Bulwafa, Shaykh Shihab al-Din, Shaykh Habib Shah, Hazrati Mir, Mustafa, and Haji Baba Bui.[46] These were the Haft-tavana, the sons of Sultan Sahak, who are the progenitors of the different ujaq sayyids of the Ahl-i Haqq.

When the four "angels" asked Sultan Sahak to identify himself from among his sons, he rose and said, "The superior essence is one:" that is, he and they were of the same divine essence. The "angels" then asked how they should treat these seven sons. Sultan Sahak answered that if the seven remained subject to the covenant of Benyamin, the meekness of Dawud, the recording pen of Pir Musi, and the communion service of Razbar, they should be treated as sayyids and sayyid zadehs (sons of a sayyid); if they did not, however, they should not be regarded as chiefs of the Barzanja clan.[47] The heads of the Kakaiyya sect in Iraq belong to the Barzanja clan, named after a village near the city of Sulaymaniyya.[48] The sayyids of the Dawudis, believe themselves to be descendants of the Hebrew prophet, King David.[49]

The line of sayyids descended from Sultan Sahak could not be maintained forever, and other lines of sayyids, especially that of the descendants of Atish Beg, the last of the seven incarnations of the Deity, came into being. Today, the important ujaq sayyids are Miri, Khamushi, Shah Ibrahimi, Baba Yadegari, and Atish Begis. The Atish Begis are usually looked down upon by the members of other ujaqs.[50] Since a sayyid is not always available, the laws and doctrines of Ahl-i Haqq may be taught by a *dalil* (guide) or khalifa (member of the religious assembly), on the premise that the dalil is in charge of the conduct of his disciple, as in Christianity the godfather is in charge of instructing the baptized.[51]

The sayyids are not priests in the Christian sense. They have no ecclesiastical hierarchy empowered by ordination or the laying on of hands. They do not receive salaries, depending instead on *fayd* (donations). They are simply instructors in the precepts of the religion. However, they have the power to decide what is lawful and unlawful, what is approved or forbidden. Their word is binding on believers.[52] They preside at the religious meetings of the Ahl-i Haqq and perform certain ceremonies, like the communal meal and initiation. Some of the sayyids are educated, but the majority are ordinary people whose only distinction is the respect they receive for serving the members of their community.

Ivanow says that in 1918, he met in Nishapur a certain Sayyid Ibrahim, a poor, illiterate man who made a living as a muleteer but was respected for his personal qualities.[53] The Ahl-i Haqq sayyids are known for their high moral standards, humility, tolerance, and hospitality.[54] Some of them carry their hospitality to the extreme, providing food and lodging to everyone, high and low, who happens to knock at their door. One sayyid even received with the utmost kindness the murderer of his father.[55]

Some sayyids, however, have resorted to juggling, magic tricks, and fire-eating. The Ali Ilahis in Persia hold festivities which feature fire-walking [walking barefoot over glowing coals] or the application of hot coals to their bodies, which they do so skillfully that they are not burned. They do so to the great delight and excitement of the people, who believe that fire has no effect on them because they are filled with divine power.[56]

20

The Ahl-i Haqq
The Jam

THE CENTER of Ahl-i Haqq worship is the Jam, or religious assembly. The word *Jam* is Arabic for "congregation" or "gathering," and the Ahl-i Haqq Jam is similar to the Ayin-i Cem of the Bektashis, Kizilbash, Shabak, and related sects. Like those sects, the Ahl-i Haqq do not have mosques, as Muslims do, although they do, according to Saeed Khan, have muezzins who call the people to prayer in Kurdish.[1]

The members of each community of Ahl-i Haqq meet in a private home, or in the house of their pir, which is transformed by their presence into the Jam. The Jam should not be understood in the Christian sense as a physical plant, with a congregation conscious of its membership in a certain denomination or in a given church belonging to that denomination. Rather, the Jam should be understood in the spiritual sense as a congregation of people bound together by belief and devotion. It is close to the Christian idea that the Church is the Body of Christ.

The Jam of the Ahl-i Haqq is a congregation of believers who meet to perform certain ceremonies, like initiation into the community or the offering of a sacrifice or communal meal. Members of the Jam are aware of other Jams held by other groups in other areas, demonstrating the importance of the Jam as evidence of their allegiance to their tribe or clan.[2]

Some communities of Ahl-i Haqq have certain houses in their districts or towns called Jam Khane, used only for religious gatherings.[3] Among these are the Jam Khane of the Thoumaris in Tabriz, and the Jam Khane of the Dawudis. This latter Jam Khane was described by Rev. Anastase al-Karmali, based on the report of an eyewitness informant, who calls it Bayt al-Salat (House of Prayer).[4]

The Jam meets frequently, especially on Thursday nights, and on the first night of lunar month.[5] According to Minorsky, the Jam convenes sixty-nine times a year; according to Saeed Khan, seventeen times a year. It also meets for three days of festivities following the three solemn days of fasting on the fifteenth, sixteenth, and seventeenth of the month of Jalal.[6] The Ahl-i Haqq call this fast Sowme-Vesul (reunion fast). Some of their young men and women abstain totally from food or drink during the three days and nights, in the hope that God may reward them by helping them choose the right marriage-partner. Mirza Karam, who lived for a long time among the Ali Ilahis, asserts that they borrowed this three-day fast from the Armenian or the Assyrian (Nestorian) Church, both of which observe the three-day fast of the Ninevites, who repented of their wicked ways after God warned them that he would destroy Nineveh after three days unless they did so.[7]

The Jam may be called at any time, morning or evening, because it is the Kaba (holy shrine) of haqiqat (Truth).[8] According to Adjarian, the Jam of Thoumaris meets every Sunday because, like the Christians, they observe Sunday as a holy day rather than the Muslim Friday.[9] They consider Sunday the best of times because it belongs to Him who is the Master of Generosity.[10] The Jam also meets on other occasions, to celebrate marriages and fraternal unions, to initiate new members, and to pray for rain or for deliverance from special calamities. In accordance with Sultan Sahak's instructions, the quorum necessary for the Jam is five people of either sex.[11] Saeed Khan, who lived among the Ahl-i Haqq for forty years, states that women are not admitted to the Jam, but a woman closely related to the man who has offered the sacrifice may be present in another room.[12] Joukovsky states that women and children are not admitted to the Jam during the ceremony of sacrifice, but that portions of the ceremonial meal are sent to their homes.[13]

Ivanow believes that stories saying women are not admitted to the Jam are false, being circulated to combat the malicious rumors that immoral sexual acts are committed at these meetings.[14] Sayyids, however, must always be male. No women can officiate at the Jam, and it is wrong for the daughter of a sayyid to offer prayer or officiate at the Jam.[15]

The Jam is sacrosanct to the Ahl-i Haqq. It is the holy of holies being to them what the Kaba is to the Muslims, because it is the house of haqiqat (Truth).[16] Utmost decorum is necessary when the Jam is in session. Even a king entering the Jam should show great humility, standing with hands folded over his breast, for "God is there."[17] According to Sultan Sahak, whenever five or more people join in the acceptance of haqiqat and bring an offering or sacrifice to the Jam, "Then we are with them."[18]

Because of its perceived sanctity, partaking in the Jam requires physical and spiritual purity. Worshippers wash and don clean clothing. To fulfill the requirement of spiritual purity, worshippers are obliged to confess their wrongdoings openly. Otherwise they risk excommunication and expulsion because, it is said, the Jam of haqiqat is the esoteric Kaba.[19]

The *Tadhkira* contains several anecdotes that vividly portray the position of women in the Ahl-i Haqq community, defined by the general attitude toward women in Middle Eastern societies. Since separation of the sexes in these societies was and still is the general rule, any mingling of men and women in public is either forbidden or looked upon as immoral. Accosting a woman with amorous intentions can lead to ostracism and, in some cases, can cost the woman her life.

One story recorded in the *Tadhkira* concerns Ali, the son of Pir Musi, one of the four "angels." Ali accosted a woman who brought curd to Sultan Sahak. Despite her protestations, Ali embraced her and kissed her on the face. At once a pimple appeared on the woman's face. Sultan Sahak found no fault with the woman. But when Ali attended the Jam, Sultan Sahak announced that one of the worshippers was a sinner. Ali stood up and confessed his sin, and he was forgiven.[20] But even after he was forgiven, Ali pursued the woman. Once he approached her while she was washing clothes on the river bank, and when she spurned his advances, he threatened to kill a child she had with her by throwing the little one into the river. She still refused, and Ali threw the child into the river.

Because of his divine omniscience, however, Sultan Sahak knew what had happened, and sent Dawud to help; he rescued the child from drowning in the river. Once again Ali attended the Jam, confessed his sins, and was forgiven. A woman present at the Jam, however, named Nariman, drew a knife to stab Ali, whose actions were a disgrace to the community. Sultan Sahak prevented Nariman from killing Ali, explaining that had she done so while swearing by the holy office of Benyamin and by the holy Kaba [the Jam], she would have committed a serious crime. Sultan Sahak went on to explain that according to the principles of haqiqat (Truth), sin must be forgiven, but the punishment due the sinner must be left to the Lord on the Day of Judgment.[21]

The immoral behavior of Ali, the son of Pir Musi, reveals him to be a habitual offender who could circumvent the law and escape punishment because of his father's eminent position in the community. Likewise, the story reveals that separate judicial standards were applied to the high and the lowly in a society which prided itself on its morality, derived from the haqiqat. Ali continued his lawless ways, for which he was repeatedly forgiven. He stole cattle from a certain tribe and blamed none other than Sultan Sahak. Upon hearing this accusation, Sultan Sahak ordered Ali to appear before him for punishment, but Ali fled to Darra Shish, a village of about fifty houses. The villagers refused to surrender Ali to Sultan Sahak because, according to their custom, handing over an offender who had sought asylum to the authorities was a betrayal of the sanctity of asylum. Sultan Sahak ordered Mustafa-i Dawudan of this village to assume the form of a cat, and to go from roof to roof at night, mewing loudly, in order to stir the villagers into delivering the culprit. Mustafa-i Dawudan did as he was commanded, but the villagers still refused to hand over the offender. Thereupon, all the villagers, including Mustafa-i Dawudan's family, died. Sultan Sahak's followers protested his harsh treatment of the villagers and the severity of their punishment. Sultan Sahak answered that their case would be postponed until Judgment Day, at which time, if the villagers were found to be in the right, they would go directly to paradise.[22]

The code of justice concerning violation of the sanctity of the Jam seems most peculiar. Offenses committed while the Jam is in session appear to be unpardonable. This is clearly exemplified by the case of a certain Iskandar (Alexander).

Once, while the Jam was in session, the four "angels" joined the other participants in singing tristichs of praise. A prominent member, Hazrat-i Mustafa, was taking part in the Jam. One of the women present looked at Mustafa and thought that it would be nice to have him as her husband. Mustafa became aware of her thoughts and, placing his hand over his eye as a gesture of consent, said he liked the idea. Sultan Sahak, however, must have considered this exchange a violation of the sanctity of the Jam, punishable by death. At the conclusion of the Jam, he called Mustafa into his presence and asked for water. When the water was brought to him, he ordered Mustafa to wash his beard and mustache in it. No sooner had Mustafa begun washing than his beard and mustache fell off. The beard and mustache are considered by many Middle Easterners to be signs of manliness to this very day; therefore, in addition to being excommunicated, Mustafa was terribly disgraced by losing his beard and mustache. He implored Razbar to intercede on his behalf, but even supplication by all four angels failed to move Sultan Sahak. He said that Mustafa's sin was unpardonable unless someone sacrificed himself on behalf of Mustafa. Otherwise, Mustafa was doomed for eternity.

Finally, a young Sayyid named Iskandar, who was preparing to be married, offered himself as a sacrifice for Mustafa. When Iskandar's mother came to collect his blood money, Sultan Sahak suggested that the wedding guests commemorate his sacrifice by arranging an elaborate communal meal since this outstanding young man had been right in the middle of wedding preparations when he sacrificed himself for Mustafa.[23] Whether there is any truth in this story or not, it demonstrates the seriousness with which the Ahl-i Haqq regard the Jam. It is the center of their worship, the sanctuary of their most sacred principle, haqiqat, and the only place where they can enjoy fraternal unity and social intercourse, much needed in a tribalistic society.

We have seen in our discussions of various sects that their communicants confess their sins either publicly, or privately to their pirs. Among the Ahl-i Haqq, there appears to be no private confession to a pir or to a sayyid. Rather, individuals stand in the Jam in a state of "Palvazheh" and confess their sins.[24] The *Tadhkira* uses the expression, "to take upon one's neck his past sin," meaning to publicly confess one's wrongdoings. Having confessed, the sinner goes unpunished, because it is believed that his punishment will be postponed until the Judgment Day. Sultan Sahak explains the reason for this: as "It is the commandment of Truth that if a man confesses his sin, we should pardon him. If punishment is demanded here, then from whom will the Lord of humanity demand the fine on the Judgment Day?"[25]

The Jam is conducted with utmost secrecy, and the place is guarded by volunteer members of the community to prevent intruders from entering the assembly. No stranger has ever been able to witness a Jam or the ceremony offering a sacrifice. Ivanow tried to attend an Ahl-i Haqq Jam and at one time almost succeeded in fulfilling this dream, but failed at the last moment.[26] This confirms the statement of Saeed Khan that "even the gaze of an unbeliever is not permitted."[27]

The meeting hall is called *maydan,* the same term used by the Bektashis for their Ayin-i Cem.[28] We have no description of a meeting hall of the Ahl-i Haqq except one given by Rev. Anastase al-Karmali of a Dawudi hall in Mandali, Iraq. Al-Karmali's description is based on the report of an informant who visited this hall, which he calls Bayt al-Salat (house of prayer). This Bayt al-Salat is an enormous structure in the middle of which stands a beautiful dome. At the end of the hall stands a huge chest, five meters long, two meters wide, and one and a quarter of a meter high. It is covered by a green cloth, and on it are rows of unlit candles stretching the length of the chest. The candles, made of baked clay, are red, yellow, green, blue, black, and white. The informant says that he was told that these candles are lit during the services, but are put out halfway through the service.[29]

The heart of the Jam is the sacred ceremony called Khidmat, with the Qurban (offering of the sacrifice). There are two kinds of offerings. One is the Niyaz, a voluntary private offering of an animal, made by an individual as a donation. The other is Khidmat, an obligatory offering made on a regular basis. In the *Tadhkira,* the term Khidmat is also used in a different context to mean serving and distributing the offerings and sacrificial meat at the Jam, but in this case it is referred to as Khayr-i Khidmat, which indicates the act of doing something good and righteous.[30]

Upon entering the Jam, every man and woman proceeds to kiss the hand of the pir before sitting down.[31] If only a few people attend the Jam, they sit in a circle; if there are many participants, they sit in two parallel rows. Everyone sits in silence while the sayyid conducts the ceremony of sacrifice and recites the necessary prayers. He is assisted by two officials, the *khalifa* (lieutenant) and the *khadim* (attendant). According to the Ahl-i Haqq, the office of sacrifice was instituted at the creation of the world when a sacrificial animal emerged from nowhere and was slain, cooked, and served at the Jam, to the accompaniment of prayers. A similar story about offering a sacrifice is told of Sultan Sahak. In this account, it was Benyamin who rose, took the right foreleg of the animal, and put it behind its right ear, saying that Yar is the first and the last. Sultan Sahak and his associates, the "angels," slaughtered the animal and cooked it. Then, having formed the Jam, they blessed the water for ablutions, spread the tablecloth on the floor, and brought the meat out, placing it before Benyamin along with bread and vegetable soup. Dawud served as a khadim. Then the ceremonial meal was divided into portions and distributed to the participants with the prayers of the king, Sultan Sahak. When the meal was over, the tablecloth was removed, and water for ablutions was passed around with Sultan Sahak's prayers. At the end, Benyamin rose to his feet and offered the *qabd,* the closing prayer of the ceremony.[32]

The *Tadhkira* does not seem to be consistent as to what animal is used for sacrifice. In two instances, the sacrificial animal is a sheep.[33] Another specifies the use of a ram.[34] On two other occasions wild goats, together with a bull, are said to be sacrificed.[35] It is significant that the ram as a sacrificial animal appears conspicuously under Sultan Sahak, who is considered the founder of the sect. When Benyamin asked what animal would be suitable for the sacrifice, Sultan Sahak said that it should be a ram without defect. This animal should be bought from any legitimate owner, by offerings collected from the members of the Ahl-i Haqq community. In fact, Sultan Sahak specified that if the pir or sayyid cheated, stealing from the offering, the offering would not be accepted.[36] We may assume, then, that the sacrificial animal is usually a ram, although some writers mention other animals or fowl being sacrificed, depending on the financial status of the participants.[37] Horatio Southgate reports that an English gentleman who lived among the Ali Ilahis of Kerind said that these people offer a hen as a sacrifice.[38]

Joukovsky, who received his information about the Ahl-i Haqq from a Guran farmer near Shiraz, states that when they offer a cock as a sacrifice, the one who offers it prays over it, saying, "O God, if you accept, accept, and if you do not accept, then do not accept." Joukovsky goes on to say that because they sacrifice a rooster, the Muslims call the Ahl-i Haqq "Khoroush-Kochan [rooster-killers]."[39]

Baron C. A. de Bode tells of a feast of the fowl observed by the Gurani, an Ali Ilahi tribe who live between Kermanshah and Zohab. He says that in every village, the head of each family brings a fowl to the shaykh or sayyid. The fowl is killed, cleaned, and then boiled in a huge kettle. When this is done, the Sayyid covers the kettle with the kerchief and then dips his hand into the kettle, taking out pieces of the cooked fowl and distributing them to the assembled company. The head of the fowl is believed to be a good luck omen, and one receiving it as his portion is believed to be most favored by Ali during the year. Baron de Bode seems to believe that this ceremony of the fowl is of Jewish origin, derived from the custom of scarificing a cock on the Day of Atonement.[40] E. B. Soane mentions a summer feast called Birkh ("lamb," in Kurdish), during which the Ali Ilahis also sacrifice fowl.[41]

Saeed Khan believes that the Ahl-i Haqq may sacrifice any kind of animal: "From an ox to a cock, sacrifices are offered."[42] Adjarian states that the Thoumaris, a branch of the Ahl-i Haqq, sacrifice a pig.[43] Ivanow is of the opinion that the Ahl-i Haqq are selective in offering animal sacrifices, and that much of what is said about their sacrifice of cocks or fish is sheer nonsense.[44]

Other kinds of food, like raisins, fruit, sweets, and rice, are served along with the sacrificial meat at Shukrana (thanksgiving).[45] In the public service of offering (Khidmat), the sayyid or another official slaughters the animal, but in the private service (Niyaz), the person who offers an animal is responsible for slaughtering it.[46] Describing the ceremony of sacrifice at the Ali Ilahi village of Ilkachi, Rev. S. G. Wilson writes that the animal, usually a lamb or sheep, is brought into the pir's house, where it is sacrificed to Ali by a man appointed formally to perform this service.

The animal is then cooked and distributed by the pir among the men, who eat it with bread in silence and reverence. Wilson compares this rite to the Old Testament rite of Passover.[47]

The sayyid of pir usually blesses the knife used for slaughtering the animal and prays that the offering be acceptable. The wish accompanying the sacrifice is granted according to the covenant of Benyamin, the acceptance (or meekness) of Dawud, the gold recording pen of Pir Musi, the pure service of Razbar, and the Karam (generosity) of Ali. Then the pir prostrates himself on the ground, touching the sacrifice with his hands.[48] G. R. Rawlinson describes one aspect of the Niyaz among the Kurds that is not related by other writers. He states that the pir who officiates at the ceremony of sacrifice holds a branch of myrtle or willow during the services. He chants prayers, especially about the divine attributes of the Ahl-i Haqq theophanies. Then he offers a sheep as a sin-cleansing sacrifice. The meat is cooked and distributed to the disciples, who creep on their knees to him to receive a portion of the sacrificial meal.[49] Although the use of a branch of myrtle or willow by the pir during the services is not practiced among the Ahl-i Haqq, M. F. Grenard writes that the pir who officiates in the Kizilbash religious ceremony, held at night, holds a cane made of willow, resembling the *barsom* of the Avesta, and dips it into some water while chanting a prayer.[50]

Mirza Karam describes the celebration of the Ahl-i Haqq supper which follows the three-day reunion fast previously mentioned. During this festival, there is no sacrificial animal such as that offered at the qurban; instead, Karam states, every family must provide a lamb or rooster cooked with rice (pilaf). Sometimes several families meet at the home of their head man, where a pir is present to officiate. Each family brings a pot of food already cooked to the Jam. After it has been blessed by the pir the people begin to eat—not a portion distributed by the pir, but a full meal. After the meal, the bones of the lambs and roosters are carefully collected and burned. Then a bottle of wine is presented, and after it is blessed by the pir, each member of the assembly takes a sip.[51] Stead writes that the supper resembles the sacramental Lord's Supper in Christianity. Bread and raisins are also distributed.[52]

The ceremony of offering a sacrifice at the Jam is a very solemn occasion, treated with utmost reverence by Ahl-i Haqq. The worshippers are encouraged to become absorbed in thoughts of haqiqat. They close their eyes and concentrate on constant remembrance of the Oneness of God. They are taught to treat the sacrificial meal with great reverence, because their partaking of it is a blessing of the pure and righteous, according to Sultan Sahak. Those partaking of the sacrificial meal never eat their fill, because to do so is a sin. However, the meal must be entirely consumed; without so much as a tiny crumb left. Otherwise the sacrifice will not be accepted and will not enter the sacred record; that is, the offering will not be recorded on Judgment Day.[53]

After the meal is entirely consumed, the bones are gathered up very carefully to prevent them from being broken, and then buried with all the solemnity and ceremony accorded a human corpse. It is believed that on the Day of Resurrection, the animal bones will be resurrected and rise in the form of a man.[54]

Some writers find similarities between the communal meal of the Ahl-i Haqq and the Paulician agape or the Armenian matal (matagh), which shall be discussed in a later chapter.

Another ritual associated with the Jam is the ceremony of initiation. Both men and women are admitted to the Jam, but only if they have been initiated are they entitled to partake of the sacrifical meal.[55] The uninitiated are similar to the catechumens in the ancient Christian church, who could not partake of the sacrament of Holy Communion until they were baptized.[56]

Initiation is required both of those born into the Ahl-i Haqq community and of converts. This fact indicates that Ahl-i Haqq is a proselytizing community, but in fact, neophytes are not readily accepted. Sultan Sahak warns against hasty acceptance of a neophyte, because it often happens that though the neophyte is attracted to the life and teachings of Ahl-i Haqq, he later finds it humiliating to accept the rules of the Jam. The neophyte, therefore, is thoroughly instructed with respect to Ahl-i Haqq customs and beliefs before being initiated.[57]

Initiation into the community can take place only when the neophyte has found a pir or sayyid to whom he will "hand over or deliver his head," in conformity with the *qarar* (rules) of the haqiqat. Like the Shiite Imam, the Ahl-i Haqq sayyid, by virtue of his position as a descendant of one of the incarnations, possesses divine authority empowering him to be the ultimate guide and leader within the community. He is the person with whom the neophyte identifies himself, and through whom he receives the necessary instruction in the faith. The sayyid becomes his god. For this reason Sultan Sahak himself set an example by handing over his head to Pir Benyamin, whom he accepted as his sayyid.[58]

The account of Sultan Sahak's submission of himself to Pir Benyamin is notable because it gives us a rare glimpse of the ceremony of initiation. This ceremony was conducted at the Jam, and the neophyte Sultan Sahak, brought with him a nutmeg, to symbolize his head. Sultan Sahak stood at the foot of the Jam, while Dawud distributed the nutmeg and Benyamin offered prayer. Sultan Sahak touched the folds of Dawud's robe and bowed to the Jam. He returned to his seat and ordered that Benyamin be given ten more nutmegs, which were distributed to the members of the Jam. Then Benyamin, Dawud, Pir Musi, and the others in turn handed over their heads to Sultan Sahak, acknowledging him as their leader. Razbar, who was also present, could not personally hand over her head, but Mustafa-i Dawudan acted for her as her *wakil* (representative). (Usually, among both Christian and Muslim marriages in the Middle East, the woman must have a wakil in attendance at the ceremony to give consent to the union, especially if she is not of age.)

Sultan Sahak concluded this rather short ceremony with a statement which showed a strong affinity with Shiism. He said that this meeting hall was the hall of Murtada Ali, the ceremony was an unutterable mystery, and the knife used to cut the nutmeg was a substitute for the sword of Ali, Dhu al-Faqar. He also said that a coin with the inscription, "There is no God but Allah, Muhammad is His Apostle, and Ali is His Wali," was the profession of faith of the five members of family of the Prophet, who were present at the Jam.[59] The coin referred to here, inscribed with the Shiite profession of faith, is a silver coin of the Safawi period. These rare coins are manufactured for the Ahl-i Haqq in the town of Huwayza (some write it Haviza) in Arabistan (Khuzistan).[60] The coin may also symbolize an offering or contribution, perhaps a pledge, made by the initiate at the Jam. According to one source, this pledge is one hundred dinars.[61] This is perhaps part of the obligatory annual pledge made by every man and woman to the Jam.[62]

Gobineau is the only writer who mentions the use of a silk handkerchief in connection with the ceremony of initiation. He states that during the ceremony a relative of the neophyte (an infant in the case being described) wraps a silk handkerchief around the neck of the neophyte while reciting some prayers. After the ceremony, the sayyid will sell the handkerchief at market and send the money to a chief pir, a descendant of the Safawi Junayd, grandfather of Shah Ismail. If this is true, then this use of the handkerchief shows the association of the Ahl-i Haqq with the Safawis, whose progenitor, Shaykh Safi al-Din, is said to have received investiture as a shaykh from Sultan Sahak. Gobineau sees in this use of a silk handkerchief traces of a Buddhist custom. But it is more probably derived from a dervish ritual, in which the pir or sayyid wraps a handkerchief around the neophyte's neck and pulls its ends tight.[63]

The initiation ceremony is taken very seriously by the Ahl-i Haqq. It establishes a close relationship, as if by blood, between the neophyte and the celebrant. As a consequence, marriage between them is prohibited.

A very interesting feature of the ceremony of initiation is the confraternal union. Because it is not clearly delineated in the *Saranjam,* or *Tadhkira,* but only mentioned rather vaguely in two separate places, writers like Gobineau, Minorsky, and Ivanow have either treated it separately or in passing in a different context.[64]

In one place in the *Takhkira,* Sultan Sahak, after establishing who may be a pir or sayyid, says that four people can make an agreement among themselves to share each other's sins and virtues on the Day of Resurrection, and live in this world in full accord with each other. In another part of the ceremony of initiation, Sultan Sahak, when choosing Benyamin as his pir according to the rules of haqiqat, said, "Group-union [*iqrar*] in haqiqat should consist of two spiritually bound brothers and one sister, not related to one another.[65] Despite the obvious discrepancies concerning the number of participants and whether they live together or separately, these two statements must be taken together before we can make any sense of the confraternal union. The important fact is that this union is an integral part of the initiation ceremony, and shows strong links with the similar traditions of the Kizilbash and the Shabak, providing evidence that all three sects have a common origin.

We have already elaborated on the confraternal union among the Shabak.[66] In the case of the Kizilbash, only married couples can be initiated into the religious assembly.[67] Among the Bektashis, the religious guide acts as a companion to the initiate.[68]

Among the Ahl-i Haqq, the confraternal union is a demonstration that everyone in the community, man, woman, and child, is a member of the whole body of haqiqat, a concept is similar to the Christian belief that the church is the visible body of Christ. This purpose was clearly illustrated by Sultan Sahak when he handed over his head to Pir Benyamin as a sign of total submission and an acknowledgment of the religious principles of the community, the haqiqat. After Sultan Sahak chose Benyamin as his pir in the covenant of Benyamin, and after he and his associates offered a sacrifice at the Jam, the haqiqat became practically binding through a "group union," that is, two brothers and a sister [or two brothers and two sisters] would live together according to the moral principles of haqiqat,[69] retaining this firm spiritual bond of "brotherhood" even to the Day of Judgment and bearing one another's sins on that day.[70]

In a religious tradition that has no concept of redemption through atonement, like that found in Christianity, redemption is totally dependent on belief and good works. In Islam, entering paradise depends on belief in God and Muhammad as His apostle, and in doing good works; so it is also with the Ahl-i Haqq. They believe in God and His seven incarnations, who established the principles of haqiqat as observed in the Jam, and in doing good works. Through their spiritual confraternal unions, members of Ahl-i Haqq try to live according to the principles of haqiqat, and on the Day of Resurrection they will help one another, through their good works in this life, to achieve safe passage to eternity. It is for this reason that Khuda Quli, Minorsky's informant, insists that each initiate who has attained adult age should have a spiritual sister. Or, as Minorsky's other informant, the Sayyid of Kalardasht, states, the confraternal unions, which are essentially moral, should consist of two brothers and one sister.[71]

The whole point is that the members of such a union act as godparents to each other, remaining in the community of haqiqat in this world and in the next. These unions must be absolutely platonic; the entertainment of any carnal thoughts or inappropriate behavior by confraternal brothers and sisters may be punishable by death.[72]

Minorsky reproduces parts of an interesting document recovered by M. A. Danon, showing that confraternal unions were known in the sixteenth century among the Safawis. The individuals who formed these unions were called Haqq-qarandash, that is, brother or sister in the truth. It is of great significance that the same document refers to the confraternal union as "the marriage of truth," as opposed to the ordinary marriage conducted according to the Shariat (law).[73] This recalls a similar practice by the Yezidis, the so-called devil-worshippers, who choose a brother or sister with whom to be united in a spiritual bond as "brothers and sisters for eternity."[74] It is not known whether confraternal unions are undertaken by Ahl-i Haqq today, but the practice has generated calumny against the sect, whose members are accused of using such unions for immoral purposes.[75] In fact, the Ahl-i Haqq, like other sects already discussed, have been accused of sexual immorality at their night meetings. Most of the rumors come from Sunnite and Shiite Muslims, who treat the Ahl-i Haqq with contempt. Gobineau writes that one branch of the Ahl-i Haqq, has been named Khamush by Muslim shaykhs because of some infamous night meeting during which they were accused of immoral sexual acts.[76]

No description of these immoral sexual acts is as graphic or wild as the one given by J. MacDonald Kinneir. Writing in 1813, Kinneir states that he was informed, most likely by outsiders, that the Ali Ilahis conduct nocturnal festivals at which women take off their dresses and throw them on a pile. Then the candles are put out, and the dresses are distributed among the men. The candles are then relit, and, according to the rules of the community, each woman must submit to the embraces of the man who has been given her dress, be it her father, son, husband, or brother. All the lights are put out once again, and for the rest of the night everybody indulges in a sexual orgy.[77] Obviously this account is based on hearsay and cannot be taken seriously. There is no evidence that any outsider has ever actually attended a meeting of the Ahl-i Haqq, and it is extremely doubtful that the Ahl-i Haqq, who emphasize morality and ethical principles at their Jam, the house of haqiqat, would turn it into a house of ill repute.

Major Henry C. Rawlinson, who refers to the midnight orgies reported by Kinneir, does not believe that the Ali Ilahis observe these rites "at present" (the first half of the nineteenth century), but he is certain that they were practiced up to the last half of the eighteenth century. He finds in their rites a worship of the principles of generation and fecundity, and relics of the orgies of Mithra and Anahita. He believes such orgies may have had their origin in the time when Sesostris made the sexual organ the object of worship and Semiramis indulged in indiscriminate pleasure in fulfillment of a religious ceremony.[78]

This rationale may seem plausible, but it is still based on sheer speculation. Although many writers have repeated rumors about night orgies by the Ahl-i Haqq or Ali Ilahis, none has concrete evidence. F. Sultanov, for example, states that the Ali Ilahis indulge in orgies at the Feast of Nawruz (New Year) on 9 March.[79] But Rev. S. G. Wilson, who witnessed the festivities of Nawruz in the village of Ilkachi, saw no such orgies. He says only that in the evening, young men on the rooftops let down ropes on their girdles. The girls tied sweetmeats to the girdles, which the boys pulled up. Sometimes the boys caught hold of the girls and pulled them up to the roof. Wilson remarks that perhaps strangers spread rumors about orgies of Venus among the Ali Ilahis because of the frolicsome play of the boys and girls.[80]

The writer Haji Zayn al-Abidin Shirvani (who is not a member of the sect), states that depravity and adultery is very rare among the Ali Ilahis.[81] According to E. B. Soane, a Persian writer, named Mirza Muhammad Husayn Isfahani Zaka al-Mulk, who lived for many years among the Ali Ilahis and challenged their doctrines, also says that there is little or no immorality among them.[82] This seems to be confirmed by the informant of Rev. Anastase al-Karmali, who lauds the honesty and moral integrity of the Dawudis, a branch of the Ahl-i Haqq.[83] It should be remembered that such infamous allegations are directed not just against the Ali Ilahis, but against all those sects that are secretive about their religious beliefs and practices.

As further evidence of the religious and moral commitment of the Ahl-i Haqq can be seen in their practice of the dhikr. This involves a constant praise of God through the chanting of Kalam, or versified mystical prayers, and the hagiolatry of saints. When the service of the communal meal at the Jam is concluded, some participants remain to engage in the dhikr. The dhikr is a Sufic practice, and Sufis and dervishes are known for their *Sama,* the performance of mystical dancing and singing with great excitement and ecstasy. There are no independent reports about the dhikr of the Ahl-i Haqq, only their own accounts of it. At one point, the *Takhkira* mentions the word dhikr in connection with the service at the Jam; in this instance the participants engaged in constant praise of the Oneness of God.[87]

According to Ivanow, no music or musical instrument, not even a hand drum (dombak) or tambourine, is allowed at the Jam.[85] Other sources, however, report that the dhikr and the ecstatic seance of the participants are accompanied by music played on the *saz* and *tar,* stringed instruments.[86] The rhythmic chant and the ceaseless recitation of certain mystical phrases excite the performers into a state of frenzy and ecstasy. It is probably at this stage that some of the participants, especially the sayyids, resort to juggling, walking on burning coals, and holding live coals in their hands. Others jump from great heights, apparently without getting hurt. One member of the Ahl-i Haqq reported that some of these sayyids beat themselves and each other without inflicting injury. To the credulous people of the Ahl-i Haqq, such extraordinary acts of endurance are miraculous and attest to the divine powers of the performers.[87]

21

The Ahl-i Haqq

The Role of Ali

IN EARLIER CHAPTERS on the Ahl-i Haqq, we have seen that the leader Sultan Sahak plays a dominant role in their religious beliefs and customs. Because of this emphasis on Sahak, and on Dawud and others, some writers have asserted that the Imam Ali is not important to this sect. Minorsky, for example, argues that since Ali is not given a dominant role in the *Saranjam,* the name Ali Ilahis (deifiers of Ali), by which the Ahl-i Haqq are often known, is not warranted. It is true that the *Saranjam,* or *Tadhkira,* contains no specific formulas of the divinity of Ali or prayers offered to him, but it does count Ali as one of the seven theophanies of the Diety. In other words, it considers him divine. According to Ahl-i Haqq tradition, Ali existed before Adam, and his coming to this world was foretold in a prophecy revealed to Adam by Gabriel. According to this prophecy, a guest was to visit Adam, riding on a horse, accompanied by a dervish carrying an axe over his shoulder. Adam met this horseman (Ali), who announced his eternal existence, saying, "Sometimes a slave, sometimes the Creator, it is We, it is We," indicating that the Creator and Ali are one. The horseman remained overnight with Adam and left the next day, telling Adam that he would come again. Adam told his son, Seth, of the coming again of the horseman, and Seth told it to his successor, and so on, until this prophecy reached the Prophet Muhammad. Ali's companion Salman al-Farisi, a Christian convert to Islam, also existed in the time of Adam. He awaited impatiently the fulfillment of this prophecy of the appearance of the horseman, Ali. He went wandering in the desert until he met the horseman on the plain of Arzhana, a thinly wooded valley between Shiraz and Kazirun in southern Iran.[1] The horseman promised Salman that he would meet him in the house of Abu Talib, Ali's father and Muhammad's uncle. His promise was fulfilled in this way:

One day, while the Prophet Muhammad was hunting, he saw a lion coming out of a grove. As he looked on, the lion laid an infant girl at his feet. The infant was Fatima bint Asad (Fatima, the daughter of the lion), the future mother of Ali. Muhammad revealed this mystery to his apparent cousin, but kept it secret from the people in order to avoid possible unrest. Later, when Ali had been manifested and was growing up, Salman al-Farisi was doubtful that the boy Ali was the same horseman whom he had seen in the time of Adam. Then one day, when the young Ali was eating dates, he threw the pits at Salman, wounding him. Salman instantly realized that this indeed was the same horseman he had met on the plain of Arzhana.[2]

Another story which portrays the preexistence of Ali and his preeminence over the Prophet Muhammad is connected with the Miraj (night journey) of the Prophet and the Chihil-Tan (forty bodies), described earlier in connection with the Abdal. Briefly stated, on his night journey to heaven, wherever he looked, Muhammad saw Ali in different forms. He also saw a doorless and windowless dome, which he tried unsuccessfully to enter. Inside the dome were assembled the Chihil-Tan with Ali. Muhammad persisted and finally was admitted, but only on the condition that he humble himself, saying that he was the servant of the poor. He was given a glass of water, which he sweetened with a single raisin he had in his pocket. After drinking the water, Muhammad was accepted by Ali as one of the forty, but when he looked around, they had become 1,001. A sheep appeared suddenly from Alam al-Ghayb (the world of mystery) and was sacrificed, amidst prayer and the shouting of "Hu!" [He, for God] Then Muhammad looked and saw that the 1,001 persons had disappeared, and only one remained. The Prophet took his leave, saying, like a dervish, "Haqq dost [lover of truth]." The one remaining person answered, "Yar dost [lover of friends—the dervishes]." On his return to earth, Muhammad heard from Ali the story of his Miraj and a description of the *Saranjam,* which is an unutterable mystery. Thus, the Prophet instituted the *qarar farmudan* (order of obedience to Ali) for the Ahl-i Haqiqat (people of truth).[3] In other words, by offering obedience to Ali, the Prophet established a rule for the Ahl-i Haqq to worship Ali, who is the haqiqat (Divine Reality).

The oneness of Ali and the mystery of his divine substance are further illustrated by a story in the *Tadhkira.* One day Ali was sitting in the mosque of Kufa, Iraq, with his associates. He wished to show the members of the Ahl-i Haqq and other people searching for the *maqam-i haqiqat* (degree of truth) the mystery of his substance and oneness, that they might not stray from the truth. He stretched his hand to the sky, holding a shell as luminous as the sun. Then he reached for the *qalam* (divine pen) and wrote on the scroll an unutterable mystery. A woman of the Ahl-i Haqq community, as was her custom, brought Ali a bowl of curd. Ali rolled up the scroll and, with his left hand, raised one of the pillars of the mosque and placed the bowl of curd and the scroll beneath it. He then said that sixty-six years later, a person from the country of the Fayli (Lurs) in western Iran would thrice bring down the sun to earth, and would also bring out "my sign" (the bowl of curd and the scroll). After saying this, Ali disappeared. Later he was manifested in Shah Kushin, who went to the mosque at Kufa, raised the pillar, and brought out the mysterious scroll and the bowl of curd. Shah Kushin showed the document, sealed at the bottom with the seal of the twelve Imams, to those present.[4]

We may infer from these stories that the principles of haqiqat (Truth) came from God through His manifestation as Ali, and were handed down to succeeding manifestations or leaders of the Ahl-i Haqq community. These principles, written on a scroll, constitute mystery known only to the different manifestations, especially Sultan Sahak, and expanded only by them. This veneration of Ali by the Ahl-i Haqq was confirmed by Sultan Sahak, who proclaimed that the hall where the Jam meets is the hall of the blessed Ali, and his knife used for breaking nutmegs at the ceremony of initiation is "the sword of Ali." Moreover, the inscription on the coin used in the ceremony is the Shiite Shahada, or profession of faith, which includes the phrase, "Ali is the vicar of God."[5] There is no doubt that these stories fall within the mainstream of Shiism in both its moderate and extreme forms.

There is sufficient evidence in the *Saranjam,* or *Tadhkira,* to assert that belief in the divine preexistence of Ali is part of the Ahl-i Haqq religious tradition. This evidence is thinly scattered throughout the *Saranjam,* in which Ali is overshadowed by the more prominent figure of Sultan Sahak. Nonetheless, the assertion of Ali's divine nature, the preexistence of Ahl al-Aba (members of the family of the Prophet), the creation of Adam's figure in "the image of God" (that is, the likeness of Ahl al-Aba), the presence of the family of the Prophet in the Jam, and the miracles wrought by Ali in the mosque of Kufa clearly show that the Ahl-i Haqq are Ghulat, or extremist Shiites, like the other sects discussed in this book. Their worship of Ali as God is asserted by every person who has had social intercourse with them, except for F. M. Stead and Mirza Karam. Stead states that the Ali Ilahis speak of Ali as divine and say although he is not God, yet he is not separate from God. He seems to believe that they do not accord Ali a prominent place in their lives, even though they claim to be his followers.[6] Likewise, Mirza Karam is of the opinion that the Ali Ilahis' veneration of Ali as God is sheer hypocrisy because they told him that they believe in Jesus Christ and no other. Karam also relates that he was once told by an old Ali Ilahi man, "Uncle Pir Verdi," who served as his family's gardener, that he was not a Muslim, and that he believed that St. John was his patron saint. For this and other reasons, Karam says he is personally convinced that the forefathers of the Ali Ilahis were nominal Christians, perhaps Armenians or Assyrians who, because of the Arabs' oppression, lost their old faith and became a sect of Islam.[7] Stead, and other writers speculate that the Ali Ilahis are of Christian or Jewish origin.[8]

The Ahl-i Haqq maintain that God manifested Himself in many forms, including Benyamin, Moses, Elias, David, Jesus Christ, Ali, and the Haft-tan (seven bodies), particularly Sultan Sahak, in whom Benyamin appeared complete.[9] The last of the seven incarnations of the Deity Khan Atish, asserted that he was Adam, Noah, Moses, and Jesus, and Ali.[10] The Ahl-i Haqq also maintain that Ali is the direct incarnation of God, and for this reason they call him Ali Allah (the Ali God).[11] He is the essence of God and coexisted with God. At the creation, God worked jointly with Ali. Although some Ahl-i Haqq maintain that Ali was not exactly God, they still assert that he is not separate either.[12]

Ali's position with reference to God is like that of silex, a stone that produces sparks but no fire. It is only for the good of mankind that Ali was separated from God and assumed the form of a man.[13] Since it is impossible for the finite to comprehend the infinite or for the divine to be related to the human, it is imperative that the divine become accessible in a human form. Only then does the invisible and incomprehensible divine entity become visible and comprehensible, as in the case of Jesus, who was born of a human being, His mother, Mary.[14]

To the Ahl-i Haqq, or Ali Ilahis, Ali is the light of God, manifested in the flesh. He is the all-powerful ruler, the savior of men, and the highest manifestation of the divine personality to whom the heavenly host bears witness.[15] Thus he is called Qasim al-Arzaq (the distributor of livelihood), a designation true only of the Almighty God, Who is the source of life.[16] In the words of the poet, Kuşcuöglu, Ali is Khavandagar as well as the Truth.[17]

As part of the "Godhead," Ali descended to earth to convert people from their evil ways, and his divine personality has dwelt in all the prophets, including Muhammad, who possesses the soul of Ali.[18] This is perhaps why the Ali Ilahis have little reverence for the Prophet of Islam, whom they consider as secondary to Ali;[19] like John the Baptist, who preceded Jesus, Muhammad is considered the forerunner of Ali.[20] Some of the Ali Ilahis assert that when Ali Allah (the Ali-God) saw that Muhammad was incapable of performing the responsibilities of prophetship, he assumed human form in order to assist Muhammad.[21]

Some Ali Ilahis believe that Ali Allah is the sun, and that the only reason he left the sun to live in a human body was to be able to help Muhammad. This is why they call the sun Ali Allah.[22] Others assert that Ali is as inseparable from God as its rays are from the sun. Perhaps because of this belief, they hold light as a sacred symbol of divine influence.[23] As shall be seen in chapter 28, the association of Ali with the sun is a major dogma of the Nusayris. The Ali Ilahis further believe that God is light, the source of life and of the whole universe, for this reason they have the custom of setting a portion of food before a candle.[24]

Because they venerate him so greatly, the Ahl-i Haqq give Ali's name, in combination with others to their male children. One commonly hears names such as Qurban Ali, Nur Ali, and Imam Ali. Some even give their children the name Kalb Ali (the dog of Ali) as a sign of utmost humility and reverence for Ali. Mirza Karam states that the famous general of Nachechevan who served Czar Nicholas II and was killed in battle with the Kurds at Ararat bore this name.[25]

The Ahl-i Haqq appear to regard Jesus Christ more highly than they regard the Prophet of Islam, considering Jesus to be divine. We have already seen that they maintain that the Deity manifested in Jesus, Ali, and Benyamin is the same, and that Jesus appeared in the form of Shah Kushin.[26] Some of them, especially the Kurdish Gurans, acknowledge Jesus Christ as a Messiah and believe that He appeared for the second time in the person of Ali. Thus Ali and Jesus are essentially the same person.[27] The Ali Ilahis acknowledge the divinity of Christ and assert that "He is God Himself."[28]

The Dawudis love Jesus Christ very much, but they believe him to be a prophet. They place Jesus in a secondary position to King David (Dawud), whom they confuse with the Dawud who served as one of the lieutenants or angels of Sultan Sahak.[29] The Dawudis are friendly toward Christians and listen with pleasure to the Gospel stories, accepting the Gospel as the Word of God. In the words of the Ali Ilahi leader Nur Ali Shah, "Friends [his followers], I can know the truth only through the law of Christ."[30] Because of this statement and the similarity between the rituals of the Ahl-i Haqq and Christians, especially the Ahl-i Haqq communal meal, which resembles the Lord's Supper, some writers consider the Ahl-i Haqq to be of Christian origin.

The Ahl-i Haqq hold the pantheistic belief that all mankind emanated from God and will at the end become unified with God, who initially created it.[31] Associated with this belief is the doctrine of metempsychosis. The *Tadhkira* contains a unique passage on the rebirth of good and evil human beings. Metempsychosis is significant in the religious system of the Ahl-i Haqq because it is associated with the worship and decorum of the Jam, as well as the haqq (Truth) which is the essence of worship. The righteous—those who adhere faithfully to the rules of the haqiqat, worship at the Jam, and partake of the sacrificial meal—will be reincarnated so that they may come to know the haqq (Truth). The wicked—those who act wrongly at the Jam or do not adhere faithfully to the principles of haqiqat—will be excommunicated from the Ahl-i Haqq community and reborn in the form of filthy animals, ultimately going to hell.[32]

We may infer from this passage in the *Tadhkira* that the reward of the righteous is their reincarnation as human beings who will retain the dignified state of righteousness which emanates from God. Eventually, the righteous will be united with the haqiqat [God]. The rebirth of the wicked as base and dirty animals symbolizes their unchaste and immoral nature; they will be eternally separated from the haqiqat. Finally, they will go to hell, because the righteous and the wicked cannot coexist.[33] It is evident, then, that the reincarnation of the righteous and the wicked in noble and ignoble forms respectively is a matter of reward and punishment. Only the righteous will be united with God in the end.[34]

The Thoumaris, however, a subgroup of the Ahl-i Haqq, seem to believe that the reincarnation of the soul of a sinner in animal form could go on for a million cycles, during which the sinner gradually attains purification, until finally he is reborn in perfect human form and approaches God.[35]

The Dawudis, another subgroup, seem to believe that death is only sleep. When a man dies, his soul leaves its prison, the body, and roams the earth, all the while keeping an eye on the body. At the completion of its wanderings, it returns to the body, and the man comes back to life once more. This cycle of the state of life and death (sleep) is continuous.[36]

The passage of the *Tadhkira* cited above reflects a mystical belief in a cycle of emanation from the haqiqat (divine reality) and return to the same reality. The *Tadhkira* says that the good or righteous person is reborn in human form as a reward for his adherence to the haqiqat. But why should a person be reborn in a human form if he was already in human form? The inference is that he should be transformed into a more perfect human form. In other words, he approaches a perfect nature which finally becomes one with God. To achieve perfection, he must go through a spiritual cycle of development. Only after he has achieved perfection by attaining the final stage of haqq (divine reality) can he be reborn into a new form of perfection. The wicked person who has lived at the animal level will go through a cycle of bestiality and ultimately be reborn in the form of a beast. This kind of metempsychosis is also a Bektashi and Nusayri doctrine.[37]

S. G. Wilson, an American missionary who lived and worked among the Ali Ilahis for many years, tells a story which illustrates their belief in metempsychosis. One day an Ali Ilahi religious instructor caught a fox while out hunting and tied it to the saddle of his horse. Before he could mount, the horse suddenly took fright and ran to the village. When the villagers saw the horse without the teacher and the fox fastened to the saddle, they shouted, "O teacher, appear to us in whatever guise you will, but do not come as a fox."[38]

Transformation of a human being into an animal does not always seem to be an act of punishment. Baron de Bode relates that a certain Ali Ilahi, Khan Guran, loved his dog, whom he believed to be the reincarnation of his grandfather.[39]

There is no clear evidence of an Ahl-i Haqq tradition of Satan and sin. Our study shows that the Ahl-i Haqq believe in the resurrection of the dead, judgment, reward and punishment, paradise and hell. Yet it is difficult to know whether they consider Satan the source of evil. Certainly, they have no concept comparable to that of the fall of Adam and original sin.[40] Available information indicates that there is no consistency among the Ahl-i Haqq on these points. Some of them maintain that evil is a principle in the heart of man, and that therefore all people except prophets and pirs are sinners.[41] According to Khuda Quli and *The Book of the Pole,* evil is of Satan, while the other informant of Minorsky, the sayyid of Kalardasht, denies the existence of Satan, who he believing him to be only a figment of the imagination of the common people.[42]

An anonymous Russian writer quoted by Minorsky states that some of the Ali Ilahis deny the existence of Satan and his temptations. He adds that they believe that human passions are the cause of evil and anxiety, or, as S. G. Wilson puts it, evil is generated by the heart of man.[43] This anonymous writer further states that the Ali Ilahis divide passions into two categories, the *ruhani* (spiritual, or good) and the *nari* (fiery, or bad). These spring from *nafs-i mutma'inna* (the noble self of man, which incites good) and *nafs-i ammara* (the base self of man, which drives him to do evil). The first is from God; the second from Satan.[44] The term *nafs-i ammara* is taken from Quran 12:53.

In the *Tadhkira,* Satan is referred to in the very specific context of the creation of Adam. When God created Adam, He asked the angels to bow down before Him, and they all obeyed except Iblis (Satan), who refused.[45] The incident is based on Quran 2:34, which shows Satan as a rebel against God's command. Satan also appears as a rebel spirit in the Shirazi fragment on the Ali Ilahis, but here he is called Malak Taus (the peacock angel). In this fragment, he looks into the box of trusts and sees that the Day of Resurrection is at hand.[46] It is interesting that the term Malak Taus is used by the Yezidis, who allegedly venerate and worship the devil and are therefore called devil-worshippers.[47] Also interesting is the fact that a branch of the Ali Ilahis is called the Tausis (the peacock sect), said to venerate the devil. F. M. Stead is, to the best of our knowledge, the only writer who has mentioned the Tausis as a branch of the Ali Ilahis. He states that while these people do not actually worship the devil, they fear him and try to please him, and no one in their presence dares to say anything disrespectful of his Satanic majesty.[48] However, Theodore Bent links the Takhtajis of Turkey with the Yezidis, because the Takhtajis believe that the peacock (Taus) is the embodiment of evil, while the Yezidis consider the peacock the god of evil. Bent further states that, like the Yezidis, the Takhtajis never use the word Shaytan (Satan) and shudder if they hear anyone else use it. Bent also links the Takhtajis with the Ali Ilahis, on the grounds that both maintain that Ali is God.[49]

Like the rest of the contemporary extremist Shiites, the Ahl-i Haqq do not conform to Muslim religious rites and rituals. They do not pray five times a day or turn toward Mecca. They do not fast for the entire month of Ramadan, but have a three-day fast. They have no mosques, but hold their services in private homes or the house of the pir. They have no muezzin (person to call them to prayer), although Saeed Khan reports that they have the Azan (call to prayer) in the Kurdish language.[50] They do not visit the Shiite holy shrines at Najaf and Karbala in Iraq or Mashhad and Qum in Iran, but instead visit the shrines of their own saints, especially the tomb of Sultan Sahak. They drink wine and, with some exceptions, eat pork,[51] even though, according to the *Tadhkira (Saranjam),* eating pork could result in excommunication from the community.[52] They have no regard for the Islamic rules regarding *tahara* (purity) or *najasa* (defilement), and thus do not perform the *wudu* (ablution) or consider eating with non-Muslims defiling, as other Shiites do.[53]

They did not traditionally allow polygamy, but do seem to allow it at present, following the example of their Muslim neighbors. Divorce is not allowed except in the case of adultery, or when the wife is a Shiite who refuses to convert to her husband's religious views and become an Ahl-i Haqq.[54]

Ahl-i Haqq men marry Shiite women, but seldom give their women in marriage to Shiites. However, some Ahl-i Haqq women voluntarily marry Shiite or Sunnite Muslim men and convert easily to Islam.[55] Like other Muslims, Ahl-i Haqq males practice circumcision, although it does not seem to have any religious significance.[56] According to Gobineau, the Ahl-i Haqq consider circumcision unnecessary although their women seem to attach great importance to the practice.[57] Adjarian states that the Thoumaris, a branch of the Ahl-i Haqq, circumcise their sons out of fear of their Muslim neighbors.[58]

Like the sects previously discussed, the Ahl-i Haqq never clip their mustaches, treating them with great veneration. Clipping the mustache is considered a great sin.[59] It is the symbol by which Ahl-i Haqq distinguish themselves from other peoples. In the *Tadhkira,* Benyamin asks Sultan Sahak what sign distinguishes the Ahl-i Haqq from other people. Sultan Sahak answers, "At the dun, or time of the incarnation of Ali, whoever loved us would not clip his mustache."[60]

Some Ahl-i Haqq tell a different legend to justify their practice of not trimming mustaches. When Ali was young, he used to visit the Prophet to learn the religious sciences of Islam from him. It was the custom for Ali to lean on the breast of Muhammad while listening to him talk. As Ali's mustache touched the holy body of Muhammad, the mustache acquired holiness, and for this reason the Ahl-i Haqq do not clip their mustaches. The Ahl-i Haqq contend that if the Christians doubt this tradition, they should be reminded that "our saint and patron, St. John, leaned on the bosom of Christ. It is the same thing."[61]

The *Tadhkira* contains another legend about the importance of keeping the mustache intact. This time, the sanctity of the mustache is connected with smoking, another of the Ahl-i Haqq taboos. A member of the Ahl-i Haqq community visited a man of another religion (most likely a Muslim), who was smoking a water-pipe. The Ahl-i Haqq was offered the water-pipe and smoked it. While smoking, he inadvertently bit off a hair from his mustache. In the evening he attended the Jam, but Khan Atish (one of the seven incarnations of the Deity), who knew the secrets of men, excommunicated him and prohibited him from ever attending the Jam again. The reason Khan Atish gave for this drastic action was that a hair from one's mustache is as sacred as the Quran, and stepping on a hair from one's mustache was considered taboo, although it seems that the Ahl-i Haqq do not observe this taboo today.[62]

Regardless of the validity of these legends, the respect with which the mustache is regarded seems to be common among the people of the Middle East, whatever their ethnic or religious origin may be. It is a social custom, associated with the belief that the mustache is a symbol of virility and masculinity, in societies where the male reigns supreme. Among many people of the Middle East, it is a grave matter to swear by one's mustache. It is like testifying under oath in the Western world.

In conclusion, our study shows that the religious code of the Ahl-i Haqq or Ali Ilahis is an agglomeration of religious systems and traditions. It is a syncretism of paganism, Christianity, and Islam. Upon careful study of these systems, however, we may discover that the evidence of extreme Shiism, especially their deification of Ali, is sufficiently obvious to classify them as Ghulat. Their Shiism is most likely a Persian Nizari Ismailism of the post-Alamut period, which ended when the Mongol Hulago occupied the Alamut Castle in 1256. According to Ivanow, Shiism whether in pure or adulterated form reached Kurdistan, the home of the Ahl-i Haqq, through missionaries or dervishes.[63] In the early fourteenth century, under Sultan Sahak, Shiism was further modified into its present state, as it appears in the *Saranjam,* or *Tadhkira,* and other available religious literature of the Ahl-i Haqq. E. B. Soane is correct when he states that Islam has not touched the Ali Ilahis, and that they are ignorant of Muslim tradition.[64]

While some writers see, among other things, a Judaic influence on the Ahl-i Haqq religion, other writers see Christian influence great enough to indicate that the Ali Ilahis had their origin in Christendom.[65] Mirza Karam, who calls the Ali Ilahis "these half-Muhammedan neighbors of ours," says that he is personally convinced that the forefathers of the Ali Ilahis were nominal Christians, perhaps Armenian or Assyrian.[66]

Ivanow attempts to show a very strong Armenian influence, especially in the celebration of the communal meal, which resembles the agape celebrated by the heretical Armenian Paulicians, the Tondrakites.[67] In fact, if we may judge the religion of the Ahl-i Haqq solely on the basis of their book, the *Saranjam* or *Tadhkira,* we find that the Christian elements are more conspicuous than those of Islamic origin. However, the fact remains that the Ahl-i Haqq have a great deal in common with the Ghulat (extremist Shiite) sects. Indeed, because they refer to themselves as Nusayris, writers like Gobineau have discussed them as Nusayris.[68]

22

The Nusayris (Alawis)
Ancient Period

Of all the Ghulat or extremist Shiite sects mentioned thus far, the Nusayris have attracted the most attention from contemporary writers of both East and West, largely because they now control the government of Syria. In 1970, a Nusayri general, Hafiz al-Asad, assumed military power in Syria, and on 22 February 1971, he became the first Nusayri president in the country's history. Al-Asad comes from the Numaylatiyya division of the Matawira, one of the major Nusayri tribes in Syria. Other key positions in the present Syrian government are also occupied by Nusayri officers.[1]

The Nusayris have been known throughout history by the name al-Nusayriyya (Nusayris), but prefer to be called Alawis (followers of Ali). When the French mandate over Syria went into effect in 1920, the French authorities created a separate Nusayri territory with its own commissioner, under the authority of the French high commissioner in Beirut. On 1 July 1922, when this Nusayri territory became a state, it was named Dawlat al-Alawiyyin (the Alawis' state); it had a seventeen-member representative council, with Nusayris holding twelve seats and Sunnites and other minorities holding five. In 1930, the political institution of this state was defined by the Organic Law and it become formally known as the Government of Latakia.

The Nusayri writer Muhammad Ghalib al-Tawail (d. 1932), who wrote a history of his sect, thanked God that after four centuries of Ottoman occupation of Syria, the Nusayris, who had been contemptuously called by this name since 1516, finally had their lawful name, Alawis, restored.[2] The fact is, however, that the sect has always been known as Nusayris, a name that has had a religious connotation since the ninth century. Moreover, it should be pointed out that Alawi is a general term frequently applied to all Shiites who follow Ali and believe him to be the heir and successor of the Prophet in leading the Muslim community.

The original habitat of the Nusaryis is the massive mountain range in northern Syria that bears their name: Jabal al-Nusayriyya (Nusayriyya Mountains), the Bargylus of the Romans.[3] The ancient Syrians called them Ukomo (Black), and, following the Syrians' practice, the Arabs called them Jabal al-Lukam (black mountains). The southern peaks of this range are called Jabal al-Summaq (sumac mountains) and Jabal Amil. The Nusayriyya Mountains stretches from al-Nahr al-Kabir (the great river, the ancient Eleutherus) on the south to a point north of the Orontes (al-Asi) River and Antioch. The range extends from Mount Lebanon along the Mediterranean, facing the island of Cyprus. The Nusayris are not confined to this mountain region, however. They are also found in great numbers in the Syrian provinces of Latakia, Hims, and Hama; in the Lebanese district of Akkar, south of Latakia; and in the Turkish provinces of Hatay (formerly the Syrian province of Alexandretta, or al-Iskandarun), Seyhan (Adana), Tarsus, and Antioch. A small number of Nusayris live in Wadi al-Taym, south of Mount Hermon, in two villages north of Nablus in the Israeli-occupied West Bank of Jordan, and in Banyas (the ancient Caesarea Philippi).[4] About thirteen Nusayri families live in Ana, a town in Western Iraq near the Syrian border. Groups of Nusayris also live in Damascus, Aleppo, and Salamiyya, south of Hama; in al-Karak, Jordan; in Istanbul, Turkey; in Yemen; and in Brazil.[5]

Until the thirteenth century, a number of Nusayri tribes lived in Sinjar, north of the city of Mosul, Iraq. These Nusayris from Sinjar, led by their Amir Hasan Yusuf al-Makzun (d. 1240), left for Syria to help their coreligionists in their struggle against their oppressors, the Kurds and Ismailis. One of these tribes was the Matawira, to which President Hafiz al-Asad of Syria belongs.[6]

With the passage of time, the religious concepts of followers of al-Makzun evolved in new directions, especially regarding Ali Ibn Ali Talib, the center of worship of all the Nusayris. Some of al-Makzun's followers came to be known as Kalazis after one of their religious leaders, Muhammad Ibn Kalazo. They also became known as Qamaris (moon-worshipers, from the Arabic *qamar,* moon) because they believe that Ali Ibn Ali Talib dwells in the moon; another group, the Shamsis (sun-worshipers), also called Shamalis, derived their name from the word *shams* (sun), because they believe that the sun, not the moon, is the abode of Ali Ibn Ali Talib. Thus, from a purely religious point of view, the Nusayris are divided into two sects whose beliefs, apart from their association of the sun or the moon with their worship of Ali, are substantially the same. We shall have more to say about these two sects in our discussion, in later chapters, of the religion of the Nusayris.

As an oppressed minority, the Nusayris found a haven for centuries in the fastness of their mountains. They avoided the urban centers of Syria; in the nineteenth century, they were not found even in Latakia, Beirut, or Damascus. They were very suspicious of other Syrian peoples and were ready to attack at the least provocation. Rev. Samuel Lyde (d. 1860), who lived among the Nusayris for six years (1853–1859), writes that, oppressed by the Ottoman government and overburdened by many taxes, the Nusayris usually took revenge on the Muslim people of the plains, whom they hated, plundering and killing without mercy.[7]

The constant internal feuds among their many tribes and clans reduced them to a state of barbarism and rendered their country a wasteland. We learn from Lyde that violence, bloodshed, treachery, and murder became a way of life with the Nusayris. He states that because of the violence, the gradual ruin of the villages, and the increasing desolation and depopulation of their country, by the middle of the nineteenth century the province of Latakia, which once had been heavily populated by Nusayris, had only a very small number of them left.[8] These chaotic conditions must have impelled the remaining Nusayri farmers to move close to the urban centers of Syria to work for landowners who lived mostly in the cities. Some of the Nusayris moved to the plains of Akkar to the south and Latakia to the west, while still others spread into the interior of Syria, especially the province of Hama.

Although Nusayris were despised by their Muslim and Christian neighbors, the landholders needed the services of the Nusayri farmers, who, because they were desperate, were subservient and hardworking, and posed no threat to their employers' interests. This explains the settlement of Nusayris in the villages in the northeastern part of the province of Hama. This migration, however, was only a trickle, because Syria, like other countries of the Middle East, was predominantly rural in nature, and the Nusayris could not make an adequate living in the urban centers of the country. Things have changed in recent years; Syria has become greatly urbanized, and movement from the countryside to the urban centers has rapidly increased. When Hafiz al-Asad rose to power in 1970, the Nusayris began to flock to the urban centers of Syria, seeking employment and education, now available thanks to the encouragement and assistance of the predominantly Nusayri government of Syria.[9]

The origin of the Nusayris is the subject of speculation among historians. Some believe that the Nusayris are descendants of the Nazerini mentioned by Pliny in his *History* (5:23), when he wrote, "Hollow Syria contains the town of Qalat al-Mudiq separated by the river Marsyas from the tetrachy of the Nazerini."[10]

In his Syriac *Chronography,* the Syrian Maphrian of the East, Bar Hebraeus (d. 1286), includes a chapter entitled "The History of Those who are Called Nusiraye."[11] He ascribes the name Nusiraye to an old man who appeared in the year A.D. 891 in the country of Aqula (al-Kufa, in southern Iraq), in a village called Nasariah.[11] In his *Tarikh Mukhtasar al-Duwal* (compendium of the history of dynasties), written in Arabic, Bar Hebraeus mentions a village called Nasrana, from which came a certain Abu al-Faraj Ibn Uthman, who belonged to the extremist sect of al-Qaramita (Carmatians). And in a third place, Bar Hebraeus mentions the Nusayriyya as an extremist Shiite sect.[12] Silvestre de Sacy, who produced Bar Hebraeus' statements about Nasariah and Nasrana, seems at first to be convinced that the name of the Nusayris derives from the village of Nasraiah or Nasrana, where their alleged founder lived. But after further contemplation, de Sacy seems uncertain of this explanation.[13]

Other writers, like Wolff, maintain that the name Nusayris is a diminutive of the Arabic word of Nasara (Christians), and that Nusayris means "little Christians." Wolff reasons that the adversaries of the Nusayris contemptuously called them by this name because of their many Christian rituals and practices.[14] Ernest Renan likewise maintains that Nusayris is a diminutive of Nasara.[15]

The Nusayri writer Muhammad Ghalib al-Tawil maintains that the name Nusayris derives from Jabal al-Nusayra (the Nusayra Mountain), where they live.[16] Another writer, Hashim Uthman, avers that the name of this mountain is Nazare, and it was so called by the Crusaders when they invaded Syria in the eleventh century.[17] This is not so; in 1099, when the Crusaders marched through Syria on their way to Jerusalem, they found Nusayris already living on the mountain called Jabal al-Nusayriyya (the Nusayris' Mountain), side by side with the Ismailis and the Druzes.[18] According to a Druze source, the Nusayris were once part of the Druze sect, later splitting off from it. The Druze catechism, probably originating in the eleventh century, speaks of the Nusayris as having been one with the Unitarian Druzes before separating themselves through the effort of a certain rector called al-Nusayri. Question forty-four of the catechism asks: "How did the Nusayris separate themselves from the Muwahhidun [Unitarians, as the Druzes called themselves] and abandon the unitarian religion?" Answer: "They became separated when al-Nusayri called them to do so. Al-Nusayri claimed to be the servant of our lord, the commander of the faithful [Ali]. He denied the divinity of our Lord al-Hakim (reigned 996–1021), the Fatimi caliph deified by the Druzes] and professed the divinity of Ali Ibn Ali Talib. He said that the Deity had manifested himself successively in the twelve Imams of the family of the Prophet, and that he had disappeared after having manifested himself in Muhammad the Mahdi, the Qaim [twelfth Imam]."[19] From this statement we learn that the name of the sect dates back to the late tenth or early eleventh century, and that the founder of the sect was a certain Nusayri, who, despite the discrepancy of the dates, was most likely Muhammad Ibn Nusayr.

The Nusayr, accepted among contemporary historians as the source of the name Nusayris, was a Persian by origin whose full name was Muhammad Ibn Nusayr al-Namiri al-Bakri al-Abdi (d. 270/883), but who was known also by his agnomen, Abu Shuayb. It is said that Muhammad Ibn Nusayr, may have been born in Khuzistan or al-Basra, Iraq. Through his association with the Arab tribe of the Banu al-Namir, he came to be known as al-Namiri. He lived in the city of Samarra, Iraq, where the eleventh Imam al-Askari lived at the same time.[20] According to Louis Massignon, the members of the sect used the name Nusayris from the time of al-Khasibi (d. 346/957), having previously been called Namiriyya.[21]

In *Kitab al-Mashyakha* (Manual for shaykhs), Muhammad Ibn Nusayr is described as the "door" to the eleventh Shiite Imam, al-Hasan al-Askari (d. 873). A substantial portion of this manuscript was translated by Rev. Samuel Lyde and incorporated into his book, *Asian Mystery* (London, 1860).[22]

In his book *Kitab al-Dala'il was al-Masa'il,* still in manuscript form, an early Nusayri writer, al-Maymun Ibn Qasim al-Tabarani (d.426/1034), relates a tradition in which the eleventh Imam al-Askari is reported to have said, "Muhammad Ibn Nusayr is my light, my door, and my proof against mankind. Whatever he related of me is true."[23]

In his *Munazara* (debate), the Nusayri Shaykh Yusuf Ibn al-Ajuz al-Halabi, known as al-Nashshabi, states that Muhammad Ibn Nusayr is "the door of God after whom there is no other door. He became the door after the ghayba (occultation) of our Lord Muhammad [the Mahdi, the last of the twelve Imams]."[24]

Muhammad Ibn Nusayr also appears as the door to the Imam al-Hasan al-Askari in *Kitab al-Majmu,* the most important source of information about the doctrines of the Nusayris. Sulayman al-Adani, a Nusayri convert to Christianity burned alive for his apostasy by leaders of his sect, first presented this work in his *Kitab al-Bakura al-Sulaymaniyya* (published in Beirut without a date, although many writers give 1863 as the date of its publication). *Kitab al-Majmu* contains sixteen chapters delineating the various doctrines of the Nusayris. Commenting on the fourth chapter, al-Adani leaves no room for doubt that the religion of the Nusayris originated with Muhammad Ibn Nusayr.[25] The identification of the Nusayris with Muhammad Ibn Nusayr is also affirmed by Shaykh Isa Suud, a former Nusayri judge of Latakia. Writing in 1930, Suud states that the name of the Nusayris derives from that of Abu Shuayb Muhammad Ibn Nusayr, the "door" to the Imam al-Hasan al-Askari. However, Suud attempts to project the Nusayris as a genuine Shiite sect originating with the Imam Ali.[26]

Writers from Ibn Nusayr's own era have noted that his teachings put him outside the mainstream of Shiite belief, however. According to the tenth-century writer Saad Ibn Abd Allah al-Qummi al-Ashari, Ibn Nusayr claimed not only that he was a prophet but that the tenth Imam, Ali al-Hadi, had appointed him as an apostle, entrusting him with the delivery of the message of the divine authority of the Imams. Al-Ashari also states that after the death of Ali al-Hadi in 868, Ibn Nusayr became associated with his son, the eleventh Imam al-Askari, and preached al-Askari's divinity. Ibn Nusayr also allowed marriage between relatives forbidden to marry under Islamic law, and considered homosexuality to be not only lawful, but one of the pleasures permitted by God, an attitude al-Ashari deplored.[27] Another tenth-century Shiite writer, Abu Muhammad al-Hasan al-Nawbakhti, seems to have used al-Ashari's book as a source, for he gives the same account, adding only that Ibn Nusayr also preached metempsychosis.[28] Yet a tenth-century Shiite, Abu Amr al-Kashshi, notes in his *Ma'rifat Akhbar al-Rijal* the existence of a sect proclaiming the prophethood of Muhammad Ibn Nusayr al-Namiri, who in turn preached the divinity of the Imam al-Askari. This was against al-Askari's wishes; al-Kashshi produced a letter written by al-Askari to a follower, totally renouncing Ibn Nusayr and his teachings.[29]

Al-Kashshi's statement is significant, for it indicates that by the end of the tenth century, there was a well-established sect (although al-Kashshi does not give its name) that followed Ibn Nusayr as a prophet. The modern Iraqi writer Kamil Mustafa al-Shaibi confirms this, asserting that a group of Shiites broke away in the time of the tenth Imam Ali al-Hadi, upholding Ali al-Hadi's imamate and proclaiming Muhammad Ibn Nusayr al-Namiri as a prophet. Al-Shaibi calls Ibn Nusayr the founder of the Nusayri sect. He says Ibn Nusayr preached the divinity of the Imams, but was lax in the application of religious duties.[30]

Another Shiite writer, Abu Jafar al-Tusi (d.460/1067), states in his *al-Ghayba* that when the eleventh Imam died, Muhammad Ibn Nusayr claimed that he had become the "door" to the twelfth Imam, al-Mahdi.[31] The same assertion is repeated by Abu Mansur al-Tabarsi (d. 620/1223) in his *Ihtijaj*,[32] and by Ibn al-Mutahhar al-Hilli (d. 726/1325) in his *al-Rijal*.[33]

The contemporary Shiite writer Shaykh Muhammad Hasan al-Zayn al-Amili discusses the Nusayris as a sect in his book *al-Shi'a fi al-Tarikh*. He states that al-Nusayriyya are the followers of Muhammad Ibn Nusayr, himself a follower of the Imam al-Hasan al-Askari. Upon the death of al-Askari, Ibn Nusayr claimed to be the agent of the son of al-Askari, the twelfth Imam, al-Mahdi. Al-Amili also mentions that al-Askari renounced and condemned Ibn Nusayr in his lifetime.[34]

It is significant that al-Amili uses the term al-Nusayriyya, the traditional name of the sect, rather than al-Alawiyyun, which is a recent appellation. The Shiite sources cited above, however, refer to this sect not as al-Nusayriyya but as al-Namiriyya, a name taken from al-Namiri, one of the most popular eponyms of Muhammad Ibn Nusayr. Turning to Sunnite sources, we find that some writers, like Abu al-Hasan al-Ashari (d. 324/935) in his *Maqalat al-Islamiyyin,* and Abd al-Qahir al-Baghdadi (d. 429/1037) in his *al-Farq bayn al-Firaq,* use the term Namiriyya for this sect.[35] The Sunnite writer al-Shahrastani (d. 548/1153), however, uses the name Nusayriyya to distinguish this sect from another heterodox sect, the Ishaqiyya, founded by Ishaq al-Ahmar.[36]

Al-Shahraslani states that these two sects asserted that a spiritual appearance in a material body cannot be denied, since Gabriel appeared in a figure of a man, and Satan in the figure of an animal. In the same way, they argued, God appeared in the form of persons. After the apostle of God (Muhammad), they believed, there is no person more illustrious than Ali, and after him, his sons (the Imams); the Divine Truth appeared in their form, spoke by their tongue, and handled with their hands. For this reason, the Nusayris and the Ishaqis both ascribe divinity to the Imams. Al-Shahrastani notes, however, that while the Nusayris stress the divine being of the Imams, the Ishaqis emphasize that, being divine, Ali should be a partner to Muhammad in the divine office of the Prophethood.[37]

Like al-Shahrastani, the Andalusian writer Abu Muhammad Ali

Ibn Hazm (d. 456/1065), uses the name al-Nusayriyya for the sect under discussion. Ibn Hazm seems to be familiar with the Nusayriyya as a sect whose members triumphed over the Jordanian army in Syria and captured Tiberius "in this our time." He quotes the Nusayris as saying that Abd al-Rahman Ibn Muljam, the murderer of the Imam Ali, will be the most excellent and noblest of all the people of the earth in the next life because, by killing Ali, he released his divinity from the darkness of his body. Ibn Hazm asserts that such a belief is sheer lunacy and utter blasphemy.[38]

From the foregoing evidence, we may deduce that the name al-Nusayriyya was not used as the proper name of this sect until the tenth century, and that prior to that time the sect was referred to as al-Namiriyya. In the thirteenth century Bar Hebraeus, already quoted, and Ibn Taymiyya (d. 1328), who issued a juristic opinion against the Nusayris as a heterodox sect, spoke of al-Nusayriyya as a sect. However, both Bar Hebraeus and Ibn Taymiyya seem to have confused the Nusayris with another heterodox Shiite group, the Qaramita (Carmatians).[39] A contemporary of Ibn Taymiyya, Abu al-Fida (d. 1331), also seems to have confused the Nusayris with the Qaramita.[40]

Modern writers offer no additional information about the origin of the Nusayris. They seem to reach the same conclusion held by ancient writers: that the Nusayris are Ghulat (extremist Shiites) whose sect was founded by Muhammad Ibn Nusayr in the ninth century. Thus, the Nusayris are one of the oldest of the Ghulat Shiite sects, and the name Alawiyyun, which they apply to themselves at present, is quite recent, dating back only to the 1920s.[41]

Most of our information about Ibn Nusayr and his teaching derives from what others wrote about him, for he left no written record or formulation of his creed. What is clearly known is that he lived in the city of Samarra, Iraq, and was a contemporary of the Imam al-Hasan al-Askari, and that after the concealment of the twelfth Imam al-Mahdi, Ibn Nusayr claimed to be the Imam and declared that his love for Ahl al-Bayt (the family of the Prophet) led him to deify the Imams. After his death, Ibn Nusayr was succeeded as the "door" to the Imams by Muhammad Ibn Jundub, about whom not much is known. Ibn Jundub was succeeded by Abu Muhammad Abd Allah al-Jannan al-Junbulani (d. 287/900), also known as al-Farisi (the Persian), from the town of Junbula, between al-Kufa and Wasit in southern Iraq. From a reference in *Kitab al-Mashyakha,* we learn that al-Junbulani was an ascetic and the teacher of al-Khasibi, a very important figure in the history of the Nusayri sect. Al-Junbulani founded a new Sufi order, al-Junbulaniyya, named after him. He went to

Egypt, where he met al-Khasibi, who became his follower. He then returned to Junbula accompanied by al-Khasibi, to whom he taught Islamic jurisprudence, philosophy, astrology, astronomy, and other sciences known at that time.[42]

After the death of al-Junbulani, the leadership of the Nusayri sect was assumed by Abu Abd Allah al-Husayn Ibn-Hamdan al-Khasibi (d. 346/957), who is highly honored by the Nusayris for unifying the sect and consolidating their teachings. The Nusayri writer Muhammad Ghalib al-Tawil describes al-Khasibi as "the great Alawi."[43] An active missionary, al-Khasibi established two Nusayri religious centers in Baghdad and Aleppo and left several books, including *Kitab-al-Hidaya al-Kubra* (The book of great guidance).[44] He is considered one of the leading Nusayri jurists who received "divine" knowledge through a chain of authorities dating back to Ali. Al-Khasibi is further credited with propagating the Nusayri religion in all lands.[45]

Al-Khasibi's importance pervades Nusayri rituals and texts. In the third Nusayri Quddas (mass), called the Quddas al-Azan (the mass of calling the people to prayer), the muezzin, after proclaiming that his religion (the Nusayri religion) has been established for eternity, that there is no god but God who is Ali, and that there is no Bab (door) but Salman al-Farisi, goes on to say that "there is no lord but my lord, our Shaykh al-Husayn Ibn Hamdan al-Khasibi. He is the ship of safety, the very essence of life. Come to prayer, come to success, O faithful ones."[46] Likewise, the ninety-eighth question of the Nusayris' *Kitab Ta'lim al-Diyana al-Nusayriyya* [catechism] asks, "Which of the shaykhs spread our faith in all lands?" The answer is, "Abu Abd Allah al-Husayn Ibn Hamdan [al-Khasibi]."[47]

Jesus Christ occupies a prominent place in al-Khasibi's teaching. Al-Khasibi held that Christ was each of the Old Testament prophets beginning with Adam, the Islamic figure al-Khadir, and Muhammad. In brief, Christ was every one of the prophets who came to this world. Christ was likewise Socrates, Plato, Galen, Nero, and many Persian and pre-Islamic Arab sages, including Luai, Kilab, Abd Manaf, and Hashim, ancestors of the Prophet Muhammad. Moreover, al-Khasibi taught that the mothers of former prophets and their wives, except for the wives of Noah and Lot, were incarnations of Salman al-Farisi, as were the Queen of Sheba and the wife of Potiphar. Salman al-Farisi also appeared, according to al-Khasibi, in inanimate objects and beasts, like the one supposed to have killed Joseph, the son of Jacob. He appeared as an ant, in winged form as a crow, and in other forms. Al-Khasibi further taught that Ali Ibn Abi Talib was incarnate in Abel, Seth, Joseph, Joshua, Asaf, Simon Peter,

Aristotle, and Hermes, and in certain wild animals, including the dog of the companions of Ahl al-Kahf (people of the cave), the camel of Salih (a pre-Islamic soothsayer), and the sacrificial cow of Moses.[48]

From Sulayman al-Adani, a Nusayri convert to Christianity, we learn that as an active missionary, al-Khasibi had fifty-one disciples, of whom the most famous were Muhammud Ibn Ali al-Jilli, Ali Ibn Isa al-Jisri, and al-Qutni. Al-Adani states that any Nusayri who traces his genealogy to one of these men is considered a "brother" of al-Khasibi.[49] It is from this al-Khasibi that the Nusayris also call themselves [*Taifat*]*al-Khasibiyya* (the Khasibiyya sect).[50] They call their religion *diyanat al-Khasibi* (the religion of al-Khasibi).[51] Question ninety-nine of their catechism asks, "Why do we bear the name of Khasibiyya?" The answer is, "Because we follow the teaching of our shaykh, Abu Abd Allah Ibn Hamdan al-Khasibi."[52] We have seen earlier that according to Massignon, the sect was also called Nusayri in the time of al-Khasibi.

To spread his teaching, al-Khasibi traveled extensively in Persia and Syria and settled in Aleppo, which in the tenth century was under the Shiite dynasty of the Hamdanis. According to Nusayri authorities, al-Khasibi won the favor of the Hamdani ruler Sayf al-Dawla (reigned 944–967), who helped him to propagate his teaching. In Aleppo he wrote *Kitab al-Hidaya al-Kubra,* dedicated to Sayf al-Dawla. Making Aleppo the center of his activity, al-Khasibi sent his disciples to Persia, Iraq, Egypt, and surrounding areas to spread his teachings. His disciples in Iraq were the Shiite Buwayhis, who ruled Baghdad from 945 to 1055, when they were overthrown by the Seljuk Turkish Sultan Tughril. The Shiite Fatimi sultans of Egypt were also among his disciples. To his disciples, al-Khasibi was erudite and deeply religious. Because of his extensive religious knowledge, he was called Shaykh al-Din (the spiritual authority of religion). After a long and eventful life, al-Khasibi died in Aleppo, where his tomb is inscribed with the name Shaykh Yabraq. It has become a holy shrine visited by many people.[53]

According to Sulayman al-Adani, the Nusayri religion began with Muhammad Ibn Nusayr, who was succeeded by Ibn Jundub, who, in turn, was succeeded by al-Junbulani who was succeeded by al-Husayn Ibn Hamdan al-Khasibi, so esteemed by the Nusayris that they consider him "superior to all his successors."[54] He is the one who perfected their prayers and taught far and wide in many countries. But, al-Adani goes on to say, al-Khasibi was not successful in winning coverts to his religious ideas.

To show his disappointment with the Syrians, who did not respond to his preaching, he satirized them in some of his poems, saying, "I dislike to stay in the land of al-Sham (Syria), may the curse of the Lord of all creatures rest upon them."[55] From Syria al-Khasibi journeyed to Baghdad, where he taught in public, but the governor of the city arrested him and threw him into prison. He managed to escape by night, claiming that Christ had delivered him from his captors, and that Christ was none other than Muhammad. According to Bar Hebraeus in his *Chronography,* al-Khasibi (who is not mentioned by name) escaped through the efforts of the jailer's maid, who felt sorry for him. When the jailer was deep in sleep, she stole the keys of the cell from him, opened the gate, let al-Khasibi out, and returned the keys to their place. When the jailer awoke and saw the prisoner had escaped, he spread the rumor that an angel had delivered him, in order to escape the governor's wrath. When al-Khasibi heard the tale of this "miracle," he became more resolute than ever in spreading his teachings.[56]

Bar Hebraeus repeats this same story in his *Tarikh Mukhtasar al-Duwal* (History of dynasties), relating it this time as the tale of a certain poor man who came from Khuzistan [Arabistan] in southwest Iran. This man went to Sawad al-Kufa in southern Iraq and, according to Bar Hebraeus, founded the Qaramita (Carmatians), another extremist Shiite group.[57] Apparently the stories told by Bar Hebraeus in his *Chronography* about the founder of the Nusayris and in *Tarikh Mukhtasar al-Duwal* about the founder of the Qaramita are related to stories related by either Jirjis Ibn al-Amid, called al-Makin (d. 1273), or Abu al-Fida (d. 1331) regarding the founder of the Qaramita.[58] From the accounts of these writers, we may gain the impression that the Qaramita and the Nusayris are one and the same sect. De Sacy concludes that the Qaramita are no different from the Nusayris because both sects are closely related with the Ismailis, and because information in Druze books about the doctrines of the Nusayris proves that these doctrines are identical with those of the Ismailis.[59] There is a great deal of truth in de Sacy's statement that the Nusayris were related to the Ismailis. Such a relationship is suggested by the effort made to unite the Nusayris and the Ismailis. The Nusayri writer Muhammad Ghalib al-Tawil states that after the death of al-Junbulani in 287/900, the Ismailis and the Nusayris, whom he calls Alawis, called an important religious meeting in the city of Ana near the Iraqi-Syrian border, attended by two representatives each from Baghdad, Ana, Aleppo, Latakia, and Jabal al-Nusayriyya (the Nusayris' Mountain). The purpose of the meeting was to unite the Alawis [Nusayris] with the Ismailis, but its result, says al-Tawil, was more disagreement and greater alienation between the two sects.[60] From this account we may infer that, since the Ismailis were the older sect, the Nusayris were an offshoot of the Ismailis.

While there is no evidence that the Nusayris and the Qaramita are identical, they do share common practices, such as prostrating themselves fifty times a day while praying, holding one-fifth of their property at the disposal of their brethren, and celebrating the feasts of the Mihrajan and Nawruz.[61] It is noteworthy, however, that Shaykh Isa Suud, former Nusayri Judge of Latakia, rejects the stories about al-Khasibi and the association of the Nusayris with the Qaramita. He blames these stories on their authors, who, "because of ignorance of the true history of the Nusayris, wrote such fables, which have no shadow of reality." However, Suud produces poetry composed by al-Khasibi while in prison in Baghdad, lamenting the fact that he was thrown into jail because he was accused of being a Qarmati (Carmatian), which indicates that there is some truth in associating al-Khasibi with the Qaramita.[62]

Among his many accomplishments, al-Khasibi established two religious centers—one in Baghdad, which he entrusted to his representative, Ali al-Jisri (whose epithet derives from *Jisr* [bridge] because of his position as the supervisor of bridges in Baghdad), and the other in Aleppo, operated by his agent, Muhammad Ibn Ali al-Jilli, from Jilliyya, near Antioch.

According to Muhammad Ghalib al-Tawil, al-Khasibi's main goal was to win people over from all creeds to the Junbulaniyya order, founded by his master, al-Junbulani. Al-Tawil goes on to say that Muslims, Christians, Jews, Byzantines, and Turks joined the Junbulaniyya order and formed the sect now called the Alawis, or Nusayris. Certainly this is a very significant testimony about the origin of the Nusayri sect, especially in that it comes from a member of that sect. Also noteworthy is al-Tawil's statement that al-Junbulani was born in 235/849 and died in 287/900. We can be quite sure that the Nusayris were already an established sect in the ninth century,[63] but they were known as Namiriyya and Junbulaniyya rather than Nusayris. In the tenth century, they were called Khasibiyya, after al-Khasibi, as well as Nusayris.

23

The Nusayris
Middle Period

THE NUSAYRI CENTER in Baghdad was eventually destroyed, together with other institutions, when the armies of the Mongol Hulago ransacked Baghdad in 1258. The center in Aleppo, after al-Khasibi died, continued under the leadership of Muhammad Ibn Ali al-Jilli, who was in turn succeeded by the prominent Nusayri, Abu Said al-Maymun Ibn Qasim al-Tabarani (d. 426/1034). Born in Tiberius, Palestine, in 968 (hence Tabarani), al-Tabarani was a more prolific writer than al-Khasibi and a distinguished Nusayri leader. Among his books was *Kitab Majmu al-A'yad* (Book of Feasts), which describes, among other festivals, the celebrations of Christmas and Nawruz (Persian New Year).[1]

Constant warfare and turmoil forced al-Tabarani to move his headquarters in 1031 to Latakia, where three years later he died and was buried. During his stay in Latakia, a conflict over religious matters arose between his sect and the Ishaqiyya, whom we have already mentioned as an extremist Shiite sect sharing with the Nusayris the concept of the apotheosis of Ali. The Ishaqiyya derive their name from Abu Yaqub Ishaq (Isaac), nicknamed al-Ahmar (the red one), who, like Muhammad Ibn Nusayr, was a follower of the eleventh Imam, al-Hasan al-Askari. Like Ibn Nusayr, Ishaq al-Ahmar claimed to be the "door" to al-Askari, and he made additions to the dogma regarding the Imams.[2]

In the time of al-Tabarani, a certain leader of the Ishaqiyya, Ismail Ibn Khallad of Balbak, nicknamed Abu Dhuhayba (from *dhahab,* gold) because of his wealth, made Jabala, south of Latakia, the headquarters of his sect. According to al-Tawil, there were no real doctrinal differences between al-Tabarani and Abu Dhuhayba," the Nusayriyya and the Ishaqiyya shared the extreme beliefs related by al-Shahrastani. However, al-

Tawil says that while al-Tabarani was known for his piety and poverty, Abu Dhuhayba was known for his wealth.[3]

Taking advantage of the piety of al-Tabarani, the ambitious Abu Dhuhayba moved his headquarters to Latakia, probably in the same year as al-Tabarani. We are informed by al-Tawil that at Latakia, Abu Dhuhayba began to antagonize and pressure the Nusayris. Had it not been for the Nusayri people of the Banu Hilal, who rushed to help their brethren, Abu Dhuhayba would have destroyed the Nusayris. When the Banu Hilal arrived in Latakia, Abu Dhuhayba escaped to Antioch. The Nusayri Diyab Abu Ghanim chief of the Banu Zughba, chased Abu Dhuhayba from place to place with eighty horsemen until finally they found him near Latakia. Abu Ghanim took him by surprise, kicked him with his stirrup, and killed him. Abu Dhuhayba was buried in Latakia, where his tomb is well known among the people of the city as the tomb of Shaykh Qarash.[4]

Al-Tabarani is so esteemed by the Nusayris that the third chapter of *Kitab al-Majmu* is entitled "The Canonization of Abu Said." This canonization, a kind of holy supplication addressed to their god, Ali Ibn Abi Talib, also "calls to mind the presence of the most illustrious, the most valiant, the lusty, the God-fearing possessor of divine knowledge, Abu Said, who avenged himself with his own hand on the head of Abu Dhuhayba, may the curse of God rest upon him."[5]

Al-Tabarani was the last religious leader to keep the whole Nusayri community united. From al-Tawil we learn that after al-Tabarani's death, the Nusayri community split into different factions ruled by independent shaykhs.[6] They remain today as they have been for centuries: a tribalistic people with a closed society. Like other persecuted minority religious groups (e.g., the Mormons in the United States in the nineteenth century), they sought a haven from their oppressors, settling in the fastness of the rugged mountain of Bargylus or al-Lukam, which bears their name, Jabal al-Nusayriyya. As noted earlier, al-Khasibi was highly favored by the Shiite Hamdanis, princes who ruled Aleppo from 944 to 1003; since they were Shiites, it was to be expected that they should support and sanction his teachings. Yet there is no evidence that the Nusayris gained any power within the Hamdani state. As extremist Shiites, the Nusayris were most likely detested by the Hamdanis, moderate Twelver Shiites who rejected the deification of Ali and the Imams. It is because of their extreme Shiite beliefs that the Nusayris retreated to the mountainous regions of northwestern Syria, where they could live in isolation, unmolested.

It was in this self-imposed isolation that the Nusayris finally developed their own syncretic religious system. As a closed society they acquired what may be called an inferiority complex, regarding themselves as a forlorn and despised people. Yet, like the children of Israel, they claimed to be a "chosen people."[7] They were in constant fear of the Sunnites, whom they considered their worst oppressors. Munir al-Sharif, who has studied the life and conditions of the Nusayris (whom he calls Alawis), states that they transmit from generation to generation the stories of the Sunnites' persecution of their people. Therefore, says al-Sharif, if an Alawi (Nusayri) knows that you are a Sunnite, he will not be as candid with you as he would be with a Christian, for the latter, like he, is weak and oppressed.[8]

This history of persecution made the Nusayris hate the Sunnites and pray for the destruction of Muslim rulers. To the Nusayris, the Muslims are an accursed people; they believe that when Muslim chiefs die, their souls assume the bodily form of asses.[9] The Nusayris' hatred of the Muslims and the fact that they are considered heretics, caused the prominent Sunnite learned man, Ibn Taymiyya (d. 1328), to issue a juristic opinion not only condemning the Nusayris as infidels who should be totally shunned by the Muslims, but also declaring that their property and blood may be lawfully taken by the Muslims unless they show repentance.[10]

When the Crusaders swept through Syria in 1097, so we are told by Bar Hebraeus, they went to Mount Lebanon and killed a great number of Nusayris.[11] But it seems that when the Crusaders learned that the Nusayris were not a truly Muslim sect, they became tolerant towards them. This explains Ibn Taymiyya's statement that the Syrian coast, where the Nusayris lived, was captured by the Crusaders with their cooperation.[12] For the services they rendered to the Crusaders, the Nusayris were able to regain most of their castles, which had been captured by the Ismailis in 1071.[13] The Ismailis remained powerful in the southern part of the Nusayri territory, however. It is strange that we do not hear as much about the Nusayris in Muslim chronicles as we do about the more powerful Ismailis and Qaramita. Perhaps because the Nusayris had religious beliefs in common with the Ismailis and had lived among the Qaramita, Muslim authors confused them with these sects.[14] The fact remains that the Nusayris remained subject to the Muslims, Crusaders, and the Assassins [Ismailis], who were the absolute rulers of several castles, including those of Qadmus and Masyaf in the southern part of the Nusayris' country. Meantime, the Kurds, who had moved into Nusayri territory, allied themselves with the Ismailis and began to challenge the very existence of the Nusayris. Faced with both Kurds and

Ismailis, the Nusayris delegated two men, Shaykh Muhammad of Banyas and Shaykh Ali al-Khayyat, to ask Shaykh Hasan al-Makzun (d. 1220), Prince of Sinjar in northern Iraq, to rush to their aid. Al-Makzun responded. In 617/1120, he marched with a force of twenty-five thousand men against the Nusayri territory but his campaign ended in failure. Learning that al-Makzun had arrived in the Nusayri territory, the Kurds and their allies congregated at Masyaf, and attacked his forces at night, defeating them. Al-Makzun returned to Sinjar.

Three years later, with a much larger force, and accompanied by women and children, al-Makzun marched once more into Nusayri territory. This time, the Ismailis deserted the Kurds and joined the Nusayris. Relieved by this defection to his side, al-Makzun drove the Kurds to Akkar in the south and returned to the citadel of Abu Qubays, which he used as headquarters. The people who accompanied al-Makzun became the ancestors of the Nusayri tribes of Haddadiyya, Matawira, Muhaliba, Darawisa, Numaylatiyya and the Banu Ali.[15] [Syrian President Hafiz al-Asad, who belongs to the Numaylatiya branch of the Matawira tribe, is, then, of Iraqi origin.]

After subduing the Kurds and the Ismailis, al-Makzun began to regulate the affairs of the Nusayris. He was a pious man and a poet, whose poetry is characterized by religious symbolism. He died in 638/1240 and is buried at Kfarsusa, near Damascus.[16] The followers of al-Makzun who hailed from Jabal Sinjar form the Kalazis, or Qamaris sect, of the Nusayris.

In 1258, the Mongol hordes, commanded by Hulago, ransacked Baghdad. A Mongol army commanded by the Christian general Kitbugha swept through northern Syria, capturing the major cities, including Hama and Aleppo.[17] Ibn Taymiyya accuses the Nusayris of helping the Mongols conquer Syria and handing over the fortresses to the enemies of Islam.[18] When the Egyptian Mamluk Sultan al-Zahir Baybars (reigned 1223–77) finally defeated the joint armies of the Mongols and the Franks at Ayn Jalut, near Nazareth, on 3 September 1260, the Nusayris according to Ibn Taymiyya, considered the triumph of the Muslims over the Mongols and the Christians (Franks) the greatest calamity.[19] The collaboration of the Nusayris with the Mongols and the Franks against Baybars explains why, after his victory, Baybars marched against the country of the Nusayris, destroying their castles. He also forced them to build mosques and ordered them to return to the religion of Islam; they did build mosques, but never worshipped in them and left them to decay.[20] The Maghribi traveler Ibn Battuta (d. 1377), who was in Syria in 1326 noticed that the mosques that Baybars had forced the

Nusayris to build were not only desolate, but had also been used as stables for cattle and sheep. Ibn Battuta said that if a stranger were to come to the Nusayris, enter a mosque, and call to prayer, they would say to him, "Don't bray, your fodder will come to you."[21] This shows that, like the other extremist Shiites we have discussed, the Nusayris had total disregard for Muslim religious duties.

The most prominent leader of the Nusayris after al-Makzun was Shaykh Imarat al-Dawla Hatim al-Tubani (d. 700/1300), from the Haddadin clan, originally from Sinjar. In his time, the Ismailis sought reconciliation and unity with the Nusayris because, as al-Tawil states, there is only one real point of difference between the Ismailis and the Nusayris: the number of Imams they accepted. While the Ismailis acknowledge the authority of only the first seven Imams, stopping with Ismail, the son of Jafar al-Sadiq, the Nusayris uphold the authority of all twelve Imams, ending with the disappearing Imam, Muhammad the Mahdi.[22] In all other matters of dogma, the Nusayris were no different from the Ismailis, which supports what has previously been said, that the Nusayris are an offshoot of the Ismailis.[23]

The leaders of the Nusayris and the Ismailis met in 690/1291 at Safita, southeast of Tartus, but resolved nothing.[24] As we have already seen, efforts to unite the two sects had begun at the meeting of Ana (287/900), which likewise ended in failure.

The fall of Baghdad to the Mongols in 1258 brought the end of the Abbasid state and caliphate, creating a political vacuum which the Mongols could not fill. As long as the Abbasid caliph was in power, he was looked upon as a symbol of Islam, at least in its Sunnite form. But the power of the Muslims suffered a setback when Hulago, influenced by his Christian wife, favored the Christians in Baghdad and Damascus. From Ibn al-Futi al-Baghdadi (d. 1323) we learn that when Hulago stormed and ravaged Baghdad, putting its inhabitants to the sword, he spared the Christians and appointed guards to protect their homes. For this reason many Muslims sought refuge with the Christians. [25] According to Imad al-Din Ibn Kathir (d. 1373), Hulago, before his defeat at Ayn Jalut, allowed the Christians to oppress the Muslims and celebrate their religious ceremonies openly.[26] He also favored the Jews, bringing some from Tiflis and appointing them as executors of Muslim bequests.[27]

Obviously, the Mongols' toleration of these minorities was meant to win over the weaker people, who would then be more willing to serve the interests of the conqueror.[28] This state of affairs changed, however, when the seventh Mongol Il-khan after Hulago, Ghazan Mahmud (reigned 1295–1304) embraced Islam. His inclination toward Shiism is revealed by the fact that he appointed a Shiite as governor of Iraq. He also visited the Shiite holy shrines in al-Najaf and Karbala.[29]

We have given this brief account to show that the Mongol rulers favored one sect over another, creating religious conflict, political rivalry, and intrigue among those men whom they appointed as their ministers. Naturally, there was a great deal of violence and bloodshed.

In this environment of religious and political turmoil, some men, driven by ambition, founded new religious sects; others claimed to be the Mahdi [the Shiite messiah], appearing after his long concealment to restore justice to the world. Ibn Kathir, in a discussion of the Nusayris' attack against the city of Jabala in the year 717/1317, relates the story of a certain Nusayri man who claimed to be the Mahdi.

At this time, according to Ibn Kathir, the Nusayris were in rebellion. Leading the rebels was a man who had at various times claimed to be Muhammad the Mahdi, Ali Ibn Ali Talib, and even Muhammad Ibn Abd Allah (the prophet of Islam). He declared that the Muslims were infidels, and the Nusayris the true believers. He deceived many people, who followed him in attacking and pillaging the town of Jabala. As they left the ravaged town they cursed the Caliphs Abu Bakr and Umar, and shouted, "There is no God but Ali, no veil but Muhammad, and no door but Salman." In their distress, the inhabitants of Jabala cried out for help, but no help came. Ibn Kathir goes on to say that this Mahdi pretender ordered his men to ravage Muslim places of worship and turn them into taverns selling wine. Whenever the Nusayris captured a Muslim, they commanded him to say, "There is no God but Ali. Worship your God Ali, who causes people to live and die, in order to spare your blood."[30]

Ibn Battuta, who arrived in Syria in 1326, gives a similar account of this Mahdi pretender. He states that an unknown man rose to prominence among the Nusayris pretending to be the Mahdi. Promising to rule the sect, he divided the land of Syria among his many followers, assigning them to conquer different parts of the country. When he commanded them to go forth, he gave them olive branches, saying, "By these conquer, for they are your authorization." He ordered his followers to attack the Muslims, beginning with the town of Jabala. They stormed the town while the inhabitants were at Friday prayers, entering the houses and ravishing the women. Some of the rebels were killed by the Nusayris, however.

When news of this Mahdi pretender reached al-Malik al-Nasir [Sultan of Egypt, 1310–40], who also controlled Syria, he ordered that the Nusayris who had killed the followers of the Mahdi pretender should themselves be put to death. But the Muslims explained that the Nusayri farmers were employed to till the land, and if they were killed, the Muslims would have no one to raise crops for them. So al-Malik al-Nasir revoked his order.[31]

The accounts of Ibn Kathir and Ibn Battuta are significant because they reveal that the Nusayris are Ghulat who deify Ali, believing that the Prohpet of Islam is only a "veil" of Ali, and who consider Sunnite Muslims to be their adversaries. Ibn Kathir, especially, implies that the Nusayris are not Muslims, but rather enemies of Islam. We shall elaborate on this point later.

From 1317, when the Nusayri Mahdi pretender appeared, until 1516, when the Ottoman Sultan Selim I, nicknamed "The Grim" (d. 1520), defeated the last of the Mamluk sultans, Qansawh, at Marj Dabiq near Aleppo, the Nusayris' country remained under the control of the Mamluks. The most important occurrence affecting the countries of the Middle East, especially Syria and Iraq, during this period was the conquest of the region by another Mongol, Timur Lang (Tamerlane, d. 1405).

In 1392, Timur conquered Iraq and parts of Syria and Turkey. Turning back to Syria, he occupied Damascus and Aleppo in 1401. The conquered peoples practiced a wide range of religious beliefs; the Muslims, who formed the majority, included Sunnites, Shiites, and Sufis. To consolidate his position, Timur exploited their differences to his own advantage.[32]

Since Sufism and the Sufi orders were prevalent in the fourteenth century, Timur established strong relations with such paragons of Sufism as the Shaykhs Shams al-Din al-Fakhuri, Abu Bakr al-Khawafi, and Muhammad Barak, who were considered saints in their time.[33] On their part, the Sufis supported Timur, praising his actions as miracles worked by divine inspiration.[34]

Timur also attempted to win over the Shiites. As a gesture of his support for them, he occupied Damascus to avenge the killing of the Imam al-Husayn in 680 by the lieutenants of the Umayyad Caliph Yazid, on the premise that Damascus was the capital of the Umayyads.[35] Timur is thought by some, including the Nusayri writer al-Tawil, to have been a Shiite. Al-Tawil maintains that Timur composed verses containing ideas conforming to those of the Junbulaniyya tariqa, a Nusayri order.[36] Whether or not Timur was a devout Shiite or had proclivities toward Shiism, the fact remains that he greatly favored and supported the Shiites, who gained the upper hand in the Islamic countries under his control.[37]

Timur's march against Syria led the Nusayris to appeal to the pro-Shiite conqueror to avenge them against their enemies, the Sunnites. We are informed by al-Tawil that before Timur stormed Damascus, an Alawi woman, Durr al-Sadaf, the daughter of Saad al-Ansar (one of the men of the Mamluk Sultan al-Zahir), accompanied by forty Alawi virgins, tearfully asked Timur to avenge the family of the Prophet particularly the daughters, including al-Husayn's sister Zaynab, who was taken as a captive after his murder to the Umayyad Caliph Yazid in Damascus.[38]

Timur promised Durr al-Sadaf that he would avenge the family of the Prophet. She accompanied him to Damascus with forty virgins, who sang songs against the Umayyads. When Timur entered Damascus, he offered amnesty to its inhabitants and asked them to find him a woman from among the dignitaries of the city to be his wife. When a maiden was found, he ordered that she be marched naked through the city. When the people refused, Timur said to them, "Who, then, gave you the right to bring the daughter of the apostle of God uncovered to your city?" Then he ordered them killed.[39] What he meant was, who had given the right to the Umayyads, in time of the Caliph Yazid, to parade the wives and sister of al-Husayn, the grandson of the Prophet of Islam, naked through the streets of Damascus?

Timur's authority in Syria did not last, however. The country fell under the rule of the Mamluks, whose power was finally destroyed in turn by the Ottoman Sultan Selim I in 1516, when Syria became an Ottoman province. The Ottoman occupation of Syria brought misfortune to the Nusayris, who had to face oppression by a powerful Sunnite enemy.

The beginning of the sixteenth century witnessed the rise of two powers, the Safawis of Persia under Shah Ismail, and the Ottomans under Selim I. The two suzerains held opposing religious views. Shah Ismail was an avowed Shiite who had established Shiism as the religion of the state, by the sword. The Ottoman Sultan Selim was a devout Sunnite who feared and loathed the fanatical Shiism of the Persians. The tension between the two rulers was exacerbated by the great number of Shiite Kizilbash in Turkey who were followers of the Safawi order in Persia. The ambitious Shah Ismail intended to extend his hegemony to Turkey and, by using his followers in that country, to make it a Shiite satellite of Persia. The animosity between Shah Ismail and Sultan Selim I broke into open hostilities which culminated at Chaldiran in 1514, with the defeat of Shah Ismail.

As extremist Shiites, the Nusayris obviously were on the side of the Safawis. The Ottoman Sultan, who was extremely suspicious of all

Shiites, naturally extended this suspicion to the Nusayris. Ottoman archives indicate that the Ottoman government took some preventive measures against the Nusayris because of their sympathies toward the Persians.[40]

After he defeated the Egyptian Mamluk Sultan Muhammad Qansawh al-Ghawri at Marj Dabiq (1516) and entered Aleppo, Sultan Selim I summoned some Sunnite religious men and obtained from them a *fatwa* (juristic opinion) to fight the "infidel Alawis," or Shiites. He also summoned the Shiite leaders to his presence, promising to confirm their authority over the town people. It is estimated that 9,400 Shiite men assembled in Aleppo; all were maliciously murdered by the order of the Ottoman Sultan on the sanction of the Sunnite religious leaders.[41]

Many Shiites did escape to the Nusayris' mountains, where it was difficult for Selim's army to wage war against them. The Turks called these Shiites who escaped to the mountains Surek (exiles), which was later distorted to Surak [the plural form being Swarik). The part of the mountain range where they settled is now called the Surak Mountain, and some Nusayris now living in the administrative districts of Sihyun (Zion), Umraniyya, and Safita, are called Surak.[42]

When their mountain refuge prevented Sultan Selim I from decimating the Nusayris, he resorted to a peaceful strategy calculated to weaken the Nusayris. He moved more than half a million members of Turkish tribes from Anatolia and as far away as Khurasan in Iran, and established them in the castles and the most desirable areas of the Nusayri territory. Soon these Turkish newcomers had spread all over the Nusayri mountains, reaching as far as Latakia and Jabala. They attacked and ravaged Latakia, driving its inhabitants to the Mediterranean, where some of them drowned. Jabala faced the same disastrous fate. According to al-Tawil, "No traces of the Nusayris were left in Latakia except the graves of their ancestors."[43] To this day, the Nusayris remember the sufferings inflicted upon them by Sultan Selim I in his effort to eradicate their sect.[44] Selim's strategem of stationing Turks in the Nusayri mountains failed to achieve this objective, however; in fact, many of the Turks from Khurasan, themselves Shiites, were absorbed by the Nusayri tribes. Because these Turks were first stationed in the Abu Qubay's castle, also called Qartal, they came to be known as Qaratila; today they are considered to be a Nusayri tribe.[45]

It should be pointed out here that the Ismailis, whose relations with the Nusayris were most precarious, allied themselves with the Ottomans, perhaps out of fear of persecution. Though fewer in number, they attacked and occupied some of the Nusayri castles in their areas. To please the Ottoman conquerors, they adopted the Ottoman dress, including having their women wear the veil in conformity with Ottoman custom.[46]

In 1760, the Nusayris were faced with another misfortune. An English physician was killed in the Nusayris' mountains, and Nusayri leaders refused to deliver the murderer to the Ottoman governor, Sulayman Pasha. Before the murder, Sulayman Pasha had imposed heavy taxes on the Nusayris, but had been unable to collect them. Using the murder of the English physician as a pretext, he led a large invasion force into the Nusayri mountains, killing many of the inhabitants. He captured seventy Nusayri leaders and after killing them, had their heads stuffed with straw.[47]

In 1807 a conflict broke out between the Nusayris and the Ismailis which resulted in a massacre of the Ismailis. In that year, three hundred Nusayris were at odds with their religious leaders, and the Ismaili chief gave them asylum in his territory. A short while later, while some Ismaili men were working in their fields, the Nusayris attacked, killing three hundred of them and ravaging their homes. The Nusayris were assisted by some of their kinsmen, who had descended from the mountains to join them, a fact indicating that the attack was preplanned. When the news of the massacre reached the Ottoman governor of Damascus, he marched with a force against the perpetrators and killed them.[48]

At the beginning of the nineteenth century, the Nusayri district of the Kalbiyya tribe was particularly notorious for its lawlessness. John Lewis Burckhardt (d. 1817), who was in Syria between 1809 and 1813, states that Berber, the Pasha (governor) of Tripoli, was in the neighborhood of Latakia, making war against some rebel Anzeyrys (Nusayris).[49] Berber was fighting to avenge the killing of a Frenchman, Captain Boutin, by the lawless Arabs called Arab al-Mulk. The murderers had escaped to the Kalbiyya district, and the Kalbiyya Nusayris, following what they believed to be a duty not to deliver anyone who had sought asylum with them, refused to hand the murderers over to Berber. This led Berber to attack the Kalbiyya district and punish the residents with marked savagery. During combat with the Kalbiyya, he is said to have beheaded seven of their men at one time. The dragoman of the English vice-consulate at Latakia told Samuel Lyde that on one of his visits to Latakia, Nusayri prisoners were taken out to meet him on the road, where Berber beheaded them and had the heads impaled. Berber, a Sunnite Muslim, hated the Nusayris, whom he must have considered worse than infidels. This dragoman told Lyde that unlike the Jews and the Christians, the Nusayris were not considered by Muslims as Ahl al-

Kitab (people of the book) under the protection of the Muslims, and that according to Islamic law, even their paying of a poll-tax in lieu of conversion to Islam is not lawful. They should be put to the sword, and their wives and children should be sold into slavery.[50]

To show the traditional hatred harbored by the Sunnite Muslims for the Nusayris, the dragoman added that a certain Shaykh Ibrahim al-Maghribi (d. 1827) issued a juristic opinion declaring that it was lawful for a Musslim to kill a Nusayri or confiscate his property. For this reason, the Nusayris curse al-Maghribi's memory.[51]

In 1832, Ibrahim Pasha, son of Muhammad Ali, viceroy of Egypt (reigned 1804–1849), invaded Syria to further the ambition of his father, who dreamed of founding an empire in the Middle East. This invasion of Syria clearly affected the Nusayris although, according to al-Tawil, Nusayri sources are not in agreement about Ibrahim Pasha. Some of these sources portray him as a saint, others as a "divine calamity" and the "worst of God's creations." Al-Tawil says that both views are correct, although he does not cite the sources by name. It seems that Ibrahim Pasha treated the Nusayri leaders as equal to their common subjects. For this reason the leaders hated him, while the commoners loved him.[52] According to Col. Paul Jacquot, many Nusayris refused to support Ibrahim Pasha, which prompted him to disarm them, chase them into the mountains, destroy their castles, and behead their leaders.[53] Ibrahim Pasha even sought the assistance of the Druzes and Maronites in order to subjugate the Nusayris. But the Nusayris captured the five hundred Druzes whom Ibrahim had sent against them and killed all of them on a round rock in Wadi al-Uyun, near al-Murayqib. To this day, this rock is called the Blood Rock.[54]

By the middle of the nineteenth century, the Nusayris' plight was decidedly serious. Rev. Samuel Lyde, an English missionary who lived among the Nuayris from 1853 to 1859 and established a mission and school in the Kalbiyya district, offers nothing but gloom about these people, their customs, and their way of life. At the end of his report, Lyde comments that even if the reader thinks that his picture of the Nusayris is a melancholy one, he may be assured that it is not exaggerated.[55]

Oppressed by the local government and exploited by the shaykhs, Nusayris sank to such a low point that their communities were rife with violence, robbery, and constant feuds. The Kalbiyya, among whom Lyde lived, constantly fought with the Muhaliba. On one occasion, the Kalbiyya attacked the Muhaliba, robbing and killing them; their women and children accompanied them and participated in the crimes. Lyde says that the women were like demons, encouraging the men and supplying them with water. When the fighting ended, the children would steal anything they could lay their hands on. Lyde says that on the hill near his house, he could see the wife of his servant stretching out her hands to Sultan Jafar al-Tayyar, oldest brother of the Imam Ali Ibn Abi Talib, praying for the success and safety of her husband, who was on one such marauding expedition.[56]

In 1857 there was fighting among the Budeh (people from the mountainous part of the Banu Ali district), the Kalbiyya, and the Amamira; the Kalbiyya were victorious. One has only to read the account given by the Nusayri writer al-Tawil of the feuds among the different Nusayri groups to realize how accurate Lyde is in his assessment of the Nusayris' life.[57]

In 1859, the government sought to burn the houses of the Juhaniyya in Latakia, and murders were committed with the connivance of government officials. So many were being killed that the population was noticeably decreasing. Brother fought against brother, and both cursed their parents, without fear or shame. The Nusayri chiefs themselves oppressed their own people, exacting double taxes from the weak and powerless. The shaykhs, says Lyde, could not offer moral exhortation to the people because they were too busy collecting taxes from them. Under these abnormal circumstances, "it is, indeed, melancholy to live under such an order of things, in which all the finer and more useful qualities of man are repressed, and the deserving and humane must go to the wall. Hence, the state of society is a perfect hell upon earth."[58]

The Nusayris rebelled against the Ottoman government in the time of the Wali (governor) Rashid Pasha in 1866, but the rebellion was suppressed; the chief rebels were hanged, and their houses destroyed. Ten years of quiet passed before the Nusayris resumed their rebellion against the government. A force from Beirut, commanded by Akif Pasha, captured the rebels, hanged some, and banished others to Akka.[59]

When Midhat Pasha, the greatest Ottoman reformer, was appointed governor of Syria from 1879–80, he held the opinion that the Nusayris were rebellious people who should be subdued by force, even though he had close friends among the Nusayris, like Hawwash Bey, the chief of the Matawira tribe. He changed his mind, however, and, instead of using force, attempted to improve the condition of the Nusayris through reform. He called a meeting in the city of Hama which was attended by five hundred Nusayri dignitaries. He told them that the Nusayris should stop rebelling against the government, pay their taxes, and respect the military conscription laws. He also told them that the

Syrians (who were mostly Sunnites) believed that the Nusayris were notorious for their bad behavior, which forced the government to discipline them. Midhat promised the Nusayris that he would open schools in their region, stop oppression by local government officials, and, best of all, grant them autonomy.[60]

These promises to the Nusayris aroused the indignation of the Sunnite dignitaries of Damascus and Hama, and they denounced Midhat to Sultan Abd al-Hamid II. The Sultan, who detested and feared Midhat for his liberal and democratic ideas, transferred him to Izmir (Smyrna) as governor of that province.[61]

It should be pointed out that the Ottoman government implemented the Millet System, which gave a certain degree of control over internal affairs to the different ethnic and religious sects within the empire. But since the Nusayris were not regarded by the Ottoman government either as Muslims or as dhimmis (like the Jews and Christians, who, according to the Islamic laws, were under the protection of the Muslims as long as they paid taxes) the Nusayris were not ruled according to the Millet System. However, some Ottoman statesmen were of the opinion that they were a forlorn and persecuted minority.[62]

One of these statesmen was Diya Bey, the Mutasarrif (provincial governor) of Latakia from 1885 to 1892 and one of Sultan Abd al-Hamid II's most obedient servants. In a report to the Sultan, Diya stated, rightly or wrongly, that the Nusayris were a tool in the hands of Persia, with which they sympathized, and that the presence of American schools (founded by missionaries) in some parts of the Nusaryi mountains was detrimental to the Ottoman government's policy. He suggested that these schools be replaced by state schools, and that the Nusayris be brought into the Islamic religion.[63]

Diya's report was apparently approved by the Sultan. Diya Bey called the Nusayri dignitaries together and had them sign in his presence a document proclaiming that they embraced the true religion of Islam, and that they had been delegated to sign this document on behalf of all the Nusayris. Thereupon, Diya Bey ordered the American schools closed (they were poor at best) and about forty state schools were built; there the Nusayri children were taught no more than elementary reading. Soon after Diya's death, however, the Nusayris closed these schools and turned them into cattle barns.[64]

24

The Nusayris
Under the French Mandate

DURING WORLD WAR I, France and Britain signed the notorious secret Sykes-Picot Agreement (1916) which divided Syria, including Lebanon, Palestine, and Iraq, among the great powers. In 1919, the League of Nations placed Syria under a French mandate which came into effect in the next year. Beginning in 1918, the French forces stationed in Cilicia, in southern Turkey, moved into parts of Lebanon and Syria, including the coastal area of the Nusayri territory. General Gouraud was appointed the general commander of the Allied occupation forces in Syria and Cilicia, and made Beirut his headquarters.

In the spring of 1919, the King-Crane Commission was sent by U.S. President Wilson to investigate the political aspirations of the Arabs, especially those in Syria. The Amir Faysal and his men declared the establishment of an Arab state in Syria at Damascus in 1920. This move was considered by France an affront to her role as trustee of the Levant. On 24 July, a French force defeated a much smaller and badly equipped Arab army at Maysalun. King Faysal abdicated the Syrian throne and fled Damascus, leaving France the master of Syria.

On 1 September 1920, General Gouraud divided the French mandate territory into four districts: Greater Lebanon, the state of Damascus (including the Druze Mountain), the state of Aleppo (including al-Iskandarun, or Alexandretta), and the territory of Latakia (Alawi territory).[1] At this time, the Nusayris were called Alawis, and their territory, which became a "state" on 1 July 1922, was called Dawlat al-Alawiyyin (the Alawis state); in 1933 it became the government of Latakia.[2]

The fragmentation of the Syrian population into many ethnic, religious, and political groups made it easier for the French to control the country, following the policy of "divide and rule." Since the urban Sunnite Muslims refused to enroll their sons in the army, the French authorities encouraged the minority groups, especially the Nusayris, to enlist. Thus, following the example of the British levy, the French formed Les Troupes Spéciales du Levant, consisting mostly of Nusayri recruits. Many Nusayris who were poor and could not afford an education for their sons had them join the army to save expenses. Once these Nusayris gained high-ranking positions in the army, they encouraged their relatives to follow suit.[3] The enrollment of the Nusayris in the army during the mandate period was the beginning of their movement toward control of the army in the 1950s and 1960s and their ultimate rise to political power in 1970. The French even used the military corps of minority groups to suppress nationalist insurrections.[4]

There is evidence that many Nusayris cooperated with the French authorities in the hope of securing the position of their sect. In a telegram sent to General Gouraud, seventy-three Nusayri chiefs, representing a great number of tribes, asked for an independent Nusayri union under French protection.[5] The writer Munir al-Sharif, a sympathizer with the Nusayris, however, claims to have played an active role in convincing the Nusayris of the north not to cooperate with the French. Al-Sharif states that some Nusayris in the northern part of the territory succumbed to the French promises of money, property, and leadership, and unwisely served the French, to the detriment of their own people.[6]

Another writer offers a different picture. Yusuf al-Hakim, who occupied a cabinet position in the Arab-Syrian government under Faysal and was a witness to the events in Syria during and after World War I states that the Nusayris were loyal to the French mandate authorities as a gesture of gratitude for the care and compassion shown them by the French.[7]

Al-Hakim goes on to say that it was to show their loyalty and gratitude to the French that the Nusayris did not send a representative to the Syrian conference.[8] In 1919, Faysal had suggested to the Arab nationalists the necessity of holding a conference of representatives from all of Syria to emphasize the desire of the Syrians for complete independence. The Arab nationalists, who would accept nothing less than complete independence, responded, and the Syrian conference met in July, 1919.[9] The Nusayris boycotted this conference. Taqi Sharaf al-Din voices the opinion that what al-Hakim said about relations between the French and the Nusayris is a significant indication of the Nusayris' antagonism toward the Arab liberation movement and the nationalist aspirations of the Syrian people.[10]

Be that as it may, the French authorities soon had to deal with the fiercest Nusayri revolt yet against French rule, led by Shaykh Salih Ahmad al-Ali (d. 1950). On 15 December 1918, al-Ali called a meeting at Nahiyat Badr, in the administrative unit of Tartus, attended by prominent Nusayri chiefs. He alerted them to the fact that the French had already occupied the Syrian coast, with the intention of separating that region from the rest of the country. He also told them that as a sign of French antagonism to the Arab nationalist movement led by Prince Faysal, whose objective was the complete independence of the Arab countries, the French authorities were tearing up the flags of the Arab rebels. He urged them to revolt and expel the French from Syria.[11]

When the French heard of this meeting, they sent a force from Qadmus (home of the Ismailis, who had allied themselves to the French) to Badr, to arrest Salih al-Ali. Salih al-Ali and his men met the French force at the village of Niha, west of Wadi al-Uyun, and the revolt began in earnest. The French force was defeated, leaving behind thirty-five casualties.[12] After this victory, al-Ali began to organize the rebels into a disciplined military force, fashioned like a regular army with its own general command, officers of various ranks, and ordinary soldiers. Some Nusayri women supported the army of revolt by supplying water and food to the combat troops and replacing the men at work in the fields.[13] Al-Ali also turned against the Ismailis, attacking them at Qadmus, Masyaf, and Nahr al-Khawabi. The French authorities rushed to the Ismailis' aid, however,[14] and attacked al-Ali on 21 February 1919, but were defeated for the second time.

Meantime, the British General Allenby, commander-in-chief of the Allied forces in the East, asked Shaykh Salih al-Ali to cease hostilities against the French. Al-Ali agreed, on condition that the French forces remain only one hour at Badr. When al-Ali withdrew his forces from Badr, however, the French broke the condition of his agreement with Allenby. As soon as they arrived in Badr, they installed cannons, took up their positions, and began shelling the villages of Shaykh Badr and al-Rastan. The fighting continued throughout the night, ending in a third defeat for the French. After this victory al-Ali turned once more against the Ismailis, attacking and plundering the town of Qadmus. He ordered his men to search the houses for Ismaili books and manuscripts, which he piled up and set fire to in the public square. The Ismailis regained Qadmus in a counterattack on 17 April 1920, however.[15] (Commenting on the hostilities between the Ismailis and the Nusayris, Col. Paul Jacquot states that they constitute separate entities and religions, yet neither is a true Muslim religion.)[16]

At this time al-Ali was joined by many Nusayri chiefs and prominent Sunnite Muslims from Latakia, al-Haffa, Tartus, Banyas, and other places, despite the fact that the French authorities had destroyed their homes and villages.[17] In July 1919, a French force attacked the rebel positions, but al-Ali retaliated by attacking and occupying the villages of the Ismailis, the allies of the French, leaving the French no alternative but to sue for peace. Al-Ali agreed to peace on certain conditions: that the Syrian seacoast be added to the state of Syria: that Nusayri captives be released; and the Nusayris be compensated for damages caused to their villages and homes by the French army. Thus, peace was concluded between the French and al-Ali. But the French were not sincere in their deal with al-Ali and violated their peace agreement by occupying and burning the village of Kaf al-Jaz. Al-Ali counteracted by occupying Qadmus from which the French conducted their military operation against him.

On 20 February 1920, al-Ali attacked the city of Tartus, but counterattacks by the French fleet off the coast caused his forces to retreat. On 3 April, the French attacked, causing heavy casualties and much damage, but Ali's forces counterattacked and forced the French to withdraw from the villages they had been occupying. Meanwhile, a French army commanded by General Gouraud defeated a small, poorly equipped Arab army at Maysalun on 24 July 1920, occupied Damascus, and ended the shortlived Kingdom of Syria under Faysal. Realizing the gravity of the situation, al-Ali attacked the town of Masyaf, which was being held by the French and their Ismalili allies. On 29 November 1920, General Gouraud sent an expedition against al-Ali near the village of Ayn Qadib, east of Qadmus, but to no avail. The French forces entered Shaykh Badr without resistance and arrested some Nusayri leaders, jailing some and hanging the others, but al-Ali escaped with his forces to the north. The French gave chase; on 15 June 1921, a great French force attacked and overran his positions in the north, but failed to capture al-Ali, who went into hiding. A court-martial was convened, and sentenced al-Ali to death in absentia. The French authorities also offered one-hundred-thousand francs as a reward in exchange for information leading to his capture, but this also was to no avail.

When the French authorities gave up hope of finding al-Ali, General Gouraud issued an edict pardoning him and had it distributed to the people by plane. Finally, after hiding out for a year, al-Ali surrendered to the French General Billote. When Billote asked why he had surrendered, al-Ali answered, "By God, if I had only ten armed men left to fight, I would not have quit." Al-Ali died at his home on 13 April 1950.[18]

Shaykh Ahmad Salih al-Ali's campaign was the first revolt against French imperialism in Syria, but some Arab writers do not see it in that light. Taqi Sharaf al-Din maintains that the revolt of al-Ali, which the Nusayris use to justify their present antagonism to the Arab nationalist movement, was not a reaction to the French occupation of the Syrian coast, although its interaction with other revolts, especially in the cities of the Syrian coast, gave it the resemblance of a nationalist revolt against French imperialism. "After all," says al-Din, "the Nusayris are not 'material' for revolt because, more than any other Syrian group, they supported the French forces' occupation."[19] In fact, he states, the French used the good offices of Nusayri chief, Ahmad al-Hamid, to prevail on Shaykh Salih al-Ali to cease hostilities and enter into negotiations with them.[20] Al-Din concludes that Salih al-Ali's revolt was the result of the long-standing conflict between the Nusayris and the Ismailis. When the Ismailis allied themselves with the French, al-Ali's attacks were directed against the Ismailis, and only incidentally against their French allies.[21] Al-Din believes that Prince Faysal, some of whose men fought alongside al-Ali's troops, supported the revolt out of fear of the French imperialistic design on Syria. In fact, Faysal would have supported anyone who revolted against French imperialism. Faysal appointed al-Ali as his representative to the Nusayris' territory and supported his revolt not because al-Ali was an Arab nationalist, but because he was openly hostile towards the French, whom Faysal considered a great impediment to the achievement of Arab independence.[22]

Mustafa Kemal also supported al-Ali against the French. Kemal was trying to oust the French army from Cilicia in southern Turkey. In order to pressure the French to withdraw from Cilicia, he furnished al-Ali with arms in his struggle against the French. Once Kemal concluded a secret peace treaty with Franklin-Bouillon in October 1921, however, he had no more use for al-Ali and ceased supporting him.[23]

The revolt of Salih al-Ali against the French authorities, therefore, was not so much an antagonistic reaction to the Arab nationalists aspirations as a Nusayri movement whose objective was independence, or at least the autonomous administration of the Nusayris in their own territory. This is why, as soon as the French mandate authorities declared the establishment of an Alawi (Nusayri) state in 1922 and chose Latakia as its capital, the Nusayris began to support France. It also explains the Nusayris' failure to support the insurrection of the Arab nationalists in Damascus in 1925–26, which was met by French bombardment from the air. It is true that some Nusayri leaders supported the Arab national movement and collaborated with Prince Faysal, but, for the most part, the Nusayris were looking to win the independence of their own territory, which they could obtain from the French authorities, rather than to become part of an all-Syrian Sunnite state. The Nusayris feared the "Sunnite Wolf,"—that is, the Arab Sunnite government in Damascus—more than the French.[24] They had suffered a great deal from the brutality and neglect of their affairs at the hands of the Ottomans. Now the French were in control of their territory, and they could exact their independence or self-rule from the French, by revolt if necessary. To achieve this aim, the Nusayris had to contend with the French mandate authorities on the one hand and the Arab-Syrian government (mostly Sunnite) on the other. They were as apprehensive of the French mandate as they were of the Syrian nationalists, who were agitating to unite all Syria and Lebanon under the sole control of a Syrian government in Damascus.

The Nusayris did not seek an end to the French mandate if the French left, they would have no protection from the Sunnites.[25] Therefore, the Nusayris' aspirations for self-rule coincided with the French objective of perpetuating the political and religious fragmentation of Syria in order to facilitate their rule of the country.

From 1920 until 1936, when France finally negotiated a treaty with the Syrian nationalists granting Syria self-government, the Nusayris opposed the incorporation of their state into a united Syria under one central government in Damascus. In 1923, the Nusayris refused to join with Damascus and Aleppo to form a "united Syria," causing General Weygand, who had succeeded Gouraud as High Commissioner, to devise a plan for uniting Damascus and Aleppo, without including the Nusayri state in this union.[26] When the Syrian nationalists revolted against the French in 1925 and demanded absolute independence for an Arab-Syrian state, the Nusayris did not participate in the insurrection. In fact, from 1925 to 1936, a period marked by nationalist riots and insurrection against French rule, the Nusayris vehemently opposed unity with Syria. On 28 April 1933, a Nusayri delegation headed by the president of the representative council of the government of Latakia (the Alawi state) arrived in Beirut to express its disagreement with the proposed union with Syria. According to Henri Ponsot, the French high commissioner, the head of the delegation said that the Nusayris opposed any union with Syria, arguing that the Nusayris had always lived separately from Syria, and that the Syrians (Sunnites) were hostile to the Nusayris because of their religion.[27]

In the face of mounting nationalist sentiment and demands for independence, France entered into negotiations with the Syrian nationalists in Paris in March, 1936. Nusayri leaders, including members of the representative council of the government of Latakia, submitted several memoranda to the high commissioner opposing union with Syria, stating that such a proposed union should be placed on the agenda of the French-Syrian negotiations.

In a memorandum dated 8 June 1936, the Nusayris said that after generations of living by themselves in the fastness of their mountains, they had developed a natural instinct for independence. Now that the French were occupying their country, some Nusayris, because of this instinct for independence, fought the French, but the majority placed their trust in the honor of the French and believed the mandate authorities would help them retain this independence, which had been affirmed by all the high commissioners in the name of France. The Nusayris were shocked, therefore, to see the French succumb to the first blow by the Syrian nationalists, forgetting their promises to keep the Nusayris from being annexed by Syria. They felt that France had no right to bargain away their independence to another country. They reminded the French of their loyalty and trust in French promises. They concluded the memorandum by stating that if France wanted to keep this trust, it should issue an official declaration respecting and guaranteeing the independence of the Nusayris under its protection and send a Nusayri delegation representing the Latakia government to Paris to defend that independence. They threatened to resort to civil disobedience if their demands were not met.[28]

In another memorandum, dated 11 June 1936, the signatories stated that the Nusayris, who formed the majority of the Alawi state, refused categorically to return to Islamic rule. France, they contended, could not determine to place a small and friendly people in bondage under the rule of their traditional religious enemies. The signatories requested the French government to delegate a parliamentary committee to their territory to investigate the great chasm separating the Nusayris from the Syrians, and to see whether it would be feasible to annex the Nusayri territory to Syria without precipitating a blood bath that would be a black spot in the history of France. They further demanded that the French-Syrian negotiations regarding the Nusayris stop at once.[29]

Still another Nusayri memorandum, dated 3 July 1936, affirmed that the signatories were most loyal to France, and that France ought never to defile its honorable history by the crime of uniting the Nusayris with Syria. The signatories reminded the French that even the Crusaders had never established a firm footing or remained very long except in northwestern Syria, the Nusayri territory.[30]

The most revealing document concerning the aspirations of the

Nusayris and their attitude toward Syria and the French is one dated 15 June 1936 and submitted to Leon Blum, head of the Popular Front government. The document was signed by six Nusayri notables, including Sulayman al-Asad, father of the current president of Syria, and Sulayman al-Murshid, who began as a humble cattle herder and become a member of the Syrian parliament in 1937. (Al-Murshid claimed to be the Rabb (Lord God) and was used by the French to further their sectarian policy in Syria. He was arrested by the Syrian authorities and hanged in Damascus in 1946.) This memorandum is so significant that we cite it in full:

> For the occasion of the current negotiations between France and Syria, we, the leaders and dignitaries of the Alawi [Nusayri] sect in Syria, take this opportunity to bring to your attention and the attention of your party the following:
>
> 1. The Alawi [Nusayri] people, who have preserved their independence year after year with great zeal and sacrifices, are different from the Sunnite Muslims. They were never subject to the authority of the cities of the interior.
>
> 2. The Alawis refuse to be annexed to Muslim Syria because, in Syria, the official religion of the state is Islam, and according to Islam, the Alawis are considered infidels.
>
> 3. The granting of independence to Syria and abolishing the mandate constitute a good example of the socialist principles in Syria. But absolute independence means the control by some Muslim [Sunnite] families of the Alawi people in Cilicia, al-Iskandarun [Alexandretta], and the Nusayri mountains. As to the presence of a parliament and a constitutional government [in Syria], that does not represent individual freedom. This parliamentary rule is no more than false appearances without any value. In truth, it covers up a regime dominated by religious fanaticism against the minorities. Do French leaders want the Muslims to have control over the Alawi people in order to throw them into misery?
>
> 4. The spirit of hatred and fanaticism imbedded in the hearts of the Arab Muslims against everything that is non-Muslim has been perpetually nurtured by the Islamic religion. There is no hope that the situation will ever change. Therefore, the abolition of the mandate will expose the minorities in Syria to the dangers of death and annihilation, irrespective of the fact that such abolition will annihilate the freedom of thought and belief.
>
> We can sense today how the Muslim citizens of Damascus force the Jews who live among them to sign a document pledging that they will not send provisions to their ill-fated brethren in Palestine. The condition of the Jews in Palestine is the strongest and

most explicit evidence of the militancy of the Islamic issue vis-a-vis those who do not belong to Islam. These good Jews contributed to the Arabs with civilization and peace, scattered gold, and established prosperity in Palestine without harming anyone or taking anything by force, yet the Muslims declared holy war against them and never hesitated in slaughtering their women and children, despite the presence of England in Palestine and France in Syria. Therefore, a dark fate awaits the Jews and other minorities in case the mandate is abolished and Muslim Syria is united with Muslim Palestine. The union of the two countries is the ultimate goal of the Muslim Arabs.

5. We appreciate the noble feeling which motivates you to defend the Syrian people and your desire to realize the independence of Syria. But at present, Syria is still far off from the noble goal you are trying to achieve, because it is still subject to the religio-feudalistic spirit. We do not think that the French government and the French Socialist Party intend to offer the Syrians an independence whose application will only mean the enslavement of the Alawi people and the exposure of the minorities to the dangers of death and annihilation.

As to the demand of the Syrians to bring the Alawi people into union with Syria, we believe it is impossible that you will accept or approve such union. For if your noble principles support the idea of freedom, such principles will never allow a people to stifle the freedom of another people by forcing it to unite with them.

6. You may think that it is possible to ensure the rights of the Alawis and the minorities by a treaty. We assure you that treaties have no value in relation to the Islamic mentality in Syria. We have previously seen this situation in the Anglo-Iraqi treaty, which did not prevent the Iraqis from slaughtering the Assyrians and the Yezidis.

The Alawi people, whom we, the undersigned, represent in this memorandum, appeal to the French government and the French Socialist Party and request from them a guarantee of their freedom and independence within their small territory, and place them in the hands of the French Socialist leaders. The Alawi people are certain that they will find a strong and faithful support for a loyal and friendly people threatened by death and annihilation and who have offered France tremendous services.

Signatories

Aziz Agha al-Hawwash
Muhammad Bey Junayd
Sulayman al-Murshid
Mahmud Agha Jadid
Sulayman al-Asad
Muhammad Sulayman al-Ahmad[31]

The memorandum reveals that the Nusayri leaders feared and detested the Sunnite Syrian nationalists, and felt that perpetuation of the French mandate was the only way to save their state from union with Syria. The most revealing thing in this historic memorandum is that the Nusayris (Alawis) speak of themselves not as Muslims, but as aliens to Islam, and that the Muslims consider them (Nusayris) to be infidels. The Nusayris clearly feared the religious fanaticism of the Muslims as a threat to their existence as a minority. They looked upon themselves as a minority with its own distinctive cultural ethos. For this reason they sympathized with the Jews in Palestine and the Assyrians and Yezidis in Iraq who were minorities already under the rule of a dominant Muslim Sunnite majority. The Nusayri leaders had no use for treaties because, as they mention, the Anglo-Iraqi treaty (1930) did not save the Assyrians from being slaughtered by the Iraqi army in the village of Summayl in 1933.

The French government was faced with a dilemma. It was trying to negotiate with the Syrian delegation to achieve the independence of Syria while simultaneously trying to allay the fears of the Nusayris, whom France suspected of planning an armed revolt. This is expressed in the memorandum dated 5 June 1936 from the French minister of foreign affairs to General Weygand, the military governor of Syria. In this memorandum, the foreign minister told Weygand that it would be better to confirm the confidence in France of the non-Muslim elements. He suggested that the military governor inform the Nusayri dignitiaries that the French government had no intention of altering the wording of the terms of their independence, as stated in the Private Regulation of 14 June 1930.[32] The national situation in Syria in the mid–1930s had changed drastically however, since the inception of the French mandate in 1920. Arab nationalist sentiment was mounting, and demands for complete independence were increasingly vehement. The use of force to suppress the Syrian nationalists and their demand for a united Syria was no longer feasible.

Following the example of Great Britain, France had to reconsider its whole situation in Syria and Lebanon, and its protection of Nusayri independence could only be interpreted by the Syrians as antagonistic to national unity. Furthermore, the confederation of the four Nusayri tribes, the Haddadin, al-Khayyatin, al-Kalbiyya and al-Matawira, whose leaders were members of the representative council of Latakia, which it was hoped would form the nucleus of an independent Nusayri state, began to lose authority, especially within the new Nusayri generation. Shortly before the outbreak of World War II, a new generation of educated

Nusayris emerged who were more flexible than their fathers with respect to joining and working with the Syrian nationalists in Damascus.

The spread of elementary and secondary education, especially among the Nusayris, began to threaten the traditional Nusayri tribal cohesion, forcing the French government to find a better and more acceptable substitute for the mandate. When Nusayri leaders found no positive response by the French government to their request for complete independence and learned that France was about to sign a treaty with the Syrian nationalists that would create a united Syria including the Nusayri state, they appealed to the French authorities to allow them to send a Nusayri delegation to participate in the Syrian-French negotiations in Paris. The French minister of foreign affairs, Delbos, informed the high commissioner in Beirut that, while the French government appreciated the Nusayris' confidence in France, it would be better not to encourage them to demand from the French government what "this government cannot fulfill." In answer to the appeal of the president of the representative council, Ibrahim al-Kinj, that a Nusayri delegation be sent to Paris, Delbos wrote to the high commissioner to inform al-Kinj that questions concerning Latakia would in time be discussed by the high commissioner and those Nusayris directly affected by those questions.[33]

The declaration by the French government in June 1936 of its intention to create a state of a united Syria apparently convinced the Nusayri leaders that they were fighting a losing battle, but still they did not give up hope. Instead, they resorted to a new strategem. On 24 June 1936, they informed the French government that if an independent Nusayri territory separate from Syria was not feasible from an international point of view, they would agree to negotiate with Lebanon concerning a possible union with that country that would guarantee them autonomy under French protection. In a letter dated 25 June 1936, the president of the representative council, Ibrahim al-Kinj, reminded French Foreign Minister Delbos that France had promised independence to the Nusayris and should not sacrifice the Nusayris to placate their enemies. Al-Kinj added that union with Lebanon would be more feasible than union with Syria because the former nation, like their own land, consisted of minorities.[34]

The Nusayris' reasons for desiring union with Lebanon were these: under Ottoman rule, the sanjaq (a province under the direct authority of the sultan in Istanbul) of Latakia and part of the sanjaq of Tripoli had been part of the province of Beirut; their country had always had strong trade relations with Lebanon; the laws of the Nusayri state and those of Lebanon were similar; and union with Lebanon would create the largest country of minorities in the Middle East, with a population of almost 1,200,000, nearly balancing that of Syria, whose population in the 1930s was 1,700,000.[35]

The Nusayris' appeal for union with Lebanon was submitted to the high commissioner in a memorandum dated 20 August 1936. The high commissioner in turn referred the memorandum to the foreign minister with a letter attached; this letter stated that the memorandum had already been submitted to the Maronite patriarch and to the president of the Lebanese Republic, but did not indicate the response of either man. It should be pointed out that two Nusayri members of the representative council of the Nusayri state favored union with Syria.[36]

The appeals of Nusayri leaders to the French government to retain the mandate and prevent the union of their state with the rest of Syria were to no avail. World War II put an end to the mandate and the French presence in Syria. At long last Syria, including the Nusayri trerritory, became an independent state, and on 5 April 1946,the last French and British toops withdrew. In that year Sulayman al-Murshid revolted against the new independent state, but was captured, tried, and hanged. Apparently, the hope of an independent Nusayri state was shattered. But, as the postwar history of Syria shows, although the Nusayris did not achieve independence, they one day became the rulers of Syria. Sulayman al-Asad, one of the signatories of the memorandum to the French government requesting that France not give up the mandate, could not have dreamed that one day his own son, Hafiz, would be the president of Syria. Thus what Sulayman al-Asad and his colleagues failed to achieve was finally accomplished by the young Nusayris. The once despised and persecuted heretical sect, whose leaders would have been satisfied with an autonomous state separate from Syria, became masters of all Syria.[37]

25

The Nusayris

Rise to Political Power

How did the downtrodden Nusayris rise to become masters of post-independence Syria? They did so through two channels: the army and the Baath Party. Their rise to preeminence in both was slow but sure: not the result of a master plan but rather of the conjunction of a variety of circumstances, including political developments and economic conditions in the postwar period, and the structure of the Nusayri community, which was based on the premises of regionalism and sectarianism. In the late 1950s, high-ranking Nusayri officers in the army realized that the circumstances in Syria were favorable to a Nusayri takeover. By the mid-1960s, the Nusayris had gained control of both the army and the Baath Party, steps culminating in their rise to national power in November 1970.

The association of the Nusayris with the army dates back to the mandate period, when the French authorities created the Troupe Spéciales du Levant, made up predominantly of Nusayri recruits.[1] The French government was aware of the importance of these Nusayri recruits in implementing a policy of "divide and rule"; it used them to quell Arab nationalist insurrections and to encourage political regionalism and division among the various minorities, isolating the Nusayris especially.[2] The Troupes Spéciales remained after the French departed in 1946. However, they then numbered only seven thousand men, and within two years this number had dwindled to twenty-five hundred. Thus, their existence alone cannot explain the present Nusayri dominance of Syria, as Hanna Batatu contends.[3] The formation of the Troupes Spéciales was, however, the humble beginning that later opened the doors for the Nusayris' rise to power.

This climb to prominence in Syria was slow and hard. In the early years after independence, the economic conditions suffered by the Nusayri peasants were deplorable. Abd al-Latif al-Yunus, a prominent Nusayri author and statesman, states that after World War I, some Nusayris in the mountain regions were forced to sell their daughters to wealthy townspeople as domestic servants because they could not support them at home.[4] Sheer poverty (the average daily income of the Syrian peasants in 1938 was the meager sum of twenty-two piasters much lower than the per capita daily income of fifty piasters) also forced the Nusayri peasants to enroll their sons in the army in large numbers. This high rate of Nusayri enrollment was also due to the fact that the majority of poor Nusayri peasants could not afford to pay the *badal,* a sum of money paid to the government in lieu of army service. Wealthy townpeople who paid the badal (ranging from five hundred Syrian liras in 1964 to three thousand liras and even up to five thousand liras recently) were exempted from military service. Many Syrian Sunnites, mostly Arab nationalists, were among them, shunning military service because of their antagonism to French imperialism.[5] The poor Nusayri peasant who could not afford to pay, however, could not escape conscription.[6] Moreover, as noted in the preceding chapter, many Nusayris were sympathetic to the French, regarding them as a bulwark against absorption into a Muslim state.

Joining the army did more than merely remove extra mouths to feed from Nusayri homes; it gave Nusayri sons opportunities that they could not have found in civilian life. Nusayri secondary school graduates for example, were able to further their education by joining the military academy, which otherwise they could not have afforded. Before their assignments as commissioned or noncommissioned officers, these Nusayris in town encouraged relatives and friends from their villages and towns to join the military.[7]

Political instability in post-independence Syria also played a part in allowing Nusayri dominance of the military. The period from 1946 to 1949 was relatively quiet internally, so the Syrian government used the interlude to try to solve some of the nation's disturbing domestic problems. In an effort to assure the territorial and demographic integrity of all Syrians, regardless of their race or creed, and to establish some kind of uniformity within the framework of Syrian and Arab nationalism, as well as to dampen or at least contain the Nusayri ambition of separation, which had been fostered by the French authorities, the government reduced and finally abolished communal representation of minorities (especially the Nusayris) in the parliament, and abrogated certain judicial rights that the French authorities had granted to the Nusayris in personal status cases.[8] The free election conducted in 1947 was only a false signal that Syria was on the way to becoming a democratic state. On 30 March 1949, Syria was rocked by the coup of General Husni al-Zaim (d. 1949), which not only shattered hopes of any further democratization, but set a precedent hitherto unknown in the Middle East, the emergence of the military as "the real source of power," a precedent that would culminate in the present military regime of Hafiz al-Asad.[9]

Two more coups followed in the same year, one headed by Colonel Sami al-Hinnawi on 14 August and another just four months later, on 19 December led by Colonel Adib al-Shishakli, who ousted al-Hinnawi and remained Syria's military dictator until he in turn was overthrown by yet another coup four years later, on 25 February 1954.[10] All three of these military men were Sunnites and after each gained power, a number of dissenting officers, mainly Sunnites who had participated in earlier coups were either purged, transferred to less sensitive positions, or forced to retire. Such "house cleanings" left Nusayri officers in important commanding positions. By the 1970s, all army strike units were effectively controlled by Nusayri personnel.[11] Thereafter, Nusayri officers dominated the Syrian army and a great number of key positions in the Syrian government.[12]

In light of the above factors, the Nusayris' military dominance was real but not too obvious. In fact, when, on 22 April 1955, Adnan al-Maliki, the Deputy Chief of staff, was assasinated by a Nusayri sergeant, Yusuf Abd al-Karim, the chief of the Intelligence Bureau, Col. Abd al-Hamid al-Sarraj, found to his astonishment that almost 65 percent of the non-commissioned officers were Nusayris.[13] This indicates that by the mid-1950s, the Nusayris had dominated the officer corps, paving the way to their ultimate control of the armed forces. These Nusayri officers had another source of leverage, too; from 1955 on they were members of the Baath Party and in control of the military section within that party.

After independence, Syria's political parties—especially the Baath, the Hizb al-Qawmi al-Suri, SSNP (Syrian Social National Party), the Communist Party, and al-Ikhwan al-Muslimun (the Muslim Brotherhood) competed for the allegiance of Syrian youth, that is, the high school and college students. Although high school students in the mandate period were politicized, after independence they gained unprecedented freedom to participate in the political life of their country by joining the political parties.[14]

The Nusayri youth were particularly attracted to the Baath Party and the SSNP because of their religious minority status. The Muslim

Brotherhood did not appeal to them because of its strict Sunnite Muslim orientation, and the Communist Party did not attract them because of its anti-religious ideology.[15] Both the SSNP and the Baath were active in recruiting members in the Nusayri area of Latakia, the former party in the late 1930s and the latter after its formation by Salah al-Din Bitar, a Sunnite Muslim, and Michel Aflaq, a Rum Orthodox Christian, in 1944.[16]

By the 1950s, equal numbers of Nusayris from both parties had joined the officer corps, but with the elimination of the SSNP by the Syrian government in the mid-1950s Nusayri membership—by civilians and officers—in the Baath Party dramatically increased, especially in the Latakia area. Although there is no strong evidence that religious or communal factors provided any impetus for the political or ideological commitments of the Nusayris, they were, in the words of Van Dusen, a "latent factor in the political equation."[17]

With the elimination of the SSNP, the Baath Party found itself competing with others, including the Arab Socialist Party of Akram al-Hawrani, from Hama, and especially the Syrian Communist Party of Khalid Bagdash, a Kurd from Damascus. As the struggle between the Baath and Communist parties intensified, the Baath leaders became suspicious of the ambitions of the Communist Party, which was making political gains and securing advantages. Baathist leaders were especially alarmed at the possibility that the Communists might win a decisive victory in the municipal and parliamentary elections projected for November 1957, and the summer of 1958, which would give them control of the government. Fearing that a showdown with the Communists might end in failure, the Baath leaders decided that the only way to beat their opponents and foil their plan of a government takeover was union with Egypt.[18]

Although it is argued that the union with Egypt was the result of a military coup masterminded by Col. Abd al-Hamid al-Sarraj; with the full understanding of Egyptian leaders, the fact remains that it was the Baath leaders, Bitar and Aflaq, who urged the Syrian army officers to negotiate a union with Cairo. After prolonged negotiations between Damascus and Cairo, the union of Syria and Egypt was finally announced on 1 February 1958, and the United Arab Republic (UAR) was born. Ironically, the Baath Party, which had been instrumental in achieving the union with Egypt, was dissolved together with other parties as a condition set by Egyptian President Nasser for the proposed union. Nasser was interested in using this union to further his ambitions as a leader of the Arab world, to consolidate his power at home, and to weaken the power of his rivals in the Arab countries. It seemed that his goals and the ideology of the Baath Party were irreconcilable. Nasser became disenchanted with the Baath Party, and dissociated himself from it.[19]

The Nusayris, especially the army officers who were members of the Baath Party, were not enthusiastic about the union of Syria with Egypt. This union was an embodiment of Arab nationalism, which aspires to bring all Arabs into one nation, sharing a common destiny and united under one leadership. Traditionally, the Nusayris, as a minority group, were separatists who suspected the Syrian Sunnite majority and feared that a union with Syria would cause them to lose their identity and their minority status. Now that Syria was united with Egypt, the Nusayri officers were even more apprehensive that the Nusayri community would be totally overwhelmed by a Sunnite majority. Of course, the Nusayri officers were well aware of the pro-Arab ideology of the Baath Party, which they considered to be a veil hiding a feeling of Islamic and Arab nationalistic superiority. They realized that with this ideology, the Baath Party would eventually rise to power in Syria. For this reason the Nusayris joined this party, which began to regroup after the dissolution of Syria's union with Egypt in September, 1961, calculating that, despite occasional setbacks, the time would come when they could use the party to promote their sectarian interests.[20]

These officers were also aware of the depressed economic conditions in the Nusayri territory, especially the Latakia area, where a few wealthy landlords from large Syrian cities controlled the land. They were afraid that immigrant farmers from Egypt might compete with or even dislodge Nusayri farmers. Their fears were compounded by rumors that the Ghab irrigation project might be turned over to Egyptian peasants. The Nusayri Baathists were especially concerned about the minority status of their own people, who formed about 10 percent of Syria's population, but would be overwhelmed by the combined majority of Syrians and Egyptians.[21] They hoped therefore, that through the Baath Party, they could fight for and achieve social equality, better economic conditions, and more human dignity for their people, still an oppressed, impoverished, and despised minority.[22] Finally, like civilians and non-Nusayri army officers in the Baath, the Nusayri officers believed that the Baath leaders, Bitar and Aflaq, had accepted the union with Egypt without consulting them and with no guarantees.[23]

Motivated by the foregoing concerns, some Nusayri officers, Hafiz al-Asad, Salah Jadid, and Muhammad Umran, and a Druze officer, Hamad Ubayd, who were stationed in Cairo in 1959 during the union with Egypt, formed a clandestine military committee within the Baath

Party, without informing party leaders.[24] This committee assured the Nusayris' dominance in the officer corps, while their control of the military section of the Baath Party afforded them the right to decide who would be admitted to the military academies, together with the power to appoint, dismiss, and transfer the personnel of all army units to suit their purposes.[25] Moreover, because of their dominance in the officer corps, the Nusayris had by 1963 assured for themselves control of all the armed forces.

The Nusayri officers who formed a military committee within the Baath Party could not have acted solely as Baathists; rather, they acted first as Nusayris. If they had been acting as loyal members of the Baath Party, why did they keep the committee secret from party leaders? In fact, they did agree with the civilian members of the party who criticized Bitar and Aflaq for failing to ask for guarantees in Syria's union with Egypt; as a result, they called for the reorganization of the party. If this was the case, their decision to keep their committee secret from the party leadership had a purpose: it is almost certain that the officers were acting not as Baathists, but as Nusayris, with the intent of using the Baath and the armed forces to rise to power in Syria. The formation of the military committee was the beginning of their plan for a future takeover of the government. Some writers of this period maintain that, during the 1950s, the communal consciousness of the Nusayris was not overriding in their struggle for power, that Nusayri officers were not always acting consciously as Nusayris, and that only after the Baathist coup of 1963 did sectarianism appear in the struggle for power among the Baathists, including the Nusayris.[26]

The formation by Nusayri officers of the secret military committee in 1959 in Cairo, followed by their attendance at a Nusayri meeting in 1960, however, is strong evidence that the Nusayri officers in the late 1950s were acting in full consciousness of communal solidarity and sectarianism. After their formation of this committee, the Nusayri officers, Hafiz al-Asad, Salah Jadid, Muhammad Umran, and Muhammad Nabhan, attended a meeting called by Nusayri leaders in 1960 in Qardaha, the native village of al-Asad. The main purpose of this meeting was to study ways of assisting Nusayri officers to join the Baath Party, in order to increase their membership in that party.[27] It was decided at the meeting that Muhammad Umran should be granted the rank of bab (door), the highest degree in the Nusayri religion. Umran was also entrusted with devising plans for the military organization and the ways and means of distributing these plans to the national organization, to be exploited for Nusayri purposes. It was also agreed that Umran should remain at least outwardly within the group of Unionists, that is, those who supported the union with Egypt. These at the meeting also resolved to entice the Druze and Ismaili army officers to cooperate with the Nusayri officers; to grant the Nusayri officer Izzat Jadid the high religious rank of naqib; to confirming another Nusayri officer, Ibrahim Makhus, in the religious rank of his father; and finally, to alert the Nusayri shaykhs and notables to call on all Nusayri young men, encouraging them to enlist in the army and to cooperate with one another.[28]

The union between Syria and Egypt was short-lived, lasting only two years and eight months. The Syrians resented their country's having become a political and economic appendage, serving the interests of Egypt. In all but name, Syria was an Egyptian colony. Matters came to a head when the army effected a coup d'etat on 28 September 1961 and the union with Egypt (UAR) collapsed, much to the shock of President Nasser. Power now lay in the hands of the Supreme Arab Revolutionary Command of the armed forces. The proclamation of a provisional constitution on 12 November 1961, the election of an assembly on 14 December and the formation of a Syrian cabinet on 1 April 1962, gave the false impression that the country was establishing a stable, constitutional life. This was not the case and Syria was plagued by the political maneuvering of many groups, namely, the Nasserites, Baathists, Secessionists, Unionists, and Communists. The Baathists, whose party in Syria had been officially dissolved, began to regroup and organize themselves. The Nusayri members of the party were especially active in reorganizing the party in the Latakia area.[29] The Nusayri army officers who had formed the secret military committee within the Baath Party, once more became active in both the party and the armed forces.[30]

The period between the collapse of the UAR on 28 September 1961 and the coup of 8 March 1963 was plagued by incessant plots and intrigues fomented by the various political factions in Syria. A coalition of Nasserites, Baathists, Arab nationalists, and Socialist Unionists prepared for the coup. The Baathists and the Nasserites, the strongest and best organized of the groups, chose Ziyad al-Hariri, a compulsive, ambitious, power-hungry army colonel to carry out the coup. Of all these groups, the Baathists emerged as the strongest, and they controlled the cabinet. Although the Secretary General of the Baath Party, Munif al-Razzaz, attempts to portray the coup as the work of the military and not of the national civilian organization of the Baath Party, he admits that the military committee of the party acted independently, as though it were a separate Baath party, a stance which later created a rift between the party and the Baathist officers within it. In fact, the Baathists received most of the credit for the coup, and their power was manifested in their control of the national council of the revolutionary command and the cabinet. The Baathists' collaboration with the Nasserites was short-lived; they soon began their purge of the Nasserites. Their clashes with Chief of Staff Ziyad al-Hariri also intensified, and he was likewise purged in July 1963.[31] The Baathists had now gained full control of Syria.

Although prominent Nusayri officers like Hafiz al-Asad, Salah Jadid, and Muhammad Umran did not play a role in the coup of 8 March 1963, shortly after the coup they were recalled and placed in important positions in the high command of the armed forces. Al-Asad was promoted from lieutenant-colonel to general and became commander of the air force. Salah Jadid became head of the Officers' Affairs Bureau and the personnel branch of the central headquarters where he had the authority to control the appointments, transfers, and dismissals of officers. Hamad Ubayd (a Druze) was given charge of the Fifth Armored Brigade, and Muhammad Umran became the commander of the Seventieth Tank Regiment, south of Damascus.

A few non-Nusayri officers filled important positions, too. A Druze, Salim Hatum, was made commander of the commando battalions; a Sunnite, Ahmad Suwaydani, became head of military intelligence, and an Ismaili, Abd al-Karim al-Jundi, head of the artillery. It should be remembered that some of the Nusayri officers promoted were members of the military committee within the Baath Party; through their positions on that committee, they were able to purge disloyal officers and fill the vacancies with loyal Nusayris or non-Nusayri officers, mostly Druzes and Ismailis, who now formed the majority of the Baath Party membership. It is estimated that seven hundred officers of various ranks were purged after the coup, their positions filled by Nusayri officers.[32]

After occupying their new military positions, the Nusayri officers began to claim that, more than any other officers, they were responsible for upholding the new government and that they were the guardians of the Baath Party. The party, which had been dissolved officially in Syria since the union with Egypt in 1958, was trying to reorganize itself after the coup of March 1963, but was hindered by many internal problems. The Nusayri officers and members of the military committee took advantage of these problems to facilitate the admission of men of their own sect as members of both the military and civilian organizations within the party, especially the former. Such tactics resulted in Nusayri control of many important positions in army brigades stationed near Damascus and unlimited military support to the civilian organization of the Latakia branch of the Baath Party, which was predominantly Nusayri, to the neglect of other branches of the party.[33]

Evidence indicates that after the coup of March 1963, some prominent Nusayri members of the Baath Party were determined to increase Nusayri membership in order to gain ultimate control of the party. The party's organizational bureau, founded after the coup and controlled by the Nusayris, admitted unqualified Nusayris and loyal non-Nusayris as active members of the party.[34] Thus, a number of blocs emerged within the Baath Party, whose members were more bound by sectarianism and regionalism than by the party's ideology of Arab socialism. Although the Nusayri members of the party were not enchanted with Arab socialism, which transcended their narrow sectarianism, they welcomed it as an ideology that would emancipate their people, who for centuries had been exploited by wealthy Sunnite landholders from the cities of the interior.[35] As Munif al-Razzaz, former secretary of the Baath Party, explains, to the Nusayri and Druze rural minorities, socialism was a revenge on the Sunnite city dwellers, intended to impoverish the Sunnite majority and reduce them to the village level of the Nusayris and Druzes. For this reason the Nusayri army officers applied, in a radical manner, the socialism imposed by the party, in order to satisfy their sectarian spirit of revenge.[36] It should also be noted in this context that in their determination to overcome obstacles to their plan to control the party, the Nusayri officers planted their own Baathists in the different military organizations and had them report on the plans and movements of their opponents.[37]

The major rivals of the Nusayri officers were the pro-Nasser groups hoping to restore the union with Egypt. On 18 July 1963, a group of Nasserite officers, led by the Sunnite officer, Jasim Alwan, attempted to overthrow the government. The coup failed, thanks to the Nusayri officer Muhammad Nabhan, who pretended to join the pro-Nasserites, but secretly reported their intentions and plans for a coup to his Nusayri colleagues.[38] The Nusayri officers took advantage of the failure of the coup to purge more than four hundred pro-Nasserite officers,[39] while sending others to the Syrian-Israeli front. They also stationed Nusayri officers of different ranks in strategic positions around the capital, Damascus. Furthermore, they made every effort to admit a great number of Nusayris to the Military Academy, the National Guard, and the Intelligence Department, and to different sections of the Baath Party.[40]

The coup of 18 July 1963, was a triumph of the Baathists over their Nasserite rivals. This triumph intensified the conflict between the regional command of the party, chosen by the Baath chapter, and the national command, which represented the party in different Arab countries. Another source of trouble was the failure of the party to define its relations with the military organization, especially the military section within the party. The Nusayri officers, together with Druze and Ismaili officers, who after 1963 outnumbered the Sunnite officers, had interests radically different from those of the national command of the party. The Baathist officers, most particularly the Nusayri officers, formed a privileged class, occupying sensitive positions in the army and the government.[41] There was evident conflict between the Baathist strongman, General Amin Hafiz (a Sunnite), now the official head of state, and the Nusayri Colonel Muhammad Umran, commander of the Seventieth Tank Regiment. Hafiz advocated an end to the Baath isolation in Syria and reconciliation with other political groups, while Umran was of the opinion that the Baath alone should rule Syria, while retaining friendship with Nasser.[42]

To show how serious the Nusayri officers in the Baath Party were in planning to assume power in Syria, a meeting was held at Hims, shortly after the abortive Nasserite coup of 18 July 1963, attended by a great number of Nusayri dignitaries and the Nusayri officers, including Hafiz al-Asad, Izzat Jadid, Muhammad Umran, and Ibrahim Makhus. After discussing the role played by Muhammad Nabhan in foiling the Nasserite coup, the conferees made the following decisions:

1. Muhammad Nabhan was promoted to the rank of Najib (a Nusayri religious rank) for his active role in aborting the Nasserite coup of 18 July 1963.

2. The degree of al-Wishah al-Babi al-Aqdas (most holy door decoration), one of the Nusayris' secret high religious degrees, was conferred on Muhammad Umran, and he was advised to continue his activity among the Nasserites.

3. The present plan for admitting more educated Nusayris to the Baath and facilitating their admission through the party to the military academies and the armed forces was to be studied. Nusayri notables were advised to call on Nusayri young men to encourage them to enlist in the armed forces.

4. Plans were made for the future establishment of a Nusayri state with the city of Hims as its capital.

5. The high religious degree of Muqaddam was conferred on Salah Jadid, and he was entrusted with the responsibility of leading and directing the Nusayri elements in the army.

6. Relocation of the Nusayris from the villages to the cities of the interior, especially Hims, Latakia, and Tartus, was to be continued.

7. Hafiz al-Asad was granted the Nusayri religious rank of Najib.

8. The Nusayri religious rank of Mukhtass was granted to Izzat Jadid and Ali Hamad.

9. The Druze and Ismaili elements in the army were to be eliminated and replaced with Nusayris.

10. Ibrahim Makhus was entrusted with the civil and political leadership, and would be prepared to become the prime minister of the future Nusayri state.[43]

These decisions obviously reveal the determination of the Nusayri officers to assume power with the blessing of the Nusayri notables. To achieve this goal, the Nusayri officers continued to create Nusayri blocs within the armed forces and to offer tremendous support to the Nusayri Major General Salah Jadid, who now occupied the sensitive position of chief of staff of the Syrian army. He was accused by General Hafiz, who had become prime minister on 4 October 1964, of promoting sectarianism among the Nusayri officers and of building a Nusayri bloc withn the Baath Party. Hafiz also told Jadid that he could not keep his position as Chief of Staff simultaneously with his other position as a member of the presidium (President's Council). Jadid gave up his position as Chief of Staff, and in 1965 he was excluded from the presidium, but continued to wield great authority in the regional command of the Baath Party. Hafiz and Lieutenant Colonel Ahmad Suwaydani, director of military intelligence, accused General Muhammad Umran of promoting sectarianism in the army. They were ostensibly supported by Jadid and Hafiz al-Asad, to dispel any suspicion of Nusayri sectarian activity in the army, although, like Umran, both Jadid and al-Asad relied heavily on their Nusayri officer colleagues to protect their positions in the armed forces.[44]

Amin Hafiz's accusation that Salah Jadid and other Nusayri officers created Nusaryi blocs in the army is true. In fact, by the mid-1960s, sectarianism in Syria had become a serious problem. Although Sami al-Jundi, an Ismaili who later became the Syrian ambassador to Paris, voices the opinion that Salah Jadid was not sectarian, he seems to contradict himself when he states that Jadid was "responsible for sectarianism. He organized and relied on it and transformed it into a 'party' lurking behind the Baath Party."[45]

But nothing reveals more the sectarianism of Salah Jadid than the following dialogue between Jadid and Sami al-Jundi:

Jadid: How should we treat the question of sectarianism?
Al-Jundi: By revolutionary measures.
Jadid: How?

Al-Jundi: Sectariansm has become a political problem, and it is becoming more complicated day after day. It will also become a social problem which will expose the country to danger. I prefer that you return to the project begun by the former Alawi generation.

Jadid: What project?

Al-Jundi: The project of publishing your secret books [of the Nusayri sect] in order that other denominations will not suspect you and maintain that you are a sect [cult]. You should tackle the problem [of sectarianism] right at the roots, and I am confident that there is nothing in your books which you are afraid to publish . . . therefore, you should not leave other people the opportunity to doubt your intentions [of Nusayri sectarianism]. It [sectarianism] has become dangerous to you [the Nusayris] and to the country.

Jadid: If we do this [publishing Nusayri secret books], the mashayikh (religious leaders) will crush us.

Al-Jundi: You are a revolutionary, and yet fear the mashayikh? How could we then fight imperialism while cowing to religious leaders?

According to al-Jundi, Jadid then fell silent and sank deep in thought. Al-Jundi goes on to say that his dissatisfaction with the government—that is, with Salah Jadid and the Nusayris in key positions in the government—began at this time. He later learned that Jadid sought the favor of the Nusayri religious leaders and even paid them religious taxes.[46]

The conflict between Amin Hafiz and Salah Jadid was, in fact, an old one that began when the Baath Party reconstituted itself a year after Syria's union with Egypt collapsed in 1961. The newly reconstituted party was divided into two rival groups, the "old guard," including men like Aflaq, Bitar, and Hafiz, and the "regionalists," mostly Nusayri officers like Salah Jadid, Hafiz al-Asad, and Muhammad Umran, who, as previously stated, formed a party within the Baath Party. By 1965, Hafiz was fully aware of the power of the Nusayri and Druze officers within the army, and he intended to stem that power. The result was a fierce conflict between the "old guard" and the "regionalists" that ultimately led to the coup of 1966.[47]

What intensified the struggle between Jadid and Hafiz was that Jadid was able to win the allegiance of a number of minority officers, like the Druzes Salim Hatum and Hamad Ubayd, and the Ismailis Ahmad al-Mir and Abd al-Karim al-Jundi. With these and other minority officers in his camp, Jadid attained a stronger position from which to challenge the Baath Party and the government. Tabitha Petran writes that the military committee, which had gained great experience in clandestine activities, was able to withhold political power from the Nasserites and the army, and enable its own Nusayri members to challenge the leadership of the Baath Party, which they had always opposed. Thus, when the Baath Party leadership decided that it was time to solidify the principles and objectives of the party, prohibit the military organization from making political policy, and establish closer relations with Egypt and Iraq the Nusayri officers, led by Jadid, opposed these measures on the grounds that the experimental union of Syria and Egypt had been a failure, and that domestic conditions in Syria should be the party's priority. The Nusayri officers seem to have won this round against the party leadership, and Jadid continued to purge a great number of Muslim Sunnite officers in 1965, replacing them with Nusayris and other minorities.[48]

The Baathist strongman Amin Hafiz was aware of the growing power of the Nusayri officers and their challenge to the party and government, and increasingly feared them; finally, he decided to curtail this power. On 19 December 1965, the Baath Party national leadership announced the dissolution of the Syrian regional leadership of the party. In an official announcement addressed to the armed forces, this leadership criticized the fact that [Sunnite] Baathists had been purged, declaring that it would protect them and that it would never allow anyone [the Nusayri officers] to control army units and convert them into sectarian military blocs. The national leadership of the party also declared that it was against sectarianism, tribal blocs, and allegiance to individuals.[49]

Amin Hafiz took another step to curtail the power of the Nusayri officers. He asked Salah al-Din Bitar to form a government in which labor unions, teachers, students, and farmers would be represented. Bitar failed because of the opposition of the Nusayri officers, who convinced prominent minority officers that the Baath national leadership intended to curb their military activities. The fierce struggle for power between Amin Hafiz and Salah Jadid took a turn for the worse when Hafiz accused Jadid of forming a new Nusayri bloc within the army. The result was the bloody and savage coup of 23 February 1966, when military units around Damascus, staffed mostly by Nusayri officers entered the city and, after four hours of battle in which Amin Hafiz was wounded in the leg, toppled Hafiz's government and with it, the "old guard" of the Baath Party.[50]

Michel Aflaq and Bitar, the founders of the Baath Party, fled the country, branded as traitors to the party. The "regionalists" and the sectarians had finally triumphed, and the long-cherished objective of the rural minority groups—the Nusayris, Druzes, and Ismailis—to reduce the authority of the socialist Sunnites had been achieved. The government was now in the hands of a new Baath Party, dominated by the Nusayris, who occupied the most sensitive positions in the new regime. Now that they were in the seat of power, these Nusayri officers had to play a subtle political game to give the impression that the coup was not sectarian but a Baathist coup, intended to serve the interests of all Syria's political groups. In the meantime, they were consolidating their power for the final elimination of their non-Nusayri rivals and the takeover of the government.[51]

It is true that on 25 February 1966, several Sunnites took key positions: Nur al-Din al-Atasi, a member of the Provisional Regional Command, was appointed head of state and secretary general of the Baath Party; Yusuf Zuayyin became prime minister, and Ahmad Suwaydani, formerly the military intelligence chief, was promoted to the rank of major general and became chief of staff. But the sensitive power positions in the new Baath regime were filled by Nusayris. Hafiz al-Asad was appointed defense minister, and Dr. Ibrahim Makhus became foreign minister, for example. The Nusayri Salah Jadid, who had engineered the coup, assumed no official position in the government, seeming content to occupy the post of assistant secretary general of the Baath Party. However, he also occupied a highly sensitive position in the provisional party command that gave him the power to appoint and dismiss the head of state and the cabinet. Why did Jadid avoid assuming the position of head of state, offering it instead to the Sunnite al-Atasi? It may have been to disarm potential opposition from non-Nusayri groups, who criticized the coup as a Nusayri scheme meant to serve Nusayri objectives. This is why, as A. R. Kelidar observes, Jadid formed a coalition of radicals who represented different political groups.[52]

After the coup of 1966, the new Baath Party, now controlled by Nusayri strongmen, began systematically to purge and arrest Sunnite Muslims, Druzes, and Ismailis in the party and the army. According to Munif al-Razzaz, former secretary general of the Baath Party, the rule of violence of the new Baath regime had no equal in the history of Syria. More than ninety officers who had disapproved of the way the regime was conducting affairs were transferred, pensioned, sacked, or arrested.[53]

At the beginning of 1967, a number of Muslim officers were accused of a coup engineered by the Syrian national leadership of the Baath Party and were court-martialed. Other prominent Sunnite Muslims, especially in the Hawran district, resigned their offices and membership in the party, in protest against the control of the party's administration and the armed forces by the Nusayris. Three cabinet ministers threatened to resign for the same reason.

After the 1967 Arab-Israeli war, many prominent civilian Muslim Baathists who had occupied key positions were dismissed from the party.[54] Meantime, quarrels and disagreements between Lt. General Hafiz al-Asad and the Sunnite Chief of Staff reached a high pitch, and on 15 February 1968, Suwaydani was released from his position.

The fate of Druze officers was no better than that of their Sunnite colleagues. When, after the 1966 coup, Hafiz al-Asad was appointed defense minister, the Druze Hamad Ubayd became dissatisfied with the new regime. He had expected to become defense minister because he had been a minister in the Zuayyin cabinet before its resignation on 22 January 1965, because he was a staunch supporter of Salah Jadid, and especially because he had helped put down the resistance against the coup in Aleppo. Ubayd was also disappointed when he was merely reappointed a member of the regional leadership of the new Baath Party. In March 1966, he was discharged from the army, and in May he attempted a coup against the regime, but the coup failed, and Ubayd and his collaborators were arrested.[55]

The fate of another prominent Druze officer, Salim Hatum, was even worse than that of Ubayd. Hatum played a major role in the February 1966 coup, personally attacking the residence of Amin Hafiz, but when he received no reward, he turned against the new regime that he had helped bring to power. As distrust and hostility between Hatum and the regime intensified, Hatum, supported by Aflaq and Bitar, attempted a coup on 8 September 1966, against the radical Baath regime. This coup also failed, and Hatum and one of his collaborators, Talal Abu Asali, escaped to Jordan, where they were given asylum. Although Jordan and Saudi Arabia were accused of supporting the plot and the editor of *al-Ahram* of Cairo implicated the CIA in the plot, it is certain that Hatum's attempted coup was the result of the conflict between the Nusayris, who were in control of the Syrian government, and the Druzes and Sunnites who were hounded by the Nusayris.[56]

While in Jordan, Hatum called a press conference at which he stated that the spirit of sectarianism had ignobly spread in Syria, especially in the Syrian army. He went on to say that the rulers in Damascus had endeavored to get rid of those who disagreed with their policies and replace them with their own supporters, with the result that key positions in the state were filled by Nusayris. Hatum estimated that the proportion of Nusayris to other groups in the army was 5 to 1.[57]

On 28 September 1966, Hatum issued a communique condemning

the ruling clique in Damascus for its intention of establishing an opportunistic regime under the slogan, "One Nusayri state with an eternal message." In this state, said Hatum, the Amid [a Nusayri religious rank] Salah Jadid and Nur al-Anwar [the light of lights, another Nusayri religious rank] Ibrahim Makhus, would shine. Hatum remained in Jordan until the Arab-Israeli war broke out in June 1967, when he returned to Syria, placing himself under the protection of the Druze leader Sultan Pasha al-Atrash, who had fought the French in 1925. Hatum then offered his services to the Syrian army. He was arrested by the new Baath leaders and sent to Damascus, where he was accused of plotting to overthrow the government. He was summarily tried and executed on 26 June 1967.[58]

Following Hatum's abortive coup, the Nusayri-controlled government forced out many Druze officers, including Fahd al-Shair, who had formed a secret military organization that refused admission to Nusayri officers. Not even the group of the Nusayri Muhammad Umran was admitted, because Umran was not trusted by Nusayri officers like Hafiz al-Asad. Many Druze officers were forced to leave the country. Furthermore, the activity of the Baath Party in the Druze area was hampered to the point that the Druze leader, Sultan Pasha al-Atrash, sent a cable to the government in Damascus, criticizing the policy of the Nusayri sectaries.[59] The criticism of al-Atrash was to no avail, and the Nusayri-controlled government continued to purge undesirable elements from the army and the party.

The Nusayris' design to take over the government was further manifested by several secret meetings, especially that of Jubb al-Jarrah on 30 January 1968. In this meeting it was decided to abolish the teaching of the Islamic and Christian religions in the schools. Another meeting convened at Sabbura on 14 April 1968, and a third at Damascus on 3 May of the same year. A fourth meeting, held at the home of Hafiz al-Asad, was attended by Salah Jadid, Ibrahim Makhus, and many other prominent Nusayris.[60] The plans of the Nusayris did not go unnoticed. The Beirut-based magazine *al-Sayyad* had sent one of its reporters to the Nusayri area in March 1966. In an article entitled, "The Alawis Today Rule Syria," the reporter said that the Alawis now openly ruled Syria after years of hiding behind the Baath Party. According to the reporter, Salah Jadid told Amin Hafiz that the loyalty of the Alawi bloc to the then current Baath regime in Syria was guaranteed. In other words, such loyalty was essential to the existence of the Baath regime. The reporter concluded that Amin Hafiz and the rest of the non-Nusayri Baathists had swallowed the bitter truth that finally the Alawis had come forward and were now ruling Syria.[61]

In fact, there is evidence that the Nusayris in the government, especially Hafiz al-Asad, who occupied the sensitive position of defense minister, handed over the Golan Heights to the Israelis in the Arab-Israeli War of 1967. According to the periodical *al-Hawadith,* two weeks before the outbreak of this war, Syrian Ambassador to France Sami al-Jundi, was instructed by his government to meet with the Israeli foreign minister, Abba Eban, in Paris. Al-Jundi says that he met with Eban for an hour and a half and made a full recording of the meeting. Al-Jundi goes on to say that Eban told him, "The Israeli forces will not go beyond Qunaytira, even though the road to Damascus will be open."[62] In fact *al-Hawadith,* in a 1968 article entitled "al-Mu'amara al-Jahanamiyyah" (The Hellish Conspiracy) states that the Syrian government affirmed the secret meeting between al-Jundi and Eban. *Al-Hawadith* further states that prior to the Israeli attack, the Syrian government had disarmed the non-Alawi units of the army. This action, says *al-Hawadith,* would ultimately allow the Alawis to achieve the takeover of the government.[63] On 1 May 1979, Anwar Sadat, then president of Egypt, affirmed that shortly before the 1967 Arab-Israeli war, the Syrian authorities removed the mines from the Golan Heights, and that the Syrian government executed an officer who had announced the fall of the Golan Heights before they actually fell to the Israelis.[64] The author was told by the late Syrian Orthodox patriarch Yaqub III (d. 1980), who lived in Damascus, that he had been personally told by the Syrian minister of health that he was in the town of Qunaytira when he heard Radio Damascus proclaim that the Golan Heights had fallen to the Israelis. The minister telephoned Damascus to tell authorities that he was in Qunaytira, and there was no sign of Israeli soldiers in the area. Nevertheless, the minister was told that the Qunaytira had already fallen.

The purpose of handing over the Golan Heights to Israel was to find in Israel a socialist ally who sympathized with Syrian Alawi socialism. Nothing reveals this purpose more than the words of the former Jordanian prime minister, Saad Jumua, in his *Al-Mu'amara wa Ma'rakat al-Masir* (The Conspiracy and Battle of Destiny). Jumua states that at noon on 5 June 1967, the ambassador of a great country (he does not name it) in Damascus contacted a responsible figure in the Syrian government and invited him to his home to discuss "an urgent matter." At the meeting, the ambassador related to the prominent Syrian the text of a telegram he had received from his government, confirming that the Israeli air force had totally destroyed the Egyptian air force and that the outcome of the war between the Arabs and Israel was obvious. The telegram also emphasized that Israel did not intend to attack the Syrian regime, and that for all intents and purposes, Israel was a "socialist" country which sympathized with the Baath's socialism in Syria. Therefore, it was in the interests of Syria and the Baath Party to carry on only token fighting in order to ensure their safety. The Syrian official immediately relayed this message to his colleagues in the national and regional commands of the Baath Party. He returned to inform the ambassador of the acceptance by the party, the government, and the national and the regional commands of the telegram.[65] Jumua laments the reluctance of the Syrian air force to enter the war on the pretext that it was not ready for combat. He asserts that the "ruling gang" in Damascus suffered from a deadly complex which he calls the "Abd al-Nasir complex." What Jumua meant is that the rulers of Syria feared the personality and popularity of the Egyptian president as an Arab national leader. They thought that once the Egyptian forces were totally destroyed by the Israelis, President Nasser would fall and they, as the apostles of the socialist left, would fill the resulting political vacuum and become the sole leaders of the Arab world. The Syrian leaders also thought that with Nasser out of the way, they would free themselves from the bonds of Arab nationalism and establish in Syria a sectarian (Nusayri) state, which would live in peace with Israel. However, concludes Jumua, "the sectarian conspiracies against Arabism and religion [Isalm] can no more be hidden.[66]

From this statement we learn that Jumua has accused the Syrian rulers of sectarian conspiracy and antagonism toward Islam and Arabism. The shadow of this accusation still hangs over the present Syrian regime and the Nusayri leaders in power.

The incident of the Golan Heights weakened Syria politically, but gave greater strength to the Nusayri-controlled army and specifically to Hafiz al-Asad. The Nusayri strike forces became so powerful that by 1970, Hafiz al-Asad was able to purge his enemies and assume full control of the government. It is true that there was a struggle for power within the Nusayri community, especially between al-Asad and Salah Jadid, but this struggle was essentially between two ambitious individuals each attempting to consolidate his local base of support in order to enhance his position and project himself as a national leader.[67] The outcome of this struggle was the triumph of Hafiz al-Asad, who had all the armed forces behind him.

On 13 November 1970, al-Asad overthrew the government and ordered the arrests of Salah Jadid and President Nur al-Din al-Atasi, who fled the country. On 22 February 1971, al-Asad became the first Nusayri president of Syria. Thus the Nusayris, who once would have been content to have autonomy in their own area, now were in control of Syria. This control has a very significant political implication. The

Nusayri community, which suffered discrimination, ridicule, rejection, and economic deprivation at the hands of the Sunnite Syrian majority, has evolved from a "backward religious community to a nationally emancipated population group in a position of dominance."[68] Today the Syrian government and army, and indeed Syria's destiny, are in the hands of Nusayris.[69]

26

The Nusayri Religious System

The Concept of God

THE FUNDAMENTAL ARTICLE of the religion of the Nusayris is the absolute oneness of God, who is self-existent and eternal. Like other Ghulat, the Nusayris believe in God without attempting to define His existence, essence, or attributes, either philosophically or theologically. Like the Ahl-i Haqq, the Nusayris believe that this God appeared on earth seven times in human form. The two sects each name seven different forms, however; the one form they both name is Ali.

In the Nusayri catechism known as *Kitab Ta'lim al Diyana al-Nusayriyya,* the fourth question asks how often our Lord (Ali) changed his form and showed himself in the likeness of man. The answer is seven times:

1. He took the name of Abel and took Adam as his veil.
2. He took the name of Seth and took Noah as his veil.
3. He took the name of Joseph and took Jacob as his veil.
4. He took the name of Joshua and took Moses as his veil.
5. He took the name of Asaf and took Solomon as his veil.
6. He took the name of Simon Peter and took Jesus as his veil.
7. He took the name of Ali and took Muhammad as his veil.[1]

As the last manifestation of the Deity, Ali was the consummate reality, in whom all the preceding manifestations found their ultimate end and completion.[2]

This God who appeared in seven human forms is a single entity, but He has three personalities, none coequal or coeternal with Himself. The first is called the Mana (Meaning); theologically, it signifies the causal determinant who is the source and meaning of all things. This Mana created the second person, the Ism (Name), who created the third person, the Bab (Door). Thus, in each of His seven manifestations, God had with Him two other persons through whom He became completely manifested to mankind. Together with God, these two persons form an indivisible trinity:

Mana	*Ism*	*Bab*
Abel	Adam	Gabriel
Seth	Noah	Yail Ibn Fatin
Joseph	Jacob	Ham Ibn Kush
Joshua	Moses	Dan Ibn Usbaut
Asaf	Solomon	Abd Allah Ibn Siman
Simon Peter	Jesus	Rawzaba Ibn al-Marzuban
Ali	Muhammad	Salman al-Farisi[3]

The last and supreme manifestation of God is Ali; his Ism is the Prophet Muhammad, and his Bab is Salman the Persian, the Prophet's companion. These three form the trinity of the Nusayris, whose mystery is represented by the initial letters of their names: A for Ali, M for Muhammad, and S for Salman, also known as Salsal. Louis Massignon speculates that the term Salsal derives from the Arabic word *silsila* (chain, or link). In this context, Salman is the link between Muhammad and Ali.[4]

Like another Ghulat sect, the Ahl-i Haqq, the Nusayris divide time into seven cycles, each corresponding to a manifestation of the deity. The concept of seven cycles dates back to the pagan Harranians, who maintained that the creator was multiple because of his manifestation in seven forms, corresponding to the seven heavenly bodies governing the universe.[5]

This concept of seven periods is also used in the Ismaili's religious system to symbolize the authority of seven Imams, beginning with Ali and ending with Ismail (d.762), son of Jafar al-Sadiq, from whom they received their name. According to Muslim sources, the Ismailis are known as Sabiyya (Seveners) because they believe in the divine authority of seven Imams.[6]

Since the Nusayri dogma of the seven incarnations of the deity is probably based on the Ismaili concept of seven emanations of the divine nature, a brief overview of the Ismaili concept follows.

In their attempt to explain the origin of the universe by means other than divine creation, and in accordance with their esoteric belief in the necessity of having a divinely inspired Imam in every generation, the Ismailis adopted the neo-Platonic doctrine of emanations, stripping it of mysticism. The neo-Platonists assert that everything that exists proceeds from God in successive emanations. The Ismailis, while maintaining seven stages of emanation, assert that God was not the immediate creator of the universe. They aver that the only thing emanating from God was the Divine Will (Amr), and that this Will is the source of everything that exists, the cause of causes.[7] This Will, which is transubstantiated into the divine word "Be" (Quran 36:82), is the first intellect, the universal reason (al-Aql al-Awwal), the first emanation of the divine nature. It is, as the Ismaili writer al-Kermani (d. 947) states, "the first Intellect or the first Existence, whose existence is not by itself but by its creation and transcendence."[8]

According to this reasoning, God has no attributes or qualities. He is an abstraction, the First Intellect or Universal Reason. As an abstract principle without attributes, God becomes so obscure that man cannot communicate with Him. This Ismaili belief seems to contradict those of Neo-Platonism, Judaism, Christianity, and Islam, which teach that God has divine attributes and that He is the primary source of existence.

Continuing their esoteric line of reasoning, the Ismailis believe that the Universal Soul created primal matter, and that space, time, and the perfect man (al-Insan al-Kamil) conclude these emanations. This perfect man comprises the sublime world, al-Alam al-Ulwi, which is the seat of creation, Dar al-Ibda.[9]

In each cycle of these emanations there exists a prophet who is the reflection of the perfect man. In Ismaili terminology this prophet is called the Natiq (speaker, or proclaimer). He is accompanied by a coadjutant called the Samit (mute) or Asas (foundation), who is the reflection of the Universal Soul in the world of senses. This Samit or Asas serves as a minister to the Natiq and is charged with the duty of proclaiming and interpreting *(tawil)* the revelation *(tanzil)* of the prophet. Al-Kermani states that this interpretation reveals the inner knowledge of the revelation (Ilm al-Batin), which is the true meaning of the divine message. Therefore, al-Kermani says, it is the function of the Imam to carry on this inner knowledge and guide the community along its lines.[10]

The cycles of the Natiqs (proclaiming prophets) began with Adam, followed by Noah, Abraham, Moses, Jesus, and Muhammad, whose coadjutants were respectively Seth, Shem, Ishmail, Aaron, Simon Peter, and Ali. Ali has a unique position in the Ismaili system because he is the Asas of the Prophet Muhammad, and his descendants, the Imams after him, have the exclusive function of interpreting the inner meaning of the divine message of Islam.

Therefore it is imperative, al-Kermani says, that an Imam should exist in every generation, whose duty is to preserve the divine message delivered by the Prophet and to protect it from distortion and alteration.[11] Thus, in his religious capacity as the Imam, the Ismaili Aga Khan III, becomes the successor of the Prophet.[12]

According to the Ismailis, six of these Natiqs and Samits have already appeared. The seventh cycle will be ushered in by the advent of the last and greatest of the Prophets, the Mahdi, or al-Qaim, who will appear before the end of the world.[13]

The concepts of the Prophet as a Natiq and of his coadjutant, the Samit, did not originate with the Ismailis. They were formulated by one of the earliest Ghulat, Abu al-Khattab Muhammad Ibn Abi Zaynab al-Asadi, killed in 138/755. According to Abu al-Hasan al-Ashari (d.935), Abu al-Khattab taught that the Imams are God's new prophets, His divine Hujjas (proofs), and messengers to mankind. Two of these remained he said; the Natiq, who was Muhammad, and the Samit, Ali Ibn Abi Talib. They possessed the knowledge of what was, what is, and what will be, and it is imperative that all men obey them.[14] Al-Ashari does not elaborate on Abu al-Khattab's concept of the Natiq and Samit, but we may speculate that the Ismailis, who were more philosophically sophisticated than Abu al-Khattab, made great use of this concept, which they combined with Neo-Platonist philosophy.

The Nusayri dogma of the seven incarnations of the deity probably derives from the Ismaili concept of seven emanations, but lacks its philosophical subtlety. René Dussaud rightly observes that, unlike the Ismailis, the Nusayris were incapable of philosophical speculation, and therefore arrived at the concept of one god not stripped of divinity and authority, as is the god of the Ismailis, who is pure intellect. They could not comprehend the abstract philosophical terminology and reasoning of the Ismailis with respect to the emanation of the divine nature and the relationship between the Natiq and the Samit, as applied to Muhammad and Ali; thus, the Nusayris readily accepted Ali as the Incarnation of God. Dussaud concludes that the Nusayris represent a remarkable example of a sect passing directly from paganism to Ismailism. This transformation, however, was not complete. It was rather a compromise between Ismaili doctrine and the Nusayri practices, resulting in the creation of a new religion.[15]

The fundamental tenet of this religion lies in the legend of Ali. Dussaud's conclusion seems to be correct, because the Nusayris exaggerate the position of Ali, regarding him as God, and as the Asas (foundation) of the Prophet Muhammad. He is the Mana, taking precedence over

Muhammad, who is the Natiq (proclaimer) of the divine message contained in the Quran.

Closely associated with their belief in the seven human manifestations of God in seven periods is the Nusayris' cosmogony. The Nusayris believe that in the beginning, before the world existed, they were brilliant, heavenly bodies and luminous stars, conscious of the distinction between obedience and disobedience. They did not eat, drink, or pass excrement. Their only activity was to behold Ali Ibn Abi Talib in a sapphire splendor. They remained in this state for 7,077 years and 7 hours. Then they boasted of themselves, saying, "Surely, he has created no more noble creatures than we are," thereby committing their first sin of pride.

Ali then created for them a Hijab (veil, or intermediary), who held them under restraint for a further 7,000 years. Ali then appeared to them and asked, "Am I not your Lord?" [Quran 7:172], to which they replied, "Certainly you are." After a while, Ali revealed to them his all-encompassing divine power (Qudra), and they fancied that they could behold him fully, supposing him to be one like themselves; this was the second sin they committed.[16]

Thereupon Ali made visible to them the Hijab, with whom they wandered 7,077 years and 7 hours. When this period was up, Ali appeared to the Nusayris in the form of an old man with white hair and a white beard; through this form, he tested the people of light, of the higher spiritual world. The Nusayris did not look beyond the form in which he appeared to them, and when he said to them, "Who am I?" they replied, "We do not know."[17] Ali then appeared to them in the form of a young man with a curled mustache, riding upon an angry-looking lion, and again in the form of a small child. In each manifestation, he called "Am I not your Lord?"

Ali was accompanied by his Ism (name), Muhammad, and his Bab (door), Salman al-Farisi, together with the people of the orders of his holiness, namely, the first seven orders constituting the great luminous world. When Ali called to the Nusayris, they imagined him to be one like themselves. They were bewildered and did not know what to do. In order to put an end to their doubt about his nature, Ali told them that he would create a lower sphere for them and cast them down into it. He would also create human forms for them and appear to them in a veil akin to their human forms. He told them that he would raise up again anyone who acknowledged him, together with his veil and his door. Anyone who rebelled against him would face an adversary created by

Ali, and anyone who denied him would be subject to *Musukhiyya* (degrading transformation) into an animal form.

The Nusayri's implored God to leave them where they were to praise, magnify, and worship Him, and not cast them into the lower sphere. But He said, "You have disobeyed me. If you had said, 'Lord, we know nothing save what you taught us, you are the inscrutable, omniscient one,' [Quran 5:109] I would have forgiven you."

Because of the disobedience of the Nusayris, Ali created the Abalisa (plural of Iblis—devil or Satan), and from the Abalisa he created woman. For this reason, the Nusayris do not teach their women any form of prayer or initiate them into the mystery of their religion. Because they are believed to have been created from Abalisa, Nusayri women are degraded and held in low esteem.[18]

After casting the Nusayris into a lower, human form, Ali appeared to them in seven Qibab (domes, tabernacles), that is, periods inhabited by al-Hinn, al-Binn, al-Timm, al-Rumm, al-Jann, al-Jinn, and al-Yunan (the Greeks).[19] In each of his seven appearances during these periods, Ali was accompanied by an Ism, a Bab, and an adversary. It is worth noting that, according to Sulayman al-Adani, in each of these seven cycles the adversary, or Satan, consisted of three persons in one (a kind of Satanic triad), namely, the "rightly guided" caliphs, Abu Bakr, Umar, and Uthman.[20] This, to be sure, expresses the implacable hatred the Shiites harbor for these men, whom they accuse of usurping the caliphate from Ali. They also accuse Umar and Uthman of burning those portions of the Quran which, they assert, included the designation of Ali by the Prophet Muhammad as his heir and successor in leading the Muslim community.

From this account; it is clear that the Nusayris believe in the existence of preadamite ages, during which the world was inhabited by different kinds of beings who worshipped Ali. The Imam Jafar al-Sadiq acknowledged the existence of seven preadamite nations. He said the Shiites aver that before God created Adam, there were seven Adams who occupied seven ages, and that the time-span of each age was fifty thousand years. Later, when God created mankind, "We, the Imams, were the first Hujjas (divine proofs) and messengers of God to mankind."

Al-Sadiq also stated that there were beings living on the earth before Adam. After they died, they were resurrected, judged, and consigned temporarily to Paradise or Hell. Finally, the people of Paradise were transformed into angels, while the people of Hell, the *qashshash* (waste heap), were transformed into such animals as pigs, bears, dogs, and jackals.[21]

The concept of seven ages is found in Zoroastrianism and may have reached the Shiites through Persia. According to a Persian legend, Zoroaster, by divine favor, saw a tree which had seven branches, one of gold, one of silver, one of bronze, one of copper, one of tin, one of steel, and one of an iron alloy. Hormizd (Ahura Mazda) revealed to him that this tree was the image of the world, and that each of these branches represented one of the periods through which he (Zoroaster) had to pass.[22] This is similar to the image King Nebuchadnezzar saw in a dream, which represented different periods of world kingdoms.[23]

These, then, are the preadamite periods, or domes as the author of *Kitab al-Bakura* calls them, whose inhabitants worshipped Ali. According to Edward Salisbury, the people of these periods represent a gradation of human existence from inferior to higher, corresponding in reverse order to the seven forms of *musukhiyya* (degrading transformation) which the Nusayris believe they had to pass through as punishment for their disobedience, or perhaps for their failure to worship Ali wholeheartedly.[24]

Salisbury further states that the period of the Greeks, the seventh and last, represents the highest point of human existence before the special manifestations of Ali in the *sab qibab dhatiyya* (seven periods of divine quality), which began after the Nusayris failed to recognize the divinity of Ali.[25] Ali manifested himself seven times in this world, as Abel, Seth, Joseph, Joshua, Asaf, and Simon Peter, and finally in his own person. In this final manifestation, Ali revealed to the Nusayris that they were the highest among mankind, and that he was the only deity to be worshipped.[26] In other words, Ali was one and the same god in each of his manifestations, and the Ism, Bab, and adversary who accompanied in each likewise appeared in successive theophanies.[27]

The concept of the seven manifestations of the deity is also found in the Druze religious system. According to the Druzes, Hamza Ibn Ali, the founder of the Druze religion, appeared seven times in this world in human form. The Formulary (catechism) of the Druzes contains the question, "How many times did Hamza appear, and under what names?" The answer is, "He appeared seven times, from Adam to the Prophet Muhammad." Then follow the names under which Hamza appeared in each of the seven periods.[28] Silvestre de Sacy doubts whether this was the original teaching of the Druzes, since he could not find the number of Hamza's appearances given in other Druze sources.[29]

The same Druze Formulary contains another question about the Fatimi Caliph al-Hakim bi Amr Allah (d.1021), considered the supreme deity of the Druzes, and his names and the maqamat (stations, or periods) in which he appeared.[30] The description of al-Hakim's manifestations shows that the Druzes, like the Nusayris, believe in a single deity who remained constant although he manifested himself in different forms. It also shows that the deity and his Hijab (veil) are so united in words and deeds that they form one person. Regardless of the number of his manifestations, the deity remains a single entity. He precedes the whole of creation and is the prototype of man. The reason al-Hakim appeared in human form was to enable man to acquire full conviction of his existence. Al-Hakim is considered by the Druzes to be the culmination of all the manifestations, which pointed to him and were completed in him.[31]

The religious systems of the Druzes and the Nusayris are strikingly similar, with one major exception: al-Hakim is God to the Druzes, while Ali is God to the Nusayris. It is not surprising, then, that the Formulary of the Druzes condemns the Nusayris for separating themselves from the Druzes.[32] It is interesting to note that both sects have their roots in Persia. Their founders, Muhammad Ibn Nusayr and Hamza Ibn Ali, were both of Persian origin, as were the founders of the Ismailis and their offshoot, the Assassins.[33] Later we shall see the influence of Persian tradition on the religious system of the Nusayris.

At the outset of this chapter, we noted that the first article of the Nusayri faith is the oneness of God, self-existent and coeternal. We also noted, however, that this God has three personalities, the Mana (Ali), the Ism (Muhammad), and the Bab (Salman al-Farisi), who form an inseparable trinity. In essence, however, these three are all Ali Ibn Abi Talib. As the Nusayri catechism explains, the Mana, the Ism, and the Bab are united as "God, the Compassionate, the Merciful," in the formula which precedes all but one of the suras of the Quran. What the author of the catechism intends is that in this formula "God" signifies the Mana (Ali), "the Compassionate" signifies the Ism (Muhammad), and "the Merciful" signifies the Bab (Salman al-Farisi).[34]

Question 12 of the same catechism asks, "Are the Mana and the Bab separate from the Ism?" The answer is, "No, they are with it—they cannot be separated."[35] This trinity, symbolized by AMS, the initial letters of the names Ali, Muhammad, and Salman, form a single divine essence. In the *Munazara* (debate) of al-Nashshabi, we read, "The one whom we saw in human form [Ali] is the M [for Muhammad], and this Muhammad, Ali, and Salman are one essence and one light."[36]

Each of these three persons manifests himself in the others, although as the "Most High" they do not change or cease to be. There is no difference between the Mana and the Ism. They are inseparable, as is the light of the sun from its sphere.[37] The tenth-century Nusayri writer Ali

Ibn Isa al-Jisri states in *Risalat al-Tawhid* (The epistle of the unity of God) that God is the Ism and the Mana. He is the Ism (Name) which was manifested in the world in order that men might come to know the Mana. The Mana cannot be separated from his Ism, and the Ism cannot be separated from his Mana.[38]

The Nusayris believe that these three persons are one, and that it is sheer ignorance, even blasphemy, to separate or differentiate them. A Nusayri who does not recognize the true relationship among the three persons of this trinity is not a true believer. This is attested to by Nusayri sources, which attribute to Jafar al-Sadiq the tradition, "He who differentiates between the Ism and the Mana has blasphemed, and he who truly worships the Ism has also worshipped the Mana, and he who worships the Ism in place of the Mana is an infidel, but he who worships the Mana through the divine reality of the Ism has in fact professed the oneness of God."[39]

This trinity forms the foundation of the Nusayris' religious system. In the ninth sura (in *Kitab al-Bakura*), called the Luminary Ayn (the initial letter of Ali's name), Muhammad Ibn Nusayr, founder of the Nusayri sect, is firmly associated with the third person of the trinity, Salman al-Farisi. This trinity is the focal point of the Nusayris' profession of faith: "There is no God but Ali Ibn Abi Talib, with the bald forehead and temples, the adorable, and no veil but the Lord Muhammad, worthy to be praised, and no door other than the Lord Salman al-Farisi, the object of desire."[40] This trinity is so sacred that in *Kitab al-Mashyakha* (Manual for shaykhs), Ali is invoked "by the truth of the Mana, the Ism, and the Bab." In this same book, reference is made to "al-Mana al-Qadim (ancient meaning), al-Ism al-Azim (great name), and al-Bab al-Karim (honorable door)."[41] In Nusayri sources, a wife of the Prophet, Umm Salama, is spoken of as being endowed with divine grace, "Through her saintliness" says one source, she "has indicated the manifestation of the Mana, the Ism, and the Bab."[42]

Thus, the trinity symbolized by the letters AMS is the center of the Nusayri worship and faith. No Nusaryi will ever swear by this trinity and then tell an untruth. Indeed, we learn from *Kitab al-Bakura* that the most binding action among the Nusayris is to place one's hand in that of another, saying, "I adjure you by your faith, the faith of the covenant of Ali, the Commander of the Faithful, and by the covenant of AMS," making it obligatory to speak the truth.[43]

Another form of this oath involves moistening a finger with saliva and placing it on the other person's neck, saying, "I am absolved of my sins and lay them on your neck, and I adjure you by the foundation of your religion, by the mystery of the covenant of AMS, to tell me the whole truth regarding [this] matter." This form also precludes the telling of a falsehood. Thus the whole life of the Nusayris—their conduct and relations with each other—is motivated by the grace of this trinity and bound by their faith in it.[44]

To the Nusayris, the letters AMS constitute a *sirr* (mystery) of their trinity, bringing to mind the mystery of the Holy Trinity in Christianity, although Christians do not use enigmatic letters to denote their Trinity. The use of cryptic letters was practiced by ancient peoples to accentuate the mysterious powers of the universe or deities.[45] Some suras of the Quran begin with cryptic letters that no one could understand or explain, except God and those Muslim scholars well versed in religious sciences (Quran 3:7).[46] Perhaps it was God's design to leave parts of His revelation enigmatic and not fully understood by mortals, as is stated in Quran 111:5: "It is He who revealed to you the Quran. Some of the verses are precise in meaning—they are the foundations of the Book—and others are ambiguous. Those whose hearts are infected with disbelief follow the ambiguous part, so as to create dissension by seeking to explain it. But no one knows its meaning except Allah."

The book of *al-Jafr,* believed by Shiites to have been revealed to the Imam Jafar al-Sadiq, contains, among other things, an esoteric explanation of the meaning of the Arabic alphabet.[47] In fact, some Nusayris, like the nineteenth-century Shaykh Muhammad Ibn Kalazo, use the letters HBQ in a spiritual sense to denote Hilal, Badr, and Qamar, indicating the different cycles of the moon.[48]

In summation, the Mana, the Ism, and the Bab form the inseparable trinity of the Nusayris, which is fashioned like the Quranic formula, "In the name of God, the Compassionate, the Merciful." The Mana, the Ism, and the Bab have threefold names: Mathaliyya (figurative), Dhatiyya (essential), and Sifatiyya (attributive). The figurative name belongs to the Mana; the attributive is that of which the Ism has made use, but which belongs peculiarly to the Mana, as when we say "the Compassionate, the Merciful, the Creator." Thus *Kitab Ta'lim al-Diyana al-Nusayriyya* (the Nusayri catechism) begins with the formula: "In the name of the ancient Mana, the great Ism, and the eternal Door, who is God, the Compassionate, the Merciful."[49]

The orthodox Muslim formula, "God, the Compassionate, the Merciful," is explained by the Nusayris in accordance with both the outward and inward meanings of the divine mysteries. So to question 98 of the catechism, "What do the outer and inner words, al-dahir and al-batin, denote?" the answer is, "The inner [signifies] the divinity of our Lord [Ali], the outer his manhood. Outwardly, we say that he is spoken of as our Lord Ali, son of Abi Talib, and this denotes inwardly the Mana, the Ism, and the Bab, one Compassionate and Merciful God."[50] Or, as Joseph Catafago has noted in his description of *Kitab Majmu al-A'yad* (Book of Feasts), its author, Abu Said Maymun Ibn al-Qasim al-Tabarani (d. 1034), distinguishes three principles in Ali: the divinity or the essence of being, the light or veil, and the door, which is the faithful spirit.[51]

The Nusayri trinity has been linked by various writers to trinities of other religions. Rev. Samuel Lyde, for example, states that the Nusayris took many things from Christianity, including the doctrine of the Trinity.[52] Rev. Henri Lammens, who seems to believe that the Nusayris are converts from Christianity, maintains likewise that they have retained many Christian tenets, including the Trinity.[54] René Dussaud, on the other hand, sees in the Nusayri trinity all the characteristics of an adaptation of the local cults, and asserts that it recalls the triads common in the ancient Syro-Phoenician cults.[53] Although we shall return to this subject later, it should be pointed out that there is no fundamental resemblance between the Nusayri trinity and that of Christianity, despite the similarity in terminology. According to Christianity, the Trinity of Father, Son, and Holy Spirit comprises three Persons who are One in essence, power, and majesty. They form one Godhead, coequal and coeternal. In this Godhead, the Son, Christ, is begotten, not made, and the Holy Spirit proceeds from the Father; the three are but one God, who is Trinity in Unity and Unity in Trinity.

The Nusayri trinity, however, is not a trinity of persons united in one godhead, for the Mana (Ali) created the Ism (Muhammad), who in turn created the Bab (Salman al-Farisi). This is made clear in a question in the Nusayri catechism, "How did the Mana create the Ism, and how did the latter create the Bab?" The answer is, "The substance of substances produced the name out of his unity."[55] According to *Kitab al-Mashyakha,* "Ali created Muhammad from the light of his unity and from the power of his eternity. And he made him a light extracted from the essence of his Mana, and called him Muhammad at the time when he conversed with him, and caused him to move out of his state of rest, and chose him, and called him by his name, and elected him. And Muhammad had no lord but him, and Ali made him his flashing light and his sharp edge and his speaking tongue, and set him over the great matter and the ancient cause, and made him the circle of existence and the center of prayer. And he said to him, 'Be the cause of causes, and the framer of the door and the Hijab [veil].' Muhammad created the door, Salman al-Farisi, by the command of the Lord [Ali] and according to his purpose. Then he commanded the door [Salman] to create the higher and lower worlds."[56]

From this passage we learn that Ali created Muhammad, and that

Muhammad has no lord but Ali. As the creature of Ali, Muhammad cannot be homologous with Ali in his divinity. He must (and does) occupy an inferior position in the trinity of the Nusayris, as is clear from the Nusayri catechism, which charges Muhammad with the duty of calling the believers to the knowledge of their Lord Ali. This catechism also asserts that Ali is the one who taught Muhammad the Quran through Gabriel.[57] Further evidence of Muhammad's inferiority to Ali is shown by his own sayings, "For I was created out of the light of his [Ali's] essence," and, "Is not Ali my Lord and your Lord?"[58] It is for this reason that we find in Nusaryi sources the Mana and the Ism coupled. We have already cited the statement attributed to the Imam Jafar al-Sadiq, "He who differentiates between the Ism and the Mana has blasphemed, and he who truly worships the Ism has also worshipped the Mana, and he who worships the Ism in the place of the Mana is an infidel, but he who worships the Mana through the divine reality of the Ism has in fact professed the oneness of God."[59] The same Jafar al-Sadiq also explains, in *Kitab al-Haft al-Sharif,* that God, the Mana, chides the believers for worshipping the Ism without the Mana, asking, "Will you, then, worship the Ism without the Mana?" This clearly indicates that the Mana alone should be their focus of worship.[60]

Thus, it is clear that the Nusayris' trinity is not a trinity of persons coequal and coeternal with God, nor is it true that in the unity of the Godhead, there are three persons of one substance, power, and eternity, as in the Christian Trinity. It is rather a trinity of partnership, in which Ali, Muhammad, and Salman are three different facets of the divine nature.

Although in essence the Nusayri trinity is different from that of Christianity, yet Sulayman al-Adani, in his commentary on *Surat al-Fath,* states that these three, Ali, Muhammad and Salman al-Farisi, form the "Holy Trinity" of the Nusayris. He explains that in this trinity, Ali corresponds to the Father, Muhammad to the Son, and Salman al-Farisi to the Holy Spirit, the three Persons of the Christian Trinity.[61] Al-Adani may be justified in suggesting this correspondence, however, for we find in ancient Nusayri writings an explicit recognition of the sonship of Christ and His consubstantiality with the Father, although these sources do not suggest an analogy between the Nusayri and the Christian trinities.

In *Kitab al-Usus* (Book of foundation), the Imam Jafar al-Sadiq describes the seven periods of the manifestations of God. He states that in each of these periods, God played a different role. In the period of Moses, for example, God commanded Moses to build a tabernacle in which He dwelt. God also gave Moses the Torah and commanded him to instruct the Israelites to observe the rules of *tahara* (purity), and to abstain from eating the flesh of certain animals which were forbidden to them. "However," says al-Sadiq, "when Christ, the Son, came, who assumed the form of the Sonship and dwelt in Mary, He altered the law of Moses and absolved the people from the obligation of purification."

Al-Sadiq continues, "Do not you who inquire see that He [Jesus] has absolved them [the Israelites] from many obligations imposed upon them by Moses?"[62] In this statement, we find the concept of a Father, and of a son who is one in being with the Father and has become incarnated through a virgin, the essence of the Christian religion. The context, however, is unmistakably Nusayri.

What, then, is the true relationship between Ali and Muhammad in the theological system of the Nusayris? We can answer this question only by examining each of the three persons of the Nusayri trinity. This we will do in the following chapters.

27

The Nusayri Religious System
The Apotheosis of Ali

To the Nusayris, Ali Ibn Abi Talib, blood cousin and son-in-law of the Prophet Muhammad, is the last and only perfect one of the seven manifestations of God, in which the Islamic religion and its Sharia (law) have been revealed. He is, as noted in the preceding chapter, the one who created Muhammad and taught him the Quran. He is the fountainhead of Islam. He is God: the very God of the Quran.

Whatever attributes the Muslims ascribe to Allah, the Nusayris ascribe to their God, Ali. Some they attribute to him in his human form, others to his Godhead.[1] The first question of the Nusayris' catechism asks, "Who is our Lord who created us?" The answer is, "He is the commander of the Faithful, Amir al-Nahl (Prince of Bees), Ali Ibn Abi Talib, who is God and the only God, the Compassionate, the Merciful." The second question asks, "Whence do we know that our Lord the Commander of the Faithful, Ali Ibn Abi Talib, is God?" The answer is, "Through his own testimony given in a public sermon which he delivered from the pulpit before many people, and which he taught to scholars and speculative thinkers. In this sermon he said, I have the knowledge of the hour (the end of the world). The apostles designated me, proclaimed my unity, and called the people to my knowledge. I have given the creation its names, flattened the earth, fixed the mountains, made the rivers flow, brought forth fruits. I have fashioned the dusk and caused the sun to rise and lightened the moon. I have created mankind and provided livelihood. I am the Lord of lords, the possesser of necks. I am al-Ali (the most high), al-Allam (the omniscient). I am Qarm al-Hadid (Almighty Lord). I am the one who commands life and death, who begat Jesus in the womb of His mother, Mary, and who sent the apostles and instructed the prophets!"[2]

The divinity of Ali is further acknowledged in the eleventh chapter (of *Kitab al-Majmu*), entitled al-Shahada (testimony) and called by the common people al-Jabal (the mountain). What is peculiar is that the testimony of divinity of Ali is associated with Islam as God's religion. The chapter begins thus: "God bears witness, the angels, too, and all those well-versed in religious sciences, that there is no God beside him, the doer of justice . . . Verily, the religion with God is Islam. O, our Lord, save us by your revelation, cause us to follow the messenger [Muhammad], and so firmly count us among those who testify to AMS."

Further on the statement is made, "I testify that there is no God but Ali Ibn Abi Talib with the bald forehead, the adorable, and no Hijab but Lord Muhammad, worthy to be praised, and no Bab but Lord Salman al-Farisi . . . I testify that the manlike form manifested among men was the end of all existence, and that it made manifest the essential light, besides which there is no God, Ali Ibn Abi Talib, and that he is immeasurable, illimitable, incomprehensible, inscrutible. I testify that I am a Nusayri in religion."[3]

The Nusayris further maintain that the proof that Ali is God is based on his own testimony in the Quran, which they claim contains an inner meaning referring exclusively to the divinity of Ali. This is evident in *Kitab al-Mashyakha,* where Ali is reported to have said, "God has described me in His precious book and said, 'He is God, beside whom there is no God, the Compassionate, the Merciful, the Holy King, the Creator. Him all things praise in heaven and earth.' Now these attributes belong to Him and are in Him, for it is necessary for Him to describe Himself (because no other being could do so), but they are in me and refer to me, and they are part of my descriptive marks. For when He says, 'He is God,' it refers to me, for I am God."[4]

The Nusayris go a step further by maintaining that the Prophet Muhammad has personally testified to the divinity of Ali. The Nusayri catechism contains the question, "Who called us to the knowledge of our Lord, the Commander of the Faithful?" The answer is, "The Apostle Muhammad (God's prayer be upon him), who in his sermon called *Bay'at al-Dar* said, 'Now hear what I am going to tell you, and never doubt it. I am calling you to Ali Ibn Abi Talib as I call you to God, except that Ali is your master and mine . . . And I call those who follow me to Ali with full understanding. Praise be to God, for I am not one of the polytheists . . . I call you to Ali by his own command. My very state of prophetship is under the dominion of Ali, because he is the one who sent me to you as a prophet. He is the one who created me from the light of his essence. He is my God and your God, my creator and your creator. Him fear and obey; declare his unity; praise, sanctify, and worship him, for there is no God beside him.' "[5]

Kitab al-Mashyakha contains a similar but more detailed testimony by the Prophet Muhammad of the divinity of Ali, related by Salman al-Farisi. Salman states that the Prophet invited him and others of his companions, including Ali, to the house of Umm Salama, one of Muhammad's wives. After the companions assembled, the Prophet told them to be of good cheer, for he had invited them for their own good to hear and mind what he, as their prophet, would tell them. The discourse is very long, so I shall give only excerpts of it.

> The Prophet began by saying, "Do you believe in God most high and in me?" We all [Salman and the companions] said, "We believe in God Most High and in you . . ." "Hear now what I tell you, and beware of doubting what you hear from me. Know that I call you to Ali, son of Abi Talib, as I call you to the great and glorious God. Is not Ali your Lord and mine? I call you to Ali with my eyes open, I and those who follow me. I call you to Ali by his command; take care not to doubt. Is not my office of prophet under the dominion of Ali, because he has sent me as a prophet to you, and because I was created from the light of his essence? Did not Ali teach me the Quran? Has not Ali sent me as an apostle to you? Is not Ali my Lord and your Lord? Is not Ali your God? Then respect him. Is not Ali your framer, your producer, your healer, your witness and lender, your balance, your keeper, your enricher? Then know him, fear him, mind him, and worship him . . . Is not Ali the Lord of the Throne? To him are all things committed. Does not Ali know what is secret and what is open in you? Is not Ali the creator of the heavens and the earth and the lord of the east and the west. There is no God but him. Then take him as your patron. Has not Ali the keys of heaven, giving bountifully and sparingly to whom he pleases, for he is all-powerful? Does not Ali (there is no God but he) quicken and kill? He is your Lord and the Lord of your ancestors. Does not Ali seize all the souls? To him all things tend. Is it not Ali to whom you return? Therefore, hear him and proclaim his unity, and praise him and sanctify him and glorify him, and say there is no God but him. He begat not nor was he begotten, neither he has any equal; neither has he been incarnate in flesh, nor taken to himself a female companion, nor a child. He has no partner in his dominion, nor any to

> protect from contempt. Therefore, magnify him [Quran 17:3]. He appears as *dahir* [outward] in revelation and is concealed in *batin* [inward] in created things. He is the lofty and great one [Quran 2:256]. He is all-powerful and all-knowing, and no one can bear his might or stand in his sight."[6]
>
> Then the Prophet turned to the Commander of the Faithful, Ali, who was sitting on his right hand, and said to him, "I ask you, by the strength of your strength and the might of your glory and the dignity of your Godhead and the greatness of your kingdom—" and before the Lord Muhammad finished his words, the Prince of the Bees (Amir al-Nahl), Ali, disappeared, and there shone upon the assembled companions a great light whose nature could not be comprehended, nor could its vision and end be understood. A swoon came upon the companions from the intensity of its shining, and they saw it, as it were, in a dream. When they saw this shining light, those assembled shouted, "Praise to you, how great is your dignity! We believe in you and believe in your apostle [Muhammad]." And there was not one of them who did not worship and see a vision from the fear and awe which had fallen upon them . . . What manifestation is more evident, and what witness and proof more just than that which is given in this information received from the greatest Lord Muhammad, and which he has manifested to the people of truth and faith [the Nusayris] in making known the unity of our Lord [Ali] and his indication of him, for the greatest of his end and Mana? May God be exalted and his name sanctified.[7]

The books of the Nusayris are replete with similar statements indicating the apotheosis of Ali. One has only to read *Kitab al-Majmu* and the Quddases (masses) incorporated in Sulayman al-Adani's *Kitab al-Bakura* to realize how fully the Nusayris have acknowledged Ali alone as their almighty God. For example, the *Quddas al-Ishara* (Indication Mass) begins thus: "Praise be to God, Ali is the light of men, Ali is the Lord of might. Ali is the cleaver of the grain. Ali is the creator of the breath of life. Ali is the fountain of wisdom. Ali is the key of mercy . . . Ali is the remover of the gate [of the Jewish fortress, Khaybar] . . . Ali is the possessor of this world and the world to come. Ali raised the heavens. Ali spread the earth . . . Ali is the creator of the night and day. Ali is the first and the last. Ali is the ancient of days. Ali is the Imam of Imams. Ali is the light of light. Ali is one. Ali is Abel, Ali is Seth, Ali is Joseph, Ali is Joshua, Ali is Simon Peter, Ali is the Commander of the Faithful. We refer to him [as divine] as former ages referred to him, and as the people who maintained the belief in the oneness of God have indicated the priority of his essence, from the beginning of creation until this time. We refer to him as did our Lord al-Husayn Ibn Hamdam al-Khasibi, his Shaykh Muhammad Ibn Nusayr, and before him Salman al-Farisi, who indicated that the archetypal divinity of Ali was shown by the Lord Muhammad, the veil, in the seven domes from Abel to Haydara Abu Turab [an appellation of Ali]. Know ye, brethren, that your God is eternal, Mana al-Maani, the ancient, the alone, the sublime Ali Ibn Abi Talib, the indivisible, the uncompounded, whom no number comprises, who is neither restricted nor finite, to whom periods and ages bring no change."[8]

The apotheosis of Ali given expression in this mass is contrary to the spirit and letter of Islam, violating both the Quran and the tradition of the Prophet. To Orthodox Muslims, such pronouncements are sheer blasphemies. However, although the Twelver Shiites renounce the Ghulat and their deification of Ali, yet their belief in the eternal preexistence of the Imams, including Ali, and their belief that these Imams are free from human sin strengthens our conviction that the Twelvers are themselves not very far from considering Ali more than mortal.

One appellation given Ali—the Mana—has a special connotation in the theologial system of the Nusayris. As noted in chapter 26 of this book, Ali is the first person of the Nusayri trinity. He is thus called the Mana (Meaning), a term theologically denoting the causal determinant, the primal element, the divine reality, and the meaning of all created things. Their use of the name Mana for Ali, then, illustrates the Nusayri belief that Ali is God, the source and the cause of all things. His *manawiyya* (archetypal divinity), revealed by Muhammad, is the very essence of God. Mana is the name for the Godhead in all its manifestations in relation to the Ism and the Bab, the second and third persons of the trinity. Because this manawiyya cannot be comprehended separately from the Ism, it was necessary that the Ism (Muhammad) become an intermediary to manifest the manawiyya of Ali. As Abu Abd Allah Ibn Harun al-Saigh relates, his master al-Khasibi, in discussing the manawiyya, states that while Ali is Muhammad, the latter is not Ali, because divinity is peculiar only to the Mana (causal determinant), just as heat is peculiar to fire. That is, fire contains heat, but heat does not contain the whole fire. Fire includes light, smoke, and activity, as well as heat, while heat alone does not contain all these elements. Thus, while Ali contains Muhammad and all that is in the Muhammadan dome (period of manifestation), Muhammad does not contain all the divine reality.[9]

The term Mana is not exclusively a Nusayri term. It was used by Baha al-Din al-Muqtana, one of the earliest Druze writers, who said,

"Praise to the Lord God, who is distinguished from all other beings, in that He alone is the Mana of all the divine manifestations." De Sacy, who reproduces this statement, says, "This expression (Mana) is especially sacred with the Ansaireeh [Nusayris] even at the present time; it signifies the divinity concealed under human form."[10]

In their desire to emphasize the divinity of Ali, the Nusayris deny that he was flesh and blood. They believe him to be a luminous appearance. This point is made clear in the catechism, where the question is asked, "If Ali be God, how did he become of the same nature with men?" The answer is, "He did not so become, but took Muhammad as his veil in the period of his transformation and assumed the name of Ali."[11] In other words, Ali was a Ghilaf (sheath) of the deity, and this sheath was concealed in another sheath, Muhammad, the veil.[12]

But if Ali is not considered flesh and blood, how do we account for the fact that in Nusayri writings Ali's human relationships are often detailed? He is spoken of as the only Hashimite on both sides of his family; his brothers—Hamza, Jafar, Talib, and Aqil—are named; his sons—Hasan and Husayn—are named; his daughters—Zaynab and Umm Kulthum—are named; and his tomb near al-Kufa in Iraq is described.[13] The explanation of this apparent contradiction is found in the fourteenth chapter of *Kitab al Majmu,* called *al-Bayt al-Ma'mur.* According to this chapter, Ali's brothers, like Ali himself, are light of light and substance of substance. Ali is far above having brothers, sisters, father, and mother; He is alone, infinite, self-existent. He is hidden yet not enveloped; that is to say, he is hidden by the nature of his divine essence. He is the mystery of the house—the roof, the grounds, and the firm underpinnings; that is, he is all and every one of the members of the house, or family of the Prophet, who with him, form but one divine unity.[14]

The *Kitab al-Haft al-Sharif,* related by al-Mufaddal Ibn Umar al-Jufi of the Imam Jafar al-Sadiq clearly indicates that the Imams, of whom Ali is chief, are not subject to the natural laws of life and death applied to the rest of mankind. According to al-Sadiq, when God desires to manifest an Imam, He sends His spirit into the future Imam, who thus becomes purified of human uncleanness, or sin.[15] According to a Nusayri manuscript acquired by Carsten Niebuhr, the Nusayris apparently believe that Muhammad, and Fatir (Fatima), together with al-Hasan, al-Husayn, and Muhsin (the three sons of Ali by Fatima, Muhsin having died in infancy), form but one unity, and all are Ali.[16] These five constitute the Ahl al-Aba or al-Kisa (family of the Prophet), considered by the extremist Shiite al-Shurayi and his followers to be divine beings.[17] In this respect, the only difference between the Nusayris and al-Shurayi's followers is that the latter count Ali among the five, while the Nusayris count Ali's son Muhsin, who died in infancy, among the five, believing them to be one divine unity denoting Ali.

The Nusayri's belief in the divinity of Ali is further manifested in their use of the many names which in the Bible and the Quran are given only to God. We have already stated that according to Nusayri sources, the Mana, the Ism and the Bab have threefold names: Mathaliyya (figurative), Dhatiyya (essential), and Sifatiyya (attributive). But a careful study of Nusayri sources shows that all these names of the three persons of the Nusayri trinity are given to Ali, and to him alone.

In the seven periods of his manifestation in human form, Ali assumed many names, although he is a single entity. In the introduction to his *Kitab al-Hidaya al-Kubra* (The book of great guidance), the prominent Nusayri teacher al-Khasibi (d. 957) states that this book contains the names of the apostle of Allah (Muhammad) and those of the Commander of the Faithful, Ali Ibn Abi Talib, his wife Fatima, and the Imams from Ali to Muhammad the Mahdi. Al-Khasibi then goes on to say that there are three hundred names for Ali in the Quran, which contradicts the Orthodox Muslims' belief that God has ninety-nine beautiful names. He gives some examples, based on Quran 11:17 and Quran 78:1 to show that Ali is the glad tidings; "Are they to be compared with these who have received a veritable word from their Lord recited by a witness from him?" and, "About what are they asking, about the great tidings (al-Naba al-Azim), the theme of their disputes?"[18] He further states that Ali's name appears in the Books of Seth, Idris (Enoch), Noah, and Ibrahim (Abraham), books which are most certainly apocryphal. In Syriac, his name is Mubin (Evident); in Hebrew, he is called Hayula (Primordial Matter), al-Amin (Faithful), Thabat (Firmness in Faith), Bayan (Divine Eloquence), Yaqin (Indisputable Truth), and Iman (Faith).

Al-Khasibi also asserts that Ali is called Elias in the Torah, and Ariah in the Psalms; that the Zanj (Black Africans) call him Habina, a distortion of Abuna, the title of the Ethiopian Metropolitan; that the Abyssinians call him Tabrik (a distortion of Batrik, or Patriarch). In Arabic he is called Haydara (lion) because he used to knock down his older brothers in their fights with him. He is also nicknamed Abu al-Hasan and al-Husayn; Abu Shibr and Abu Shabir (the sons of Aaron in Islamic tradition); Abu Turab (a nickname given to him by the Prophet); Abu al-Nur (father of light); and Abu al-Aimma (father of the Imams).[19]

So far this list of names is only slightly different from the one given in *Kitah al-Mashyakha*.[20] But further on, al-Khasibi gives other names of

Ali, some of which are current both among the Nusayris and among mainstream Shiites. Ali is called, for example, the Dividing Line between Paradise and the Fires of Hell, the Judge of Religion, the Fulfiller, the Promise, the Great Destroyer of Jinn, the Dispeller of Sorrow, the Ship of Safety, and the Firm Foundation who forever appears new in God.[21]

Al-Khasibi also gives Ali the epithet of Amir al-Nahl (Prince of Bees, i.e., of the [Shiite] believers), a name peculiar to the Nusayris and the one most constantly used in their books. The Nusayris base this appellation on a tradition related by Jafar al-Sadiq of the Prophet Muhammad, who reportedly said, "The believer is like the bee, it sucks nectar and produces honey."[22] This is echoed in Quran 16:68, "And your Lord has revealed to the bees." In these cases, "the bees" are interpreted by the Nusayris to mean the believers.

In the Nusayri catechism, we find still more names given to Ali along with a few already cited by al-Khasibi. These names were given to Ali by many peoples including the Arabs, Hebrews, Hindus, Africans, Armenians, Daylamites (inhabitants of the mountain region south of the Caspian Sea), and even beings believed by Nusayris to have pre-existed Adam.[23] Obviously, what al-Khasibi and the author of the catechism intended is to establish the universal recognition of Ali as God of all nations in conformity with the Nusayris' belief of the apotheosis of Ali.

Through a linguistic manipulation of the term Ali, which literally means "high," the author of *Kitab al-Usus* states that the term Ali means "Most High," above every name and triumphant over every name.[24] Obviously, the intention of the author is to ascribe divine attributes to the name Ali, which was and still is commonly used by Muslims and non-Muslims alike, with no spiritual connotations.

According to Dussaud, the Nusayris call Ali Ali Allah (God-Ali), recalling the name of another extremist sect, the Ali Ilahis or Allahis, and the name Ali al-Ala (Ali the Most High).[25] Dussaud does not mention any Nusayri sources for the name Ali al-Ala; rather, he refers to de Sacy, who states that this name was used in a Druze text dealing with the manifestation of the divinity in human form.[26] Dussaud then proceeds to offer an etymological explanation for this name. He does not believe that it is of Arabic origin, because if it were, it would be written Ali Taala, which is the name of God meaning Most High in Arabic. Dussaud conjectures that the name Ali al-Ala instead derives from the old divine epithet El-Elioun, which is equivalent to the Greek Zeus Ophistos, and the Phoenician god known by the Greeks as Adonis.[27] I find Dussaud's reasoning unconvincing, however. The name Ali al-Ala is used by Jafar al-Sadiq in *Kitab al-Haft al-Sharif*, page 147, in reference to God. Al-Ala is certainly an authentic Arab term and forms the title of Sura 87 of the Quran.

A study of the Nusayris' religious system reveals the existence of deep-rooted Persian elements which give the Persians a prominent place in the divine economy of the cult of Ali. This is a vital point because Ali was an Arab, a pure Hashimite like his blood cousin, the Prophet Muhammad, and most likely had nothing to do with the Persians or their kings. Yet he is called by the Nusayris the Crown of Kisras, from Khosraw (Chosroes), as the Sassani kings of Persia were called by the Arabs.[28] Among the figurative (mathaliyya) names given to Ali from Adam to Muhammad the Mahdi, we find the names of two Persian kings, Ardashir and Sapor.[29]

The seven appearances of the deity from Abel to Ali are said to have taken place in seven domes or periods, including the period of Abraham, the Arab period, the period of Muhammad and the Persian period, in which Ali manifested himself.[30] In Persian books Ali is called Numayr, the word for fire.[31] This is an indication that Ali is connected with the Persian worship of fire, as shall be seen shortly.

The association of Ali with the Persian kings is more than fortuitous. It is the result of a deliberate attempt by Nusayri writers to project, through Ali, the supremacy of the Persians over the Arabs, by maintaining that the Persian kings were the medium through whom Ali, his Name, and his Door were manifested in the world of light. This is indicated by al-Tabarani in his *Kitab Majmu al-A'yad* (Book of feasts) when he discusses the celebration of the festival of Nawruz (the New Day), which begins the Persian New Year. Al-Tabarani states: "The Lord (Ali, may he be glorified!) manifested himself in the person of the Persian kings, and it is in them that he effected the manifestation of his Names, his doors, and his sacred hierarchies, which constitute the great world of light."

Al-Tabarani then goes on to say, "Our Lord al-Khasibi (may God sanctify his soul) has explained this point in one of his treatises called *Risala fi al-Siyaqa*."[32]

In this *Risala,* al-Khasibi discusses the manifestations of Ali since Adam in different periods, especially the Persian period. He states that in this period, Ali (who was also Adam) manifested himself in the person of Ardashir, son of Babek, the first of the Persian Sassani kings of the line of Khosraw (Chosroes), the Sassani kings, and then manifested himself in the person of Sapor, son of Ardashir. Afterwards, Ali manifested himself among the Arabs in the person of Luay, son of Kilab (an ancestor of the Prophet Muhammad and of his cousin, Ali). Luay, al-Khasibi explains, means "he who turns," signifying that he turned the light from the land of the Persians to the land of the Hijaz, where the Mana, the Ism, and the Bab were manifested.

Al-Khasibi further explains that when the divinity (Ali) left the Persians to manifest himself among the Arabs, he delegated to the Persians the *maqamat* (stations) of his wisdom, to be transmitted successively to their kings, whom he designated as the personifications of the Mana, the Ism, and the Bab. However, a change took place in the time of Kisra [Khosraw, or Chosroes] Anushirwan; because of pride, he disobeyed the Lord Muhammad, and through his disobedience, the Persians lost their royalty.[34]

What al-Khasibi means is that the Persian kings were the personification of the divine religion, manifested from the time of Adam in Ali. But when Ali manifested himself in the period of Muhammad, which ushered in the religion of Islam, whose source is Ali, the religious light was transferred through Ali from the Persians to the Arabs. The Persian king, Anushirwan, disobeyed the new revelation and consequently lost his dominion to the Arabs. However, al-Khasibi attempts to minimize the Persians' loss of supremacy to the Arabs by stating that they continued to observe the festivals of the Nawruz and Mihrajan, which had been instituted by their kings, just as the Arabs celebrate the three festivals of Id al-Fitr, Id al-Adha, and Id al-Ghadir, instituted by the Lord Muhammad. All of these festivals, then, will be celebrated until the future manifestation of the Qaim bi al-Amr, the last Imam (the Mahdi).[35] This must mean that the Persians were foremost in the divine manifestation of Ali, his Ism, and his Bab, and never lost their spiritual position, even after Ali manifested himself among the Arabs in the Muhammadan period, and that the Persians continued the tradition of the divine Ali through the celebration of their pagan festivals, which became the counterpart to the Islamic festivals instituted by Muhammad. This argument by al-Khasibi becomes pointless, however, when we realize that Id al-Ghadir was not instituted by Muhammad, and that its observance corroborates the Shiites' claim that the Prophet appointed Ali as his successor at Ghadir Khumm.

In a special chapter of his *Risala fi al-Siyaqa,* al-Khasibi shows the supreme spiritual wisdom and position of the Persian kings, whom he considers the manifestations of the Nusayri trinity, the Mana, the Ism, and the Bab. He ascribes great honor to the Persians because the Bab (Salman) was Persian and the wisdom he possessed derives from the Persians. Furthermore, this Persian Bab, together with the other two persons of the trinity, the Mana and the Ism, was manifested in two maqamat (stations) of the first two Sassani Persian kings, Aradashir, son of Babek, and Ardashir's son Sapor. Al-Khasibi asserts that through these manifestations the Persian kings received divine wisdom, which was transmitted in an unbroken line to the last three kings, whom al-Khasibi calls Sharwin, Kharwin, and Khosraw. He goes on to say that through this manifestation, these kings too, came to occupy the place of the Mana, the Ism, and the Bab, because they were the servants of the Mana (Ali) and possessed full knowledge of him. This is indeed a very significant statement. Al-Khasibi means here that the Nusayri trinity, which is the essence of the Nusayri religion, has become a symbol of Persianism because the Bab (Salman) is Persian. Al-Khasibi also implies that divine wisdom and revelation are not the possession of the Arabs exclusively, but of the Persians too. Al-Khasibi concludes that on quitting the Persians, the Lord (Ali) deposited his wisdom with them, promising to return.[36]

While al-Khasibi seems in error in making these three Persian kings "the last trinity," his intention is quite clearly to show that these Persian kings are the embodiment of the three persons of the Nusayri trinity. In other words, they are Ali, Muhammad, and Salman the Persian, which means that the Persians are as much part of the divine economy of the god Ali as the Arabs are. At the same time, al-Khasibi establishes the spiritual supremacy of the Persians over the Arabs by asserting that the Arabs (and here he most likely means Sunnite Muslims) have lost the divine mystery, while the Persians preserved it: "The Most High [Ali] deposited his wisdom with the Persians and then left, being pleased with them. He promised to return to them. He is the one who said that God Almighty has deposited His mystery with you [the Arabs], manifested Himself amongst you, and destined you to receive it. But you have lost it while the Persians have preserved it even after its disappearance, by means of fire and light, in which He manifested Himself."[37]

Thus, the religious system of the Persians, based on their worship of fire and light, becomes the forerunner of the revelation of Muhammad. This statement becomes even more important when we realize that in the treatise of *Fiqh* (Jurisprudence), mentioned by al-Tabarani, "The Persians have sanctified fire, from which they await the manifestation of the deity. This manifestation will take place among the Persians, for they never cease to keep lighted the fire from which they await this same manifestation, and the accomplishment of the promise of the deity in that event." Since the divinity manifested itself in the form of Ali, Ali becomes the personification of fire and the god of the Persians, not the Arabs. The Arabs, al-Khasibi states, lost their spiritual privileges when they refused to believe in the divine mystery of Ali while the Persians preserved it. This mystery is the manifestation of Ali in fire and light, which al-Khasibi likens to the fire of the burning bush which Moses saw when speaking to God.[38]

Al-Tabarani then cites a tradition related by al-Mufaddal Ibn Umar al-Jufi of the Imam Jafar al-Sadiq, who is reported to have said, "The Mana [Ali] manifested himself in the time of the Persians twice each year, at the time of the change from cold to heat, and from heat to cold. The change from cold to heat was called Nawruz, and that from heat to cold was called Mihrajan. These two days are held sacred by the Persians because the Mana manifested himself in transmigration among them."[39]

The spiritual supremacy of the Persians over the Arabs is also maintained in *Kitab Ta'lim al-Diyana al-Nusayriyya,* in connection with the celebration of the Nawruz. Question ninety, about the nature of the Nawruz, is answered in a poem by al-Khasibi, who states that the Nawruz is the truth established by the authority of the most noble Hashimite. It is the day on which God [Ali] manifested himself in the periods of the Persians before he did so in the periods of the Arabs and raised these periods of the Persians to high heaven.[40] We shall give a full translation of this poem in the discussion of the celebration of the Quddas.

The several passages cited above reveal many Persian elements in the religious system of the Nusayris. As Rev. Samuel Lyde has rightly observed, they contain "wild conceits which are probably due to some Persian." Lyde goes on to say that these passages are contained in a section of *Kitab al-Mashyakha* entitled, "The Traditionary Sayings of [the Persian] Abu Ali of Basra, in his Dwelling in Shiraz in the year of the Hijra 327 [A.D. 938]"[41]

The fact that these passages glorify the Persians over the Arabs convinces us of the Persian origin of the Nusayris and their religious system. As Abd al-Husayn Mahdi al-Askari rightly observes, these passages betray "the Nusayri partisanship toward the Persians and indicate the hatred (Shuubiyya) which non-Arabs, especially the Persians, harbor toward the Arabs."[42] Such hatred is also observed by Sulayman al-Adani, who states, "No member of any Arab sect is admitted into their [the Nusayris] fraternities for the first time unless he be of the Ajam [Persians], because, like the Nusayris, the Persians believe in the divinity of Ali Ibn Abi Talib, and without doubt, their progenitors were from Persia and Iraq."[43] Al-Adani seems to be correct, because the founder of the Nusayri sect, Muhammad Ibn Nusayr was of Persian origin.

The Persian element is most conspicuous in the association of light and fire with the manifestation of the deity. Light and fire constitute an essential part of the ancient Persian religious system. We have already seen in the description of the merits of the Nawruz that upon leaving the Persians to manifest himself among the Arabs, the deity deposited his wisdom with the Persians and promised to return to them. According to al-Khasibi, God, as Ali, then deposited his mystery [his manifestation as God] with the Arabs and ordered them to preserve it, but they failed to do so. After the deity left the Persians, however, they perpetuated his manifestation through their sanctification of light and fire, from which they awaited the manifestation of the deity.[44] This manifestation, according to *Risalat al-Fiqh,* will take place among the Persians because they do not cease to keep lighted the fire from which they look for this manifestation and the accomplishment of the promises made by the deity during his appearance.[45]

We have summarized these passages in order to show the lengths to which the Nusayri writers went in order to appropriate Ali as the manifestation of God and make his manifestation an "exclusively Persian" privilege, associated with the worship of light and fire, which are part of the Persian tradition. The Nusayri writers, who are mostly of Persian origin, have Persianized Ali as a divinity to allow the Persians to boast to the Arabs that the Arab Hashimite Ali had become a "Persian" deity, whom the Arabs had lost because they were not worthy of him. Making Ali a Persian deity also offered the Persians the opportunity to boast that, although the Arabs, have Muhammad as their Prophet, the Persians have their God, Ali, who created Muhammad from the light of his essence. Hence, the Persians and the Nusayris can claim spiritual superiority over the Arabs.

28

The Nusayris Concept of Light
Shamsis and Qamaris

Reverence for light forms an essential part of the Nusayri religious system. Among the Nusayris, light is symbolized by the sun, considered the light of light. This light, according to *Kitab Ta'lim al-Diyana al-Nusayriyya,* is the mystery of God. It is the ancient Mana [Ali], who was veiled by the light. The sun is the light of light because it is the abode of the eternal, the everlasting, the mystery of mysteries, and Ali, who is veiled in the light which is the eye of the sun from which he shall appear again. Thus, the sun is the Qibla (holy place) toward which the Nusayri believer (Ahl al-Wala) should turn his face when he prays.[1]

It should be pointed out that there is dissension among the Nusayris over the connection of the sun with the adoration of their God Ali. They are divided by this question into two groups, the Shamsis, whose name is taken from Shams (sun), and the Qamaris, whose name derives from Qamar (moon). The Shamsis are also called Mawakhisa, Ghaybis, or (most often) Shamalis (from Shamal, whose connotation shall be explained later), and the Qamaris are known as Kalazis. The Shamsis are the original and oldest people of the mountains, while the Qamaris came from the east, from Jabal Sinjar (Sinjar Mountain) in northern Iraq in the thirteenth century, led by Hasan al-Makzun.[2]

The Shamsis and the Qamaris disagree over whether Ali and Muhammad should be associated with the sun or with the moon, and this disagreement causes a great deal of confusion. The Shamsis believe that Ali is the source of the morning sun, and that the sun is his abode. It is also their belief that Ali is the creator of the luminous full moon. Therefore, the sun, as the abode of the creator, should be reverenced in greater measure than the moon, a created object. The Qamaris, who reverence the moon, answer that Ali created the moon as a place to live, just as man builds a house to live in. They claim that the black spots which appear on the moon are the personification of the worshipped [Ali], who has a body, arms, and legs, and who wears a crown on his head and carries a sword named Dhu al-Faqar.[3]

To prove they are correct in honoring the moon, the Qamaris cite the eleventh chapter of *Kitab al-Majmu,* which states that Ali shall appear out of the eye of the sun. Commenting on this chapter, Sulayman al-Adani states that the Qamaris claim that the appearance of Ali out of the eye of the sun (Ayn al-Shams) must mean that the moon's light issues forth from the sun.[4]

Al-Adani further comments that those who worship the twilight (he does not identify them) believe that it comes from the eye of the sun, while at the same time they maintain that the reddening of the sky at twilight results in the appearance of the sun. The Shamsis' answer to this assertion is that the sun in this context is only a symbol for Fatima bint Asad, Ali's mother, and the other Fatima, daughter of the Prophet and wife of Ali, who are closely connected with the expressed deity, that is, Muhammad, who they maintain is symbolized by the sun.[5]

Al-Adani goes on to say that, based on the fourteenth chapter of *Kitab al-Majmu,* called al-Bayt al-Mamur, the Nusayris all agree that Muhammad is the sun, and disagree only regarding the Mana and the Bab. While the Qamaris believe that the moon is the Mana (Ali), the Shamsis hold that the moon is the Bab (Salman al-Farisi). In other words, the Shamsis recognize the divinity of the sun under the name of Muhammad; as the abode of Ali, the sun also represents Muhammad. What this really means is that the Shamalis believe that in their association with the sun, Ali and Muhammad are the same deity. Such a belief is expressed in the seventh chapter, called al-Salam (Salutation).

While the Shamsis believe in the divinity of Muhammad, the elect, the Qamaris maintain the divinity of Ali. The Qamaris assert that the Shamsis have fallen into error by ascribing divinity to Muhammad and Ali indiscriminately. The Shamsis reply that Muhammad and Ali are allied, not opposed. While Ali is the First Cause (al-Ghaya al-Kubra), they say, Muhammad is also a creator, and it is not an error to believe in Muhammad's divinity: the Shamsis and the Qamaris share the same doctrine of the trinity.[6] The Shamsis also cite the fifth chapter of *Kitab al-Majmu*, entitled al-Fath (the victory), to demonstrate that Ali and Muhammad are one in their divinity. According to this chapter, Ali created Muhammad out of the light of his essence and called him his Ism (name), his self, his throne, his seat, and his attribute. Muhammad is thus united with Ali as the sun's rays are to its disk.[7] Whatever their reasoning, there is evidence that the Qamaris pray to the sun and the moon because they are very much afraid of them. It is also common among their women and children to consider the moon the face of Ali, and the sun the face of Muhammad.[8]

Another point of difference between the Shamsis and the Qamaris is that while the former believe that heaven is the Mana (Ali) and the moon is the Bab (Salman al-Farisi), the latter believe that the moon is heaven.[9] The Shamsis' apparent identification of Ali with heaven (the sky) was a matter for reproach, according to an ancient Druze source.[10]

Where did the Nusayris get these beliefs, which are certainly neither Biblical nor Islamic? Chapter 13 (of *Kitab al-Majmu*), entitled *al-Musafara* (the journey), offers a clue but not much detail. In it, we read about the mystery of Lord Abu Abd Allah (al-Khasibi) and his elect children, drinkers from the sea of AMS (the trinity of Ali, Muhammad and Salman), who are fifty-one in number. Of these, seventeen were from Iraq, seventeen from Syria, and seventeen of unknown origin, all stationed at the gate of the city of Harran.[11]

Commenting on this chapter, al-Adani states that whenever a city was mentioned in the Nusayris' secret books, they interpreted it figuratively as signifying the heavens and supposed that its inhabitants were the stars. So it is with the city of Harran, at whose gates stand the fifty-one disciples of al-Khasibi, believed to be stars of the order of the small spirit world.[12] This explanation by al-Adani of the Nusayri interpretation of this chapter may shed a revealing light on the source of many of the astral beliefs of the Nusayris. We are indebted to René Dussaud, who traced a connection between some of these beliefs and the astral cult of Harran, to which he traced the origin of the name Shamalis (a common name for the Shamsis).[13]

The Harranians are an Aramaic people who, like the ancient people of Syria, spoke the Aramaic-Syriac language. During the Muslim period, they came to be known as Sabeans, a name by which they are still known today. Their earlier name derives from their city, Harran, situated on a tributary of the Euphrates in upper Mesopotamia. It is the place in which Terah, Abraham's father, settled with his household after leaving his house in Ur, in the southern part of present-day Iraq (Genesis 11:31–32). The Sabeans were not confined to the city of Harran alone, however. They spread all over Syria, including the area inhabited by the Nusayris. In the tenth century, there were Sabeans living in Baalbak and Hierapolis (Manbij).[14]

Daniel Chwolsohn maintains that these Sabeans were a remnant of the Hellenized pagans of Syria.[15] Their religion was based on worship of the sun, the moon, and five planets. In his *Fihrist,* Abu al-Faraj Muhammad Ibn Ishaq, known as Ibn al-Nadim (d. 995), devotes several pages to the religion and festivals of the Sabeans of Harran, reproduced from earlier sources. He quotes a report by Ahmad Ibn al-Tayyib (al-Sarakhsi) of the account of the Arab philosopher al-Kindi (d. 873), indicating that the Sabeans worship the sun at its rising and setting. Ibn al-Nadim also quotes another, writer, Said Wahb Ibn Ibrahim al-Nasrani (the Christian), who states that the Harranians offer sacrifices every day of the week to a certain god. One of these gods is the sun god, Helios, to whom they offer sacrifice on Sunday. Another is a moon god, Sin, to whom they offer sacrifice on Monday.[16] The Harranians also recognize five principles, as did the Neo-Platonists, the Gnostics, the Cabbalists, and, later, the Ismailis.[17]

Ibn al-Nadim's account of the Sabeans' religious practices is of the utmost importance to our subject. On several occasions throughout the year, he says, the Harranians would fast, pray,and celebrate a mystery (a kind of sacrament), offering sacrifices to their gods, including the god Shamal (Chief of the Jinn and their greatest god). They observed the birth of their lord, the moon on 24 January and celebrated for Shamal, offering sacrifices. In February, they fasted seven days for their great god of good, the sun; for the rest of the month, they would pray only to Shamal, the Jinn, and devils. On the first day of May, they celebrated the sacrificial mystery for Shamal, and on 27 June, they celebrated the same sacrament in honor of the god Shamal, to Jinn, and devils. On 8 August, they would sacrifice a newborn infant, mix his flesh with flour and spices, and bake it in a new oven, as a mystery for the people of Shamal. In September, the Harranians would bathe in boiled water as part of a celebration of the mystery of Shamal. They would also offer eight sheep, seven for their gods and one for the god Shamal. On the twenty-seventh and twenty-eighth of the same month, they would hold many celebrations of sacraments, offering sacrifices and oblations to Shamal and to the devils and the Jinn, who protect them and bring them good luck.[18]

It is quite important to note that, according to Ibn al-Nadim's account, the feasts, fasting, prayer, and sacrificial offerings to the god Shamal are often associated with the sun cult and the seven planet gods of the Harranians. Most of these celebrations take place shortly before sunrise. For example, on 26 September, after they have offered sacrifices to Shamal, the Harranians climb the mountain to receive the sun.[19] Thus, in the lists of feasts, we find the same characteristics attributed to both Shamal and sun god, "the greatest god."[20] Does this mean that the

Shamsis derive their more common name of Shamalis and some of their religious practices from the ancient solar cult of Harran?

It is true that the word Shamalis means "northerners" (from Shamal, "north"), but these Nusayris are not called Shamalis because they live in the northern part of their country. If this were the case, then the Nusayris who live in the south (Janub) of that country should be called Janubis; no such name appears in the Nusayri books or tradition. Rev. Samuel Lyde, who lived for many years among the Nusayris, observed that the Shamalis are not confined to the northern part of the country, as the name suggests, but are dispersed throughout the land, some living even in the extreme south, near Mount Hermon.[21] In fact, the only time the word Shamal, here meaning "left," is used in *Kitab al-Majmu* is to distinguish Abu Dharr al-Ghifari from al-Miqdad, who is called the Yamin (righthand side). Although Abu Dharr and al-Miqdad are considered by the Nusayris to be two of the five Aytam (incomparables) created by Salman al-Farisi,[22] the word Shamal, as used in this context, does not appear to have any religious connotation; even if it does, we are forced to speculate that the term derives from the Harranian cult, for otherwise, characterizing these men as Shamal (left) and Yamin (right) makes no sense.

We need not elaborate on this point any more. The few examples cited clearly show the correlation between the Nusayris' cult and that of Harran.[30] The Nusayri conception of God does not differ greatly from that of the Harranians, to whom God was unique in essence, but multiple in his manifestations as the seven heavenly bodies governing the world.[31]

29

The Nusayri "Trinity"

Ali, Muhammad, and Salman al-Farisi

As noted in chapter 26, the Nusayri trinity comprises the Mana (Ali), the Ism (Muhammad), and the Bab (Salman al-Farisi). The position of Ali in this trinity was discussed in chapter 27; here we shall discuss the positions of its other two members.

The second person of the Nusayri trinity is the Ism, Muhammad, whose manifestations took place in the period of Ali, considered the consummate period of the seven manifestations of God. The first appearance of the Ism in human form was Adam, and the last was Muhammad. The Shamalis consider Muhammad, as the Ism, to be their Lord, yet he occupies a position secondary to that of Ali. It was Ali, as God, who created Muhammad from the light of his essence and taught him the Quran. Ali made Muhammad a light, extracted from the essence of his meaning; he called him by his name Muhammad, and elected him. He said to him, "Be the cause of causes, and the framer of the Bab (door) and the Hijab (veil).[1] The phrase "cause of causes" suggests that the office of Muhammad as the Ism is like that of a demiurge, through whom God [Ali] created the worlds, and to whom He entrusted the administration of the universe.[2] In a way, Muhammad occupies the same position as the Logos in Christianity. Yet, unlike the Logos, who is begotten, not made, and who is of one substance with the Father, Muhammad, as stated in *Kitab al-Mashyakha,* is the "best of created beings."[3]

The Nusayri catechism lists many names under which Muhammad appeared. Some indicate the divine attributes of Muhammad, and others are merely abstract names. Among the divine names listed are the mysterious "Madd al-Madd" in the Torah, the "Redeemer" in the Zabur (psalms), the "Paraclete" in the gospels (the Holy Spirit is known by this name in the New Testament), and Muhammad in the Quran. The most important abstract names given Muhammad are "Will," "Perception," and "Might."[4]

The Ism is also the Hijba (veil, or intermediary) through whom the God Ali revealed himself to mankind. It is the Ism who veils the brightness of their God from the eyes of human beings. The Hijab is frequently mentioned and elaborated on in Nusayri writings in association with the deity.[5] Question 4 of the catechism asks, "If Ali is God, how did he take man's nature?" The answer is, "He did not take it, but he veiled himself in the period of his change of forms and took the name of Ali."[6] This means that the divinity of Ali is so bright that no mortal can look at it directly, without a veil. Thus, Muhammad became the veil of the God, Ali, in whom Ali was concealed and through whom He manifested Himself to mankind.[7]

According to al-Khasibi, God is inwardly Muhammad, and Muhammad is outwardly God. God represents the power of the divinity, and Muhammad, the weakness of humanity. For this reason men are allowed to be named Muhammad or Ali, but no one is permitted to be named God.[8] As al-Nashshabi explains in his *Munazara,* Muhammad and Ali are but two mortal names of the Godhead; the God, Mana, revealed His essence to no one but Muhammad, and Muhammad was the only one worthy to be the veil of God.[9]

In *Risalat al-Tawhid* (Treatise on the unity of God), as related by the Nusayri writer Ali Ibn Isa al-Jisri, a disciple of al-Khasibi, there is a tradition in which the Prophet Muhammad reportedly said, "I am from Ali and Ali is from me," meaning that Muhammad is Ali's name, spirit, soul, and word. In essence, the Mana is one, the Ism is one, and the Bab is one, no matter how their names and attributes change. The Mana, the Ism, and the Bab are one.[10]

Muhammad is the pathway that leads to Ali, in accordance with the sayings, "No one knows God except God Himself," "God can only be known by God Himself," and "No one can indicate God except he who is for God."[11] In summation, when Ali as the divine Mana wanted to call mankind to himself, he inspired and guided the people through Muhammad, who became the intermediary between God and man.[12] Whatever Muhammad's position in the religious system of the Nusayris, they believe Ali and only Ali to be worthy of their adoration.

The third person of the Nusayri trinity is the Bab. In the time of Adam, the Bab was the angel Gabriel, and in the time of Ali, Salman al-Farisi (the Persian). In the third Nusayri (mass), entitled Quddas al-Adhan (call to prayer) is the statement, "I testify that there is no God but

Ali, the Prince of Bees, with the bald forehead, the adorable, and no Hijab but Lord Muhammad, the unsurpassed, the all-glorious, the august, the worthy-to-be-praised, and no Bab but Lord Salman al-Farisi, the pattern." In this same mass, Salman is also called "God's noble Bab, whereby alone one comes to God," and "Salsal, Salsabil." (Both these words mean sweet water. The latter is believed by Muslims to refer to the Spring of Sweet Water in Paradise.)[13] In another source, the same Salman is called not only Salsal and Salsabil, but Gabriel. (Divine Guidance and Indubitable Truth); it is even said, "He is truly the Lord of all worlds."[14]

As we have already indicated, Massignon seems to believe that Salsal derives from silsila (chain, or link) and is applied to Salman, who is considered the "lost link" between Muhammad and Ali. He also quotes a Druze source to show that the Druzes consider Salman the silsila (chain) of the Aqsa Mosque, at which people make their oaths.[15]

But why should a man from far-away Persia, whose history and personality are shrouded in mystery, occupy such a prominent position in Islamic tradition and serve as a link between the Prophet of Islam and Ali? Salman al-Farisi (the Persian) has been and still is a subject of controversy in the history of Islamic tradition.

In the accounts he published between 1909 and 1913, Clement Huart denied the historical existence of Salman al-Farisi, although he admitted that there was a Salman present at the Battle of the Khandaq (ditch), fought by the Prophet of Islam in 627 against the Meccan confederate tribes (Ahzab).[16]

In 1922, Josef Horovitz attempted to establish that a tradition in which Salman al-Farisi advised the Prophet to have a ditch dug to halt the advance of the attacking Meccan tribes is nothing but a fable created by Muslim writers to embellish the victory of the Muslims over the Meccans and make this Salman the Persian, about whom nothing is known, a Persian engineer and Mazdakian convert to Islam who became the private counselor of Muhammad. Massignon, who disagrees with this opinion, tries to demonstrate that Salman al-Farisi was a true historical figure. He bases his analysis and conclusion on early Islamic sources, from Abu Ishaq al-Subayi and Ismail al-Suddi (both of whom died in 127/744) to Ali Ibn Mehzayar (d. 210/825).[17]

According to these sources, Salman was born to a noble Persian family and was raised in the Mazdakian religion, an offshoot of Zoroastrianism. He is identified as either Mabah, son of Budkhashan, or Rawzabah, son of Marzaban. While on a hunting trip, he passed a Christian monastery, where he heard the chanting of hymns and prayers and became fascinated with Christian worship. He converted to Christianity and decided to live a pious life, abstaining from drinking wine and eating the flesh of animals slaughtered by the Mazdakians.[18] Salman traveled from city to city, stopping at Hims, Damascus, Jerusalem, Mosul, Nisibin, Antioch, Amuriya, and Alexandria in Egypt, always staying with the people of Zuhd (piety). While in Alexandria, he learned that the imminent appearance of a prophet was expected in Arabia. Leaving Alexandria to meet the new prophet, he was betrayed by his guides, who sold him to some Arabians, who in turn sold him to a Jew named Uthman al-Ashhal, of the Qurayza tribe. (Some sources say he was sold as a slave to either a Jewish or an Arabian woman.) Eventually, Salman heard of Muhammad and went to Mecca to look for him, believing that he was the new prophet. When he saw Muhammad, he searched his body and saw the sign of his prophetship in the form of a fleshy growth on his right shoulder. Upon recognizing Muhammad as the newly-sent Prophet of God, Salman converted to Islam. He was emancipated and became the first Persian convert to Islam, and the Prophet called him Salman.[19]

The improbability of this story notwithstanding, Salman occupies a prominent position in the early history of Islam. His wisdom, piety, and knowledge of the religions of Persia and of Christianity were undoubtedly assets to the new Prophet Muhammad and his small band of followers. This wisdom was manifested when he advised the Prophet to dig a ditch to foil the attack of the Meccans against Medina. His advice must have been well-received, for both the Muslims of Medina (the Supporters) and the Muslims of Mecca (the Immigrants) claimed Salman as one of their own. The Prophet solved the problem by proclaiming Salman a member of the family of the Prophet; hence the tradition, "Salman minna Ahl al-Bayt," meaning Salman is counted as a member of the Prophet's family.[20]

Salman's close relationship with the Prophet and his religious knowledge must have caused the Arab pagans of Mecca to accuse Salman of teaching the Quran to Muhammad, but God refutes their allegation in Quran 16:103: "The tongue of him they wickedly point to is notably A'jami [foreign], while this is Arabic, pure and clear."[21] An early commentator on the Quran, al-Dahhak Ibn Muzahim (d. 105/723), states that the Ajami in this Quran verse is none other than Salman. Al-Dahhak asserts that Salman assisted the Prophet by acquainting him with the earlier religious books from which the Prophet derived the Quran.

The Ismailis go a step further, maintaining that Salman delivered the whole Quran to Muhammad, and that the Angel Gabriel, through whom God revealed the Quran to Muhammad, was none other than

Salman, who carried this divine revelation.[22] Thus, from the earliest period of Islam, Salman was considered a pious Muslim who possessed al-Ilm al-Laduni (knowledge imparted directly by God through mystic intuition). Because of this knowledge, and because he is counted as a member of Ahl al-Bayt, we can understand the prominent position of Salman in the traditions of Islam. This is attested to by Ali, who likened Salman to the Quranic figure Luqman the Sage, affirming that he was "one of us [the family of the Prophet] who has known the first and the last Ilm [divine knowledge], and read the first and last books. He is an inexhaustible sea."[23]

Salman was not only a pious Zahid convert to Islam, a favorite companion and advisor of the Prophet, and a member of Ahl al-Bayt, but also one of the pioneer Muslims (Ahl al-Suffa) who were the Shia (partisans) of Ali. These included Ammar Ibn Yasir, Abu Dharr al-Ghifari, al-Miqdad Ibn al-Aswad, and others who saw in Ali the worthiest Muslim to be the heir of the Prophet. Recognized for their piety, humility, selflessness, and devoted to Islam as a sublime spiritual movement opposed to the materialistic extravagance of the Quraysh (the enemies of the Prophet), they supported Ali as the champion of the weak, the poor, and the helpless. Thus, Shiism began in the time of the Prophet as a spiritual movement whose champions were Ali and the companions who supported him.[24]

To the Shiites, Salman is probably the most important figure after Ali. Not only was he known as one of the Shiites (partisans) of Ali and a member of Ahl al-Bayt, but he was also the first to defend Ali's right to succeed the Prophet, a right considered by the Shiites to be the foundation of the imamate. It is also reported that while in Kufa, Iraq, the headquarters of Ali, Salman formed an alliance with the tribe of the Banu Abd al-Qays and was able to win their support, together with that of their allies of al-Hamra, for Ali's right to succeed the Prophet.[25]

Other early Muslims maintain the divine origin of the imamate of Ali, considering it to be as one with the imamate of Adam. Thus, we find Sasaa Ibn Sawhan in the year 33/653 in the presence of Muawiya, the enemy of Ali, undauntedly proclaiming that the imamate of Ali and that of Adam are one, meaning that both derive from the same divine origin (cf. Quran 2:28, where God appointed Adam as Khalifa [Imam]).[26]

The relation of Salman with Ali was so strong that Salman became the most trusted witness of Ali's excellences. He is reported to have told the Muslims, "If I tell you everything of what I know about the excellences of the Commander of the Faithful [Ali], peace be upon him, some of you would say he is insane. Others would say, 'May God forgive the one who would kill Salman.' "[27] The "excellences" of Ali, in this context, are his exclusive spiritual traits and the divine knowledge he received from the Prophet, which, the Shiites believe, made him the worthiest successor of the Prophet.

From the time of Muhammad, Salman was associated with other companions of the Prophet who figure greatly in the religious system of the Nusayris. These Aytam (incomparables) as the Nusayris call them, were the first Shiites (supporters of Ali). According to one tradition, the Prophet said, "Paradise longs to meet four: Ali, Ammar, Salman, and al-Miqdad."[28] These supporters of Ali are so important that the Shiites chose four men whom they called Nuqaba and later Arkan (pillars), namely, Salman, Abu Dharr, al-Miqdad Ibn al-Aswad, and Hudhayfa Ibn al-Yaman. They, so Ali Ibn Ibrahim (al-Qummi) maintains, are the ones referred to in the Quran verse: "The true believers are those whose hearts are filled with awe at the mention of God. . . . They are those who put their trust in their Lord, pray steadfastly, and bestow the alms which we have given them" (Quran 8:2).[29] As shall be seen later, the Nusayris maintain that the Aytam were created by Salman al-Farisi.

In the light of this account of Salman, his portrayal as one of the first Muslims to support Ali's right to the imamate is of utmost significance to the Shiites. They consider him no ordinary man, but one who possessed of divine wisdom and knowledge of prior religions. According to Islamic legend, he lived early enough to have been the contemporary of Jesus Christ and His disciples. In this sense, it is believed that Salman became the link between Christianity and Islam, and the one who proclaimed the appearance of the new Prophet, that is, Muhammad. Ibn Ishaq, the earliest biographer of the Prophet, relates a tradition in which Muhammad is reported to have said to Salman, "If you trust me, O Salman, I believe that you met Isa [Jesus], the son of Mary."[30] To the Shiites, the longevity of Salman (he is believed to have lived since the time of Christ) and his possession of divine knowledge established him as a witness of the prophets of old and their message, especially the relations between Moses and Aaron, which Muhammad cited to show the relation between himself and Ali, in the tradition, "You [Ali] are in the same position to me as Aaron was to Moses, except that there will be no Prophet after me."[31] The Shiites often cite this tradition to show that Muhammad designated Ali as his successor through the Wasiyya (testamentary trust) and confirmed him in the office of the imamate, as Moses designated Aaron as his successor.

The witness to this tradition is Salman, who lived an uncommonly long time and acquired divine knowledge that qualified him to proclaim

Ali as the rightful heir to the Prophet.[32] It is in this sense that Salman becomes the "lost link" of divine authority between Ali and Muhammad. It is in the same sense that the Shiites give great weight to Salman's association with both Ali and the Prophet especially with the latter, who counted Salman as a member of Ahl al-Bayt to legitimize their claim that the Prophet appointed Ali as his successor and leader (Imam) of the Muslim community. Salman not only was considered the example of a faithful, true, and pious Muslim; he was, as the Prophet said, "the Ibn [son] of Islam."[33]

In sum, to the Twelver Shiites, who maintain the divine authority of twelve Imams, Salman is the divine counselor whom the Prophet left for Ali, so that all Muslims should recognize Ali as the sole Imam and heir to the Prophet, based on the divine testimony of Salman, and so that they should realize that the office of the imamate, or caliphate, was meant exclusively for Ali. Through the machinations of some of the companions of the Prophet (Abu Bakr, Umar, and Uthman), however, this office was usurped from Ali. The witness again was Salman, who unleashed his resources to defend Ali's right to the imamate.[34]

In the early period of Islam, then, Salman was honored as a counselor of the Prophet, one of the zuhhad (ascetics) later called Sufis, a possessor of divine knowledge, a member of Ahl al-Bayt, and the Son of Islam. To Ibn Arabi, in his *al-Futuhat al-Makkiyya* (I, 255–56), Salman was infallible because, as a member of the family of the Prophet, he was sanctified and cleansed from sin by God.

To the Shiites, he was also honored as the witness of Ali's right to the imamate. But as time went on and the struggle between the Shiites and their opponents intensified, a group of Ghulat or extremist Shiites emerged, including Muhammad Abu al-Khattab (d. 138/755), who deified the Imams. It was also natural for them to deify Salman, the arch-defender of Ali's right to the imamate, and to call him Salsal and Salsabil, the two epithets which begin with the letter S, as does the name Salman.[35]

Thus, we find Abu al-Hasan al-Ashari (d. 324/935) stating, "In our time, there are those who assert the divinity of Salman al-Farisi."[36] Some of these Ghulat (extremist) sects evidently regarded Ali, Muhammad, and Salman al-Farisi as divine, and placed great spiritual importance on their names, referring to them by their initial letters, AMS.

We learn from the Ismaili writer Abu Hatim al-Razi (d.934), in his *Kitab al-Zina,* that the Ayniyya, (from *ayn* the initial letter of Ali), asserted the divinity of both Ali and Muhammad, giving preference to the former, while the Mimiyya, (from *mim* the initial letter of Muhammad), asserted the divinity of both Ali and Muhammad but preferred Muhammad to Ali.[37]

Al-Razi goes on to say that one of the Ghulat is the Salmaniyya sect, whose adherents maintain that Salman al-Farisi was a prophet. Others, al-Razi continues, proclaim that he was divine. They base their belief in Salman's divinity on Quran 43:45, where God tells Muhammad, "Question our apostles whom we sent before you," Salman being an apostle having been sent before Muhammad. They justify this allegorical interpretation by saying that the name Salman sounds identical to the Arabic words Sal man ("question whom"). Al-Razi concludes that some of the Ghulat exaggerated Salman's role to the point of giving him precedence over Ali.[38]

One of these Ghulat sects must have been the Nusayris, who assert that Ali, Muhammad, and Salman al-Farisi are a triune God symbolized by the letters ayn, mim, and sin. They must have emerged as a Chulat group in the second century of the Islamic era (eighth century A.D.), and mixed with other Ghulat groups such as the Siniyya (already mentioned), the Alyaiyya, and the Khattabiyya, founded by Abu al-Khattab, a contemporary of the Imam Jafar al-Sadiq (d. 765). They remained without a distinct identity until the next century, when Muhammad Ibn Nusayr, who claimed to be the Bab of the eleventh Imam, al-Hasan al-Askari (d.873), became independent of the latter and founded Nusayrism. The great apostle and propagator of Nusayrism, al-Khasibi (d. 957), has left us very important evidence indicating that the Prophet Muhammad called Salman al-Farisi the Bab, the very position the Nusayris assign to Salman in their trinity.

According to al-Khasibi's account, Muhammad Ibn Abi Zaynab al-Asadi, known as Abu al-Khattab, one of the Ghulat already mentioned, was in the company of the Imam Jafar al-Sadiq, when the latter turned to him, saying that he wanted to address him as his great-grandfather, the Prophet, had addressed Salman. Al-Sadiq went on to say that one day Salman was in the company of the Prophet, who addressed him thus: "Salman, you have become the vessel of our knowledge, the mine of our mystery, the central point of our commands and interdicts, and the educator of the believers in our religious practices and moral conduct. By Allah! You are the Bab who transmitted our knowledge, and from you emanates the divine knowledge of revelation (tanzil) and the allegorical interpretation (tawil) of the Quran, and the hidden mystery and the secret of this mystery. Blessed are you at the beginning and the end, outwardly and inwardly, living and dead. I am addressing you, O Muhammad [Abu al-Khattab], as my great-grandfather the Prophet addressed Salman."[39]

Later we shall see the significance of Abu Khattab, an extremist Shiite, in the discussion of Nusayri festivals.

It is clear from this tradition that the Prophet Muhammad was the first to call Salman the Bab, through whom the divine knowledge of the ancients was transmitted. Salman was also recognized by the Prophet as the source from whom this knowledge emanated. He was a trusted transmitter of the tradition of the Prophet; He was the first and most illustrious of the Muslims. He was called, as has been stated earlier, the Son of Islam. The Nusayris made Salman, whom they called Salsal and Salsabil, the Fountain of Water in Paradise, according to Islamic tradition. In *Kitab al-Mashyakha* we find the following references to Salman: "O God, be favorable to our Lord Muhammad and the family of our Lord Muhammad, and to Salsal and the family of Salsal, the light that disperses the darkness," and, "May God cause us and you, O brethren, to drink a draught from the palm of Salsal."[40]

In his introduction to *Kitab Majmu al-A'yad,* al-Tabarani, invoking the God Ali to pray over his Name [Muhammad], states, ". . . and also pray over the most shining light, the brightest lamp, the path, the Bab, the cause of causes, the faithful spirit, the refreshing water, the deliverance of those who seek him, the destroyer of tyrants, the possessor of plain [divine] ways, the audience and guidance, the one who sets up stations [of men], the creator of clouds, the great Bab Salsal, through whom the gnostic attains to the God Ali."[41] Indeed, there is hardly a supplicatory prayer appended to the different festivals in this book which does not praise Salman and invoke his divine aid, along with that of Ali and Muhammad. In the discourse for the Fitr festival, the Nusayri believers invoke the God Ali to pray to "the Bab of your mercy and the beginning of your wisdom," and in the Khutba (sermon) for the Adha festival, after invoking the God Ali and Muhammad, the believers bear testimony that "the Lord Salman is the path of deliverance and the cause of life for all the learned believers."[42]

In the Nusayri religious system, Salman like the Mana and the Ism, appears under different names in the seven periods of the manifestation of the deity. Questions 22 to 42 of *Kitab Ta'lim al-Diyana al Nusayriyya* furnish the names of Salman. He is called the Faithful Spirit, the Holy Ghost, the Universal Soul, the Lord of Men, Mount Sinai, the Ark of Noah, the Throne of God, Gabriel, the Evidence, the Apostle, the Omniscient (the perfect soul) and the Cow [in the second chapter of the Quran], just to mention a few.[43]

Salman is also identified with Zakat, or alms (religious tithes), as the Prophet is with Salat (prayer). According to a verse ascribed to al-

Khasibi, "Salman is Zakat [alms], the Door (who is also the angel Gabriel), besides whom there is no guide to the Apostle [Muhammad]."[44] Such symbolism is used by the Nusayris to show that Muhammad and Salman represent spiritual as well as worldly concerns.

It is important to point out that the Nusayris believe Salman appeared in the Persian period, one of the periods of the seven manifestations, in the persons of the Persian Bahmans (kings), among whom were Firuz, Anushirwan, Bahram, Feridun, and others.[45] Once more we see the Persian roots of some of the Nusayris' tradition, although there is no evidence that Salman impressed his Persianism on the Prophet or on Islamic tradition.

Above all, in the Nusayri religious system, Salman is the Bab, created by Muhammad in obedience to the command of his Lord, the End and Mana (Ali). For this reason, Salman calls the Prophet "my most great Lord."[46] He is the only Door which leads to the Mana, the causal determinant (Ali), through the Name (Muhammad). No one comes to the God Ali except through him.[47] He is the teacher of men, a guide to the Apostle Muhammad, whose office is only that of an intermediary between Ali and Salman.[48] In this sense, the office of the Bab seems to complete the Nusayri system of the threefold manifestation of the deity. Indeed, this office is essential to the Nusayri system, because without the Bab no one can know or approach the Mana. In the judgment of the author, the office of the Bab forms the cornerstone of the Nusayri belief in the divine and infallible authority of the twelve Imams and the perpetuation of this authority in the person of Muhammad Ibn Nusayr, founder of Nusayrism, as the Bab and heir of the Imams.

30

The Nusayri Religious System
The Twelve Imams

According to the Nusayris each of the Imams has a Bab (door), who serves as the path leading believers to him. They base this belief on a tradition in which the Prophet Muhammad is reported to have said, "I am the city of knowledge, and Ali is its gate," and, "He who seeks divine knowledge must go through the gate."[1]

Because each Imam possessed the divine knowledge of former Prophets and messengers of God, it was necessary that each should have a Bab able to transmit this divine knowledge to the faithful of his age. The office of the Bab was best explained by the Imam Jafar al-Sadiq, who said that the Bab is the one who, at will, knows the affairs of the Imams. Nothing can conceal the Imam from him—no high mountain, deep sea, or surrounding wall.[2] The Bab acts as the testamentary trustee and heir to the Imam and, like the Imam, possesses divine knowledge and the capacity for allegorical interpretation (tawil) of the inward and outward meanings of the Quran. This explains the necessity of a Bab for every Imam. In the Nusayri religious system, the Imams and their Babs are as follows:

Imam	*Bab*
Ali	Salman al-Farisi
Al-Hasan	Qays Ibn Waraqa, known as al-Safina
Al-Husayn	Rashid al-Hijri
Ali Zayn al-Abidin	Abd Allah al-Ghalib al-Kabuli, nicknamed Kankar
Muhammad al-Baqir	Yahya Ibn Muammar Ibn Umm al-Tawil al-Thumali
Jafar al-Sadiq	Jabir Ibn Yazid al-Jufi

Musa al-Kazim	Muhammad Ibn Abi Zaynab al-Kahili
Ali al-Rida	Al-Mufaddal Ibn Umar al-Jufi
Muhammad al-Jawad	Muhammad Ibn Mufaddal al-Jufi
Ali al-Hadi	Umar Ibn al-Furat, known as al-Katib
Al-Hasan al-Askari	Abu Shuayb Muhammad Ibn Nusayr

Since the twelfth Imam, Muhammad (the Mahdi), had no Bab when he disappeared, Abu Shuayb Muhammad Iby Nasayr, who was still living when the Mahdi disappeared and who had been the Bab of the Mahdi's father, al-Askari, became the heir, representative, and guide of the Mahdi. In short, Ibn Nusayr became the Bab; he was succeeded by Muhammad al-Jannan al-Junbulani, who in turn was succeeded by al-Khasibi (d. 957), already mentioned. It was al-Khasibi, more than his predecessors, who established a firm foundation for the Nusayri sect and spread Nusayrism throughout all the lands. Thus, according to the Nusayri writer al-Tawil, the office of the Bab forms a fundamental part of the religious system of the Nusayris.[3]

The twelve Imams also constitute an essential part of the Nusayri system. In *Kitab al-Mashyakha,* they are spoken of as the culmination of the sixty-three personifications of the Ism (Muhammad). This work also states that the Imams are part of the divine economy of God. In a supplicatory prayer, the Nusayris ask their God Ali to establish them in obedience to Him, to His apostle Muhammad, to His Wali (vicegerent) Salsal (Salman al-Farisi), and to "the Imams, who are yours, you had named yourself by them; they are not empty of you, but you are of them."[4]

Like the Twelver Shiites, the Nusayris maintain that the twelve Imams existed before all of creation. The Imam Jafar al-Sadiq is reported to have said that God created the Imams thousands of years before He created Adam. They were spirits around the throne of God, praising Him, and were joined by all the heavenly host in their praise. Later the Imams descended to earth in physical bodies; there they continued to praise God, joined in their praise by the people on earth, as is related in the Quran 37:165–66: "and we are verily ranged in rank [for service]; and we are verily those who declare [God's] glory."[5]

The Imams were also God's first delegates to His people. They acted as God's spokesmen, repositories of His divine knowledge and storehouses of His secrets, the heirs of His prophets and messengers, His light, His proof against mankind, and the trustees of His creation. In the words of the fifth Imam, Muhammad al-Baqir, the Imams are the vicegerents of God on earth. No part of God's knowledge on earth and in heaven escapes them. They are the arm, the hand, the face, the eye, and the side of God. Wherever the believer turns his face, he sees them. Whatever is God's will is also that of the Imams. Al-Baqir concludes by saying, "Praise be to God, who chose us from the light of His power, granted us the secret of the knowledge of His will, and commanded us to inculcate in our partisans [Shia] the truth of His creed in order to redeem their souls from eternal torment through adherence to Him."[6]

The Nusayri representation of the Imams as preexistent celestial beings having divine status, seems no different from the view of the Twelver Shiites. In the treatise entitled *al-Tawjih* (Direction) in *Kitab al-Mashyakha,* for example, the eleventh Imam, al-Hasan al-Askari, is portrayed as a divine being. It is reported that a certain Yahya Ibn Muin al-Samiri went to see al Hasan al-Askari and found him sitting on a throne of light, with rays of light before him and a light between his eyes which filled the east and west. Al-Samiri said, "When I saw him, I fell on my face in adoration; then I raised my head and stood praising and thanking my Lord [al-Askari] and said, 'My Lord is to be praised. He is holy. Our Lord is the Lord of the angels and of the spirit.' "[7]

This spiritual preeminence of the Imams is further asserted by Jafar al-Sadiq, who is reported to have said that God created seven heavens, the first being the abode of the Imams. Al-Sadiq also said that whenever a believer (Shiite) dies, his soul is carried to the Imam Ali to be examined, in order that Ali may determine whether the soul is that of a true believer and may decide whether it should be sent to Paradise or to Hell. Indeed, so magnificent is the spiritual position of the Imam that al-Sadiq interpreted Quran 41:10, "He set on the earth mountains standing firm and high above it," to mean that the mountains are the Imams, without whom the believers (Shiites) would have doubted their religion and gone astray.[8]

The same Jafar al-Sadiq also said that when mentioning an Imam, "the speaker should observe silence, and on mentioning God, [he] should fall silent and attentive."[9]

Such, then, is the lofty spiritual plane occupied by the Imams in the religious system of the Nusayris. They are divine beings chosen to guide believers to knowledge of the God Ali through the medium of their Babs. This role is the reason the Imams are considered leaders of their communities and are so highly honored.

According to Sulayman al-Adani, the common people among the Nusayris regard their Imams as infallible and not subject to the laws of nature.[10] They also believe that their Imams have knowledge of the future; they consult them in any matter on which they need advice, such as the building of a house, or marrying, or moving from the village.[11]

The religious hierarchy of the Nusayris embraces seven ranks. They are the Babs, the five Aytam of Salman al-Farisi, the Naqibs, the Najibs, the Mukhtassun, the Mukhlisun, and the Mumtahanun. The Babs are the highest of these, followed by the Aytam.[12] The Aytam number 500, all of whom are connected with the different Isms (names) of Salman al-Farisi, five with Muhammad, five with Muhammad's daughter Fatima, five with Muhammad's wife Umm Salama and five with one of al-Fairsi's close associates Abu Abd al-Rahman Ibn Waraqa al-Riyahi nicknamed al-Safina (the Ark).[13] In the Nusayri's religious system, however, al-Miqdad Ibn al-Aswad, Abu Dharr al-Ghifari, Abd Allah Ibn Rawaha, Uthman Ibn Madun and Qanbar Ibn Kadan, are considered the five Aytam par excellence who exclusively belong to Salman al-Farisi and are believed by Nusayris to have been created by al-Farisi.[14]

It is strange that women are mentioned as Aytam, since they have no place in the Nusayri's religious system. Like the extremist Shiites, however, the Nusayris regard Fatima, daughter of Muhammad, as a male and give her the name of Fatir.[15] We shall further discuss the Aytam in the following chapter.

Fatima/Fatir holds an interesting place in the Nusayri religious system, serving to exalt the imamate. In *Kitab Majmu al-A'yad* (The Book of Feasts), Fatima-Fatir is described as a personification of Laylat al-Qadr (the Night of Power), during which the Quran was first revealed to the Prophet Muhammad. Quran 97:1–5 states, "We have revealed the Quran in the Night of Power. Do you realize what the Night of Power is? The Night of Power is better than a thousand months. On it the angels and the Spirit, by their Lord's leave, descend with His decrees. That night is peace till break of dawn." Al-Khasibi explains that Laylat al-Qadr, which falls in the middle of Shaban (the eighth month of the Islamic calendar), is a noble night during which God rewards and answers the prayers and fasting of His people [the Nusayris] for the glorification of Fatir [Fatima], al-Hasan, al-Husayn, and Muhsin, who are the light and essence of Muhammad. He adds that the Qadr (power) is Muhammad, and the night of that power is Fatima-Fatir, who is the mystery of Muhammad. Fatima, he says, appeared in a feminine form to delude the wretched created beings.

Another Nusayri writer, al-Jilli, reiterates al-Khasibi's interpretation, stating the Fatima is the Night of Power. People believed that

Fatima appeared in feminine form, says al-Jilli, but God dispelled this belief when He asked [Quran 97:1], "Do you realize what the Night of Power is?" Al-Jilli explains that this Night of Power is Fatima-Fatir, who created all mankind. He goes on to interpret "better than a thousand months" to mean better than a thousand prophets, "angels" as those who possess knowledge of Fatima's reality and "the Spirit" as her magnification and the call to know and obey her. Al-Jilli interprets the final sentence of the passage to mean that Fatima will uphold justice and manifest herself on behalf of the Imams until the day of the appearance of the Mahdi.

From the preceding evidence we are able to state that to the Nusayris, Fatima is divine. She is the creator of mankind. She is not only the daughter of the Prophet, but homologous with him. They are the same essence. It is in this sense, as shall be seen later, that the Prophet addresses Fatima as *umm Abiha* (mother of her father). Furthermore, Fatima-Fatir is the manifestation of the Imams, who emanated from her, and she is acting on their behalf until the day when the Mahdi shall appear and bring justice to the earth. Just as Laylat al-Qadr is exalted as the time when the Quran was first revealed to the Prophet, so Fatima-Fatir is exalted because she is the mother of the Imams, the one from whose essence they emanated. In other words, as the prophethood was exalted through the divine revelation of the Quran, so the imamate was exalted through divine Fatima, who is the very essence of Muhammad. Thus, the Nusayris believe that the prophethood and the imamate are coequal; on this point they are in complete agreement with the Twelver Shiites, although the Twelvers do not regard Fatima as divine.[16]

The preceding evidence also indicates that the Nusayris are one of the ancient Ghulat sects called the Mukhammisa (Fivers), who maintained that the five members of the family of the Prophet are the incarnation of God, and who prefer to call Fatima by the masculine name of Fatir. Among the Fivers mentioned by al-Razi are the al-Shurayiyya and al-Namiriyya sects.[17] But in fact, as we have seen earlier, al-Namiriyya is none other than the Nusayriyya, founded by Muhammad Ibn Nusayr.

31

The Nusayri Religious System
Role of the Aytam and Spiritual Hierarchies

As EXPLAINED IN CHAPTER 26, the Nusayris believe that the deity manifested himself seven times in seven human forms, beginning with Adam and ending with Ali Ibn Ibi Talib. Each manifestation as a Mana was accompanied by corresponding manifestations of an Ism, a Bab, and an adversary to the deity. The Bab was entrusted with the creation through five Aytam (incomparables) who, as their name indicates, are unique. In cosmological essence, they are the principles of the universe and the cause of all that exists, visible and invisible. The Aytam appeared in new incarnations in each of the seven cycles. But the Nusayri believe that in the seventh and last cycle, when the Mana was Ali, the Ism, Muhammad, and the Bab, Salman, the five Aytams were created by Salman. We read in *Kitab al-Mamju* that the Lord Salman created the five noble Incomparables, al-Miqdad Ibn Aswad al-Kindi, Abu Dharr al-Ghifari, Abd Allah Ibn Rawaha al-Ansari, Uthman Ibn Madun al-Najashi, and Qanbar Ibn Kadan al-Dawsi, as servants of Ali.

The Aytam are the creators of this world: the dry land and the oceans; every plain and every mountain; the southern regions and the northern; the Orient and the occident; everything spanned by the blue vault of heaven.[1]

Not only did the Aytam create this whole world as it now exists, however; they also hold the government of the heavens and the earth in their hands. Al-Miqdad controls thunder, lightning, and earthquakes; Abu Dharr al-Ghifari supervises the gyrations of the stars and constellations; Abd Allah Ibn Rawaha directs the winds and is in charge of the arrest of human spirits (in Islamic tradition, he is the Angel of Death); Uthman Ibn Madun controls stomachs, the heat of the body, and human diseases; and Qanbar Ibn Kadan al-Dawsi is responsible for the introduction of spirits into the body.[2]

Like the Bab, the Incomparables form a part of the Nusayri hierarchy. But why should these five men be given such sublime positions in the Nusayri system? Like Salman, they were pioneer converts who saw in Islam a spiritual force that would change the carnal life of the pagan Arabs. Pious mystics (zuhhad), they totally surrendered their souls to God, condemning the worldliness and extravagance of the Quraysh as sinful. These men saw in Ali Ibn Ibi Talib the exemplary Muslim, possessed of sublime spiritual ideals. They considered him to be the only one qualified to succeed the Prophet in leading the Muslim community. They became, therefore, the first supporters (Shia) of Ali's right to this leadership (the imamate), and through this support, they came to be connected with Salman al-Farisi, who was greatly venerated by the Prophet, who was considered, like Ali a member of the family of the Prophet, and who supported Ali as the Prophet's successor. This is why the Aytam are frequently referred to as the "five luminous bodies," and occupy the second rank in the world of light in the Nusayris' religious hierarchy.

The Nusayris' primal belief in the seven manifestations of God and the threefold divinity is closely associated with their system of spiritual hierarchies. According to the Nusayris, there are countless worlds known to God. Chief among them are the great luminous world (al-Alam al-Kabir al-Nurani) and the little earthly world (al-Alam al-Saqhir al-Turabi). The first is heaven, the "light of light," and the second is the residence of men. The great luminous world contains seven hierarchical orders, each having its representatives on earth. Chief among these ranks are the Babs (doors), who number 400 and the Aytam, who number 500. Below them in the hierarchy are the Naqibs, or princes, numbering 600; the Najibs, or excellent ones, numbering 700; Mukhtassun, or peculiars, numbering 800; the Mukhlisun, or pure in faith, numbering 900; the Mumtahanun, or the tried, number 1,100; in all these orders number 5,000 strong.[3]

These heavenly ranks appeared in the little earthly world together with the manifestations of God in human form and were personified in the Nusayri dignitaries. These ranks are represented by twelve Naqibs and twenty-eight Najibs, who possess complete knowledge of the functions of the ranks beneath them, and knowledge of the God Ali, His Name, and His Bab. They have other counterparts in apostles and prophets who are also representative of the deity because they have partially emanated from Him.[4]

These ranks seem to represent natural phenomena. The five Aytam who form the second order represent the East, the West, the moon, the new moon, the stars, thunder, and lightning. The seven degrees of the third order, Naqibs, are prayer, Zakat (alms), pilgrimage, fasting, Hijra (immigration), Jihad (holy war), and Dua (supplication). The seven degrees of the fourth order, the Najibs, are mountains, rain clouds, seas, rivers, winds, clouds, and thunderbolts. The seven degrees of the fifth order, the Mukhatassun are night, day, lunch, supper, the morrow, sunset, and torrential streams. The seven degrees of the sixth order, the Mukhlisun, are cattle, riding beasts, camels, bees, fowl, monks' cells, and churches. And lastly, the seven degrees of the seventh order, the Mumtahanun, are home, places of worship, palm trees, berries, pomegranates, olives, and figs.[5]

The Earthly World contains seven degrees of believers. There are 14,000 Muqarrabun (near ones), 15,000 Cherubim, 16,000 Ruhiyyun (spiritual or sanctified), 17,000 Muqaddasun, 18,000 Saihun (wandering ascetics), 19,000 Mustamiun (listeners), and 20,000 Lahiqun (followers). In all, they number 119,000.[6]

These hierarchies are held in such great reverence that the Nusayris believe that their mere invocation is a means of gaining the remission of sin. According to one tradition, the Prophet said, "When a congregation of true believers assembled in the east, west, north, or south of the earth, and made mention of the Most High, his Name, his Door, his Aytam, his Naqibs, his Najibs, Mukhatassun, Mukhlisun, Mumtahanun and all the people of his hierarchies, then a crier from above would proclaim, 'Rise with your sins forgiven, and your bad deeds changed into good ones.' "[7]

In addition to the hierarchies, the Nusayris are required to honor a host of apostles and prophets who, together with the hierarchies, number 124,000. These include 28 Najibs, or excellent ones, the greatest of whom is Abd Allah Ibn Saba, believed to have been the first to assert the divinity of Ali during his lifetime.[8]

Other illustrious characters honored by the Nusayris include Jafar al-Tayyar, brother of Ali, and the legendary figure al-Khidr, more correctly called al-Khadir (the ever-verdant), so named because of his eternal youth and because he caused a rod to break forth in blossom. The Nusayris also honor Christian saints and apostles, including Matthew, Paul, Peter, and Saint John Chrysostom, who are believed to be the Aytam (incomparables) of Rawzabah, the Bab in the time of Jesus, when Peter (Simon Cephas) was the Mana.[9]

Advancement within these hierarchies from the earthly world, to the great luminous world (heaven) is possible through instruction and training; the gnostic, who is well-versed in the science of religion, prepares the seeker, or neophyte. A neophyte desiring to attain the world of light must first become a mumtahan (one who is tried). From this stage the neophyte advances to the following rank of mukhlis (faithful one). When he attains all the knowledge of the mukhlis and of the mumtahan, then his spiritual guide advances him to the rank of mukhtass (peculiar). When he has absorbed the knowledge of the mukhtass, his instructor advances him to the rank of najib, or excellent. If he absorbs the knowledge of the najib and without doubting, he moves up the rank of naqib (prince), and if he proves himself steadfast in the knowledge of the naqib, he is advanced to the rank of Yatim (singular of Aytam), or Incomparable.

Upon attaining the rank of naqib, the seeker is given into the hands of the Bab, who will then entrust him to the Hijab (veil), or intermediary, Muhammad, who will then lead him to the Mana (Ali). The seeker, who has by now gone through a very rigorous examination of his faith, will be considered a mumin (believer) and will be presented to the Mana. The Mana talks with him and examines him further, hoping to find that his good deeds outweigh his bad ones; even if they do, however, the Mana then reveals to him only those mysteries which he deems fit to disclose to him.

Now the believer is given the opportunity to intercede on behalf of a brother or another relative, that he may likewise attain the knowledge of Ali as the Mana by going through these stages and appearing before the Mana. The Mana will then respond to the believer's appeal, purifying his relative and raising him unto himself.[10]

Finally, the believer asks his Lord and God (Ali) to remove the veil from his eyes, so that he may behold the upper and lower worlds, the heavens and the earth, and all things therein. Then God will disclose Himself to the believer and empower him with His Spirit, so that the believer becomes, like the angels, not subject to human necessities like eating or drinking. The believer is then emancipated from human nature and transformed into an immortal being, a shining celestial star, having his own will. He becomes able to ascend to the heavens or descend to the earth, and can traverse the world from east to west at will.[11]

In *Kitab al-Haft al-Sharif,* the Imam Jafar al-Sadiq states that believers may advance from one hierarchical rank to another and from one virtue to another until they become like the angels of heaven, free from human limitations and the needs of human nature. Al-Sadiq asked his interlocutor, al-Mufaddal al-Jufi, whether he had seen one of these believers in the spiritual state. Al-Jufi replied he had not. But Muhammad Ibn al-Walid, who was in the presence of al-Sadiq, told him that he had seen a man in this form.

Al-Walid said that while he was sitting in the mosque praising God, he saw a stranger in travel-stained clothes guiding a female camel. He invited the stranger to his home and gave him a supper of meat and bread. When supper was over and a servant came to remove the dishes, al-Walid was astounded to see that the food on his guest's plate was untouched. The servant asked the reason for this. Al-Walid was speechless. He became even more startled when he looked at his guest and found him to be someone else, not the man he had invited to dine with him. His guest now had a long mustache. Al-Walid was disturbed, but his guest told him not to be frightened because of his changed appearance. He explained that when a believer has passed through all the degrees of spiritual growth and reached the end, he became a spiritual being like the angels, no longer subject to the limitations of human nature. The guest declared that he had just experienced such a transformation.

Al-Sadiq turned to al-Walid and al-Jufi and said, "This same man came to see me three times this week while you were sitting here with me, but you neither saw nor heard him."[12] Belief in such spiritual transformation and transcendentalism is an integral part of the Nusayris' belief that, in the beginning, before the world was created, the Nusayris existed as shining lights and luminous stars beholding Ali in sapphire splendor, conscious of the distinction between obedience and disobedience, yet not drinking, eating or excreting. They lost this spiritual existence because of their disobedience,[13] but the stages of spiritual advancement which the Nusayri neophyte must undergo are seen as a means of regaining it, the same by the grace of their God, Ali.[14] Thus a Nusayri neophyte, who passes successfully through these spiritual stages finally becomes transformed into a celestial being emancipated from human nature, exactly like the Abdal and others discussed in chapter 10 of this book. In other words, the believer can attain immortality without experiencing death by passing through the different stages of the Nusayri hierarchy. Al-Walid's transformed guest tells him, "I am only a believer like you, but I have been able to achieve this final stage [of spiritual transformation]."[15] There is no evidence that the guest passed through death before he attained the supernatural change from a human to a celestial form.

32

The Nusayri Religious System

Metempsychosis

THE DOCTRINE OF METEMPSYCHOSIS, or transmigration of souls, is an integral part of the Nusayri religious system. This doctrine is not new, and may have been adopted from the early religions of the East. From al-Nawbakhti (tenth century) we learn that a certain Abd Allah Ibn al-Harith (late seventh century), whose father was Zindiq (freethinker) from al-Madain (Ctesiphon), enticed some Muslims to adopt the doctrine of metempsychosis.[1] Al-Shahrastani (d. 1153) also affirms this, stating that the Ghulat are unanimous in their belief in metempsychosis, having received it from the Mazdakians, Brahmans, Philosophers, and Sabeans.[2]

It is evident that metempsychosis is not an Islamic doctrine based on the Quran. Rather, it is a belief held by the early Ghulat, who interpreted certain passages of the Quran in their own way to justify their belief in it.

Metempsychosis (in Arabic, *tanasukh*) is referred to by the Nusayris as Taknis or Tajayyul [from *Jil* (generation] and means reappearance in successive generations.[3] The Nusayris maintain that the soul of man passes from one body to another several times. But the soul of a good Nusayri will enter into a body more perfect than his own, while the soul of a sinful Nusayri will enter the body of an unclean beast.[4]

From the second chapter of *Kitab-al Majmu,* we learn that there are seven kinds of metempsychosis:

1. Naskh: the passing of the soul into another human body
2. Maskh: the passing of the human soul into that of an animal
3. Faskh: the passing of the soul into a plant
4. Raskh: the passing of the soul into a short plant

5. Waskh: the passing of the soul into dirt or trash
6. Qashsh: the passing of the soul into a dry plant or straw
7. Qashshash: the passing of the soul into insects such as flies or ants.[5]

The Nusayris' belief in metempsychosis is attested to by both Nusayri and non-Nusayri (especially Druze) sources. Hamza Ibn Ali, the great Druze apostle and author (d. 1030), wrote that a Nusayri book entitled *Kitab al-Haqa'iq wa Kashf al-Mahjub* (The book of truth and the manifestation of that which is veiled) had fallen into his hands. He condemns everyone acquiring this book as a servant of the devil because its Nusayri author believed in metempsychosis. Apparently the author attributed this doctrine, together with the telling of falsehoods and the practice of sexual immoralities, to the Druzes. Hamza declares, "God forbid that the religion of our Lord [the Fatimi Caliph al-Hakim bi Amr Allah (d. 1021), deified by the Druzes], should authorize criminal action."[6] He goes on to say that the Nusayris assert that the souls of the Nawasib (Sunnite Muslims) and the *addad* (adversaries of Ali) will pass into dogs and such other unclean beasts as pigs, monkeys, owls, and fowl, till they enter fire to be burned and beaten under the hammer. Hamza rejects the belief that human souls enter the bodies of animals as preposterous and utterly false, and warns that anyone believing in metempsychosis will suffer the loss of both this world and the next.[7]

Hamza is correct in asserting that the Nusayris believe in Musukhiyya, the transmigration of human souls into dreadful forms, especially those of animals. But what is the origin of Musukhiyya? Why should human beings be transformed into unclean animals like dogs, pigs, and monkeys, as the Nusayris maintain?

According to Jafar al-Sadiq, Musukhiyya occurs as the result of the disobedience of Iblis (Satan) to God. When God created Adam, He asked all the angels to prostrate themselves before Him. They all did so except Iblis, who disobeyed God and refused to worship Adam. When God asked why he refused to worship Adam, Iblis replied that he was nobler than Adam, who was created from clay, while he, Iblis, was created from fire (see Quran 7:12 and 38:75–77). Thus, from the disobedience of Satan and his posterity, God initiated Musukhiyya. Satan looked at the state of Musukhiyya and said, "What is this?" God answered, "This is your state and the state of your posterity, who will be transformed into all kinds of beasts." So God clothed Satan and his posterity with animals' skins, and clothed Adam and his posterity in human forms. Musukhiyya, then, is the punishment inflicted on the infidels or unbelievers, who are the posterity of Satan. For this reason, says al-Sadiq, it is difficult to distinguish between those infidels who are still in human form and those who have been transformed into animals. He states that one may see a man and believe that he is a human being, when in reality he is a monkey, a bear, or a dog in human form. Or a man may pass by a strange dog that follows him or jumps at him. This man, al-Sadiq says, may be unknowingly married to the wife of this dog, once a human being, whom God has punished by transforming him. The "dog" sees this man living with his wife, and in his home, and tries to harm him.[8]

Al-Sadiq gives another example, of a female beast biting or kicking or trampling a man until he is dead for no apparent reason. Al-Sadiq explains that this beast in life was probably an infidel who was wronged by a believer, without having the opportunity to avenge the wrong done him. The infidel, transformed after his death into a female beast, seeks to take revenge on the believer. By the same token, one may see a believer kill a female beast with his sword or break one of her limbs. The reason is that the female beast, in a previous life was an infidel who had wronged the believer, and therefore deserves to be wounded or killed for its bad deeds.[9]

Here we find the law of retaliation implemented in both spirit and fact. In *Kitab al-Sirat,* we find that when a man is killed in this life by a beast, he will later be transformed into a beast to enable him to kill the beast that had killed him in his human form. Thus, while it appears that people kill lions and lions kill people, in fact, "no one kills a lion except a lion." Thus, if one creature gets satisfaction by killing another, the victim in turn gets satisfaction by killing the killer.[10]

The point here is that the state of Musukhiyya, or transformation into animal forms, does not rob the transformed person of his reason or humanity. He retains his empathy toward people and animals alike. Thus—so it is stated in *Kitab al-Sirat*—one finds some people like to raise dogs, cats, pigeons, and other creatures, because they have previously had the forms of these animals. Thus, what happens to a man in his transformed (animal) state because of disease or misfortune has already happened to him in his human form.[11]

In this same work, a certain Muhammad Ibn Sinan states that there is no bird or fowl which does not have human antecedents. He then points to a carpenter working on his house and says that this carpenter was, in his first *dawr* (period), a rooster. The Nusayris use the terms *dawr* and *kawr* to indicate the cycles of rebirth into this world, the revolution of time, and particularly the manifestations of Ali in human form.[12]

According to Sulayman al-Adani, all Nusayris believe that the spirits of Muslim dignitaries well-versed in religious science are reborn after death in the form of asses; the souls of learned Christian men enter the bodies of swine; and the souls of learned Jewish men take the forms of monkeys. The souls of wicked Nusayris, however will enter the bodies of cattle, especially those used for food. The souls of persons of mixed character, partly good and partly bad, return in the bodies of persons from other sects that deviate from the Nusayri religion. When a person outside the Nusayri sect recants his belief and joins the Nusayris, they believe that in past generations this person was one of them, and that, because of sins he had committed, he had renounced the Nusayri faith and joined another sect.[13] However, the metempsychosis of "wicked Nusayris" related by al-Adani seems to be qualified by other Nusayri sources, as shall be seen shortly.

Rev. Samuel Lyde relates that he often heard the Nusayris laugh and say, when the jackals howled toward dusk, "Those are the Muslims calling [the faithful] to afternoon prayer, for the souls of Muslims passed into jackals."[14]

The souls of the adversaries of Ali, as Hamza, the Druze apostle, said, will enter into dogs and other unclean beasts. An episode related by al-Khasibi seems to confirm Hamza's statement. Al-Khasibi says that when, on the day of Ghadir Khumm, the Prophet Muhammad cited Ali to him and told those present, "This is your God, worship him, and this is your Lord, proclaim his oneness," some of the host from heaven and earth who could not fully comprehend the oneness of the Lord of creation (Ali) were disturbed. Others who had full knowledge of the oneness of God became more firm in their belief and praised and thanked their God (Ali). Those of the heavenly host who denied the Prophet's proclamation of Ali as Lord and God were transformed by Ali into toads and sent, croaking, through the clouds to earth. Ali also hardened their hearts so that they could not remember the proclamation of the oneness of the Commander of the Faithful. In his wrath over their unbelief, the sad Ali, carried by the clouds, descended to earth and slaughtered these unbelievers with his sword, Dhu al-Faqar. When Salman al-Farisi saw Ali with his unsheathed sword dripping with blood, he asked him the reason for the carnage. Ali answered that some of the heavenly host had denied his oneness (as God), so he punished them with his sword.[15]

The Nusayris' belief in metempsychosis is connected with the concept of reward and punishment. The souls of the wicked are punished by being made to assume the forms of unclean animals, like pigs, dogs, and monkeys, while the souls of the righteous will enter human bodies more perfect than their own.[16]

The Nusayris do not apply the term "wicked" to themselves,

applying it rather to non-Nusayris, who occupy a status much inferior to their own; for their wickedness—that is their denial of Nusayri beliefs—such non-Nusayri shall be forced to assume forever the forms of such beasts as pigs, bears, dogs, jackals, and weasels. While it is true that there are wicked Nusayris, they will not be punished by transformation into beasts; rather, their souls will enter human bodies (most likely Nusayri bodies) more perfect than theirs. They become purified by passing through a number of revolutions, as many as twenty-one, each lasting for 1,077 years. After their purification, the Nusayris join the heavenly host, becoming luminous stars and angels of light, because the spirits of believers and those of angels are one and the same.[17] For this reason the Nusayris pray to their God Ali to clothe the brethren in *qumsan* (literally, shirts), or envelopes of light.[18]

We do find in some Nusayri sources, however, instances of Nusayris being transformed into unclean animals, without evidence that these people were wicked or that their reappearance in animal form was a punishment. One such case concerns a carpenter who turned into a rooster. Another, related by Dussaud, was derived from a Druze source; although it was meant to caricature the Nusayris' belief in metempsychosis, it nevertheless corroborates this belief, especially with regard to the transformation of human beings into animals.

According to this story, a Nusayri husbandman had a vineyard. After his death, his son took care of the vineyard. The son noticed that during the grape season, a wolf visited the vineyard to eat grapes. He grew tired of the wolf's damage to the vineyard and decided to kill him.

One day, therefore, the owner tried to shoot the wolf when he visited the vineyard. But just as he was about to shoot, the wolf spoke in a human voice, saying, "Would you kill your own father, who has spent his whole life tending the vineyard, just because he ate a few grapes?"

The son was startled to hear the wolf speak like a man and, turning to the wolf, he asked, "Who are you?" The wolf said, "I am your father. I have been transformed into a wolf, and this is my vineyard, which you and I worked together." The son could not believe his ears. He decided to test the wolf to see whether it really was his father. He remembered that before his death his father had hidden a sickle somewhere in the vineyard; the son had tried his utmost to find it, but had failed. He turned to the wolf and asked, "Well, if you are really my father, tell me, where is the sickle that my father and I used to trim the vines?" The wolf asked the son to follow him, and when they reached the place in the vineyard where the father had hidden the sickle, the wolf picked it up and handed it to the son, saying, "This is it." Now the son was convinced that the wolf was his father, and he allowed him to visit the vineyard and eat the grapes unmolested.[19]

The doctrine of metempsychosis also serves to support the superior position held by Nusayri men over Nusayri women. It is quite clear from *Kitab al-Haft al-Sharif* that a Nusayri woman can be transformed into another woman if God wills it, but never into the form of a male believer. Jafar al-Sadiq is reported to have said that God was too gracious to allow the transformation of a woman into a man. God would not degrade any Nusayri man, let alone a believing Nusayri, by permitting a Nusayris woman to assume the form of a man. This is so because the Nusaryi believe that God created women from devils, and therefore accord them a low status in Nusayri society.[20]

Metempsychosis also reinforces the position of the catamite in Nusayri society. When asked why some women are used as catamites by men, al-Sadiq asserted that the state of being a catamite is an abomination with which God afflicts non-Shiites and those who deny that Ali is the Vicegerent of God. Al-Sadiq concludes that the catamite *(mabun)* was a harlot in his first incarnation who in his second was transformed into a man and came to be used as a catamite by men.[21]

It is evident, then, that according to their belief in metempsychosis, the Nusayris, whether wicked or righteous, will pass through many stages of transformations in human form, leading ultimately to total purification and transformation into luminous stars. The infidels and the damned will be transformed into unclean animals, and will continue to be reborn as animals until the Mahdi returns. Their transformation into animals is a lesser punishment, however; the final punishment will come when the Mahdi appears and kills these infidels by the sword. He will also kill the *taghut* (the Quranic term for idols, or false gods) and destroy the cross (the symbol of Christianity), in order to establish the one and only religion of God: Shiite Islam.[22]

The Nusayris seem to take their belief in transmigration seriously, citing examples to support it. Lyde relates many such examples. If a villager died and a child was born at the same time in another village, Lyde often heard the Nusayris say that the soul of the dead man had returned in the form of the child. He also heard a certain healer of snake bites claim that he had been a healer throughout all the generations. Lyde even heard a peculiar story of a Christian woman who claimed that she had been a Nusayri in a former age, and that she could describe what she did in that age. Another woman, so Lyde says, claimed that she had appeared in seven forms, and that she went to a village where she had lived in a previous state to tell the people where to dig for water. The villagers listened to her advice, and when they dug at the spot she pointed out, they found water. Lyde seems to dismiss these anecdotes as lies and fancy, however.[23]

The Nusayris support their belief in metempsychosis by citing passages such as Quran 6:38: "There is no beast on earth nor fowl which flies with its wings but communities like you. We have not omitted anything from the Book [Quran], and they [beasts and fowl] shall all be gathered [on the Day of Resurrection] before their Lord." This and other passages from the Quran believed to confirm metempsychosis are found in *Kitab al-Haft al-Sharif.*[24]

According to Muslim heresiographers, these passages were also cited by the ancient Ghulat to justify their belief in the transmigration of souls. In this context, al-Nawbakhti notes the passage from the Quran cited above together with another (35:24), "and there never was a people without a warner (a prophet who carries a divine message) having lived among them [in the past]." He comments that the Kaysaniyya, Harithiyya, Abbasiyya, and Khurramdiniyya sects, which believe in the transmigration of souls, interpret these passages to mean that beasts and fowl were formerly people and communities. Those good among them who died were reborn in bodies more perfect than their own, while the wicked were transformed after death into grotesque and dirty forms.[25] Thus, the state of beasts and human beings in this context seems to be the same.

Among other passages cited by the Nusayris to support their belief in metempsychosis is Quran 6:27: "If you could see them when they stand before the fire of Hell, they would say, 'Would that we could return. Then we would not deny the revelation of our Lord.'" In *Kitab al-Sirat,* the author seems to have twisted this passage to read, "Would that we could return in order to do other than what we did." The author apparently takes the passage to mean that people facing the fire of Hell shall return to the world once more in human form, in order to act justly and be purified of their former sinful ways, finally being drawn to heaven.[26]

Another passage, Quran 40:11, states, "They shall say, 'Lord, twice you have made us die, and twice you have given us life. We now confess our sins. Is there no escape from Hell?'" Again, the Nusayri author of *Kitab al-Sirat* cites this passage to show that God's causing people to die and live again is a continuous cycle; sensing that this cycle of life and death is continuous, the people in this passage are asking whether there is any escape from it.[27]

Still another passage, Quran 4:56, says, "Those that deny our revelations, we will burn in Hell-fire. No sooner will their skins be consumed than we shall give them new skins, so that they may truly taste our scourge." Quran 17:50–51 adds: ". . . Say: You shall; whether you turn to stone or iron, or any other subsance which you may think unlikely to be given life." The author interprets these passages, taken together, to mean that those people who after death assumed human form (skins) but were not sufficiently purified would be transformed into inanimate substances, like stone or metal.[28]

In *Kitab al-Haft al-Sharif,* the Imam Jafar al-Sadiq cites several Quranic verses to support metempsychosis. One of these is Quran 10:31—"Who brings forth the living from the dead, and the dead from the living"—which al-Sadiq interprets to mean that people will pass through seven stages of metempsychosis in seven bodies. The believer shall assume a human form, while the infidel shall assume an animal form. Another passage is Quran 95:4–5—"We molded man into a most noble image, and in the end we shall reduce him into the lowest of the low"—which al-Sadiq interprets as meaning that the infidel shall assume an animal form in perpetuity, while the righteous shall be free from such transformations.[29] Thus the destinies of the wicked infidel and the believing Nusayri are predetermined: the infidel will become an animal, while the believing Nusayri will go through a process of purification by metempsychosis, finally becoming a luminous star, or angel.

Do the Nusayris embrace a concept of eschatology, including resurrection and a day of judgment? Nusaryi sources imply that the Nusayris do expect a kind of millenium in the world, for they speak of the Resurrection and Judgment. But the significance of these events in the Nusayri religious system seems to be allegorical rather than literal. In *Kitab Majmu al-A'yad,* Iblis (Satan) is said to have asked God to postpone his punishment to the Day of Resurrection, but he was granted a shorter postponement: to the day of the appearance of the Mahdi, who shall kill Iblis.[30] Such a mention of the Day of Resurrection is purely Islamic and conflicts with the Nusayri belief, as stated in the catechism, that after leaving their graves, the souls of Nusayri believers will go to the great world of light, while those of the godless and polytheists will be tormented and suffer for all ages. We learn from *Kitab Ta'lim al-Diyana al-Nusayriyya* that Ali will manifest himself once more without any transformation, in pomp and glory, to claim for himself the world from one end to the other. He will become the Lord of all. In this last manifestation, without veil or intermediary, he shall reclaim the souls of the deceased believers from their flesh and blood coverings and clothe them in eternal light.[31]

There is no evidence here of a real resurrection or judgment. There is only an indication of a state in which perfect souls become part of the divine essence (the essence of light). The Nusayris believe that stars are perfected souls. Hence, they pray to their God Ali to draw the believers to his presence, that they may enjoy the bliss of being near him and his might.[32] Another prayer says, "Remember God with a due remembrance, and remember His Name, and His Door, and His Incomparables and all the people of His hierarchies, that they may release you from your graves, and the envelopes of flesh and blood in which you are now enclosed."[33]

The Nusayris believe that at death, the soul leaves the body of the dying person through the mouth. For this reason, the Nusayris object to the hanging of criminals, believing that hanging prevents the soul from quitting the body. Thus, whenever the government of Latakia in the last century condemned a Nusayri to die by hanging, his relatives offered considerable sums of money to have him impaled instead. Lyde relates that he often saw in the houses of the Nusayris two holes over the door, so that when the soul of a departed Nusayri left the body, it would not meet an evil spirit entering the house through a single hole.[34]

The day of the appearance of Ali is called Yawm al-Kashf (the Day of Manifestation). On this day all the kings and rulers of the earth shall stand in the presence of Ali, who shall subdue his adversaries by the sword, destroy the unjust, and conquer all regions. The earth will be in great turmoil, but Ali will come and save all the worthy ones.[35]

After Ali, the Mahdi shall appear and possess all the earth. He shall conquer kings, rulers, and Kharijites [those who turned against Ali in his struggle with Muawiya, the Umayyad governor of Syria]; control the seven regions of the earth by his sword; establish justice; destroy oppression; banish the corruptors; and alter the laws and ordinances. Then will follow the judgment of people according to their deeds. Those who have done good deeds shall go to paradise, but the wicked who passed through many periods of transformation and still failed to become totally purified shall be cast into eternal fire.[36]

This concept of reward and punishment is allegorical, however; in the Nusayri system, the bliss of Paradise and the torment of the fires of Hell are not to be understood in the Islamic sense. Paradise or eternal bliss is to know Ali and acknowledge him as God, and to honor and acknowledge the mystery of the Nusayri trinity of Ali, Muhammad, and Salman al-Farisi. He who knows these three is in Paradise, while he who does not know or acknowledge them is in Hell. Thus, the infidels, atheists, and polytheists of all sects and religions who do not know or who deny Ali shall be in Hell.[37] The ultimate state of happiness, then, is to know the trinity without an intermediary and to live eternally in one of the seven heavens according to one's position. According to Jafar al-Sadiq in *Kitab al-Haft al-Sharif,* the first heaven is for the Imams, the second for the Natiqs (proclaiming prophets), the third for the Najibs (excellents), the fourth for the Mukhlisun (peculiars), the fifth for the Aytam (incomparables), the sixth for the Hujub (intermediaries), and the seventh for the Babs (doors).[38]

33

The Nusayri Religious System

Initiation

Like other Ghulat, the Nusayris are very secretive about their religious beliefs. They will not divulge them to strangers.[1] We learn from the accounts of Muslim heresiographers that ancient extremist sects, usually called *batinis* (from *batin,* inward religious meaning) for their allegorical or esoteric interpretations of the Quran, kept their teachings absolutely secret to protect their communities from the intrusion of foreign ideas. Abd al-Qahir al-Baghdadi (d. 1037) gives an account of the different stages through which these sects passed on their teachings to the neophyte. When a neophyte advanced to the last degree, he was asked to state under oath that he would keep the teachings secret, never divulging anything without the authorization of the leader or his representative.[2]

In this sense all of the Ghulat sects, particularly the Ismailis, Bektashis, Kizilbash, Shabak, Ahl-i Haqq, and Nusayris, functioned as secret societies, disclosing their teachings only to fully initiated and fully participating members sworn to keep those teachings secret. The reason for this secrecy, al-Baghdadi explains, is that the founders of these esoteric religions were Majus (adherents of Mazdaism) who did not dare proclaim their religion openly, for fear of the Muslims' swords. They resorted to secrecy to preserve their ancient religion (especially the belief in the principles of good and evil, symbolizied by light and darkness), which depended on allegorical interpretation of parts of the Quran and of the traditions of the Prophet Muhammad.[3] For this reason, initiation into the mysteries of the sect is an extremely important ceremonial process in the Nusayri religious system.

There are two main versions of the Nusayris' initiation ceremony agreeing in general but differing on minor points. One is contained in ancient Nusayri sources; the other is described by Sulayman al-Adani in his *Kitab al-Bakura*. The differences between them arise from the fact that the account of ancient Nusayri writers is based on the tradition of the Nusayri subgroup called the Qamaris (also known as Haydaris or Kalazis), while al-Adani derives his account from the tradition of the Shamsis (or Shamalis). The differences between the beliefs of these two groups were discussed at length in chapter 28.

Among the Nusayris, only males are initiated, because religious knowledge is the exclusive privilege of the male. Instruction is also confined to those who were born to Nusayri parents. Nusayri males of mixed marriages, especially of non-Nusayri mothers, cannot be initiated. The ceremony of initiation is conducted by a religious shaykh selected by the father of the initiate. Usually the shaykh belongs to a family of shaykhs whose function is to conduct the ceremony of initiation. Thus, the solemn duty of imparting religious mysteries to the initiate is restricted to certain families. The shaykhs (religious teachers) are called *Uqqal* (initiates), while the laity are called *ammis* (commoners). The Nusayris' ceremony of initiation consists of two parts. The first part is called al-Taliq, also called al-Dukhul, which ushers the initiate in the community of the chosen [Nusayris]. The second is called Rutbat al-Sama (listening), which directs the attention of the neophyte to the teaching and guidance of his instructor in the mysteries of the faith.[4]

The initiate must be eighteen years old, or sixteen if he is the son of a shaykh. On the day of initiation, the neophyte brings with him an animal for sacrifice. He is accompanied by the shaykh, usually of the rank of Naqib, who partakes of the sacrifice. The shaykh, known as the *amm* (uncle) of the initiate, begins the ceremony of initiation in the presence of two or three witnesses, who testify that the initiate is of good conduct and will never betray the secrets of his religion.

After delivering a sermon, the officiating shaykh stands with the neophyte to his right. The shaykh orders the young man to place the slippers of his Imam on his head as a sign of humility.[5] Then the initiate implores the congregation to ask his shaykh and his lord to accept him as his child, to free his neck from the yoke of bondage, to direct him to the right knowledge of God, and to deliver him from the darkness of blindness and from the mushabihiyya (anthropomorphists and polytheists). The congregation stands and tells the shaykh that this disciple has implored them, in the most perfect manner, to ask him to grant the disciple's wish and accept him. After accepting their intercession, the Naqib removes the slippers from the neophyte's head and asks him to sit before the Imam. The Imam turns to the neophyte and recites the following passage (Quran 53:3–5): "He does not speak out of his own fancy. This is an inspired revelation. He is taught by one who is powerful and mighty."

Then the Imam recites a tradition in which the Prophet says, "Unite in marriage and multiply, for I will be boastful of you before the nations on the Day of Resurrection." (This passage is strikingly similar to Genesis 9:1: "And God blessed Noah and his sons and said unto them. 'Be fruitful and multiply and replenish the earth.' ")[6]

The Imam explains that the ceremony of initiation just conducted is a consummation of Nikah al-Sama, a kind of spiritual marriage between the neophyte and his Naqib or shaykh, and that the reason the congregation attended the ceremony was to sanction his *nikah* (marriage) to his religious guide. If the neophyte rejects this "spiritual marriage," the Imam then figures out the amount of money the neophyte has spent on his initiation ceremony and asks those present to reimburse him. If the neophyte obeys, then the Imam holds his right hand and says, "I unite you in marriage by the order of God and His will, and according to the tradition of His apostle, to your master . . . because God has put you in his trust. It is a trust delivered according to God's order. Certainly God has established something which cannot be doubted—the light of knowledge and the truth of the faith."[7]

The Imam goes on to tell the neophyte that this light will grow and its sanctity become greater because of the thirst the neophyte will develop for the spiritual instruction of his religious shaykh, or guide, and because of his readiness to accept the shaykh's words much as a fetus is formed and begins to develop in its mother's womb. Then the Imam asks the neophyte whether he has accepted this marriage. If he says he does, the Imam blesses the neophyte for accepting the marriage.[8]

The so-called marriage concluded between the neophyte and the Sayyid, his religous instructor, should be understood only as a spiritual bond uniting the two men in the fundamental mysteries of the Nusayri religion, the manifestation of the God Ali in human form and his representation in the trinity with Muhammad and Salman al-Farisi.

It is believed that in this spiritual union, the word of the initiator fertilizes the soul of the neophyte. According to a Nusayri source, in this spiritual marriage, the neophyte becomes a "woman," that is, a "spiritual wife" to the instructor, whose teaching he will carry as a woman carries a fetus in her womb.[9] The new spiritual relationship between the neophyte and his instructor (Sayyid) becomes exactly like a blood relationshp between close relatives which forbids intermarriage between them. The neophyte is forbidden to marry a daughter of his instructor, for she is considered his real sister. The neophyte cannot desert his instructor except with the instructor's consent. If the instructor goes on a journey or moves to another locality, he should first inform the Imam, so that another instructor can be found to continue teaching the neophyte and complete his initiation.[10]

The Imam's use of symbolism during the initiation ceremony, when he reminds the neophyte that God has established in him the light of knowledge, which will grow and develop like a fetus in its mother's womb, helps to illuminate the Nusayris' belief system.[11]

Why should the mystery of religion be symbolized in terms of light, and its development likened to that of a fetus? We have already discussed the importance of light in the religious system of the Nusayris, who maintain that before the world began, they were themselves luminous lights. As we shall see later that the Nusayris also associate wine with light, calling wine Abd al-Nur (the servant of light).

Edward Jurji sees a strong connection between the Nusayri process of instruction, the concept of light in Sufism, and the mysticism of the Ishraqis, followers of the Islamic school of philosophy called Hikmat al-Ishraq (wisdom of illumination). The concept of illumination among the Sufis, especially Shihab al-Din Suhrawardi (d. 1191), is greatly influenced by the philosophy of Hellenism, which reached the Near East through Neo-Platonism. As for the Ishraqis, one of the fundamental characteristics of their mystical theosophy is the theory that a spiritual light constitutes the reality of all things. Light is the essence of all beings; even God Himself is light. Therefore, superior intellects coming from God are also light. Since God is the Light of Light, the Ishraqis believed, the whole of existence is light which, through "irradiation" (in Arabic, *ishraq*) from its primary source, illuminates the world of darkness. The concept of light may have reached the Nusayris through the Ismailis and Illuministic Sufis and thus may be ultimately traceable to Neo-Platonism and Zoroastrianism.[12]

When the first stage of the initiation, symbolized by the "marriage" of the neophyte to his instructor, has been accomplished, the neophyte then waits for nine months, the period of a normal pregnancy, at the end of which the final stage of the initiation, called Rutbat al-Sama, is celebrated. During this nine-month period, the neophyte receives instruction in the Nusayri faith. This faith, which is being nurtured in his soul as the fetus is in the mother's womb, will grow during the nine months, until the neophyte is ready to deliver his spiritual 'baby,' that is, his developed faith, and join the fraternity of Nusayri believers.[13] This view of initiation is also held by the Ismailis and the Druzes.[14]

The second and final stage of initiation is a solemn occasion for the neophyte. If the neophyte comes from a rich family, a great deal of money will be spent for this occasion. The ceremony is conducted in the presence of three religious dignitaries, representing the Nusayri trinity. The first of these dignitaries is the Imam, who represents Ali; the second, the Naqib, represents Muhammad; and the third, the Najib, represents Salman al-Farisi. The Naqib, it should be pointed out, is the *amm* (uncle) who participated in the instruction of the neophyte.

Beside these dignitaries the initiation ceremony is also attended by twelve other Naqibs, representing the twelve Apostles of Jesus and twenty-four men, twelve of whom, also called Najibs, act as witnesses. The other twelve, called Hawariyyun (apostles), act as the guarantors of the first twelve. Dussaud raises the question of whether these twenty-four men suggest the twenty-four elders in the Book of Revelation, who sit on twenty-four thrones in God's presence. He later dismisses this notion of borrowing from Christianity, however; maintaining instead that the Abbasids instituted twelve Naqibs when they were operating clandestinely against the Umayyads. Dussaud also states that Quran 5:15 institutes twelve Naqibs to correspond to the captains of the twelve houses of Israel.[15] Recalling Exodus 19:28, we may speculate, then, that the twelve Naqibs of Islam (and thus the twelve Nusayri Naqibs) are connected with the twelve captains of Israel in the Old Testament and the twelve Apostles of Jesus in the New Testament.

This second part of the ceremony of initiation is very lengthy, containing many prayers, invocations, and oaths. Thus we will describe only its essentials, following the description in Arabic MS. 1450, in the Bibliothèque Nationale. The Imam asks the neophyte what his ideas are, what seems right to him after serious consideration, and what he requires from his Sayyid.

If the neophyte answers that his wish is to have his neck freed from the yoke of bondage and to be directed to the right path, the Naqib warns him once again that he has prepared himself for the demands of a great matter, the "mystery of mysteries and the article of the faith of the righteous."[16] The Imam then recites the words of the Imam Jafar al-Sadiq: "If anyone readily receives our instruction, it opens for him the door of the heart so that he becomes an able man. But he who receives it with doubt will only be removed by it to a great distance from us."[17]

The Imam further warns the neophyte that if he reveals the doctrine, he will be counted among the brethren of devils and transformed into a succession of horrid creatures. He will also be tortured in every revolution of time. The Imam advises him, therefore, to consider his choice carefully.[18]

If the neophyte agrees to the Imam's exhortation the Imam will bind him with the following contract.[19] "In the name of the Lord, the compassionate, the merciful; in the name of the ancient Mana and the great Ism and the lasting Bab, and the high road of those rightly directed, and the eye of certainty, and the foundation of religion, I make between you (with your full consent, and with freedom of determination with respect to what is mutually agreed upon between you and these notables who are present) a free and unconstrained contract . . . I have made a contract between you and your religious guide, the contract of AMS, the weapon of the pious." The Imam follows this by reciting Quran 48:10, cited earlier.[20] After further instructions, the Imam asks the Naqib to present a cup of wine to the neophyte, who drinks "the mystery" of the Imam. He hands him a second cup to "drink the mystery" of his instructor, and a third one to "drink the mystery" of the congregation. Thereupon, each one present rises and drinks the "mystery of acceptance," indicating the admission of the neophyte into the fraternity of the Nusayris. All those present then kiss the Imam, one by one.[21]

A different account of the ceremony of initiation is given by Sulayman al-Adani, who was himself initiated into the Nusayri fraternity. His account derives from the tradition of the Shamsis, while the account given above derives from the tradition of the Qamaris.

Al-Adani states that his initiation took place in the city of Adana, Turkey, when he was eighteen years old. The people of his community began to disclose to him the mysteries of their religion, which are withheld from anyone under eighteen (or in some cases twenty) years of age. One day a crowd of high and low Nusayris gathered in Adana and called al-Adani to come to them. When he appeared, they presented a cup of wine to him. The Naqib, who stood next to him, asked him to say, "By the mystery of your benevolence, O my uncle, my Sayyid and the crown of my head, I will be your disciple, and your shoes will be upon my head." When al-Adani drank the wine, the Imam turned to him saying, "Would you take up the shoes of those here present upon your head to do honor to your Lord?" Al-Adani answered that he would put on his head only the shoes of his Lord, the Imam. This response made the audience laugh, because it was not according to the rules of the initiation ceremony. The attendant was ordered to bring the shoes of al-Adani's Sayyid, the Naqib, to which they fastened a white cloth. They uncovered al-Adani's head and placed the shoes upon it. The Naqib then chanted a prayer that al-Adani might accept the mystery of religion. When the prayer ended, the shoes were removed from al-Adani's head, and he was instructed to keep the ceremony secret. Then everyone dispersed. Al-Adani calls this gathering the Assembly of Consultation.[22]

After forty days another crowd assembled and called al-Adani to join them. The Sayyid, or Naqib, handed al-Adani a cup of wine, which he drank, and then commanded him to recite the mystery of AMS, which (al-Adani explains) stands for Ali, Muhammad, and Salam al-Farisi. The Imam then commanded al-Adani to recite the symbolic letters ayn, mim, and sin five hundred times a day. Before he was dismissed, al-Adani was once again enjoined to keep the ceremony a secret. This second gathering is called Jamiyyat al-Malik, which may mean the Adoption Assembly. After seven months (more commonly the interval is nine months), al-Adani was called for the third time and was made to stand at some distance from the group. A deputy from the assembly stood with the Naqib on his right and the Najib on his left, each carrying a cup of wine. Turning their faces toward the Imam, they chanted the third hymn by al-Husayn Ibn Hamdan al-Khasibi and then walked toward the Murshid (religious guide), chanting, "I inquired about the location of the dwelling-place of the traits of noble character, and certain men directed me to you. By the truth of Muhammad and his family, have mercy on him who has come to kiss your hand. I have sought you, so do not disappoint my belief in you, for we are all today in your charge."[23]

The three men laid their hands on the Murshid's head and then seated themselves. The Murshid rose, took the cup from the deputy and, prostrating himself, chanted the sixth chapter (prostration) of *Kitab al-Majmu,* and lifting his head, he read the chapter of the Ayn. Then he drank the contents of the cup and recited the seventh chapter (al-Salam).[24]

The Murshid then walked toward the Imam, saying "Yes, yes, yes, my Lord the Imam." The Imam replied, "May it be gracious to you and to those around you. You have done what this assembly could not have done. You have received the cup with your own hand, drunk it, prostrated yourself, and made the necessary greeting. To God alone worship is due. Tell me, what is your need, and what is it that you want?" The Murshid answered, "I want to have a blessed evening by looking at my Master's face." Having said that, he retired, looked toward the heavens, and returned to the Imam, the deputy, the Naqib, and the Najib, and repeated, "Yes, yes, my Lord." As before, the Imam asked him what he wanted. The Murshid said he had a need that he wanted to see fulfilled. The Imam told him to go and fulfill his need. The Murshid then approached al-Adani and asked him to kiss his hands and feet, which al-Adani did. The Murshid returned to the Imam, and the Imam asked him once more about his need. The Murshid said that a person had appeared to him on the way, and that that person was this man (al-Adani) who had come here in order to be initiated "in your presence." "Who directed him to us?" asked the Imam. The Murshid replied, "The ancient Mana, the great Ism, and the noble Bab, signified by AMS." The Imam asked the Murshid to bring the man in, that he might see him. The Murshid took al-Adani by his right hand and led him toward the Imam. When al-Adani drew near, the Imam stretched out his feet, which al-Adani kissed. Al-Adani also kissed his hands. The Imam asked al-Adani what his need was. Thereupon the Naqib rose, stood next to al-Adani, and instructed him to say, "I ask for the mystery of your faith and your believers." The Imam looked sternly at al-Adani and asked what had made him seek this mystery, crowned with jewels and pearls, which no one can carry except an angel or a prophet sent by God. The Imam went on to tell al-Adani that though angels are numerous, only those near to God can carry this mystery; though prophets are many, only those charged with God's mission can carry it; and though believers are many, only those who are tested can carry it. The Imam then warned sternly, "Do you accept the condition that your head, hands, and feet be cut off rather than you disclose this mystery?" Al-Adani replied that he accepted. The Imam then added that he demanded one hundred witnesses, to which those present replied that the Imam should implement the law. The Imam agreed and reduced the number of witnesses required to twelve. When they were appointed, the Murshid and al-Adani hurried to kiss the Imam's hands. They told him that if the initiate [al-Adani] disclosed or betrayed the mystery, they would bring him to the Imam, cut his body into pieces, and drink his blood. The Imam, not quite sure of their pledge, asked for two notable witnesses to guarantee the first twelve. When the two were found, they told the Imam that they would guarantee the twelve sureties and the initiate. They pledged that if the initiate escaped or betrayed the mystery before he had fully learned the form of their prayer, they would bring him to the Imam to be killed.

The Imam then called al-Adani to him and asked him to swear by the heavenly bodies that he would not disclose the mystery. He also handed him *Kitab al-Majmu,* which al-Adani held in his right hand. The Naqib asked him to swear on this book that he would never betray this mystery, and that if he did, the Naqib would be absolved of his sin. The Imam took the book from al-Adani and told him that he was made to take an oath not because of material concerns, but because of the mystery of God, which his elders and lords had sworn him to keep. Al-Adani says that he placed his hand on the book and swore three times that he would never disclose the mystery. The Imam warned him that the earth would not suffer him to be buried in it if he should disclose the mystery, and that he would never be reborn in human form but would wear the garments of degrading transformation, from which there would never be deliverance.

Then they seated al-Adani and, uncovering his head, threw a veil over it, while the sponsors placed their hands on his head and began to recite prayers from *Kitab al-Majmu*. After that, they all drank wine. The amm (uncle) from the first ceremony al-Dukhul, delivered al-Adani to his Murshid. The amm gave al-Adani a cup of wine, which he drank, and then taught him to say, "In the name of God, and by God, and by the mystery of the lord Abu Abd Allah (al-Khasibi), possessor of divine knowledge, by the mystery of his blessed memorial, may God make happy his mystery." The assembly then dispersed, and the Naqib took al-Adani aside, teaching him chapters from *Kitab al-Majmu,* and acquainting him with the Nusayri prayer that pays divine homage to Ali Ibn Abi Talib.[25]

We learn from this account that initiation is not a trivial ceremony to be observed like a festival. It is, rather, a most serious matter by which the Nusayri neophyte is introduced to the mystery and the holy of holies of this religion. After his initiation, the neophyte is entitled to partake in the celebration of the mass and to receive the consecrated wine in which the God Ali has manifested himself.

Question 82 of *Kitab Ta'lim al-Diyana al-Nusayriyya* asks, "What is the mystery of the faith of the Unitarians, which is the mystery of mysteries and doctrine of the righteous?" The answer is, "It is the mystery of the Tintayn [colloquial Arabic for "two"], which is the true knowledge of God. It is a noble mystery, a great message, a magnificent perception, and a heavy responsiblity which mountains cannot bear because of its position and nobility. It is a healing antidote for him who keeps the mystery, and a killing poison for him who discloses it. It is the two fold [tintayn] mystery of the veiling of our Lord Ali in light, that is, the eye of the sun, and his manifestation in his servant Abd al-Nur (servant of light)."[26]

The servant of light is, in fact, the consecrated wine which only Nusayri initiates may partake of in the celebration of their Quddas mass during certain festivals.[27] Wine occupies a prominent place in the religious system of the Nusayris; they believe that the God Ali has manifested Himself in it.[28] According to Ibn Fadl Allah al-Umari (d.

749/1348), the Nusayris glorify wine and believe it to be light itself. They hold the grapevine in such high esteem that they will not uproot it.[29]

On the margin of page 16 of Arabic MS. 6182, Bibliothèque Nationale, opposite question 82, the Nusayri copyist added the following: "Know ye that this mystery is also called the mystery of good and evil, light and darkness, water and fire, flesh and blood, eating and drinking, life and death, heat and cold, and it is the mystery of the Nawruz and Mihrajan."[30] This is indeed a significant addition since it emphasizes the duality of principles, revealing the Persian, Zoroastrian, Mithraic, and Manichean influences, and connects the Nusayris' mystery with the Nawruz and the Mihrajan, two Persian festivals.

It is the solemn duty of the Nusayri initiate to keep the mystery of his religion secret. He is believed to lose the favor of God and invite death if he does not do so.[31] This is exactly what happened to al-Adani, who recanted his Nusayri religion and converted to Christianity, for which he was burned to death by his own people.[32]

Before leaving the subject of initiation, we should point out that in his short article on the Nusayris, Victor Langlois states that the ceremony of initiation is also called Tazneer (putting on a sash), and that the neophyte has been "tazannara," that is, he has put on a sash when initiated in the presence of two godfathers. Of all the sources discussed thus far, Langlois is the first to mention the use of a sash as part of the initiation ceremony. Since Langlois states that his account derives from a Nusayri manuscript in the library of the Mufti of Tarsus, there is no reason to doubt the truth of his account.[33]

34

Nusayri Ceremonies

Festivals

THE NUSAYRIS CELEBRATE many festivals of varied origins: Arabian, Persian, and Christian. One major source of information about these festivals is the *Kitab Majmu al-A'yad* (Book of feasts), by the prominent Nusayri, Abu Said Maymun Ibn al-Qasim al-Tabarani (d.1034), described because of his religious knowledge as al-Shabb al-Thiqa (the authoritative young man).[1]

From al-Tabarani we learn that the information about the Nusayri festivals is derived from the Imam Jafar al-Sadiq. It is reported that one day Muhammad Ibn Sinan, who attended the assembly of al-Sadiq, asked him to explain the Arabian and Persian feasts that God had mentioned in the Quran. Al-Sadiq gave an account of the festivals, beginning with the Arabian ones.[2]

The association of the Imam Jafar al-Sadiq with the religious system of the Nusayris, and especially with their festivals, is very significant. It demonstrates that the Nusayris are Shiites who recognize al-Sadiqs authority. This Imam is considered as an outstanding jurist and religious authority; indeed, a special juristic and theological school, al-Madhhab al-Jafari, bears his name. To obtain legitimacy as sound and moderate Shiites, the Nusayris capitalized on the name of this Imam. It is no wonder that *Kitab al-Haft al-Sharif,* one of the secret books of the Nusayris, is believed to have been related by al-Mufaddal Ibn Umar al-Jufi about the Imam Jafar al-Sadiq.[3]

But we should not be misled by the Nusayris' association with the Imam al-Sadiq into believing that they are moderate Shiites like the Twelvers, who constitute the majority of Shiites. The Nusayris were and still are Ghulat, or extremist Shiites, who have exceeded the religious bounds of Shiism by deifying the Imam Ali. Indeed, the purpose and celebration of the many feasts found in *Kitab Majmu al-A'yad* constitute clear evidence that the Nusayris are Ghulat. Some of their festivals may seem similar to those of the orthodox Sunnite Muslims, but in reality they demonstrate the Nusayris' extreme Shiite beliefs. The account of each of their festivals given in *Kitab Majmu al-A'yad* is followed by supplicatory prayers or sermons in praise of the God Ali and His divine attributes.

In one section of this book the Imam Jafar al-Sadiq associates the Nusayris with one of the earliest Ghulat, Muhammad Ibn Abi Zaynab, known as Abu al-Khattab. According to *Kitab Majmu al-A'yad,* Muhammad Ibn Sinan asked the Imam al-Sadiq about the day on which Abu al-Khattab proclaimed his *dawa* (call or message). Al-Sadiq answered that that day, a Monday, the tenth of the month of Muharram, is a great day glorified by God. Therefore, believers should spend that day praising God and praying for Abu al-Khattab and his companions.[4]

Who was this Abu al-Khattab, and why was his message so significant to the Nusayris that the Imam al-Sadiq considered the day of its proclamation to be a festival among the Nusayris?

Abu al-Khattab was a Persian client of the Arab tribe of the Banu Asad; for this reason, he was called al-Asadi. He was one of the many Ghulat who lived in al-Kufa, in southern Iraq, which in the eighth century was a hotbed of extreme Shiite teachings.[5]

Abu al-Khattab was a contemporary and acquaintance of the Imam Jafar al-Sadiq. His extreme teaching included the deification of the Imam al-Sadiq. It is said that he pitched a tent in a certain district of al-Kufa and began to call for the worship of the Imam al-Sadiq as God. He also preached that the Shiite Imams were gods and the sons of gods. When the Imam Jafar al-Sadiq learned that Abu al-Khattab was deifying him, he cursed and expelled him.[6]

Abu al-Khattab and his followers revolted against the Abbasid governor of al-Kufa, Isa Ibn Musa (d. 783), who sent a force against them. Abu al-Khattab was captured and crucified in 755. After his death, his followers taught that, although the Imam Jafar al-Sadiq was God, yet Abu al-Khattab was more excellent than he and the Imam Ali.[7] Thus it is clear that Abu al-Khattab's followers considered him to be divine.

In chapter 26, we discussed the Nusayri belief that, in each of the seven cycles of divine emanation, a prophet called the Natiq existed, who was a reflection of the perfect man, and who was accompanied by a Samit who would proclaim and interpret the prophet's revelations. If, as we suggested earlier, this belief, thought to have been created by the Ismailis and adopted by the Nusayris, was in fact generated by Abu al-Khattab, there must have been a close connection between his followers and the Nusayris. It is significant that al-Nawbakhti considers the Ismailis and the Khattabiyya (named after Abu al-Khattab) to be one and the same sect.[8]

Arabian Festivals

Among the Arabian (Islamic) festivals celebrated by the Nusayris is Id al-Fitr, the feast of breaking the fast. Muslims celebrate this feast at the end of the fasting month of Ramadan. But to the Nusayris, it does not have the same significance, for there is no evidence in their Book of Feasts that they fast in the month of Ramadan. There is, however, a prayer in this book for the month of Ramadan; a plea to the God Ali to help, protect, and guide the believers (Nusayris). According to al-Khasibi, Id al-Fitr, much like prayer and alms, is believed to be a personification of the lord Muhammad.[9]

Another Arabian feast is Id al-Adha (the feast of sacrifice), which the Nusayris celebrate on the tenth of the Islamic month of Dhu al-Hijja. The Muslims celebrate Id al-Adha on the twelfth of the same month. To the Nusayris, this festival marks the day on which the Mahdi will appear wielding a sword and causing much bloodshed. To the Muslims, it is the commemoration of Abraham's offering his son, Ismail, as a sacrifice.[10]

Another feast is celebrated in honor of Salman al-Farisi, the third person of the Nusayri trinity. It is observed on the second al-Ahad (Sunday) of the month of Dhu al-Hijja. It is reported that on that Sunday, Ali ordered Salman al-Farisi to enter the house of worship, preach to the people, and, through Ali, expose the false gods and the apostates (those who rejected Ali's divinity). It is also the day on which Ali told Salman that if he asked, he would endow him with eloquence and give him evidence of his (Ali's) divinity. Ali declared Salman to be a distinguished luminary and told the believers, "Salman is a tree, and you are the branches."[11] This is further evidence of the prominent position Salman the Persian occupies in the religious system of the Nusayris.

The Nusayris also celebrate three Shiite festivals, but these observances are characterized by their extreme Shiite beliefs. The first of these festivals is Id al-Ghadir, which is named after Ghadir Khumm (Khumm Pond), the spot where the Prophet is believed to have appointed Ali as his lawful successor to lead the Muslim community, thus confirming the divine office of the imamate.

According to Shiite tradition, in the year 632 A.D., when the Prophet was returning to Medina from Mecca, where he performed his last pilgrimage, he camped near the Ghadir Khumm. Making a pulpit of camel saddles, he began to preach. His followers fraternized with one another, joined in a bond of brotherhood. Ali was not invited to join this circle, however, and that broke his heart. Noticing that Ali was unhappy, the Prophet called him and, holding his hand, he raised it, saying, "He who recognizes me as his master: for him, Ali, too, is master. May Allah love those who love him and be the enemy of those who hate him."[12]

According to the Nusayri version of this event, the Prophet Muhammad said, "He who recognizes me as his Master, for him Ali is his Mana," indicating that the Prophet was revealing the manawiyya (divine reality) of Ali as God, the causal determinant of the entire creation. According to this version, when Muhammad called Ali to him that day, he knew that he was standing before his Lord Ali and his Bab (Salman), but he wanted to reveal the reality of Ali as the Mana (causal determinant) to the world. This is confirmed by al-Khasibi, who declares in a lengthy poem entitled "al-Qasida al-Ghadiriyya" (The Ghadir's Ode) that this feast is called the Feast of al-Ghadir because the lord Muhammad there revealed the divinity of his master, Ali, by saying, "This is your Lord, God and creator; therefore, know and worship him. He is the only one, the architect, the first and the last, the one who causes life and death, the compassionate. I am his apostle servant, sent to you with a divine book [the Quran]. He commanded me to inform his creation that he is their lord and master. He is truly God, and you who have denied this truth shall remain to be transformed, generation after generation."[13] For this reason, says the author of *Kitab Majmu al-A'yad,* the Nusayris (whom he calls Ahl al-Tawhid) celebrate this feast with joy, eating and drinking.[14]

Another Shiite feast is the Feast of the Mubahala, which the Nusayris celebrate on the 21st day of Dhu al-Hijja. As we have already seen in chapter 7, the Prophet Muhammad debated with a group of Arab Christians from Najran, in southern Arabia, as to whether Jesus was the Son of God. Muhammad, asserting that this belief was blasphemy, asked the Christians of Najran for a mubahala; that is, the disputants would supplicate *(bahala)* God over this matter and God, as judge, would strike dead those who were in error. The Shiites used this incident to prove that Ali, Fatima, al-Hasan, and al-Husayn are the family of the Prophet par excellence, and therefore the imamate (leadership of the Muslim community) should be confined to Ali and his descendants. This imamate is a divine office that no other Muslim, no matter how excellent his qualities, can occupy. Moreover, since the members of the family of the Prophet are preexistent and their names are inscribed on the throne of God, Ali and his descendants, the Imams, are the only ones who possess the right, pre-ordained by God, to rule over the Muslim community.

The Nusayri account of the mubahala is a little different from the Shiite account. It expresses the Nusayris' theological dogma of the trinity of Ali, Muhammad, and Salman. According to this version, the mubahala took place near al-Kathib al-Ahmar (the red hillock). The hillock was ablaze with lightning flashes, and when the lightning subsided, Muhammad, Ali, Fatima, al-Hasan, al-Husayn, and Salman al-Farisi appeared. Then, together with some companions, all were covered with a mantle. When the leaders of the Arab Christians of Najran were asked to draw near the shrouded figures to begin the mubahala, they found they were unable to move. They tried three times to draw near, but failed each time. This greatly astonished them. One of the Christian leaders, Shihab Ibn Abi Tammam, called to his companions in rhyme, asking whether they were seeing the same thing he saw, the deity covered with a mantle. The only sense that can be made of this episode is that the Christians of Najran were greatly surprised to realize that they were appealing to Ali, Muhammad, and Salman al-Farisi, the Nusayri trinity, which was identical in makeup to their own Trinity of God the Father, God the Son, and God the Holy Spirit.[15]

Still another Shiite feast is the Feast of the Firash (bed), which the Nusayris observe on 29 Dhu al-Hijja, to commemorate the night when Ali slept in Muhammad's bed to save him from being killed by his enemies, the people of the Quraysh tribe. In the year 622, Muhammad decided to emmigrate with his companions to Medina, to escape the persecution of his enemies, the polytheists of Quraysh. Fearing that his enemies would kill him, Muhammad asked Ali to sleep in his bed, and Ali agreed. When the men of Quraysh stormed into the bedroom, they found Ali in Muhammad's bed. Realizing that they had been tricked, the men gave chase to Muhammad, but he escaped on his camel.[16]

According to one version of this episode, God blinded the attackers and poured dust on their heads. They spent the night in pain and confusion. Then when morning came, Ali went out to them, and they suddenly realized that Muhammad had already escaped to safety.[17] Appended to this version of the episode is an ode by Ibn Harun al-Saigh.[18]

One of the most revered festivals of the Nusayris is Dhikr Id Ashur, or the Commemoration of Ashur, as the title appears in *Kitab Majmu al-A'yad.*[19] Ashur, or Ashura, is the tenth day of the month of Muharram in the Islamic year 61 (10 October 680), on which al-Husayn, second son of Ali, was brutally murdered with his entourage at Karbala, twenty-five miles northwest of al-Kufa in present-day Iraq. To the Shiites, this day is a day of grief and mourning over al-Husayn, who was murdered by his enemies, the Umayyads. Muawiyya, the Umayyad governor of Syria, had challenged Ali, al-Husayn's father, for the office of the caliphate in 661. Ali was killed by a Kharijite, Abd al-Rahman Ibn Muljam, and instantly became a canonized martyr to his partisans, the Shiites. In that year, Muawiyya was proclaimed caliph in Jerusalem. He made Damascus his capitol, and with him began the Umayyad caliphate (661–750).

The Shiites of Iraq declared al-Hasan, eldest son of Ali, as caliph. However, al-Hasan was not interested in becoming a caliph; abdicated the office in favor of Muawiyya and retired to Medina, where he died in 669 at the age of forty-five.

Al-Husayn, the younger brother of al-Hasan, refused to acknowledge Muawiyya and his son, Yazid, who succeeded his father as caliph in 680. The same year, the Shiites of Iraq invited al-Husayn to come to Iraq and be their caliph. Al-Husayn travelled to Iraq with a small entourage. It was at Karbala, where they camped, that al-Husayn and his band were brutally murdered by a contingent of four thousand Umayyad troops commanded by Umar, son of the prominent Arab army commander, Saad Ibn Abi Waqqas. Al-Husayn's head was cut off and sent to the Caliph Yazid in Damascus. The Shiites consider al-Husayn as Sayyid al-Shuhada (the chief of martyrs). With the murder of al-Husayn, Muslim politics triumphed over Muslim brotherhood.

While the tenth day of Muharram (Ashura) is a day of mourning to the Shiites, it is a day of jubilation, of praising God, and affirming His unity, to the Nusayris. The reason for the jubilation is that the Nusayris believe that al-Husayn like Jesus Christ, was not killed: that his murderers merely thought they had killed him. Concerning Jesus' crucifiction, Quran 4:157 states "They [the Jews] declared, 'We have put to death the Messiah Jesus, the Son of Mary, the Apostle of God.' They did not kill Him, nor did they crucify Him, but they thought they did."[20] According to Islamic tradition, Jesus was neither killed nor crucified, but was made to resemble another man, a substitute, whom the Jews really killed. So it was with al-Husayn. His murderers thought they had killed him, but in fact he was concealed from their eyes and they killed another man, Hanzala Ibn Asad, instead: one who resembled al-Husayn. The Imam Jafar al-Sadiq, believed to be the source of the account of the

Nusayris' festivals, states that this episode of al-Husayn is similar to that of Jesus Christ, who the Christians maintain was crucified, but who in fact was not. Likewise the Muslims [Sunnites] and Shiites believe that al-Husayn was killed, but in fact he was not, because, "Our Lord al-Husayn is Christ, and Christ is al-Husayn."[21]

In accordance with the Nusayris' belief, al-Sadiq maintains that all the names from Adam to the Qaim [the twelfh Imam, the Mahdi], including Jesus and Muhammad, denote one and the same manifestation of the Prophethood and the imamate. In other words, al-Husayn is believed to be one of the manifestations of God which appeared in the period of Muhammad, and one of the five members of Ahl al-Bayt (the family of the Prophet), who are considered by the Nusayris to be deities.[22]

In *Kitab al-Haft al-Sharif,* Jafar al-Sadiq states that al-Husayn escaped being killed because he was an Imam and a vicar of God; indeed, God was veiled in him. God showed His grace in not allowing al-Husayn, as one of His chosen, to suffer death at the hands of infidels. This, says al-Sadiq, is a great mystery which is incomprehensible to unbelievers, who do not have vicars of God. But, al-Sadiq continues, "Our own followers, the Shiites, who hear from us the inner knowledge of God, His vicar Ali, and His apostle Muhammad, understand this mystery and deliver it to their believing brothers . . . As Ismail, son of Abraham, was ransomed by a ram when his father tried to offer him as a sacrifice, so al-Husayn was ransomed by the old man, Adlam, of the Quraysh tribe, who was transformed into a ram and was sacrificed instead of al-Husayn."[23]

Al-Sadiq further explains that the would-be murderers of al-Husayn could not have killed him because, as an Imam, al-Husayn had the power to transform himself from a physical to a spiritual body (and vice-versa) at his own discretion. When the attackers of al-Husayn tried to kill him, he simply left his physical body; God lifted him up to prevent his enemies from killing him.[24]

Moreover, al-Sadiq asserts, al-Husayn could not have been killed because God was veiled in him; he was God. This statement confirms to the Nusayris' belief in the divinity of the Imams. Al-Sadiq states that when the enemies of al-Husayn advanced to kill him, he called the angel Gabriel and said to him, "Brother, who am I?" Gabriel answered, "You are God; there is no God but He, the Everlasting, the Everliving, the One Who is the author of life and death. You are the one who commands the heavens and the earth, the mountains and the seas, and they will obey you. You are the one whom no one can deceive or harm." Al-Husayn asked, "Do you see those wretched people who intend to kill their Lord because of their weakness? But they will never achieve their aim nor be able to kill any of God's vicars, just as they failed to kill Jesus and the Commander of the Faithful, Ali. However, they intended to kill these vicars of God, and their intention might be proof convicting them of torture." Following the command of al-Husayn, Gabriel assumed the form of a stranger and went to see Umar Ibn Saad Ibn Abi Waqqas, who had orders from the Umayyad governor Ubayd Allah Ibn Ziyad to kill al-Husayn.

In this guise, Gabriel appeared before Saad, who, though surrounded by guards and generals, was frightened by his looks. Saad asked the stranger what he wanted. Gabriel told him that he was one of God's servants who had come to ask Saad who it was that he intended to fight. Saad replied that he had orders to fight al-Husayn, son of Ali. Gabriel said, "Woe to you. You want to kill the Lord of the Worlds and the God of those who are first and last, the creator of the heavens and the earth and all therein."

When Saad heard these words, he became frightened and ordered his men to attack Gabriel. Just as they were about to strike, Gabriel spat in their faces, causing them to fall to the ground unconscious. When they regained consciousness, Gabriel had disappeared.[26]

Saad and Muawiya (the Umayyid caliph) suffered metempsychosis as their punishment for their plan to murder al-Husayn. They were transformed first into ugly giants, and then into rams. When they appeared as rams before the Lord of Mercy [al-Husayn] and asked him to restore them to human form, al-Husayn refused to do so. He commanded that they remain in the musukhiyya (metempsychotic state) for a thousand years, saying, "I will never forgive you or have compassion for you. I forgive and have compassion for the holy and chosen people only."[27] According to this account, the angel Gabriel, whom al-Husayn dispatched to Umar Ibn Saad, was none other than Abu al-Khattab, who talked to Saad and spat in his face and the faces of his men and caused them to fall to the ground unconscious; and he is the one in charge of their torment forever.

This demonstrates the mind-set of the Nusayris. Religion is the focal point of their lives, directing their every action, at home and in their community, even extending into their government. The story clearly demonstrates the Nusayri belief that Abu al-Khattab existed from the beginning, together with Adam, Noah, Abraham, Moses, David, Jesus, and Muhammad. It is a tenet of the Nusayris' faith, and their sincere belief, that Abu al-Khattab appeared in different forms and was known by different names in every one of the generations of the Imams, and that he controls life and death and provides for mankind by the order of his Lord (al-Husayn).[28]

The story of Abu al-Khattab is also significant from another standpoint. It shows that the Nusayris were among the early Ghulat (extremist Shiites). Abu al-Khattab, whose full name is Muhammad Ibn Abi Zaynab al-Asadi (d. 755), was one of the early extremist Shiites who proclaimed the divinity of the Imams, especially Jafar al-Sadiq. Earlier we discussed the association of Abu al-Khattab with Jafar al-Sadiq and the tradition which al-Khasibi related, indicating that al-Sadiq called Abu al-Khattab the Bab (door), just as his great-grandfather, the Prophet Muhammad, had called Salman al-Farisi the Bab.[29]

Al-Husayn's divinity and his freedom from death are reaffirmed by al-Khasibi, the great apostle of Nusayrism. He states that al-Husayn was Christ and the Mana and that death therefore had no power over him. He also attributes divinity to al-Husayn in a lengthy ode, asserting that divinity could not be killed. After asserting that there is no difference between Jesus Christ and al-Husayn, al-Khasibi goes on to say, "How is it possible to kill the one [al-Husayn] by whose power and mercy people live?" He laments over those (Shiites) who weep over their Lord (al-Husayn), saying, "I will never be party to those who weep over their Lord, whom they think of as having been murdered at Karbala. Such thought is false because, like Jesus, al-Husayn was not killed."[30]

Thus the Shiites' observance of the murder of al-Husayn on the tenth of Muharram (Ashura) as a day of sorrow and lamentation is transformed by the Nusayris into a day of festivity and joy because, being divine, al-Husayn has triumphed over death. Their celebration of this day affirms that the Nusayris are extremist Shiites.

We close the subject of the Nusayris' celebration of Ashura with the following supplicatory prayer, entitled Ziyarat Yawm Ashura, which Nusayris recite upon visiting a holy shrine on the day of Ashura. It epitomizes the Nusayri assertion of the divinity of al-Husayn, over whom death has no power.

ZIIYARAT YAWM ASHURA

> Peace upon you, O brilliant light, radiant beam, shooting star, the Proof against mankind, the Insoluble Bond, the Veritable Door, and the Strong Kernel (of faith). I testify that you have not been killed or vanquished, you have not died or slept, but that you concealed yourself by your power and hid from human eyes by your wisdom.

> You are my Lord, present and absent, witnessing and hearing what people ask, and you provide them with answers. My Lord, upon you and from you is peace. I have come visiting in knowledge and recognition of your excellence, professing your manifestation, seeking refuge in you, worshipping your forms, renouncing those who set themselves to fight against you. You are greater than their will and purpose, and through your power you are far from being subject to killing, captivity, defeat, and persecution. You cause to die whom you will. You provide livelihood to whom you will, without account. You are glorified and highly exalted above the falsehood of the iniquitous, who claim that on this spot (in Karbala) you were buried and vanquished. For you are the creator of death and annihilation. You are the everlasting, everliving, the ancient of days. You are the lord of lords and god of gods. How could you be killed when you are he who authorized life? Or how could your enemies lay hands on you while you are the one who caused them to live and die, whatever you will and wherever you will? Exalted are you above those who say that you were killed, vanquished, persecuted, contained, and buried on this spot. Nay, you have cast your form on your chosen one, Hanzala, who came to resemble you, and for this reason you promised through your forgiveness your Garden (Paradise) and offered him a lofty rank and position. May your greeting, salutation, prayer, and peace be upon Hanzala and upon the Unitarian believers [the Nusayris], who recognize their creator forever and ever.[31]

Another festival celebrated by the Nusayris is called the Remembrance of the Middle of Shaban Night. Shaban is the last month of the Nusayri calendar; the first being the month of Ramadan. The Nusayri calendar was arranged by al-Khasibi, and for this reason it is called in *Kitab Majmu al-A'yad* the year of the Muwahiddin (Unitarians), who are "the noble sect of al-Khasibiyya al-Jiliyya."[32]

In a discourse called the *Rastbashiyya,* al-Khasibi extols the Night of Shaban as a blessed night celebrated for the glory of Fatir (Fatima), al-Hasan, al-Husayn, and Muhsin (a third son of Ali and Fatima who died in infancy), who are the light and essence of Muhammad. Al-Khasibi cites Quran 44:2–3 to show that this night is blessed because in it, God revealed the Quran. To al-Khasibi, it is the Night of Power (Laylat al-Qadr), in which, Muslims maintain, Quran was revealed to Muhammad.

The Muslims celebrate the revelation of the Quran during the night of the 26th and 27th of Ramadan, not during Shaban as the Nusayris do. The Nusayris, desiring to stand apart from the rest of the Muslim community, give the celebration of this night a dogmatic meaning suited to their own extreme Shiite beliefs. Thus, al-Khasibi interprets the Qadr to mean Muhammad, and the night to mean Fatir (Fatima), Muhammad's daughter. Further, he interprets Quran 44:1–2—"We revealed it [the Qur'an] on a blessed night . . . in that night is made distinct every affair of wisdom,"—to refer to al-Hasan, al-Husayn, and Muhsin, through whom the legitimacy of the Imamate was established. Al-Khasibi considers Fatima one of the Imams, asserting that it was only through sheer confusion that she appeared among them in a feminine form.[33]

Here al-Khasibi is in fact reiterating a belief held by some ancient extremist Shiite sects, the Alyaiyya, the Dhamiyya, and the Mukhammisa, who maintain that the members of the family of the Prophet (that is, Muhammad, Ali, his wife Fatima, and their sons, al-Hasan and al-Husayn) are gods, and that Fatima (whom they call by the masculine form Fatim), is one of the Imams.[34]

Persian Festivals

The Nusayris celebrate two solemn festivals of Persian origin, the Nawruz and the Mihrajan. The feast of Nawruz and the Mihrajan. The feast of Nawruz (New Year) is celebrated in April. A very solemn and holy feast, it is the source of great merit to those who have received the faith (the Nusayris).[35]

The Nusayris celebrate this day because of their belief in the spiritual supremacy of the Persians over the Arabs. They believe that the Mana, Ai, appeared in the persons of Persian (Sassani) kings, and that the Persians preferred the divine mystery thus revealed to them after the Arabs, Ali's own people rejected him. As discussed at length in chapter 27, the Nusayris' observance of the Nawruz reveals the Persian origin of the Nusayri religion.[36]

The Festival of Mihrajan is celebrated on 16 October. Although the *Kitab Majma al-Ay'ad* refers to it as one of the finest of feasts, it contains no description of its observance or of its benefits to believers. This book does contain, however, two lengthy invocations describing the divinity of Ali and his appearance in the Persian periods, the second of which states clearly that the Mihrajan is a Persian holiday: "O great Lord Ali, this is a Persian day and a Bahman feast [Bahman is a Persian word for king], which you have instituted and revealed to your chosen ones, offering the Mihrajan to your creation in order that they may receive forgiveness by the knowledge of its inward and outward truth."[37]

Christian Festivals

The Nusayris celebrate many Christian feasts, of which al-Tabarani, in *Kitab Majmu al-A'yad,* lists only one, Dhikr Laylat al-Milad (Remembrance of Christmas Eve).[38] Sulayman al-Adani also describes only the Christmas festival, but he lists many other Christian feasts observed by the Nusayris, including the Epiphany, Pentecost, Palm Sunday, and the feasts of Saint John the Baptist, Saint John Chrysostom, Saint Barbara, and Saint Mary Magdalene.[39]

The festival of Epiphany, which the Nusayris call Ghattas (immersion), is celebrated on 6 January, following the custom of the Eastern Churches. It is the celebration of the baptism of Jesus by John the Baptist in the River Jordan. Jesus was completely immersed in the water during His baptism, and for this reason the Christians, especially the Syrians and Lebanese, call this festival "Ghattas." It is also for this reason that the Eastern Churches baptize by immersion—in the font in the case of an infant, or in a deep receptable with an adult.[40]

The Nusayris have a tradition of adorning trees on the eve of Epiphany, believing that by doing so they will receive anything they have prayed for. On their way back from the ceremony of immersion, they pick branches of myrtle. They dip these branches in water and put them in containers filled with corn, which they then place in various parts of the house. They also bring in stones from their sacred sources of water and place them on fruit trees; this, they believe, will assure them of a bountiful harvest of fruit.[41]

The festival of Saint Barbara is celebrated on 16 October. Some Nusayris have a tradition of lighting bonfires in the village square or in special containers at home on the eve of this feast. On the same evening, young men gather and choose from among themselves one whom they call Arandas (the lion). They dress him in grotesque clothes and blacken his face with charcoal. Then they take him from house to house, shouting, "Biseyyat Barbara, biseyyat Barbara [supposedly the name of the Egyptian cat-headed goddess Bast]"[42] This feast is a combination of Christian and pagan traditions.

The Nusayris celebrate the Feast of Christmas Eve (Dhikr Laylat al-Milad) on 24 December according to one version of *Kitab Majmu al-*

A'yad, and on 25 December according to another version.[43] Their purpose in celebrating Christmas is to affirm their belief in the different manifestations of God, of which Ali was the final one. The Nusayris' Christmas is outwardly Christian, but closer examination shows it to be a demonstration of their extremist Shiite beliefs. Furthermore, we should not be misled by the Nusayri narrative of the birth of Jesus, based on the Quran, to conclude, as did Abd al-Rahman Badawi, that this narrative is Islamic. Badawi maintains that the Nusayris celebrate the birth of Jesus as a manifestation of God because he miraculously spoke like a grown-up, when a newborn in the cradle. Badawi concludes that the Nusayri celebration of the birth of Jesus is not Christian, but Islamic, and in full conformity with the story of the birth of Jesus as recorded in the Quran.[44] This conclusion seems faulty, however. The Nusayris did utilize the Quranic rather than the Biblical narrative of the birth of Jesus, but they did so to affirm their own extremist belief in the different manifestations of God, which is not an Islamic belief. The *Kitab Majmu al-A'yad* provides evidence for this view.

According to this Book of Feasts, Christmas Eve falls on 24 December, the last day of the Greek year. On this night God manifested Himself through birth to the holy Virgin Mary. In Quran 66:12, Mary is described as "Mary, daughter of Imran, who preserved her chastity, and into whose womb he breathed our Spirit. She believed in the word of her Lord, gave credence to His books, and was obedient." To the Nusayris, however, Mary is none other than Amina, the daughter of Wahb and mother of the Lord Muhammad. In other words, in the Muhammadan period, Mary was manifested in the person of Amina. Many Nusayris believe that this Mary-Amina was also manifested in Fatir (Fatima), Muhammad's daughter, because Muhammad reportedly addressed her once by saying, "Come in, O you who are the mother of her own father (umm Abiha)." A more moderate interpretation is that the Prophet used this language merely to indicate that his daughter Fatima was the mother of his grandsons, al-Hasan, al-Husayn, and Muhsin.[45]

The Nusayris belief that Muhammad's mother appeared in the form of Mary in the Christian period is affirmed by the prominent Nusayri writer Abu al-Husayn Ahmad Ibn Ali al-Jilli. Al-Khasibi also speaks of the sanctity of Christmas Eve, in which the Lord Jesus Christ manifested himself: "On a hill where peace sojourns and pure water flows, Mary brought forth Jesus Christ, the Messiah, for whom I sacrifice myself and whom I love sincerely."[46]

The author of *Kitab Majmu al-A'yad* concludes his description of Christmas Eve by stating that ever since the Lord Christ spoke and manifested himself during that night, it has been sanctified and honored.[47] Although this narrative does not mention Ali by name, it does indicate that since Amina, the mother of Muhammad, was none other than Mary, the mother of Jesus, Muhammad is the manifestation of Jesus. In other words, Muhammad, the Ism of Ali in the Nusayri trinity, is also Jesus, who was the Ism of another: of the seven manifestations of God. As the Ism of Ali, Muhammad had to be born miraculously, like Jesus, or else the sequence of manifestations of God asserted by the Nusayris would have been interrupted. That is why the author of *Kitab Majmu al-A'yad* considers Muhammad's mother homologous with the mother of Christ.

One prayer from the Feast of Christmas Eve tells how, on that eve, Ali manifested himself in human form as a child and proved to men his eternity and divinity, as he had done before in different forms in his periodic manifestations. What is significant is that Ali manifested not only himself on Christmas night, but also his Name, Muhammad (who is his Soul, his Veil, and his Throne), and his Bab, Salman al-Farisi.[48]

Another Christmas Eve prayer seems to be more emphatic in stating that Ali appeared in the person of Jesus, and that, as the veil of Ali, Muhammad was manifested in the preceding prophets, including Moses and Jesus. Thus Ali, like his veil, Muhammad, became manifested in Jesus, who is intimately associated with the Nusayri trinity. The prayer contains invocations of Christian personages and describes rituals incomprehensible to any who are not familiar with Christian terminology.

The following prayer, written in very difficult Arabic (in one place it uses the Syriac term Sullaq [Ascension]), particularly illustrates the Christian elements in the Nusayri religion:

> O Lord, I adjure you by the shining light of your awe-inspiring majesty and the tongue which utters the mysteries of your wisdom and explains truths through the mouths of your saints. I adjure you by him who spoke miraculously in the cradle and raised the dead from the grave; by him who binds and looses, threatens and promises; by him whom minds cannot comprehend except by the knowledge and understanding supported by divine miracles and extracted from the universal elements of the divine world and the transcendent spirit manifested in Yasu [Jesus] whose manifestation was Greek and whose speaking [in the cradle] was Jacobite, who appeared as Lord, was lifted up while he was veiled and concealed when he was crucified, and is the same to all those who see him. O Lord, my Master, I adjure you by the celebration of Easter, by the Sullaq [the

> Ascension of Jesus to heaven], by the Anathemas [Hurum] in assertion of the Christian orthodox faith, by the Epiphany, by the great sprinkling of water associated with the Epiphany, and by the innermost [mystery] of Christmas Eve and in honoring it, that you purified the hearts of your saints by fire and spirit.
>
> I adjure you by the glorification of the Great Cross and the Holy Mary and by what is said in the Church; by the magnificent words uttered on the Shaanin [Palm Sunday]; by the monks; by Saint Simon and his light; by the Figs and Olives [Quran 95:1]; by what was dwelt in Peter [probably the words of Christ delivering to him the Keys of the Kingdom] and thy Saint George, who outdid him in the truth; by the crucifixion and Him who was lifted on the cross, by the gospel and him who reads it, by Christ and him who sees Him, by Him "Who is God in heaven and God on earth" [Quran 43:84], there is no God but Him our Lord, the Prince of Bees, Ali, who is manifest in John and Simon Peter, and no Hijab [veil] except our Lord Muhammad, who is manifest in Jesus, Moses, and Saint George, and no Bab except Salman. I adjure you by your self (for there is nothing greater than you) to bring us to full knowledge of you in every transmigration and revolution; inspire us with your guidance, confirm us in following your command, open for us the treasures of your bounty and knowledge; increase generously our livelihood in order to extend the same to our brethren and friends, and do not decrease it or offer it to us with a tight hand. Protect us from all evil and perils, you who control the affairs of heaven and earth, O benevolent and gracious, O Ali, O great.[49]

In essence, the prayer is in affirmation of the Nusayris' belief in Ali's divinity. The Christian terms and the names of saints it contains have been borrowed from the Eastern Churches of Syria, to assert the Nusayris' belief in the many manifestations of God in different periods of time, the last and the most important of which, of course, is Ali.

The various festivals celebrated by the Nusayris, whatever their origins, are transformed within the Nusayri culture into testaments of their belief in the divinity and eternity of Ali. It should be remembered that in Middle Eastern societies, be they Islamic or Christian, religious dogma and doctrine play a very insignificant role in directing the people's lives. Rather, it is the outward aspects of religion—traditions, customs, and ceremonies—that govern the lives of these people.

The importance of these various festivals as an affirmation of the Nusayris' popular beliefs can scarcely be overestimated. Given their importance, it is not surprising that during the seasons of these festivals, the Nusayris visit many *Ziyaras* (holy shrines) of their saints, there celebrating the great mystery, the secret of secrets, the consecration of wine, in a mass called "Quddas," the very word used by the Eastern Churches for the celebration of the sacrament of the Holy Eucharist. This mass will be discussed at length in the following chapter.

Among the Christians, Muslims, and Yezidis (the so-called devil-worshippers), saint worship has exercised a great influence on the religious life of the people.[50] This is true among the Nusayris also. They visit many holy shrines; some commemorating Biblical figures such as the prophet Yunus (Jonah), Rubayl (Reuben), Saint Yuhanna (John), Saint Jirjis (George), and the Sayyida (the Blessed Virgin Mary), while others commemorate Shiite notables: Saykh Badr al-Halabi, Ahmad al-Kirfas, a Nusayri holy man; Jafar al-Tayyar, brother of the Imam Ali and a Shiite personage; and al-Arbain, the forty Martyrs of Sebaste. These holy shrines and tombs are generally situated on hilltops, amid groves of evergreens and oak, with springs nearby, recalling the Canaanite shrines situated on high hills under evergreens. Lyde believes that many of the Nusayri groves are very, very old, perhaps as old as the Canaanites. The shrine typically consists of one square room, topped with a white plastered dome, although some like that of Jafar al-Tayyar, consist of three rooms.[51]

The Nusayris believe in the divine power of the holy men buried in these shrines to cure many diseases. Nusayris also take oaths by these shrines, which they take very seriously, firmly believing that a false oath leads to calamities.[52]

Munir al-Sharif relates that one of the shrines in the village of Rabo, in the district of Masyaf, has a very narrow window. An oathtaker whose veracity is in doubt is made to try to pass through the window; if he has told a falsehood, he cannot pass through it. However, al-Sharif says, many Nusayris mock the miraculous power of the window; they commit immoral acts and then pass through the window purportedly proving that their denials about these acts were truthful.[53]

Other Nusayris believe that some of these shrines warded off bullets fired by the French. Still others, particularly young Nusayri men and women, look to the saints in the shrines to find them the right partner. Childless couples invoke the saints to grant them offspring; farmers pray to them for abundant crops; and householders ask for blessings on their homes.[54] It should be remembered, however, that invoking the divine aid of saints is a universal custom among the people of the Middle East, regardless of their religious convictions.

35

The Nusayri Mass

As noted in the last chapter, the celebration of the Quddas (mass), or consecration of wine, forms an integral part of observance of Nusayri festivals, and thus holds an important place in their religious system.

Since the Nusayris have no place of worship, like those of the Muslims, they celebrate their festivals and perform their Quddas in private homes or out-of-the-way places.[1] According to Sulayman al-Adani, every rich Nusayri man is bound to celebrate one to three festivals every year with his family, relatives, and friends, and to bear the entire cost. The amount he spends on food, drink, and entertainment on these occasions is a measure of his religious zeal.[2]

The consecration of the wine is conducted with utmost secrecy. Watchmen are posted at the meeting place to make sure no stranger gets in. Lyde mentions that many times Nusayris would ask Christians living near their meeting place to leave their homes, because the Nusayris did not want them anywhere near the place where the wine was to be consecrated.[3]

Al-Adani tells us that the meetings are held in the evening and only in towns, because extreme secrecy is not practical in a village.[4] Only initiated male members of the community partake of this Nusayri mystery; women and children are prohibited from attending.

The celebration of the consecration of the wine is extremely important; this writer is convinced that nothing else in the whole Nusayri religious system so fully reveals the essence of their creed than their belief in the manifestation of their God Ali in the consecrated wine.

We have two sources of information regarding the Quddas, or

sacrament, and the prayers recited during this service. One is *Kitab al-Bakura,* by Sulayman al-Adani; the other is *Kitab Ta'lim al-Diyana al-Nusayriyya,* the Nusayris' catechism. The information in the two sources is nearly identical except for some prayers which al-Adani had either abbreviated or merely mentions in passing. But the catechism is concerned not so much with the mechanics of the celebration of the Quddas as with its mystical meaning and theological connotation as a *sirr* (mystery): the manifestation of the God Ali in the wine, which is called Abd al-Nur (the servant of light). Significantly, the concept of light is associated with the Persian Nawruz (New Year). The subject of the Quddas is covered by several questions in the catechism:

> Question 76: What is the Quddas?
> Answer: It is the consecration of the wine, which is drunk in the mystery of the Naqibs and Najibs [religious ranks of Nusayri shaykhs].
> Question 77: What is the Qurban?
> Answer: It is the bread offered by the believers for the souls of their brethren, and for this reason the Quddas is read.
> Question 79: What is the great mystery of God?
> Answer: It is the sacrament of the flesh and blood which Christ offered to His disciples, saying, "Eat and drink thereof, for it is eternal life. . . .
> Question 82: What is the mystery of the faith of the Unitarians? What is the secret of secrets and chief article of the righteous?
> Answer: It is the knowledge of God . . . It is the mystery of the vesting of our Lord [Ali] in the light [i.e., the eye of the sun and his manifestation in wine, his servant Abd al-Nur, the servant of light]. . . .[5]
> Question 91: What is the consecrated wine called which the believers drink?
> Answer: It is called Abd al-Nur [Servant of light].
> Question 92: Why is it called Abd al-Nur?
> Answer: Because God has manifested himself in the same.

Here follows a very important poem by al-Khasibi which associates the Nawruz with the manifestation of Ali in wine:

> The Nawruz of truth is full of benefits and bounty.
> It is realized by the allegiance to the most noble Hashimite [Ali].
> It is the day when God manifested His theophany in the
> Persian period, before he did in the Arab period.

> He exalted the Persian period towards heaven,
> where they [the Persians] saw His excellence.
> And on that day Salsal [Salman al-Farisi] manifested
> himself with authority, who was conformable to an
> Ancient One [Ali], the predecessor.
> Drink, then, from the pure wine, for
> It is the day whose light has shone through the clouds,
> Namely, the day of al-Ghadir [the Khumm Pond],
> where Muhammad
> Intentionally referred to [Ali] as the all-knowing God and
> Lord. . . .[6]

We have elaborated on the Nusayri concept of light and its possible sources in chapter 28 and so shall not repeat that discussion here.[7] It is worth emphasizing, however, that the celebration of the Quddas by the Nusayris is an affirmation of their belief, not in Jesus as Lord and Saviour as the Christians hold, but in Ali as God, who manifested Himself in wine. As noted earlier, the Nusayris believe Ali appeared in the Persian period in the persons of the Sassani kings before he appeared among the Arabs.[8] Thus the implication in this catechism is that the Persians are more favored by the God Ali than the Arabs, although Ali was a pure-blooded Arab from the house of Hashim, to which Muhammad belonged. This belief in the spiritual superiority of the Persians over the Arabs allows as a corollary the belief that Nusayrism is far superior to orthodox Islam, since Ali is the eternal God who was veiled in light, but then appeared in the Muhammadan period and created Muhammad from the essence of his light.

There is a great, irreconcilable difference between orthodox Islam and Nusayrism. In Quran 24:35, God is the light of the heavens and the earth; in Nusayrism, Ali is the eternal light who manifested Himself in wine. To the Nusayris wine is a sacred substance, a personification of the God Ali. When he calls it Abd al-Nur (the servant of light) al-Khasibi is actually considering it as a person. Thus because of its sacred nature, the Nusayris refrain from mentioning wine; they associate it exclusively with themselves. For this same reason, they glorify the grapevine.[9]

There are two versions of the celebration of the Quddas, or consecration of wine, one given in *Kitab al-Mashyakha,* the other in *Kitab al-Bakura*. The order of the service is quite different in the two versions, although they contain some identical prayers. According to *Kitab al-Mashyakha,* the service begins with a prayer of direction, followed by the reading of the first Quddas, called Quddas al-Ishara (the Indication Mass). A second Quddas, containing the prayer of al-Khasibi quoted earlier as the answer to Question 92, is followed by several prayers and chapters from *Kitab al-Majmu*. The partakers of the wind drink the mystery of the host in whose home the ceremony is conducted, and the mystery of the Imams, Naqibs, Najibs, Abd Allah Ibn Saba (a contemporary of Ali believed to be the first to proclaim his divinity), and the pillars of the Nusayri religion, such as Khasibi.[10] In *Kitab al-Bakura,* the service begins with Quddas al-Tib (the Perfume Mass), Quddas al-Bakhur (the Incense Mass), and Quddas al-Adhan (the Mass of the Call to Prayer). These are followed by several prayers and then Quddas al-Ishara, which comes first in the order given in *Kitab al-Mashyakha*.[11]

The two versions essentially agree, however, on the main purpose of the ceremony, which is the consecration and partaking of the wine. Indeed, the purpose of the celebration of the Quddas is to praise and glorify the God Ali and the Nusayri trinity of Ali, Muhammad, and Salman al-Farisi. It also reminds the people that the eternal God Ali is ever-present in the community in the form of wine, and that he is the only God. Here follows a summary of al-Adani's account of the Quddas in *Kitab al-Bakura*. It should be remembered that this mass is conducted during the Nusayri festivals in private homes, because the Nusayris have no places of worship like those of the Muslims.

When the day of festival comes, the people assemble at the house of the sponsor of the feast. The Imam takes his seat, and before him is placed a white cloth, on which are laid mahlab-berries, camphor, candles, and myrtle or olive branches, and a vessel filled with wine or with grape or raisin juice.[12] Two Naqibs (Nusayri religious officers) seat themselves on either side of the Imam. The sponsor of the feast designates another Naqib to act as minister for the occasion, and then the sponsor kisses the hands of the Imam and the Naqibs.

The Naqib designated to conduct the service then rises and, placing his hand on his chest, bids the people good-evening. He asks them whether they want him to minister for them at the feast. When the people agree to his ministering, the Naqib kisses the ground. Then he distributes myrtle leaves while reciting the prayer called Myrtle-String. This prayer is actually a eulogy to some of the early Shiite companions of Ali, including Sasaa Ibn Sawhan and Ammar Ibn Yasir. The prayer is likewise recited by those present, who rub the myrtle leaves and smell them. Afterward the officiating Naqib takes a bowl of water, puts in the mahlab-berries and the camphor, and reads Quddas al-Tib. In this Quddas, those assembled are enjoined to put away hatred and malice from their hearts and remember that Ali is ever-present among them, and that he is the omniscient God, to whom sincere worship is due.

The minister (or officiating Naqib) then pours a spoonful of perfume on the Imam's hand and passes the bowl to another Naqib who pours perfume upon the hands of those present. The minister then reads the prayer called Sitr al-Rayhan, based on Quran 21:31 and 3:43. Those present recite these same passages while washing their faces. Then the minister takes a censor, stands up, and recites the second Quddas of the Bakhur. This mass refers to the wine as Abd al-Nur, and describes it as a mystery. The believers are instructed to incense their cups and light their lamps. They are told to believe that the person of Abd al-Nur is lawful to them and unlawful to others. Al-Adani comments that wine is thus presented as an image of Ali.

After this, the minister incenses the Imam, the two Naqibs seated at his side, and then each of those present while reciting the Sitr al-Bakhur. The receivers of the incense likewise recite this prayer, invoking the names of the Prophet Muhammad and the Imams. When they finish reciting, the minister takes a cup of wine in his hand and, rising, recites the third Quddas, al-Adhan. This service is an exaltation of Ali, the Mana; his wife Fatir (Fatima); their sons; Muhammad as the Veil of Ali; and Salman as his Bab. This is a succinct illustration of the Nusayris' extremist belief. This prayer states that at the time of the call to prayer, Salman proclaimed that there is no God but Ali, no Veil but the Lord Muhammad, and no Bab but Salman al-Farisi, and that the Lord Muhammad as Ali's Veil, is bound to Him, His sent prophet, His revealed book (the Quran), His great throne and firm seat.

The believers are also enjoined to say this prayer, that they may enter the Garden, be delivered from bodily grossness and corporeal darkness, and behold their glorious Lord, Ali. The officiating Naqib then presents the cup he has filled to the Imam, and presents another to each Naqib. They drink the wine and recite the following prayer: "I testify that my master and yours is the Prince of Bees, Ali Ibn Abi Talib, who is unchanging and imperishable and does not proceed from one state to another. I testify that his Hijab is the Lord Muhammad and his Bab is the Lord Salman, and that there is no separation between the Mana, the Ism, and the Bab."

The minister then says, "Brother, take this cup in your right hand and implore your Lord Ali Ibn Abi Talib to help and support you." To this each one replies, "Give, O my brother, that which is in your right hand, and implore your Lord and creator to help and guide you in the affairs of your religion. May God make it to flourish by the sanctity of Muhammad and the members of his family."

Then they kiss each other's hands. Afterwards the minister rises and, placing his hands upon his breast, he says, "May God grant you a good evening, O brothers, and a good morning, O people of the faith. Forgive us any errors and negligence, for man is so called only because he lapses into error. Absolute perfection belongs only to our Lord Ali, the Glorious and Omniscient." He then kisses the ground and sits down.

At this point the Imam stands to officiate. Facing the assembly, he says, "May God grant you a good evening, O brothers, and a pleasant morning, O people of the faith. Is it your pleasure that I should minister to you on this blessed day on behalf of the sponsor?" He kisses the ground, and, doing the same, the assembly salutes him, saying, "We have accepted you as our lord and shaykh (chief)." The Imam then recites the following tradition:

> It is reported on the authority of Jafar al-Sadiq, the Samit [mute] and Natiq [proclaimer], the pure and preeminent, that he said, "At prayer time it is forbidden to take or give, to sell or to buy, to talk or gossip, to make noise or tell stories over the myrtle [considered a religious symbol]. Let every man then be silent, listening, attentive, and saying Amen.
>
> Know, O my brothers, that if anyone bears a black turban on his head [meaning Muslims] or a thimble (Kustaban) on his finger [indicating Christian bishops, who wore rings on their fingers], or has at his waist a two-edged sword [indicating the Druzes and Ismailis, who kill with poisoned knives], his prayer is not valid, because the greatest sin is the one against the myrtle. It is the duty of the messenger to deliver what he has been charged with.

At the end of the prayer, those present prostrate themselves, kiss the ground, raise their hands to their heads, and say, "To God, may He be exalted, be your obedience, O our shaykh and lord."

At this point, the Imam recites what is termed Tabarri, a condemnation by Muhammad Ibn Nusayr of those Sunnite Muslims whom the Nusayris consider their accursed enemies, among whom are the first three rightly guided Caliphs, Abu Bakr, Umar, and Uthamn. After adjuring Ali, to make this an hour of favor, acceptance, and forgiveness for those present, the Imam says, "It is related of Abu Shuayb Muhammad Ibn Nusayr al-Abdi al Bakri al-Namiri that he said, 'Whoever desires salvation from the glow of infernal fire, let him say, "O Lord, curse that company of iniquitous men, oppressors, and those who turned against Ali and who shall end up in hell." ' Chief among these men are the accursed Abu Bakr, the iniquitous adversary Umar Ibn al-Khattab, and that Satan, Uthman Ibn Affan. Others are Talha: Saad; Said; Khalid Ibn al-Walid (handler of the sword); Muawiya and his son Yazid; al-Hajjaj Ibn Yusuf al-Thaqafi, the Wretched; Abd al-Malik Ibn Marwan, the Stupid; and Harun al-Rashid, the Abbasid caliph. May the curse of God rest upon them until the Day of Judgment, when Jahannam [hell] is asked whether it has been filled and it replies, 'There is room for more.' Ibn Nüsayr's condemnation of all the enemies of the Nusayris continues, naming such enemies as Ishaq al-Ahmar, founder of the Ishaqiyya sect; Ismail Ibn Khallad and other prominent Sufis, including the two shaykhs Ahmad al-Rifai and Abd al-Qadir al-Gilani; the four Islamic schools of jurisprudence, the Hanafis, Shafiis, Malikis, and Hanbalis; and every Jew and Christian, including the Maronites, who follow the Patriarch John Marun. In brief, this condemnation is directed against all those who regard Ali as begotten rather than divine and subject to natural needs such as eating and drinking. The condemnation ends with Ibn Nusayr entreating Ali to curse all those who, while feeding themselves on his bounties as God, worshipped other gods. Ibn Nusayr beseeches Ali to rid the Nusayris completely of those accursed enemies as flesh is stripped from bone, by the sanctity of Ali, Muhammad, and Salman, and by the mystery of Ayn, Mim, Sin. Apparently, the latter part of this condemnation is an interpolation by a later Nusayri because both al-Rifai and al-Gilani lived more than two centuries after Ibn Nusayr.

The service does not end here, but continues with more drinking of wine and the recitation of many more prayers, the longest of which is Quddas al-Ishara. This Indication Mass epitomizes the whole theological concept of the Nusayris. It proclaims the divine attributes of Ali, who is alpha and omega, the beginning and the end, the personification of all the Biblical patriarchs from Adam to Shamun al-Safa (Simon Cephas, or Peter), the embodiment of religion and Islam.

The Quddas al-Ishara is followed by the recitation of still more prayers and poems, including a number by al-Khasibi. Two of these prayers, the Right-Hand Invocation and the Left-Hand Invocation, are contained in *Kitab al-Mashyakha*. It is not clear what source al-Adani followed, but it seems that he omitted many prayers in his account, recording only what he thought was most necessary.

The ceremony, as described by al-Adani, ends when all the prayers, including the Right-Hand and Left-hand Invocations, have been recited. The Imam closes by saying, "This homage to God and to you, O brethren, and to all those present." Then he and each member of the assembly kisses the ground and the hands of the persons to the right and the left. They rise and uncover their heads, and the Imam directs the asembly to recite the Fatiha (opening chapter of the Quran), so that the Ottoman state will fall, the rulers of the Muslims perish, and the Khasibiyya-Nusayriyya sect triumph. At the end of the mass, the ministers rise and place food before those present, giving a good part of it to the Imam, who distributes some of it to those sitting near him. Then all eat and finally disperse.[13]

The Christian elements in the Nusayri religion are unmistakable. They include the concept of trinity; the celebration of Christmas, the consecration of the Qurban, that is, the sacrament of the flesh and blood which Christ offered to His disciples, and, most important, the celebration of the Quddas. How did these Christian elements find their way into the Nusayri religion? Are the Nusayris Christian converts to extreme Shiism? Rev. Samuel Lyde (d. 1860), who worked among the Nusayris, states that they received their sacraments from Christianity.[14] Father Henry Lammens (d. 1937) who wrote at length on the Nusayris goes a step further, asserting (in an article entitled "Les Nosairis Furent-Ils Chrétiens?" [Paris, 1901]) that the Nusayris were formerly Christians who converted to extreme Shiism.[15] Lammens wrote this article in response to René Dussaud, who, in *Histoire et Religion des Nosairis* (Paris, 1900), rejected the hypothesis that the Nusayris were of Christian origin. Dussaud maintains that the trinity of the Nusayris is a vestige of the divine trinities worshipped by the Syro-Phoenicians. Furthermore, this is not a real trinity, says Dussaud, for Muhammad and Salman are regarded as lesser beings than Ali. He gives as evidence the phrase "Ali Most High," used by the Nusayris.[16]

As to the celebration of the sacraments and the consecration of wine, Dussaud rejects any Christian influence on the grounds that there are only superficial similarities. Furthermore, he states, the Nusayris do not use the two elements, bread and wine, that characterize the Christian Mass; they use only wine in their service. Thus, Dussaud concludes, one should not pay attention to "certain Nusayri writings" whose authors attempt to show the excellence of the Nusayri religion by identifying it with Christianity.[17]

Dussaud also observes that the tradition of Christmas was transmitted to the Nusayris through the Muslims, not the Christians. With respect to Christian names, Dussaud remarks that such names are also common among the Yezidi tribesmen. His final argument rests in the theory of "religious syncretism, which postulates that two religions living side by side "have a fatal influence on each other." This, he avers, supports his conclusion that the Nusayris were originally Muslims.[18]

Lammens disagrees with most of Dussaud's opinions. He states that he personally visited fourteen Nusayri areas and found many vestiges of Christian churches, sculptures, inscriptions, crucifixes, and tombstones. Lammens does not produce any convincing evidence that the Nusayri trinity is based on the Christian trinity; he makes a rather weak argument that while the author of the Nusayri catechism reveals the incoherence and inconsistence of his ideas, this is characteristic of all Nusayri writing. To Lammens, such inconsistency is an insufficient reason to deny the Christian origin of the Nusayri trinity.

Lammens also states that on one of his visits to the house of a Nusayri shaykh, someone brought a jar of oil, intended for a sick person, for the shaykh to bless. Lammens was able to jot down part of the blessing the shaykh said over the oil. One phrase, "The Messiah, who brought dead persons back to life . . ." led Lammens to compare it with the Christian sacrament of Extreme Unction.

Lammens also believes that the initiation ceremony of the Nusayris has replaced Christian baptism. According to the Nusayris, the initiate becomes the son of the initiator, creating between the two a spiritual relationship identical to a real blood kinship, prohibiting the initate from marrying the daughter of the initiator because she has become like his real sister.

Finally Lammens presents as proof of the Christian origins of the Nusayris their observance of traditional Christian feasts such as the Epiphany, Easter, and Pentecost, and the feast days of some saints, including John the Baptist, John Chrysostom, Mary Magdalene, and Barbara. Moreover, says Lammens, Christian names such as Matthew, Helen, Gabriel, and Catherine are common among the Nusayris.

In conclusion, Lammens maintains that the Nusayris were originally Christians who did not bend under the pressure of Muslim conquest but stuck firmly to the Christian ideas and traditions they had adopted very early in the Christian era. The Muslim customs evident among the Nusayris, he believes, were superimposed on this Christian framework as the result of dogmas spread by the Ismailis and Persian Shiites.[19]

Abu Musa al-Hariri dismisses Lammens' arguments on the grounds that he did not consult a single Nusayri source, but based his opinions solely on physical evidence of Christian practices—Christian ruins and vestiges of Christian faith—observed on his visits to Nusayri villages, evidence that al-Hariri dismisses as misleading.

Al-Hariri states that many villages in the Middle East once had Christian inhabitants who were, for one reason or another, evicted and replaced by non-Christians (most likely Muslims). A man like Father Lammens, with his European mentality, says al-Hariri, is unable to understand this pattern of successive evictions and settlements common to the Middle East.[20]

Abd al-Rahman Badawi agrees with Dussaud that the Nusayri celebration of Christmas is inspired not by the Christian but by the Muslim tradition, based on the Quranic narrative of the birth of Jesus. He observes that the Nusayris celebrate the feast of Christmas because Jesus manifested Himself on Christmas Day and spoke in the cradle, in accordance with the Quranic, not the Biblical, narrative.

Furthermore, Mary is portrayed in the Quran as the daughter of Imran and has no relation to the Mary of the Bible; the Nusayris believe that Mary was none other than Amina, the mother of Muhammad. Finally, Badawi asserts that the Nusayri invocation of Christmas is addressed to the God Ali and not to Jesus. He concludes that the Nusayris' celebration of Christmas is free from Christian influence.[21]

Whether the Nusayris were originally Christians or not, the fact that their religious system and traditions contain many Christian elements cannot be overlooked. Although it may be argued that Father Lammens fails to produce convincing evidence for many of his views, he does pinpoint a significant weakness in Dussaud's argument when he questions the latter's assertion that the reason for the many Christian elements in the religious traditions of the Nusayris is "religious syncretism." What Dussaud means by this is that since the Nusayris lived side by side with their Greek and Maronite Christian neighbors for many centuries, they were likely to have been influenced by Christian tradition. Lammens forcefully retorts that the Ismailis, and especially the Druzes, also had prolonged and close contact with Maronite Christians. Why, he asks, didn't Dussaud's "religious syncretism" affect them?[22]

Dussaud's "religious syncretism" theory is further undermined by the fact that the Nusayris, like the Druzes, are very secretive about their religion and do not divulge anything to strangers. Both groups are closed religious communities. Why, then, should the Druzes show so little evidence of Christian influence and the Nusayris show so much?

Our own study has shown that the Nusayris are one of the ancient Ghulat, or extremist Shiite sects, founded by Abu Shuayb Muhammad Ibn Nusayr, a follower of the eleventh Imam, al-Hasan al-Askari (d. 873). Ibn Nusayr taught that al-Askari was God, and that he was His apostle and the Bab leading to Him. Ibn Nusayr also believed in the transmigration of souls, and he declared incest and homosexuality to be commendable and lawful. These beliefs led al-Askari to condemn and renounce Ibn Nusayr.[23] Although the Nusayri sect takes its name from Ibn Nusayr, it is also known by other names such as al-Namiriyya, al-Khasibiyya, and al-Jiliyya.[24]

The Nusayris, Sunnites, and Twelver Shiites

Outwardly, the Nusayris, like the rest of the Ghulat, seem to be an Ithnaashari (Twelver) sect; Shiites who believe in the divine authority of twelve imams. Like the Twelvers, the Nusayris believe that Ali and his descendants, the Imams, are the only legitimate heirs and successors to the Prophet of Islam in governing the Muslim community. They maintain that the imamate is a divine office that only Ali, whom the Prophet appointed as his successor, should occupy. However, the Nusayris and other Ghulat differ from the moderate Twelvers on many fundamental issues, paramount among them the deification of Ali.

To the Ghulat, including the Nusayris, Ali is God, the very God of the Bible and the Quran, who created the heavens and the earth. They maintain that this God manifested Himself in this world seven times, the last time as Ali. The Nusayris also believe that He is manifested in sacramental wine, which they call Abd al-Nur (the servant of light).

The Nusayris asserted that this God created Muhammad from the light of His essence and made him His Name, the reflection of His essence. They also believe in a trinity of Ali, Muhammad, and Salman al-Farisi. And they share with other Ghulat, especially the Ahl-i Haqq (or Ali Ilahis), belief in metempsychosis, or the transmigration of souls. Finally, they believe that the five persons who constitute the family of the Prophet are deities. These beliefs separate the Nusayris from moderate Shiites and demonstrate that their creed is a syncretism of the astral pagan religious system of the Harranians, Christianity, and extremist Shiism.

We have shown in earlier chapters that the Nusayris do not share the Muslim emphasis on fulfilling Islamic religious obligations, such as prayer and fasting in the month of Ramadan and pilgrimage to Mecca.

They have no mosques or muezzins, as the Muslims do, instead conduct their religious meetings in private homes, most often in the homes of their shaykhs. Moreover, they consider Sunnite Muslims to be their enemies and pray for their damnation.

Like the rest of the Ghulat, the Nusayris are very secretive about their religious practices and beliefs, refusing absolutely to divulge them to strangers. This secretiveness has led outsiders to accuse them of nocturnal sexual orgies.[1] But since no outsiders have ever been admitted to these nocturnal meetings, and since the reports of sexual misconduct came from enemies of the Nusayris, they should be considered groundless calumnies meant to besmirch the name of the Nusayris, who are hated by the Sunnites as heretics.

The former Nusayri Sulayman al-Adani does state, however, that one branch of the Nusayris, the Kalazis, have a custom that stands to support such rumors: when one imam visits another, the host is expected to offer his wife as a bed partner to his guest. Al-Adani says that the Kalazis believe anyone violating this practice will be forbidden to enter Paradise. They seem to base this practice on a figurative interpretation of Quran 33:49, which states, "Prophet, we have made lawful to you the wives to whom you have granted dowries . . . and the other women who gave themselves to you, and whom you wished to take in marriage." Al-Adani goes on to say that when he visited a shaykh from a village near Antioch, woman (whom he does not identify) entered his room at night and lay down beside him, reminding him of his solemn and imperative duty.[2]

Closely related to the secrecy with which the Nusayris surround their religious beliefs and ceremonies are the use of taqiyya (dissimulation) and of conventional signs which suggest a connection between Freemasonry and Nusayrism.

The taqiyya is a strategy by which a person is permitted to conceal, lie about, and deny his true religious beliefs, and even to profess the beliefs of his adversaries, in order to escape persecution or save his life. The practice of taqiyya, which dates back to the earliest period of Islam and was once used by many different Muslim sects, has come to be exclusively connected with the Shiites. The reason is that the Shiites, more than any other sect in Islam, have been the target of persecution by Sunnite Muslims, because of their belief that the imamate is a divine office assigned only to the members of the family of the Prophet.[3] Indeed, ancient and contemporary Muslim writers consider the Ghulat (the Nusayris included) to be subversive elements whose objective is to destroy Islam and Arabism. Ibn Hazm accuses the Persians of deliberately creating the different Ghulat sects in order to destroy Islam. He states that when the Muslim Arabs occupied Persia and converted the Persians to Islam (not without coercion), the Persians lost their state and power to the Arabs, whom they considered inferior to themselves. As a result of this calamitous loss, the Persians became vindictive and went on to fight against Islam. Some of them, who had embraced Islam hypocritically, began to lure the Shiites by pretending that, like them, they loved the family of the Prophet and decried the injustice done to Ali by his enemies, who had denied his exclusive right to the imamate. In this manner, says Ibn Hazm, the Persians were able to inculcate the Shiites with heretical teachings and eventually lure them out of the domain of Islam.[4] This same idea is expressed by contemporary Sunnite Muslim writers, who refer to the anti-Arab and anti-Islamic attitude of the Persian converts to Islam as Shuubiyya, meaning the movement which denigrates the privileged religious and cultural position of the Muslim Arabs. These writers affirm that the Shuubiyya's objective is to destroy both Islam and the Arab entity.[5]

The first instance of taqiyya is associated with Ammar Ibn Yasir, one of the pioneer Shiites and the staunchest supporter of Ali's right to the imamate. It is reported that the banu Quraysh, enemies of Muhammad, captured and tortured Ammar's parents because they had converted to the new religion of Islam. The Quraysh also captured Ammar intending to kill him as they had his parents, for having recanted the idol gods of the Quraysh and embraced Islam. Ammar, fearing torture and death, recanted Islam, cursed the Prophet Muhammad, and professed the idol gods of the Quarysh, whereupon he was set free. When the Prophet Muhammad was told that Ammar had denied Islam and blasphemed, the Prophet did not believe what he heard, but insisted that Ammar was a true Muslim body and soul. Ammar went to see the Prophet with tears running down his face. The Prophet wiped Ammar's tears, saying, "What is the matter with you? How do you find your heart?" Ammar told the Prophet of his encounter with the Quraysh and affirmed that his heart was still filled with faith in Islam. The Prophet said, "If the Quraysh do this to you again, do the same thing you did before."[6] The Prophet therefore approved Ammar's dissimulation under duress as a means of saving his life. As the Prophet was talking to Ammar, the following verse of the Quran was instantly revealed to Muhammad; "Those who are forced to recant while their hearts remain loyal to the faith shall be absolved." (Quran 16:106).[7] We may deduce, then, that taqiyya is sanctioned by the Quran. It has also been sanctioned by the imams, especially Jafar al-Sadiq, who reportedly said, "the taqiyya is of my religion and that of my forefathers; he who has no taqiyya has no religion." Al-Sadiq also asserted on another occasion, "The believer shall be raised to the highest spiritual state by four qualities: faithfulness, truthfulness, decorum, and taqiyya."[8] To the Shiites, taqiyya is the religion of God, and protection is His sword, without which He could not be worshipped. God could not be better worshipped than by taqiyya; thus, it is an essential part of their religion, and neglecting it is the same as neglecting prayer.[9]

To the Nusayris, the taqiyya is a very serious matter. They are admonished to keep their religious beliefs and practices absolutely secret from outsiders. We have already pointed out that, according to *Kitab Ta'lim al-Diyana al-Nusayriyya,* the Nusayris are not supposed to reveal the secrets of their religion except to their brethren. We have also shown that the neophyte makes a solemn oath not to betray the secret of his religion, else he will be punished by death. Indeed, in *Kitab al-Haft al-Sharif,* the Imam Jafar al-Sadiq constantly tells his interlocutor to keep secret the "mysteries of God," and the "knowledge of God, which God has kept secret from His angels."[10]

When they are in the company of members of other sects, especially Sunnite Muslims, the Nusayris profess similar views in order to escape embarrassment or harassment. They swear to the Sunnites that, like them, they fast and pray. Then enter a mosque or masjid with Sunnites and pretend to be praying. They genuflect and prostrate themselves and seem to be reciting prayer, when in reality they are cursing the first three rightly guided caliphs, Abu Bakr, Umar, and Uthman. They justify such behavior by a metaphor; they are the body, and the other sects are clothing, and whatever clothing man may put on will not harm him. In fact, they seem to believe that anyone who does not dissemble in this manner is a fool. However, it is a very serious matter for a Nusayri to abandon his religion or reveal its secrets. According to al-Khasibi, "Whosoever betrays our testimony is forbidden our garden."[11]

The Nusayris seem to interpret the Islamic Jihad (holy war against the infidels) as a form of taqiyya, concealing their faith from non-Nusayris, even if such concealment exposes them to grave danger.[12] Obviously, the reason for such strict emphasis on the taqiyya is the historical religious conflict between the Nusayris and orthodox Muslims, who consider the Nusayris to be infidels.

Like the rest of the Ghulat and batini (esoteric) sects, the Nusayris form a secret society and are classified as such by some Western writers like Heckethorn and Springett.[13] Springett, a Freemason, attempts to establish a connection between the ancient esoteric sects of the East, especially the Nusayris of Syria, and the freemasonic movement.[14] He seems to base this idea on the conventional signs the Nusayris use to recognize one another. Springett's attempt to connect Freemasonry with the Nusayris is not novel. He derives his idea from the accounts of Rev. Samuel Lyde and from Salisbury's translation of al-Adani's *Kitab al-Bakura,* which he has copied. Other Western writers have alluded to the conventional signs used by the Nusayris, without specifying these signs. F. Walpole, who visited Syria in the first half of the nineteenth century, states that the Ansayrii (Nusayris) have signs and questions by which they salute and examine each other as a means of recognizing one another. Walpole says that these signs are little used and known only to a few Nusayris, however, and he does not indicate their nature.[15] Victor Langlois also states that the Nusayris have conventional signs by which they recognize each other, but, like Walpole, he does not describe these signs.[16] It was left to Sulayman al-Adani, a Nusayri convert to Christianity, to provide specific examples of these conventional signs. He states that when a stranger (looking for a relative) comes among his fellow believers, the Nusayris, he inquires, "I have a relative; do you know him?" They ask, "What is his name?" He says, "al-Husayn." They follow up, saying, "Ibn Hamdan." He answers, "al-Khasibi." Thus, through question and answer, the stranger is recognized as a Nusayri by the naming of al-Husayn Ibn Hamdan al-Khasibi, the great apostle of Nusayrism. The second conventional sign of recognition is similar. The Nusayris ask the stranger who is looking for a relative among them: "How many folds has the turban of your uncle?" If he answers that it has sixteen folds, they receive him as one of them. In a third case, the Nusayris ask the stranger, "If your uncle is thirsty, from where do you give him water to drink?" The correct answer is "From the fountain of Ali the divine." the fourth sign is also a question: "If your uncle relieved himself, what would you give him [to wipe himself with]?" The response should be, "The beard of Muawiya [the enemy of Ali]."[17] A fifth question asks: "If your uncle were lost, how would you find him?" the answer is, "By al-Nisba," which in this context could only mean tracing the relationship of the uncle to the host of the apostles of Nusayrism mentioned in chapter 4, *al-Nisba,* of *Kitab al-Majmu.*[18] The seventh sign takes the form of a riddle: "Four and two fours, three and two, and twice these numbers—in your religion, what is the answer? "The answer is, "In al-Musafara." The *Musafara* (Journeying), forms the thirteenth chapter of *Kitab al-Majmu.* It mentions disciples of al-Khasibi, divided into three groups, each from a different country. If one considers the numbers of this puzzle, four and two fours make twelve, and three and two make five, for a total of seventeen, which, added to twice that number, yields a total of fifty-one.[19] If the stranger has guessed this number, he is further asked to state the groups into which these are divided, where they are stationed, and what they do. If he states, in accordance with the Sura of the Musafara, that the fifty-one stand at the gate of the city of Harran, and that seventeen of them are from Iraq, seventeen from al-Sham [Syria], and seventeen are hidden or unknown, and that their duty is to receive justly and render justly, he is received as a genuine Nusayri.[20] It is in these signs that Springett tried to find a connection between Freemasonry and Nusayrism. He states, "Here we have in all probability, the source of the Masonic custom of 'lettering, or halving' passwords in perambulating the lodge during certain ceremonies.[21] Lyde states that in their books the Nusayris use the double interlacing triangle, or seal of Solomon, also used by Freemasons, but he provides no source.[22]

The relation between modern Freemasonry and the ancient esoteric cults of the East requires more investigation, which lies beyond the boundaries of this book. Suffice it to say that the connection between the ancient cults of the Assassins, the Ismailis, and the Templars is more than accidental. Von Hammer indicates many points of similarity among these groups, including the white mantle and red cross of the templars.[23] Lyde states that the Nusayris dress is white and they are fond of red jackets and red handkerchiefs. He further states that there is a degree of Freemasonry called that of the Templars. The Templars lived next to these secret sects, including the Nusayris of Syria, and must have been influenced by their customs and tradition.[24] In investigating the sources of Masonic tradition and ritual, Springett affirms, one should look to Asia in general and to Syria in particular.[25]

The Nusayris have been denounced by Sunnite Muslims as infidels. Shaykh al-Islam Ibn Taymiyya (d. 1328) issued a juristic opinion condemning the Nusayris as infidels. He stated, "Those people who are called Nusayriyya, together with the Qaramita, are more infidels than the Jews and Christians; nay, they are more infidels than many polytheists, and their harm to the nation of Muhammad is greater than that of the infidel Turks and Franks. They appear to be ignorant Muslim lovers of Ahl al-Bayt (the family of the Prophet), but in reality they do not believe in God, His messenger (Muhammad), or His book (the Quran). Nor do they believe in reward and punishment, the Garden (Paradise) or Hell, or in any messenger who preceded Muhammad."[26]

The Ghulat have also been condemned by Twelver Shiites for their extreme beliefs. Among these Shiites we may cite Ibn Babawayh al-Qummi (d.991), who, although he does not mention the Nusayris specifically, condemns all the Ghulat as "infidels and worse than the Jews, Christians, and polytheists."[27]

Ibn Shahr Ashub (d.1192) condemned the Nusayris as nihilists (Ibahiyya), saying, "Muhammad Ibn Nusayr revived ghuluw [extremism] by claiming that the most High God is Ali. The band of Nusayris who followed him are nihilists who relinquished Islamic worship and religious duties and permitted immoral and forbidden acts."[28]

A modern writer, Abd al-Husayn Mahdi al-Askari, avers that the Nusayris should not be considered Shiites as long as "they renounce the Ithnaashari Shiites and their beliefs."[29] In recent times, however, some Sunnite and Ithnaashari writers have tended to consider the Nusayris to be "true Muslims," either because they were persecuted or in conformity with the true spirit of Muslim brotherhood. Al-Hajj Amin al-Husayni, the Grand Mufti of Palestine (d. 1974), issued a juristic opinion in 1936 calling on Muslims to cooperate with the Nusayris. He stated, "These Alawis [Nusayris] are Muslims, and it is the duty of all Muslims to cooperate with them and stop antagonizing each other for reasons of religion . . . because they [the Nusayris] are brothers who have common roots and interests with the Muslims and, according to Islamic brotherhood, Muslims should love for others what they love for themselves."[30]

Munir al-Sharif, who lived for many years among the Nusayris and visited their villages, especially in and around Latakia, states that the Alawis (Nusayris) are a Muslim sect who continue to read the Quran with great respect, and that their rituals are the same as those of the Muslims, although they "have no mosques and maintain some of the ignorant extremist beliefs among them."[31]

It is evident that although al-Sharif considers the Nusayris to be Muslims, he admits that they have no mosques and that they harbor extremist religious beliefs; thus his statement confirms what has been said earlier, that the Nusayris are Ghulat who lie outside the pale of orthodox Islam.

Another writer, al-Shaykh Mahmud al-Salih, considers the Nusayris a true Shiite Muslim sect and says that everything written about them by Orientalists or other writers is sheer fabrication.[32]

In 1956, Muhammad Rida Shams al-Din, a Shiite living in Lebanon, was delegated by the highest Twelver Shiite authority in al-Najaf (Iraq) to go among the Nusayris and study their conditions and religious beliefs. Shams al-Din visited the Nusayris and wrote an account in which he tried to portray the Nusayris as true Shiite Muslims, although he remarks with obvious regret that he found the Nusayris to be lax regarding Islamic religious duties such as prayer and pilgrimage. He also notes that the Nusayris have no mosques, but excuses them on the grounds of poverty and politics, by which he means that the Syrian government is against them.[33]

Several Nusayri writers have also written in defense of their people and religious beliefs. One of these is Arif al-Sus, who tried to show that the Nusayris are Shiite Muslims who believe in God and His apostles, and in the walaya (vicegerency) of Ali as the "brother" and cousin of the Prophet. Al-Sus further states that the Nusayris observe all the Muslim religious duties, such as prayer, pilgrimage to Mecca, and the offering of zakat (religious tax).[34]

Another Nusayri, Abd al-Rahman al-Khayyir, wrote several articles defending the Nusayris as true Muslims, although he admits that many superstitions have crept into their beliefs because of their cultural decline and manipulation by their shaykhs. However, al-Khayyir relates an incident which shows that as far back as the beginning of the nineteenth century, the Nusayris had no mosques and did not perform the pilgrimage to Mecca. He states that in 1838 a prominent Nusayri, Shaykh Abd al-Al, known as Hajj Mualla, went to Mecca to perform the pilgrimage. On his way back to Syria (then under the rule of Muhammad Ali, viceroy of Egypt), Hajj Mualla stopped in Egypt and obtained permission to build a mosque in this village.[35]

In 1938, the magazine *al-Nahda* published a special issue about the Nusayris in which some Nusayri authors wrote articles in defense of their people as true Muslims. One of these writers, Ahmad Sulayman Ibrahim, lamented the bad luck of his people. He said they were constantly persecuted, for no reason other than that "we were and will ever be in relation to Islam as the roots are in relation to the trunk."[36] In this same issue of *al-Nahda* another writer, Muhammad Yasin, emphatically states that the Nusayris are Muslim Shiites and seems greatly surprised by those who say that they are not Muslims.[37]

In addition to these defenses, Nusayri religious leaders issued several declarations to prove their innate Islamism. Perhaps they were encouraged by the juristic opinion of the Grand Mufti al-Hajj Amin al-Husayni, which affirmed they were true Muslims.

In 1936, Nusayri religious men published a pamphlet in which they stated emphatically that the Nusayris were Shiite Muslims, and that any Nusayri who did not recognize Islam as his religion and the Quran as his holy book would not be considered a Nusayri according to the Sharia [Islamic law].[38]

In 1938, Nusayri religious leaders issued a proclamation entitled,

"Decidedly, religion with God is Islam." In it, they stated that their religion was Islam, according to the Jafari Theological School, named in honor of the Imam Jafar al-Sadiq. In June 1956, after twenty days of deliberation with the Nusayri religious men, the Mufti of Syria agreed to license Nusayri religious men to teach their faith and allowed them to wear religious garb like other Muslim religious men. But the most significant proclamation was that issued by Nusayri religious men at their meeting in 1392/1972. In this proclamation they elaborated on the articles of their faith, their belief in God, the office of the imamate, the Quran, the Sunna, eschatology, and other doctrines. As a matter of fact, these Nusayri religious men reiterated the Twelver Shiite doctrines and affirmed that they held the same beliefs. The proclamation was signed by eighty Nusayri religious men.[39]

The Nusayris' identification with true Islam was further strengthened by President Hafiz al-Asad of Syria. In the mid-1970s, after only a few years in power, al-Asad asked Syrian Sunnite Muslim religious men to declare him a true Muslim, which they did. He also persuaded Lebanese Shiite religious men to declare the Nusayris true Muslims.[40] Furthermore, the Nusayri-controlled Syrian government published a book to prove that the Nusayri community was an inseparable part of the main body of Islam. This book was distributed on a grand scale by various government agencies. It was followed by the publication of an edition of the Quran carrying a picture of al-Asad on its front page, which the people called "al-Asad Quran." In the meantime, al-Asad made a change in the Syrian constitution, inserting a new article stating, "Islam shall be the religion of the head of state."[41]

One might ask why the Nusayris have this penchant for identifying themselves with Islam. If the Nusayris are true Orthodox Muslims, why is there such urgency to prove it? Our study of the history and religion of the Nusayris shows that they were not and still are not regarded by Sunnites and Twelver Shiites as true Muslims, despite the efforts of some writers to exonerate them of heterodoxy.

In the 1930s, under the French mandate, the Nusayris stated they were not Muslims and declared the Sunnites their enemies. Some of them, however, witnessing the rise of Arab nationalism and the liberation of Syria at the end of World War II, attempted to identify themselves with Arab nationalism and true Islam to escape alienation and persecution by Sunnite Muslims. Some of the more prominent Nusayris must have believed that identification with true Islam would assure them of positions in the Syrian government and would expedite their rise to power. When they finally achieved control of the government in 1971, when Hafiz al-Asad became the first Nusayri president of Syria, the Nusayris were still considered heretics by the Sunnite Muslim majority in Syria, as well as opponents of both Arab nationalism and Islam.

In order to protect their position and power, the Nusayri rulers resorted to secularization and socialism as a means of diminishing the role of Islam and the position of the Sunnite religious men in the state. These efforts enraged the Sunnite community, especially in the city of Hama, where riots broke out in the spring of 1973 because the government had not included an article in the newly proposed constitution stating that Islam was the religion of the state.[42]

The Sunnite uprising motivated Hafiz al-Asad to declare himself a true Muslim and amend the constitution, declaring Islam to be the state religion. Peter Gubser remarks rightly that al-Asad's objective in identifying himself with Islam was to broaden his base in the Syrian society, rather than to lessen Nusayri consciousness or distinctiveness.[43]

The measures taken by al-Asad failed to convince the Sunnite majority of his true allegiance to Arab nationalism and to Islam. The Nusayris continued to be considered a heterodox minority that had usurped power from the Sunnite majority. Key positions in both the army and the civilian sector of the government were occupied by Nusayris, while the few positions in the cabinet filled by Sunnites were mere window dressing.

The bubble of tension, suspicion, and antagonism towards the Nusayri-controlled government finally burst in March 1980; Sunnite Muslims in the major cities and towns went on strike. Demonstrations against the government began in Aleppo and then spread to other cities. The strikers demanded an end to sectarianism and sectarian rule. Government's answer was the use of force and the dissolution of both labor and professional unions. For a while the situation seemed to have calmed down, but riots broke out in 1982 in Hama, and al-Asad retaliated by ordering the destruction of most of the city.[44]

In conclusion, based on their own writings and literature, the Nusayris (or Alawis, as they are known today), are a heterodox sect, called Ghulat or extremists by Muslim Sunnites and Twelver Shiites. Their religion is a syncretism of extreme Shiite, pagan, and Christian beliefs, and they fall outside the pale of orthodox Islam. The very fact that some of them deify Mujib and Saji, the sons of Sulayman al-Murshid (who, because he declared himself God, was executed by the Syrian authorities in 1946) is a demonstration that the Nusayris believe in the continuous manifestation of the deity, a belief repulsive to orthodox Islam.[45]

37

Pagan, Christian, and Islamic Elements in the Beliefs of the Ghulat

REFERENCES HAVE BEEN MADE throughout this study to pagan, Christian, and Islamic elements in the beliefs of contemporary extremist Shiite sects, and especially to such Christian elements as the celebration of festivals, the private and public confession of sins, and the partaking of a ceremonial meal resembling the Lord's Supper. In this chapter we shall discuss the sources of these elements and show how they found their way into the worship and rituals of extremist Shiite sects, particularly the Kizilbash Kurds of Turkey.

It would be easy to dismiss the members of these sects as heterodox Shiites who have deviated from orthodox Islam, but the fact remains that they maintain many religious beliefs and rituals not only alien but blasphemous to orthodox Islam. Thorough investigation surprisingly reveals a Christian origin for some of these beliefs. Al-Sarraf, who discussed the confession of sins and the ceremonial meal observed by the Shabak, states that these practices are of Christian origin, but fails to explain how such non-Islamic rituals came to be practiced by the Shabak. Although he avers that these rituals are common among such other groups as the Bektashis, Kizilbash, Nusayris, and Ahl-i Haqq (Ali Ilahis), he admits to puzzlement as to how they found their way into the worship of these extremist Shiites.[1]

We have pointed out throughout this study that the contemporary Ghulat are mostly of Turkoman, Persian, Kurdish, or Arab origin. Despite their common belief in the deification of Ali, their names, languages, and locations vary widely. The Ahl-i Haqq are found mainly in Western Iran; the Shabak, Bajwan, Ibrahimiyya, and Sarliyya-Kakaiyya live in Iraq; the Nusayris live in Syria and Lebanon; and the Bektashis, Kizilbash (Alevis), Çepnis, and Takhtajis in Turkey.[2] Generally, the names of these sects indicate a religious rather than an ethnological identity. The study of their religious tenets reveals a syncretism of Islamic Shiism, Sufism, and Christianity, along with traces of animistic and heathen superstitions. But one should be careful not to confuse these sects with the greater body of Shiites, especially the Twelvers, who do not deify Ali. These sects are extremists whose apotheosis of Ali is the cornerstone of their belief. Their belief in a trinity of God, Muhammad, and Ali (or Ali, Muhammad, and Salman al-Farisi in the case of the Nusayris) and in metempsychosis also separates them from Twelver Shiism and from orthodox Islam.

There is a great deal of fluidity and divergence in the religious practices of the Ghulat sects, due perhaps to the ignorance of their religious leaders, their lack of substantial body of religious literature, and the utter secrecy with which they guard their beliefs. Nevertheless, the investigation of these beliefs shows that they derive partly from heathenism, partly from Shiite Islam, and partly from Christianity.

Writers have observed idolatrous practices among these groups, especially the Kizilbash. Dunmore writes that whenever the Kizilbash find a piece of black wood, they worship it, saying it is a relic of some holy man or of a horse.[3] Herrick considers them heathens because they revere their religious leaders to the point of worship. He reports some of these idolatrous practices, for example, their practice of bowing before wands cut from a certain tree and kept in the house of their shaykh, or religious leader.[4] In this sense the Kizilbash are no different from the Ahl-i Haqq, who deify their shaykhs.[5] J. G. Taylor speaks of a rock that is the object of idolatrous worship by some Kizilbash in the district of Dersim (Tunceli), in the upper Euphrates valley. He also reports that some Kizilbash worship fire, the sun at its rising and setting, and the sources of rivers, practices he believes are remnants of old Armenian paganism.[6] Taylor thus implies that the Kizilbash Kurds of Dersim are of Armenian origin; this, as shall be seen shortly, has a great bearing on the presence of Christian elements in the worship of extremist Shiite groups. Similar traces of paganism among the Kizilbash have also been observed by Grenard, who reports that they worship the sun and the moon, and subscribe to the cults of the goddesses Anahit, Artemis, Aphrodite, Astarte (Ishtar), and others.[7] This has also been observed by G. E. White, who points out that in ancient Anatolia, the female principle in the divine nature was primary, while the male principle was secondary, accounting for the worship of goddeseses.[8] Devil worship is reported among a branch of the Ahl-i Haqq as well as among the Yezidis of northern Iraq. It may be more accurate, however, to say that the Ahl-i Haqq and Yezidis do not worship Satan as a deity, but honor him from fear of his evil power. Like the Yezidis, some Ahl-i Haqq honor Taus Malak, the peacock angel that they believe guards the gates of paradise; they are therefore known as the Tausis, or peacock sect.[9] Pantheistic beliefs are also reported among some of the Ahl-i Haqq. S. G. Wilson, a longtime missionary in Persia, states that some Ahl-i Haqq (whom he calls Ali Ilahis) maintain that "not only prophets and Imams, but also all of God's creation (including angels), emanate from Him and are an integral part of His essence. This belief is closely associated with the doctrine of metempsychosis and the ultimate absorption of all things in the infinite."[10] Although specific pagan practices are not reported among the extremist Shiites of northern Iraq, it is certain that the Shabak share with their neighbors the Yezidis a veneration for some holy shrines (the shrine of Hasan Fardosh in the village of al-Darawish, east of Mosul, Iraq, for one) in addition to celebrating of some Yezidi festivals.[11] The Ghulat also believe in the transmigration of souls, a doctrine which has a major place in the belief systems of the Ahl-i Haqq (Ali Ilahis), the Kakaiyya, and the Nusayris.

On the Shiite side, we may note the exalted position these groups give to the Imam Ali, whom they deify. They consider him part of a trinity along with God and Muhammad or among the Nusayris, with Muhammad and Salman al-Farisi. They exalt Ali above the Prophet Muhammad, who they maintain was the forerunner of Ali. To them Ali is God incarnate. He is the divine being that dwelt in the biblical prophets Abraham, Moses, and David, and even in Christ. As an expression of their worship of Ali, they offer him prayer and sacrifice.[12] To the Nusayris Ali is God Himself, the Lord of Lords, the creator of mankind and the source of the livelihood of His creation. The author of the Nusayri *Kitab al-Mashyakha* (Manual for shaykhs) states that Ali/God created Muhammad from the light of His unity and from the power of His eternity. This book contains traditions in which Muhammad himself attests to the divinity of Ali, demonstrating that Ali is superior to Muhammad.[13] The extremist Shiites also exalt the Imams, considering them infallible, sinless, and divine.

Such hyperbole is totally foreign to orthodox Islam. In fact, to orthodox Muslims, the majority of the Shiites, and especially the Ghulat, are heretics. The Ghulats' total disregard for religious duties and obligations moreover, drive them still farther from orthodox Islam. They do not pray or perform the ablution (purification by washing) before prayer.

They do not fast during the month of Ramadan or make the pilgrimage to Mecca. They do not recognize the Quran as the only sacred book—they have their own sacred books—or accept Muhammad as a prophet. Some of them prohibit divorce, a practice sanctioned by the Quran. They have a religious hierarchy of elders, or shaykhs, who they believe are the descendants of Ali and are infallible regarding religous matters.[14]

The most striking phenomenon about the extremist Shiites is the Christian elements in their belief and rituals; those elements are noted by almost every writer who has come in contact with them. Most of the writers focus on the Bektashis and Kizilbash of Asia Minor and on smaller groups like the Takhtajis and Çepnis; Sir Charles Wilson was the first to classify the Shabak and Bajwan as Kizilbash, who have many things in common with the Ahl-i Haqq of western Iran.[15]

Christian elements are prevalent in both the beliefs and the rituals of the extremist Shiite groups. The Nusayris celebrate Christmas and other Christian festivals, and their catechism affirms their belief in the Holy Eucharist. Some extremist Shiites believe that Jesus is the Son of God or even God Himself, although they maintain that He appeared under the name of Ali. They believe that as God is Christ, so Ali is the one who spoke through Moses and the prophets. To them Jesus is also the Word of God and the Savior of men, who intercedes with the Father on behalf of sinful humanity.

Like the Christians, they maintain that God comprises a trinity, although unlike the Christian trinity, the three persons of their trinity do not seem to be equal. Some of them baptize their children, but in the name of Ali. They believe that Mary is the mother of God, and that her conception of Jesus was an act of divine will. Like the Roman Catholics and all the Eastern Churches, they maintain that Mary was a virgin before and after she gave birth to Christ. They celebrate a rite resembling the Lord's Supper, partaking of a cup of wine which they call the Cup of Love; Those guilty of sin are not allowed to partake of this cup. They confess their sins to their pirs and once a year hold a ceremony of public penance.

The religious hierarchy of the Ghulat is quite similar to that of Christianity. They observe several Christian holidays and honor several Christian saints. Finally, some of them accept the Bible rather than the Quran as a sacred book.[16] Nutting, who attended an open prayer meeting of some Kizilbash in Turkey, writes that at the end of their worship, men and women kissed one another in the most modest manner. This practice resembles the Christian kiss of peace, performed during the celebration of the liturgy by the Eastern Churches to this day. Nutting also found other practices among the Kurdish Kizilbash which he believed had a Christian origin. Among these were phrases and concepts contained in their songs and hymns proclaining such Christian truths as the duty of humility and the necessity of forgiving injuries inflicted by others.[17]

Before baking their bread, the Kizilbash women around Marsovan, Turkey, mark every loaf with the sign of the cross.[18] Christian traits among the Kizilbash of the Hermus valley in the neighborhood of Sardis were noted by Sir William M. Ramsay. He states that while the men of these villages bore Muslim names, the women had such common Christian names as Sophia, Ann, and Maryam. The villagers drank wine and were monogamous. They accepted Christian holy books and were visited by an itinerant religious official, a kind of priest, called a Karabash (one who wears a black headdress). Ramsay's informant told him that these villagers were Christians with a veneer of Muhammadanism.[19]

Their beliefs and practices have led many writers to regard extremist Shiites as crypto-Christian or, as Grenard puts it, "Islamic Protestants."[20] Some writers have maintained that these extremist Shiites are closer to Christianity than to Islam.[21] S. G. Wilson states that one of the beliefs of the Ahl-i Haqq of Persia is that as a god incarnate, Ali manifested himself in Christ. Therefore, Ali and Christ are identical; like Christ, Ali becomes the Redeemer. For this reason the Ahl-i Haqq receive Christians as their brethren and listen to the gospel. Wilson further relates that one time, when he attended the celebration of the Persian New Year, a part of the end of the celebration was omitted, and at that point he was invited to read from the Injil (gospel).[22]

F. M. Stead relates that once, when he was preaching the gospel to the Ahl-i Haqq in Western Iran, they asked him, "Why do you come to us with this message? We are already near you in belief. You should go to the Muslims, who are far removed in faith."[23] This corroborates the statement of de Gobineau, who wrote in the middle of the nineteenth century that the Muslims of Persia consider the Ahl-i Haqq close to the Christians, for just as the Christians believe that Jesus is God incarnate, the Ahl-i Haqq believe that Ali is the manifestation of God.[24] Such evidence illustrates how far these deifiers of Ali are from orthodox Islam and how near they are to Christianity. G. E. White, for many years a missionary in Turkey with many friends among the Kizilbash (whom he calls the Shia Turks), rightly states that there is much truth in their claim that "less than the thickness of an onionskin separates [them] from Christians."[25]

Our study of the extremist Shiite sects of northern Iraq shows that their rituals, like those of the Bektashis and Kizilbash, contain unmistakably Christian elements. There is no evidence that these rituals were introduced by the small Christian communities in Iraq (namely, the Assyrians or Nestorians), whose members were converted to Catholicism in the eighteenth and nineteenth centuries and were renamed Chaldeans by the Church of Rome. To determine the effect of Christianity on the extremist Shiites of northern Iraq, we should look for evidence instead among the Shiite heterodox groups of Turkey, especially the Bektashis and the Kizilbash. These groups, Turkoman by origin, lived in Anatolia and held the same religious beliefs as the Shabak and related sectaries in Iraq. But how were these extremist Shiites in Turkey influenced by Christian beliefs and rituals?

To answer this question, it is necessary to trace the spread of Christianity among the Turks and Mongols. In the apostolic and post-apostolic eras, Christianity spread into Central Asia and China, taking especial hold among the Turks and Mongols. There is ample evidence in Greek, Latin, and Syriac sources to attest to this historical fact. From Bardaysan (154–222), Eusebius of Caesarea (263–339), and St. Jerome (347–420) to the Syrian Maphrian Bar Hebraeus (1226–86) and the Venetian traveler Marco Polo (1254–1324), we learn about the spread of Christianity among the Scythians, Parthians, Chinese, Turks, and Mongols.[26]

It is difficult, however, to determine the extent to which Christianity influenced these people, especially the Turks, among whose beliefs Christian elements persisted even after their conversion to Islam. One could dismiss the whole question by saying that after the Byzantines were defeated at the battle of Malazgirt in 1071 and the hordes of Muslim Turkoman tribes rushed from Persia to Iraq to dwell in Asia Minor, there ensued a mass conversion of the Christian population to Islam. One can also speculate that the Ghazis—zealot Muslim religious warriors motivated by the Islamic tenet of Jihad (holy war) against the Christian "infidels"—were instrumental in spreading Islam in Asia Minor and establishing a number of Muslim Turkish states. There is evidence that the leaders of these Ghazis, the Danishmends, were Armenian converts to Islam,[27] which explains the emergence of crypto-Christian communities like the extremist Shiites. On the surface this may be true, and there is no denying that cases of forced conversion among the population of Asia Minor can be cited. But there is no evidence of forcible mass conversion under the Seljuk Turks.

As the Ottomans consolidated their power toward the end of the thirteenth century, a large number of conquered people converted to Islam, and a new army, the Janissaries, was recruited from captured

Christian children. Many of the Christians retained their religion and were recognized as independent ethnic or religious communities under the millet system.[28] From a purely economic point of view, mass conversion of these rayas (subjects) was not in the interest of the Ottomans, because as soon as the rayas became Muslims they were exempt from the taxes imposed on non-Muslims according to Islamic law. There were, however, Christians who converted to Islam but retained most of their religious practices in secret. They are most likely the same people from Trebizond and the neighboring mountains mentioned by W. J. Hamilton. He calls them "Greek Turks" or "Turkish Greeks" and says that they profess to be Muslims and, observe such Muslim religious duties as circumcision and attending the mosque, but are secretly Christians.[29] According to Ramsay, these crypto-Christians "have now ceased to be under the necessity of practicing this sham Mohammedanism."[30]

Rev. Horatio Southgate also refers to these people in describing a visit to the district of Trebizond in 1841. He states that in the city of Trebizond, there are several hundred people of Greek origin called Croomlees who are outwardly Muslims, but secretly Christians. They baptize their children, receive Holy Communion, and welcome priests to their homes, but in public they profess to be Muslims and wear the white turban of the Turks. Southgate also writes that in the vicinity of Trebizond there are many Muslims of Greek descent; indeed, they make up the majority of the Muslim population between Trebizond and Gumuşhane.[31]

Vital Cuinet mentions the crypto-Christians of Trebizond in the district of Rize, who, though Muslims by faith, have preserved some Christian rituals, such as baptism.[32] Many of these crypto-Christians speak not Turkish but Armenian, indicating their Armenian origin. Southgate states that in the district east of Trebizond live some thousand Muslim families of Armenian origin who still speak the Armenian language.[33] The influence of Armenian Christianity on the extremist Shiites, particularly the Kizilbash, will be explored later. Suffice it to say here that incidents of conversion to Islam did exist. The conversion to Islam of the crypto-Christians of Trebizond, however, was recent (the seventeenth century), and they were most likely converted to Sunnite rather than to Shiite Islam.[34]

Tracing the history of the transition from Christianity to Islam in Asia Minor is difficult and complex, due mainly to the dearth of information available about the Christian cults in Asia Minor at the time of the Turkish conquest, except for the heterodox Paulicians in Armenia and eastern Anatolia, who shall be discussed later. There is, however, ample evidence of religious interrelations between Christians and Muslims and of the usurpation of many Christian sanctuaries and saints by Muslims.[35] Like the orthodox Muslims, the Bektashis, Kizilbash, and Mevlevis appropriated a number of Christian sanctuaries, saints, and burial grounds, but in their dealings with the Christians of Asia Minor they followed a policy of tolerance, in order to win the Christian peasantry to their fold.

It should be remembered that the difference between the Bektashis and Kizilbash is less in their teachings than in their organization,[36] and if we realize that the Shabak and other related sects in northern Iraq are of both Bektashi and Kizilbash origin, we can safely state that what applies to the Bektashis and Kizilbash regarding their association with Christianity applies also to the Shabak and related sects. One difference is that while the Bektashis and Kizilbash in Asia Minor continued to revere Christian saints and sanctuaries, the Shabak and related sects, who since the sixteenth century had lived as an isolated group in northern Iraq, lost faith. Their neighbors were either Sunnite Muslims or Yezidis, and the Shabak and related sects found themselves drawn more toward the Yezidis than to the Sunnite Muslims, with whom they had sharp religious differences. This explains their sharing of some shrines and festivities with the Yezidis. From the defeat of the Byzantine army at the battle of Malazgirt (1071) until the rise of the Ottomans to power at the end of the thirteenth century, Christians and Turks lived side by side. The establishment of the Seljuk state of Rum in 1077 may be regarded as the beginning of a long association between Muslim Turks and Christians. The Seljuk sultans of Rum were patrons of the liberal arts, literature, and science, and left behind them the most beautiful architecture in Asia Minor. Many of them were familiar with Christianity and treated their Christian subjects with tolerance.[37]

The Seljuks may also have been influenced by the Crusaders from Europe, who in 1096 marched through Asia Minor on their way to the Holy Land to wrest Jerusalem from Muslim hands. In 1190 Frederick Barbarossa captured Konya, the capital of the Seljuks, forcing Konya to furnish him with guides and provisions. Six years later, the Seljuk Sultan Rukn al-Din Sulayman (reigned 1196–1206) coined money in imitation of Christian money. The opponents of the Seljuks, the Danishmends of Malatya (Melitene) and Sivas, even minted coins with the image of Christ on them. Many of the coins minted by Rukn al-Din Sulayman had a portrait of a horseman carrying a mace on his shoulders, in imitation of the coin minted by Roger of Antioch one hundred years earlier.[38]

The Seljuk Sultan Ala al-Din Kaykubad I (reigned 1219–36) became acquainted with Christianity during his eleven years of exile in Constantinople. One of his predecessors, Ghiyath al-Din Kaykhosraw I (reigned 1192–1196 and 1204–10), who was obliged to take refuge in Lesser Armenia, Trebizond, and Constantinople, fell in love with a Greek woman while in the Byzantine capital, a lady of noble birth, the daughter of Manuel Movrozomas.[39] At one time Ghiyath al-Din was accused of apostasy by his more strict Muslim neighbors of Aleppo.[40] It is even said that Giyath al-Din's son Izz al-Din Kaykaus I (reigned 1210–19), while in Constantinople, was admitted to the Sacraments.[41] Many Seljuk sultans married Christian wives and had Christian mothers, some of whom had great influence on the Seljuk court. One of these women was the Georgian Princess Russudana, wife of Ghiyath al-Din Kaykhosraw II (reigned 1236–45). Kaykhosraw's II intention to stamp a portrait of his wife on his coin met with public opposition, and he was forced to abandon the idea.[42] His partiality toward the Christians also enraged his Muslim subjects. His chief judge accused him of loving and admiring the Byzantine [Christian] way of life. Angered by the audacity of the judge, Ghiyath al-Din had him killed instantly.[43]

In the latter part of the thirteenth century, the prevalence of Christian elements among the Turks of Asia Minor caused Anthimus, Patriarch of Constantinople, to believe that Izz al-Din Kaykaus II (1246–83) had secretly converted to Christianity, and that there were many converts among the Bektashis and the Ismailis. It is not certain whether Izz al-Din Kaykaus II was converted to Christianity, but there is no doubt that his youngest son, Malik Constantine, lived in Constantinople, converted to Christianity, and married a Greek woman.[44] At Konya, headquarters of the Mevlevi (Mawlawi) order of dervishes, Christians (both Greek and Armenian) and Jews were treated with tolerance. Scholars and physicians among them were welcomed at the court of the Seljuk sultans, as were their Muslim counterparts. Some Greeks and Armenians converted to Islam for convenience, in order to seek favor with the Sultans or to protect their property, but they continued to adhere to certain Christian practices which eventually became part of the Seljuk tradition. With the state of Lesser Armenia to the east and the Greeks and the Crusaders to the west of their sultanate, and with many Christians living amongst them, the Seljuks could hardly have escaped Christian influence.[45]

Such tolerance was perhaps one factor giving rise to the dervish orders of the Mevlevis (Mawlawis) and the Bektashis. The period of the Seljuk state of Rum at Konya, especially during the rule of Ala al-Din Kaykubad I, was marked by great upheavals in art and literature and the fusion of Christian and Muslim cultures. In fact, the rise of the Seljuks of

Rum to power coincides with the rise of the state of Lesser Armenia in 1180. For 300 years this state fought on all fronts against the Byzantines, Arabs, and Seljuks.

The impact of Armenian legends and beliefs is most evident among the Kizilbash Kurds and the Ahl-i Haqq, as shall be seen in the following chapter. Under the Seljuk sultans of Rum, especially during the thirteenth century, constant warfare, the mingling of population and ideas, and especially religious tolerance were the major factors in the emergence of the dervish orders, whose religion combined pagan, Christian, and Muslim beliefs.[46] It was during this period that numerous holy men and mystics from Bukhara, Khurasan, and other parts of Persia, driven by Mongol pressure at home, left for Anatolia. Most notable among them were the mystic poet Jalal al-Din Rumi, who left Bukhara and arrived in Konya in 1233, and his friend Shams al-Din Tabrizi (d. 1246), who arrived in the same city in 1244. There they founded the Mevlevi Order. Rumi was tolerant toward Christians and even had Christian disciples.[47]

The Bektashis were one of the dervish orders which flourished at this time; unlike the Mevlevis (Mawlawis), they began to propagate their beliefs among different people, including the Christian peasantry. Under Ala al-Din I, Konya became the focus of ideas and a culture wholly derived from Persia. Many of these dervishes were probably already Shiites or influenced by Shiite beliefs. There is evidence that in Asia Minor, missionaries from Konya preached Shiism to the common people. The objects of Shiite propaganda were the Takhtajis of Lycia and the Alawi (Kizilbash) Kurds of Diyarbakr. According to Hamd Allah Mustawfi (1340), the inhabitants of Senusa, near Amasia, were fanatic Shiites.[48] Other streams of Shiism flowed from neighboring Syria. We have noted earlier that a certain Baba Ishaq, originally from the town of Kfarsud on the Syrian border, preached extreme Shiite beliefs to the Turkoman tribes and instigated an insurrection by these tribes against the Seljuk Sultan Ghiyath al-Din Kaykhosraw II (reigned 1236–45).[49]

The rise of the dervish orders may also be attributed partially to the rise of the Ottomans to power near the end of the thirteenth century and their establishment of a theocratic state based on the Islamic Sharia. Although Turkoman in origin, the Ottomans were nevertheless distinct from the rest of the Turks of Asia Minor in character, outlook, and political ambition.[50] The Ottomans were the ruling class, and their objective was to build a strong empire. They were political pragmatists, more concerned with their destiny as a military elite than with the religious duty of converting non-Muslims, which motivated the Turkish Ghazis. To the Ottoman rulers the non-Muslims, whether of Greek,

Armenian, or any other origin, were taxpayers, and their conversion to Islam would deprive the state of substantial revenue. This is why the Ottomans based their state not on race but on religious denominationalism (the millet system), offering the Christian communities the freedom to manage their own cultural and religious affairs as long as they accepted the status of *rayas* (subjects) and paid the Jizya (poll-tax).[51]

Most significant, however, is that the Ottomans adopted orthodox Islam according to the Hanafite school as the formal religion of their state. The reason may be that they found in orthodox Islam a workable judicial and administrative system able to meet the needs of the new state. The Islamic Sharia served also as a convenient solution to the problems caused by the many different religious groups in the Ottoman state. Non-Muslisms had to pay the Jizya and Kharaj (land-tax) to receive protection from the state. Thus, the relationship between the non-Muslim subjects and the state was more concerned with economics than with allegiance. The elaborate and intricate judicial system of Islam was based on the Quran and the interpretation of jurists, the Ulama (men learned in religious science). They were the guardians of the Sharia and its application to the lives of the Muslim believers. The chief of these Ulama was Shaykh al-Islam, who advised the Ottoman sultans on the operation and actions of the government, to ensure that they were in conformity with the tenets of the Quran and the Sharia. The juristic opinions of Shaykh al-Islam ranged from determining the fast of Ramadan to the declaration of war on a foreign state. The reverence of the Ulama and their sultans for the Islamic Sharia was boundless, since, according to Islam, its source was God, not man. Hence, to the Ulama, the Sharia was divinely instituted, and no mortal could tamper with it. The Ulama, the upholders of the Sharia, became a separate caste, and along with the ruling class and the military were the backbone of the Ottoman state. One of the results of their adherence to Islamic orthodoxy was that the Ottomans came to employ more and more Arabic words and usages, which caused their language to diverge increasingly from the old Turkish. According to Ziya Gökalp (d. 1924), it was the official language of the Ottomans, but not of the Turkish masses.[52] In fact, at one time some sultans wanted to adopt Arabic, the language of the Quran, as their formal tongue. By the fourteenth century, the dichotomy between the Ottomans and the Turkish masses began to widen, and it continued to do so until the fall of the empire in 1918. According to some authorities, from the beginning of their political career in the latter part of the thirteenth century, the Ottomans called themselves only Ottomans, never Turks. They also considered themselves different from the Turks.[53]

The American missionaries Eli Smith and G. H. O. Dwight, who traveled through Turkey at the beginning of the nineteenth century, observed that the Turkomans were generally called Turks by the Ottomans, who abhorred the name Turk and preferred to be called Musulmans (Muslims).[54]

To the Ottomans, "Turk" was a name that belonged to the people of Turkestan and the nomadic hordes who roamed the steppes of Khurasan. They considered themselves civilized Ottomans, and could not understand why Europeans called them Turks. As a sophisticated ruling class, the Ottomans looked down upon the Turkish peasantry, calling them Eşek Turk (the donkey Turk) and Kaba Turk (stupid Turk).[55] Expressions like "Turk-head" and "Turk-person" were contemptously used by Ottomans when they wanted to denigrate each other.[56]

The Turkish peasantry, although Muslim, was little affected by the Ottomans' Islamic orthodoxy, with its intricate scholastic theology, its religious schools, the juristic opinions of the Ulama, and the Arabic terminology that inundated the Ottoman literary language. To the masses, the Ottomans were as alien as the Greeks. The strict and complex orthodoxy adopted by the Ottomans appealed little to the Turkish peasant who, although Islamized, was still influenced by the shamanistic origin of his culture. Their God was Tanri, the old pagan deity who symbolized love and beauty. According to Halide Edib, the Muslim preacher who threatened the masses with hellfire and the torture of Ifrits (demons) was less popular among the masses than those who talked of Tanri as the symbol of beauty and love. It is against this background that many dervish orders and heterodox sects emerged in Asia Minor, in reaction to strict Islamic orthodoxy. Among these were the Kizilbash, the Mevlevis (Mawlawis), and the Bektashis, whose simple spiritual teaching and emphasis on mystical love and universal brotherhood appealed tremendously to the Turkish masses.[57] To them, true religion was the internal enlightenment of the heart, rather than a formal application of ritual. This is why they rejected the religious dogmatism and ritualism of the orthodoxy sponsored by the state.

In the thirteenth and fourteenth centuries, the Bektashis were actively competing with other orders to win the majority of the populace to their fold. There is evidence that they encroached upon the tribal sanctuaries and holy places of other orders. This encroachment extended to Christian sanctuaries, churches, saints, and tombs.[58] In order to win the Christian peasantry to their fold, the Bektashis opened their own holy places to the Christians.[59] At the beginning of the fifteenth century

Badr al-Din, son of the judge of Samawna, led a socio-religious rebellion which was connected with the Bektashi sect. There is evidence that in the wake of this rebellion, Christian converts to Bektashism were enthusiastically welcomed, and the equality of Christians with Muslims in their worship of God was so emphasized that leaders of the rebellion proclaimed that any Turk who denied the truths of the Christian religion was himself irreligious.[60] Thus, in time, the simple and illiterate folk of Anatolia, both Christian and Muslim, came to honor the same saints, visit the same shrines, and share common burial grounds. For example, the Haji Bektash lodge near Kirşehir is visited not only by members of the Bektashi order, but also by Christians, who, on entering the shrine, make the sign of the cross. For this reason, local tradition associates the tomb of Haji Bektash with the Greek Saint Charalambo, and the Bektashi dervishes who guard the shrine seem to encourage this association. It is said that many Bektashi dervishes consider Haji Bektash to be the incarnation of St. Charalambo, whom they honor so much that they do not hesitate to kill any Muslim who blasphemes him or Christ.[61] The Haji Bektash lodge has also become the religious center for all Bektashis, Kizilbash, and other extremist Shiite sects in Asia Minor. To these extremist Shiites, the holy shrines of Karbala and Najaf in Iraq were too far to visit as a religious duty; they found it more convenient to perform the pilgrimage to the Haji Bektash lodge.[62] A similar shrine is in the village of Haydar al-Sultan, near Angora (Ankara), where a Muslim saint is buried. He is identified as Khoja Ahmad (Karaja Ahmad), presumably a disciple of Haji Bektash. His wife Mene was a Christian from Caesarea. Local tradition indicates that this tekke stands on the site of a Christian monastery. The inhabitants of the village are Kizilbash, indicating that the differences between the Bektashis and Kizilbash are minor.[63]

38

Armenian Elements in the Beliefs of the Kizilbash Kurds

Throughout this study, we have identified the Kizilbash as Turkoman and Kurdish tribes who held extreme Shiite beliefs and became adherents of the Safawi Sufi Order of Persia. They share common religious beliefs and practices with the Bektashis. In many parts of Asia Minor, the Kizilbash and the Bektashis are considered one and the same.[1] The Kizilbash are divided into several subgroups living in many parts of Turkey. These subgroups are known by different names—including the Takhtajis (woodcutters) and Çepnis—although generally they share the common name of Kizilbash, indicating their association with the Safawis of Iran.[2] In some parts of Turkey they call themselves Alawis (Alevis—worshippers of Ali) and are usually connected with the Bektashi order of dervishes.[3] The Kizilbash Kurds live in Dersim (Tunceli), an area of about seven thousand square miles in the upper Euphrates valley, lying mostly between the Furat Su and the Murad Su, two tributaries of the Euphrates.[4] Until World War I the whole area was populated by multi-ethnic groups, Kurds and Armenians comprising the majority, but as a result of the massacre of Armenians and their deportation by the government of the Young Turks in 1915, the Armenian population of Dersim, indeed of all of eastern Turkey, was extremely diminished. The Kizilbash Kurds spread farther east to western Iran, around Kermanshah, Kerind, Sahna, and Kengavar, where they are called Ahl-i Haqq (Ali Ilahis), that is, deifiers of Ali.[5] A racial and religious affinity between Kurds and Armenians have been noted by those who have come in contact with these peoples. Like the Armenians, the Kurds are of Indo-European origin, and are akin to the Armenians. The Mamakanli Kurds are said to be descendants of the Armenian Mamigonians.[6] Kurds in the Haimanah district southwest of Angora (Ankara), and around Sivas are divided into Sunnites and Shiites. The latter are known as Kizilbash. One of the Kurdish tribes in the province of Sivas is possibly of Armenian origin. The Kizilbash Kurds retain certain Christian practices and sometimes call themselves Christians.[7] There is evidence that some of the Kizilbash Kurds of Dersim came originally from Armenia. These Kizilbash are of two groups. The Sayyid Hasanalis, who inhabit the plains and are said to have come originally from Khurasan in Persia, lived in the vicinity of Malatya (Melitene) and then immigrated to Dersim. The second group, the true Dersimlis who inhabit the mountainous area of the Muzur Dagh and Kuzichan, are believed to be descended from the pagan Armenians who lived in Dersim before the Christian era. These true Dersimlis speak a Kurdish dialect (Zaza), interspersed with Armenian words, not used by other Kurds living in the same region.[8] This is confirmed by E. B. Soane, who states that the Balaki tribesmen of Dersim, who live among Kurds and Zaza, speak a language that is a mixture of Kurdish, Armenian, and Arabic.[9] There is some truth in this assumption, which is supported by the ancient Armenian chronicler Moses Khorenantsi (Khoren). From Khorenantsi's chronicle, we learn that Dersim constituted a part of Armenia. He relates that after Xisuthra and his sons sailed to Armenia and went ashore there, one of his sons, Sim, went northwest to explore the land. Sim arrived at a plain penetrated by a river which flowed down to Assyria (present-day Iraq). He lingered at the bank of the river for two moons and gave his name to the mountain.[10] The river is the Euphrates, which flows through the district of Dersim to Iraq. We may assume that Dersim is named after Xisuthra's son Sim: *Der* in Armenian means "lord and master," and Dersim indicates that this area belonged to Lord Sim.

Some of these Kizilbash may have been Armenians converted to Shiism. Taylor is of the opinion that the Dersimlis were Christian Armenians converted to Shiite Islam. They influenced the Hasanalis with Christian customs, which the Dersimlis retained after their conversion. He observes that some characteristics of the Dersimlis resemble those of the Armenians, especially among the inmates of convents around Lake Van and parts of Kurdistan.[11] Ellsworth Huntington also maintains that the inhabitants of the Harput mountains were Christian Armenians who, because of persecution by the Persians who occupied their homeland, became nominal Muslims and intermarried with the invaders.[12] Among these Armenian converts are the Kizilbash. According to the thirteenth-century traveler Yaqut al-Hamawi (d. 1229), the inhabitants of Erzinjan in the upper Euphrates valley were Armenians, and there were some

Muslims among them.[13] Another traveler, Ibn Battuta, who visited this city in the following century (1330), states that most of the inhabitants are Armenian Muslims, but that the Turks among them speak Turkish.[14] There is some evidence that the Sunnite Afshars of the Anti-Taurus are of Armenian descent,[15] but this is only an isolated case of the conversion of Armenians to Sunnite Islam.

A great number of Armenians were converted to extremist Shiite Islam and joined the Kizilbash while retaining many christian practices. It is important to note that only the Armenians in Asia Minor, and not the Greeks, converted to the extreme Shiism of the Kizilbash.[16] Some Armenians believe that the Kizilbash in the mountains of Dersim were Armenians who fled to these mountains for refuge from the Assyrians, and that the present Kurds are their descendants. This assumption probably motivated Armenian bishops and priests in the nineteenth century to try to lead these Kurdish descendants of Armenians back to Christianity.[17] Regardless of this assumption, the fact remains that since time immemorial Anatolia has been populated by the Armenian people. Religious traditions and the observations of modern writers reveal the connection between the Kizilbash and Armenians. The writers already quoted are unanimous in their belief that the Kizilbash of Anatolia were Christians who for some reason, most likely persecution, embraced Islam but secretly retained many Christian practices.[18] This is confirmed by the claim of the Kizilbash and other extremist Shiites themselves, related by White, that "less than the thickness of an onionskin separates them from the Christians."[19] There is evidence that two or three centuries ago the Armenians of Hamshen, east of Trebizond between Rize and Batum (the ancient Armenian province of Daik), were so brutally massacred by Muslims that many of the survivors converted to Islam. Although they have become Turkified, their Turkish dialect contains unmistakable traces of their Armenian origin.[20] It is also reported that in the year 1751, thousands of Armenian families in Turkey, especially in the province of Oudi, were forced to embrace Islam because of the persecution inflicted upon them by a certain fanatic Çelebi and his collaborators, the Persian Muslims. To this day, many people in that province have names betraying Armenian origin. The Armenian villagers of Luristan have also converted to Islam because of persecution, and traces of Christianity can be seen among them, as among the villagers of the Oudi province. The Turkish women of Gis, for example, invoke the name of St. Elisaeus (probably Elijah), whose sanctuary is venerated by both Muslim Turks and Armenians in that city. Also, when a Muslim Turkish mother in Gis puts her child to bed, she makes the sign of the cross over the child while uttering the name of Jesus.[21]

Another interesting theory regarding the existence of elements of Armenian Christianity in the beliefs of the Ahl-i Haqq (Ali Ilahis) is advanced by W. Ivanow, who in 1953 published an English translation and analysis of a religious document of the Ahl-i Haqq. We have partly discussed Ivanow's theory in connection with Sultan Sahak, a prominent figure in the religious traditions of the Kakaiyya and the Ahl-i Haqq. Ivanow showed that Sahak is an Armenian name, used exclusively for Isaac. If the Ahl-i Haqq (and, for that matter, the Kakaiyya) wanted to write this name in the correct Arabic manner, they should have written it as Ishaq, and not Sahak. One must conclude, then, that the term Sahak demonstrates an unmistakable Armenian influence.[22] Although Ivanow is discussing the Ahl-i Haqq, his theory of Armenian influence applies equally to the Kizilbash Kurds of Dersim and to neighboring sects in adjacent Iraq, such as the Shabak, because of the striking similarities of their beliefs.

Ivanow argues that Armenian Christianity has exerted a significant influence on the beliefs of the Ahl-i Haqq and other extremist Shiite sects. A careful study of the doctrines and religious practices of these sects shows that they derive, not from orthodox but from heterodox Armenian Christianity—in this case, from the Paulicians. But who are these Armenian Paulicians, and what is their association with the Muslims, and particularly with heterodox Shiite sects?

The Paulician heresy dates back to the third century, when Armenian votaries established a strong foothold in Armenia and came to be known as Paulicians. The origin of the term Paulician is somewhat obscure. Some writers associate it with St. Paul;[23] others maintain that it derives from a certain Paul, an Armenian son of a Manichean woman named Callinice from Samosata, who sent Paul and her other son John to Armenia to propagate the Manichean heresy. The Manichean heresy takes its name from Mani, who lived in Persia in the third century and preached a combination of Gnosticism, Zoroastrianism, Buddhism, Christianity, and other religious beliefs. Still others hold that the term Paulician derives from another Paul, who lived in Armenia during the reign of the Byzantine Emperor Justinian II Rhinotmetus (reigned 669–711).[24] According to the Armenian writer Karapet Ter Mekerttschian, when the name Paulician is used in Armenian as a diminutive form, it means "followers of little Paul," but Mekerttschian offers no explanation as to who this little Paul is.[25]

From the latter part of the third century, the Paulicians were considered exponents of the Manichean heresy, which was condemned by the Council of Nicea (325). They considered themselves "true Christians," however, and called other Christians "Romanists." They denied any association with Manicheism or with Paul and John, the sons of Callinice.[26] In fact, Armenian heretics seldom associate the Paulicians with Manichaeanism, or attribute to them Manichean teaching. The Armenian writer Gregory Magistros (d. 1058) was the first to relate that the Paulicians received their name and teaching from Paul of Samosata, a patriarch of Antioch condemned for heresy in 269. Magistros states, "Here then you see the Paulicians, who got their poison from Paul of Samosata."[27] The heresy of Paul of Samosata was essentially that of the Adoptionists, who maintained that Jesus Christ received divinity at His baptism, and that the Virgin Mary gave birth not to God, but to Christ the man. In other words, Christ was not the Word made flesh through whom the whole creation came into existence, but was a creature who became the Head of all creation. He became an adopted Son when the Spirit of God rested upon him at baptism.

After their condemnation by the Council of Nicea (A.D. 325), the Paulicians seem to have faded from the empire, but they reemerged in Armenia in the seventh century. In the time of the Armenian Catholicos Nersis III, "the Builder" (641–661), they established their headquarters in Jrga, north of the city of Bitlis.[28] They also spread into Syria, where their leader, Theodore Rushduni, died at Damascus in 654.[29] In the next century (about 717), they made Miyafarqin (present-day Diyarbakr in Turkey) their headquarters and attracted the attention of the Umayyad governor al-Walid.[30] According to John the Philosopher, who became the Armenian Catholicos in 719, the Paulicians were dissenters [heretics] who, because of oppression by the Orthodox Armenian Church, had sought the protection of the Arabs—who had challenged the hegemony of the Byzantines in Armenia since 650.[31] This explains the interest of the Umayyads in these Paulicians and the collaboration between the two peoples. We should not assume, however, that these Armenian Paulicians betrayed the Christian Church and allied themselves with the Arabs. It was the cruel treatment of both church and state that forced the Paulicians to seek the protection of the Muslims. The Byzantines' persecution of the Paulicians may have destroyed a strong bulwark that might otherwise have thwarted the advance of the Muslim Arabs into Armenia.[32]

Like the Byzantine Church, the Byzantine emperors were determined to eradicate the Paulicians. Throughout the seventh and eighth centuries, they hunted the Paulicians down. Under Constantine

Pogonatus (reigned 668–85) one Paulician leader was put to death, while under Justinian Rhinotmetus another leader was burned alive.[33] Another emperor, Leo III Isaurian, called the Syrian (reigned 717–41), tried to decimate the Paulicians but failed. It was not until the time of Nicephorus Logotheta (802–811) that the harried Paulicians found respite from persecution.[34]

The persecution was renewed, however, under Emperors Michael I (reigned 811–13) and Leo V, the Armenian (813–20). Leo ordered the bishop and civil governor of Neo-Caesarea (present day Niksar, north of Tokat, Turkey) to investigate the state of the Paulicians in eastern Asia Minor. The Paulicians killed the emperor's commissioners and fled to Melitene, where they enjoyed the protection of the Muslim governor, who treated them kindly and settled them in the small town of Argaeum. From Melitene the Paulicians began to raid Byzantine territory.[35] But as the Byzantine hostility abated, the Paulicians returned to their homes in Byzantine territory, only to suffer the severest persecution they had yet faced at the hands of Empress Theodora (841–55). Theodora ordered that the Paulicians be restored to the Byzantine Church or exterminated by any means. Commissioners were sent to Armenia to carry out her orders, which they did with such zeal that about ten thousand Paulicians were killed, and their property confiscated. Those who escaped the wanton butchery sought refuge with the Muslims, who gave them full protection. This time the Paulicians built for themselves the city of Tephrike. They allied themselves with the Muslims and continued to fight the Byzantines throughout the ninth century. Their attacks against the Byzantines culminated in an attack by Karbeas, an Armenian army officer whose father had died because of the persecution; leading an army of Paulicians, he captured several cities, including Tephrike, which had fallen into Byzantine hands. He was supported by his father-in-law Chrysochir, a convert to Islam. One of the captured cities was Ephesus, whose Church of St. John was turned into a stable. Emperor Basil I, the Macedonian (867–86), desiring to reestablish peace with the Paulicians, in 870 delegated Peter Siculus [the Sicilian] to approach the Paulicians of Tephrike to negotiate peace and exchange of prisoners of war. Peter's mission failed, mainly because of the extravagant demands of Chrysochir, and the persecution and war were resumed.[36] Basil fought against the Paulicians, with the result that Chrysochir was slain in battle, Karbeas was reconciled, and Tephrike was recaptured (873); the power of the Paulicians seemed to have been completely destroyed.

According to Armenian sources, the Paulicians came to be known as Tondraketsi (Tondrakites), after the town of Tonrak in the district of Manzikert, where they set up their headquarters. Both Gregory of Nareg (late tenth century) and Gregory Magistros (d. 1058) state that the leader of the Tondrakites was a certain Smbat Spartapet, but offer no significant information about him except that he rejected the doctrines of the Orthodox Armenian Church.[37] Magistros simply calls him Smbat and says that he appeared in the time of the Lord John, the overseer of Armenia, and of Smbat Bagratuni. He came from the village of Zarehaven, in the district of Tsalkotn, and lived in Tonrak.[38] Conybeare identifies Smbat as the same Smbat Bagratum [Bagratuni] who founded a petty Armenian dynasty in Bagratum in the upper Euphrates valley of Murad-Chai. This dynasty extended from southeast of the Euphrates valley to the east of the city of Harput, in present-day Turkey.[39] To his enemies the Orthodox Armenians, Smbat was a heretic and Antichrist, but he considered himself "light, life, and truth."[40] He interfered in the internal affairs of the Orthodox Armenian Church, installing and deposing their Catholicoi. In 849, the Abbasid Caliph al-Mutawakkil (d. 861) dispatched Yusuf Ibn Muhammad al-Marwazi, who lived in the Armenian marches, to conquer the Armenian Prince Ashot, who ruled the province of Vaspurakan southeast of Van, and Prince Bagart, who ruled Taron.[41] When al-Marwazi reached Khilat (Akhlat), he encountered and routed Ashot and then invited Smbat to have an audience with him. It was a trick; when Smbat appeared before al-Marwazi, he was treacherously captured and sent to Samarra in Iraq.[42] (According to al-Baladhuri [d. 892], it was Buqrat Ibn Ashot [the Bagratid Ashot] whom al-Marwazi captured and sent to Samarra.)[43] Seeing the treachery of the Muslim commander, Smbat's followers, the Tondrakites, rallied their forces to avenge the capture of their leader. In 852, they stormed the city of Muş and killed al-Marwazi, who had sought refuge on the roof of the great church built by Smbat in Muş. Some Armenian chronicles state that after his capture, Smbat converted to Islam, and that other Armenians, especially the Artsruni princes, followed his example. However, according to the Armenian chronicler Vardan (d. 1270), Smbat Sparapet was captured by the Abbasid Amir (prince) Bouha (Bugha, the Turkish commander) and taken to Baghdad in 855. Bugha promised to restore to him the Kingdom of Armenia if he recanted his Christian faith, but Smbat always answered that he could not leave Christ or forsake the Christian faith, which he had received by the grace of baptism. Because of his refusal to recant, Smbat was tortured and slain. His followers asked the Caliph al-Mutawakkil to give them his body, which he did. They carried the body to the vicinity of ancient Babylon and laid it in a shrine built on the site of the lion's den into which the prophet Daniel was cast.[44]

The death of Smbat in 855 by no means put an end to the Tondrakites. They were as strong as ever in the middle of the eleventh century, when Magistros recorded the names of their leaders up to his time.[45] They occupied the country south of Erzerum to Muş, and were predominant in the entire upper valley of the Tigris and Euphrates.[46] It is significant that this region included the district of Dersim (Tunceli), where the Kurdish extremist Shiites also lived.

Considered heretics, the Paulicians (by the eleventh century called Tondrakites) were persecuted by both church and state and became friends with the Muslims, who offered them protection. Gregory Magistros credits himself with the persecution of the Tondrakites. In 1050, Magistros, who was offered the title of Duke of Vaspurakan and Taron by the Byzantine Emperor Constantine IX Monomachus (reigned 1042–54), was dispatched to the southeast region of Armenia to investigate the state of affairs, especially that of the Tondrakites. Magistros heaps invective on the Tondrakites and relates that when he reached Mesopotamia, he rid the land of the tares sown by them. He also says he forced many of those who lived in Tonrak to recant their heresy and return to orthodoxy. He claims that he did not inflict bodily harm on the Tondrakites.[47] However, the Tondrakites suffered the severest persecution at the hands of the catholicoi of the Orthodox Armenian Church, whose favorite form of torture was to brand their foreheads with the image of a fox.[48] It is surprising that while the Paulicians were being persecuted in Armenia and Mesopotamia, their heresy spread to Europe and was kept alive by heretical groups like the Bogomiles of Bulgaria, the Patrini, the Cathars, the Albigenses, and the Waldensians—reaching as far as Oxford in 1160.[49]

Despite persecution, a remnant of the Tondrakites survived until modern times. Writing in the nineteenth century, the Armenian Orthodox Paul W. Meherean states that a small group of the Tondrakites survived between Erzerum and Muş.[50] He tells of a certain Hovannes, who came from the Monastery of Bordshimasur and falsely styled himself a bishop. Hovannes was a Paulician (Tondrakite) who between 1774 and 1781 spread his heresy in Constantinople. He visited Venice and then returned to Erzerum and Muş to propagate his heretical teachings. He escaped the persecution of the Orthodox Armenian Church only by converting to Islam. He is the one who in 1782 made a copy of *The Key of Truth,* a manual of the Paulician-Tondrakite heresy. In his excellent introduction to this book, Conybeare vividly relates the story of the late survivors of the Tondrakites, numbering only twenty-five families. They were refugees from the village of Jewiurm, in the district of Khnus, who settled in the village of Arkhweli, in the province of Shirak. Conybeare also describes the investigation of their belief by the Orthodox Armenian Church; they confessed that they were Paulicians and that *The Key of Truth* was their authoritative book, and some of them renounced the Paulician heresy and returned to orthodoxy.[51]

We may conclude that the Paulicians, who were persecuted by both church and state as heretics, always found refuge in Muslim territories and allied themselves with the Muslims. This Paulician-Muslim alliance facilitated the Arab invasion of Byzantine territory. Armenia became a hotbed of revolt against the Byzantines, while from the ninth century onward the Paulicians and the Muslims were close friends.[52]

Of great significance to our discussion is the fact that these Paulicians (Tondrakites) lived together with the Kurds and also with the Turkomans, who rushed en masse into the Byzantine country, especially after the defeat of the Byzantine army by the Seljuks at Malazgirt in 1071. It is also likely that many Paulicians embraced Islam to escape persecution by church and state. One such convert was the Paulician leader Chrysochir.

The social intercourse between the Paulicians and the Muslims may explain the fact that the Turkoman and Kurdish Shiite Kizilbash adopted from these Paulicians some Christian beliefs and practices. Otherwise, how can we explain the fact that until the nineteenth century a tribe of Kurds who lived in the district of Bayezid near Tonrak, the headquarters of the Tondrakites, were called Manicheans?[53] Why these Kurds, the neighbors of the heretical Tondrakites, are called Manicheans i.e., followers of Mani (216–76) is unknown. Mani's doctrine was a synthesis of Gnosticism, Zoroastrianism, Buddhism and Christianity, and Mani claimed himself to be the Paraclete (comforter, or holy spirit) promised by Jesus. The question becomes all the more important when we realize that the Armenian Paulicians were accused of being Manichean heretics, an accusation that set both church and state against them.

Throughout the whole history of the Muslim people, we find no Muslim religious sect or group accused of being Manichean or even called by this name. Since these Kurds who were called Manicheans lived in the vicinity of Tonrak, headquarters of the Paulicians or Tondrakites, the possibility becomes greater that they were once Paulicians who converted to Islam to escape persecution by both church and state. It is probable that these Tondrakites converted to Islam in its Shiite form, already the faith of a number of Turkomans, in order to preserve their traditional tenets and practices and to avoid the rigid form of Sunnite Islam, commonly hostile to Christian beliefs.

As heretics, the Tondrakites renounced most of the tenets and rituals of the traditional Christian church as non-Biblical. They rejected the virgin birth of Christ, maintaining that Mary gave birth to a mere man who at His baptism became the Messiah, the Son by adoption. They objected to the worship of the cross and even to the signing of the cross, and denied the intercession of Saints and the efficacy of the Eucharist (Holy Communion). There are, however, striking similarities between some of the practices of the Paulicians-Tondrakites and those of extremist Shiites. Like the Ghulat, the Tondrakites had no churches, believing that the real church was not a structure of wood or stone but the invisible communion of the faithful. They conducted their rituals, especially the celebration of the Eucharist, in private homes, cellars, stables, or wherever else they could. This, to be sure, may have been an ancient Armenian practice retained by these heretics. In his canons of the church (c. 425), the Armenian Catholicos Sahak states that out of ignorance, Armenian elders celebrated the Agape and Eucharist in their homes. He insists that these rituals should be celebrated in the church.[54]

Because they rejected the great mystery of the sacrifice of Christ and refused to honor the Cross, the Tondrakites interpreted their sacrament "less as a sacrifice offered for the sins of men than as a meal symbolic of the unity of the faithful."[55] This unity was symbolized by the use of only one loaf of unleavened bread, laid on a wooden table. This recalls the type of communion performed by all extremist Shiite groups which, in the case of the Kizilbash, G. E. White says, "is a debased form of the Lord's Supper."[56] It may be that this concept of the Eucharist and the abhorrence of altars of stone led them to eat in an ordinary room off an ordinary table of wood.[57] The Eucharist was always preceded by the Agape, which may have been a continuance of the Jewish Paschal meal (in which meat was consumed, preferably the flesh of pigeons and sheep) in the earliest Armenian Church.[58] According to Frédéric Macler, this kind of sacrifice, called Matal or Matagh, is still practiced by Armenians, with such offerings as a cock, a sheep, or fruits.[59] In the communal meal of the Shabak and Ahl-i Haqq, a cock or a sheep is sacrificed.[60] It is interesting that these practices survived until the beginning of the nineteenth century in the village of Arkhweli in the province of Shirak, in the present state of Soviet Armenia. The village's population included twenty-five families who were Paulician-Tondrakites. The Armenian Orthodox priest of the village, who discovered these heretics, wrote to the consistory of Yerevan on 23 May 1841, describing their "wicked practices." One of these practices was the communion, in which every member of the congregation received a piece of bread and drank a sip of wine.[61]

There are also similarities between the religious hierarchy of the Paulicians and that of the extremist Shiites. The Paulician-Tondrakites had no church organization and no priests, but did have elders, called the "elect ones," who had the power to bind and loose men from their obligations. They held no particular office and were not charged with any special function in the church, but were believed to be those in whom the spirit of God dwelt and thus to be of the same nature as Christ Himself, the only difference between them and Christ being a matter of degree.[62] This recalls the spiritual powers of the religious leaders of the extremist Shiites, who are no more than "elders" but are held in utmost honor, and, in the case of the Ahl-i Haqq, are worshipped as God.[63] These leaders are called the manifestation of the Truth and considered the only ones in the community with the right to bind and loose men from their obligations. They not only hear confession of the sins of the laity, but also offer them absolution.[64]

A number of traditions may serve to demonstrate that the Kizilbash Kurds are akin to the Armenians. One of these is a Kizilbash legend which represents the fifth Imam, Muhammad al-Baqir, as being born of the virgin daughter of an Armenian priest. This legend, preserved for us by Capt. Molyneux-Seel, is maintained by the Kizilbash Kurds of Dersim (Tunceli), who believe that the Imam al-Baqir is the founder of their sect.

When al-Husayn, son of Ali, was killed at Karbala, Iraq (October 680), his murderers cut off his head and took it to the Umayyad Caliph Yazid Ibn Muawiya in Damascus. En route to Damascus, they stopped to rest at the house of an Armenian priest named Akh (Brother) Murtaza Keshish. The priest noticed that al-Husayn's head showed supernatural signs and wanted to keep it. He tried to devise a way to retain this precious relic, but failed to do so. While he was deep in thought, his oldest son entered and asked why he was so pensive. The priest told his son about his desire to keep the head of al-Husayn. The son offered a solution, asking his father to cut off his head and give it to the "Turks" (meaning the Sunnite Muslims who killed al-Husayn) instead of al-Husayn's head. Without hesitation the priest cut off his son's head and offered it to the "Turks," but they refused to take it, insisting on taking the head of al-Husayn. The priest happened to have seven sons, six of whose heads he cut off successively to satisfy the murderers of al-Husayn, but these endeavors failed. While deeply distressed over what to do next, he heard a voice saying to him, "Smear the head of your last son with the blood of the head of al-Husayn." This he did, and when he offered the head of his last son to the murderers, they accepted it without hesitation, believing that they had carried off the head of al-Husayn. Thus the head of al-Husayn was kept by the Armenian priest. When he was in possession of this precious treasure, the priest placed the head in a special compartment and adorned it with gold, silver and silk.

This priest had a single daughter. One day she entered the compartment where al-Husayn's head had been placed, and to her astonishment she found a golden bowl filled with honey; apparently the head of al-Husayn had been transformed. She took a taste of the honey and immediately became pregnant. Her father, noticing her pregnancy, determined to kill her. But she was able to convince him that she had miraculously become pregnant when she tasted the honey into which the head of al-Husayn had been transformed. The father believed her and was appeased.

One day the maiden complained of a cold, and when she sneezed, her father noticed a bright flame coming out of her nose. The blame was immediately transformed into a child, who was the Imam al-Baqir. When the "Turks" learned that a descendent of Ali had been born, they sent men to find and kill the child. When they came to the priest's house, the child's mother was busy washing the household linen. Suspecting the men intended to kill al-Baqir, she hid him in a copper cauldron which was on the fire and covered him with linen. Now these men were magicians and knew through their magic that the child was hidden in a copper cauldron, but they could not find the house in which he was hidden. Totally baffled, they left, and thus the life of the child was saved. Because of this incident, the child was called Bakir, which in Turkish means "copper."[65] It is true that in the Turkish language *bakir* means "copper," but this meaning does not apply to the fifth Imam, Muhammad Ibn Ali; he was nicknamed al-Baqir because of his profound knowledge of religious sciences. However, the fact remains that the originator of this story, whoever he was, wished to establish a strong relationship between the Kizilbash Kurds and the Armenians by designating a young Armenian virgin, the daughter of a priest, as the mother of the Imam al-Baqir.

According to a slightly different version of this story related by G. E. White, when Ali was murdered by his enemies, his head was cut off and by some chance was entrusted to a Christian priest for safekeeping. Afterwards the murderers wanted to abuse the head of Ali, but the priest refused to deliver it up to them. The priest offered the heads of his seven sons instead of Ali, but they were refused. Finally his wife asked him to cut off her head; he did so, and it was accepted by the persecutors. The authenticity of this story is not important; what is important is the respect the extremist Shiites have for Christianity, to the point of trusting the head of Ali or his son al-Husayn to a Christian priest, as related in both versions of the story. As White rightly remarks, the story is exceedingly suggestive in showing the Alevi (Kizilbash) belief that when their hero suffered death and abuse by his persecutors, a passionate Christian priest did not hesitate to sacrifice his own sons and wife in order to save the suffering hero from indignity.[66]

The story also vividly recalls another tale, relating the miraculous birth of Balim Sultan, the second founder of the Bektashi order. Like al-Baqir in the legend just mentioned, Balim Sultan was born of a virgin Christian princess, who conceived him after eating bal (Turkish for honey). It is not sheer coincidence that both the Bektashis and Kizilbash should attribute miraculous birth to their patrons, and that in both cases these patrons were born of Christian virgins.[67] Regardless of their truth or lack of it, both legends are suggestive of the strong Christian (and in the case of the Kizilbash story, Armenian) influence on the beliefs of the extremist Shiite sects. They also indicate the deep hatred the extremist Shiites harbor for the Sunnites, a hatred which the Umayyads inspired by their killing of al-Husayn.

Several stories connected with the carrying off of al-Husayn's head to Damascus and with the compassion Christian priests and monks had for al-Husayn have become a part of Shiite folklore. According to one of these stories, after leaving the town of Baalbak in Syria, the murderers of al-Husayn rested for the night near the cell of a Christian monk. At night, the monk looked through the window and saw a pillar of light reaching up to heaven, issuing forth from al-Husayn's head. He also saw a door open in heaven and hosts of angels descend upon al-Husayn's head. On the next day, the monk appealed to the carriers of al-Husayn's head to let him keep it at least for one hour, but they would not do so unless he paid them a certain sum of money. The monk gave them money and the leader of the company handed him the head, fixed on a lance. Holding the head in his hands, the monk kissed it and broke into tears. Addressing the head, he implored al-Husayn to tell his grandfather, the prophet Muhammad, when he met him in heaven, that he [the monk] bears testimony that there is no God but Allah, that Muhammad is His apostle, and that Ali is His Wali (vicar). Then the monk returned the head of al-Husayn to the murderers. When they proceeded to divide the money which the monk paid them, they found to their bewilderment that the pieces of coin had turned into pieces of clay, with an inscription stating "the wrongdoers still know what fate awaits them."[68] There is also a tradition still current among the Shiites of Iraq that an Englishman rushed to save al-Husayn from his enemies and offered him water when his murderers tried to drive him and his company to death by thirst, by preventing them from reaching the waters of the Euphrates River. This is most likely British propaganda meant to win the sympathy of the Shiite tribes in southern Iraq who were opposed to the British occupation of Iraq.

Another tradition connecting the Kizilbash with the Armenians is that of the legendary figure al-Khadir (known by common people as Khidr). Although the Quran does not mention al-Khadir by name, Islamic traditions associate him with Moses (Quran, Sura 18). Once, when Moses was preaching with great eloquence to the Israelites, he was asked whether another man wiser than he existed. He answered in the negative. God appeared to Moses in a vision and rebuked him for saying that no other man was wiser than he. He told Moses that His servant the Khadir was surely wiser than he, and that he would find him at the confluence of the two seas. Taking with him his lieutenant Joshua, son of Nun, Moses proceeded on a long journey until he came to the place described by God, and there he saw the Khadir. The story then goes on to tell of the feats the Khadir performed, which proved to Moses that the Khadir was wiser than he. The Khadir had been permitted to drink from the fountain of life, and thus had become immortal; hence he was named Khadir (ever-verdant).[69] Usually the Khadir is associated with Phineas, Elijah, Alexander the Great, and St. George. He is considered a saint by both Muslims and Christians, and many mosques and religious sites in Jerusalem, Nablus, Damascus, Baghdad, and Mosul are associated with his name.[70] Armenian tradition associates him with St. Sarkis (Sergius).[71] The Kizilbash of Turkey call him Khidr Elias and make pilgrimages to Armenian churches whose patron is St. Sarkis.[72] They also celebrate a feast in his name on 9 February, preceded by one week of fasting.[73] The Khadir also had a prominent place among other extremist Shiites, like the Bektashis and the Nusayris of Syria.[74] The tradition of the Khadir serves as an important link between the extremist Shiites (especially the Kizilbash Kurds) and Christianity.

The link between the Kizilbash and the Armenians is strengthened by the honor and respect the Kizilbash show for Armenian churches and relics. At the Armenian church in Muş an old parchment copy of the New Testament was discovered written in Armenian. The Armenian countrymen and the Kizilbash Kurds believed in its miraculous healing power.[75] The Armenian monastery Surp Garabet Vank (St. John the Baptist Monastery), situated to the north of Hozat, seat of the government in Dersim (Tunceli), is greatly honored by the Kizilbash Kurds. It is believed by the people in that region that when the Kurds once tried to destroy the monastery, they were repelled by the miraculous relics of St. John the Baptist. Realizing the divine power of the saint, the Kurds began making pilgrimages to the monastery to seek healing from sickness.[76] It is also reported that the Kizilbash attend Christian church services and kneel and bow with the rest of the worshipers. Showing an even closer association with the Armenians, the Kizilbash do not decline to bury their dead next to those of Armenians, a practice most offensive to Sunnite Muslims. Ellsworth Huntington reports that behind the village of Kala in Dersim, on a steep slope of the Mushar Mountain, there are several shrines. One of these is said to house the grave of an Armenian girl who took care of the great church at the top of the mountain. The Kizilbash aghas (chiefs) were honored by being buried in the same graveyard, next to this Armenian girl.[77]

The socioreligious relationship between the Kizilbash and the Armenians seems to be an established fact. Armenians and Kurds, who are ethnically and perhaps anthropologically homogeneous, have been living side by side in Anatolia since time immemorial.[78] In fact, the Kizilbash population has been dense in the Armenian provinces of eastern Turkey, with many villages inhabited by both Armenians and Kizilbash Kurds.[79] Sometimes this coexistence was disrupted by flareups of violence, or by the common social conflict instigated by idiosyncratic social customs. The ancient Armenian church of St. Nerses at Rumkale, on the upper Euphrates River, was forcibly occupied by Muslims in the latter part of the seventeenth century.[80] Likewise, at the village of Hozat in Dersim, the original Armenian inhabitants have been driven out by Kizilbash Kurds. The graveyard of the village's church is full of tombstones bearing the elaborate flowery cross commonly used for Armenian clergy.[81] In some cases the Kurds stay close to Armenian villages, where they abduct and marry Armenian women.[82]

In conclusion, it seems fairly clear that the religion of the Kizilbash, who live mostly in eastern Turkey but are also scattered from Erzerum in the east to Aydin and Smyrna (Izmir) in the west, belongs to the Shiite sect of Islam, although their beliefs and rituals contain considerable pagan and Christian elements, placing them outside the pale of orthodox Islam. Some of the Kizilbash are Kurds, and they are mostly found in Dersim in the upper Euphrates valley. This area was at one time heavily populated by Armenians, as is evident from the many ruins of Armenian villages and churches. The religious beliefs and practices of the Kizilbash are shared by several other Shiite groups known by different names: the Nusayris in Syria; the Shabak, Bajwan, Sarliyya-Kakaiyya, and Ibrahimiyya in Iraq; and the Ahl-i Haqq (Ali Ilahis) in western Iran.

Sometimes the Shabak are identified with the Kizilbash and are in fact called by this name. Some of these sects, whose communicants live in the area stretching from Anatolia to Syria, Iraq, and Iran, not only possess religious beliefs with only slight variations, but have anthropological similarities revealing a common ethnic origin. This area forms a melting pot for several ethnic groups, especially for the Persians, Kurds, and Armenians.[83] This area became a border between Turkey and Persia and has witnessed the activities of Shiite propagandists since the thirteenth century. Shiite propaganda was carried by the nomadic Turkoman and Kurdish tribes to Armenian Christians, with the result that a heterodox religion emerged whose veneer is Shiite Islam, but whose core is a syncretism of paganism, Mithraism, Armenian Christianity, and perhaps Mazdaism.[84] By their own admission, members of these heterodox Shiite sects claim a strong association with Christianity, predominantly Armenian Christianity. They were most probably converted to extreme Shiism, either through conviction or compulsion, but retained most of their Christian practices and beliefs. A good example of such a conversion from Armenian Christianity to Kizilbashism is found among the inhabitants of the villages in the district of Rizeh, in the province of Trebizond, who, although they profess Islam, have preserved the rite of baptism and speak Armenian rather than Turkish.[85] The majority of the Ghulat sects studied here fall into the same category as the extremist Shiites of Turkey. They form a vital part of the population in the area between Anatolia and Persia, which they have traversed for centuries.[86]

Notes

Introduction

1. See the standard Arabic dictionary of Muhammad Ibn Abd al-Karim Ibn Manzur, *Lisan al-Arab* (Beirut: Dar Sadir, 1955–56), 15: 131–34; and Hans Wehr, *Dictionary of Modern Written Arabic*, ed. J. Milton Cowan (Ithaca: Cornell University Press, 1961), 682.

2. Abu al-Hasan al-Ashari, *Kitab Maqalat al-Islamiyyin wa Ikhtilaf al-Musallin*, ed. Hellmut Ritter (Wiesbaden: Franz Steiner, 1980), 5; Abu Muhammad al-Hasan al-Nawbakhti, *Firaq al-Shi'a* (al-Najaf: al-Matbaa al-Haydariyya, 1389/1969), 59–61; Abd al-Qahir al-Baghdadi, *al-Farq bayn al-Firaq*, ed. Muhyi al-Din Abd al-Hamid (Cairo: Matbaat al-Madani, n.d.), 23; Abu Muhammad Ali Ibn Hazm, *Kitab al-Fisal fi al-Milal wa al-Ahwa wa al-Nihal*, (Cairo: Muassasat al-Khanji, 1321/1903) 2: 114–15; and Abd al-Karim al-Shahrastani, *Kitab al-Milal wa al-Nihal*, 2:10–11 printed on the margin of Ibn Hazm's book.

3. Ibn Manzur, 8:187–92; Abu al-Muzaffar al-Isfarayini, *al-Tabsir fi al-Din wa Tamyiz al-Firqa al-Najiya an al-Firaq al-Halikin*, ed. Muhammad Zahid al-Kawthari (Cairo: Maktabat al-Khanji, 1955), 16–17; Julius Wellhausen, *The Arab Kingdom And Its Fall* (Beirut; Khayat, 1963), 66–68 of the Introduction; and Kamil Mustafa al-Shaibi, "Kalimat shi'a fi al-Lugha wa al-Tarikh," *Majallat Kulliyyat al-Tarbiya fi al-Jamia al-Libiyya* no. 3 (1972), 171–204.

4. Abu Jafar Ibn Abi Abd Allah Ahmad al-Barqi, *al-Rijal* (Tehran: Chap Khanah Daneshgah, 1342/1923), 1; and Muhammad al-Hurr al-Amili, *Amal al-Amil fi Ulama Jabal Amil* (n.p., 1306/1888), 7.

5. Ali Ibn Ibrahim (al-Qummi), *Tafsir Ali Ibn Ibrahim* (lithographed Tabriz: 1315/1897), 93–94 and 159; Muhammad al-Zahri known as Ibn Saad, *al-Tabaqat al-Kubra* ed., E. Sachan (Leiden: E. J. Brill 1904), 3: 14; Ahmad Ibn Abi Yaqub Ibn Wadih al-Yaqubi, *Tarikh al-Yaqubi* (al-Najaf: Matbaat al-Ghari, 1358/1939), 2:93: Al-Shaykh al-Saduq Abu Jafar Muhammad Ibn Babawayh (al-Qummi), *Ilal al-Shara'i* (al-Najaf: al-Matbaa al-Haydariyya, 1383/1963), 1:137, 161–63 and 202; Abu al-Husayn Muslim, *Sahih Muslim* (Cairo, Matbaat Muhammad Sabih, 1334/1915) 7:120–22.

6. Al-Shaykh Abu Hatim Ahmad Ibn Hamdan al-Razi, *Kitab al-Zina*, edited and appended by Abd Allah Sallum al-Samarrai to his book, *al-Ghuluw wa al-Firaq al-Ghaliya fi al-Hadara al-Islamiyya*, 2nd ed. (Baghdad and London: Dar Wasit li al-Nashr, 1982), 259.

7. Julius Wellhausen, *The Religio-Political Factions in Early Islam*, ed. R. C. Ostle,

translated by R. C. Ostle and S. M. Walzer (Amsterdam: North Holland Publishing Company, 1975), 95. William Montgomery Watt is of the opinion that the Shiites appeared as a definite group after Ali's return from the battle of Siffin (33/657). See William Montgomery Watt, *Islam and the Integration of Society* (London: Rutledge and Kegan, Paul, 1961), 104; and M. G. S. Hodgson, "How Did The Early Shi'a Become Sectarian," *Journal of the American Oriental Society* 75 (January–March 1955): 1–13.

8. Abu Jafar Muhammad Ibn al-Hasan al-Tusi (Shaykh al-Taifa), *Talkhis al-Shafi fi al-Imama* (al-Najaf: Maktabat al-Alamayn 1383/1963), 3:96. For more information see below chapter 9, "The Twelve Imams," and Wilfred Madelung, "Bemerkungen zur imamitischen Firaq-Literatur," *Der Islam* 43 (1967): 37–52, and idem, "Imama," *The Encyclopedia of Islam* 3 (Leiden and London: E. J. Brill, 1971), 1163–69.

9. Abu al-Hasan al-Masudi, *Muruj al-Dhahab wa Ma'adin al-Jawhar,* (Cairo: dar al-Raja 1357/1938) 2:307–9; and Abu al-Faraj al-Isfahani, *Maqatil al-Talibiyyin wa Akhbaruhum* ed. Sayyid Ahmad Saqar (Cairo: Dar Ihya al-Kutub, 1368/1948), in entirety.

10. Al-Ashari, *Maqalat al-Islamiyyin,* 15.

11. Al-Baghadi, *al-Farq bayn al-Firaq,* 225 and 233.

12. Ibn Hazm, *al-Fisal* 4:186. For the English translation of this verse see Samuel Lyde, *The Asian Mystery* (London: Longman Green, Longman and Roberts, 1860), 31.

13. Ibn Hazm, ibid., Abu Said Nashwan al-Himyari, *al-Hur al-In,* ed. Kamal Mustafa (Cairo: al-Khanji, 1368/1948), 154; Shihab al-Din Abu al-Fadl ibn Hajar al-Asqalani, *Lisan al-Mizan* (Haydarabad: Matbaat Majlis Dairat al-Maarif al-Nizamiyya, 1329–31/1911–13), 3:289–90; Israel Friedländer, "Abdallah b. Saba, der Begründer der Schi'a und sein jüdischer Ursprung," *Zeitschrift für Assyriologie* 23 (1909): 296–327 and 24 (1910): 1–46, and idem, "The Heterodoxies of the Shiites in the Presentation of Ibn Hazm," *Journal of the American Oriental Society* 28 (1907): 1–80 and 19 (1908): 1–185; M. Houtsma, "Abd Allah b. Saba," *The Encyclopedia of Islam* 1 (Leiden: G. J. Brill, 1913): 29; G. Van Vloten, *Recherches sur la Domination arabe, le Chiitisme et les Croyance messianiques sous le Khalifat des Omayades* (Amsterdam: Johannes Müller, 1894), 40–42; and M. G. S. Hodgson, "Abd Allah b. Saba," *The Encyclopedia of Islam,* 1 (Leiden and London: E. J. Brill, 1960), 51. For a contemporary analysis of Ibn Saba see Dr. Ali al-Wardi, *Wu'az al-Salatin* (Baghdad: n.p., 1954), entire chapter 5, 147–79, and idem; *Mahzalat al-Aql al-Bashari* (Baghdad: Matbaat al-Rabita, 1955), 296 and 322–24; and Abd al-Rahman Badawi, *Madhahib al-Islamiyyin* (Beirut: Dar al-Ilm li al-Malayin, 1973)2:16–44.

14. Saad Ibn Abd Allah al-Ashari, *al-Maqalat wa al-Firaq,* ed. Muhammad Jawad Mashkur (Tehran: Matbaat Haydari, 1963), 21; and al-Nawbakhti, *Firaq al-Shi'a,* 40.

15. Abu Jafar Muhammad Ibn Jarir al-Tabari, *Tarikh al-Umam wa al-Muluk* (Cairo: Matbaat al-Istiqama, 1357/1939), 3:378–79; and al-Nawbakhti, *Firaq al-Shi'a,* 40.

16. Al-Nawbakhti, *Firaq al-Shi'a,* 41.

17. Israel Friedländer, "Abdallah b. Saba, der Begründer der Shi'a und sein jüdischer Ursprung," 296–327; Julius Wellhausen, *Skizzen und Vorarbeiten* (Berlin: Georg Reimer, 1884–99), 6:124; and Leone Caetani, *Annali dell'Islam* (Milano: U. Hoepli, 1918), 8:42–50.

18. Murtada al-Askari, *Abd Allah Ibn Saba wa Asatir Ukhra* (Beirut: Dar al-Kutub, 1968), 29–30, 37–59 and 62–64; idem, *Khamsun wa Mi'at Sahabi Mukhtalaq* (Beirut: Dar al-Kutub, 1968), 12 and al-Wardi, *Wu'az al-Salatin,* 147–49.

19. Al-Wardi, *Wu'az al-Salatin* 273–79. See Ihsan Ilahi Zahir, *al-Shi'a Ahl al-Bayt* (Lahore: Idarah Tarjuman al-Sunna, 1982), 117–27 in which the author provides evidence that Ibn Saba was a real person.

20. Al-Wardi, *Wu'az al-Salatin,* 274–78; al-Tabari, *Tarikh al-Umam wa al-Muluk,*

3:335, Taha Husayn, *al-Fitna al-Kubra* (Cairo: Dar al-Maarif, 1953), 131–37; and al-Shaibi, *al-Sila bayn al-Tasawwuf wa al-Tashayyu* (Cairo: Dar al-Maarif, 1969), 40–42.

21. See sources in the previous footnote.

22. Muhammad Jabir Abd al-Al, *Harakat al-Shi'a al-Mutatarrifin* (Cairo: Dar al-Maarif, 1954), 26–90.

23. Al-Shaibi, *al-Sila bayn al-Tasawwuf wa al-Tashayyu,* 121.

24. W. Montgomery Watt, *Islam and the Integration of Society,* 104.

25. Taha Husayn, *Ali wa Banuh* (Cairo: Dar al-Maarif, 1953), 188; and al-Wardi, *Wu'az al-Salatin,* 40.

26. Abd Allah al-Fayyad, *Tarikh al-Imamiyya wa Aslafihim min al-Shi'a* (Beirut: Muassasat al-Alami li al-Matbuat, 1975), 89.

27. Abu Jafar Muhammad Ibn al-Hasan al-Tusi, *al-Ghayba* (al-Najaf: Matbaat al-Numan, 1385/1965), 241–42.

28. Ibn Babawayh, *Ilal al-Shara'i,* 1: 227; and al-Shaykh al-Mufid, *Kitab Sharh Aqa'id al-Saduq aw Tashih al-I'tiqad,* printed together with his *Awa'il al-Maqalat fi al-Madhahib wa al-Mukhtarat* (Tabriz: Matbaat Ridai, 1371/1951), 257.

1—The Shabak

1. Rev. Anastase Marie al-Karmali, "Tafkihat al-Adhhan fi Ta'rif Thalathat Adyan," *al-Mashriq* 5 (1902): 576–82. The same article is reproduced in Ahmad Hamid al-Sarraf, *al-Shabak* (Baghdad: Matbaat al-Maarif, 1954), 218–25.

2. Al-Karmali, ibid., 582, and idem, "al-Yazidiyya," *al-Mashriq* 2 (1899): 395.

3. Al-Karmali, "Tafkihat al-Adhhan," 578.

4. Vladimir Minorsky, "Shabak," in *The Encyclopedia of Islam* 4 (Leiden: E. J. Brill 1934): 238–39. See also Amal Vinogradov (Rassam), "Ethnicity, Cultural Discontinuity and Power Brokers in Northern Iraq: The Case of the Shabak," *American Ethnologist* (June 4, 1973): 207–18; and Saad Ibrahim al-Adami, *al-Aqaliyyat al-Diniyya wa al-Qawmiyya wa Ta'thiruha ala al-Waqi al-Siyasi wa al-Ijtima'i fi Muhafazat Ninawa* (n.p., 1982), 95–117.

5. Amkah (pseudonym used by al-Karmali), "al-Shabak," *al-Muqtataf* 54 (1921); 230–32.

6. Kamil Mustafa al-Shaibi, *al-Tariqa al-Safawiyya wa Rawasibuha fi al-Iraq al-Mu'asir* (Baghdad: Maktabat al-Nahda, 1967), 54 n. 191.

7. Dawud al-Chalabi in al-Sarraf, *al-Shabak,* 8–11.

8. Ibid.

9. Abbas al-Azzawi, *al-Kaka'iyya fi al-Tarikh* (Baghdad: Sharikat al-Tibaa wa al-Tijara al-Mahduda, 1949), 95–99.

10. Abd al-Munim al-Ghulami, *Baqaya al-Firaq al-Batiniyya fi Liwa al-Mawsil* (Mosul: Matbaat al-Ittihad al-Jadida, 1950), 2 of introduction; 23; 45–48. Al-Ghulami's monograph was originally published as a series of articles in *al-Majalla* (1939) nos. 21–23 dated August 1, and August 16, and September 1 respectively. Cf. al-Azzawi, *al-Kaka'iyya fi al-Tarikh,* 96–8.

11. A. Layard, *Nineveh and Babylon* (London: John Murray, 1867), 216; Gertrude Lowthian Bell, *Amurath to Amurath* 2nd ed. (London: Macmillan, 1924), 270, who quotes Layard in full. Cf. Saad Ibrahim al-Adami, *al-Aqaliyyat,* 98–101.

12. Bell, *Amurath to Amurath,* 270.

13. Al-Sarraf, *al-Shabak,* Introduction, 2.

14. Ibid., 3–4 and 6–7 of Introduction.

15. For the Turkish and Arabic versions of the *Buyruk,* see al-Sarraf, 146–217.

16. Al-Sarraf, *al-Shabak,* 1, 11, and 89.

17. Ibid., 90. Cf. Al-Azzawi, *al-Kaka'iyya fi al-Tarikh,* 95.

18. Al-Azzawi, Ibid., 12–13, 90–91. On the Ak Koyunlu clan, see John E. Woods, *The AQ Qoynlu Clan Confederates Empire* (Chicago: Bibliotheca Islamica, 1976).

19. Al-Sarraf, 12–13, 90–91.

20. Ibid., 13, 91.

21. Al-Shaibi, *al-Tariqa al-Safawiyya wa Rawasibuha fi al-Iraq al-Mu'asir,* 45–46, and idem, *al-Fikr al-Shi'i wa al-Naza'at al-Sufiyya hatta Matla al-Qarn al-Thani Ashar al-Hijri* (Baghdad: Maktabat al-Nahda, 1966), 405–6. Al-Shaibi's authority here is *Samuel Purchas His Pilgrimage* 4th ed. (London: printed by W. Stansby for H. Fetherstone, 1626), Book 4:382. The original source here is not Purchas but Ioao de Barros, *Daasiade Ioao De Barros Dos Feitos Que Ospar, Decada Secunda* (Em Lisboa: Impressa per Iorge Rodriguez, 1628), Book 10:231–33. See also Clement Hurat, "Kizil-Bash," in *The Encyclopedia of Islam* 2 Leiden: G. J. Bill, (1927): 1053, and narrative of a journey in Persia by an anonymous Venetian merchant in Charles Grey, trans., *A Narrative of Italian Travels in Persia, in the Fifteenth and Sixteenth Centuries* (London: Hakluyt Society, 1873), 206; Edward G. Browne, *A Literary History of Persia: Modern Times* 1500–1924, (Cambridge: at the University Press, 1959, 4: 47–48; and Frederick W. Hasluck, *Christianity and Islam under the Sultans,* ed. Margaret M. Hasluck (Oxford: At the Clarendon Press, 1929), 1:139–59.

22. Al-Shaibi, *al-Tariqa al-Safawiyya,* 45–46; al-Shaibi, *al-Fikr al-Shi'i,* 405–6.

23. Hasluck, *Christianity and Islam,* 1:140. Cf. Armin Vámbéry, *Das Türkenvolk in seinen ethnologischen und ethnographischen Beziehungen geschildert* (Leipzig: F. A. Brockhaus, 1885), 607.

24. Al-Shaibi, *al-Tariqa al-Safawiyya,* 46–47.

25. Al-Azzawi, *al-Kaka'iyya fi al-Tarikh,* 91. On Haji Bayram, see Evliya Efendi, *Narrative of Travels in Europe, Asia, and Africa in the Seventeenth Century,* tr. Ritter Joseph von Hammer, (London: Oriental Translation Fund Publication, 1846–50), 2:231–34; E. J. W. Gibb, *A History of Ottoman Poetry,* (London: Luzac, 1901), 1:299; and John P. Brown, *The Darvishes or Oriental Spiritualism,* ed. H. A. Rose (London: Frank Cass, 1968), 61–62 n. 2, 269, and 459, Appendix 3.

26. Al-Shaibi, *al-Fikr al-Shi'i,* 373–85; and idem, *al-Tariqa al-Safawiyya,* 45–46. On the Babaiyya, see C1. Cahen, "Baba'i" *The Encyclopedia of Islam,* 1 (Leiden and London: E. J. Brill, 1960):843–44. According to the anonymous *History of Shah Isma'il* contained in Cambridge University Turkish MS Add. 200, fol. 27, on his march from his place of seclusion at Lahijan to Ardabil, Shah Ismail was joined by many devoted disciples and supporters from Syria and Asia Minor. Cf. E. G. Browne, *A Literary History of Persia,* 4:51.

27. Al-Shaibi, *al-Tariqa al-Safawiyya,* 48–49 and Halil Inalcik, *The Ottoman Empire: The Classical Age 1300–1600,* tr. Norman Itzkowitz and Colin Imber (New York: Praeger, 1973), 33. Inalcik states that thousands of Turkomans migrated to Iran and Azerbayjan and became the core of the Safawi army. For the wars of the Ottoman Sultan Selim I against the Safawis, including his massacre of thousands of Kizilbash on his march eastward and his victory over Shah Ismail at Chaldiran, see Joao De Barros, 231–33 and J. R. Walsh, "Chaldiran," *The Encyclopedia of Islam,* (Leiden and London: E. J. Brill, 1965):2:7–8

28. Al-Sarraf, *al-Shabak,* 13, 91 139.

29. Laurence Lockhart, *The Fall of the Safawi Dynasty and the Afghan Occupation of Persia* (Cambridge: The University Press, 1958), 19.

30. Lockhart, 19; and John E. Woods, *The AQ Quyunlu Clan Confederates Empire,* 173–74.

31. Al-Sarraf, 13, 91; and al-Shaibi, *Al-Tariqa al-Safawiyya,* 48–49.

32. Lockhart, 19.

33. Al-Shaibi, *al-Tariqa al-Safawiyya,* 48–49. For an account of the strained relations between the Ottoman sultans and Shah Ismail that led to the battle of Chaldiran, see De Barros, 57–77.

34. Claude Cahen, *Pre-Ottoman Turkey,* tr. J. Jones Williams (New York: Taplinger Publishing Company, 1968), 64–72; and Frederick W. Hasluck, *Christianity and Islam under the Sultans,* 1:158.

2—The Bektashis

1. F. W. Hasluck, *Christianity and Islam under the Sultans, ed. Margaret M. Hasluck* (Oxford: Clarendon Press, 1929), 1:341 and 2:488–90.

2. Eviya Efendi, *Narrative of Travels in Europe, Asia and Africa in the Seventeenth Century,* trans. Ritter von Hammer (London: Oriental Translation Fund Publication, 1846–50), 2:20–21. See also John P. Brown, *The Darvishes or Oriental Spiritualism* (London: Frank Cass, 1968), 214–16; John Birge, *The Bektashi Order of Dervishes* (London: Luzac & Co., 1937), 26–51; Georg Jacob, *Beiträge zur Kenntnis des Derwisch-Ordens der Bektaschis,* (Berlin: Mayer & Müller, 1908), Introduction 1–2; R. Tschudi, "Bektashiyya," in *The Encyclopeida of Islam* (Leiden and London: E. J. Brill, 1961): 1:1161–62; W. Barthold, *Tarikh al-Turk fi Asiya al-Wusta* (History of the Turks in Central Asia), trans. Ahmad al-Said Sulayman (Cairo: Maktabat al-Anglo Misriyya, 1958), 142–43; Nur Yalman, "Islamic Reform and the Mystic Tradition in Eastern Turkey," *Archives Européennes de Sociologie* 10 (1969): 41–42; M. Fuad Köprülü, "Anadoluda Islamiyet," *Edebiyat Fakultesi Mecumasi* no. 2 (Istanbul, 1338/1919), 295; Köprülü, "Les Origines du Bektachisme," *Actes des Congrès Internationale d'Histoire des Religions* 2 (Paris, 1925):391–411; Abdulbaki Golpinarli, "Bektasilik ve Haci Bektas," *Aylik Ansiklopedi* no. 41 (September, 1947), 1194–95; and idem, "Bektas" (Manuscript, 1982).

3. Shams al-Din Ahmad al-Arifi al-Aflaki, *Manaqib al-Arifin,* ed. Tahsin Yazici (Ankara: Milli Egitim Basimevi, 1953–54), 1:381. Cf. Halil Inalcik, *The Ottoman Empire: The Classical Age 1300–1600* (New York, Praeger, 1973), 194.

4. Evliya Efendi, *Narrative of Travels* 2:20–21. Cf. John Kingsley Birge, *The Bektashi Order of Dervishes,* 51.

5. Aşikpaşazada, *Tevarih-i Al-i Osman* (Istanbul: Matbaa-Yi Amire, 1332/1913), 206. Some Bektashis maintain that Haji Bektash appeared in the time of the Ottoman Sultan Orhan. See Ahmad Sirri Dede Baba, *al-Risala al-Ahmadiyya fi al-Tariqa al-Bektashiyya* (Cairo: Matbaat Abduh wa Anwar Ahmad, 1959), 7.

6. See Oruc Ibn Adil, *Tarih-i Al-i Osman,* ed. by Franz Babinger, *Die Frühosmanichen Jahrbücher des Urudsch* (Hanover: H. Lafaire, 1925), 15, 22, 89, 93 and Birge, *Bektashi Order of Dervishes,* 46–47.

7. M. Fuad Köprülü, "Andoluda Islamiyet," *Edebiyat Fakultesi Mecmuasi* no. 1 (Istanbul, 1338/1919), 297–98; W. Ivanow, *The Truth-Worshippers of Kurdistan* (Leiden: E. J. Brill, 1953), 57–58, and 60 n. 1 (In this note, Ivanow relates his effort to find a clue to the origin of the term *Qalandar*). Cf. John P. Brown, *The Darvishes or Oriental Spiritualism* (London: Luzac & Co., 1937), 169–72 n. 1.

8. Ivanow, *Truth-Worshippers,* 48, 60–62; and Paul Wittek, "The Rise of the Ottoman

Empire," *The Royal Asiatic Society of Great Britain and Ireland* 23 (London, 1938, reprinted 1965), 18. Cf. C. Cahen, *Pre-Ottoman Turkey* 66–72; and Inalcik, *Ottoman Empire,* 5–8.

9. Wittek "Rise of the Ottoman Empire," 18–21; and W. Barthold, *Tarikh al-Turk fi Asiya al-Wusta,* trans. Ahmad al-Said Sulayman (Cairo: Maktabat al-Anglo-Misriyya, 1958), 108–9.

10. Wittek, "Rise of the Ottoman Empire," and idem, "Zur Geschichte Angoras im Mittelalter," in *Festschrift Georg Jacob* (Leipzig: O. Harrassowitz, 1932), 339. There is also some evidence that the Danishmends' coins bore Christian representations, such as, the head and shoulders of Jesus Christ. See Cahen, *Pre-Ottoman Turkey,* 169.

11. Wittek, "Rise of the Ottoman Empire," 21–23; Abu al-Muzaffar Yusuf al-Baghdadi (Known as Sibt Ibn al-Jawzi), *Mir'at al-Zaman fi Tarikh al-A'yan* (Haydarabad India: Matbaat Dairat al-Maarif al-Uthmaniyya, 1950), 293; and Cahen, *Pre-Ottoman Turkey,* 96–106.

12. Wittek, ibid., 24–25; and Cahen, *Pre-Ottoman Turkey,* 247. Some scholars believe that the term *Turkoman* has a religious connotation. When the Turks were converted to Islam their chief, Salur, called them "Turk-iman," (Turks of faith), to distinguish them from the rest, who remained heathens. See Sadik Shahid Bey, *Islam, Turkey and Armenia and How They Happened* (St. Louis: G. B. Woodward Co., 1898), 101–2.

13. Köprülü, "Anadoluda Islamiyet" 297–98 and J. Spencer Trimingham, *The Sufi Orders of Islam* (Oxford: Oxford University Press, 1971), 67–69.

14. Barthold, "Turgai" *The Encyclopedi of Islam* 4 (Leiden: E. J. Brill, 1934):894–96; René Grousset, *The Empire of the Steppes,* trans. Naomi Walford (Rutgers University Press, 1970), 120, 141; and H. R. Gibb, *The Arab Conquest of Central Asia* (London: The Royal Asiatic Society, 1923), 96–97.

15. Grousset, *Empire of the Steppes,* 120; R. N. Frey, "The Samanids," in *The Cambridge History of Iran* (Cambridge: Cambridge University Press, 1975), 4:150; and Barthold, *Tarikh al-Turk,* 57–59, 68–71.

16. Abu Jafar Muhammad Ibn Jarir al-Tabari, *Tarikh al-Umam wa al-Muluk* (Cairo: Matbaat al-Istiqama, 1938), 8:167; Abu al-Hasan al-Masudi, *Muruj al-Dhahab wa Ma' adin al-Jawhar* ed. Muhyi al-Din Abd al-Hamid, (Cairo: Dar al-Raja 1938), 4:179–80; Arminius Vámbéry, *History of Bokhara* (1873; reprinted, New York: Arno Press, 1973), 55–72; and Frey, "The Samanids," 4:150, 155.

17. Grousset, *Empire of the Steppes,* 144–45; and Barthold, *Tarikh al-Turk,* 71–77.

18. Frey, "The Samanids," 155.

19. Al-Masudi, *Muruj al-Dhahab,* 4:294–296. See also Abu al-Fath Abd al-Karim al-Shahrastani, *Kitab al-Milal wa al-Nihal,* printed on the margin of Ibn Hazm *Kitab al-Fisal* (Cairo: Muassasat al-Khanji, 1321/1903), 1:211; Jalal al-Din al-Suyuti, *Tarikh al-Khulafa* (Cairo: 1952; reprinted Matbaat Munir, Baghdad: 1983), 381; Anastase Marie al-Karmali, *Khulasat Tarikh Baghdad* (Basra: Matbaat al-Hukuma, 1919), 110; W. Madelung, "The Minor Dynasties of Northern Iran," in *The Cambridge History of Iran* (Cambridge: Cambridge University Press, 1975), 4:208; S. M. Stern, "The Early Isma'ili Missionaries in North-West Persia and in Khurasan and Transoxiana", *Bulletin of the School of Oriental and African Studies* 23 (1960): 76; idem, *Studies in Early Isma'ilism* (Jerusalem: The Hebrew University, 1983), 216; and Vámbéry, *History of Bokhara,* 74.

20. Izz al-Din Ibn al-Athir, *al-Kamil fi al-Tarikh* (Leiden: E. J. Brill 1870), 8:149; and Muhammad Ibn Ali Ibn Tabataba (known as Ibn al-Tiqtiqa), *al-Fakhri fi al-Adab al-Sultaniyya wa al-Duwal al-Islamiyya* (Cairo: al-Maktaba al-Tijariyya al-Kubra, 1927), 204.

21. Abu al-Rayhan al-Biruni, *Kitab al-Jamahir fi Ma'rifat al-Jawahir* (Haydarabad: Matbaat Jamiyyat Dairat al-Maarif al-Uthmaniyya, 1355/1936–37), 22–23; Ibn al-Athir, ibid.; and al-Shaibi, *al Fikr al-Shi'i* (Baghdad: Maktabat al-Nahda, 1966), 43–44.

22. Al-Masudi, *Muruj al-Dhahab,* 4:196, 296. Cf. Stern, "The Early Isma'ili Missionaries in North-West Persia and in Khurasan and Transoxiana," *Bulletin of the School of Oriental and African Studies* 23 (1960), 71; and idem, *Studies in Early Isma'ilism* (Jerusalem: The Hebrew University, 1983), 216.

23. Abd al-Qahir al-Baghdadi, *al-Farq Bayn al-Firaq,* ed. Muhammad Muhyi al-Din Abd al-Hamid (Cairo: Matbaat al-Madani n.d.), 283.

24. Imad al-Din Muhammad Ibn Hamid al-Isfahani, *Kitab Tarikh Dawlat Al Seljuk,* ed. Ali Ibn Muhammed al-Bandari (Cairo: Matbaat al-Mawsuat, 1318/1900), 88; and Stern, *Studies in Early Isma'ilism,* 216–23.

25. R. Levy, "The Account of the Isma'ili Doctrines in the Jami al-Tawarikh of Rashid al-Din Fadlallah," *Journal of the Royal Asiatic Society* (1930): 509–36; and Taqi al-Din Abu al-Abbas al-Maqrizi, *Itti'az al-Hunafa bi Akhbar al-A'imma al-Khulafa,* ed. Jamal al-Din al-Shayyal (Cairo: Dar al-Fikr al-Arabi, 1367/1947), 247.

26. Abd al-Qahir al-Baghdadi, *al-Farq Bayn al-Firaq,* 282.

27. Grousset, *Empire of The Steppes,* 142; and Frey, "The Samanids," 4;153.

28. C. E. Bosworth, "The Early Ghaznavids," in *The Cambridge History of Iran* (Cambridge: Cambridge University Press, 1975), 4:177.

29. Philip K. Hitti, *History of the Arabs,* 10th. ed. (New York: MacMillan St. Martin's, 1970), 446–48.

30. Barthold, *Tarikh al-Turk,* 142–43.

31. Vladimir Minorsky, *Notes sur la Secte des Ahlé-Haqq* (Paris: Ernest Leroux, 1921), 56–57.

32. Henri Lammens, *Islam Beliefs and Institutions,* trans. Sir E. Denison Ross (New York: E. P. Dutton, 1926), 177–78.

33. Hasan Ibn Ali Ibn Muhammad al-Tabari, *Kamil-i Baha'i* (Bombay: 1323/1905), 7; and Ivanow, *Truth-Worshippers,* 15.

34. Birge, *Bektashi Order,* 29.

35. Franz Babinger, "Der Islam in Kleinasien, Neue Wege der Islamforschung," *Zeitschrift der deutschen morgenländischen Gesellschaft* 76 (1922):128.

36. F. W. Hasluck, *Christianity and Islam,* 1:158; Köprülü, *Türk Edebiyatinda Ilk Mutesavviflar* (First mystics in Turkish literature) (Istanbul: Matbaa-Yi Amire, 1918), 232–34; and Claude Cahen, *Pre-Ottoman Turkey,* 259–60.

37. Bar Hebraeus (Ibn al-Ibri), *The Chronography of Gregory Abu' L-Faraj Known as Bar Hebraeus,* trans. Ernest A. Wallis Budge (Oxford: Oxford University Press, 1932), 1:405; and idem; *Tarikh Mukhtasar al-Duwal,* 2nd ed., ed. Anton Salhani (Beirut: al-Matbaa al-Katholikiyya, 1958), 251.

38. Birge, *Bektashi Order,* 28–33; and Abu al-Abbas Ahmad Ibn Sinan al-Dimashqi al-Qaramani, *Akhbar al-Duwal wa Athar al-Uwal* (lithographed Baghdad: 1282/1865), 293.

39. Nasir al-Din al-Husayn Yahya Ibn Muhammad Ibn Ali al-Jafari al-Raghdi (known as Ibn Bibi), *al-Awamir al-Ala'iyya fi al-Umur al-Ala'iyya,* ed. Adnan Sadiq Erzi (Ankara: Türk Tarih Kurumu Basimevi, 1956), 498–510.

40. Cahen, *Pre-Ottoman Turkey,* 136.

41. Bar Hebraeus, *Chronography,* 1:405.

42. Ibn Bibi, *al-Awamir al-Ala'iyya,* 502; al-Aflaki, *Manaqib al-Arifin,* 1:381; Köprülü, *Türk Edebiyatinda,* 233; and al-Baghdadi (Sibt ibn al-Jawzi), *Mir'at al-Zaman* (Haydarabad, Matbaat Dairat al-Maarif al-Uthmaniyya, 1950), 773.

43. Bar Hebraeus, *Chronography,* 1:405.

44. Claude Cahen, "Baba'i" In *The Encyclopedia of Islam* (1960), 843–44; Idem, *Pre-Ottoman Turkey,* 136–37; al-Aflaki, *Manaqib al-Arifin,* 1:381; al-Qaramani, *Akhbar al-Duwal,* 293; Bar Hebraeus, *Chronography,* 1:406, and Idem, *Tarikh Mukhtasar al-Duwal,* 251.

45. Imad al-Din Abu al-Fida Ismail al-Qurashi al-Dimashqi (known and Ibn Kathir), *al-Bidaye wa al-Nihaya* (Cairo: Matbaat al-Saada, 1351–58/1932–39), 13:198.

46. Al-Shaibi, *al-Fikr al-Shi'i, 375.*

47. *Birge, Bektashi Order,* 40–41.

48. Ibid., 32–33.

49. Ignaz Goldziher, *Vorlesungen über den Islam* (Heidelberg: C. Winter, 1910, reprinted 1963), 167; Georg Jacob, *Beiträge zur Kenntnis des Derwisch-Ordens der Bektaschis,* (Berlin: Mayer & Müller, 1908), Introduction, passim; and Jacob, "Die Bektaschijje in ihrem Verhältnis zu verwandten Erscheinungen," *Abhandlungen der philosophisch-philologischen Klasse der Königlich Bayerischen Akademie der Wissenschaften,* sect. 3 (München: 1909), 42–44.

50. Al-Hajj Masum Ali (al-Nimat Ilahi al-Shirazi), *Tara'iq al-Haqa'iq* (Tehran: 1319/1901), 155–56; al-Shaibi, *al-Fikr al-Shi'i,* 378 n. 42; and Birge, *Bektashi Order,* 36.

51. For *Maqalat Haji Bektash,* see E. G. Browne Papers, Turkish MS. 20, fol. 48b, Cambridge University; and R. Tschudi, "Bektashiyya," in *The Encyclopedia of Islam* (Leiden and London: J. Brill, 1960), 1161–62. Cf. Rüştü Şardağ, *Her Yönü ile Haci Bektas-i Veli* (Izmir: Karinca Matbaacilik, 1985), 124–81.

52. Hasluck, *Christianity and Islam,* 1:60 and 2:565–66.

53. Browne, "Further Notes on the Literature of the Hurufis and their Connection with the Bektashi Order of Dervishes," *Journal of the Royal Asiatic Society* (1907): 533–38; and Birge, *Bektashi Order,* 60–62.

54. Birge, *Bektashi Order,* 50–51.

55. Joseph von Hammer-Purgstall, *Histoire de l'Empire Ottoman,* trans. J. J. Hellert (Paris: Bellizard, Barthes, Dufour et Lowell, 1835–43), 4:91.

56. See *Maqalat Haji Bektash* in E. G. Browne Papers, Turkish Ms. 20, fol. 1a–2a, Cambridge University.

57. Brown, *The Darvishes,* 162–64; and Birge, *Bektashi Order,* 51–53 and 74–78.

58. Birge, *Bektashi Order,* 56–58.

59. Al-Shaibi, *al-Fikr al-Shi'i,* 381.

60. Birge, *Bektashi Order,* 56, 58–62, 73; Browne, "Some Notes on the Literature and Doctrines of the Hurufi Sect," *Journal of the Royal Asiatic Society* (January 1898), 61–94; Clement Hurat, *Textes Houroufis* (Leiden: E. J. Brill, 1909); 226, 228, 238; Brown, *The Darvishes,* 223; and Appendix to chapter 7 by H. A. Rose; and al-Shaibi, *al-Fikr al-Shi'i,* 211–44.

3—The Safawis and Kizilbash

1. *History of Shah Isma'il,* MS. Add. 200, fol. 3a, Cambridge University. See also Ismail Tawakkuli known as Ibn Bazzaz, *Safwat al-Safa* (Bombay: 1329/1911), 3; Cf. Shaykh Husayn Ibn Shaykh Abdal-i Zahidi, *Silsilat al-Nasab Safawiyya,* E. G. Browne Papers, MS. H. 12, fol. 5b, Cambridge. Edward G. Browne published a summary of this work in English, entitled, "Notes on an apparently unique Manuscript History of the Safawi Dynasty of Persia," *Journal of the Royal Asiatic Society,* (1921): 395–418; Michel Mazzaoui, *The Origins of the Safawids: Shi'ism, Sufism and the Gulat* (Wiesbaden: Franz Steiner, 1972), 41–82; and I. P. Petrushevsky, *Islam in Iran,* trans. Hubert Evans (Albany, New York: State University of New York at Albany Press, 1985), 303–26.

2. Zahidi, *Silsilat al-Nasab Safawiyya,* E. G. Browne Papers, MS. H 12, fols. 5b and

6a, Cambridge: Browne, "Manuscript History of the Safawi Dynasty of Persia," 396, 398; Idem, *A Literary History of Persia 1500–1924* (Cambridge, 1959), 4:36; and al-Shaibi, *al-Fikr al-Shi'i,* 39, 391.

3. Ibn Bazzaz, *Safwat al-Safa,* 12; Zahidi, *Silsilat,* MS. H 12, fols. 6a; al-Shaibi, *al-Fikr al-Shi'i,* 391; Browne, "Manuscript History of The Safawi Dynasty," 398.

4. *History of Shah Isma'il,* MS. Add. 200, fol, 14b, Cambridge University. For the Georgians' invasion of Azerbayjan, see Ibn al-Ibri (Bar Hebraeus), *Tarikh Mukhtasar al-Duwal,* 228–29.

5. *History of Shah Isma'il,* MS. Add. 200, fol. 14b.

6. Bazzaz, *Safwat al-Safa,* 12, 21; and al-Shaibi, *al-Fikr al-Shi'i,* 392. E. G. Browne, following Zahidi, refers to Amin al-Din Jabrail as the son of Qutb al-Din. See Browne, *Literary History,* 4:37. Cf. Browne, "Manuscript History of the Safawi Dynasty," 398.

7. Bazzaz, in his *Safwat al-Safa,* 13 errs in referring to this spiritual leader as Kamal al-Din Masud Ibn Abd Allah al-Khajandi; the latter most probably died in the last decade of the fourteenth century, while Amin al-Din Jabrail lived and died in the thirteenth century. Cf. Zahidi, *Silsilat,* MS. H 12, 8b; Browne, "Manuscript History of the Safawi Dynasty," 339; idem, *Literary History,* 4:37.

8. *History of Shah Isam'il,* MS. Add. 200, fol. 5a.

9. Brown, *Literary History,* 4:37. See also Bazzaz, *Safwat al-Safa,* 12; Zahidi, *Silsilat,* MS. H 12, fol. 8a; Browne, "Manuscript History of the Safawi Dynasty," 399; and al-Shaibi, *al-Fikr al-Shi'i,* 393.

10. Zahidi, *Silsilat,* MS. H 12, fol. 9a. See also al-Shaibi, *al-Fikr al-Shi'i,* 393.

11. There is certainly a discrepancy between the dates of Safi al-Din's arrival in Shiraz and of the death of Shaykh Najib al-Din Buzghush. See Browne, *Literary History,* 4:42 n. 1; and al-Shaibi, *al-Fikr al-Shi'i,* 393.

12. *The History of Shah Isma'il,* MS. Add. 200, fol. 7a; Bazzaz, *Safwat al-Safa,* 15; and al-Shaibi, *al-Fikr al-Shi'i,* 394.

13. Browne, *Literary History,* 4:43, and Idem, "Manuscript History of the Safawi Dynasty," 403.

14. Bazzaz, *Safwat al-Safa,* 89–90, 335–58; and Browne, ibid., 403.

15. Hamd Allah Ibn Bakr Ibn Ahmad Ibn Nasr Mustawfi, *Tarih-i Guzida,* ed. Abd al-Husayn Hawai (Tehran: n.p., 1336–39/1357–60), 675; and Michel M. Mazzaoui, *The Origins of the Safawids* (Wiesbaden: Franz Steiner, 1972), 46.

16. Bazzaz, *Safwat al-Safa,* 95, 105, 242–43; and Khwand Amir, *Habib al-Siyar fi Akhbar Afrad al-Bashar* (Tehran: Intisharat Kitabkhane Khayyam, 1315/1897), 3:220 and 4:421.

17. See Letter 45, from Rashid al-Din to Shaykh Safi, in Browne, *Literary History,* 3:85.

18. Bazzaz, *Safwat al-Safa,* 105.

19. Ibid., 11. This genealogy is also given in Zahidi, *Silsilat,* MS. H 12, fol. 5b; and Browne, *Literary History,* 4:32–33 n. 1. Cf. Ghulam Sarwar, *History of Shah Isma'il Safawi* (1939; reprinted, New York: A.M.S. Press, 1975), 17–29, which contains the genealogy of Shah Ismail back to the Imam Musa al-Kazim as well as a brief history of the ancestors of Shah Ismail. Samuel Purchas, *Purchas His Pilgrimage* (London: printed by William Stansby for Henry Fetherstone, 1617), 430, calls Shaykh Safi al-Din a "Nobleman called Sophi, Lord of the City of Ardabil reporting himself to be of the blood of Ali Descended from Musa 'Cazin' al-Kazim."

20. See *Manaqib al-Awliya aw Buyruk,* Turkoman MS. 14706/1, Iraqi Museum. This Manuscript consists of a school notebook of 111 pages. It is written in Arabic script but the

language is Turkoman, or old Turkish, interspersed with Persian and Arabic words and phrases. At the end of the manuscript is a colophone written in a different hand. This addition may be by a man from the town of Tallafar north of Mosul, Iraq. It states that the book was completed by the grace of God, and that it is the book in which the Sufis of Tallafar believe. Then follows the date December 28, 1953, indicating the completion of the transcription of the manuscript. An insignia on the front page shows that it was in the possession of an Iraqi Shiite attorney-at-law, Sadiq Kammuna, who donated it to the library of the Iraqi Museum in 1975.

21. Ahmad Kasrawi, "Nijad va Tabari-i Safaviyah," *Ayandah* 11 (1926–28), nos. 5 and 7, 357ff., 389ff., and 801. For a detailed account, see Mazzaoui, *The Origins of the Safawids: Shi'ism, Sufism, and The Gulat* (Wiesbaden: Franz Steiner, 1972), 47–48. Cf. I. P. Petrushevsky, *Islam in Iran,* trans. Hubert Evans (Albany, New York: State University of New York at Albany, 1985), 314–15.

22. Al-Shaibi, *al-Fikr al-Shi'i,* 395 n. 39.

23. Bazzaz, *Safwat al-Safa,* 11–12; and al-Shaibi, *al-Fikr al-Shi'i,* 395.

24. Al-Shaibi, *al-Fikr al-Shi'i,* 395, 397, 398.

25. Bazzaz, *Safwat al-Safa,* 95, 105, 242–43; Browne, *Literary History,* 4:43–44; al-Shaibi, *al-Fikr al-Shi'i,* 396; and Mazzaoui, *Origins of the Safawids,* 47–51.

26. Fadl Allah Ibn Ruzbihan Khunji, *Tarikh-i alam ara-yi Amini* abridged and translated as *Persia in A.D. 1470–1490,* trans. V. Minorsky (London: The Royal Asiatic Society of Great Britain, 1957), 62.

27. Browne, "Manuscript History of the Safawi Dynasty," 403.

28. Ibid.

29. Bazzaz, *Safwat al-Safa,* 4.

30. Zahidi, *Silsilat,* MS. H 12, fols. 26–28; Amir, *Habib al-Siyar,* 4:521–23; and al-Shaibi, *al-Fikr al-Shi'i,* 398.

31. Bazzaz, *Safwat al-Safa,* 97, 101–2.

32. Nur Allah al-Tustari, *Majalis al-Mu'minin* (Tehran: Sayyid Hasan Tehrani, 1299/1881), 273.

33. Browne, "Manuscript History of the Safawi Dynasty," 407 and idem, *Literary History,* 4:46. Cf. Sir John Malcolm, *The History of Persia from the Most Early Period to the Present Time.* (London: John Murray, 1815), 1:321.

34. Zahidi, *Silsilat,* MS. H 12, fols. 32a–44b; and Browne, "Manuscript History of the Safawi Dynasty," 407.

35. Browne, "Manuscript History of the Safawi Dynasty," 407 n. 1.

36. *History of Shah Isma'il,* MS. Add. 200, fol. 10b.

37. Ioao De Barros, *Daasiade Ioao De Barros Dos Feitos Que Ospar,* Decada Secunda, (Lisboa: Impressa par Iorge Rodriguez, 1628), Book 10, chapter 4, fol. 230.

38. Samuel Purchas, *Purchas His Pilgrimage* (London: printed by W. Stanby for H. Fetherstone, 1617), Book 4, chapter 8, 431 and the 1626 edition of the same, 382.

39. *History of Shah Isma'il,* MS. Add. 200, fols. 10–11b; Zahidi, *Silsilat,* MS. H 12 fol. 41b; Browne, "Manuscript History of the Safawi Dynasty," 408–9; De Barros, *Daasiade,* fol. 230, states that Timur's release of these captives of war took place in the time of Iune (Junayd). Browne, in his *Literary History,* 4:46, states that Shaykh Sadr al-Din was the one who interceded with Timur to free the Turkish Prisoners. Cf. Malcolm, *History of Persia,* 321.

40. *History of Shah Isma'il,* MS. Add. 200, fol. 11a; and Zahidi, *Silsilat,* Ms. H 12, fol. 32b.

41. De Barros, *Daasiade,* fol. 230.

42. Ibid. Cf. Purchas, *Purchas His Pilgrimage,* 431.

43. Purchas, *Purchas His Pilgrimage,* 431.

44. Shams al-Din Muhammad Ibn Abd al-Rahman al-Sakhawi, *al-Daww al-Lami li Ahl al-Qarn al-Tasi* (Cairo: Maktabat al-Quds, 1353–55/1934–36), 4:29–30.

45. Isam al-Din Ahmad Ibn Mustafa Taşköprüzade, *al-Shaqa'iq al-Nu'maniyya fi Ulama al-Dawla al-Uthmaniyya,* printed on the margin of Ibn Khallikan, *Wafayyat al-A'yan* (Cairo: al-Taba al-Maymaniyya, 1310/1892), 1:155.

46. Muhammad Raghib al-Tabbakh, *I'lam al-Nubala bi Tarikh Halab al-Shahba* (Ḥalab: al-Matabaa al-Ilmiyya, 1923–26), 3:56; Zahidi, *Silsilat* MS. H 12, fols. 36a and 45a; *History of Shah Isma'il,* MS. Add. 200, fol. 11a; Amir, *Habib al Siyar,* 4:424; and al-Shaibi, *al-Fikr al-Shi'i,* 402.

47. Browne, Literary History, 4:46; Zahidi, *Silsilat,* MS. H 12, fol 46b; idem, "Manuscript History of the Safawi Dynasty," 411; al-Shaibi, *al Fikr al-Shi'i,* 403, 406 R. M. Savory, "Djunayd," in *The Encyclopedia of Islam* 2 (Leiden and London, E. J. Brill, 1965):598; Idem, "The Development of the Early Safawid State under Isma'il and Tahmasp", (Ph.D. Diss., University of London, 1958), 54–55.

48. Al-Tabbakh, *I'lam al-Nubala,* 5:337.

49. Khunji, *Persia in A. D. 1478–1490,* 66; Mazzaoui, *Origins of the Safawids,* 72. Cf. al-Tabbakh, *I'lam al-Nubala,* 5:337.

50. Mazzaoui, *Origins of the Safawids,* 72.

51. Abbas al-Azzawi, *Tarikh al-Iraq bayn Ihtilalayn* (The history of Iraq between two occupations) (Baghdad: Sharikat al-Tijara wa al-Tibaa, 1935), 3:110–11. On Muhammad Ibn Fallah (known as al-Mushasha), see Abd Allah Ibn Fath Allah al-Baghdadi, *al-Tarikh al-Ghiyathi,* ed. Tariq Nafi al-Hamdani (Baghdad: Matbaat Asad, 1975), 273–76; and Jasim Hasan Shubbar, *Tarikh al Musha'sha'iyyin wa Tarajim A'lamihim* (al-Najaf: Matbaat al-Adab, 1965), 22–23.

52. Mustafa Abd al-Qadir al-Najjar, *al-Tarikh al-Siyasi li Imarat Arabistan al-Arabiyya 1897–1925* (The political history of the Arab principality of Arabistan), (Cairo: Dar al-Maarif, 1971), 227–49; and Matti Moosa "Ahwaz: An Arab Territory," in *The Future of the Arab Gulf and the Strategy of Joint Arab Action,* (Kuwait: Fourth International Symposium of the Center for Arab Gulf Studies, 3:1982), 12–49.

53. Al-Tabbakh, *I'lam al-Nubala,* 3:56; and al-Azzawi, *Tarikh al-Iraq,* 2:332 and 5:336–37.

54. *History of Shah Isma'il,* MS. Add. 200, fol. 11b.

55. Ibid., 15a and Zahidi, *Silsilat,* MS. H 12, fol. 46b.

56. Khunji, *Persia in A. D. 1478–1490,* 66; Petrushevsky, *Islam in Iran,* 315.

57. *History of Shah Isma'il,* MS. Add. 200, fol. 11b.

58. Al Tabbakh, *I'lam al-Nubala,* 2:56 and 5:337; al-Azzawi, *Tarikh al-Iraq* 3:332 and 5:326–27.

59. Khunji, *Persia in A. D. 1478–1490,* 64–65. Browne, *Literary History,* 4:47, sets the date of Junayd's death at 1456. In fact, Junayd was killed in 1460. See Savory, "Djunayd" 2:598. Cf. Mazzaoui, *Origins of the Safawids,* 75.

60. Al-Shaibi, *al-Fikr al-Shi'i,* 404; and Mazzaoui, *Origins of the Safawids,* 72–73.

61. Browne, *Literary History,* 4:64.

62. Browne, *Literary History,* 4:55, following *Ahsan al-Tawarikh,* lists twelve of these potentates who dominated Persia.

63. Al-Tabbakh, *I'lam al-Nubala,* 5:337; Khunji, *Persia in A.D. 1478–1490,* 66; and Mazzaoui, *Origins of the Safawids,* 73.

64. *History of Shah Isma'il,* MS. Add. 200, fol. 13a.

65. Zahidi, *Silsilat,* MS. H 12, fol. 47b; Browne, "Manuscript History of the Safawi Dynasty," 411; idem, *Literary History,* 4:47; "The Travels of a Merchant in Persia," in *A Narrative of Italian Travels in Persia in the Fifteenth and Sixteenth Centuries,* trans. Charles Grey (London: Hakluyt Society, 1873), 178–79; Khunji, *Persia in A.D. 1478–1490,* 65–82; al-Shaibi, *al-Fikr al-Shi'i,* 406; Savory, "Haydar," in *The Encyclopedia of Islam,* (Leiden and London: 1971), 3:315; and E. D. Ross, "The Early years of Shah Isma'il, Founder of the Safawi Dynasty," *Journal of the Asiatic Society of Great Britain and Ireland* (April, 1896), 253.

66. Al-Sakhawi, *al-Daww al-Lami,* 9:283; al-Azzawi, *Tarikh al-Iraq,* 3:276 and 361; and al-Shaibi, *al-Fikr al-Shi'i,* 407.

67. Letter from Yaqub of the AK Koyunlu dynasty to the Ottoman Sultan Bayazid II, in Browne, *Literary History,* 4:67.

68. "Travels of a Merchant in Persia," 185.

69. "Travels of a Merchant in Persia," 186; Browne, *Literary History,* 4:48; Zahidi, *Silsilat,* MS. H 12, fol. 48a; idem, "Manuscript of the Safawi Dynasty," 412; al-Azzawi, *Tarikh al-Iraq,* 3:270; Savory, "Haydar," 3:316; and al-Shaibi, *al-Fikr al-Shi'i,* 407 n. 134. Cf. Carl Brockelmann, *History of the Islamic People,* trans. Joel Carmichael and Moshe Perlmann (New York: Capricorn, 1960), 320.

70. Khunji, *Persia in A.D. 1478–1490,* 64; and Mazzaoui, *Origins of the Safawids,* 73–76.

71. On the role of the Ghazis in the establishment of the Ottoman state, see Wittek, "Rise of the Ottoman Empire," 16–51; and Mazzaoui, *Origins of the Safawids,* 76–77.

72. Stephen Van Renesselaer Trowbridge, "The Alevis, or Deifiers of Ali," *Harvard Theological Review* (1909), 340. Cf. Hasan Rashid Tankut, *al-Nusayriyyun wa al-Nusayriyya* (Ankara: Devlet Matbaasi, 1938), 61.

73. *History of Shah Isma'il,* MS. Add. 200, fol. 13b; Ross, "Early Years of Shah Isma'il," 254–55; Browne, *Literary History,* 4:48; Theodor Nöldeke, "Haidar," in *the Encyclopedia of Islam* (Leiden and London: 1927), 2:218–19; and Clement Huart, "Kizil-Bash," in *The Encyclopedia of Islam* 2 (Leiden and London: 1927):1053–54.

74. Ross, "Early Years of Shah Isma'il," 255.

75. A. Houtum-Schindler, "Shah Isma'il" *Journal of the Royal Asiatic Society of Great Britain and Ireland* (1897): 114–15.

76. Giovanni Tommaso Minadoi, *Historia della Guerra fra Turchi et Persiana* di Giovanni Thomaso Minadoi da Rouige divisa in libri noue (Venetia: Appresso Andraea Muschio & Barezzo Barezze, 1594), 45. For an English translation of this book, see Abraham Hartwell, trans., *The History of the Warres Between the Turkes and the Persians* (London: John Wolfe, 1595), 47. See also Purchas, *Purchas His Pilgrimage,* 431.

77. Minadoi, *Historia della Guerra,* 45; Hartwell, *History of the Warres,* 46.

78. Minadoi, *Historia della Guerra,* 48.

79. Houtum-Schindler, "Shah Isma'il," 114–15.

80. "Travels of a Merchant in Persia," 206.

81. *History of Shah Isma'il,* MS. Add. 200. fol. 13b.

82. "Travels of a Merchant in Persia," 194–95.

4—The Bektashis, the Kizilbash, and the Shabak

1. F. W. Hasluck *Christianity and Islam,* 1:140.

2. Ibid., 1:140–41; M. F. Grenard, "Une Secte Religieuse D'Asie Mineure: Les Kyzyl-Bachs," *Journal Asiatic,* 10th ser., 3 (1904); 511, and 521–22; and Muhammad Ghalib al-Tawil, *Tarikh al-Alawiyyin,* 4th ed. (Beirut: Dar al-Andalus, 1981), 535.

3. See Richardson, report dated 14 July 1856, *Missionary Herald* 52 no. 10 (October 1856): 298.

4. Ibid., 298; and Dunmore, report dated 24 October 1854, *Missionary Herald* 51 (2 February 1855): 55–56.

5. Wilson, Major-General Sir Charles, *Handbook for Travellers in Asia Minor, Transcaucasia Persia, etc.,* (London: John Murray, 1895), 62–63.

6. F. W. Hasluck, *Christianity and Islam,* 1:140–41; Grenard, "Une Secte Religieuse." 520–21; and Ivanow, *Truth Worshippers,* 48–57.

7. Felix von Luschan, "The Early Inhabitants of Western Asia," *Journal of the Royal Anthropological Institute* 41 (1911): 230–31; and F. W. Hasluck, *Christianity and Islam,* 1:142.

8. J. G. Taylor "Journal of a Tour in Armenia, Kurdistan and Upper Mesopotamia, with Notes of Researches in the Deyrsim Dagh in 1866," *Journal of the Royal Asiatic Society* 38 (1868): 312.

9. J. W. Crowfoot, Survivals Among the Kappadokian Kizilbash (Bektash)," *Journal of the Royal Anthropological Institute* 30 (1900): 305.

10. Grenard, "Une Secte Religieuse," 512.

11. Von Hammer-Purgstall, *Histoire de l'Empire Ottoman,* 4:91.

12. F. W. Hasluck, *Christianity and Islam,* 1:142, 158; Abbes al-Azzawi, *al-Kaka'iyya fi al-Tarikh,* 88; Minorsky, *Notes sur le Secte des Ahlé-Haqq,* 40; G. E. White, "Some Non-Conforming Turks," *The Moslem World* 8, no. 3 (July 1918): 242–48; idem, "The Alevi Turks of Asia Minor," *The Contemporary Review Advertiser* 104 (November 1913): 690–98; Trowbridge, "The Alevis, or Deifiers of Ali," 340; Lammens, *Islam Beliefs and Institutions,* 177; and Mehmet Eröz, *Türkiye'de Alevilik-Bektaşilik* (Istanbul: N.P., 1977), 52, 80–81.

13. Grenard, "Une Secte Religieuse," 511.

14. Horatio Southgate, *Narrative of a Tour Through Armenia, Kurdistan, Persia, and Mesopotamia* (London: Tilt & Bogue, 1840), 2:297; and idem, *Narrative of a visit to the Syrian (Jacobite) Church* (New York: D. Appleton and Co., 1844), 75.

15. F. W. Hasluck, *Christianity and Islam,* 1:159.

16. Grenard, "Une Secte Religieuse," 514–21.

17. See for example White, "Alevi Turks," 696–98; L. Molyneux-Seel, "A Journey in Dersim," *Geographical Journal* 44 (1914): 64–66; and Trowbridge, "The Alevis or Deifiers of Ali," 253.

18. See Dunmore, report dated 22 January 1857, *Missionary Herald* 53, no. 7 (July 1857): 220. For the Kizilbash hatred of the Sunnite Turks, See Rev. Henry Fanshawe Tozer, *Turkish Armenia and Eastern Asia Minor* (London: Longmans, Green, and Co., 1881), 259–60.

19. See Ball, report dated 8 August 1857, *Missionary Herald* 53, no. 12 (December 1857): 394–95.

20. Ellsworth Huntington, "Through the Great Canon of the Euphrates River," *The Geographical Journal* 20, no. 2 (August 1901): 186–87.

21. Nur Yalman, "Islamic Reform and the Mystic Tradition in Eastern Turkey," *Archives Européennes de Sociologie* 10 (1969): 52.

22. Dunmore, report dated 24 October 1854, 56; idem, report dated 22 January 1857, 220; Ball, report dated 8 August 1857, 394–95; and G. E. White, "The Shia Turks," *Faith and Thought, Journal of the Transactions of the Victoria Institute* 43 (1908): 288, 230. Cf. Charles Wilson, *Handbook for Travellers,* 68; F. W. Hasluck, *Christianity and Islam,* 1:165; Grenard, "Une Secte Religieuse," 512; Trowbridge, the "Alevis, or Deifiers of Ali," 351; Ellsworth Huntington, "Through The Great Canon," 187–88; and Yalman, "Islamic Reform," 51–52.

23. Horatio Southgate, *Narrative of A Tour,* 1:232.

24. Sir William Ramsay, *Impressions of Turkey During Twelve Years' Wanderings* (New York: Putnam's Son, 1897), 268.

25. Yalman, "Islamic Reform," 49–50, 55.

26. Eröz, *Türkiye' de Alevilik-Bektaşilik* (Istanbul: p.p., 1977), 15–16, 114–15.

27. Grenard, "Une Secte Religieuse," 513.

28. Dunmore, report dated 24 October 1954, 55. This chief is probably Ali Gako, mentioned in J. G. Taylor, "Journal of a Tour," 317–18.

29. See Jewett, report dated 16 December 1857, *Missionary Herald* 54, no. 4 (April 1858): 109, Cf. the reports of other missionaries, including Richardson, report dated 14 July 1856, 296; and Winchester, report dated 28 November 1860, *Missionary Herald* 57 (March 1861): 71.

30. Winchester, report dated 28 November 1860, 72.

31. See Herrick, report dated 16 November 1865, *Missionary Herald* 62, no. 3 (March 1866): 68–69.

32. See Livingstone, letter dated 30 March 1869, *Missionary Herald* 65 (7 July 1869): 224.

33. Grenard, "Une Secte Religieuse," 515.

34. See Georg Jacob, *Beiträge zur Kenntnis,* 9:73; and Georg Jacob, "Die Bektaschijje," 33.

35. Jafar Ibn Mansur al-Yaman, *Kitab al-Kashf,* ed. R. Strothmann (Oxford: Oxford University Press, 1952), 8–9; and Henry Corbin, *Cyclical Time and Ismaili Gnosis* (London: Routledge Kegan Paul, 1981), 186, where this quotation is produced in full.

36. Dunmore, report dated 22 January 1857, 220.

37. See Parson, report dated 17 September 1857, *Missionary Herald* 54 (18 January 1858): 24.

38. White, "The Shia Turks," 230.

39. Grenard, "Une Secte Religieuse," 515.

40. Trowbridge, "The Alevis, or Deifiers of Ali," 341.

41. Molyneux-Seel, "Journey in Dersim," 65. Cf. Trowbridge, "The Alevis, or Deifiers of Ali," 341 and 344–46.

42. This portion of Virani's poem is quoted by Georg Jacob, in his "Die Bektaschijje," 39. Cf. Ibn Babawayh, *Ma'ani al-Akhbar* (Tehran: Matbaat al-Haydari, 1379/1959), 55, where Ibn Babawayh states that the Name of Ali derives from Ali al-A'la (The Most High).

43. See Nutting, report dated 30 July 1860; *Missionary Herald* 56 (November 1860), 345.

44. F. W. Hasluck, *Christianity and Islam,* 1:162–63.

45. T. Gilbert, 'Notes sur les Sectes dans le Kurdistan," *Journal Asiatique* 7th ser., 11 (July 1873): 393–94; G. R. Driver, "The Religion of the Kurds," *Bulletin of the School of Oriental Studies* 11 (1921–23): 198; and Sir Richard Carnac Temple, "A Commentary," appended to R. H. Empson, *The Cult of the Peacock Angel* (London: H.F.&G. Witherby, 1928), 173.

46. White "Alevi Turks," 693; F. W. Hasluck, *Christianity and Islam,* 1:161–64; and Birge, *Bektashi Order,* 58, 64 n. 4.

47. Birge, *Bektashi Order,* 58, 64 n. 4; and J. Spencer Trimingham, *Sufi Orders,* 82–83.

48. White, "Alevi Turks," 694; F. W. Hasluck, *Christianity and Islam,* 1:162–63, 2:502–3; and Birge, *Bektashi Order,* 57–58. For the definition of the term *Chalabi,* see Brown, *The Darvishes,* appendix C of chapter 7: 216–18, by H. A. Rose.

49. Birge, *Bektashi Order,* 57–58.

50. Eröz, *Túrkiye' de Alevilik-Bektasilik,* 52, 64 n. 4.

51. F. W. Hasluck, *Christianity and Islam,* 1:162.

52. Grenard, "Une Secte Religieuse, 514.

53. Feridun Bey quoted in Browne, *Literary History,* (Cambridge, 1959), 4: 67–68.

54. F. W. Hasluck, *Christianity and Islam,* 1:169–72; Browne, *Literary History,* 4:70–72; Birge, *Bektashi Order,* 66; and Stanford Shaw, *History of the Ottoman Empire* (Cambridge: Cambridge University Press, 1976), 1:78.

55. Browne, *Literary History,* 4:72–74.

56. Richard Knolles, *The Turkish History: from the origin of that nation, to the growth of the Ottoman Empire with the lives and conquests of their princes and emperors,* 6th ed. with continuation by Sir Paul Ricaut (London: printed by Charles Browne, 1687–1700), 1:315; and Browne, *Literary History,* 4:70.

57. Knolles, *Turkish History,* 1:316–24; Von Hammer-Purgstall, *Histoire de l'Empire Ottoman,* 90–95.

58. Browne, *Literary History,* 4:67–69; and al-Tawil, *Tarikh al-Alawiyyin,* 403.

59. Edward W. Creasy, *History of the Ottoman Turks* (Beirut: Khayat, 1961), 131–32; and Shaw, *History of the Ottoman Empire,* 1:67–68.

60. Von Hammer Purgstall, *Histoire de l'Empire Ottoman,* 3:255, 5:95; F. W. Hasluck, *Christianity and Islam,* 1:163–74.

61. See Eugenio Albèri ed., *Relazioni degli ambasciator veneti al Senato,* 3rd ser., (Firenze: Societa Editrice Fiorentina, 1839), 1:338; J. W. Zinkeisen, *Geschichte des Osmanischen Reiches in Europa,* (Gotha: F. A. Perthes, 1855), 567; F. W. Hasluck, *Christianity and Islam,* 1:174; and Knolles, *Turkish History,* 1:324.

62. Al-Shaibi, *al-Tariqa al-Safawiyya,* 46–49.

63. Al-Ghulami, *Baqaya al-Firaq,* 50, 54–55.

64. See Dawud al-Chalabi's letter in al-Sarraf, *al-Shabak,* 8.

65. Al-Azzawi, *al-Kaka'iyya fi al-Tarikh,* 95.

66. Charles Wilson, *Handbook for Travellers,* 68.

67. Al-Sarraf, *al-Shabak,* 45–48, and 103–4.

68. Ibid., Introduction 3–7; al-Azzawi, *al-Kaka'iyya fi al-Tarikh,* 44–46, 51; and al-Ghulami, *Baqaya al-Firaq,* 44.

69. Al-Sarraf, *al-Shabak,* 45–48, 103–4.

70. Birge, *Bektashi Order,* 210–11.

71. F. W. Hasluck, *Christianity and Islam,* 2:570.

72. On this point, see G. E. White, "Saint Worship in Turkey," *The Moslem World* 9 (1919): 8–18.

73. F. W. Hasluck, *Christianity and Islam,* 2:569.

74. Birge, *Bektashi Order,* 210–11.

75. Ibid., 73.

76. Ibid., 198.

77. Brown, *The Darvishes,* 202.

78. Yalman, "Islamic Reform," 52.

5—The Ghulat's "Trinity"

1. Al-Sarraf, *al-Shabak,* 57, 100, 104, 112, 114, 118. For evidence of the deification of Ali by the Bektashis, see Birge, *Bektashi Order,* 132–40, 54. On the Bektashi "Trinity," see Birge, *Bektashi Order,* 132–34.

2. See this book chapter 18. See also René Dussaud, *Histoire et Religion des Nosairis* (Paris: Librairie Émile Bouillon, 1900), 64–65; and Rev. Canon Sell, *The Cult of Ali* (London: The Christian Literature Society for India, 1910), 28.

3. Wilson, *Handbook for Travellers,* 66.

4. Birge, *Bektashi Order,* 132.

5. Ibid.

6. See the *Buyruk* in al-Sarraf, *al-Shabak,* 148 of the Turkish version and 193 of the Arabic translation. In *Mishkat al-Masabih* (Niche of lamps), this tradition is related as follows: "I am the house of wisdom and Ali is its door." The compiler of the *Mishkat* states that this tradition is transmitted by Tirmidhi on the authority of Sharik. See Abu Muhammad al-Baghawi, *Mishkat al-Masabih,* trans. James Robson, (Lahore: Ashraf Press, 1975), 2; Book 26, 1341. According to the tenth-century Shiite authority Muhammad Ibn Yaqub al-Kulayni, this hadith is related as follows: "I am the city and Ali is its gate." See Abu Jafar Muhammad Ibn Yaqub Ibn Ishaq al-Kulayni, *al-Usul min al-Kafi,* 3rd ed. (Tehran: Dar al-Kutub al-Islamiyya, 1388/1968), 2:239. See also the entire book of al-Imam Ahmad Ibn Muhammad al-Siddiq al-Maghribi, *Fath al-Malik al-Ali bi Sihhat Hadith Bab Madinat Ali* (Cairo: al-Matbaa al-Islamiyya, 1354/1935), and Ibn Babawayh, *Ma'ani al-Akhbar,* 58.

7. Birge, *Bektashi Order,* 134. See also *Maqalat Haji Bektash* in E. G. Browne Papers, Turkish MS. 20, fol. 79, Cambridge University.

8. See the *Buyruk* in al-Sarraf, *al-Shabak,* 148, 193; for elaboraton on the belief that Muhammad and Ali are of one light, see al-Hafiz Rajab al-Bursi, *Kitab Mashariq Anwar al-Yaqin fi Asrar Amir al-Mu'minin,* 10th ed. (Beirut: Muassasat al-Alami, n.d.), 39–41, 160–61; and Mutahhar Ibn Tahir al-Maqdisi (late tenth century), in *al-Bad wa al-Tarikh,* ed. Clement Huart (Paris: E. Leroux 1899–1919), 150.

9. Muhammad Baqir al-Majlisi, *Hayat al-Qulub* (Life of Hearts), trans. Rev. James L. Merrick (Boston, Phillips, Sampson, 1850; reprinted, San Antonio, Texas: Zahra Press, 1982), 170–71.

10. Al-Majlisi, *Bihar al-Anwar* (Oceans of lights), (Tehran: Dar al-Kutub al-Ilmiyya, 1376/1966), 1:97.

11. For this poem, see al-Masudi, *Muruj al-Dhahab,* 2:48–49. See also al-Qasim Ali Ibn al-Hasan Ibn Hibat Allah Ibn Asakir, *Tarikh Dimashq* (History of Damascus), ed. Salah al-Din Munajjid (Damascus: al-Majma al-Ilmi al-Arabi, 1371/1951), 1:149; idem, *Tahdhib al-Tarikh Ibn Asakir* (Revision of the history of Ibn Asakir), ed. Abd al-Qadir Ahmad Badran (Damascus: Rawdat al-Sham, 1329/1911), 1:348; Kamal al-Din al-Damiri, *Hayat al-Hayawan al-Kubra* (The greater life of animals) (Cairo: Matbaat al-Istiqama, 1383/1963), 2:350; Abu Abd Allah Ibn Muslim Ibn Qutayba, *Ta'wil Mukhtalif al-Hadith,* ed. Muhammad Zuhdi al-Najjar (Cairo: Maktabat al-Kuliyyat al-Azhariyya, 1966), 88–89; and Kamil Mustafa al-Shaibi, "al-Wahi lada al-Samiyyin wa al-Islamiyyin," *Bayn al-Nahrayn* 10, nos. 37–38 (1982): 38. For more information on al-Haqiqa al-Muhammadiyya, see Corbin, *En Islam iranien: Aspects spirituels et philosophiques* (Gallimard Edition; 1978), 1:53, 187–218, 278–79, 3:209, 295–347, and 4:70–71, 207–14, 328; and Tor Andrae, *Die Person Muhammeds In Lehre Und Glauben Seiner Gemeinde* (Stockholm: Kngl-Boktryckeriet, P. A. Norstedt & Söner, 1918), 333–57.

12. Abu al-Fath Abd al-Karim al-Shahrastani, *Kitab al-Milal wa al-Nihal,* printed on the margin of Ibn Hazm, *Kitab al-Fisal fi al-Milal wa al-Ahwa wa al-Nihal* (Cairo: Muassasat al-Khanji, 1321/1903), 2:26. Cf. Sell, *The Cult of Ali,* 5; and Ata Muhy-Ud-Din, *Ali the Superman,* 2nd ed. (Lahore: Muhammad Ashraf Press, 1980), 324.

13. Sayyiduna Tahir Ibn Ibrahim al-Harithi al-Yamani, *Kitab al-Anwar al-Latifa,* in Muhammad Hasan al-Adami, *al-Haqa'iq al-Khafiyya an al-Shi'a al-Fatimiyya wa al-Ithnay*

'ashariyya (Cairo: al-Haya al-Misriyya al-Amma li al-Talif wa al-Nashr, 1970), 75–182. The reference here is to 127.

14. Al-Shahrastani, *Kitab al-Milal,* 2:26.

15. Abu Jafar Muhammad Ibn Yaqub Ibn Ishaq al-Kulayni, *al-Usul min al-Kafi,* 1:376–77; and Muhammad Baqir al-Khwansari, *Rawdat al-Jannat fi Ahwal al-Ulama wa al-Sadat,* 2nd ed., ed. Muhammed Ali Hawzati (Tehran: 1367/1947), 703.

16. Ali Ibn Ibrahim (al-Qummi), *Tafsir Ali Ibn Ibrahim,* (Commentary on the Quran), (lithographed Tabriz: 1315/1897), 270; and al-Shaibi, *al-Sila bayn al-Tasawwuf wa al-Tashayyu,* 2nd ed. (Cairo: Dar al-Maarif, 1969), 423; Goldziher, *Vorlesungen über den Islam,* 165–67.

17. *Islam and Revolution: Writings and Declarations of Imam Khomeini,* trans. Hamid Algar (Berkeley: Mizan Press, 1981), 64–65.

18. R. A. Nicholson, *The Idea of Personality in Sufism* (Reprint, Lahore: Ashraf Press, 1970), 81, and idem, *Studies in Islamic Mysticism* (Cambridge: Cambridge University Press, 1921), 106–7.

19. See the litany at the end of the *Buyruk,* in al-Sarraf, *al-Shabak,* 189. Cf. Nicholson, *The Idea of Personality in Sufism,* 80.

20. Quran Suras 4:105, 17:93, 18:110, 40:55, 41:6, 47:18, and 48:1–2.

21. Goldziher, "Neuplatonische und gnostische Elemente im Hadit," *Zeitschrift für Assyriologie* 22 (1921): 323. Cf. Sayyid Hussein Nasr, *Ideals and Realities of Islam* (New York: Frederick Praeger, 1967), 88.

22. Taqi al-Din Abu al-Abbas (Shaykh al-Islam) Ibn Taymiyya, *Majmu Fatawa Shaykh al-Islam Ahmad Ibn Taymiyya,* 1st ed., (Beirut: Dar al-Arabiyya, 1398/1977), 17:369–70; and al-Hasan Ibn Yusuf Ibn al-Mutahhar al-Hilli, *Kitab Minhaj al-Karama fi Ma'rifat al-Imama,* printed together with Ibn Taymiyya, *Minhaj al-Suna al-Nabawiyya, fi Naqd Kalam al-Shi'a wa al-Qadiriyya,* ed. Muhammad Rashad Salim, (Cairo: Matbaat al-Madani, 1962), 1:77, 202.

23. Goldziher, "Neuplatonische und gnostische," 323, quoting Ibn Taymiyya.

24. For different versions of this tradition, see *Ibid.,* 324–26.

25. Al-Kulayni, *al-Usul min al-Kafi,* 1:440; and Abu Jafar Muhammad Ibn al-Hasan al-Tusi (Shaykh al-Taifa), *Talkhis al-Shafi fi al-Imama* (al-Najaf: Matbaat al-Adab, 1383/1963), passim; and al-Bursi, *Kitab Mashariq,* 39–42.

26. Al-Masudi, *Muruj al-Dhahab,* 1:22–24; Dwight M. Donaldson, *The Shiite Religion A History of Islam in Persia and Irak* (London: Luzac, 1933), 137–39; and Sell, *The Cult of Ali,* 4–5.

27. *Kitab al-Haft al-Sharif,* ed. Mustafa Ghalib (Beirut: Dar al-Andalus, 1964), 92–93, 221–22.

28. L. Veccia Vaglieri, "Fatima," *The Encyclopedia of Islam* (Leiden and London: J. Brill, 1965), 845–50. For more on Fatima, see Ali Shariati, *Fatima is Fatima,* trans. Laleh Bakhtiar (Brooklyn, N.Y.: Muslim Students Council, n.d.).

29. Baha al-Din Haydar Ibn Ali Haydar al-Ubaydi al-Amuli, *Jami al-Asrar wa Manba al-Anwar,* Arberry Arabic MS 1349, fol. 5a, Indian Office, London. For detailed account of the religious concepts of al-Amuli, see Corbin, *En Islam iranien: Aspects spirituels et philosophiques,* London: Routledge Kegan Paul, Gallimard edition, 1978), 3:147–213; and al-Shaibi, *al-Fikr al-Shi'i,* 120–33.

30. Al-Amuli, *Jami al-Asrar,* 1349, fols. 5a; and al-Shaibi, *al-Fikr al-Shi'i,* 120–33. For an analysis of *"Khutbat al-Bayan,"* see Louis Massignon, "L'Homme Parfait en Islam et Son Originalité Eschatologique," *Eranos Jahrbuch* 15 (1947): 311–14; and the Arabic translation of the same in Abd al-Rahman Badawi, *al-Insan al-Kamil fi al-Islam* (The perfect man in

Islam) (Kuwayt: Wakalat al-Matbuat, 1976), 133–38, and 139–42, which contains the Arabic text of *"Khutbat al-Bayan."* See also Corbin, *En Islam Iranien,* 4:166–67, and John Birge, *Bektashi Order,* 140–45. Birge gives a detailed analysis of this speech. On the concept of the Perfect Man, see R. A. Arnaldez, "al-Insan al-Kamil," *The Encyclopedia of Islam* (Leiden: E. J. Brill, 1971), 3:1239–41.

31. Al-Majlisi, *Hayat al-Qulub,* 4. Cf. Muhammad Ibn al-Fattal al-Nisaburi, *Rawdat al-Wa'izin wa Basirat al-Mutta'izin,* (al-Najaf: al-Matbaa al-Haydariyya, 1386/1966), 1:77; and W. A. Rice, "Ali in Shi'ah Tradition," *The Moslem World* 4, no. 1 (January 1914):29.

32. Abu Abd Allah al-Husayn Ibn Hamdan al-Khasibi, *Kitab al-Hidaya al-Kubra* in Hashim Uthman, *al-Alawiyyun bayn al-Ustura wa al-Haqiqa* (Beirut: Muassasat al-Alami, 1980), 237; al-Majlisi, *Hayat al-Qulub,* 4–5; Ibn Babawayh, *Ma'ani al-Akhbar,* 56; and Rice, "Ali in Shi'ah Tradition," 29–30.

33. Al-Hajj Masum Ali, *Tara'iq al-Haqa'iq,* (Tehran 1319/1901), 7:43.

34. Ibid., and al-Bursi, *Kitab Mashariq,* 161–62.

35. For the concept of the Perfect Man, see al-Shaykh Abd al-Karim Ibn Ibrahim al-Jili, *al-Insan al-Kamil fi Ma'rifat al-Awakhir wa al-Awa'il* (The perfect man in knowing the first and last things), 4th ed. (Beirut: Dar al-Fikr, 1975); Nicholson, *Islamic Mysticism,* 68–141; and Badawi, *al-Insan al-Kamil fi al-Islam.*

36. Abu al-Mughith al-Husayn Ibn Mansur al-Hallaj, *Kitab al-Tawasin,* ed. Louis Massignon (Paris: P. Geuthner, 1913), 9, 11–12. Cf. A. E. Affifi, *The Mystical Philosophy of Muhyid Din-Ibnul Arabi* (1938; reprint, Lahore: Ashraf Press, 1964), 86.

37. Al-Hallaj, *Kitab al-Tawasin,* 130–34; and Nicolson, "Mysticism," in *The Legacy of Islam,* ed. Thomas Arnold and Alfred Guillaume (Oxford: Oxford University Press, 1931), 216.

38. Al-Hallajj, *Kitab al-Tawasin,* 136.

39. Muhyi al-Din Ibn Arabi, *al-Futuhat al-Makkiyya* (The Meccan revelations), (Cairo: Bulaq al-Matbaa al-Amiriyya, 1293/1876), 1:114, 186.

40. Muhyi al-Din Ibn Arabi, *Fusus al-Hikam* (The bezels of wisdom), trans. R. W. I. Austin (New York: Paulist Press, 1980), Introduction: 38, and 66–68; and Affifi, *Mystical Philosophy,* 66–92.

41. Ibn Arabi, *Fusus al-Hikam,* 97, 167, 200, 272, 284; and Affifi, *Mystical Philosophy,* 66–92, especially 73–74.

42. Al-Jili, *al-Insan al-Kamil fi Ma'rifat al-Awakhir wa al-Awa'il,* 2:29–30, 59–60, entire chapter 60. Cf. Arnaldez, "al-Insan al-Kamil," 3:1240–41.

43. Nicholson, *Islamic Mysticism,* 87. cf. Tor Andrae, *Die Person Muhammeds in Lehre Und Glauben Seiner Gemeinde,* 335–57.

44. Nicholson, *Islamic Mysticism,* 87–88.

45. Affifi, *Mystical Philosophy,* 59–145, passim.

46. E. H. Palmer, *Oriental Mysticism* (London: F. Cass, 1969), 43.

47. Ibid., 43–44

48. Ibn Arabi, *Fusus al-Hikam,* Introduction: 38, and 168; and Affifi, *Mystical Philosophy,* 92–103. The verses cited are Quran, 2:257 and 42:28 respectively.

49. Ibn Arabi, *al-Futuhat al-Makkiyya,* 1:318–19; idem, *Fusus al-Hikam,* Introduction: 38; and Affifi, *Mystical Philosophy,* 92–102.

50. Muhyi al-Din Ibn Arabi, *Anqa Maghrib fi Khatm al-Awliya wa Shams al-Maghrib* (Cario: n.p., 1954), 42; and Affifi, *Mystical Philosophy,* 72–77.

51. Al-Shaibi, *al-Sila bayn al-Tasawwuf wa al-Tashayyu,* 376–77.

52. Birge, *Bektashi Order,* 253, under Alevi.

53. Al-Kulayni, *al-Usul min al-Kafi,* 1:441.

54. Nicholson, *Islamic Mysticism,* 159–61.

55. Palmer, *Oriental Mysticism,* 44, including n. 1.

56. *Nahj al-Balaqha,* ed. Muhyi al-Din Abd al-Hamid with comments by Muhammad Abduh, (Cairo: Matbaat al-Istiqama, n.d.), 1:24–25; and Ali Ibn Ibrahim, *Tafsir,* 281, quoting the Imam Jafar al-Sadiq; and Ibn Babawayh, *Ma'ani al-Akhbar,* 35–103.

57. Al-Kulayni, *al-Usuul min al-Kafi,* 1:443.

58. Al-Bursi, *Kitab Mashariq,* 144–45.

59. Muhammad Baqir al-Sadr, *Bahth Hawl al-Walaya* (A treatise on the Walaya), 2nd ed. (Beirut: Dar al-Tarif bi al-Matbuat, 1399/1978), 1–96.

60. Al-Kulayni, *al-Usul min al-Kafi,* 1:443; and al-Shahrastani, *Kitab al-Milal,* 1:195.

61. Murtaza Mutahhari, *Master and Mastership,* 2nd ed., trans. Mustajib A. Ansari, (Tehran: Foreign Department of Bethat Foundation, 1982), 40–48.

62. Abu Nuaym al-Isfahani, *Hilyat al-Awliya* (Cairo: Maktabat al-Khanji, 1351/1932), 1:79; Muhammad Ibn Ali Abi Talib, *Qut al-Qulub fi Mu'amalat al-Mahbub* (Cairo: Mustafa al-Babi al-Halabi, 1933), 1:134; Abu al-Qasim Ali Ibn al-Hasan Ibn Hibat Allah Ibn Asakir, *Tahdhib Tarikh Ibn Asakir,* ed. Abd al-Qadir Ahmad Badran (Damascus: Rawdat al-Sham, 1329/1911), 4:83.

63. Abu Mansur Ahmad Ibn Ali al-Tabarsi, *al-Ihtijaj* (al-Najaf: Matbaat al-Numan, 1386/1966), 1:384–85; Ali Ibn Ibrahim, *Tafsir,* 327.

64. Al-Bursi, *Kitab Mashariq,* 140.

65. Abu Nasr al-Sarraj al-Tusi, *al-Luma,* ed. R. A. Nicholson (Leiden: E. J. Brill, 1914), 378.

66. Al-Amuli, *Jami al-Asrar,* MS 1349, fols. 108b–109a; and al-Shaibi, *al-Fikr al-Shi'i,* 123.

67. Al-Sarraj, *al-Luma,* 129.

68. Ibid., 129–132.

69. See *Diwan Ibn al-Farid* (Anthology of Ibn al-Farid), 2nd ed. (Cairo: al-Maktaba al-Husayniyya, 1352/1933), 60.

70. See *Kuliyyat Shams-i Tabrizi: Diwan-i ghazaliyyat* (Tehran: Amir Kabir, 1336/1957), 372–74.

71. Nicholson, *Islamic Mysticism,* 11.

72. Goldziher, *Vorlesungen über den Islam,* 251–53 and the Arabic translation of the same: idem, *al-Aqida wa al-Shari'a fi al-Islam,* 2nd ed., trans. Muhammad Yusuf Musa et al. (Cairo: Dar al-Kutub al-Haditha, 1959), 157–58. Cf. al-Shaibi, *al-Sila bayn al-Tasawwuf wa al-Tashayyu,* 46; and al-Bursi, *Kitab Mashariq,* 155–62.

6—The Miraculous Attributes of Ali

1. Sayyid Muhammad Kazim al-Qazwini, *Ali min al-Mahd ila al-Lahd,* 7th ed. (Beirut: Dar al-Turath al-Arabi, n.d.), 18–25.

2. This episode is related in Muhammad Ibn al-Fattal al-Nisaburi, *Rawdat al-Wa'izin wa Basirat al-Mutta'izin* (al-Najaf: al-Maktaba al-Haydariyya, 1966), 1:76–81. For more on the miracles of Ali see Rice, "Ali in Shi'ah Tradition," 30–36.

3. Al-Shaykh al-Mufid Abu Abd Allah Muhammad Ibn al-Numan al-Baghdadi al-Karkhi al-Ukbari, *Kitab al-Irshad ila Fada'il al-Amjad,* trans. I. K. A. Howard, (New York: Tahrike Tarsile Quran, Inc., 1981), 229–67, quotation in 230.

4. *Ibid.,* 231–32, 235–50; and *Sharh Nahj al-Balagha,* ed. Izz al-Din Abd al-Hamid

(known as Ibn Abi al-Hadid), (Beirut: Dar al-Fikr li al-Jami, 1388/1968), 1: 207–8 and the Cairo edition, Dar al-Kutub al-Arabiyya, 1329/1911.

5. Al-Mufid, *Kitab al-Irshad*, 1, 251–58, 261–63; and Ibn Asakir, *Tarjamat al-Imam Ali min Tarikh Dimashaq*, ed. al-Shaykh Muhammad Baqir al-Mahmudi (Beirut: Muassasat al-Mahmudi li al-Tibaa, 1980), 2:287.

6. Birge, *Bektashi Order*, 136–37.

7. See al-Ghulami, *Baqaya al-Firaq*, 35–36.

8. Ibid., 33.

9. S. G. Wilson, *Persian Life and Customs* (New York: Fleming H. Revell, 1900), 213,

10. Al-Shaykh Abu Hatim Ahmad Ibn Hamdan al-Razi, *Kitab al-Zina*, part 3, edited and appended by Abd Allah Sallum al-Samarrai to his *al-Ghuluw wa al-Firaq al-Ghaliya fi al-Hadara al-Islamiyya* (Baghdad: Dar Wasit li al-Nashr, 1982), 247–312; the reference here is to 305–6; al-Nawbakhti, *Firaq al-Shi'a*, 4th ed. (al-Najaf: al-Matbaa al-Haydariyya, 1969), 40–41; Abd al-Qadir al-Baghdadi, *al-Farq Bayn al-Firaq;* 234; Ibn Hazm, *Kitab al-Fisal fi Milal wa al-Ahwa al-Nihal* (Cairo: 1321/1903), 4:176, 180; al-Shahrastani, *Kitab al-Milal* 2:11, and M. G. S. Hodgson, "Abd Allah B. Saba," *The Encyclopedia of Islam* (Leiden and London: E. J. Brill, 1960), 1:512 and the bibliography on Ibn Saba.

11. Al-Razi, *Kitab al-Zina*, part 3, 297, 307; al-Shahrastani, *Kitab al-Milal*, 1:204, 2:12–13; al-Nawbakhti, *Firaq al-Shi'a*, 50–51. For more information, see Muhammad Jabir Abd al-Al, *Harakat al-Shi'a al-Mutatarrifin* (Cairo: Matbaat al-Sunna al-Muhammadiyya, 1954), 33–36; and M. G. S. Hodgson, "Bayan b. Sam'an al-Tamimi," *The Encyclopedia of Islam* (Leiden and London: E. J. Brill, 1960), 1:146–47. Cf. al-Imam Abu al-Hasan Ali Ibn Ismail al-Ashari, *Kitab Maqalat al-Islamiyyin wa Ikhtilaf al-Musallin*, 3rd ed., ed. Hellmut Ritter (Wiesbaden: Franz Steiner, 1980), 14. Al-Ashari does not mention the extremist Shiite sect that he says "insults the Prophet," 123–25.

12. Al-Shahrastani, *Kitab al-Milal*, 2:13; al-Baghdadi, *al-Farq Bayn al-Firaq*, 234; Ibn Hazm, *Kitab al-Fisal*, 4:176, 180; and al-Imam Abu al-Hasan Ali Ibn Ismail al-Ashari, *Maqalat*, 14.

13. Al-Ghulami, *Baqaya al-Firaq*, 34.

14. Jamal al-Din Abu al-Faraj Ibn al-Jawzi, *Talbis Iblis* (The devil's delusion), (Beirut: Dar al-Kutub al-Ilmiyya, 1368/1948), 22, 98.

15. W. C. Taylor, *The History of Muhammedanism and its Sects* (London: John W. Parker, 1834), 198–99; and Southgate, *Narrative of a Tour*, 1:43.

16. *Le Cabous-Name ou Livre de Cabous*, trans. A. Querry (Paris: E. Leroux, 1886), 5; and Minorsky, *Notes Sur la Sect des Ahlé-Haqq*, 17.

17. Haji Zayn al-Abidin Shirvani, *Bustan al-Siyaha*, ed. Ali Asghar Khan Atabeg (Tehran: printed at the expense of Sayyid Abd Allah Mustawfi, 1315/1897), 378–79; and F. M. Stead, "The Ali Ilahi Sect in Persia," *The Moslim World* 22, no. 2 (April 1932), 184. On the deification of Ali by the Ali Ilahis, see S. G. Wilson, *Persian Life and Customs*, 239–40, and chapter 21 of this book.

18. Al-Kulayni, *al-Usul min al-Kafi*, 1:234. For more information on Ali's sword, see E. Mittwoch, "Dhu l'Fakar," *The Encyclopedia of Islam* (Leiden and London: E. J. Brill, 1965), 2:233.

19. Al-Ghulami, *Baqaya al-Firaq*, 33.

20. Molyneux-Seel, *"Journey in Dersim,"* 52.

21. Nicholson, *The Mystics of Islam* (New York: Schocken Books, 1975), 153.

22. *Umm al-Kitab*, ed. Ivanow in *Der Islam* 223 (1936): 61–62 of the original Persian text and 46–47 of the periodical. Cf. Ivanow, *Truth-Worshippers*, 49. For information and

analysis of *Umm al-Kitab,* see Ivanow, "Notes sur l' Ummu'l-Kitab," *Revue des Études Islamiques* (1932): 419–82; and Corbin, *Cyclical Time amd Ismaili Gnosis,* 168–73.

23. Donaldson, *The Shi'ite Religion,* 44.

24. Al-Mufid, *Kitab al-Irshad,* 86–87; Donaldson, *The Shi'ite Religion,* 44; al-Majlisi, *Hayat al-Qulub,* 275; Ibn Shahr Ashub, *Manaqib Al Abi Talib* (al-Najaf: al-Matbaa al-Haydariyya, 1376/1956), 1:125–28; al-Sayyid Muhsin al-Amin, *Siyar al-A'imma* (Beirut: Dar al-Taaruf, 1980), 1:239–46; and al-Qazwini, *Ali min al-Mahd ila al-Lahd,* 137–44.

25. Abu Jafar Muhammad Ibn Ali al-Tabari, *Bisharat al-Mustafa li Shi'at al-Murtada,* 2nd. ed. (al-Najaf: al-Maktaba al-Haydariyya, 1963), 191; and al-Shahrastani, *Kitab al-Milal,* 2;25–26.

26. Al-Bursi, *Kitab Mashariq,* 110; and al-Majlisi, *Hayat al-Qulub,* 273–76.

27. Al-Bursi, ibid., al-Majlisi, ibid., and al-Shahrastani, *Kitab al-Milal,* 1:204, 2:25.

28. Ibn Ibrahim, *Tafsir,* 63. According to a tradition related by al-Shaykh al-Mufid in his book, *Kitab al-Irshad,* 58, an angel called Ridwan was the one who shouted "No chivalrous youth but Ali and no sword but Dhu al-Faqar." For the killing of Marhab see al-Mufid, *Kitab al-Irshad,* 87–88.

29. Al-Bursi, *Kitab Mashariq,* 110.

30. Abu al-Fadl Sadid al-Din Shadhan Ibn Jabrail ibn Ismail Ibn Abi Talib al-Qummi known as Ibn Shadhan, *al-Fada'il* (Exemplary acts), (al-Najaf: al-Matbaa al-Haydariyya, n.d.), 64–65.

31. Al-Khasibi, *Kitab al-Hidaya,* 274–75; Ibn Shahr Ashub, *Manaqib Al Abi Talib,* 2:123–24; al-Nisaburi, *Rawdat al-Wa'izin,* 1:114–15.

32. Al-Ghulami, *Baqaya al-Firaq,* 33, states that he tried very hard to explain to the Shabak and others who held the same belief that the "three in this Quranic verse meant Kab Ibn Malik, Hilal Ibn Umayya and Marar Ibn al-Rabi who tarried in joining the Prophet in his raid against Tabuk and not the three Caliphs who were first to join the forces of the Prophet in that skirmish."

33. Abu Ali al-Fadl Ibn al-Hasan al-Tabarsi, *Majma al-Bayan fi Tafsir al-Qur'an,* ed. Ahmad Arif al-Zayn (Sayda: Matbaat al-Irfan, 1333/1914), 5:201.

34. Al-Shaykh Mumin Ibn Hasan al-Shabalanji, *Nur al-Absar fi Manaqib Al Bayt al-Nabi al-Mukhtar,* (Baghdad: Maktabat al-Sharq al-Jadid, 1984), 112.

35. Al-Ghulami, *Baqaya al-Firaq,* 35.

36. Shaykh Muhsin Fani, *Dabistan or School of Manners,* trans. David Shea and Anthony Troyer 2 (Paris: Allen & Co., 1843), 368–69; W. St. Clair Tisdall, "Shi'ah Additions to the Koran," *The Moslem World* 3, no. 3 (July 1913), 227–41; and Abd al-Aziz al-Dihlawi, *Mukhtasar al-Tuhfa al-Ithnay 'ashariyya,* 2nd ed., ed. Mahmmud Shukri al-Alusi (Cairo: al-Matbaa al-Salafiyya, 13878/1967), 30–32.

37. Al-Mufid, *Kitab al-Irshad,* 256–58; and Mutahhar Ibn Tahir al-Maqdisi, *Kitab al-Bad wa al-Tarikh,* ed. Clement Huart (Paris: E. Leroux, 1899), 1: 150.

7—The Family of the Prophet

1. Ibn Ibrahim, *Tafsir,* 304. See also, al-Kulayni, *al-Usul min al-Kafi,* 1:287; Abu al-Husayn Ibn al-Hajjaj Muslim, *Sahih Muslim* (Collection of traditions by Mulsim) (Cairo: Maktabat Muhammad Ali Sabih wa Awladihi, 1334/1915), 8:121, 130; and Abu al-Abbas Shihab al-Din Ahmad Ibn Hajar al-Haythami, *al-Sawa'iq al-Muhriqa fi al-Radd ala Ahl al-*

Bida wa al-Zandaqa, 2nd ed., ed. Abd al-Wahhab Abd al-Latif (Cairo: Sharikat al-Tibaa al-Muttahida, 1965), 143.

2. Ibn Ibrahim, *Tafsir,* 93; and Ibn Babawayh, *Ma'ani al-Akhbar,* 90–3. See also Abu al-Husayn Muslim, *Sahih Muslim,* 7: 123; and Abu Muhammad al-Baghawi, *Mishkat al-Masabih,* trans. James Robson, 1:47.

3. Abu al-Qasim Abd al-Karim Ibn Hawazin al-Qushayri, *al-Risaia al-Qushayriyya,* ed. Abd al-Halim Mahmud and Mahmud al-Sharif (Cairo: Dar al-Kutub al-Haditha 1966), 1: 277; Sayyid Muhammad Taqi al-Hakim, *Ahl al-Bayt wa Mawadi Ukhra* (Beirut: Dar al-Zahra, 1978), 21; and al-Shabalanji, *Nur al-Absar,* 111–12.

4. Abd al-Qadir al-Jili, *al-Fath al-Rabbani wa al-Fayd al-Rahmani* (Beirut: Dar Sadir, 1972), 218; and Ibn Arabi, *al-Futuhat al-Makkiyya,* 2:126.

5. Abd al-Qadir al-Jili, *Kimya al-Sa'ada,* Arabic MS. Add. 422, fol. 229, Cambridge University; al-Shaibi, *al-Sila bayn al-Tasawwuf wa al-Tashayyu,* 351–52; al-Shabalanji, *Nur al-Absar,* 110; and al-Shaykh Ahmad al-Sabban, *Is'af al-Raghibin fi Sirat al-Mustafa wa Fada'il Ahl Baytihi al-Tahirin,* printed on the margin of al-Shabalanji, 104–108.

6. Jamal al-Din Abu al-Faraj Ibn al-Jawzi, *Sifat al-Safwa,* ed. Muhammad Fakhuri (Halab: Dar al-Wai, 1969), 1:535, 546; and Ibn Arabi, *al Futuhat al-Makkiyya,* 2:167. See also the tradition concerning the fifth Imam al-Baqir by Jabir Ibn Zayd al-Jufi in Corbin, *Cyclical Time and Ismaili Gnosis,* 144.

7. Abu al-Husayn Ibn al-Hajjaj Muslim, *Sahih Muslim,* 1:123.

8. See sources in note 1 of this chapter. See also Ibn Hajar al-Haythami, *al-Sawa'iq al-Muhriqa fi al-Radd ala Ahl al-Bida wa al-Zandaqa,* 144; al-Shabalanji, *Nur al-Absar,* 110–11; al-Sabban, *Is'af al-Raghibin,* 104–6; and Ihsan Ilahi Zahir, *al-Shi'a wa Ahl al-Bayt* (Lahore: Idarah Tarjuman al-Sunna, 1982), 16–19.

9. Ibn Ibrahim, *Tafsir,* 56. See also Abu Jafar Muhammad Ibn Abi al-Qasim al-Tabari, *Bisharat al-Mustafa li Shi'at al-Murtada,* (al-Najaf: al-Matbaa al-Haydariyya, 1383/1963), 16; and Ibn Shadhan, *al-Fada'il,* 95; 155–56.

10. For the episode of *al-Mubahala,* see Abu Jafar Muhammad Ibn Jarir al-Tabari, *Jami al-Bayan fi Tafsir sl-Qur'an* (Commentary on the Quran) (Cairo: al-Matbaa al-Maymaniyya, 1322–30/ 1904–11), 192–93; Nizam al-Din Hasan Ibn Husayn al-Qummi al-Nisaburi, *Ghara'ib al-Qur'an wa Ragha'ib al-Furqan,* printed on the margin of al-Tabari, *Jami al-Bayan,* 192–93; Abu al-Rayhan al-Biruni, *al-Athar al-Baqiya an al-Qurun al-Khaliya,* ed. C. Edward Sachau (Leipzig: Harrassowitz, 1923), 333; and Massignon, *Le Mubahala Étude sur la Proposition d'ordalie faite par le Prophète Muhammad aux Chrétiens Balharith du Nejràn en l'an* 10/631 *à Médine* (Melun: 1944).

11. Abu al-Faraj al-Isfahani, *Kitab al-Aghani,* (Cairo: Bulaq, 1285/1868), reprint, Beirut: Dar al-Fikr li al-Jami, 1970), 10:144.

12. Al-Mufid, *Kitab al-Irshad,* 116–18.

13. Imad al-Din Ibn Kathir, *al-Bidaya wa al-Nihaya* (Cairo: Matbaat al-Saada, 1351–58/1932–39), 5:54. This episode of the Mubahala is reproduced in Muhammad Ibn Abd al-Wahhab, *Mukhtasar Sirat Rasul Allah* (Riyad: Maktabat al-Riyad al-Haditha, 1375/1956), 442–48. For a Nusayri version of the Mubahala, see chapter 34 of this book.

14. Ibn Arabi, *al-Futuhat al-Makkiyya,* 1:256, 2:126, 4:139.

15. *Nahj al-Balagha,* ed. Muhammad Muhyi al-Din Abd al-Hamid with comments by al-Shaykh Muhammad Abduh (Cairo: Matbaat al-Istiqama, n.d.), 24:25; Abu Jafar Muhammad Ibn Ali al-Qasim al-Tabari, *Bisharat al-Mustafa,* 49.

16. Al-Shaibi, *al-Sila bayn al-Tasawwuf wa al-Tashayyu,* 59.

17. Muhammad Jawad Cherri, *The Brother of Muhammad* (The Imam Ali) (Detroit,

Michigan: Islamic Center, 1979). See Ibn Ibrahim, *Tafsir*, 63, where it is stated that a voice from the throne of God said that Ali was the brother of Muhammad.

18. Al-Kulayni, *al-Usul min al-Kafi*, 1:196–98.

19. Ibid., 1:196.

20. Al-Mufid, *Kitab al-Irshad*, 119. The verse of the *Mubahala* is found in Quran 33:33. For more information on this episode, see note 4 of this chapter.

21. Ibn Ibrahim, *Tafsir*, 342.

22. Al-Bursi, *Kitab Mashariq*, 60–61.

23. Al-Majlisi, *Hayat al-Qulub*, 203; and Donaldson, *The Shi'ite Religion*, 52.

24. Abu Jafar Muhammad Ibn al-Hasan al-Tusi, *Kitab al-Ghayba* (al-Najaf: Matbaat al-Numan, 1385/1965), 2–3; and al-Suyuti, *Tarikh al-Khulafa*, (Baghdad: Matbaat Munir, 1983), 170. Al-Suyuti describes a tradition in which the Prophet tells Ali, "You are my brother in this life and the one to come."

25. Al-Hajj Masum Ali (al-Nimat Ilahi al-Shirzal), *Tara'ia al-haqa'iq*. (Tehran: 1319/1901), 1:211.

26. Abu al-Faraj Abd al-Rahman Ali Ibn al-Jawzi, *al-Muntazam fi Tarikh al-Muluk wa al-Umam* (Haydarabad al-Dakan: Matbaat Dairat al-Maarif al-Uthmanivya, 1357–61/1938–42), 6:370–71; Adam Mez, Die Renaissance des Islams (Heidelberg: Carl Winter, 1922), 59; and the English translation, idem, *The Renaissance of Islam*, trans. Salahuddin Khuda Bakhsh and D. S. Margoliouth (London: Luzac, 1937), 62–67.

27. Al-Bursi, *Kitab Mashariq*, 151–52. Cf. Rev. S. G. Wilson, *Persian Life and Customs*, 213.

28. Al-Suyuti, *Tarikh al-Kulafa*, 173.

29. Ibn Ibrahim, *Tafsir*, 328.

30. This verse is cited in al-Shaibi, *al-Sila bayn al-Tasawwuf wa al-Tashayyu*, 61.

31. Muhammad Ibn al-Fattal al-Nisaburi, *Rawdat al-Wa'izin*, 101–2; and Abu Jafar Muhammad Ibn Ali al-Qasim al-Tabari, *Bisharat al-Mustafa*, 20, 24, 96.

32. Ibn Ibrahim, *Tafsir*, 222; and al-Tabari, *Bisharat al-Mustafa*, 40, 63.

33. Al-Hasan al-Askari, *Tafsir al-Imam Hasan al-Askari*, printed on the margin of Ibn Ibrahim, *Tafsir*, 73–74; and Goldziher, "Neuplatonische und gnostische," 327. Cf. Ibn Ibrahim, *Tafsir*, 19, 21; and al-Shahrastani, *Kitab al-Milal*, 2:26.

34. Golsdizher, "Neuplatonische und gnostische," 327.

35. Ibid.

36. Abu Hatim Ahmad Ibn Hamdan al-Razi, *Kitab al-Zina*, part 3, 307; Saad Ibn Abd Allah al-Aashari, *al-Maqalat wa al-Firaq*, ed. Muhammad Jawad Mashkur (Tehran: Matbaat Haydari, 1963), 56. Cf. al-Shahrastani, *Kitab al-Milal*, 2:13, 26.

37. Abu al-Hasan al-Ashari, *Kitab Maqalat al-Islamiyyin*, 14–15; and al-Shahrastani, *Kitab al-Milal*, 2:13.

38. Al-Razi, *Kitab al-Zina*, 307; and al-Shahrastani, *Kitab al-Milal*, 2:13. Cf. similar verses related in Mumin al-Shabalanji, *Nur al-Absar*, 113, 115. On al-Razi and his book *Kitab al-Zina*, see Ivanow, *A Guide to Ismaili Literature* (London: Royal Asiatic Society, 1933), 32–33.

39. Abu al-Faraj Abd al-Rahman Ali Ibn al-Jawzi, *al-Muntazam fi Tarikh al-Muluk wa al-Umam* (Haydarabad: Matbaat Dairat al-Maarif al-Uthmaniyya, 1357/1938), 6:370–71; Mez, *Die Renaissance des Islam*, 58; and idem, *The Renaissance of Islam*, 62, and al-Suyuti, *Tarikh al-Khulafa*, 399.

40. Ibn Babawayh (al-Qummi), *Ilal al-Shara'i*, introduced by M. S. Bahr al-Ulum (al-Najaf; al-Matbaa al-Haydariyya, 1383/1963), 1:181; and idem, *Ma'ani al-Akhbar, 63;*

Mez, Die Renaissance des Islam, 59; and idem, *The Renaissance of Islam,* 63 n. 2. On Fatima as Maryam al-Kubra (the Great Mary), see al-Yaman, *Kitab al-Kashf,* 97–98; Corbin, *Cyclical Time and Ismaili Gnosis,* 183; and Mahmud Ayoub, *Redemptive Suffering in Islam: A Study of the Devotional Aspects of Ashura in Twelver Shi'ism* (The Hague: Mouton Publishers, 1978), 35.

41. Al-Sarraf, *al-Shabak,* 56.

42. Birge, *Bektashi Order,* 187 n.1, 193, 195, 197, 198.

43. Evliya Efendi, *Siyahatname* (Istanbul: Devlet Matbaasi, 1357/1938), 8:740. Cf. Birge, *Bektashi Order,* 71.

8—Religious Hierarchy

1. Al-Sarraf, *al-Shabak,* 52–55; and Birge, *Bektashi Order,* 162–65. For the degrees of the Bektashi order, see Baba, *al-Risala al-Ahmadiyya,* 69–70. For more information on the *qalandar,* see Gibb, *History of Ottoman Poetry* (Leyden: E. J. Brill, 1900), 1:357; and Brown, *The Darvishes,* 169–72, especially the note by H. A. Rose.

2. Al-Sarraf, *al-Shabak,* 55. For further information on the *Qutb* in the different Dervish orders, see Rev. Edward Sell, *The Religious Orders of Islam* (London: Sympkin, Marshall, Hamilton and Kent Co., 1914), 23.

3. Birge, *Bektashi Order,* 97.

4. Al-Ghulami, *Baqaya al-Firaq,* 30–31.

5. Ibid., 31, and Saad Ibrahim al-Adami, *al-Aqaliyyat al-Diniyya wa al-Qawmiyya* (n.p., 1982), 108–11.

6. See Barnum, report dated 22 July 1863, *Missionary Herald* 59 (1863), 310.

7. White, "Alevi Turks," 695–96; idem, "The Shia Turks," 231; and idem, "Some Non-Conforming Turks," 245.

8. Grenard, "Une Secte Religieuse," 518.

9. White, "Some Non-Conforming Turks," 245.

10. Al-Ghulami, *Baqaya al-Firaq,* 31–32.

11. Nur Yalman, "Islamic Reform," 54.

9—The Twelve Imams

1. For the most comprehensive Shiite source on the twelve Imams, see al-Mufid, *Kitab al-Irshad,* trans. I. K. A. Howard (New York: Tahrike Tarsile Quran, Inc., 1981); al-Bahrani, *Ghayat al-Maram wa Hujjat al-Khisam fi Ta'yin al-Imam min Tariq al-Khass wa al-Amm* Tehran: 1321/1903); al-Kulayni, *al-Usul min al-Kafi,* 1:286–553; and Hashim Maruf al-Hasani, *Sirat al-A'imma al-lthnay'ashar,* 2 vols. 2nd ed. (Beirut: Dar al-Qalam, 1398/1978).

2. W. C. Taylor, *History of Muhammedanism,* 218.

3. Abu Jafar Muhammad Ibn al-Hasan al-Tusi, *Kitab al-Ghayba* (al-Najaf: Matbaat al-Numan, 1385/1965), 3–4; and al-Mufid, *Kitab al-Irshad,* 524.

4. See al-Shaykh Yusuf Ibn al-Ajuz al-Halabi (known as al-Nashshabi), *Munazara* (Debate), in Arabic MS. 1449, fol. 120, Bibliothèque Nationale.

5. Al-Mufid, *Kitab al-Irshad,* 525.

6. Al-Majlisi, *Hayat al-Qulub,* 305; Donaldson, *The Shi'ite Religion,* 229; and Hus-

ayn Ibn Muhammad Taqi al-Tabarsi al-Nuri, *Kashf al-Sitar an Khabar al-Gha'ib an al-Absar* Tehran: 1318/1900).

7. Al-Shahrastani, *Kitab al-Milal,* 1:22.

8. Al-Kulayni, *al-Usul min al-Kafi,* 1:199; Ibn Ibrahim, *Tafsir,* 211, 306–7; Abu al-Hasan al-Ashari, *Maqalat,* 2–3; and W. Madelung, "Imama," *The Encyclopedia of Islam* 3 (Leiden: E. J. Brill, 1971):1163–69.

9. Al-Shahrastani, *Kitab al-Milal,* 1:22; Abd al-Rahman Ibn Khaldun, *al-Maqaddima* (Cairo: Matbaat Mustafa Muhammad, n.d.), 9; H. R. Gibb, "Constitutional Organization," in *Law in the Middle East,* ed. Majid Khadduri and Herbert J. Liebesny (Washington D.C.: The Middle East Institute, 1955), 1:4.

10. Al-Ashari, *Maqalat al-Islamiyyin,* 5; al-Shahrastani, *Kitab al-Milal,* 1:195; Abu Muhammad al-Hasan Ibn Musa al-Nawbakhti, *Firaq al-Shi'a* (Shiite Sects), 4th ed. (al-Najaf: al-Matbaa al-Haydariyya, 1969), 22.

11. Muhammad Ibn al-Fattal al-Nisaburi, *Rawdat al-Wa'izin,* 2:293–94; al-Haythami, *al-Sawa'iq al-Muhriqa,* 161.

12. For this tradition, see al-Shaykh al-Saduq Ibn Babawayh (al-Qummi) *Amali al-Suduq* (al-Najaf: al-Matbaa al-Haydariyya, 1389/1969), 79, 84–85; and Muhammad al-Husayn Al Kashif al-Ghita, *Asl al-Shi'a wa Usuluha,* 3rd ed. (Beirut: Muassast al-Alami li al-Matbuat, 1397/1977), 43–44.

13. See Muhammad Baqir al-Sadr, *Bahth Hawl al-Walaya,* 9–96; and idem, *Dawr al-A'imma fi al-Hayat al-Islamiyya* (Tehran: al-Maktaba al-Islamiyya al-Kubra, 1400/1979), 3–16; *Nahj al-Balaqha,* ed. Muhyi al-Din Abd al-Hamid with comments by Muhammad Abduh, 2:82. Cf. Muhammad Jawad Mughniya, *Falsafat al-Tawhid wa al-Walaya* (Qumm: Dar al-Tabligh al-Islami, 1971), passim.

14. See the Ismaili writer Hamid al-Din Ahmad al-Kermani (Hujjat al-Iraqayn), *Rahat al-Aql,* ed. Mustafa Ghalib (Beirut: Dar al-Andalus, 1967), 574–76; and al-Shaibi, *al-Sila bayn al-Tasawwuf wa al-Tashayyu,* 55–68.

15. Al-Shahrastani, *Kitab al-Milal,* 2:51; Horatio Southgate, *Narrative of a Tour,* 2:304, and appendix 8.

16. Al-Kulayni, *al-Usul min al-Kafi,* 1:292–93; al-Nawbakhti, *Firaq al-Shi'a,* 36–37; al-Ashari, *Maqalat,* 16, 17, 24, 26, 30, 64, and 67–69; al-Shahrastani, *Kitab al-Milal,* 1:195, 218–19. Regarding the imamate, the Zaydis maintain that although a descendant of Ali and Fatima should have priority in becoming an Imam, the public interest of the Muslim community demands that other Muslims also be able to become Imams. For this reason the Zaydis accept Abu Bakr, Umar, and Uthman as lawful caliphs or Imams,

17. Ibn Ibrahim, *Tafsir,* 94; al-Bahrani, *Ghayat al-Maram,* 28–92; al-Razi, *Kitab al-Zina,* part 3; Ibn Babawayh, *Ma'ani al-Akhbar,* 67–74.

18. Al-Shahrastani, *Kitab al-Milal wa al-Nihal,* 1: 220–21.

19. Yahya Ibn al-Husayn, *Kitab al-Ifada fi Tarikh al-A'imma al-Sada,* Arabic MS. 1647, fols. 55a and b, Leiden University Library. See also al-Mufid, *Kitab al-Irshad,* 108–9; Abu al-Husayn Muslim, *Sahih Muslim,* 7:120–21; *Sahih al-Bukhari,* trans. Muhammad Assad (Gibraltar: Dar al-Andalus, 1981), 65; Ali Ibn Ibrahim, *Tafsir,* 159 and 282; and Ibn Babawayh, *Ma'ani al-Akhbar,* 76–9.

20. Al-Nisaburi, *Rawdat al-Wa'izin,* 1:112–13. Cf. Rice, "Ali in Shi'ah Tradition," 32.

21. See this sermon in *Nahj al-Balaqha,* ed. Muhyi al-Din Abd al-Hamid with comments by al-Shaykh Muhammad Abduh, 2:182–83.

22. Al-Kulayni, *al-Usul min al-Kafi,* 1:181–85. See also Abu Hanifa al-Numan Ibn Mansur Ibn Ahmad Ibn Hayyun al-Tamimi al-Maghribi, *Da'aim al-Islam wa Dhikr al-Halal*

wa al-Haram wa al-Qadaya wa al-Ahkam an Ahl Bayt Rasul Allah, ed. Asaf A. A. Fayzi (Cairo: Dar al-Maarif, 1951), 1:3; Sami Nasib Makarem, *The Doctrine of the Ismailis* (Beirut: The Arab Institute for Research and Publishing, 1972), 15.

23. Al-Razi, *Kitab al-Zina,* 257.

24. Ibn Shahr Ashub, *Manaqib Al Abi Talib,* 1:212 and 2:290–92; Ibn Ibrahim, *Tafsir,* 327; Ibn Babawayh, *Ma'ani al-Akhbar,* 96–103 especially 97–98; and Sell, *The Religious Orders of Islam,* 2.

25. Al-Kulayni, *al-Usul min al-Kafi,* 1:202, 269–74; al-Bahrani, *Ghayat al-Maram,* 152–613; Donaldson, *The Shi'ite Religion,* 347–56, E. Tyan, "Isma," in *The Encyclopedia of Islam* (Leiden and London: E. J. Brill, 1973), 4:182–84; and Muhammad Rida al-Muzaffar, *Aqa'id al-Shi'a al-Imamiyya* (al-Najaf, Matabi al-Numan, 1381/1961), 53–54 and 76.

26. For a thorough analysis of Wilayat al-Faqih according to the Iranian Constitution, see Ali Ahmad Matlub, et al., *Nahj Khomeini fi Mizan al-Fikr al-Islami* (Baghdad: Dar Ammar, 1985), especially the first three chapters. See also articles 5, 57 and 107 of the Constitution of the Islamic Republic of Iran. For a pioneering study of Wilayat al-Faqih see al-Shaykh Ali Al Kashif al-Ghita, *al-Nur al-Sati fi al-Fiqh al-Nafi* (al-Najaf: Matbaat al-Adab, 1381/1961), 1:340–407.

27. See "Gilani Shaw," *al-Dustur, The International Arab Weekly,* No. 340, 28 November 1983, London, 19.

28. Abd al-Jabbar Mahmud al-Umar, *al-Khomeini bayn al-Din wa al-Dawla* (Baghdad: Dar Afaq Arabiyya, 1984), 6, 50–51.

29. Al-Majlisi, *Hayat al-Qulub,* 3:23–24; Tyan, "Isma," in *The Encyclopedia of Islam* 4 (Leiden and London: E. J. Brill, 1974):183–84; and al-Muzaffar, *Aqa'id al-Shi'a al-Imamiyya,* 65–67.

30. Al-Kulayni, *al-Usul min al-Kafi,* 1:199–200, 203–5; and al-Bahrani, *Ghayat al-Maram,* 270–73.

31. Al-Mufid, *Awa'il al-Maqalat fi al-Madhahib wa al-Makhtarat* (Tabriz: Matbaat Ridai, 1371/1951), 35, 37–39; and idem, *Kitab Sharh Aqa'id al-Saduq aw Tashih al-I'tiqad* (Tabriz: Matbaat Ridai, 1371/1951), 60–62.

32. Donaldson, *The Shi'ite Religion,* 330–38.

33. Ibn Ibrahim, *Tafsir,* 115, 222, 368.

34. Al-Tusi, *Kitab al-Ghayba,* 119.

35. Al-Haythami, *al-Sawa'iq al-Muhriqa,* 134–35.

36. Al-Bahrani, *Ghayat al-Maram,* 224–50.

37. Al-Kulayni, *al-Usul min al-Kafi,* 1:190–92; and *Kitab al-Haft al-Sharif,* 92–93, 114.

38. Hasan al-Askari, *Tafsir,* 82–3.

39. See P. M. Sykes, ed. and trans., *The Glory of the Shia World: The Tale of a Pilgrimage* (London: Macmillan, 1910), 240. Cf. Petrushevsky, *Islam in Iran,* trans. Hubert Evans (Albany: State University of New York Press, 1985), 227.

40. Al-Kulayni, *al-Usul min al-Kafi,* 1:198–206, 292–97; al-Ghita, *Asl al-Shi'a wa Usuluha,* 65–71; and Muhammad al-Husayn al-Adib, *al-Mujmal fi al-Shi'a wa Mu'taqadatihim,* 3rd ed. (al-Najaf: Matbaat al-Numan, 1381/1961), 38–39.

41. See al-Mufid, *Kitab al-Irshad,* passim, and the religious book of the Shabak, the *Buyruk,* in al-Sarraf, *al-Shabak,* 214–17.

42. Al-Sarraf, *al-Shabak,* 108, 115, 126, 127; and al-Ghulami, *Baqaya al-Firaq,* 36.

43. J. G. Taylor, "Journal of a Tour," 319.

44. Birge, *Bektashi Order,* 145–46.

45. Al-Sarraf, *al-Shabak,* 138–39.

46. Ibid., 183–88.

47. Ibid., 183–88. There is some resemblance between this account and that of Fatima seated on a throne in the proto-Ismaili source, *Umm al-Kitab,* 211.

48. Al-Sarraf, *al-Shabak,* 153–88.

49. Muslims usually confound the Prophet Elijah or Elias with a legendary figure al-Khadir or Khidr, and consider him the Chief Saint or Qutb, that is, pole or highest degree in the Sufi hierarchy. They claim that the Khadir is immortal because he drank from the fountain of life. On the Khadir, see Abu al-Husayn Muslim, *Sahih Muslim,* 7:103–8; Ibn Kathir (d. 774/1372) treats al-Khadir and Elias as two different persons. See Ibn Kathir, *al-Bidaya wa al-Nihaya,* 1:321–26, 355–67, and 367–76; and idem, *Qisas al-Anbiya,* (Baghdad: Matbaat al-Wisam, 1983), 449–71. See also Muhammad Ibn Ahmad Ibn Iyas, *Bada'i al-Zuhur fi Waqa'i al-Duhur* (Baghdad: Matbaat Hisam, 1983), 205–11; and A. J. Wensinck, "al-Khadir (al-Khidr)," in *The Encyclopedia of Islam* 2 (Leiden: E. J. Brill, 1927): 861–65; P. N. Boratav, "Khidr-Ilyas," in *The Encyclopedia of Islam,* (Leiden: E. J. Brill, 1979), 5:5.

50. See the *Buyruk* in al-Sarraf, *al-Shabak,* 188–89 and 216–17.

51. Al-Kulayni, *al-Usul min al-Kafi,* 1:525–26.

52. Brown, *The Darvishes,* 173–75, especially the lengthy footnote by H. A. Rose.

53. See the Gospel according to St. Matthew 11:10–15; and Brown, *The Darvishes,* 175 n. 10 by H. A. Rose.

54. Sami Nasib Makarem, *The Doctrine of the Ismailis,* 27–28; and Arif Tamir, *al-Imama fi al-Islam* (Beirut: Dar al-Kitab al-Arabi, n.d.), 145–55.

55. For these sub-periods, see Tamir, 156–61.

56. Joseph Arthur Comte de Gobineau, *Les Religions et les Philosophie dans l'Asie Centrale* (Paris: Dedier, 1865), 60.

57. Ivanow, *Truth-Worshippers,* (Leiden: E. J. Brill, 1953), 52.

58. On the Adoptionists' views, see Adolph Harnack, *History of Dogma* (New York: Dover, n.d.), 1:120, 191–97, as well as the rest of the volume in passim.

59. Ivanow, *Truth-Worshippers,* 52. Cf. Corbin, *Cyclical Time and Ismaili Gnosis,* 102–17; and idem, *The Man of Light in Iranian Sufism,* 131–38.

60. See chapter 5 of this book, especially the discussion of the concept of al-Haqiqa al-Muhammadiyya.

61. Al-Sarraf, *al-Shabak,* 50.

62. Birge, *Bektashi Order,* 147–48, 150–51; and al-Sarraf, *al-Shabak,* 51.

63. For a detailed account of the Shaykhis, see Corbin, *En Islam iranism,* 4:205–300; Ali al-Hairi, *Aqidat al-Shi'a* (Karbala: 1348/1964), 9–11; Ali al-Wardi, *Lamahat Ijtima'iyya min Tarikh al-Iraq al-Hadith* (Baghdad: Matbaat al-Irshad, 1971), 130–31.

64. *Sirat al-Shaykh Ahmad al-Ahsa'i,* ed. Husayn Mahfuz (Baghdad: Matbaat al-Maarif, 1957), 17–19; and al-Wardi, *Lamahat Ijtima'iyya.*

10—The Abdal

1. Al-Sarraf, *al-Shabak,* 51.

2. Birge, *Bektashi Order,* 251; Brown, *The Darvishes,* 199 n. 2; and Sell, *The Religious Orders of Islam,* 24–25. For more on the Abdal, see al-Shaibi, *al-Sila bayn al-Tasawwuf wa al-Tashayyu,* 458–61; Muhammad Husayn Sulayman al-Alami, *Da'irat al-Ma'arif al-Musammat bi Muqtabis al-Athar wa Mujaddid ma Duthir,* (Qumm: Matbaat al-Hikma, 1375/1957), 2:275–77; and Goldziher, "Abdal," in *The Encyclopedia of Islam* (Leiden and London: E. J. Brill, 1960), 1:94–95.

3. Ibn Arabi, *al-Futuhat al-Makkiyya,* 2:9; and al-Karmali, "al-Abdal," *al-Mashriq* 12 (1909): 197, in which the author states that Abdal is the plural of *badil.*

4. Abu al-Hasan Muhammad Ibn al-Husayni Ibn Musa al-Alawi (known as al-Sharif al-Jurjani), *al-Ta'rifat* (Cairo: al-Babi al-Halabi, 1357/1938), 37.

5. Abd al-Aziz Ibn Abd al-Salam, *Risala fi al-Radd ala man Yaqul bi Wujud al-Abdal.* This treatise is probably lost but is mentioned under *Abdal* in Abu al-Fayd Muhammad al-Murtada al-Zubaydi, *Taj al-Arus min Sharh Jawahir al-Qamus,* 10 vols. (Cairo: al-Matbaa al-Khayriyya, 1306–7/1888–89).

6. Jalal al-Din al-Suyuti, "al-Khabar al-Dall ala Wujud al-Qutb wa al-Awtad wa al-Nujaba wa al-Abdal," edited with extensive footnotes by Miqdad Mansiyya, and published in *al-Nashra al-Ilmiyya li al-Kuliyya al-Zaytuniyya li al-Shari'a wa Usul al-Din,* no. 5 (Tunis: The Tunisian University, 1979), 319–91. Cf. al-Karmali, "al-Abdal," *al-Mashriq* 12 (1909): 194–204, in which al-Karmali made use of al-Suyuti's treatise.

7. Ibn Taymiyya, *Majmu'at al-Rasa'il wa al-Masa'il,* ed. Muhammad Rashid Rida (Cairo: Matbaat al-Manar, 1341–49/1923–30), 1:51; al-Sarraf, *al-Shabak,* 51; Brown, *The Darvishes,* 91–93, 202–3; and Lucy M. Garnett, *Mysticism and Magic in Turkey* (New York: Charles Scribner's Sons, 1912), 37. See also the introduction by Miqdad Mansiyya to al-Suyuti, "al-Khabar al-Dall," 319–23; and Goldziher, "Abdal," 1:94.

8. Nicholson, *The Mystics of Islam,* 123–24. Al-Sarraf gives another variant of this Sufi hierarchy. See al-Sarraf, *al-Shabak,* 51.

9. Al-Arif bi Allah Sayyid Afif al-Din Abd Allah Ibn Asad al-Yafii, *Kifayat al-Mu'taqid fi Nikayat al-Muntaqid aw Nashr al-Mahasin al-Ghaliya fi Fadl Mashayikh al-Sufiyya,* printed on the margin of Yusuf Ibn Ismail al-Nabhani, *Jami Karamat al-Awliya* (Cairo: al-Matbaa al-Maymaniyya, 1329/1911), 275–76, 336–37, and 338–39; Muhammad Amin Ibn Umar (known as Ibn Abdin), "Ijabat al-Ghawth bi Bayan Hal al-Nuqub wa al-Nujaba wa al-Abdal wa al-Awtad wa al-Ghawth," in idem, *Rasa'il Ibn Abdin* (al-Asitana, Constantinople: Muhammad Hashim al-Kutubi, 1325/1907), 2:214, 274; Abu al-Hasan Ali Ibn Uthman al-Julabi al-Hujwiri, *Kashf al-Mahjub,* trans. R. A. Nicholson (1911 reprint, Lahore: Islamic Book Foundation, 1974), 214; al-Jurjani, *al-Ta'rifat,* 155; and Sell, *The Religious Orders of Islam,* 22.

10. Al-Jurjani, *al-Ta'rifat,* 155; Ibn Abdin, "Ijabat al-Ghawth," 2:269 and 274; al-Hujwiri, *Kashf al-Mahjub,* 214; and Sell, *The Religious Orders of Islam,* 22.

11. Mez, *Die Renaissance des Islam,* 281; and idem *The Renaissance of Islam,* 294.

12. Affifi, *Mystical Philosophy,* 89–92.

13. Al-Shaibi, *al-Sila bayn al-Tasawwuf wa al-Tashayyu,* 463.

14. For this speech, see *Nahj al-Balagha,* ed. Muhyi al-Din Abd al-Hamid with comments by Muhammad Abduh, 1:25–33. Cf. Ibn Babawayh, *Ma'ani al-Akhbar,* 361.

15. Al-Hujwiri, *Kashf al-Mahjub,* 214; al-Suyuti, "al-Khabar al-Dall," 368–69; Sell, *The Religious Order of Islam,* 23–25; and Nicholson, *The Mystics of Islam,* 123–24.

16. Ibn Arabi, *al-Futuhat al-Makkiyya,* 2:2–16; al-Suyuti, "al-Khabar al-Dall," passim, and Goldziher, "Abdal," 1:94–95.

17. See *Kitab al-Haft al-Sharif,* 137–38.

18. Al-Hujwiri, *Kashf al-Mahjub,* 214; *Kitab al-Haft al-Sharif,* 137; and Nicholson, *The Mystics of Islam,* 124.

19. Ibn Arabi, *Muhadarat al-Abrar wa Musamarat al-Akhyar fi al-Adabiyyat wa al-Nawadir wa al-Akhbar* (Damascus: Dar al-Yaqza al-Arabiyya, 1388/1968), 1:418–19; and al-Suyuti, "al-Khabar al-Dall," 344, 372.

20. Ibn Arabi, *al-Futuhat al-Makkiyya,* 2:9.

21. Al-Suyuti, "al-Khabar al-Dall," passim.

22. Abu Nuaym al-Isfahani, *Hilyat al-Awliya,* 8–9; al-Suyuti, "al-Khabar al-Dall," 343; Abu Abd Allah Muhammad Ibn Husayn al-Hakim al-Tirmidhi, (d. 898) *Nawadir al-Usul fi Ma'rifat Akhbar al-Rasul* (Beirut: Dar Sadir, 1972), 69–71; Ibn Asakir, *Tarikh Dimashq,* ed. Salah al-Din al-Munajjid (Damascus: al-Majma al-Ilmi al-Arabi, 1951), 1:278; and al-Majlisi, *Bihar al-Anwar,* 13:402.

23. Ibn Taymiyya, *Majmu'at al-Rasa'il wa al-Masa'il,* 1:51; al-Suyuti, "al-Khabar al-Dall," 372; al-Hujwiri, *Kashf al-Mahjub,* 213; and al-Majlisi, *Bihar al-Anwar,* 13:402.

24. F. W. Hasluck, *Christianity and Islam,* 2:391–93.

25. See William Francis Ainsworth, *Travels and Researches in Asia Minor, Mesopotamia, Chaldea and Armenia* (London: John W. Parker, 1842), 2:12; Afram Barsoum, *al-Lu'lu al-Manthur,* (Halab: n.p., 1956), 179; and F. W. Hasluck, *Christianity and Islam,* 2:393, 394, especially 393, n.8.

26. Al-Shaibi, *al-Sila bayn al-Tasawwuf wa al-Tashayyu,* 460.

27. Ibn Asakir, *Tarikh Dimashq,* 1:278, 322; al-Suyuti, "al-Khabar al-Dall," 337, 339.

29. Ibn Arabi, *al-Futuhat al-Makkiyya,* 2:9.

30. Al-Suyuti, "al-Khabar al-Dall," 334–47, 349, 358, 365–66; idem, *al-Jami al-Saghir fi Ahadith al-Bashir al-Nadhir* (Cairo: al-Matbaa al-Khayriyya, 1306/1888), 1:103, 106; Ibn Asakir, *Tarikh Dimashq,* 1:285; *Kitab al-Haft al-Sharif,* 137–38; and Goldziher, "Abdal," 1:95.

31. Al-Suyuti, "al-Khabar al-Dall;," quoting Abu Muhammad al-Khallal, *Karamat al-Awliya,* 334–35, 345–46 and 359–60.

32. Al-Hujwiri, *Kashf al-Mahjub,* 213; Ibn Asakir, *Tarikh Dimashq,* 1:885; al-Suyuti, "al-Khabar al-Dall," 365; and al-Karmali, "al-Abdal," 195, where the author quotes al-Tayyibi, *Sharh al-Mishkat,* as saying that the Abdal are the Awliya (saints) and the Ubbad (worshipful).

33. Al-Suyuti, "al-Khabar al-Dall," 348, 350, 353, 368–69.

34. Ibid., 369 where al-Suyuti mentions this tradition without giving a source. This tradition is reproduced on the authority of Ibn Abi al-Dunya in Ibn Asakir, *Tarikh Dimashq,* 1:291.

35. Al-Tirmidhi, *Nawadir al-Usul fi Ma'rifat Akhbar al-Rasul,* 69–71.

36. Al-Hujwiri, *Kashf al-Mahjub,* 213.

37. Ibid.

38. Al-Alami, *Da'irat al-Ma'arif,* 2:275–76.

39. For this tradition of the forty, see al-Sarraf, *al-Shabak,* 50, 126.

40. M. F. Grenard, "Une Secte Religieuse," 516.

41. For this tradition see Birge, *Bektashi Order,* 266.

42. Ibid., 137–38.

43. *Tadhkira-i A'la,* in Ivanow, *Truth Worshippers,* 165.

44. Ibid., 62 and 165. On Sultan Mahmud Patili, see Hajj Nimat Allah (Mujrim) Mokri, *Shah Nama-ye Haqiqat,* ed. Muhammad Mokri, (Tehran: Departement D'Iranologie De L'Institute Franco-Iranien; Paris: Librairie D'Amerique et D'Orient Adrien-Maisonneuve, 1966), 1:232–35.

45. Minorsky, *Notes Sur la Secte des Ahlé-Haqq,* 14–15. For the names of the forty, see 15–16.

46. Samuel Graham Wilson, *Persian Life and Customs,* 241.

47. M. H. Adjarian, "Gyorans et Thoumaris," trans. Frédéric Macler, *Revue De*

L'Histoire Des Religion 93, no. 3, (May–June 1926): 296–97.

48. H. J. Kissling in his postscript to Goldziher, "Abdal," 1:95; and Nur Yalman, "Islamic Reform," 49.

11—Rituals and Ceremonies

1. Al-Sarraf, *al-Shabak,* 97–98. Haji Bektash was not fully obedient to the Islamic religious law (Sharia). For example, he was criticized for not performing formal prayer as a religious duty. See also, al-Aflaki, *Manaqib al-Arifin,* 381; Dunmore, report dated 24 October 24, 1854 in *Missionary Herald* 51 (2 February): 56; Perkins letter 30 May 1855 in Ibid., 297; and Birge, *Bektashi Order,* 42, 49.

2. Al-Ghulami, *Baqaya al-Firaq,* 32. The Caliph Ali was struck on the forehead with a poisoned sword by his assassin the Kharijite Abd al-Rahman Ibn Muljam while he was on his way to pray at the mosque in al-Kufa. He was buried in al-Najaf, Iraq where a magnificent shrine was built over his remains.

3. Al-Sarraf, *al-Shabak,* 96. The Kizilbash have no mosques but pray at the house of a Sayyid (pir) on Fridays. See Molyneux-Seel, "Journey in Dersim," 66; and White, "Some Non-Conforming Turks," 246–47.

4. Al-Sarraf, *al-Shabak,* 96–97.

5. Ibid., 96. Although the term *Hu* in this and other prayers means "He," that is, "God," yet generally it is used as an expression of adoration and intercession. It is one of the most common expressions used by the Bektashis. See Birge, *Bektashi Order,* 167.

6. Birge, *Bektashi Order,* 168.

7. Al-Ghulami, *Baqaya al-Firaq,* 32, and al-Sarraf, *al-Shabak,* 97.

8. F. W. Hasluck, *Christianity and Islam,* 2:559; and Grenard, "Une Secte Religieuse," *Journal Asiatique,* 10th ser., 3 (1904): 514.

9. Birge, *Bektashi Order,* 169; and Donaldson, *The Shi'ite Religion,* 91.

10. Al-Ghulami, *Baqaya al-Fraq,* 32; and al-Sarraf, *al-Shabbak,* 97.

11. This is reported in al-Sarraf, *al-Shabak,* 97.

12. Ibid.

13. Al-Ghulami, *Baqaya al-Firaq,* 32; and al-Sarraf, *al-Shabak,* 97. For the Bektashi-Kizilbash pilgrimage see Molyneux-Seel, "Journey in Dersim," 66; and Grenard, "Une Secte Religeuse," 519.

14. Al-Ghulami, *Baqaya al-Firaq,* 33.

15. Birge, *Bektashi Order,* 91–92.

16. al-Karmali, "Tafkihat al-Adhhan fi Ta'rif Thalathat Adyan," *al-Mashriq* 5 (1902): 582; al-Ghulami, *Baqaya al-Firaq,* 38, 43; and al-Sarraf, *al-Shabak,* 11, 104.

17. Birge, *Bektashi Order,* 72.

18. Al-Sarraf, *al-Shabak,* 98, 101–3.

19. See Birge, *Bektashi Order,* 173–74. The "reverence of the threshold" is a Bektashi custom. One explanation of this custom is that given by Birge: "Since Ali is considered the Gate or Door of the city of knowledge, any doorway is symbolic of Ali's spiritual significance." The "reverence of the threshold" probably originated as an old Semitic custom. The author has often observed that members of the Syrian churches in the Middle East, whether Nestorians, Chaldeans, and Syrian Orthodox (especially in the villages north of Mosul), kiss both portals and the threshold of the church before entering to worship.

20. For the Shabak celebration of the New Year's day see al-Sarraf, *al-Shabak,* 99–100.

21. For the commemoration of Ashura by the Shabak and their mourning of al-Husayn, see al-Sarraf, *al-Shabak,* 117–18. Cf. Birge, *Bektashi Order,* 169.

22. Al-Sarraf, *al-Shabak,* 118–20.

23. White, "The Shia Turks," 231; idem, "Survival of Primitive Religion Among the People of Asia Minor," *Journal of the Transactions of the Victoria Institute* 39 (1907): 161; and Eröz, *Türkiye de Alevilik-Bektaşilik* (Istanbul, n.p. 1977), 115.

24. For an elaboration of Gökalp's opinion, see Eröz, *Türkiye de Alevilik-Bekasilik,* 292–104; and Erisen and Samancigil, *Haci Bektaş Veli Bektaşilik ve Alevilik Tarihi* (Istanbul: Ay Yayinevi, 1966), 21.

25. G. Jacob, "Fortleben von antiken Mysterien und Alt-Christlichen im Islam," *Der Islam* 11 (1911): 232; and F. W. Hasluck, *Christianity and Islam,* 1:151, who follows Jacob. For the Bektashi "ritual meal," see Birge, *Bektashi Order,* 169.

26. Grenard, "Une Secte Religieuse," 517, 518.

27. Georg Jacob, "Beiträge zur Kenntnis," 9:88–90; and idem, "Fortleben von Antiken Mysterien," 232.

28. Yalman, "Islamic Reform," 54–55.

29. Molyneux-Seel, "Journey in Dersim," 66; and F. W. Hasluck, *Christianity and Islam,* 1:148. For the sacrament celebrated by eastern Kizilbash, see White, "Alevi Turks," 696.

30. Al-Sarraf, *al-Shabak,* 118. Among the Kizilbash, neglect of confession of sins is punishable by fines; F. W. Hasluck, *Christianity and Islam,* 1:148–49.

31. According to Islamic sources, the Jews of Khaybar made an alliance with Muhammad to withhold support from his enemies of the Quraysh tribe. It is reported that the Jews violated this alliance and were considered by Muslims to be hypocrites. See Hitti, *History of the Arabs,* 117, 169.

32. Al-Sarraf, *al-Shabak,* 119.

33. Ibid., 119–20. For a similar prayer, see Brown, *The Darvishes,* 100. *Ishq* is an Arabic term meaning "passionate love." But to the Bektashis or Kizilbash and to other dervish orders, it means a passionate yearning for God. It is probably in this sense that it is used in this hymn. Khatai is the pen name of Shah Ismail al-Safawi, who signed his poems with it; why he chose it as a pen name is not known.

34. For this hymn, see al-Sarraf, *al-Shabak,* 131–34.

35. Ibid., 134–35, especially 134 n. 1.

35. Ibid., 135–36.

37. *History of Shah Isma'il,* fols. 22b and 71a; al-Shaibi, *al-Fikr al-Shi'i,* 413; and Said Amir Arjomand, "Religion, Political Action and Legitimate Domination in Shi'ite Iran: fourteen to eighteenth centuries," *European Journal of Sociology* 20 (1979): 79–80.

38. The learned Shaykh Ali Ibn Abd al-Ali al-Karaki (d. 1534) wrote a treatise in which he stated that it was permissible to worship the *abd* (man) in order to justify the worship of Shah Ismail by his followers. See Mirza Makhdum, *al-Nawaqid li Bunyan al-Rawafid,* Arab MS. Or. 7991, fol. 98b, British Museum; *A Narrative of Italian Travels in Persia in The Fifteenth and Sixteenth Centuries* trans. Charles Grey (London: Hakluy Society, 1873), 206; and Arjomand, "Religion, Political Action, and Legitimate Domination," 59–109.

39. For this hymn, see al-Sarraf, *al-Shabak, 136–38.* From the name Hilmi, we may assume that it was composed by the Bektashi poet Hilmi; see al-Sarraf, *al-Shabak,* 129. The term Ayin-i Cem refers to the principal ritual ceremonies of the Bektashis and Kizilbash.

40. For the Shabak "Night of Forgiveness," see al-Sarraf, *al-Shabak,* 98, 103–10. For the Bektashi Forgiveness of Sins, see Birge, *Bektashi Order,* 170.

41. Al-Sarraf, *al-Shabak,* 101–3.

42. The practice of placing the big toe of the right foot over the big toe of the left foot is reported by al-Ghulami as part of the Shabak's ceremony of initiation. See al-Ghulami, *Baqaya al-Firaq,* 42. This practice is also part of the Bektashi ceremony of initiation; see Birge, *Bektashi Order,* 184.

43. Al-Sarraf, *al-Shabak,* 105.

44. Ibid., 107, 108.

45. Ibid., 108. The Erenler of the Rum means those Bektashi or Kizilbash spiritual guides who have attained a complete understanding of the Divine Reality (God), and who originally came from Rum (Anatolia or Asia Minor).

46. For the whole ceremony of the Night of the Forgiveness of Sins, see al-Sarraf, ibid., 103–10.

47. See Ziya Bay's account of the Bektashi *Maghfireti Zunub* (forgiveness of sins) in Birge, *Bektashi Order,* 170.

48. Grenard, "Une Secte Religieuse," 17; White, Alevi Turks," 696; Hugo Grothe, *Meine Vorderasienexpedition 1906 and 1907* (Leipzig: Hiersimann, 1911–12), 155; F. W. Hasluck, *Christianity and Islam,* 1:148–49; al-Sarraf, *al-Shabak,* 109–10; and H. J. Van Lennep, *Travels in Little-Known Parts of Asia Minor* (London: John Murray, 1870), 1:293, 295.

49. Grenard, "Une Secte Religieuse," 517.

50. Ivanow, *Truth-Worshippers,* 64–65.

51. Al-Sarraf, *al-Shabak,* 140–41.

52. F. W. Hasluck, *Christianity and Islam,* 1:149; and Grenard, "Une Secte Religieuse," 516–17.

53. Al-Sarraf, *al-Shabak,* 141.

54. al-Karmali, "Tafkihat al-Adhhan," 579, 582; al-Azzawi, *Al-Kaka'iyya fi al-Tarikh,* 68–69, 74; al-Ghulami, *Baqaya al-Firaq,* 18; al-Sarraf, *al-Shabak,* 104, 140–41; and Minorsky, "Shabak," *The Encyclopedia of Islam* (Leiden and London: E. J. Brill, 1934), 4:238–39, who follows al-Karmali.

55. Al-Karmali, "Tafkihat al-Adhhan," 579.

56. Al-Shaibi, *al-Tariqa al-Safawiyya,* 55.

57. See particularly al-Sarraf, *al-Shabak,* 140–41. See al-Shaibi, *al-Tariqa al-Safawiyya,* 54 n. 191.

58. Al-Rahib (Monk) Behnam al-Mawsili al-Suryani, "Maqala fi al-Yazidiyya," *al-Mashriq* 46 (1952): 38 and n. 1. This article, which appeared in *al-Mashriq* in two parts; vol. 45 (1951); 533–48 and vol. 46 (1952): 29–40, is—except for the statement that Behnam personally attended the night of the Kafsha at the village of Bashiqa—a verbatim copy of Rev. Anastase al-Karmali's article "al-Yazidiyya," *al-Mashriq* 2 (1899), beginning on 32.

59. F. W. Hasluck, *Christianity and Islam,* 1:153. See *The Itinerary of Benjamin of Tudela,* trans. Marcus Nathan Adler (New York: Phillipp Feldheim, 1907), 18.

60. Van Lennep, *Travels in Little Known Parts of Asia Minor,* 1:293–95.

61. Gilbert, "Notes Sur Les Sectes Dans le Kurdistan," 393–95. Gilbert's article is summarized in Driver, "The Religion of the Kurs," 196–213, especially 198.

62. Felix von Luschan, "Die Tahtadji und andere Reste der alten Bevölkerung Lykiens," *Archives für Anthropologie* 19 (1892): 31–53; idem, "Early Inhabitants of Western Asia," 230; E. A. H. Peterson and Von Luschan, *Reisen in Lykien* (Wien: Gerold, 1889), 198; Crowfoot, "Survivals Among the Kappadokian Kizilbash," 312; and Jacob, "Fortleban von Antiken Mysterien," *Der Islam* 2 (1911):232–34.

63. Ramsay, *Impressions of Turkey,* 268; and Theodore Bent, "The Yourouks of Asia Minor," *Journal of the Royal Anthropological Institute of Great Britain and Ireland* 20 (1890–91): 270.

64. Yalman, "Islamic Reform," 55.

65. Robert L. Canfield, "What They Do When The Lights are Out: Myth and Social Order in Afghanistan" (Paper presented to the ACLS/SSRC Joint Committee on the Near and Middle East Conferences on Symbols of Social Differentiation, Baltimore, Maryland, 25–28 May 1978.

66. Abu al-Hasan Ali Ibn Muhammad al-Shabushti, *al-Diyarat,* ed. G. Awwad (Baghdad: Matbaat al-Maarif, 1966), 983; and al-Karmali, "Laylat al-Hashush wa al-Mashush," *Lughat al-Arab* 8 (1930): 368–73.

67. Baha Sait, "Türkiyede Alevi Zumreleri," *Türk Yurdu* 22 (1926–27): 332–55; and Birge, *Bektashi Order,* 182 n. 3.

68. Al-Sarraf, *al-Shabak,* 111.

69. Ibid., 111–12.

70. According to Muslims, *Salsabil* is the name of a spring in paradise. *Zanjabil* is a ginger drink. I don't see the significance of *Zanjabil* in this context except for the rhyme with *Salsabil* and the fact that it is a pleasant and refreshing drink.

71. Al-Sarraf, *al-Shabak,* 112–13.

72. Ibid., 114.

73. For the beliefs of the *Ghulat* and their refutation, see a summary of the book *Aqa'id al-Shi'a,* by Ali Akbar Ibn Ali Asghar (which he wrote in the time of the Qajari Shah Muhammad) in Browne, *Literary History,* 385.

74. For the whole ceremony of initiation see *al-Sarraf, al-Shabak,* 111–15.

75. Al-Ghulami, *Baqaya al-Firaq,* 42–43.

76. This song was first reported by al-Ghulami, *Baqaya al-Firaq,* and later by al-Sarraf, *al-Shabak.*

77. For an elaboration of the ceremony of initiation, see Birge, *Bektashi Order,* 175–102. Cf. Brown, *The Darvishes,* 206–7; Garnett, *Mysticism and Magic in Turkey,* 97–102; and al-Sarraf, *al-Shabak,* 104–10.

78. Brown, *The Darvishes,* 208; and Garnett, *Mysticism and Magic in Turkey,* 98. Cf. al-Sarraf, *al-Shabak,* 111.

79. See chapter 3 n. 37 and 38 of this book for more information on the Kizilbash cap.

80. Al-Ghulami, *Baqaya al-Firaq,* 40–41; and al-Sarraf, *al-Shabak,* 115–16.

81. For an account of Ali Zayn al-Abidin and his poetry, see al-Shaibi, *al-Sila bayn al-Tasawwuf wa al-Tashayyu,* 147–62.

82. Al-Sarraf, *al-Shabak,* 116.

83. Al-Shaibi, *al-Tariqa al-Safawiyya,* 51.

84. Al-Ghulami, *Baqaya al-Firaq,* 38, 40.

85. Al-Shaibi, *al-Tariqa al-Safawiyya,* 51.

86. Al-Tabari, *Tarikh al-Umam wa al-Muluk,* 4:258; al-Masudi, *Muruj al-Dhahab,* 3:6.

87. Al-Ghulami, *Baqaya al-Firaq,* 42; and al-Sarraf, *al-Shabak,* 117. Ubayd Allah Ibn Ziyad was killed by Ibrahim Ibn al-Ashtar in the year 67/686 near the lower Khazir, a tributary of the Tigris near Mosul in a battle called Ayn al-Warda. See al-Tabari, 4, 555; and al-Masudi, *Muruj al-Dhahab,* 3:41.

88. Al-Ghulami, *Baqaya al-Firaq,* 40; al-Sarraf, *al-Shabak,* 116.

12—Social Customs

1. Al-Karmali, "Tafkihat al-Adhhan," 582; and al-Azzawi, *al-Kaka'iyya fi al-Tarikh,* 95.

2. Vital Cuinet, *La Turquie d'Asie,: géographie, administrative, statistique, descriptive, et*

raisonnée de chaque province de l'Asie Mineure (Paris: E. Leroux, 1890–95), 2:767, and al-Shaibi, *al-Tariqa al-Safawiyya,* 49.

3. Al-Azzawi, *al-Kaka'iyya fi al-Tarikh,* 70–71; and al-Ghulami, *Baqaya al-Firaq,* 12.

4. *Tadhkira-i Ala,* quoted in Ivanow, *Truth-Worshippers,* 97–98, 161.

5. Al-Azzawi, *al-Kaka'iyya fi al-Tarikh,* 71; Minorsky, *Notes Sur la Secte des Ahlé-Haqq,* 124 n.3; and Grenard, "Une Secte Religieuse," 511.

6. *Tadhkira-i Ala,* quoted in Ivanow, *Truth-Worshippers,* 98.

7. Al-Sarraf, *al-Shabak,* 121.

8. Ibid., 123.

9. Al-Ghulami, *Baqaya al-Firaq,* 32.

10. Al-Sarraf, *al-Shabak,* 122.

11. For the procedures of divorce see al-Sarraf, *al-Shabak,* 122–23.

12. White, "The Shia Turks," 228; Idem, "Some Non-Conforming Turks," 224; idem, "Alevi Turks," 692; Trowbridge, "The Alevis, or Deifiers of Ali," 348; Grenard, "Une Secte Religieuse," 518.

13. Trowbridge, "The Alevis or Deifiers of Ali," 348; and White, "Some Non-Conforming Turks," 245.

14. For more on this topic, see al-Wardi, *Dirasa fi Tabi'at al-Mujtama al-Iraqi* (Baghdad: Matbaat al-Ani, 1965), 213–21; idem, "al-Faradiyyat al-Thalath Hawl al-Mujtama al-Iraqi," *al-Qadisiyya* 1868 (29 June 1968): 5.

15. See *Qanun al-Uqubat al-Iraqi,* ed. Kamil al-Samarrai (Baghdad: Matbaat al-Maarif 1957), 133.

16. Al-Sarraf, *al-Shabak,* 139. For article 216 of the Iraqi Penal Code, see *Qanun al-Uqubat al-Iraqi,* 133.

17. Al-Sarraf, *al-Shabak,* 139.

18. Al-Ghulami, *Baqaya al-Firaq,* 18.

19. Al-Sarraf, *al-Shabak,* 123.

20. Ibid. See also Saad Ibrahim al-Adami, *al-Aqaliyyat al-Diniyya,* 110–11.

21. al-Ghulami, *Baqaya al-Firaq,* 27.

22. Grenard, "Une Secte Religieuse," 512; White, "Some Non-Conforming Turks," 244. See also Eröz, *Türkiye' de Alevilik-Bektaşilik,* 60, 95–97, 304, where the author relates the opinion of Ziya Gökalp that the Bektashi-Kizilbash custom of drinking wine is an ancient custom dating back to the time when the Turks were pagans.

23. Birge, *Bektashi Order,* 172–73; White, "Some Non-Conforming Turks," 245; Ihsan Mesut Erisen and Kemal Samancigil, *Haci Baktaş Veli: Bektaşilik ve Alevilik Tarihi* (Istanbul: Ay Yayinevi, 1966), 20.

24. Erisen and Sasmancigil, *Haci Bektaş Veli,* 20.

25. Ibid., and Birge, *Bektashi Order,* 173.

26. Erisen and Samancigil, *Haci Bektaş Veli,* 20.

27. Al-Ghulami, *Baqaya al-Firaq,* 27.

28. Ibid.

29. Ibid.

28; and al-Sarraf, *al-Shabak,* 125, following al-Ghulami.

30. Al-Ghulami, *Baqaya al-Firaq, 20.*

31. Ibid., 28–29.

32. Ibid., 30.

13—Religious Books

1. Birge, *Bektashi Order,* 68, and chapter 3, 87–161, on Bektashi doctrines and beliefs.

2. Ibid., 68, and Baha Sait in *Türk Yurdu* (Istanbul: 1926–27) 28:320 quoted in Birge, 68.

3. Birge, *Bektashi Order,* 68.

4. J. G. Taylor, "Journal of a Tour," 320.

5. See Dunmore, report dated 22 January in *Missionary Herald* (1857): 219–20.

6. M. F. Grenard, "Une Secte Religieuse," 514 n. 1.

7. Al-Sarraf, *al-Shabak,* 3–6, 141–43, 144 n.1, 146–91.

8. In the summer of 1981, the author obtained a copy of this manuscript which had been deposited in the Iraqi Museum Library as Turkoman MS 14706/1. It bears the private seal of the attorney Sadiq Kammuna dated 1975. The manuscript is entitled *Manaqib al-Awliya aw Buyruk* (Exemplary acts of saints of commandments). It consists of two parts, the first containing the biography of Shaykh Safi al-Din and an account of his acts and religious instructions, and the second containing collections of Turkish poems and hymns in praise of Ali and the rest of the Imams. It is written in blue ink and was completed at Tallafar on 28 December 1953. A colophone reads, "This is the book in which the Sufis of Tallafar believe."

9. Ibid., 142–43.

10. Al-Shaibi, *al-Tariqa al-Safawiyya,* 52.

11. Ibn Bazzaz, *Safwat al-Safa.* For a detailed description of this book, see Basil Nikitin, "Essai D'Analyse du Safvat-us-Safa," *Journal Asiatique,* 5th ser., 245 (1957): 385–93; and Browne, *Literary History,* 32–34.

12. Al-Azzawi, *al-Kaka'iyya fi al-Tarikh,* 89–90.

13. Ibid., 49, 90–91.

14. Dunmore, report dated 22 January 1857, 219–20.

15. J. G. Taylor, "Journal of a Tour," 320.

16. See the introduction to the *Buyruk* in al-Sarraf, *al-Shabak,* 146 and 192.

17. Ibid., 192, 193.

18. Ibid., 209. For the connotations of these two terms, see Birge, *Bektashi Order,* 270.

19. Ibn Bazzaz, *Safwat al-Safa,* 11, 140, 146, 152.

20. For sections 7 to 35 of the *Buyruk,* see al-Sarraf, *al-Shabak,* 149–68 of the Turkish text and 194–206 of the Arabic translation.

21. For sections 37 and 38 of the *Buyruk* see ibid., 169–71 of the Turkish text and 207–8 of the Arabic translation.

22. For sections 39 to 42 of the *Buyruk,* see ibid., 171–75 of the Turkish text and 208–11 of the Arabic translation.

23. For the anecdote of *Ghadir Khumm* in the *Buyruk,* see ibid., 177–81 of the Turkish text and 211–13 of the Arabic translation.

24. For section 50 of the *Buyruk,* see ibid., 181–82 of the Turkish text and 213–14 of the Arabic translation. On Najm al-Din Kubra, see notes by H. A. Rose in John P. Brown, *The Darvishes,* 2nd. ed. (London: Cass, 1968), 423–24; Browne, *History of Persian Literature,* 11:491–94, 579; Trimingham, *Sufi Orders,* 55–57; and Corbin, *The Man of Light in Iranian Sufism* (Boulder and London: Shambhala, 61–97.

25. For sections 51–52 of the *Buyruk,* see al-Sarraf, *al-Shabak,* 182–91 of the Turkish text and 214–17 of the Arabic translation.

26. For this statement in section 49 of the *Buyruk,* see al-Sarraf, *al-Shabak,* 180–81 of the Turkish text and 213 of the Arabic translation.

27. Al-Azzawi, *al-Kaka'iyya fi al-Tarikh,* 63; and al-Shaibi, *al-Fikr al-Shi'i,* 225.

28. Al-Hajj Masum Ali, *Tara'iq al-Haqa'iq* (Tehran: 1319/1901), 2:2; and al-Shaibi, *al-Sila bayn al-Tasawwuf wa al-Tashayyu,* 23.

29. Al-Shaibi, ibid., 11, 109; Massignon, *Salman Pàk et les premices de l'Islam iranien* in Abd al-Rahman Badawi, ed., *Shakhsiyyat Qaliqa fi al-Islam* (Cairo: Dar al-Nahda al-Arabiyya, 1964), 49 n.1; and al-Shaibi, *al-Sila bayn al-Tasawwuf wa al-Tashayyu,* 32.

30. Yamini Baba, *Fadilat Nama,* in Browne Papers, Turkish MS. 16, fols., 102–4b and 107b, Cambridge University; and al-Shaibi, *al-Fikr al-Shi'i,* 383.

31. Birge, *Bektashi Order,* 147–48.

32. On Salman al-Farisi see Ibn al-Jawzi, *Sifat al-Safwa,* 1:523–56; Massignon, *Salman Pàk et les premices de l'Islam iranien,* 3–58; Abd Allah al-Subayti, *Salman al-Farisi,* 2nd ed (Baghdad, Matbaat al-Azhar, 1969). On the conversion of Salman to Islam, see Muhammad Ibn al-Fattal al-Nisaburi, *Rawdat al-Wa'izin,* 2:275–78. For the spiritual position of Salman al-Farisi, see *Umm al-Kitab,* 132, 138–39, 170–74, and 179; and Corbin, *Cyclical Time and Ismaili Gnosis,* 72–76, 124–25 and 142–144.

14—The Bajwan and Ibrahimiyyap

1. Minorsky, "The Guran," *Bulletin of the School of Oriental Studies* (1943): 85.

2. Al-Karmali, "Tafkihat al-Adhhan," 580.

3. Al-Chalabi, letter in al-Sarraf, *al-Shabak,* 9.

4. Al-Azzawi, *al-Kaka'iyya fi al-Tarikh,* 95–96. Cf. Minorsky, "The Guran," 76, 85. Minorsky uses the name Bajilan for these people, and states that they speak a dialect similar to the Gurani.

5. Al-Ghulami, *Baqaya al-Firaq,* 15, 24, 27.

6. Al-Azzawi, *al-Kaka'iyya fi al-Tarikh,* 98.

7. Al-Ghulami, *Baqaya al-Firaq,* 46–47.

8. Al-Karmali, "Tafkihat al-Adhhan," 580. For the source of his information about the Bajwan and related groups see page 578.

9. Minorsky, "Ahl-i Hakk," in *The Encyclopedia of Islam* 1 (Leiden and London: E. J. Brill, 1960):260; and Stead "The Ali Ilahi Sect."

10. Al-Karmali, "Tafkihat al-Adhhan,", 580.

11. Al-Shaibi, *al-Tariqa al-Safawiyya,* 31–32.

12. Ibid., 50. Al-Shaibi's intention in quoting al-Karmali is to show that by glorifying Ismail the Shabak as a sect reflect the "Safawi order under Shah Isma'il."

13. Al-Karmali, "Tafkihat al-Adhhan," 580–81.

14. Ibid., 581.

15. Ibid.

16. Al-Sarraf, *al-Shabak,* 283.

17. Al-Sarraf, *al-Shabak,* 51. This story has been confirmed as a part of the Ibrahimiyya tradition by Tawfiq Wahbi, an Iraqi statesman who has served several times in the Iraqi Cabinet. Cf. *Mathnawi of Jalalu'ddin Rumi,* ed. and trans. Reynold A. Nicholson (Cambridge: Cambridge University Press, 1926; reprinted 1977), 1:161 and 2:108, when Muhammad Himself calls Ali "the Lion of God."

18. See chapter 10 of this book on the Abdal.

19. *Manaqib al-Awliya aw Buyruk,* passim, especially 8 and 24.

20. Husayn Ali Razmara, *Farhang Gughrafia-i Iran* (Geographical Dictionary of Iran) (Tehran: Chap Khanah Artish, 1331/1952), 5:362, and al-Shaibi, *al-Tariqa al-Safawiyya,* 60.

21. *Manaqib al-Awliya aw Buyruk,* 14, 25, and 34.

22. Al-Sarraf, *al-Shabak,* 55.

23. Al-Azzawi, *al-Kaka'iyya fi al-Tarikh,* 33–34, 39–40.

24. Abd al-Hujja al-Balaghi, *Maqalat al-Hunafa fi Maqamat Shams al-Urafa* (Tehran: Chap Khanah Mazahri, 1327/1948), 197; and al-Shaibi, *al-Tariqa al-Safawiyya,* 61.

25. Al-Sarraf, *al-Shabak,* 55.

15—The Sarliyya-Kakaiyya

1. Al-Azzawi, *al-Kaka'iyya fi al-Tarikh,* 45–46.

2. Rev. Anastase al-Karmali, "Tafkihat al-Adhhan," 579; Minorsky, "Shabak," 4:238–39, who follows al-Karmali; al-Azzawi, *al-Kaka'iyya fi al-Tarikh,* 32, 78; Saad Ibrahim al-Adami, *al-Aqaliyyat al-Diniyya,* 117–22.

3. Al-Azzawi, *al-Kaka'iyya fi al-Tarikh,* 78.

4. Al-Ghulami, *Baqaya al-Firaq,* 12.

5. *Al-Tarikh al-Ghiyathi: al-Fasl al-Khamis min Sanat 656 to 689/1258 to 1290,* ed. Tariq Nafi al-Hamdani (Baghdad: Asad Press, 1975), 184–85.

6. Al-Azzawi, *al-Kaka'iyya fi al-Tarikh,* 4.

7. Ivanow, *Truth-Worshippers,* 66.

8. Taha al-Hashimi, *Mufassal Jughrafiyyat al-Iraq* (Elaborate Geography of Iraq), quoted in al-Azzawi, *al-Kaka'iyya fi al-Tarikh,* 7.

9. Al-Azzawi, *al-Kaka'iyya fi al-Tarikh,* 8.

10. Ibid., 9. On the *Akhiyya* or *Akhi,* see Fr. Taeschner, "Akhi," in *The Encyclopedia of Islam* (Leiden and London: E. J. Brill, 1960), 1:321–23 and 966–69. For Futuwwa, see Corbin, *En Islam iranien* 4:410–60; and Cahen, *"Futuwwa,"* in *The Encyclopedia of Islam* (Leiden and London: E. J. Brill, 1965), 2:961–65.

11. Ibn Babawayh, *Ma'ani al-Akhbar,* 119; and Cahen, "Futuwwa," 2:961. For the noble qualities of the Futuwwa, see al-Qushayri, *al-Risala al-Qashayriyya,* ed. Abd al-Halim Mahmud and Mahmud Ibn al-Sharif (Cairo: Dar al-Kutub al-Haditha, 1966), 2: 472–79.

12. Ibn Babawayh, *Ma'ani al-Akhbar,* 119; and al-Hasan Ibn Yusuf Ibn al-Mutahhar al-Hilli, *Kashf al-Haqq wa Minhaj al-Sidq* (Revelation of the truth and path of truthfulness), Arabic MS. 437, fol. 78b, The India Office, Loth, London.

13. Al-Azzawi, *al-Kaka'iyya fi al-Tarikh,* 24–25.

14. See Ahmad Ibn Elias al-Naqqash (of Khartbart), *Tuhfat al-Wasaya,* Arabic MS. 2049, Hagia Sophia, in which the author discusses al-Futuwwa and its rejuvenation by the Abbasid Caliph al-Nasir; Cahen, "Futuwwa," 2:946–65; and al-Azzawi, *al-Kaka'iyya fi al-Tarikh,* 14–17.

15. Cahen, "Futuwwa," 2:964; and al-Shaibi, *al-Fikr al-Shi'i,* 66–67.

16. Cahen, "Futuwwa," 2:964; and Bernard Lewis, *The Assassins: A Radical Sect in Islam* (New York: Weidenfeld & Nicholson, 1967), 91.

17. Köprülü, *Türk Edebiyatinda,* 231; Lewis, *The Assassins,* 91.

18. Al-Azzawi, *al-Kaka'iyya fi al-Tarikh,* 20–22.

19. *The Travels of Ibn Battuta A.D. 1325–1354* trans. H. A. R. Gibb from the Arabic text edited by C. Defrémery and B. R. Sanguinetti (Cambridge: Cambridge University Press, 1962), 2:418–21, and Köprülü, *Türk Edebiyatinda,* 237.

20. Fr. Taeschner, "Futuwwa, Post Mongol Period," *The Encyclopedia of Islam,* 2:966–67.

21. Al-Azzawi, *al-Kaka'iyya fi al-Tarikh,* 21–22. For the distribution of the Kakaiyya, see pages 31–40, and for the distribution of the Sarliyya, see pages 32–33; See also al-Ghulami, *Baqaya al-Firaq,* 13–14.

22. Al-Azzawi, *al-Kaka'iyya fi al-Tarikh,* 45–46.

23. Al-Azzawi, *al-Kaka'iyya fi al-Tarikh,* 31; and al-Ghulami, *Baqaya al-Firaq,* 17.

24. Al-Azzawi, *al-Kaka'iyya fi al-Tarikh* 33, 40, 51–55, 89.

25. Ibid., 56.

26. On the dogma of the Nusayris, see chapters 26 to 35 of this book and René Basset, "Nusairis," *The Encyclopedia of Religion and Ethics* ed. James Hastings (New York: Charles Scribners, & Son, 1917), 9:417–19. For more on the Ahl-i Haqq, see Minorsky, "Ahl-i Hakk," 1:260; and the religious book of Ahl-i Haqq entitled *Tadhkira-i A'la* in Ivanow, *Truth-Worshippers,* 102. According to *Tadhkira-i A'la,* the creator first created a pearl *(durr)* in which were manifested five images in his image. Thereafer 1001 persons *(surat)* manifested themselves and formed an assembly *(jam).* See also al-Azzawi, *Tarikh al-Iraq,* 2:18 and 3:151 and 153.

27. Murtada Al Nazmi, *Jami al-Anwar,* quoted in al-Azzawi, *al-Kaka'iyya fi al-Tarikh,* 77.

28. Al-Azzawi, *al-Kaka'iyya fi al-Tarikh,* 60–61.

29. Ibid., 58–59.

30. I. Goldziher, "The Influence of Buddhism Upon Islam," trans. T. Duka, *Journal of the Royal Asiatic Society of Great Britain and Ireland* (January 1904): 127–28. Goldziher also associates metempsychosis with the Islamic concept of fatalism.

31. Al-Azzawi. *al-Kaka'iyya fi al-Tarikh,* 62.

32. Ibid.

33. Ibid., 62. For the tradition of Munkar and Nakir, see Abu Muhammad al-Baghawi, *Mishkat al-Masabih,* trans. James Robson (Lahore: Sh. Muhammad Ashraf Press, 1975), 35–37. It is interesting that the Yezidis have a similar burial tradition, except that the Faqir (a religious rank) tells the deceased person that if Munkar and Nakir are not satisfied with an offering of bread and cheese, the deceased person should beat them with the Faqir's *gopal;* (stick). See W. B. Heard, "Notes on the Yezidis," *Royal Anthropological Institute of Great Britain and Ireland* 41 (1911): 211.

34. Al-Azzawi, *al-Kaka'iyya fi al-Tarikh,* 73, 88, and 273; al-Karmali, "Tafkihat al-Adhhan," 578; and Ivanow, *Truth-Worshippers,* 85–86. Cf. Minorsky, "Ahl-i Hakk," 261.

35. Al-Azzawi, *al-Kaka'iyya fi al-Tarikh,* 73; and al-Ghulami, *Baqaya al-Firaq,* 18.

36. Al-Azzawi, *al-Kaka'iyya fi al-Tarikh,* 68 and 73–74; and al-Karmali, "Tafkihat al-Adhhan," 578, who states that only the Sarliyya do not fast.

37. Al-Azzawi, *al-Kaka'iyya fi al-Tarikh,* 67.

38. Ibid., 67; and al-Ghulami, *Baqaya al-Firaq,* 17.

39. Al-Azzawi, *al-Kaka'iyya fi al-Tarikh,* 67, 69; and al-Ghulami, *Baqaya al-Firaq,* 16–18.

40. Al-Azzawi, *al-Kaka'iyya fi al-Tarikh,* 69.

41. Ibid.

42. al-Karmali, "Tafkihat al-Adhhan," 578–79.

43. This ceremonial Meal of Love is related by al-Karmali, ibid., 579; and by al-Azzawi *al-Kaka'iyya fi al-Tarikh,* 72–73 with slight differences.

44. Al-Karmali, "Tafkihat al-Adhhan," 579.

45. See chapter 11 of this book.

46. Al-Karmali, "Tafkihat al-Adhhan," 579, and idem, "Laylat al-Hashush," 241, 368.

47. Mirza Makhdum, *al-Nawaqid li Bunyan al-Rawafid* quoted in al-Azzawi, *al-Kaka'iyya fi al-Tarikh,* 76.

48. Al-Azzawi, *al-Kaka'iyya fi al-Tarikh,* 66; and al-Ghulami, *Baqaya al-Firaq,* 15.

49. *Tadhkira-i A'la,* in Ivanow, *Truth-Worshippers,* 125–27.

50. Al-Azzawi, *al-Kaka'iyya fi al-Tarikh,* 71. Cf. F.M. Stead, "The Ali Ilahi Sect in Persia," *The Moslem World* 22 (April 1932): 186–87 where the author mentions the custom of the Ali Ilahi shaykhs of collecting donations.

51. Al-Ghulami, *Baqaya al-Firaq,* 15; and stead, "The Ali Ilahi Sect," 186.

52. Al-Ghulami, *Baqaya al-Friaq,* 15; and Stead, "The Ali Ilahi Sect," 186.

53. Al-Azzawi, *al-Kaka'iyya fi al-Tarikh,* 44.

54. Al-Ghulami, *Baqaya al-Firaq,* 15–16.

55. Ibid.

56. Al-Azzawi, *al-Kaka'iyya fi al-Tarikh,* 62.

57. For "Khutbat al-Bayan," see Birge, *Bektashi Order,* 140–45. For more on the origin of Khutbat al-Bayan, see Massignon, "L'Homme Parfait en Islam," 309–14; Badawi, *al-Insan al-Kamil fi al-Islam* (Kuwayt: Wakalat al-Matbuat, 1976, 131–38 and portions of "Khutbat al-Bayan," are found in a Nusayri source still in manuscript form: Arab MS. 5188. Bibliothèque Nationale.

58. Birge, *Bektashi Order,* 141–45; and Badawi, *al-Insan al-Kamil fi al-Islam,* 135–38.

59. See the lengthy ode entitled *al-Ta'iyya al-Kubra,* composed by the Egyptian Sufi Umar Ibn al-Farid, in *Diwan Ibn al-Farid,* 60, where Ibn al-Farid states that through the Wasiyya (testamentary trust) of Muhammad, Ali had the authority to interpret problematic questions of the Islamic faith.

60. See for example René Dussaud, *Histoire et Religion des Nosairis* (Paris: Libraire Émile Bouillon, 1900), 162.

61. On the Hurufis and their doctrine, see Browne, "Some Notes on the Literature and Doctrines of the Hurufi Sect," 16–94; idem, "Further Notes on the Literature of the Hurufis," 533–81; Clement Hurat, *Textes Persans relatifs a la secte des Houroufis* in E. G. W. Gibb Memorial Series 9 (1909): 1–41. See also al-Shaibi, *al-Fikr al-Shi'i,* 179–244.

62. Al-Azzawi, *al-Kaka'iyya fi al-Tarikh,* 53.

63. Minorsky, "Ahl-i Hakk," 262.

64. Al-Azzawi, *al-Kaka'iyya fi al-Tarikh,* 54. Al-Azzawi states that the book of *Saranjam* has been translated into Arabic by Baha al-Din Nuri but that the translation has not been published.

65. Ibid., and al-Ghulami, *Baqaya al-Firaq,* 16.

66. Al-Azzawi, *al-Kaka'iyya fi al-Tarikh,* 53, 57. On Fuduli al-Baghdadi, see Husayn Mujib al-Misri, *Fi al-Adab al-Islami: Fuduli al-Baghdadi Amir al-Shi'r al-Turki al-Qadim* (On Islamic literature: Fuduli al-Baghdadi, the prince of ancient Turkish poetry) (Cairo: Dar al-Fikra li al-Tab wa al-Nashr, 1966).

67. Al-Ghulami, *Baqaya al-Firaq,* 19; and al-Azzawi, *al-Kaka'iyya fi al-Tarikh,* 43.

68. Al-Ghulami, *Baqaya al-Firaq,* 19.

69. Al-Azzawi, *al-Kaka'iyya fi al-Tarikh,* 41, 43; and Minorsky, *Notes Sur la Secte des Ahlé Haqq,* 24. See also chapters 16–21 of this book on the Ahl-i Haqq or Ali Ilahis.

70. Al-Azzawi, *al-Kaka'iyya fi al-Tarikh,* 41. This must by the same Ibrahim Shah of Ahl-i Haqq. Cf. *Tadhkira-i A'la,* in Ivanow, *Truth Worshippers,* 7 and 164; and Mokri, *Shah Nama-ye Haqiqat,* 1:514–24.

71. Al-Azzawi, *al-Kaka'iyya fi al-Tarikh,* 41–42. See also chapters 16–21 of this book on the Ahl-i Haqq or Ali Ilahis.

72. Huntington, "Through the Great Canyon," 43.

73. Al-Azzawi, *al-Kaka'iyya fi al-Tarikh,* 42, 43.

74. Ibid.

75. Ibid.

76. Al-Ghulami, *Baqaya al-Firaq,* 12.
77. Al-Azzawi, *al-Kaka'iyya fi al-Tarikh,* 70.
78. Ibid.
79. Ibid.
80. Ibid.; al-Karmali, "Tafkihat al-Adhhan," 579; and al-Ghulami, *Baqaya al-Firaq,* 12.
81. Al-Ghulami, *Baqaya al-Firaq,* 12; and al-Azzawi, *al-Kaka'iyya fi al-Tarikh,* 70–71.
82. Al-Karmali, "Tafkihat al-Adhhan," 579–80.
83. Al-Azzawi, *al-Kaka'iyya fi al-Tarikh,* 71–73.

16—The Ahl-I Haqq (Ali Ilahis): *Origin and Identity*

1. For these names and the authors who used them, see Minorsky, *Notes Sur la Secte des Ahlé-Haqq,* 60–84; idem, "Ahl-i Hakk," 1:26–283; *Tadhkira-i A'la* in Ivanow, *Truth-Worshippers,* 136, 137, and 168–69; Stead, "The Ali Ilahi Sect," 184; Wilson, *Persian Life and Customs,* 239; and Clement Huart, "Ali Ilahi," in *The Encyclopedia of Islam* (Leiden and London: E. J. Brill, 1913), 1:292–93.

2. Mirza Karam, "The Sect of the Ali Ilahis or the Ahl-i Haqq," *The Moslem World* 29, no. 1 (January 1939): 73; and the note by Rev. James L. Merrick in his translation of Muhammad Baqir al-Majlisi, *Hayat al-Qulub,* 440, where Merrick mentions the Lak as Ali Ilahis.

3. De Gobineau, *Trois ans en Asie, 1855 à 1858* (Paris: Librarire de L. Hachette, 1859), 337–70. Cf. Minorsky, *Notes Sur la Secte des Ahlé-Haqq,* 8.

4. For this legend, see *Shah Nama-ye Haqiqat,* 1:236–39; al-Majlisi, *Hayat al-Qulub,* 44; Karam, "Sect of the Ali Ilahis," 74–75; Bent, "Azerbeijan," *The Scottish Geographical Magazine* (1890), 6:81–82, where the author writes the name Nusayr as Nazeyr; Minorsky, *Notes Sur la Secte des Ahlé-Haqq,* 8; and S. G. Wilson, *Persian Life and Customs,* 239. See also Charles R. Pittman's translation of a version of *Saranjam,* entitled "The Final Word of Ahl-i Haqq," *The Moslem World* (1937), 27:161; and Ivanow, *Truth Worshippers,* 2; Southgate states that the common name of the Ali Ilahis is Nesouri. See Southgate, *Narrative of a Tour,* 2:141.

5. Minorsky, *Notes Sur la Secte des Ahlé-Haqq,* 8; and idem, "Ahl-i Hakk," 1:260.

6. De Gobineau, *Trois ans en Asie,* 339–41.

7. See the section entitled :Haqiqat" in Ivanow, *Truth-Worshippers,* 155–56; and al-Majlisi, *Hayat al-Qulub,* 440.

8. Gobineau, *Trois ans en Asie,* 342–44. Gobineau states that by Ahl-i Tariqa the Ahl-i Haqq mean those whose are different from them and who reject their dogma.

9. Al-Shahrastani, *Kitab al-Milal,* 2:31, where al-Shahrastani discusses the beliefs of the Ismailis; von Hammer-Purgstall, *The History of the Assassins,* trans. Oswald Charles Wood (London: Smith and Elder Cornhill, 1840), 108–9; Hodgson, *The Order of Assassins* (The Hague: Mouton, 1955), 148–59 and 299–304; Corbin, *En Islam iranien,* 1:77–78 and 2:187; idem, *Cyclical Time and Ismaili Gnosis,* 117–18; Lewis, *The Assasins* 71–74; Azim Nanji, *The Nizari Isma'ili Tradition in the Indo-Pakistan Subcontinent* (Delmar, New York: Caravan Books, 1978), 108–10 and Ivanow, *Truth-Worshippers,* 70.

10. Von Hammer-Purgstall, *History of the Assassins,* 109; Ivanow, *Truth-Worshippers,* and idem, *Studies in Early Persian Isma'ilism,* 2nd ed. (Bombay: Ismaili Society, 1955), 110.

11. Ivanow, *Truth-Worshippers,* 71.

12. De Gobineau, *Trois ans en Asie,* 339; Charles Wilson and H. C. Rawlinson,

"Kurdistan," in *The Encyclopedia Britannica,* 11th ed. (Leiden and London: E. J. Brill, 1911), 15:950; S. G. Wilson, *Persian Life and Customs,* 240; Shaykh Muhsin Fani, *The Dabistan or School of Manners,* trans. David Shea and Anthony Troyer 2 (Paris: Allen & Co., 1843), 451–60; Karam "Sect of the Ali Ilahis," 75; Stead, "The Ali Ilahi Sect," 184; and Petrushevsky, *Islam in Iran,* trans. Hubert Evan (Albany: State University of New York Press, 1985), 262–64.

13. Minorsky, "Ahl-i Hakk," 1:260–62; and idem, *Notes Sur la Secte des Ahlé-Haqq,* 8 and 17.

14. Sayyid Muhammad Ibn al-Sayyid Ahmad al-Husayni, *Rihlat al-Munshi al-Baghdadi,* trans. Abbas al-Azzawi (Baghdad: Sharikat al-Tirjara wa al-Tibaa, 1367/1947), 38–39, 40, 45, 47, 51, 53–56, and 64.

15. A copy of *Saranjam* dated 1259/1843 was first discovered and translated into Russian by V. Minorsky in 1911. The text remains unedited. Another copy dated 1291/1874, entitled *Tadhkira-i A'la* was translated into English by W. Ivanow and published with a detailed introduction and commentary in his book, *The Truth-Worshippers of Kurdistan,* already cited. Yet a third copy was translated into English by Charles R. Pittman in his article, "The Final Word of The Ahl-i Haqq," *The Moslem World* (1937), 27–147–63. This copy lacks a beginning, starting only with the miraculous birth of Shah Kushin, Cf. *Shah Nama-ye Haqiqat,* 1:187, where Ali is called God and Haqq (Truth).

16. *Shah Nama-ye Haqiqat,* 1:422–232, and 8 of the Introduction by Muhammad Mokri. For more on Nimat Allah, see Saeed Khan, "The Sect of Ahl-i Haqq (Ali Ilahis)," *The Moslem World* 17(1927):34; and Stead, "The Ali Ilahi Sect," 188–89.

17. Ivanow, *Truth-Worshippers,* 28.

18. Minorsky, "Ahl-i Hakk," 1:262–63; and *Shah Nama-ye Hqqiqat,* 1:33–50.

19. Ivanow, *Truth-Worshippers,* 2.

20. Minorsky, *Notes Sur la Secte des Ahlé-Haqq,* 33.

21. Minorsky, "Ahl-i Hakk," 1:262. Cf. Ivanow, *Truth-Worshippers,* 70.

22. Minorsky, *Notes Sur la Secte des Ahlé-Haqq,* 33; and G. S. F. Napier, "The Road from Baghdad to Baku," *The Geographical Journal* 52, no. 1 (January 1919): 10.

23. De. Gobineau, *Trois ans en Asie,* 345; and Huart, "Ali Ilahi," 1:293.

24. S. G. Wilson, *Persian Life and Customs,* 239.

25. Napier, "Baghdad to Baku," 10.

26. Khan, "The Sect of Ahl-i Haqq (Ali Ilahis)," 40.

27. Stead, "The Ali Ilahi Sect," 186.

28. Khan, "The Sect of Ahl-i Haqq (Ali Ilahis), 32; and Minorsky, *Notes Sur la Secte des Ahlé-Haqq,* 35.

29. Major H. S. Rawlinson, "Notes on a March from Zohab, at the foot of Zagros, along the Mountains to Khuzistan (Susiana), and from these through the Province of Luristan to Kirmanshsh, in the year 1836," *Journal of the Royal Asiatic Society* (1839), 9:36. Cf. E. B. Soane, *To Mesopotamia and Kurdistan in Disguise* (London: John Murray, 1920), 383.

30. Stead, "The Ali Ilahi Sect," 186–87, and H. C. Rawlinson, Notes on a March from Zohab," 110.

31. Karam, "Sect of the Ali Ilahis," 73; Khan, "The Sect of Ahl-i Haqq (Ali Ilahis)," 40; Minorsky, *Notes Sur la Secte des Ahlé- Haqq,* 42–59; Haji Zayn al-Abdin Shirvani, *Bustan al-Siyaha,* ed. Ali Asghar Atabeg (Tehran: Printed at the expense of Abd Allah Mustawfi, 1315/1897), 378–79. Cf. Muhammad Mokri's French introduction to *Shah Nama-ye Haqiqat,* 1:11 On the Ali Ilahis in Luristan see M. H. Louis Rabino, *Les Tribes de Louristan* (Paris: E. Leroux, 1916), 1–46.

32. See M. H. Louis Rabino, "Kermanchah," *Revue du Monde Musulman* 38 (March 1920): 1–40, in which he gives information about different communities of Ahl-i Haqq living in that region; and Minorsky. *Notes Sur la Secte des Ahlé-Haqq*, 46.

33. H. C. Rawlinson, "Notes on March from Zohab," 36.

34. Napier, "Baghdad to Baku," 10.

35. Minorsky, *Notes Sur la Secte des Ahlé-Haqq*, 57.

36. F. Sultanov, "Some information on the Sect of the Ali Ilahis," (in Russian), *The Caucasus* (Tiflis: 1893), quoted in Minorsky, *Notes Sur la Secte des Ahlé-Haqq*, 57–58, and 78.

37. De Gobineau, *Trois ans en Asie*, 341–42; and Khan, "The Sect of Ahl-i Haqq (Ali Ilahis)," 42; and anonymous article signed Ch., "The Ali Ilahis," quoted in Minorsky, *Notes Sur la Secte des Ahlé-Haqq*, 75; and al-Karmali, "Al-Dawuda aw al-Dawudiyyun," *al-Mashriq* 8(1903): 63–64.

38. Karam, "Sect of the Ali Ilahis," 78.

39. H. Adjarian, "Gyorans et Thoumaris," trans. Frédéric Macler, *Revue de l'Histoire des Religions* 93, no. 3 (May–June 1926): 294–307; and Minorsky, "Études sur les Ahl-i Haqq, 1, "Toumari"—Ahl-i Haqq," *Revue de l'Histoure des Religions* (1928): 90–105. On the Guran see Rabino, "Les Provinces Caspiennes De La Perse," *Revue du Monde Musulman* 38 (March 1920): 23–25; Minorsky, "The Guran," *Bulletin of the School of Oriental Studies* 9 Part 1 (1943): 75–103; and Soane, *To Mesopotamia and Kurdistan in Disguise*, 382.

40. Adjarian, "Gyorans et Thoumaris," 298. Ivanow observed the same exaggeration of Ahl-i Haqq about the volumes they possess of their religious book. See Ivanow, *Truth-Worshippers*, 25.

41. Ivanow, *Truth-Worshippers*, 30–33. *The Shah Nama-ye Haqiqat* is a recent source that adds no significant information on the Ahl-i Haqq.

42. Karam, "Sect of the Ali Ilahis," 76.

17—The Ahl-I Haqq: *Cosmology and Cosmogony*

1. *Tadhkira-i A'la*, in Ivanow, *Truth-Worshippers*, 100 Cf. Muhammad Mokri, "La naissance du monde chez les Kurdes Ahl-e Haqq," *Trudy 25 (Moscou: Mezhdunarodonogo Kongress Vortokovedow* 2, 1963): 159–68.

2. De Gobineau, *Trois ans en Asie*, 346; and *Qutb Nama*, in Minorsky, *Notes Sur la Secte des Ahlé-Haqq*, 12.

3. *Tadhkira*, in Ivanow, *Truth-Worshippers*, 100–1.

4. Ibid.

5. Ibid.

6. Khan, "The Sect of Ahl-i Haqq (Ali Ilahis)," 32; and Muhammad Mokri, "Le symbole de la Perle dans le folklore Persan et chez les Kurdes Fidèles de Vérité (Ahl-e Haqq), *Journal Asiatique* (1960): 436–81.

7. *Tadhkira*, in Ivanow, *Truth-Worshippers*, 102; Ivanow, *Truth-Worshippers*, 42; Minorsky, *Notes Sur la Secte des Ahlé-Haqq*, 12; de Gobineau, *Trois ans en Asie*, 347; and Khan, "The Sect of Ahl-i Haqq (Ali Ilahis)," 35.

8. Shaykh Muhsin Fani, *Dabistan or School or Manners*, trans. David Shea and Anthony Troyer, 1(Paris: Allen & Co., 1843), 6–7.

9. Rev. Ignatius Abduh Khalifa al-Yasui, "al-Yazidiyya: Tarjamat al-Suryaniyya fi Ahwal al-Firaqa al-Yazidiyya al-Shaytaniyya" (Account of the Devil-Worshipping Yezidi Sect), *al-Mashriq* 47 (1953): 580.

10. Minorsky, "Ahl-i Hakk," 1:263; referring to Nöldeke's letter to him.

11. Brown, *The Darvishes*, 104; and Birge, *Bektashi Order*, 102.

12. De. Gobineau, *Trois ans en Asie,* 346; and *Tadhkira,* in Ivanow, *Truth-Worshippers,* 100–1.

13. For this tradition, see Birge, *Bektashi Order,* 109–10. Cf. Gibb, *History of Ottoman Poetry,* 1:15–23.

14. *Tadhkira,* in Ivanow, *Truth-Worshippers,* 153–56, 158.

15. Minorsky, *Notes Sur la Secte des Ahlé-Haqq,* 12 and 130.

16. Khan, "The Sect of Ahl-i Haqq (Ali Ilahis)," 35; and Ivanow, *Truth-Worshippers,* 167.

17. *Tadhkira,* in Ivanow, *Truth-Worshippers,* 167.

18. Minorsky, *Notes Sur la Secte des Ahlé-Haqq,* 12, Cf. Chapter 7 of this book on the family of the Prophet.

19. Gobineau, *Trois ans en Asie,* 347.

20. Ibid., 348; Minorsky, *Notes Sur la Secte des Ahlé-Haqq,* 12, 124; idem, "Ahl-i Hakk," 1–260; Ivanow, *Truth-Worshippers,* 73 and 168; and H. Adjarian, "Gyorans et Thoumaris," 296.

21. See chapter 12 of this book. Cf. Vital Cuinet, *La Turquie d'Asie,* 2:767; Karam, "Sect of the Ali Ilahis," 76; and Minorsky, *Notes Sur la des Ahlé-Haqq,* 124 n. 3.

22. Minorsky, "Ahl-i Hakk," 1:260; and Gobineau, *Trois ans en Asie,* 348.

23. Minorsky, *Notes Sur la Secte des Ahlé-Haqq,* 10; idem, "Ahl-i Hakk," 1:261 and Haji Zayn al-Abidin Shirvani, *Bustan al-Siyaha,* ed. Ali Asghar Khan Atabeg (Tehran: printed at the expense of Sayyid Abd Allah Mustawfi, 1315/1897), 379.

24. De Gobineau, *Trois ans en Asie,* 348–51.

25. Adjarian, "Gyorans et Thoumaris," 296–300; and Ivanow, *Truth-Worshippers,* 164–65.

26. Reynold A. Nicholson, *The Mystics of Islam,* 153.

27. Al-Kulayni, *al-Usul min al-Kafi,* 1:234; and E. Mittwoch, "Dhu l'Fakar," 2:233.

28. See Frédéric Macler's comments in Adjarian, "Gyarans et Thoumaris," 305–6.

29. Rawlinson, "Notes on a March from Zohab," 95.

30. Khan, "The Sect of Ahl-i Haqq (Ali Ilahis)," 32.

31. Stead, "The Ali Ilahi Sect," 185.

32. Sami Nasib Makarem, *The Doctrine of the Ismailis* (Beirut: The Arab Institute for Research and Publishing, 1972), 34–41.

33. Ivanow, *Truth-Worshippers,* 72–73.

34. For a full development of this concept, see Birge, *Bektashi Order,* 116–17.

35. Ibid., 102.

36. Minorsky, "Ahl-i Hakk," 1:260.

37. De Gobineau, *Trois ans en Asie,* 342–45.

38. Khan, "The Sect of Ahl-i Haqq (Ali Ilahis)," 35. Cf. W. Ivanow, "An Ali Ilahi Fragment," *Collectanea* (Leiden: E. J. Brill, published for the Ismaili Society, 1948), 1: 173–74 of the English translation and 181 of the Persian text.

39. Stead, "The Ali Ilahi Sect," 183.

40. Ibid.

41. Julius Heinrich Petermann, *Reisen im Orient* (Leipzig: Veit & Co., 1860–61), 2:202–5.

42. Stead, "The Ali Ilahi Sect," 186.

43. Ivanow, *Truth-Worshippers,* 9 of the Introduction.

44. *Tadhkira,* in Ivanow, *Truth-Worshippers,* 102. Cf. Rawlinson, "Note on a March from Zohab," 36.

45. Minorsky, "Ahl-i Hakk," 1:261.

46. *Tadhkira,* in Ivanow, *Truth-Worshippers,* 106.

47. Ibid., 104. Cf. *Shah Nama-ye Haqiqat,* 1:253–60.

48. *Tadhkira,* in Ivanow, *Truth-Worshippers,* 104. Cf. Ivanow, *Truth-Worshippers,* 47 of the Introduction. In *Shah Nama-ye Haqiqat,* 1:253–160, the Saj-i Nar is considered a mythical tree. Ivanow, "An Ali Ilahi Fragment," 1: 167, ft. 1, seems to believe that the Saj-i Nar resembles the sky.

49. Khan, "The Sect of the Ahl-i Haqq (Ali Ilahis)," 38.

50. *Tadhkira,* in Ivanow, *Truth-Worshippers,* 104–5.

51. See Quran, 52:24, 56:17, and 76:19.

52. *Tadhkira* in Ivanow, *Truth-Worshippers,* 104–7.

53. Birge, *Bektashi Order,* 130.

54. Ibid., and *Tadhkira,* in Ivanow, *Truth-Worshippers,* 104.

55. Minorsky, *Notes Sur la Secte des Ahlé-Haqq,* 13.

56. Ivanow, "An Ali Ilahi Fragment," 1:173, 179; and idem, *Truth-Worshippers,* 45, fol. 3.

57. Brigham Young, *Journal of Discourses,* 1:50, quoted in Walter Martin, *The Rise of the Cults* (Grand Rapids, Michigan: Zondervan, 1961), 52; and Anthony Hoekema, *The Four Major Cults,* 5th ed. (Grand Rapids, Michigan: Wm. B. Eerdmans, 1976), 40–41.

58. De Gobineau, *Trois ans en Asie,* 347–48.

59. *Tadhkira,* in Ivanow, *Truth-Worshippers,* 106–7, Minorsky, "Ahl-i Hakk," 1:261 and idem, *Notes Sur la Secte des Ahlé-Haqq,* 17, where he calls Razbar a "feminine principle." Cf. de Gobineau, *Trois ans en Asie,* 347; and Adjarian, "Gyorans et Thoumaris," 296.

60. *Tadhkira,* in Ivanow, *Truth-Worshippers,* 44 and 106; and Minorsky, *Notes Sur la Secte des Ahlé-Haqq,* 12, 17.

61. *Tadhkira,* in Ivanow, *Truth-Worshippers,* 47, 104–6; Minorsky, *Notes Sur la Secte des Ahlé-Haqq,* 12, 17; de Gobineau, *Trois ans en Asie,* 350.

62. De Gobineau, *Trois ans en Asie,* 350; and Ivanow, *Truth-Worshippers,* 81–84.

63. Ivanow, *Truth-Worshippers,* 86; and de Gobineau, *Trois ans en Asie,* 350.

64. Ivanow, *Truth-Worshippers,* 86.

65. See Frédéric Macler's comments, in Adjarian, "Gyorans eet Thoumaris," 305.

66. Ivanow, *Truth-Worshippers,* 38, 44.

67. *Tadhkira,* in Ivanow, *Truth-Worshippers,* 43 and 104.

68. Ivanow, *Truth-Worshippers,* 54–55. For the celebration of the Eucharist by the Paulicians or Tondrakites see F. C. Conybeare, *The Key of Truth: A Manual of The Paulician Church of Amenia* (Oxford: Oxford University Press, 1898), 183.

69. For the list of these names see *Saranjam,* trans. Pittman in "The Final Word of the Ahl-i Haqq," 147; and Minorsky, *Notes Sur la Secte des Ahlé-Haqq,* 10–11. There are differences in the transliterations of names between the lists of Pittman and Minorsky. Furthermore, Minorsky's list contains names not found in Pittman's, such as Nusayr and Fatima, who belong to Ali's manifestation.

70. Minorsky, *Notes Sur la Secte des Ahlé-Haqq,* 10–11.

71. Ivanow, *Truth-Worshippers,* 8 of the Introduction.

72. Ibid.

73. See *Tadhkira-i A'la,* in Ivanow, *Truth-Worshippers,* 122. Cf. Muhammad Mokri, "Le idée de l' incarnation chez les Ahl-e Haqq," Akten des Internationalen Orientalisten Kongr., 24, (München, Wiesbaden: 1959):496–98.

74. H. C. Rawlinson, "Notes on a March from Zohab," 36; Soane, *To Mesopotamia and Kurdistan in Disguise,* 383; William Kennett Loftus, *Travels and Researchers in Chaldea and Susiana* (London: James Nisbet, 1857), 386 together with the footnote on that page; Stead, "The Ali Ilahi Sect," 186–87. Cf. Charles Wilson and Rawlinson, "Kurdistan," 950; and *Shah Nama-ye Haqiqat,* 1:521–23 and 256–27 on Baba Yadegar.

75. Minorsky, *Notes Sur la Secte des Ahlé-Haqq*, 23.

76. Khurshid Efendi, *Siyahat Nama Hudud,* in Minorsky, *Notes Sur la Secte des Ahlé-Haqq*, 23.

77. Minorsky, *Notes Sur la Secte des Ahlé-Haqq*, 23. Cf. *Shah Nama-ye Haqiqat,* 1:521–23, 526–27.

78. Loftus, *Travels and Research in Chaldea and Susiana*, 386.

79. Stead, "The Ali Ilahi Sect," 186–87.

80. S. G. Wilson, *Persian Life and Customs,* 234–35.

81. Stead, "The Ali Ilahi Sect," 188–89. Khan, "The Sect of Ahl-i Haqq (Ali Ilahis)," 34. Cf. *Shah Nama-ye Haqiqat,* 1:422–23 and 8 of the Introduction.

82. Khan, "The Sect of Ahl-i Haqq (Ali Ilahis)," 34.

83. Minorsky, *Notes Sur la Secte des Ahlé-Haqq*, 53.

84. Stead, "The Ali Ilahi Sect," 188; and Petrushevsky, *Islam in Iran,* 263, where the author states that the Ahl-i Haqq considered Shah Ismail, founder of the Safawi dynasty, an incarnation of God. Cf. *Shah Nama-ye Haqiqat,* 1:526–267 and 533–57 on Shah Hayyas.

85. See *Saranjam,* trans. Pittman, in "The Final Word of the Ahl-i Haqq," 148–49; *Tadhkira,* in Ivanow, *Truth-Worshippers,* 111; and *Shah Nama-ye Haqiqat,* 1:273–97 and 301–3.

86. *Saranjam,* trans. Pittman, in "The Final Word of the Ahl-i Haqq," 159–60; *Tadhkira,* in Ivanow, *Truth-Worshippers,* 121; and *Shah Nama-ye Haqiqat,* 1:317–43.

87. *Tadhkira,* in Ivanow, *Truth-Worshippers,* 134 (Ivanow gives the name as Shah Ways-Quli); and *Saranjam,* trans. Pittman, in "Final Word of the Ahl-i Haqq," where this episode is too brief and only contains the name of Qirmizi as Shah Vali-Quli.

88. *Tadhkira,* in Ivanow, *Truth-Worshippers,* 143.

89. Ibid., 115 and 120–22.

90. V. A. Joukovsky, *People of the Truth,* in Minorsky, *Notes Sur la Secte des Ahlé-Haqq*, 76.

91. *Saranjam,* trans. Pittman, in "The Final Word of the Ahl-i Haqq," 151; and *Tadhkira,* in Ivanow, *Truth-Worshippers,* 111–12. Shakkak Ahmad does not appear in Minorsky's list as one of the Four angels of Shah Kushin. See Minorsky, *Notes Sur la Secte des Ahlé-Haqq*, 11; and idem, "Ahl-i Hakk," 1:260.

92. H. C. Rawlinson, "Notes on a March from Zohab," 110.

93. Minorsky, *Notes Sur la Secte des Ahlé-Haqq*, 22; Ivanow, *Truth-Worshippers,* 112 n.26; Rawlinson, "Notes on a March from Zohab," 95; and Joukovsky, *People of the Truth,* 215.

94. Loftus, *Travels and Researches in Chaldea and Susiana,* 386.

95. *Saranjam,* trans. Pittman, in "The Final Word of the Ahl-i Haqq," 152–54; *Tadhkira,* in Ivanow, *Truth-Worshippers,* 112–14.

96. Ivanow, *Truth-Worshippers,* 11.

97. *Tadhkira,* in Ivanow, *Truth-Worshippers,* 113.

98. Ibid., 12, 113, 117–18; and *Saranjam,* trans. Pittman, in "The Final Word of the Ahlé-Haqq," 152.

99. *Tadhkira,* in Ivanow, *Truth-Worshippers,* 115–16.

100. Ivanow, *Truth-Worshippers,* 9.

101. *Tadhkira,* in Ivanow, *Truth-Worshippers,* 115 and *Saranjam,* trans. Pittman, in "The Final Word of the Ahl-i Haqq." 154.

18—Sultan Sahak: *Founder of the Ahl-I Haqq*

1. Ivanow, *Truth-Worshippers,* 10.

2. See Frédéric Macler's note in Adjarian, "Gyorans et Thoumaris," 297 n. 1, 305; and Ivanow, *Truth-Worshippers,* 8, 9, n.1, and 20.

3. Ivanow, *Truth-Worshippers,* 8–9.

4. Ibid., 48–49, 51–53.

5. Ibid., 12, 125; Khan, "The Sect of Ahl-i Haqq (Ali Ilahis)," 31, 32, 38–39; Minorsky, *Notes Sur la Secte des Ahlé-Haqq,* 24; and al-Azzawi, *al-Kaka'iyya fi al-Tarikh* 41.

6. Adjarian, "Gyorans et Thoumaris," 297.

7. Minorsky, *Notes Sur la Secte des Ahlé-Haqq,* 36; Khan, "The Sect of Ahl-i Haqq (Ali Ilahis)," 32; and *Tadhkira,* in Ivanow, *Truth-Worshippers,* 63.

8. *Tadhkira,* 62–66; Ivanow, *Truth-Worshippers,* 121; and *Saranjam,* trans. Pittman, in "The Final Word of the Ahl-i Haqq," 159–60.

9. Khan, "The Sect of Ahl-i Haqq (Ali Ilahis)," 32; and Minorsky, *Notes Sur la Secte des Ahlé-Haqq,* 25.

10. *Tadhkira,* in Ivanow, *Truth-Worshippers,* 124.

11. Ivanow, *Truth-Worshippers,* 155.

12. Ibid.

13. Al-Kulayni, *al-Usul min al-Kafi,* 1:181–85. For more information on this subject, see chapter 9 of this book.

14. *Tadhkira,* in Ivanow, *Truth-Worshippers,* 124. For detailed information about Safi al-Din, his religious guide Zahid of Gilan, and the Safawi Order, see chapter 3 of this book.

15. Ibid., 130–31. Cf. *Shah Nama-ye Haqiqat,* 1:474–79.

16. Ivanow, *Truth-Worshippers,* 130–31.

17. For the question of whether Shaykh Safi al-Din was Shiite, see chapter 3 of this book.

18. Hasan Ibn Ali Muhammad al-Tabari, *Kamil-i Baha-i,* 7; and Ivanow, *Truth-Worshippers,* 25, 61–62.

19. Khan, "The Sect of Ahl-i Haqq (Ali Ilahis)," 32.

20. *Tadhkira,* in Ivanow, *Truth-Worshippers,* 144.

21. For more information see Ivanow, *Truth-Worshippers,* 57–69.

22. Amir, *Habib al-Siyar,* (1315/1897), 3:220 and 4:421; and al-Shaibi, *al-Fikr al-Shi'i,* 396. Cf. Ivanow, *Truth-Worshippers,* 170 n. 20.

23. *Tadhkira,* in Ivanow, *Truth-Worshippers,* 6, 37, 137, 146, 157, 170 n. 20; and *Shah Nama-ye Haqiqat,* 1:462–65, on Benyamin.

24. Minorsky, *Notes Sur la Secte des Ahlé-Haqq,* 12 and *Tadhkira,* in Ivanow, *Truth-Worshippers,* 167.

25. *Tadhkira,* in Ivanow, *Truth-Worshippers,* 167–68.

26. Ivanow, *Truth-Worshippers,* 13.

27. Minorsky, *Notes Sur la Secte des Ahlé-Haqq,* 19.

28. Khan, "The Sect of Ahl-i Haqq (Ali Ilahis)," 39.

29. *Saranjam,* trans. Pittman, in "The Final Word of the Ahl-i Haqq," 155–56; and *Tadhkira,* in Ivanow, *Truth-Worshippers,* 120.

30. Ivanow, *Truth-Worshippers,* 13.

31. *Tadhkira,* in Ivanow, *Truth-Worshippers,* 122.

32. I personally heard such stories from the Iraqi army commander at the city of Muhammara when I visited the battle front there in March 1981.

33. Ivanow, *Truth-Worshippers,* 122.

34. *Tadhkira,* in Ivanow, *Truth-Worshippers,* 137–38.

35. Ibid., 146. Cf. *Shah Nama-ye Haqiqat,* 1:534–35, on Muhammad Beg.

36. *Tadhkira,* in Ivanow, *Truth-Worshippers,* and *Shah Nama-ye Haqiqat,* 536–38.

37. *Tadhkira,* in Ivanow *Truth-Worshippers,* 13 and 168.

38. Ivanow, *Truth-Worshippers,* 37.

39. Ibid.

40. Stead, "The Ali Ilahi Sect," 185.
41. Khan, "The Sect of Ahl-i Haqq (Ali Ilahis)," 34.

19—The Ahl-I Haqq: *The Cult of Dawud*

1. Al-Karmali, "al-Dawuda aw al-Dawudiyyun," 60–67. Cf. Stead, "The Ali Ilahi Sect," 186; and Minorsky, *Notes Sur la Secte des Ahlé-Haqq,* 37–38.
2. Minorsky, *Notes Sur la Secte des Ahlé-Haqq,* 37.
3. Al-Karmali, "al-Dawuda aw al-Dawudiyyun," 61.
4. Stead, "The Ali Ilahi Sect," 185.
5. Ibid., 184; and Minorsky, *Notes Sur la Secte des Ahlé-Haqq,* 37, and the anonymous author (C.) whom he quotes.
6. Stead, "The Ali Ilahi Sect," 184.
7. Al-Karmali, "al-Dawuda aw al-Dawudiyyun," 62.
8. Ibid.
9. Louis Cheikho, "Some Moslem Apocryphal Legends," trans. Josephine Spaeth, *The Moslem World* 2 (January 1912): 47–59.
10. S. M. Zwemer, "A Moslem Apocryphal Psalter," *The Moslem World* 5, no. 4 (October 1915): 399–403.
11. Ivanow, *Truth-Worshippers,* 57. The Author of *Shah Nama-ye Haqiqat* seems to consider King David and Dawud of the Ahl-i Haqq as two separate persons. See *Shah Nama-ye Haqiqat,* 1:160–63 and 449–62.
12. Minorsky, *Notes Sur la Secte des Ahlé-Haqq,* 37–38.
13. See *Shah Nama-ye Haqiqat,* 1:236–39. Al-Majlisi, *Hayat al-Qulub,* 44; Karam, "Sect of the Ali Ilahis," 74–75; Bent, "Azerbeijan," *The Scottish Geographical Magazine* 6 (1890):81–82, where the author writes the name Nusayr as Nazeyr; Minorsky, *Notes Sur la Secte des Ahlé-Haqq,* 8; and S. G. Wilson, *Persian Life and Customs,* 239. See also Charles R. Pittman's translation of a version of *Saranjam,* entitled "The Final Word of Ahl-i Haqq," *The Moslem World* 27(1937):161; and Ivanow, *Truth-Worshippers,* 2. Southgate states that the common name of the Ali Ilahis is Nesouri. See Southgate, *Narrative of a Tour,* 2:141.
14. *Tadhkira,* in Ivanow, *Truth-Worshippers,* 124.
15. De Gobineau, *Trois ans en Asie,* 349.
16. Khan, "The Sect of Ahl-i Haqq (Ali Ilahis)," 37.
17. Minorsky, *Notes Sur la Secte des Ahlé-Haqq,* 12; idem, "Ahl-i Hakk," *The Encyclopedia of Islam* (Leiden and London: E. J. Brill, 1960) 1:260–62; de Gobineau, *Trois ans en Asie,* 348; and Ivanow, *Truth-Worshippers,* 73, 152–53, and 168.
18. H. C. Rawlinson, "Notes on a March from Zohab," 36; S. G. Wilson, *Persian Life and Customs,* 239; and Loftus, *Travels and Research in Chaldea and Susiana,* 386.
19. Stead, "The Ali Ilahi Sect," 184.
20. *Tadhkira,* in Ivanow, *Truth-Worshippers,* 151 and 168; and idem, "An Ali Ilahi Fragment," 1: 174–75 and 182.
21. Stead, "The Ali Ilahi Sect," 184–85.
22. Southgate, *Narrative of a Tour,* 2:241; and Soane, *To Mesopotamia and Kurdistan in Disguise,* 383.
23. Al-Karmali, "al-Dawuda aw al-Dawudiyyun," 64.
24. *Tadhkira,* in Ivanow, *Truth-Worshippers,* 128.
25. Ibid., 151.
26. Ibid.

27. Ibid., 80, 151.

28. Ibid., 153.

29. Ibid., 151.

30. Khan, "The Sect of Ahl-i Haqq (Ali Ilahis)," 34–35. On Kuşcuöglu, see *Shah Nama-ye Haqiqat,* 1:503–5.

31. H. C. Rawlinson, "Notes on a March from Zohab," 39; and Loftus, *Travels and Researches in Chaldea and Susiana,* 386.

32. H. C. Rawlinson, "Notes on a March from Zohab," 384; Minorsky, *Notes Sur la Sect des Ahlé-Haqq,* 38–39; and al-Azzawi, *al-Kaka'iyya fi al-Tarikh,* 41–42.

33. See chapter 15 of this book; and al-Azzawi, *al-Kaka'iyya fi al-Tarikh,* 41–42.

34. J. T. Bent, "Azerbeijan," 86; and Ivanow, *Truth-Worshippers,* 5.

35. De Gobineau, *Trois ans en Asie,* 345; and J. T. Bent, "Azerbeijan," 87.

36. Khan, "The Sect of Ahl-i Haqq (Ali Ilahis)," 39.

37. Shirvani, *Bustan al-Siyaha,* 378–79; and Soane, *To Mesopotamia and Kurdistan in Disguise,* 386.

38. Soane, *To Mesopotamia and Kurdistan in Disguise,* 383 no. 1.

39. Stead, "The Ali Ilahi Sect," 186–87.

40. ibid.

41. S. G. Wilson, *Persian Life and Customs,* 234–35, 241.

42. Ivanow, *Nasiri-i Khusraw and Isma'ilism,* (Bombay: Ismaili Society, Ser, B., no. 5, 1948), 20; and idem, *Truth-Worshippers,* 5.

43. Wilson, *Persian Life and Customs,* 242; and Stead "The Ali Ilahi Sect," 186–87.

44. *Tadhkira,* in Ivanow, *Truth-Worshippers,* 125.

45. Khan, "The Sect of Ahl-i Haqq (Ali Ilahis)," 32. It is mentioned in *Saranjam,* trans. Pittman, in "The Final Word of the Ahl-i Haqq," 160, that Sultan Sahak married an unnamed girl from a noble family in his district.

46. The list of names followed here is based on the *Saranjam,* trans. Pittman, in "The Final Word of the Ahl-i Haqq," 160. Other lists differ slightly from this one. One such list is produced by Minorsky in *Notes Sur la Secte des Ahlé-Haqq,* 35 and reproduced in Ivanow, *Truth-Worshippers,* 126. Another list is taken from a poem by the fourteenth-century poet Shayda reproduced in Ivanow, *Truth-Worshippers,* 163–64.

47. *Tadhkira,* in Ivanow, *Truth-Worshippers,* 126.

48. Al-Azzawi, *al-Kaka'iyya fi al-Tarikh,* 4, 7, and 27.

49. Al-Karmali, "al-Dawuda aw al-Dawudiyyun," 65.

50. Ivanow, *Truth-Worshippers,* 7.

51. De Gobineau, *Trois ans en Asie,* 355; and *Tadhkira,* in Ivanow, *Truth-Worshippers,* 154.

52. Shirvani, *Bustan al-Siyaha,* 378–79; and Soane, *To Mesopotamia and Kurdistan in Disguise,* 386.

53. Ivanow, *Truth-Worshippers,* 7.

54. Al-Karmali, "al-Dawuda aw al-Dawudiyyun," 65.

55. Stead, "The Ali Ilahi Sect," 187.

56. Ibid., de Gobineau, *Trois ans en Asie,* 368–68; J. T. Bent, "Azerbeijan," 87; and Minorsky, *Notes Sur la Secte des Ahlé-Haqq,* 38.

20—The Ahl-I Haqq: *The Jam*

1. Khan, "The Sect of Ahl-i Haqq (Ali Ilahis)," 38. Cf. *Shah Nama-ye Haqiqat,* 1: 420–22.

2. Khan, ibid., and Ivanow, *Truth-Worshippers,* 75–78.

3. Bent, "Azerbeijan," 87; and Minorsky, *Notes Sur la Secte des Ahlé-Haqq,* 95.

4. Al-Karmali, "al-Dawuda aw al-Dawudiyyun," 62–63; and Adjarian, "Gyorans et Thoumaris," 301.

5. *Tadhkira,* in Ivanow, *Truth-Worshippers,* 158.

6. Khan, "The Sect of Ahl-i Haqq (Ali Ilahis)," 37 and 39; and Minorsky, *Notes Sur la Secte des Ahlé-haqq,* 95. Cf. Ivanow, *Truth-Worshippers,* 78.

7. Karam, "Sect of the Ali Ilahis," 77.

8. *Tadhkira,* in Ivanow, *Truth-Worshippers,* 158.

9. Adjarian, "Gyorans et Thoumaris," 302.

10. Khan, "The Sect of Ahl-i Haqq (Ali Ilahis)," 37.

11. Ibid., and *Tadhkira,* in Ivanow, *Truth-Worshippers,* 158.

12. Khan, "The Sect of Ahl-i Haqq (Ali Ilahis)," 39.

13. See Joukovsky, *People of the Truth,* in Minorsky, *Notes Sur la Secte des Ahlé-Haqq,* 92; Khan, in "The Sect of Ahl-i Haqq (Ali Ilahis)," 40, states that women are not admitted to the Jam but placed in a special compartment. Cf. *Tadhkira,* in Ivanow, *Truth-Worshippers,* 158.

14. Ivanow, *Truth-Worshippers,* 78.

15. *Tadhkira,* in Ivanow, *Truth-Worshippers,* 160.

16. *Tadhkira,* in Ivanow, *Truth-Worshippers,* 158.

17. Khan, "The Sect of Ahl-i Haqq (Ali Ilahis)," 36.

18. *Tadhkira,* in Ivanow, *Truth-Worshippers,* 158.

19. Ibid., 149.

20. Ibid., 127.

21. Ibid., 128.

22. Ibid., 150–51.

23. See appendix 2 in Ivanow, *Truth-Worshippers,* 180–81; and Minorsky, *Notes Sur la Secte des Ahlé-Haqq,* 91.

24. Khan, "The Sect of Ahl-i Haqq (Ali Ilahis)," 37.

25. *Tadhkira,* in Ivanow, *Truth-Worshippers,* 128.

26. Ivanow, *Truth-Worshippers,* 77.

27. Khan, "The Sect of Ahl-i Haqq (Ali Ilahis)," 37.

28. Birge, *Bektashi Order,* 177.

29. Al-Karmali, "al-Dawuda aw al-Dawudiyyun," 62–63.

30. *Tadhkira,* in Ivanow, *Truth-Worshippers,* 140, 149, 158; and Minorsky, *Notes Sur la Secte des Ahlé-Haqq,* 88–89.

31. Bent, "Azerbeijan," 87.

32. *Tadhkira,* in Ivanow, *Truth-Worshippers,* 102, 122–23; de Gobineau, *Trois ans en Asie,* 350; and Minorsky, *Notes Sur la Secte des Ahlé-Haqq,* 92.

33. *Tadhkira,* in Ivanow, *Truth-Worshippers,* 109, 119, and 147.

34. Ibid., 115. In Minorsky, *Notes Sur la Secte des Ahlé-Haqq,* 92, it is yellow ram.

35. *Tadhkira,* in Ivanow, *Truth-Worshippers,* 135 and 145. De Gobineau, in his *Trois ans en Asie,* 350 and 356, mentions a cow as a sacrifice.

36. *Tadhkira,* in Ivanow, *Truth-Worshippers,* 159. Cf. J. T. Bent, "Azerbeijan," 87, where the author describes the sacrificing of a sheep.

37. Khan, "The Sect of Ahl-i Haqq (Ali Ilahis)," 37; and Minorsky, *Notes Sur la Secte des Ahlé-Haqq,* 92.

38. Southgate, *Narrative of a Tour,* 2:141.

39. Joukovsky, *People of the Truth,* 76, 91. Minorsky, in his *Notes Sur la Secte des Ahlé-Haqq,* follows Joukovsky; and Huart, "Ali Ilahi," 293.

40. Baron C. A. De Bode, *Travels in Luristan and Arabistan* (London: J. Madden and Co., 1845), 2:180.

41. Soane, *To Mesopotamia and Kurdistan in Disguise* (London: John Murray, 1912), 384.

42. Khan, "The Sect of Ahl-i Haqq (Ali Ilahis)," 37. Cf. Minorsky, *Notes Sur la Secte des Ahlé-Haqq*, 88.

43. Adjarian, "Gyorans et Thoumaris," 302.

44. Ivanow, *Truth-Worshippers*, 85.

45. *Tadhkira*, in Ivanow, *Truth-Worshippers*, 158–59; de Gobineau, *Trois ans en Asie*, 357–58; and Adjarian, "Gyorans et Thoumaris," 302.

46. Minorsky, *Notes Sur la Secte des Ahlé-Haqq*, 91.

47. S. G. Wilson, *Persian Life and Customs*, 241.

48. Minorsky, *Notes Sur la Secte des Ahlé-Haqq*, 91.

49. G. Rawlinson, *History of Herodotus* (New York: Appleton and Company, 1889), 1:258; Minorsky, *Notes Sur la Secte des Ahlé-Haqq*, 93–94; and Southgate, *Narrative of a Tour*, 2:141.

50. Grenard, "Une Secte Religieuse," 517.

51. Karam, "Sect of the Ali Ilahis," 77.

52. Stead, "The Ali Ilahi Sect," 185.

53. *Tadhkira*, in Ivanow, *Truth-Worshippers*, 159, 161, 169.

54. Ibid., 89, 154, and 159; and Minorsky, *Notes Sur la Secte des Ahlé-Haqq*, 9. Cf. Southgate, *Narrative of a Tour*, 2:141; and G. Rawlinson, *History of Herodotus*, 1:258.

55. *Tadhkira*, in Ivanow, *Truth-Worshippers*, 158–59.

56. Ivanow, *Truth-Worshippers*, 89.

57. *Tadhkira*, in Ivanow, *Truth-Worshippers*, 160–61.

58. Ibid., 157 and 160; and Minorsky, *Notes Sur la Secte des Ahlé-Haqq*, 104–5.

59. *Tadhkira*, in Ivanow, *Truth-Worshippers*, 157–58; and *Shah Nama-ye Haqiqat*, 1:414–17, on Jawz.

60. Khan, "The Sect of Ahl-i Haqq (Ali Ilahis)," 38; Minorsky, *Notes Sur la Secte des Ahlé-Haqq*, 106–7; Ivanow, *Truth-Worshippers*, 91 n. 2; and *Tadhkira*, in Ivanow, *Truth-Worshippers*, 157–58.

61. Shirvani, *Bustan al-Siyaha*, 378–79.

62. Ibid.; Khan, "The Sect of Ahl-i Haqq (Ali Ilahis)," 38; Minorsky, *Notes Sur la Secte des Ahlé-Haqq*, 107; and S. G. Wilson, *Persian Life and Customs*, 241.

63. De Gobineau, *Trois ans en Asie*, 355–56; Minorsky, *Notes Sur la Secte des Ahlé-Haqq*, 168; and Ivanow, *Truth-Worshippers*, 91, n. 3.

64. De Gobineau, *Trois ans en Asie*, 361–62; Minorsky, *Notes Sur la Secte des Ahlé-Haqq*, 108–12; and Ivanow, *Truth-Worshippers*, 39–41.

65. *Tadhkira*, in Ivanow, *Truth-Worshippers*, 129, 159.

66. See chapter 11 of this book.

67. Birge, *Bektashi Order*, 182 n. 3.

68. Ibid.

69. *Tadhkira*, in Ivanow, *Truth-Worshippers*, 129 and 159.

70. De Gobineau, *Trois ans en Asie*, 361–62; and Minorsky, *Notes Sur la Secte des Ahlé-Haqq*, 108–12.

71. Minorsky, *Notes Sur la Secte des Ahlé-Haqq*, 110.

72. De Gobineau, *Trois ans en Asie*, 362.

73. Minorsky, *Notes Sur la Secte des Ahlé-Haqq*, 111.

74. Ibid., 18; and Mark Lidzbarski, "Ein Exposé der Jesiden," *Zeitschift der deutschen morgenländischen Gesellschaft* 51 (1897): 492–604.

75. Minorsky, *Notes Sur la Secte des Ahlé-Haqq,* 111.

76. De Gobineau, *Trois ans en Asie,* 345–46.

77. J. MacDonald Kinneir, *A Geographical Memoir of the Persian Empire* (London: John Murray, 1813), 141 including the footnote.

78. H. C. Rawlinson, "Notes on a March from Zohab," 110.

79. F. Sultanov, "Some Information on the Sect of the Ali Ilahis," quoted in Minorsky, *Notes Sur la Secte des Ahlé-Haqq,* 78.

80. S. G. Wilson, *Persian Life and Customs,* 236.

81. Shirvani, *Bustan al-Siyaha,* 379.

82. Soane, *To Mesopotamia and Kurdistan in Disguise,* 386.

83. Al-Karmali, "al-Dawuda aw al-Dawudiyyun," 64–66.

84. *Tadhkira,* in Ivanow, *Truth-Worshippers,* 161; and Minorsky, *Notes Sur la Secte des Ahlé-Haqq,* 112–16.

85. Ivanow, *Truth-Worshippers,* 96.

86. De Gobineau, *Trois ans en Asie,* 359; and Minorsky, *Notes Sur la Secte des Ahlé-Haqq,* 114, who draws his information from Joukovsky, *People of the Truth.*

87. Minorsky, *Notes Sur la Secte des Ahlé-Haqq,* 115–16; Stead, "The Ali Ilahi Sect," 187; de Gobineau, *Trois ans en Asie,* 368; and Ivanow *Truth-Worshippers,* 96.

21—The Ahl-I Haqq: *The Role of Ali*

1. *Tadhkira,* in Ivanow, *Truth-Worshippers,* 107–10. In *Shah Nama-ye Haqiqat,* 1: 187, Ali is called God and Haqq (Truth).

2. *Tadhkira,* in Ivanow, *Truth-Worshippers,* 108.

3. Ibid., 108–9.

4. Ibid., 109–10 and 116 respectively, and *Saranjam,* trans. Pittman in "The Final Word of the Ahl-i Haqq," 154.

5. *Tadhkira,* in Ivanow, *Truth-Worshippers,* 157–58.

6. Stead, "The Ali Ilahi-Sect," 184.

7. Karam, "The Sect of the Ali Ilahis," 74.

8. Stead, "The Ali Ilahi Sect," 185.

9. Soane, *To Mesopotamia and Kurdistan in Disguise,* 383; Khan,, "The Sect of Ahl-i Haqq (Ali Ilahis)," 35; and J. E. Polak, *Persien, das Land und seine Bewohner,* (Leipzig: F. A. Brockhaus, 1865), 1:349; and H. C. Rawlinson, "Notes on a March from Zohab," 36.

10. Ivanow, *Truth-Worshippers,* 176.

11. Fani, *Dabistan or School of Manners,* 2, 451 and 456–58; Bent, "Azerbeijan," 87–88; H. T. Colebrooke, "On the Origin and Peculiar Tenets of Certain Muhammedan Sects," *Asiatic Researches* 7 (1807): 337; and Polak, *Persien,* 1:349.

12. See the anonymous article in Russian signed Ch. entitled, "The Ali Ilahis," in *The Caucasus* (Tiflis, 1876), 27, 29, and 30, summarized in Minorsky, *Notes Sur la Secte des Ahlé-Haqq,* 75; J. T. Bent, "Azerbeijan," 87–88; Shirvani, *Bustan al-Siyaha,* 378–79; and Stead, "The Ali Ilahi Sect," 184.

13. See the anonymous article in Russian signed Ch. entitled, "The Ali Ilahis," in *The Caucasus* (Tiflis, 1876), summarized in Minorsky, *Notes Sur la Secte des Ahlé-Haqq,* 75.

14. Soane, *To Mesopotamia and Kurdistan in Disguise,* 384–85.

15. Ibid., 385; and S. G. Wilson, *Persian Life and Customs,* 283–40.

16. Soane, *To Mesopotamia and Kurdistan in Disguise,* 185.

17. See the poems of Kuşcuöglu (Quschi Oghli) translated by Minorsky in Ivanow, *Truth-Worshippers,* 201.

18. J. T. Bent, "Azerbeijan," 87–88; and Fani, *Dabistan or School of Manners,* 2: 457–58.

19. Khan, "The Sect of Ahl-i Haqq (Ali Ilahis), 36; and de Gobineau, *Trois ans en Asie,* 339.

20. S. G. Wilson, *Persian Life and Customs,* 239.

21. Fani, *Dabistan or School of Manners,* 2: 457; and Colebrooke, "Certain Muhammedan Sects," 338.

22. Fani, *Dabistan or School of Manners,* 2: 458.

23. Soane, *To Mesopotamia and Kurdistan in Disguise,* 385.

24. S. G. Wilson, *Persian Life and Customs,* 241.

25. Karam, "The Sect of the Ali Ilahis," 77. Cf. H. Rawlinson, "Notes on a March from Zohab," 52, where the author mentions that an infamous chief, Kalb Ali Khan, had murdered the English Captains Grant and Fotheringham for refusing to pronounce the Muslim profession of faith: "There is no God but Allah and Muhammad is His Prophet." The mere pronunciation of this formula is considered by Muslims sufficient testimony of an embrace of the Islamic religion.

26. *Tadhkira,* in Ivanow, *Truth-Worshippers,* 115–16.

27. George Thomas Keppel (Albemarie), *Personal Narrative of a Journey from India to England, by Bussorah, Baghdad, the Ruins of Babylon, Curdistan, the Court of Persia, the western shores of the Caspian Sea, Astrakhan, Nishny Novogorod, Moscow, and St. Petersburgh in the year 1824* (London: H. Colburn, 1827), 2:61.

28. Stead, "The Ali Ilahi Sect," 185.

29. Al-Karmali, "al-Dawuda aw al-Dawudiyyun," 63.

30. Khan, "The Sect of Ahl-i Haqq (Ali Ilahis)," 34; de Gobineau, *Trois ans en Asie,* 340; and S. G. Wilson, *Persian Life and Customs,* 236 and 240.

31. S. G. Wilson, *Persian Life and Customs,* 241; de Gobineau, *Trois ans en Asie*. 364; and Minorsky, *Notes Sur la Secte des Ahlé-Haqq,* 128.

32. *Tadhkira,* in Ivanow, *Truth-Worshippers,* 160. Cf. Khan, "The Sect of Ahl-i Haqq (Ali Ilahis)," 36, where he states that Sultan Sahak believed and preached Pythagorean metempsychosis.

33. Cf. Ivanow, *Truth-Worshippers,* 73–74.

34. De Gobineau, *Trois ans en Asie,* 363.

35. Adjarian, "Gyorans et Thoumaris," 301.

36. Al-Karmali, "al-Dawuda aw al-Dawudiyyun," 64–65.

37. Birge, *Bektashi Order,* 130. On the metempsychosis of the Nusyaris, see chapter 32 of this book.

38. S. G. Wilson, *Persian Life and Customs,* 240.

39. See "The People of Baron De Bode" (in Russian), quoted in Minorsky, *Notes Sur la Secte des Ahlé-Haqq,* 71.

40. Ivanow, *Truth-Worshippers,* 44.

41. S. G. Wilson, *Persian Life and Customs,* 240–41.

42. Minorsky, *Notes Sur la Secte des Ahlé-Haqq,* 130, in which Minorsky produced verses 75–78 of *The Book of the Pole.*

43. See the anonymous article in Russian signed and entitled "The Ali Ilahis," in *The Caucasus* (Tiflis, 1876), quoted in Minorsky, *Notes Sur la Secte des Ahlé-Haqq,* 129; and S. G. Wilson, *Persian Life and Customs,* 240.

44. Minorsky, *Notes Sur la Secte des Ahlé-Haqq,* 129.

45. *Tadhkira,* in Ivanow, *Truth-Worshippers,* 106.

46. See Ivanow, "An Ali-Ilahi Fragment," 1:177, 184; and idem, *Truth-Worshippers,* 47 and 169 n. 12.

47. The bibliography on the Yezidis is extensive. Here I will give for the benefit of the common reader two sources: Isya Joseph, *Devil Worship* (Boston: Richard G. Badger, 1919), 147–58 and Empson, *The Cult of the Peacock Angel* 134–35, appended by Sir Richard Carnac Temple, "A Commentary," 161–219.

48. Stead, "The Ali Ilahi Sect," 186.

49. Theodore Bent, "The Yourouks of Asia Minor," 270.

50. Khan, "The Sect of Ahl-i Haqq (Ali Ilahis)," 38.

51. Khurshid Efendi, *Siyahat Nama Hudud,* quoted in Minorsky, *Notes Sur la Secte des Ahlé-Haqq,* 74; Soane, *To Mesopotamia and Kurdistan in Disguise,* 383; Karam, "The Sect of Ali Ilahis," 77–78; Minorsky, *Notes Sur la Secte des Ahlé-Haqq,* 36, 45, 136; Ivanow, *Truth-Worshippers,* 97; and al-Karmali, "al-Dawuda aw al-Dawudiyyun," 64.

52. *Tadhkira,* in Ivanow, *Truth-Worshippers,* 152.

53. S. G. Wilson, *Persian Life and Customs,* 236; de Gobineau, *Trois ans en Asie,* 341; and Minorsky, *Notes Sur la Secte des Ahlé-Haqq,* 136.

54. Khan, "The Sect of Ahl-i Haqq (Ali Ilahis)," 42; Karam, "The Sect of the Ali Ilahis," 78; de Gobineau, *Trois ans en Asie,* 341–42; al-Karmali, "al-Dawuda aw al-Dawudiyyun," 63–64; and Adjarian, "Gyorans et Thoumaris," 300.

55. De Gobineau, *Trois ans en Asie,* 342; and Minorsky, *Notes Sur la Secte des Ahlé-Haqq,* 116.

56. Keppel, *Journey from India to England,* 2:61; Karam, "The Sect of the Ali Ilahis," 77; and S. G. Wilson, *Persian Life and Customs,* 241.

57. De Gobineau, *Les Religions et les Philosophies dans l'Asie Centrale* (Paris: Dedier, 1865), 17; and Minorsky, *Notes Sur la Secte des Ahlé-Haqq,* 125.

58. Adjarian, "Gyorans et Thoumaris," 300.

59. Al-Karmali, "al-Dawuda aw al-Dawudiyyun," 66.

60. *Tadhkira,* in Ivanow, *Truth-Worshippers,* 161.

61. Karam, "The Sect of the Ali Ilahis," 76. Cf. Minorsky, *Notes Sur la Secte des Ahlé-Haqq,* 124, and the sources he gives in footnote 4.

62. *Tadhkira,* in Ivanow, *Truth-Worshippers,* 149.

63. Ivanow, *Truth-Worshippers,* 74.

64. Soane, *To Mesopotamia and Kurdistan in Disguise,* 384.

65. H. C. Rawlinson, "Notes on a March from Zohab," 36; Petermann, *Reisen im Orient* 2:202–5; Stead, "The Ali Ilahi Sect," 185.

66. Karam, "The Sect of the Ali Ilahis," 73 and 74.

67. Ivanow, *Truth-Worshippers,* 48–57. Cf. Adjarian, "Gyorans et Thoumaris," 300 and 302.

68. De Gobineau, *Trois ans en Asie,* 338–71.

22—The Nusayris (Alawis): *Ancient Period*

1. Hanna Batatu, "Some Observations On The Social Roots Of Syria's Ruling Military Group And The Causes For Its Dominance," *The Middle East Journal* 35, no. 3 (Summer 1981): 331–32.

2. Muhammed Ghalib al-Tawil, *Tarikh al-Alawiyyin* (Beirut: Dar al-Andalus, 1981), 446–49; and Col. Paul Jacquor, *L'État des Alaouites Terre d'art, de souvenirs et de mystère* (Beirut: Emp. Catholique, 1929), 15–16.

3. Pliny, *Natural History,* Book 5, 17.

4. For a thorough description of the Nusayris habitat, see Lyde, *The Asian Mystery* (London, Longman, 1860), 1–24. This is the first major work in English on the Nusayris.

Lyde lived for many years among the Nusayris and his knowledge about them is first hand. In his preface, he states that he attempted with the sect of the Ansaireeh (Nusayris) what De Sacy had already effected with that of the Druzes. For a lengthy review of Lyde's book see Charles Henry Brigham, "The Asian Mystery," *North American Review* 93, no. 193 (October, 1861): 342–66.

5. Al-Tawil, *Tarikh al-Alawiyyin,* 521–24; Hashim Uthman, *al-Alawiyyun bayn al-Ustura wa al-Haqiqa* (Beirut: Muassasat al-Alami, 1980), 39–43; and Peter Gubser, "Minorities in Power: The Alawites of Syria," in *The Political Role of Minority Groups in the Middle East,* ed. R. D. McLaurin (New York: Praeger, 1979), 17–18.

6. Al-Tawil, *Tarikh al-Alawiyyin,* 416; Munir al-Sharif, *al-Alawiyyun: Man Hum Wa Ayna Hum* (Damascus: al-Maktaba al-Kubra li al-Talif wa al-Nashr, 1946), 69–71; Abu Musa al-Hariri, *al-Alawiyyun al-Nusayriyyun* (Beirut: n.p., 1980), 196; and Abd al-Rahman Badawi, *Madhahib al-Islamiyyin* (Beirut: Dar al-Ilm li al-Malayin, 1973), 2:497–98. Al-Makzun al-Sinjari was a prominent Nusayri mystical poet. For his poetry see Asad Ahmad Ali, *Ma'rifat Allah wa al-Makzun al-Sinjari,* 2 vols. (Beirut: Dar al-Raid al-Arabi, 1972).

7. Lyde, *The Asian Mystery,* 23 and 193–232.

8. Jacques Weulersse, *Le Pays des Alouites* (Tour: Arrault, 1940), 1:121.

9., Gubser, "The Alawites of Syria," 20.

10. Cf. Lyde, *The Asian Mystery,* 55–56; and the sources the author cites.

11. Bar Hebraeus, *Chronography,* 1:150.

12. Bar Hebraeus *Tarikh Mukhtasar al-Duwal,* 97, 150. Cf. Abu al-Fida, *Kitab al-Mukhtasar fi Akhbar al-Bashar* (Beirut: Dar al-Fikr and Dar al-Bihar, 1959), 3:70; and Jamal al-Din Abu al-Faraj Ibn al-Jawzi, *Talbis Iblis* (Beirut: Dar al-Kutub al-Ilmiyyam, 1368/1948), 104.

13. Antoine Isaac Silvestre De Sacy, *Exposé de la Religion des Druzes,* (Paris: L'Impremerie Royale, 1838), 2:565 and 567.

14. Wolff, "Auszüge aus dem Katechismus der Nossairier," *Zeitschrift der deutschen morgenländischen Gesellschaft* (1849). 3:302. The Arabic original of this Nusayri catechism, entitled *Kitab Ta'lim al-Diyana al-Nusayriyya,* is found in Arab MS. 6182, Bibliothèque Nationale. For an abridged English translation of the same, see Lyde, *The Asian Mystery,* 270–80.

15. Ernest Renan, *Mission de Phénicie* (Paris: Impremerie, Impériale, 1864), 114; and Dussaud, *Histoire et Religion des Nosairis,* 9. For further information on the etymology of the name of the Nusayris, see Massignon, "Nusairi," *The Encyclopedia of Islam* (Leiden and London: E. J. Brill, 1936), 3:963.

16. Al-Tawil, *Tarikh al-Alawiyyin,* 446–47.

17. See Uthman, *al-Alawiyyun,* 35–36; and Muhammad Kurd Ali, *Kitat al-Sham* (Beirut: Dar al-Ilm li al-Malayin, 1971), 6:260, whose idea about the origin of the term of Nusayris was misunderstood by Uthman.

18. Lyde, *The Asian Mystery,* 68.

19. See the Druze Catechism (Formulary) in Arab MS. 5188, fols. 51–52, Bibliothèque Nationale. Other copies are found in Arab MSS. 1445, 1446, and 1447, Bibliothèque Nationale; and De Sacy, *Exposé,* 2:260.

20. Sulayman al-Adani, *Kitab al-Bakura al-Sulaymaniyya fi Kashf Asrar al-Diyana al-Nusayriyya* (Beirut: n.p., n.d.), 14–16. Although the book contains no date of publication, many authors accept the year 1863 as the date of its publication. For an English translation of the same, see Edward Salisbury, "Notes on the Book of Sulaiman's First Ripe Fruit Disclosing the Mysteries of the Nosairian Religion," *Journal of the American Oriental Society* 8 (1864): 227–308; the reference here is to page 242. See also, Rev. Louis Cheihho, "Jawla fi al-Dawla al-Alawiyya," *al-Mashriq* 22, No. 7 (Beirut, 1924): 481–95; Abd al-Husayn Mahdi

al-Askari, *al-Alawiyyun aw al-Nusayriyya* (n.p., 1980), 31, n.1; Taqi Sharaf al-Din, *al-Nusayriyya: Dirasa Tahliliyya* (Beirut: n.p., 1983), 111; Badawi, *Madhahib al-Islamiyyin,* 2:441; and al-Hariri, *al-Alawiyyun al-Nusayriyyun,* 27–30.

21. Louis Massignon, "Les Nusairis," *Opera Minora* (Beirut: Dar al-Maarif, 1963), 1:619; and idem, "Nusairi," 963.

22. Lyde, *The Asian Mystery,* 58–59 and 235. Lyde states that the copy of *Kitab al-Mashyakha* (Manual for Shaykhs) in his possession contains 188 pages transcribed in the handwriting of a certain Shaykh Muhammad of the village of Bishargo, which he had transcribed from an old copy in the year 1239/1824. It contains all the chief parts of the religion of the Nusayris. The First reference to this manuscript was made by Joseph Catafago, dragoman of the Prussian Consulate in Beirut; for his description of it, see the *Journal Asiatic* (July 1848), 72–78.

23. R. Strothmann, "Seelenwanderung bei den Nusairi," *Oriens* 12 (1959): 104. In this article, Strothmann published Arabic excerpts from two books, *Kitab al-Ma'arif and Kitab al-Dala'il wa al Masa'il,* by the Nusayri writer Maymun Abu al-Qasim al-Tabarani (d. 1034), using as his source a rare manuscript. See MS. Orient 304, fol. 81, Hamburger Staats-und Universität-Bibliothek.

24. Al-Shaykh Yusuf Ibn al-Ajuz (known as al-Nashshabi), *Munazara* (debate) in Arab MS. 1450, fols. 68–155, Bibliothèque Nationale. The reference here is to fols. 118–119; and al-Jisri, *Risalat al-Tawhid,* Arab MS 1450, fol. 44.

25. *Kitab al-Majmu* contains sixteen suras (chapters) incorporated by Sulayam al-Adani in his *Kitab al-Bakura.* The reference here is to page 15 in al-Adani, *Kitab al-Bakura.* See also page 16. *Kitab al-Majmu* was published with a French translation by René Dussaud in his *Histoire et Religion des Nosairis,* 161–98. The Arabic text of the same is found in Abu Musa al-Hariri's *al-Alawiyyun al-Nusayriyyun,* 234–55, and in al-Husayni Abd Allah, *al-Judhur al-Tarikhiyya li al-Nusayriyya al-Alawiyya* (Dubai: Dar al-Itisam, 1980), 145–74. Because of his conversion to Christianity, al-Adani was lured by his own people to the city of Latakia, where he was burned to death. See Farid Wajdi, *Da'irat Ma'arif al-Qarn al-Ishrin,* 2nd ed. (Cairo: Matbaat Dairat Maarif al-Qarn al-Ishrin, 1925), 10:252.

26. Shaykh Isa Suud, "Ma Aghfalahu al-Tarikh: al-Alawiyyun aw al-Nusayriyya," *Majallat al-Amani,* nos. 1–3 (October–November and December 1930), nos. 6–7 (March–April 1931), and no. 8 (May 1931). This article is reproduced in Uthman, *al-Alawiyyun,* 156–73; see especially pages 157 and 161. Cf. Mustafa Ghalib, *al-Harakat al-Batiniyya fi al-Islam* (Beirut: Dar al-Andalus, 1982), 272.

27. Saad Ibn Abd Allah al-Ashari, *al-Maqalat wa al-Firaq,* 100–1.

28. Al-Nawbakhti, *Firaq al-Shi'a,* 102–3.

29. Abu Amr Muhammad Ibn Abd al-Aziz al-Kashshi, *Ma'rifat Akhbar al-Rijal,* ed. Ahmad al-Husayni (Karbala: Muassasat al-Alami, n.d.), 438.

30. Al-Shaibi, al-Fikr al-Shi'i, 18.

31. Abu Jafar al-Tusi, *al-Ghayba,* 244.

32. Abu Mansur Ahmad Ibn Ali al-Tabarsi, *al-Ihtijaj,* 2:290–91.

33. Al-Hasan Ibn Yusuf Ibn al-Mutahhar al-Hilli, *al-Rijal,* (al-Najaf: al-Matbaa al-Haydariyya, 1961), 245–57.

34. Shaykh Muhammad Hasan al-Zayn al-Amili, *al-Shi'a fi al-Tarikh,* 2nd ed., (Beirut: Dar al-Athar li al-Tibaa wa al-Nashr, 1979), 95 and 219–25. For more information see al-Askari, *al-Alawiyyun aw al-Nusayriyya,* 33–42.

35. Al-Ashari, *Maqalat,* 15; and Abd al-Qahir al-Baghdadi, *al-Farq bayn al-Firaq,* 252 and 255.

36. Al-Shahrastani, *Kitab al-Milal,* printed on the margin of Ibn Hazm's *Kitab al-Fisal,* 2:24–26.

37. Al-Shahrastani, *Kitab al-Milal,* 24–26; and Abbas al-Azzawi, *al-Kaka'iyya fi al-Tarikh,* 64.

38. Ibn Hazm, *Kitab al-Fisal,* 4:188.

39. Bar Hebraeus, *Chronography,* 1:150; and idem, *Tarikh Mukhtasar al-Duwal,* 149–50. This fatwa by Ibn Taymiyya entitled "Fatwa fi al-Nusayriyya," was published by Stanislas Guyard, "Le Fatwa d'Ibn Taimiyyah sur Les Nosairis," *Journal Asiatique* 17 (August–September, 1871), 158–98. The reference here is to p. 162 of the Arabic text. This fatwa is reproduced in several sources especially those of Badawi, *Madhahib al-Islamiyyin,* 2:449–57; Uthman, *al-Alawiyyun bayn al-Ustura wa al-Haqiqa,* 52–58; al-Husayni Abd Allah, *al-Judhur al-Tarikhiyya,* 28–51; and Mujahid al-Amin, *al-Nusayriyya, (al-Alawiyyun), Aqa'iduhum, Tarikhuhum, Waqi'uhum* (Beirut: Dar al-Fikr, n.d.), 47–66.

40. Imad al-Din Ismail Abu al-Fida, *Kitab al-Mukhtasar,* 3:70.

41. As an example of the opinions of contemporary writers we give those of al-Shaibi, *al-Sila bayn al-Tasawwuf wa al-Tashayyu,* 145–56; and idem, *al-Fikr al-Shi'i,* 18 and 36; Muhammad Abu Zahra, *Tarikh al-Madhahib al-Islamiyya* (Cairo: Dar al-Fikr al-Arabi, n.d.), 1:67–68; and Mustafa al-Shaka, *Islam bila Madhahib* (Beirut: al-Dar al-Misriyya li al-Tibaa, 1971), 301–18.

42. *Kitab al-Mashyakha,* in Lyde, *The Asian Mystery,* 60; al-Adani, *Kitab al-Bakura,* 14; al-Tawil, *Tarikh al-Alawiyyin,* 256, 258; and al-Hariri, *al-Alawiyyun al-Nusayriyyun,* 30–31.

43. Al-Tawil, *Tarikh al-Alawiyyin,* 256, 258.

44. Ibid., and al-Khasibi, *Kitab al-Hidaya al-Kubra* appended to Uthman, *al-Alawiyyun,* 229–96.

45. *Kitab al-Mashyakha,* in Lyde, *The Asian Mystery,* 60–61; al-Adani, *Kitab al-Bakura,* 14–16, 27, and 47; *Kitab Ta'lim al-Diyana al-Nusayriyya,* question 98 and its answer Arab MS 6182, fol. 16, Bibliothèque Nationale; Wolff, "Auszüge aus dem Katechismus der Nossairien," 3:303; and Lyde, *The Asian Mystery,* 280.

46. Joseph Catafago, "Drei Messen der Nosairier," *Zeitschrift der deutschen morgenländischen Gesellschaft* (1848), 2:388–94. The Arabic version of these masses are also found in Badawi, *Madhahib al-Islamiyyin,* 2:490–94; al-Askari, *al-Alawiyyun aw al-Nusayriyya,* 105–9; and Victor Langlois, "Religion et Doctrine des Noussaries," *Revue d'Orient et d' l'Algerie et des Colonies* in *Societe Orientale De France,* (Paris: Juin 1856), 3:435–37.

47. Wolff, "Auszüge aus des Katechismus der Nossairien," 303–9. For Arabic versions of *Kitab Ta'lim al-Diyana al-Nusayriyya,* see Arab MS. 6182, Bibliothèque Nationale; Badawi, *Madhahib al-Islamiyyin,* 474–87; and al-Askari, *al-Alawiyyun aw al-Nusayriyya,* 82–96.

48. Al-Adani, *Kitab al-Bakura,* 17.

49. Ibid.

50. *Kitab al-Mashyakha,* in Lyde, *The Asian Mystery,* 62.

51. Al-Adani, *Kitab al-Bakura,* 90.

52. Arab MS. 6182, fol, 19, Bibliothèque Natioanle; Wolff, "Auszüge aus dem Katechismus der Nossairien," 308–9; Lyde, *The Asian Mystery,* 280; Badawi, *Madhahib al-Islamiyyin,* 2:487; and al-Askari, *al-Alawiyyun aw al-Nusyriyya,* 96.

53. Al-Tawil, *Tarikh al-Alawiyyin,* 256–60; and Suud, "Ma Aghfalahu al-Tarikh," in Uthman, *al-Alawiyyun,* 157.

54. Al-Adani, *Kitab al-Bakura,* 16.

55. Ibid.

56. Bar Hebraeus, *Chronography,* 150; idem, *Tarikh Mukhtasar al-Duwal,* 14–50; Ibn al-Jawzi, *Talbis Iblis,* 104; Lyde, *The Asian Mystery,* 63–64; and al-Hariri, *al-Alawiyyun al-Nusayriyyun,* 33.

57. Bar Hebraeus, *Tarikh Mukhtasar al-Duwal,* 149–50.
58. Abu al-Fida, *Kitab al-Mukhtasar,* 3:70; and De Sacy, *Exposé,* 2:567.
59. De Sacy, *Exposé,* 1:183.
60. Al-Tawil, *Tarikh al-Alawiyyin,* 258.
61. Abu al-Fida, *Kitab al-Mukhtasar,* 3:70; and Lyde, *The Asian Mystery,* 66.
62. Shaykh Isa Suud in Uthman, *al-Alawiyyun,* 168–69.
63. Al-Tawil, *Tarikh al-Alawiyyin,* 258, 261.

23—The Nusayris: *Middle Period*

1. Al-Tawil, *Tarikh al-Alawiyyin,* 264–65; *Kitab al-Bakura,* 17; Massignon, "Nusairi," 3:966–67; and Joseph Catafago, "Notices sur Les Anserien," *Journal Asiatique* (February 1848): 149–56. The entire work was published by R. Strothmann in *Der Islam,* 27 (1943–44), 1–60 and (1946), 160–273. Cf. Badawi, *Madhahib al-Islamiyyin,* 2:462–66.
2. Al-Tawil, *Tarikh al-Alawiyyin,* 262–64.
3. Ibid., 262–63 and Massignon, "Nusairi," 966.
4. Al-Tawil, *Tarikh al-Alawiyyin,* 262–64.
5. Al-Adani, *Kitab al-Bakura,* 11–12.
6. Al-Tawil, *Tarikh al-Alawiyyin,* 264.
7. Weulersse, *Le Pays des Alaouites,* 49, 54, 73, and 288; and al-Din, *al-Nusayriyya,* 52–56.
8. Munir al-Sharif, *al-Alawiyyun: Man Hum wa Ayna Hum,* 93.
9. Al-Adani, *Kitab al-Bakura,* 53–54, 81.
10. Stanislas Guyard, "Le Fatwa d'Ibn Taimiyyah sur Les Nosairis," *Journal Asiatique,* 17 (1871): 158–98. The reference here is to page 175.
11. Bar Hebraeus, *Chronography,* 1:235.
12. See the Fatwa of Ibn Taymiyya published in Guyard, "Les Fatawa d'Ibn Taimiyyah," 169.
13. Al-Hariri, *al-Alawiyyun al-Nusayriyyun,* 210. For the castles the Ismailis captured from the Nusayris, see Lyde, *The Asian Mystery,* 64.
14. Lyde, *The Asian Mystery,* 69.
15. Al-Tawil, *Tarikh al-Alawiyyin,* 359–63.
16. Ibid., 363.
17. Philip Hitti, *History of Syria* (New York: MacMillan, 1951), 631.
18. See the Fatwa of Ibn Taymiyya in Guyard, "de Fatawa d'Ibn Taimiyyah," 169.
19. Ibid., 169, 174.
20. Ibn Battuta, *The Travels of Ibn Battuta* A.D. 1325–1352, translated with revision and notes from the Arabic text edited by C. Defrémery and B. R. Sanguinetti by H. A. R. Gibb (Cambridge: at the University Press, 1962), 1:111–12, Cf. Abu al-Mahasin Ibn Taghri Birdi, *al-Nujum al-Zahira fi Muluk Misr wa al-Qahira* (Cairo: Dar al-Kutub al-Misriyya, 1938), 7:150.
21. *The Travels of Ibn Battuta,* 1:112.
22. Al-Tawil, *Tarikh al-Alawiyyin,* 365, 377–78.
23. Hitti, *History of Syria,* 631.
24. Al-Tawil, *Tarikh al-Alawiyyin,* 365 and 378.
25. Kamal al-Din al-Fadl Abd al-Razzaq Ibn al-Futi, *al-Hawadith al-Jami'a wa al-Tajarib al-Nafi'a fi al-Mi'a al-Sabi'a,* ed. Mustafa Jawad (Baghdad: al-Maktaba al-Arabiyya, 1351/1932), 329; and Imad al-Din Ibn Kathir, *al-Bidaya wa al-Nihaya,* 13:203.

26. Ibn Kathir, *al-Bidaya wa al-Nihaya,* 8:219; and Abu al-Fida, *Kitab al-Mukhtasar,* 3:273–74.

27. Ibn al-Futi, *al-Hawadith al-Jami'a,* 455.

28. Al-Shaibi, *al-Fikr al-Shi'i,* 80.

29. Ibn al-Futi, *al-Hawadith al-Jami'a,* 478; Ibn Kathir, *al-Bidaya wa al-Nihaya,* 14:121; Ibn Hajar al-Asqalani, *al-Durar al-Kamina fi A'yan al-Mi'a al-Thamina* (Haydarabad: Matbaat Majlis Dariat al-Maarif al-Nizamiyya, 1348–50/1929–32), 1:501.

30. Ibn Kathir, *al-Bidaya wa al-Nihaya,* 14:83–84; Abu al-Fida, *Kitab al-Mukhtasar,* 7:97; and Abu al-Falah Abd al-Hayy Ibn al-Imad, *Shadharat al-Dhahab fi Akhbar man Dhahab* (Cairo: Maktabat al-Qudsi, 1350–51/1931–32), 1:43. Cf. Lyde, *The Asian Mystery,* 70–71; and al-Shaibi, *al-Fikr al-Shi'i,* 89.

31. *The Travels of Ibn Battuta,* 1:112–13.

32. Al-Shaibi, *al-Fikr al-Shi'i,* 168.

33. Ahmad Ibn Muhammad Ibn Abd Allah al-Dimashqi known as Ibn Arabshah, *Aja'ib al-Maqdur fi Akhbar Timur* (Cairo: Bulaq, 1285/1868), 7; al-Sakhawi, *al-Daww al-Lami,* 3:15; Ibn al-Imad, *Shadharat al-Dhahab,* 7:43.

34. Abd al-Razzaq Ibn Ishaq al-Samarqandi, *Matla al-Sa'dayn,* Cambridge Persian MS. Add. 185(12), fol. 272, Cambridge University; Abu Talib al-Husayni, *Malfuzat Sahib Qiran,* Persian MS. 7575, fol. 2, British Museum; and al-Shaibi, *al-Fikr al-Shi'i,* 169.

35. Al-Samarqandi, *Matla al-Sadayn,* fol. 34b.

36. Al-Tawil, *Tarikh al-Alawiyyin,* 388.

37. Al-Husayni *Mulfuzat Sahib Qiran,* fol. 34b. For more on this subject consult al-Shaibi, *al-Fikr al-Shi'i,* 167–73.

38. Al-Tawil, *Tarikh al-Alawiyyin,* 390–91.

39. Ibid., 391.

40. See the Ottoman Baş Vekalet Muhimmat Defteri Arsif(7), 80, Stautes 1835, 1984 and 2021; and al-Din, *al-Nusayriyya,* 60.

41. Al-Tawil, *Tarikh al-Alawiyyin,* 394–95; and Sati al-Husri, *al-Bilad al-Arabiyya wa al-Dawla al-Uthmaniyya* (Beirut: Dar al-Ilm li al-Malayin, 1965), 16–17.

42. Al-Tawil, *Tarikh al-Alawiyyin,* 396.

43. Al-Tawil, *Tarikh al-Alawiyyin,* 397.

44. See *al-Sayyad,* no. 1123 (24 March 1966), 21; and al-Hariri, *al-Alawiyyun al-Nusayriyyun,* note a.

45. Al-Tawil, *Tarikh al-Alawiyyin,* 399 and 434–36.

46. Ibid., 399.

47. Ibid., 442.

48. John Lewis Burckhardt, *Travels in Syria and the Holy Land* (London: John Murray, 1822), 152–53.

49. Ibid., 71.

50. Lyde, *The Asian Mystery,* 195–96.

51. Ibid.

52. Al-Tawil, *Tarikh al-Alawiyyin,* 452.

53. Jacquot, *L'Etat des Alaouites,* 15.

54. Ibid., al-Tawil, *Tarikh al-Alawiyyin,* 451; and al-Hariri, *al-Alawiyyun al-Nusayriyyun,* 215–16.

55. Lyde, *The Asian Mystery,* 199–200 and 231; and al-Tawil, *Tarikh al-Alawiyyin,* 421–25.

56. Lyde, *The Asian Mystery,* 199–200 and 208.

57. Al-Tawil, *Tarikh al-Alawiyyin,* 418–38.

58. Lyde, *The Asian Mystery,* 209, 211, 214, 216, 222–23.

59. Badawi, *Madhahib al-Islamiyyin,* 2:498.

60. Al-Tawil, *Tarikh al-Alawiyyin,* 454–58.

61. Ibid., 458.

62. Wajih Kawtharani, *Bilad al-Sham* (Beirut: Mahad al-Inma al-Arabi, 1980), 79.

63. Farid Wajdi, *Da'irat Ma'arif al-Qarn al-Ishrin,* 2nd. ed. (Cairo: Matbaat Dairat Maarif al-Qarn al-Ishrin, 1925), 10:252; Badawi, *Madhahib al-Islamiyyin,* 2:499; al-Hariri, *al-Alawiyyun al-Nusayriyyun,* 217; and al-Din, *al-Nusayriyya,* 63–64.

64. Wajdi, *Da'irat Ma'arif,* 10:252; Yusuf al-Hakim, *Suriyya wa al-Ahd al-Faysali,* 2nd ed., (Beirut: al-Matbaa al-Katholikiyya, 1980), 70–71; Muhammad Kurd Ali, *Khitat al-Sham,* 3:108; and al-Din, *al-Nusayriyya,* 64–65.

24—The Nusayris: *Under the French Mandate*

1. For the territorial division of Syria, consult A. Hourani, *Syria and Lebanon: A Political Essay* (London: Oxford University Press, 1946); Hasan al-Hakim, *al-Wath'iq al-Tarikhiyya al-Muta'alliqa bi al-Qadiyya al-Suriyya* (Beirut: Dar Sadir, 1974), 254; Kawtharani, *Bilad al-Sham,* 220–21; Dhuqan Qarqut, *Tatawwur al-Haraka al-Wataniyya fi Suriyya* (Beirut: Dar al-Talia, 1975), 61; and Archives du Ministère des Affaires Étrangères, Serie E-Levant-Syrie-Lebanon, Paris vol. 125.

2. Yusuf al-Hakim, *Suriyya,* 52–53; and Cheikho, "Jawla fi al-Dawla al-Alawiyya," *al-Mashriq* 22, no. 7 (1924), 481–95.

3. Gubser, "The Alawites of Syria," 40.

4. Tabitha Petran, *Syria: A Modern History* (London: Ernest Ben Ltd., 1972), 62; and Nikolas Van Dam, *The Struggle for Power in Syria* (London: Croom Helm, 1979), 18.

5. Kawtharani, *Bilad al-Sham,* 211.

6. Shaykh Mahmud al-Salih, *al-Naba al-Yaqin an al-Alawiyyin* (n.p.: n.p., 1961), 127.

7. Al-Hakim, *Suriyya,* 14 and 91.

8. Ibid., 14; and al-Din, *al-Nusayriyya,* 68–69.

9. Qarqut, *Tatawwur al-Haraka,* 32.

10. Al-Din, *al-Nusayriyya,* 69.

11. Abd al-Latif al-Yunus, *Thawrat al-Shaykh Salih al-Ali* (Damascus: Dar al-Yaqza al-Arabiyya, 1961), 107; Badawi, *Madahhib al-Islamiyyin,* 2:500–1; al-Sharif, *al-Alawiyyun: Man Hum wa Ayna Hum,* 110–11; al-Salih, *al-Naba al-Yaqin,* 125–26; al-Hariri, *al-Alawiyyun al-Nusayriyyun,* 221–26; and Ali Rida, *Qissat al-Kifah al-Watani fi Suriyya Askariyyan wa Siyasiyyan hatta al-Jala* (Halab: al-Matbaa al-Haditha, 1979), 23.

12. Badawi, *Madhahib al-Islamiyyin,* 2:501; and al-Yunus, *Thawrat al-Shaykh Salih al-Ali,* 107.

13. Al-Yunus, *Thawrat al-Shaykh Salih al-Ali,* 72–85.

14. Badawi, *Madhahib al-Islamiyyin,* 2:500.

15. Ibid., 501.

16. Jacquot, *L'État des Alaouites,* 15.

17. Al-Sharif, *al-Alawiyyun: Man Hum wa Ayna Hum,* 110–11.

18. Al-Yunus, *Thawrat al-Shaykh Salih al-Ali,* 219–28; Badawi, *Madhahib al-Islamiyyin,* 2:503–05; and al-Hariri, *al-Alawiyyun, al-Nusayriyyun,* 223–24.

19. Al-Din, *al-Nusayriyya,* 73.

20. Ibid.; and Rida, *Qissat al-Kifah,* 34.

21. Al-Din, *al-Nusayriyya,* 74–75.

22. Al-Din, *al-Nusayriyya,* 74; and Kawtharani, *Bilad al-Sham,* 372.

23. Rida, *Qissat al-Kifah,* 32; Kawtharani, *Bilad al-Sham,* 372–73; and Weulersse, *Le Pays des Alouites,* 118.

23. Al-Din, *al-Nusayriyya,* 74–75.

24. See the report of the British consul in Damascus to his government in British Archive Fo 225/226, dated 10 October 1944, and in the Arabic magazine *al-Tadamun,* 2, no. 68 (28 July 1984): 36–37.

25. Ibid.

26. Kawtharani, *Bilad al-Sham,* 235–36; Qarqut, *Tatawwur al-Haraka,* 56–58; and al-Din, *al-Nusayriyya,* 81–82, 85, 88.

27. Archives du Ministère des Affaires Étrangères, Levant, Syrie-Leban, Paris, file no. 510, 114, document 124.

28. Ibid., file 492, p. 193, Document 412.

29. Ibid.

30. Ibid., file 492, 53.

31. On Sulayman al-Murshid, see Khayr al-Din al-Zirrikli, *Qamus al-A'lam* (Beirut: Dar al-Ilm li al-Malayin, 1979), 3:170; *al-Tadamun* 2, no. 68, 28 July 1984, 36–37; and Stephen Longrigg, *Syria and Lebanon,* (New York: Octagon Books, 1972), 344, where the author describes al-Murshid as "the obese and half-shrewd, half crazy god Sulayman al-Murshid." For the memorandum submitted to Blum, see Archives du Ministère, Paris, file 3547; al-Hariri, *al-Alawiyyun al-Nusayriyyun,* 228–35; and Mujahid al-Amin, *al-Nusayriyya (al-Alawiyyun), Aqa'iduhum, Tarikkukum, Waqi'uhum* (Beirut: Dar al-Fik, nod.), 72–73. Cf. Gubser, "The Alawites of Syria," 24.

32. Archives du Ministère, files 492 and 493, which contains cable no. 347–49, dated 2 July 1936, sent by the French minister of foreign affairs to the French high commissioner in Beirut. Cf. al-Din, *al-Nusayriyya,* 92.

33. Archives du Ministère, file no. 492 and 493, including cable no. 557 from Delbos to the French high commissioner, dated 25 August 1936; Arabic excerpts of the same are in al-Din, *al-Nusayriyya,* 90, 92–93.

34. Archives du Ministère, E. 412.2, file 393, 8 and file 493, 7; and al-Din, *al-Nusayriyya,* 94.

35. Archives du Ministère, file no. 493, 229. The letter of the high commissioner to the foreign minister is no. 852, dated 28 August 1936.

37. Al-Hariri, *al-Alawiyyun al-Nusayriyyun,* 233–34.

25—The Nusayris: *Rise to Political Power*

1. Batatu, "Social Roots of Syria's Ruling Group," 341.

2. Archives du Ministère, file 419, 1940, document 2619 dated 4 October 1935. This document contains the letter of the French minister of war to the French foreign minister. Cf. Petran, *Syria: A Modern History,* 62; Van Dam, *The Struggle for Power in Syria,* 18; Gubser, "The Alawites of Syria," 40.

3. Batatu, "Social Roots of Syria's Ruling Group," 341.

4. Ibid., 334; and al-Yunus, *Thawrat al-Shaykh Salih al-Ali,* 178.

5. Batatu, "Social Roots of Syria's Ruling Group," 334, 342; and Gubser, "The Alawites of Syria," 40.

6. Batatu, "Social Roots of Syria's Ruling Group," 342; and Gubser, "The Alawites of Syria," 40.

7. Gubser, "The Alawites of Syria," 40; Gordon H. Torrey, "Aspects of the Political Elite in Syria," in *Political Elite in the Middle East,* ed. George Lenczowski (Washington, D.C.: The American Enterprise Institute for Public Policy Research, 1975), 157; Van Dam, *The Struggle for Power in Syria,* 41; Michael Van Dusen, "Political Integration and Regionalism in Syria," *The Middle East Journal* 26, no. 2 (Spring, 1972): 133–34; and al-Din, *al-Nusayriyya,* 164–65.

8. Gubser, "The Alawites of Syria," 39–40; and Moshe Maoz, "Attempts at Creating a Political Community in Modern Syria," *The Middle East Journal* 26, no. 4 (Autumn 1972); 399; and idem "The Emergence of Modern Syria," in *Syria under Asad,* ed. Moshe Maoz and Avner Yaniv (New York: St. Martin's, 1986), 22–34.

9. Umar F. Abd Allah, *The Islamic Struggle in Syria* (Berkeley: Mizan Press, 1983), 50. For a concise account of the political process in Syria 1945–70 see R. Hrair Dekmejian, *Islam in Revolution: Fundamentalism in the Arab World.* (Syracuse: Syracuse, University Press, 1985), 110–12.

10. For these coups of 1949, see Alford Carleton, "The Syrian Coups d'Etat of 1949," *The Middle East Journal,* 4 no. 1 (January 1950): 1–11; George M. Haddad, *Revolution and Military Rule in the Middle East: The Arab States* (New York: Robert Speller & Son, 1971), 2:195–204; Petran, *Syria: A Modern History,* 96–98; Richard F. Nyrop, ed., *Syria: A Country Study* (Washington D.C.: American University Foreign Area Studies, 1979), 29.

11. Haddad, *Revolution and Military Rule,* 2:204–15; Gubser, "The Alawites of Syria," 40; Van Dam, *The Struggle for Power in Syria,* 41–42.

12. A. R. Kelidar, *"Religion and State in Syria," Journal of the Royal Central Asian Society* 41, (New Series, vol. 5, part 1) (February 1974): 17.

13. Batatu, "Social Roots of Syria's Ruling Group," 341.

14. Van Dusen, "Integration and Regionalism in Syria," 126.

15. Gubser, "The Alawites of Syria," 41.

16. Petran, *Syria: A Modern History* 74 and 89–92; Nyrop, *Syria: A Country Study,* 162–63; John F. Devlin, *The Ba'th Party: A History from its Origin to 1966,* (Stanford: Hoover Institution Press, 1976), 162–63; and Van Dusen, "Integration and Regionalism in Syria," 134.

17. Van Dusen, "Integration and Regionalism in Syria," 134.

18. Petran, *Syria: A Modern History,* 106 and 111–20; Haddad, *Revolution and Military Rule,* 2:231 and 233; Devlin, *The Ba'th Party,* 65–73; and Abd Allah, *The Islamic Struggle in Syria,* 52.

19. Haddad, *Revolution and Military Rule,* 2:237–38.

20. Van Dam, *The Struggle for Power in Syria,* 32; and al-Din, *al-Nusayriyya,* 183.

21. Gubser, "The Alawites of Syria," 41.

22. Van Dusen, "Integration and Regionalism in Syria," 132–33.

23. Haddad, *Revolution and Military rule,* 2:231.

24. Ibid,; Petran, *Syria: A Modern History,* 146 and 171; Batatu, "Social Roots of Syria's Ruling Group," 343; Abd Allah, *The Islamic Struggle in Syria,* 56; Bernard Vernier, *Armée et Politique au Moyen Orient* (Paris: Payot, 1966), 144; and al-Din, *al-Nusayriyya,* 166–67.

25. Petran, *Syria: A Modern History,* 146 and 171; Batatu, "Social Roots of Syria's Ruling Group," 343; and Abd Allah, *The Islamic Struggle in Syria,* 56.

26. Haddad, *Revolution and Military Rule,* 2:321; Gubser, "The Alawites of Syria," 42–43; and Batatu, "Social Roots of Syria's Ruling Group," 343.

27. Michael Hudson, *Arab Politics* (New Haven: Yale University Press, 1977), 64, where the author states that not until the 1960s that the Alawite political identity became a factor in Syrian politics. Cf. al-Hariri, *al-Alawiyyun al-Nusayriyyun,* 234–35.

28. Al-Hariri, *al-Alawiyyun al-Nusayriyyun,* 234–35.

29. Avraham Ben-Tzur, "The Neo Ba'th Party in Syria," *New Outlook* 12, no. 1 (January 1969): 27.

30. Gubser, "The Alawites of Syria," 42 and Van Dam, *The Struggle for Power in Syria,* 41–42.

31. Munif al-Razzaz, *al-Tajriba al-Murra* (Beirut: Dar Ghandur, 1967), 86–90; Haddad, *Revolution and Military Rule,* 11, 2:309–12, 391–94; Itamar Rabinovich, *Syria Under the Ba'th 1963–1966* (Tel Aviv: Israel Universities Press, 1977) 43–74; and H. Hrair Dekmejian, *Islam in Revolution: Fundamentalism in the Arab World* (Syracuse: Syracuse University Press, 1985), 111.

32. Van Dam, *The Struggle for Power in Syria,* 43; Petran, *Syria: A Modern History,* 171; Abd Allah, *The Islamic Struggle in Syria,* 58; al-Din, *al-Nusayriyya,* 167–68.

33. Van Dam, *The Struggle for Power in Syria,* 43; Petran, *Syria: A Modern History,* 171; and al-Din, *al-Nusayriyya,* 168.

34. Petran, *Syria: A Modern History,* 171.

35. Van Dam, *The Struggle for Power in Syria,* 36.

36. Al-Razzaz, *al-Tajriba al-Murra,* 158; and Haddad, *Revolution and Military Rule,* 2:190–91.

37. Batatu, "Social Roots of Syria's Ruling Group," 343. For this coup see Haddad, *Revolution and Military Rule,* 2:312–19.

38. Van Dam, *The Struggle for Power in Syria,* 40; and Petran, *Syria: A Modern History,* 170.

39. Al-Hariri, *al-Alawiyyun al-Nusayriyyun,* 325.

40. Van Dam, *The Struggle for Power in Syria,* 51–53.

41. Al-Razzaz, *al-Tajriba al-Murra,* 62–64, 94–96; and Haddad, *Revolution and Military Rule,* 2:320–23.

42. Haddad, *Revolution and Military Rule,* 2:322–23.

43. Al-Hariri, *al-Alawiyyun al-Nusayriyyun,* 235–36. Al-Hariri states that he was able to obtain classified materials on the decisions of several Nusayri meetings including the one under discussion, but he gives no information of how he received such classified information.

44. Haddad, *Revolution and Military Rule,* 2:342–51; and Rabinovich, *Syria Under the Ba'th,* 160–64, 180–83; Van Dam, *The Struggle for Power in Syria,* 54–56.

45. Sami al-Jundi, *al-Ba'th* (Beirut: Dar al-Nahar, 1969), 144.

46. Ibid., 144–45.

47. Petran, *Syria: A Modern History,* 239–48; Devlin, *The Ba'th Party, 281 and 303; Nyrop, Syria: A Country Study,* 33–34; Abd Allah, *The Islamic Struggle in Syria,* 53–54 Rabinovich, *Syria Under the Ba'th,* 195–204.

48. Petran, *Syria: A Modern History,* 167, 169; and Batatu, "Social Roots of Syria's Ruling Group," 343.

49. Van Dam, *The Struggle for Power in Syria,* 60; and al-Din, *al-Nusayriyya,* 173–74.

50. Petran, *Syria: A Modern History,* 239–48; Devlin, *The Ba'th Party,* 281–303; Haddad, *Revolution and Military Rule,* 2:352–58; and Van Dam, *The Struggle for Power in Syria,* 60–62.

51. Ibid.

52. Kelidar, "Religion and State in Syria," 17.

53. Al-Razzaz, *al-Tajriba al-Murra,* 200–4; and Haddad, *Revolution and Military Rule,* 360.

54. Van Dam, *The Struggle for Power in Syria,* 78.

55. Ibid., 69–70; and Haddad, *Revolution and Military Rule,* 362–64.

56. Van Dam, *The Struggle for Power in Syria,* 67–70; and Haddad, *Revolution and Military Rule,* 2:362–64.

57. Van Dam, *The Struggle for Power in Syria,* 75.

58. Ibid.

59. Haddad, *Revolution and Military Rule,* 2:364.

60. Al-Hariri, *al-Alawiyyun al-Nusayriyyun,* 236–37.

61. Ibid., 236; and *al-Sayyad,* no. 1123 (24 March 1966), 18–21.

62. *Al-Hawadith,* no. 518 (14 October 1966) and no. 608, (5 July 1968), no. 610 (19 July 1968) and no. 614 (8 August 1968); and al-Hariri, *al-Alawiyyun al-Nusayriyyun,* 237–39.

63. *Al-Hawadith,* no. 614 (16 August 1968).

64. Al-Hariri, *al-Alawiyyun al-Nusayriyyun,* 238.

65. Saad Jumua, *al-Mu'amara wa Ma'rakat al-Masir* (Beirut: Dar al-Katib al-Arabi, 1968), 109–10; and al-Amin, *al-Nusayriyya (al-Alawiyyun),* (Beirut: Dar al-Fikr, n.d.), 31–32.

66. Jumua, *al-Ma'amara,* 191–94.

67. Van Dam, *The Struggle for Power in Syria,* 83–84; and Gubser, "The Alawites of Syria," 37.

68. Van Dam, *The Struggle for Power in Syria,* 88.

69. Batatu, "Social Roots of Syria's Ruling Group," 331–33.

26—The Nusayri Religious System: *The Concept of God*

1. See *Kitab Ta'lim al-Diyana al-Nusayriyya* (catechism), Arab MS. 6182, fol. 4, Bibliothèque Nationale; and the English translation in Lyde, *Asian Mystery,* 271. See also, Dr. Wolff's German translation in Wolff, "Auzüge aus dem Katechismus der Nossairien," 303–9. Cf. al-Hariri, *al-Alawiyyun al-Nusayriyyun,* 49.

2. Lyde, *Asian Mystery,* 110; and Bar Hebraeus, *Tarikh Mukhtasar al-Duwal,* 97.

3. See questions 9 to 33 of *Kitab Ta'lim al-Diyana al-Nusayriyya,* Arab MS. 6182, fols. 4–15, Bibliothèque Nationale; and Carsten Niebuhr, *Travels,* reproduced with an English translation in Lyde, *Asian Mystery,* 295–97. Niebuhr's information is based on a Nusayri book that fell into his possession. The book, says Niebuhr, was found by Turkish officials in the room of a Nusayri whom they had surprised in the night and taken to prison. The seven manifestations of the deity in human form is also found in the Druze religion but in the case of the Druzes it was Hamza Ibn Ali, founder of their religion and considered by the Druzes to be their God, who had appeared seven times in this world. See the Formulary or Catechism (Instruction of the Druze Religion) in Arab MS. 5188 questions 24 and 25 fols. 58, Bibliothèque Nationale; and de Sacy, *Exposé,* 1:66.

4. See Suras in chapters 5 and 8 of *Kitab al-Majmu* in al-Adani, *Kitab al-Bakura al-Sulaymaniyya,* 3, 19–20 and 23–24. For an explanation of the term *Salsal,* see Massignon, *Salman Pak et les Prémices Spirituelles de l'Islam iranien,* 37, including no. 3.

5. De Sacy, *Exposé,* 1:471; Dussaud, *Histoire et Religion des Nosairies,* 45 and von Hammer-Purgstall, *The History of the Assassins,* 35.

6. Jamal al-Din Abu al-Faraj Ibn al-Jawzi, *Talbis Iblis,* 103; al-Sahrastani, *Kitab al-Milal,* 2:38; Arif Tamir, *Khams Rasa'il Isma'iliyya* (Beirut: Dar al-Insaf, 1956), 147–50; Petrushevsky, *Islam in Iran,* 244; and al-Shaibi, *al-Sila bayn al-Tasawwuf wa al-Tashayyu,* 200–3

7. Abu Yaqub Ishaq al-Sijistani, *Tuhfat al-Mustajibin* in Tamir, *Khams Rasa'il Isma'il-iyya,* 143–50; and Sami N. Makarem, *The Doctrine of the Isam'ilis,* (Beirut: The Arab Institute for Research and Publishing, 1972), 17.

8. Al-Kermani, *Rahat al-Aql,* 158. For elaboration on cyclical time in Ismailism, see Corbin, *Cyclical Time and Ismaili Gnosis,* 30–58 and 184.

9. Petrushevsky, *Islam in Iran,* 245.

10. Al-Kermani, *Rahat al-Aql,* 252–54; Makarem, "The Philisophical Significance of the Imam in Isma'ilism," *Studia Islamica* 28 (1967): 47–48; Idem, *The Doctrine of the Isma'ilis,* 29–30; von Hammer-Purgstall, *The History of the Assasins,* 35; and Corbin, *Cyclical Time and Ismaili Gnosis,* 42, 45, 47, 98, 157, and 184.

11. Al-Kermani, *al-Masabih fi Ithbat al-Imama,* ed. Mustafa Ghalib (Beirut: Manshurat Hamad, 1969), 80–95; and Makarem, *The Doctrine of the Isma'ilis,* 37–39. Cf. Corbin, *En Islam iranien,* 3:231, 257, and 4:281–86.

12. *The Memoirs of Aga Khan* (London: Cassel and Company, 1954), 3:178–79.

13. Petrushevsky, *Islam in Iran,* 235.

14. Abu al-Hasan Ali Ibn Ismail al-Ashari, *Kitab Maqalat,* 10–11; and Abd al-Qahir al-Baghdadi, *al-Farq bayn al-Firaq,* 247–48.

15. Dussaud, *Histoire et religion des Nosairis,* 45 and 51.

16. Ibid., 70–71. See also, al-Mufaddal Ibn Umar al-Jufi, *Kitab al-Sirat,* in Arab MS. 1449, fol. 86a, Bibliothèque Nationale; al-Adani, *Kitab al-Bakura,* 59–69 and the English translation of the same in Salisbury, "Notes on the Book of Sulaiman's First Ripe Fruit," 280; and al-Hariri, *al-Alawiyyun al-Nusayriyyun,* 67.

17. See *Kitab al-Usus* in Arab MS. 1449, fol. 9a Bibliothèque Nationale; al-Adani, *Kitab al-Bakura,* 60; Dussaud, *Histoire et Religion des Nosairis,* 71; and al-Hariri, *al-Alawiyyun al-Nusayriyyun,* 67.

18. Al-Adani, *Kitab al-Bakura,* 60–61; Dussaud, *Histoire et Religion des Nosairis,* 72; al-Hariri, *al-Alawiyyun al-Nusayriyyun,* 68.

19. See *Kitab Ta'lim al-Diyana al-Nusayriyya* in Arab MS. 6182, question 52, Bibliothèque Nationale; *Kitab al-Mashyakha* (manual for Shaykhs), quoted in Lyde, *The Asian Mystery,* 61; and Dussaud, *Histoire et Religion des Nosairis,* 74–75.

20. Al-Adani, *Kitab al-Bakura,* 17 and 62.

21. *Kitab al-Haft al-Sharif,* 186–88; and al-Hariri, *al-Alawiyyun al-Nusayriyyun,* 69. Cf. Ali Ibn Ibrahim, *Tafsir,* 19 and 21, on al-Sadiq, who maintains the existence of pre-Adamite beings.

22. E. Blochet, "Études Sur l'Histoire Religieuse de l'Iran," *Revue de l'Histoire des Religion* (1899), 2:15; and Dussaud, *Histoire et Religion des Nosairis,* 75. Cf. "Cyclical Time in Mazdaizm," in Corbin, *Cyclical Time and Ismaili Gnosis,* 1–30.

23. See the Book of Daniel 2:31–45. Cf. Frédéric Macler, *Les Apocalypse Apocryphes de Daniel,* (Paris: C. Noblet, 1895); and Dussaud, *Histoire et Religion des Nosairis,* 75.

24. See Edward Salisbury's translation of al-Adani's *Kitab al-Bakura* in "Notes on the Book of Salaiman's First Ripe Fruit," note on 287.

25. Ibid.; and al-Adani, *Kitab al-Bakura,* 85–86.

26. Al-Adani, *Kitab al-Bakura,* 11, 47 and 59–63, and al-Hariri, *al-Alawiyyun al-Nusayriyyun,* 70.

27. See the Nusayri catechism in Arab MS. 6182 fols. 3–4, Bibliothèque Nationale; and *Kitab al-Mashyakka,* cited in Lyde, *The Asian Mystery,* 118.

28. See the Formulary of the Druzes in the Arab MS. 5188, fol. 58, Bibliothèque Nationale; and Lyde, *The Asian Mystery,* 87.

29. De Sacy, *Exposé,* 1:65–67.

30. Arab MS. 5188, fols. 59, Bibliothèque Nationale.

31. For the details, see De Sacy, *Exposé,* 1:66.

32. See the Formulary of the Druzes in Arab MS. 5188, fols. 5152, question 44, Bibliothèque Nationale.

33. De Sacy, *Exposé,* 1:66.

34. See *Kitab Ta'lim al-Diyana al-Nusayriyya,* Arab MS. 6182, fols. 4, Bibliothèque Nationale.

35. Ibid.

36. See *Munazara,* Arab MS. 1450, fol. 139, Bibliothèque Nationale.

37. Ibid., fols. 96–97.

38. *Risalat al-Tawhid,* Arab MS. 1450, fol. 47, Bibliothèque Nationale.

39. Ibid., fols. 6–7; *Masa'il,* related by Abu Abd Allah Ibn Harun al-Saigh of his master Abu Abd Allah Ibn al-Husayn Ibn Hamdan al-Khasibi, Arab MS. 1450, fol. 50, Bibliothèque Nationale; Abu Abd Allah Shuba al-Harrani, *Kitab al-Usayfir,* Arab MS. 1450, fols. 7b and 8a, Bibliothèque Nationale, where the author quotes Jafar al-Sadiq. Cf. De Sacy, *Exposé,* 2:581.

40. See Sura 4 of *Kitab al-Majmu* in al-Adani, *Kitab al-Bakura,* 14; and Dussaud, *Histoire et Religion des Nosairis,* 166.

41. For these passages, see *Kitab al-Mashyakha* in Lyde, *The Asian Mystery,* 121; Sura 6 of *Kitab al-Majmu* in al-Adani, *Kitab al-Bakura,* 21; and the preamble to *Kitab Ta'lim al-Diyana al-Nusayriyya,* Arab MS. 6182, Bibliothèque Nationale.

42. *Kitab Ta'lim al-Diyana al-Nusayriyya,* Arab MS. 6182, question 22, fol. 6, Bibliothèque Nationale; and *Kitab al-Mashyakha,* in Lyde, *The Asian Mystery,* 121 and 136.

43. Al-Adani, *Kitab al-Bakura,* 83.

44. Ibid.; and al-Hariri, *al-Alawiyyaun al-Nusayriyyun,* 43.

45. Dussaud, *Histoire et Religion des Nosairis,* 65.

46. Theodor Nöldeke, *Sketches from Eastern History,* trans. John Sutherland Black (Beirut: Khayat, 1963), 47–48.

47. Abd al-Rahman Ibn Khaldun, *al-Muqaddima,* (Cairo: Matbaat Mustafa Muhammad, n.d.), 334 and 338. Cf. Dussaud, *Histoire at Religion des Nosairis,* 67.

48. Al-Adani, *Kitab al-Bakura,* 64; and Dussaud, *Histoire et Religion des Nosairis,* 67.

49. *Kitab Ta'lim al-Diyana al-Nusayriyya,* Arab MS. 6182, fols. 1 and 4, Bibliothèque Nationale.

50. Ibid., MS. 6182, fol. 19.

51. Abu Said Maymun Ibn al-Qasim al-Tabarani al-Nusayri (known as al-Tabarani), *Kitab Sabil Rahat al-Arwah wa Dalil al-Surur wa al-Afrah ila Faliq al-Isbah, known as Majmu al-Ayad.* This second title shall be used throughout. This manuscript was discovered by Joseph Catafago, chancellor of the Prussian General Consulate in Beirut, who published in French the titles of the Nusayri feasts and some prayers, especially those of the Nawruz and Christmas Eve. See Catafago, "Notices Sur Les Anseriens," 149–68. An English translation of the same can be found in Lyde, *The Asian Mystery,* 289–90. The whole text was later published by R. Strothmann in three parts; see al-Tabarani, *Kitab Majmu al-A'yad,* ed. R. Strothmann, in *Der Islam,* 27 (1943–44): 1–60 and (1946): 161–273.

52. Lyde, *The Asian Mystery,* 118. Cf. Dussaud, *Histoire et Religion des Nosairis,* 64.

53. Dussaud, *Histoire et Religion des Nosairis,* 64.

54. Henri Lammens, "Les Nosairis Furent-Ils Chrétiens?" *Revue de l'Orient Chrétien* 6 (1901): 33–50; and idem, "Les Nosairis, Notes sur leur Histoire et leur Religion," *Études*

Religieuses (1899): 482–83; and idem, "Au Pay des Nosairis," *Revue de l'Orient Chrétien* (1899): 572, Seq and (1900): 99, Seq; and Edward J. Jurji, "The Alids of North Syria," *The Moslem World* 29, no. 4 (October 1939): 337, no. 30.

55. *Kitab Ta'lim al-Diyana al-Nusayriyya,* Arab MS. 6182, fol. 4, Bibliothèque Nationale.

56. *Kitab al-Mashyakha,* in Lyde, *The Asian Mystery* 125–25; and al-Adani, *Kitab al-Bakura,* 19–20.

57. *Kitab Ta'lim al-Diyana al-Nusayriyya,* Arab MS. 6182, questions 3 and 73, fols. 2 and 15, Bibliothèque Nationale, 271 and 278.

58. *Kitab al-Mashyakha,* in Lyde, *The Asian Mystery,* 124.

59. See the works cited in note 39 above. See also De Sacy, *Exposé,* 2:158; and Dussaud, *Histoire et Religion des Nosairis,* 67 n. 7, who follows De Sacy.

60. *Kitab al-Haft al-Sharif,* 209.

61. Al-Adani, *Kitab al-Bakura,* 19–20.

62. *Kitab al-Usus,* in Arab MS. 1449, fols. 56b–57a, Bibliothèque Nationale, and al-Hariri, *al-Alawiyyun al-Nusayriyyun,* 50–51.

27—The Nusayri Religious System: *The Apotheosis of Ali*

1. *Risalat al-Tawhid,* Arab MS. 1450, fol. 47 Bibliothèque Nationale; al-Nashshabi, *Munazara,* ibid., fols. 80–81 and 103; and Lyde, 113.

2. See *Kitab Ta'lim al-Diyana al-Nusayriyya,* Arab MS. 6182, fol. 2, Bibliothèque Nationale; and Lyde, *The Asian Mystery,* 271. Cf. al-Hariri, *al-Alawiyyun an-Nusayriyyun,* 55. According to Ali Ibn Ibrahim, *Tafsir,* 283, the bees are Shiites.

3. This Sura is in al-Adani, *Kitab al-Bakura,* 26–27, and in *Kitab al-Mashyakha,* in Lyde, *The Asian Mystery,* 114.

4. *Kitab al-Mashyakha,* in Lyde, *The Asian Mystery,* 114.

5. *Kitab Ta'lim al-Diyana al-Nusayriyya,* Arab MS. 6182, question 3 fol. 2–3, Bibliothèque Nationale; *Munazara,* MS. 1450, fol. 95, Bibliothèque Nationale. Cf. al-Hariri, *al-Alawiyyun al-Nusayriyyun,* 55–56.

6. *Kitab al-Mashyakha,* in Lyde, *The Asian Mystery,* 237–42.

7. Ibid.

8. Al-Adani, *Kitab al-Bakura,* 46–48; Lyde, *The Asian Mystery,* 246–48; *Risalat al-Bayan li Ahl al-Uqul wa al-Afham wa man Talaba al-Huda ila Ma'rifat al-Rahman,* in Arab MS. 1450, fol. 54b, Bibliothèque Nationale; and *Kitab al-Usus,* Arab MS. 1449, fol. 54, Bibliothéque Nationale.

9. See *Masa'il,* related by al-Saigh of his master Abd Allah Ibn al-Husayn Ibn Hamdan al-Khasibi, Arab MS. 1450, fols. 52–53, Bibliothèque Nationale.

10. De Sacy, *Exposé,* 1:60.

11. *Kitab Ta'lim al-Diyana al-Nusayriyya,* Arab MS. 6182, question 4, fol. 3, Bibliothèque Nationale.

12. *Kitab al-Mashyakha,* in Lyde *The Asian Mystery,* 116.

13. *Kitab al-Mashyakha* ibid., 87–88; and *Kitab Ta'lim al-Diyana al-Nusayriyya,* Arab MS. 6182, questions 45–48, Bibliothèque Nationale.

14. See this Sura in al-Adani, *Kitab al-Bakura,* 30.

15. *Kitab al-Haft al-Sharif,* 114.

16. See an English translation of this manuscript acquired by Niebuhr in Lyde, *The*

Asian Mystery, 294–98; *Kitab Ta'lim al-Diyana al-Nusayriyya,* Arab MS. 6182, question 21, fol. 6, Bibliothèque Nationale; and *Risalat al-Tawhid,* Arab MS. 1450, fols. 45–46 Bibliothèque Nationale.

17. Abu al-Hasan Ali Ibn Ismail al-Ashari, *Kitab Maqalat,* 14–15; and al-Shahrastani, *Kitab al-Milal,* reprinted together with Ibn Hazm's *Kitab al-Fisal fi al-Milal wa al-Ahwa wa al-Nihal* (Cairo: Muassasat al-Khanji, 1321/1903), 2:13.

18. Al-Shaykh Abu Abd Allah al-Husayn Ibn Hamdan al-Khasibi, *Kitab al-Hidaya al-Kubra,* appended to Uthman, *al-Alawiyyun,* 229–97, especially 229 and 230.

19. Ibid., 230–31. Cf. Ibn Babawayh, *Ma'ani al-Akhbar,* 59–60.

20. *Kitab al-Mashyakha,* in Lyde, *The Asian Mystery,* 115.

21. Al-Khasibi, *Kitab al-Hidaya al-Kubra,* in Uthman, *al-Alawiyyun,* 231–32.

22. Ibid., 230; *Kitab al-Haft al-Sharif,* 93; and *Risalat Fitrat al-Munsan wa Nuzhat al-Qalb wa al-Ayan,* fols. 38–39 in Uthman, 28 of the introduction; *Kitab al-Mashyakha,* In Lyde, *The Asian Mystery,* 87–88; questions 45 and 50 of *Kitab Ta'lim al-Diyana al-Nusayriyya,* Arab MS. 6182, Bibliothèque Nationale; and most of the Suras of *Kitab al-Majmu* in al-Adani, *Kitab al-Bakura,* 7, 10–11, 21, 23.

23. *Kitab Ta'lim al-Diyana al-Nusayriyya,* Arab MS. 6182, questions 43 and 50, fol. 11 and 12, Bibliothèque Nationale; *Kitab al-Mashyakha,* in Lyde, *The Asian Mystery* 115; and the first Sura of *Kitab al-Majmu* in al-Adani, *Kitab al-Bakura,* 8.

24. *Kitab al-Usus,* Arab MS. 1449, fol. 42b, Bibliothèque Nationale; and al-Hariri, *al-Alawiyyun al-Nusayriyyun,* 59.

25. Dussaud, *Histoire et Religion des Nosairis,* 51.

26. Ibid., 51–52; and De Sacy, *Exposé,* 1:31–32.

27. Dussaud, *Histoire et Religion des Nosairis,* 52. There is evidence that Fatima, daughter of the Prophet, claimed that she was divine and called herself Ali al-A'la. See Corbin, *Cyclical Time and Ismaili Gnosis,* 145–46, n. 214. In his *Ma'ani al-Akhbar,* 55, Ibn Babawayh states that God derived the name of Ali from His name, Ali al-A'la.

28. Lyde, *The Asian Mystery,* 115.

29. *Kitab Ta'lim al-Diyana al-Nusayriyya,* Arab MS. 6182, question 14, fol. 5, Bibliothèque Nationale.

30. *Kitab al-Mashyakha,* in Lyde, *The Asian Mystery,* 118; and *Kitab Ta'lim al-Diyana al-Nusayriyya,* Arab MS. 6182, question 5, Bibliothèque Nationale.

31. *Kitab Ta'lim al-Diyana al-Nusayriyya,* Arab MS. 6182, question 43, fol. 11, Bibliothèque Nationale.

32. Al-Tabarani in Catafago, "Notices Sur Les Anseriens," 161–62.

33. Ibid. 161–62.

34. Ibid., 163.

35. Ibid.

36. Ibid., 164–65. Cf. al-Askari, *al-Alawiyyun aw al-Nusayriyya,* 104–5.

37. Al-Tabarani, *Majmu al-A'yad,* in Catafago, "Notices Sur Les Anseriens," 165.

38. See al-Tabarani, *Kitab Majmu al-A'yad,* ed. Strothman, 190; and Lyde, *The Asian Mystery,* 292.

39. Al-Tabarani, *Majmu al-A'yad,* in Catafago, "Notices Sur Les Anseriens," 167.

40. *Kitab Ta'lim al-Diyana al-Nusayriyya,* Arab MS. 6182, question 90, fol. 17, Bibliothèque Nationale.

41. Lyde, *The Asian Mystery,* 137–38.

42. Al-Askari, *al-Alawiyyun aw al-Nusayriyya,* 105.

43. Al-Adani, *Kitab al-Bakura,* 81–82.

44. Al-Tabarani, *Majmu al-A'yad,* in Catafago, "Notices Sur Les Aseriens," 165.

45. Ibid., 167; idem, *Kitab Majmu al-A'yad,* ed. Strothman, 190; and Lyde, *The Asian Mystery,* 292.

28—The Nusayri Concept of Light: *Shamsis and Qamaris*

1. *Kitab Ta'lim al-Diyana al-Nusayriyya,* Arab MS. 6182, questions 82 and 95, fols. 16 and 18, Bibliothèque Nationale; *Kitab al-Mashyakha,* in Lyde, *The Asian Mystery,* 295; al-Adani, *Kitab al-Bakura,* 27–28; *Munazara,* Arab MS. 1450, fol. 126, Bibliothèque Nationale; and De Sacy, *Exposé,* 2:561.

2. *Kitab al-Majmu,* in al-Adani, *Kitab al-Bakura,* 20–23, 28, 31 and 85.Cf. Dussaud, *Histoire et Religion des Nosairis,* 78–79; al-Tawil, *Tarikh al-Alawiyyin,* 361–66, and Lyde, *The Asian Mystery,* 50–54, and 138.

3. *Kitab al-Majmu,* Sura 6, in al-Adani, *Kitab al-Bakura,* 20–21, 85, and 91. Cf. Lyde, *The Asian Mystery,* 39, especially the argument on this point between representatives of the Shamsis and the Qamaris.

4. This Sura is in al-Adani, *Kitab al-Bakura,* 26–27.

5. Al-Adani, *Kitab al-Bakura,* 28.

6. Ibid., 22, 31.

7. *Kitab al-Majmu,* Sura 5, in al-Adani, *Kitab al-Bakura* 18–19. Cf. Dussaud, *Histoire et Religion des Nosairis,* 87–88.

8. Lyde, *The Asian Mystery,* 139.

9. Al-Adani, *Kitab al-Bakura,* 31 and 91.

10. De Sacy, *Exposé,* 2:561; and Dussaud, *Histoire et Religion des Nosairis,* 79.

11. *Kitab al-Majmu,* Sura 13, in al-Adani, *Kitab al-Bakura,* 29.

12. Ibid.

13. Dussaud, *Histoire et Religion des Nosairis,* 82–92.

14. Ibid., 82; and Daniel Chwolsohn, *Die Ssabier und der Ssabismus* (St. Petersburg: Buchdruckerei der Kaiserlichen Akademie der Wissenschaften, 1856), 1:489–91.

15. Chwolsohn, *Die Ssabler und der Ssabismus,* 1:180, and Dussaud, *Histoire et Religion des Nosairis,* 82.

16. Abu al-Faraj Muhammad Ibn Ishaq Ibn al-Nadim, *Kitab al-Fihrist,* ed. Gustav Flügel (Halle, University of Halle, 1871–72; reprinted, Beirut: Khayat, n.d.), 320–21; Chwolsohn, *Die Ssabier und der Ssabismus* 2:32–34; and Dussaud, *Histoire et Religion des Nosairis,* 83.

17. Chwolsohn, *Die Ssabier und der Ssabismus,* 1:748; and Dussaud, *Histoire et Religion des Nosairis,* 83.

18. Ibn al-Nadim, *al-Fihrist,* 322–24.

19. Ibid., 323.

20. Dussaud, *Histoire et Religion des Nosairis,* 84.

21. Lyde, *The Asian Mystery,* 50–55.

22. *Kitab al-Majmu,* Suras 11 and 15, in al-Adani, *Kitab al-Bakura,* 26–27 and 32.

23. Dussaud, *Histoire et Religion des Nosairis,* 82.

24. Ibid., 88; and al-Adani, *Kitab al-Bakura,* 19.

25. Dussaud, *Histoire et Religion des Nosairis,* 86 and 88.

26. Ibid., 85 and Chwolsohn, *Die Ssabier und der Ssabismus,* 2:59–60.

27. Ibn al-Nadim, *al-Fihrist,* 323.

28. *Kitab al-Majmu,* Sura 1, in al-Adani, *Kitab al-Bakura,* 8.

29. Al-Adani, *Kitab al-Bakura,* 10.

30. For further examples of the relations between the Nusayri cult and that of the Harranians, see Dussaud, *Histoire et Religion des Nosairis,* 87–92.

31. Al-Shahrastani, *Kitab al-Milal.* 2:97–99.

29—The Nusayri "Trinity": *Ali, Muhammad, and Salman as-Farisi*

1. *Kitab al-Mashyakha,* in Lyde, *The Asian Mystery,* 124; and *Kitab Ta'lim al-Diyana al-Nusayriyya,* Arab MS. 6182, questions 11 and 72, Bibliothéque Nationale.

2. See the review of Lyde's, *The Asian Mystery* by Charles Henry Brigham in *North American Review* 93 (1861): 355.

3. *Kitab al-Mashyakha,* in Lyde, *The Asian Mystery,* 124, n. 2.

4. *Kitab Ta'lim al-Diyana al-Nusayriyya,* questions 16 and 18, Arab MS. 6182, Bibliothèque Nationale.

5. *Kitab al-Mashyakha,* in Lyde, *The Asian Mystery,* 122.

6. *Kitab Ta'lim al-Diyana al-Nusayriyya,* question 4, Arab MS. 6182, Bibliothèque Nationale.

7. Cf. al-Hariri, *al-Alawiyyun al-Nusayriyyun,* 51.

8. See *Masa'il,* related by al-Saigh of his master, Arab MS, 1450, fol. 53, Bibliothèque Nationale.

9. *Munazara,* Arab MS. 1450, fols. 95–96, Bibliothèque Nationale.

10. Ibid., fol. 47; *Risalat al-Tawhid,* related by Jisri, Arab MS. 1450, fol. 46, Bibliothèque Nationale; and al-Hariri, *al-Alawiyyun al-Nusayriyyun,* 63.

11. See *Kitab al-Usus,* Arab MS. 1449, fol. 1, Bibliothèque Nationale; *Kitab al-Usayfir,* Arab MS. 1450, fols. 11 and 18, Bibliothèque Nationale. Cf. Al-Hariri, *al-Alawiyyun al-Nusayriyyun,* 47.

12. *Munazara,* Arab MS. 1450, fols. 95–96, Bibliothèque Nationale.

13. See this third Quddas in al-Adani, *Kitab al-Bakura,* 40; and the anonymous tract, Arab MS. 1450, fol. 55, Bibliothèque Nationale.

14. *Kitab al-Majmu,* Sura 5, in al-Adani, *Kitab al-Bakura,* 18; and Catafago, "Drei Messen der Nosairier," 393 and *Kitab al-Sirat,* Arab MS. 1449, fol. 122, Bibliothèque Nationale.

15. Massignon, *Salman Pàk et les Prémices Spirituelle de l'Islam,* 37, n. 3.

16. Ibid., 8.

17. Ibid., 8; 13–14; and I. Horovitz "Salman al-Farisi," *Der Islam* 12 (1922): 178–83. Other sources Massignon cites are Ubayd al-Muktib (d. 140/757), Ibn Ishaq (d. 150/767), Abd al-Malik al-Khathami (d. 180/796), and Sayyar al-Anzi (d. 199/814).

18. Massignon, *Salman Pàk et les Prémices Spirituelle de l'Islam iranien,* 13–14; Muhammad al-Zahri known as Ibn Saad, *al-Tabaqat al-Kubra,* 4:53–57; Ibn Hisham, *al-Sira al-Nabawiyya,* ed. Mustafa al-Saqqa et al. (Cairo: Mustafa al-Babi al-Halabi, 1375/1955), 214–17; Masum Ali; *Tara'iq al-Haqa'iq,* 2:2; and al-Shaibi, *al-Sila bayn al-Tasawwuf wa al-Tashayyu,* 25.

19. Massignon, *Salman Pàk et les Prémices Spirituelles de l'Islam iranien,* 14, Ibn Saad, *al-Tabaqat al-Kubra,* 4:53–57; Ibn Hisham, *al-Sira al-Nabawiyya,* 1:218–20, Jamal al-Din Abu al-Faraj Ibn al-Jawzi, *Sifat al-Safwa,* 1:523–56; Abu Nuaym al-Isfahani, *Hilyat al-Awliya,* 1:192; Masum Ali, *Tara'iq al-Haqa'iq,* 2:2; al-Subayti, *Salman al-Farisi,* 2nd. ed. (Baghdad: Matbaat al-Azhar, 1969), 22.

20. Jamal al-Din Abu al-Faraj Ibn al-Jawzi, *Sifat al-Safwa,* 1:535, Massignon, *Salman Pàk et les Premices Spirituelles de l'Islam iranien,* 16–17; al-Subayti, *Salman al-Farisi,* 26–27; Ibn Hisham, *al-Sira al-Nabawiyya,* 1:70; and al-Shaibi, *al-Sila bayn al-Tasawwuf wa al-Tashayyu,* 19, 26, and 30–31.

21. Al-Tabari, *Jami al-Bayan fi Tafsir al-Qur'an,* 14:111; Masum Ali, *Tara'iq al-Haqa'iq, 2:2; and Massignon, Salman Pàk et les Prèmices Spirituelles de l'Islam iranien,* 33.

22. Massignon, *Salman Pàk et les Prémices Spirituelles de l'Islam iranien,* 33. On Salman as the angel Gabriel, see Corbin, *Cyclical Time and Ismaili Gnosis,* 72 and 124–26.

23. Jamal al-Din Abu al-Faraj Ibn al-Jawzi, *Sifa al-Safwa,* 1:546. For the tradition related of the fifth Imam al-Baqir by Jabir al-Jufi, see Corbin, *Cyclical Time and Ismaili Gnosis,* 144.

24. Al-Shaibi, *al-Sila bayn al-Tasawwuf wa al-Tashayyu,* 22.

25. Massignon, *Salman Pàk et les Prémices Spirituelles de l'Islam iranien,* 29.

26. Ibid. According to al-Masudi, Sasaa said in the presence of Muawiya that "Ali and His companions are among the righteous Imams." See Abu al-Hasan al-Masudi, *Muruj al-Dhahab,* 2:341. For more on Adam, especially in Ismailism, see Corbin, *Cyclical Time and Ismaili Gnosis,* 42–43, 66–69 and 79–80.

27. Masum Ali, *Tara'iq al-Haqa'iq,* 1:211.

28. For the Aytam see *Risalat al-Tawhid,* Arab MS. 1450, fols. 55–57 and Abu Nuaym al-Isfahani, *Hilyat al-Awliya,* 1:139.

29. Ibn Ibrahim, *Tafsir,* 287.

30. Ibn Hisham, *al-Sira al-Nabawiyya,* 1:222. On the continued presence of Salman from Christ down to Muhammad, see Corbin, "Le Livre du Glorieux de Jabir Ibn Hayyan," *Eranos-Jahrbuch,* 18 (1950): 47–114.

31. Al-Masudi, *Muruj al-Dhahab,* 2:301; Abu al-Husayn Muslim, *Sahih Muslim* (Cairo: Matbaat Muhammad Ali, 1334/1915), 7:120–21; and Ibn Ibrahim, *Tafsir,* 159.

32. Al-Shaibi, *al-Sila bayn al-Tasawwuf wa al-Tashayyu,* 28.

33. Al-Nawbakhti, *Firaq al-Shia,* 58.

34. Massignon, *Salman Pàk et les Prémices Spirituelles de l'Islam iranien,* 35.

35. Ibid., 37. On Abu al-Khattab, see al-Ashari, *Kitab Maqalat,* 10–11; Abd al-Qahir al-Baghdadi, *al-Farq bayn al-Firaq,* 247–48; and al-Razi, *Kitab al-Zina,* 289.

36. Al-Ashari, *Kitab Maqalat,* 13.

37. Al-Razi, *Kitab al-Zina,* 307; and al-Shahrastani, *Kitab al-Milal,* 2:13.

38. Al-Razi, *Kitab al-Zina,* 306; and Massignon, *Salman Pàk et les Prémices Spirituelles des l'Islam iranien,* 42–49. It is interesting that although al-Razi is an Ismaili writer, he appears neutral as a heresiographer. This becomes more puzzling when we realize that in *Umm al-Kitab,* a proto-Ismaili source of the eighth century, Salman appears as a divinity who is God's messenger, His Bab (door), His Book (the Quran), His Throne, His Right Hand, His Trustee, and His Hijab (veil). See *Umm al-Kitab,* 139 and 172; and Corbin, *Cyclical Time and Ismaili Gnosis,* 171.

39. This tradition, related by al-Khasibi, appears in Husayn Muhammad Taqi al-Tabarsi al-Nuri, *Nafas al-Rahman fi Ahwal Salman* (Tehran, 1285/1868), part 5, 53; see also, Massignon, *Salman Pàk et les Prémices Spirituelles l'Islam iranien,* 48.

40. *Kitab al-Mashyakha,* in Lyde, *The Asian Mystery,* 130.

41. Al-Tabarani, *Kitab Majmu al-A'yad,* ed. Strothman, in *Der Islam,* 27:23.

42. Ibid., 23 and 67. In *Risalat al-Tawhid,* Arab MS. 1450, fol 47 Bibliothèque Nationale, Salman is considered as the Creator of the World.

43. *Kitab Ta'lim al-Diyana al-Nusayriyya,* Arab MS. 6182, question 23, fol. 6, Bibliothèque Nationale. In the prologue of *Shah Nama-ye Haqiqat,* Salman Pak (pure) appears as

the terrestrial typification of Gabriel. See also Corbin, *Cyclical Time and Ismaili Gnosis,* 72, no. 3.

44. *Kitab al-Mashyakha,* in Lyde, *The Asian Mystery,* 129.

45. Ibid., in Lyde, *The Asian Mystery,* 131; and al-Tabarani, *Kitab Majmu al-A'yad,* ed. Strothman, 209–22.

46. *Kitab al-Mashyakha,* in Lyde, *The Asian Mystery,* 131.

47. See Arab MS. 1450, fol. 55, Bibliothèque Nationale and the Third Quddas (called Quddas al-Adhan) in al-Adani, *Kitab al-Bakura,* 41.

48. *Kitab Ta'lim al-Diyana al-Nusayriyya,* Arab MS. 6182, questions 24–29; Bibliothèque Nationale; and *Kitab al-Mashyakha,* in Lyde, *The Asian Mystery,* 131.

30—The Nusayri Religious System: *The Twelve Imams*

1. Al-Tawil, *Tarikh al-Alawiyyin,* 254. See also chapter 5 of this book, notes 10 and 15.

2. *Kitab al-Haft al-Sharif,* 67; and al-Hariri, *al-Alawiyyun al-Nusayriyyun,* 24–26.

3. Al-Tawil, *Tarikh al-Alawiyyin,* 254–59.

4. *Kitab al-Mashyakha,* in Lyde, *The Asian Mystery,* 132.

5. *Kitab al-Haft al-Sharif,* 205.

6. Ibid., 190, 192–93, 196, 201, 221. In his *Ma'ani al-Akhbar,* 35, Ibn Babawayh relates similar statements by the Imam Ali Zayn al-Abidin.

7. For this treatise of *al-Tawjih,* see Arab MS. 6182, fols. 21–22, Bibliothèque Nationale; and *Kitab al-Mashyakha,* in Lyde, *The Asian Mystery,* 133.

8. *Kitab al-Haft al-Sharif,* 102, 105.

9. *Kitab al-Mashyakha,* in Lyde, *The Asian Mystery,* 265 and 132.

10. Al-Adani, *Kitab al-Bakura,* 56.

11. Al-Hariri, *al-Alawiyyun al-Nusayriyyun,* 100.

12. C. Niebuhr gives the names of these Aytam at the seven appearances of the Deity. See the English translation of Niebuhr's manuscript in Lyde, *The Asian Mystery,* 294–98.

13. *Kitab Ta'lim al-Diyana al-Nusayriyya,* Arab MS. 6182, questions 23–43, and 70, fols. 7–11 and 15, Bibliothèque Nationale; and *Kitab Majmu al-A'yad,* ed. Strothman, 23 and 69. Cf. *Kitab al-Mashyakha,* in Lyde, *The Asian Mystery,* 133.

14. *Kitab Ta'lim al-Diyana al-Nusayriyya,* questions 56–63, and 70, Arab MS. 6182, Bibliothèque Nationale; *Risalat al-Tawhid,* fol. 55; and *Kitab al-Mashyakha,* in Lyde, *The Asian Mystery,* 134.

15. *Kitab Ta'lim al-Diyana al-Nusayriyya,* Arab MS. 6182, question 70, fol. 15 which refer to Fatima in the masculine as al-Sayyid Fatir; al-Razi, *Kitab al-Zina,* 307; and al-Shahrastani, Kitab al-Milal, 2:14. In the proto-Ismaili source *Umm al-Kitab,* Fatima declares that she is the Creator-Fatir, of heaven and earth and the spirit of the true believers. See *Umm al-Kitab,* ed. W. Ivanow, 39–40; and Corbin, *Cyclical Time and Ismaili Gnosis,* 146, the note carried from the previous page.

16. Al-Tabarani, *Kitab Majmu al-A'yad,* ed. Strothmann 155–56 and *Risalat al-Tawhid,* Arab MS. 1450, fol. 45, Bibliothèque Nationale. Cf. Corbin, *Cyclical Time and Ismaili Gnosis,* 101; and Shariati, *Fatima is Fatima,* 134–36, where the author produces a tradition in which the Prophet states that Fatima is part of his body and that she is the final link in the chain of divine justice. Cf. Ibn Babawayh, *Ma'ani al-Akhbar,* 55–56.

17. Al-Razi, *Kitab al-Zina,* 307; al-Ash'ari, *Kitab Maqalat,* 14; and al-Shahrastani, *Kitab al-Milal,* 2:14.

31—The Nusayri Religious System: *Role of the Aytam and Spiritual Hierarchies*

1. *Kitab al-Majmu,* Sura 5, in al-Adani, *Kitab al-Bakura,* 19. Cf. *Umm al-Kitab,* 172.
2. Al-Adani, *Kitab al-Bakura,* 19–20.
3. *Kitab al-Sirat,* Arab MS. 1449 fols. 93b–98a, Bibliothèque Nationale; *Risalat al-Bayan,* Arab MS. 1450, fols. 55a–60b, Bibliothèque Nationale; *Kitab Ta'lim al-Diyana al-Nusayriyya,* questions 55, and 59–68, Arab MS. 6182, Bibliothèque Nationale; Lyde, *The Asian Mystery,* 111–12; and al-Hariri, *al-Alawiyyun al-Nusayriyyun,* 103–8.
4. *Kitab al-Sirat,* Arab MS. 1449 fols. 93b-98a, Bibliothèque Nationale; and Lyde, *The Asian Mystery,* 112.
5. *Kitab Ta'lim al-Diyana al-Nusayriyya,* questions 58, 59, 61, 62, 63. Cf. al-Hariri, *al-Alawiyyun al-Nusayriyyun,* 105–6.
6. *Kitab Ta'lim al-Diyana al-Nusayriyya,* questions 55 and 65, Arab MS. 6182, Bibliothèque Nationale; and *Risalat al-Bayan,* Arab MS. 1450, fols. 58a–60b. Cf. al-Hariri, *al-Alawiyyun al-Nusayriyyun,* 107–8.
7. *Kitab al-Mashyakha,* in Lyde, *The Asian Mystery.,* 135.
8. Ibid., 136.
9. Ibid., 136; and *Kitab Ta'lim al-Diyana al-Nusayriyya,* question 29, Arab MS. 6182, Bibliothèque Nationale.
10. See *Risalat al-Bayan,* Arab MS. 1450, fols. 58b–60a, Bibliothèque Nationale; and al-Hariri, *al-Alawiyyun al-Nusayriyyun,* 109–10.
11. *Risalat al-Bayan,* Arab MS. 1450, fols. 58b–60a, Bibliothèque Nationale.
12. *Kitab al-Haft al-Sharif,* 74–78.
13. Al-Adani, *Kitab al-Bakura,* 59–60.
14. *Kitab al-Mashyakha,* in Lyde, *The Asian Mystery,* 142.
15. *Kitab al-Haft al-Sharif,* 77.

32—The Nusayri Religious System: *Metempsychosis*

1. Al-Nawbakhti, *Firaq al-Shi'a,* 51. For more on the Nusayris' concept of musukhiyya, see Strothmann, "Seelenwanderung Bei Den Nusairi," *Oriens,* 113, especially 104–13.
2. Al-Shahrastani, *Kitab al-Milal,* 2:12. For a detailed account of metempsychosis, especially the transformation of human beings into animal forms, see Abd al-Qahir al-Baghdadi, *al-Farq bayn al-Eiraq,* 272–76; and Strothmann, "Seelenwanderung Bei Den Nusairi," 107.
3. Lyde, *The Asian Mystery,* 140.
4. *Risalat al-Bayan,* Arab MS. 1450, fol. 57, Bibliothèque Nationale.
5. *Kitab al-Majmu,* in al-Adani, *Kitab al-Bakura,* 10–11; *Kitab al-Haft al-Sharif,* 175–76; Neibuhr, *Travels,* in Lyde, *The Asian Mystery,* 140; al-Hariri, *al-Alawiyyun al-Nusayriyyun,* 72; al-Shahrastani, *Kitab al-Milal,* 2:12; and Dussaud, *Histoire et Religion des Nosairis,* 122 and 124.

6. See Hamza Ibn Ali, *al-Risala al-Damigha wa al-Radd, ala al-Nusayri al-Fasiq* (refutation of the Nusayris), Arab MS. 1419, fols. 5 and 14 and MS. 1449, fol. 2, Bibliothèque Nationale; De Sacy, *Exposé,* 2:561–68.

7. Hamza Ibn Ali, *al-Risala al-Damigha,* Arab MS. 1419, fols. 5 and 14, and MS. 1449, fol. 2, Biliothèque Nationale; and De Sacy, *Exposé,* 2:579. Cf. Lyde, *The Asian Mystery,* 140.

8. *Kitab al-Haft al-Sharif,* 59–61, 144–45. There is evidence that Jafar al-Sadiq considered metempsychosis to be one of the Ghulat's errors and deceptions. See Abu Mansur Ahmad Ibn Ali al-Tabarsi, *al-Ihtijaj,* ed. Muhammad Baqir al-Khirsan, (al-Najaf: Matbaat al-Numan, 1386/1966), 2:89.

9. Ibid.

10. *Kitab al-Sirat,* Arab MS. 1449, fols. 117–18, Bibliothèque Nationale.

11. Ibid., fols. 114, and 118, 173b.

12. *Kitab al-Haft al-Sharif,* 205; *Kitab al-Mashyakha* in Lyde, *The Asian Mystery,* 141; and al-Tabarani, *Kitab Majmu al-A'yad,* ed. Strothmann, 67.

13. Al-Adani, *Kitab al-Bakura,* 81; and *Kitab al-Haft al-Sharif,* 97.

14. Lyde, *The Asian Mystery,* 141.

15. Al-Tabarani, *Kitab Majmu al-A'yad,* ed. Strothmann, 71–72.

16. Al-Adani, *Kitab al-Bakura,* 81, 85–86; and Lyde, *The Asian Mystery,* 140.

17. *Kitab al-Haft al-Sharif,* 146–47 and 152–53; and *Kitab al-Mashyakha,* in Lyde, *The Asian Mystery,* 141–42.

18. *Kitab al-Mashyakha,* in Lyde, *The Asian Mystery,* 141–42.

19. Arab MS. 4291, fol. 56, Berlin Royal Library, quoted in Dussaud, *Histoire et Religion des Nosairis,* 35.

20. *Kitab al-Haft al-Sharif,* 166–67; and Strothmann, "Seelenwanderung bei den Nusairi," 113, in which he quotes al-Tabarani as stating that God created women from the disobedience of Iblis (Satan).

21. *Kitab al-Haft al-Sharif,* 164–65.

22. Ibid., 152–54.

23. Lyde, *The Asian Mystery,* 144.

24. *Kitab al-Haft al-Sharif,* 88–90.

25. Al-Nawbakhti, *Firaq al-Shi'a,* 52–53.

26. *Kitab al-Sirat,* Arab MS. 1449, fols. 112–13, Bibliothèque Nationale.

27. Ibid., fol. 126.

28. Ibid., fol. 146.

29. *Kitab al-Haft al-Sharif,* 62.

30. Al-Tabarani, *Kitab Majmu al-A'yad,* ed. Strothmann, 198; and *Journal Asiatic* (February 1848), 166.

31. *Kitab Ta'lim al-Diyana al-Nusayriyya,* Arab MS. 6182, question 7, fol. 4 and questions 80 and 81, fol. 16, Bibliothèque Nationale; and al-Tabarani, *Kitab Majmu al-A'yad,* ed. Strothmann, 67.

32. *Kitab al-Mashyakha,* in Lyde, *The Asian Mystery,* 141.

33. *Risalat al-Tawhid,* Arab MS. 1450, fol. 46, Bibliothèque Nationale.

34. Burckhardt, *Travels in Syria and the Holy Land,* 156; and Lyde, *The Asian Mystery,* 143.

35. See al-Nashshabi, *Munazara,* Arab MS. 1450, fols. 140–41, Bibliothèque Nationale.

36. Ibid.

37. Ibid., fol. 132.

38. *Kitab al-Haft al-Sharif,* 102.

33—The Nusayri Religious System: *Initiation*

1. Al-Adani, *Kitab al-Bakura,* 81–82.

2. Al-Baghdadi, *al-Farq ban al-Firaq,* 298–305.

3. Ibid., 284–85. Cf. M. Jan De Goeja, *Memoire Sur Les Carmathes du Bahrein* (Leiden: E. J. Brill, 1886), 170–72; Dussaud, *Histoire et Religion des Nosairis,* 104; and Bandali Jawzi, *Min Tarikh al-Harakat al-Fikriyya fi al-Islam* (Beirut: Dar al-Rawai, n.d.), 138–41, where the author discusses the Ismailis' allegorical interpretation of the Quran.

4. See "Ma'rifat al-Taliq," Arab MS. 1450, fols. 158–63, and "Ma'rifat al-Sama," fols. 163–67.

5. "Ma'rifat al-Sama," fols. 158–59; Dussaud, *Histoire et Religion des Nosairis,* 107. Dussaud states that the initiate places the slippers of all the onlookers on his head.

6. See Hamza Ibn Ali, *al-Risala al-Damigha,* Arab MS. 1419, fols. 5 and 14 and MS. 1415 fol. 2, Bibiothèque Nationale; De Sacy, *Exposé,* 2:561–68; Lyde, *The Asian Mystery,* 258; Arab MS. 1450, fol. 15, Bibliothèque Nationale; and Dussaud, *Histoire et Religion des Nosairis,* 108–9.

8. Arab MS. 1450, fol. 160, Bibliothèque Nationale; and Dussaud, *Histoire et Religion des Nosairis,* 112.

9. See Arab MS. 5188, fol. 132, Bibliothèque Nationale. Cf. Jurji, "The Alids of North Syria," 340.

10. See the rubric entitled *Khitab al-Tilmidh ba'd al-Su'al* (The discourse of the disciple after being questioned), in Arab MS. 6182, Bibliothèque Nationale. This part of the manuscript immediately follows a portion of *Kitab al-Mashyakha.* Cf. Lyde, *The Asian Mystery,* 160.

11. See "Ma'rifat al-Ta'liq," in Arab MS. 1450, fol. 160, Bibliothèuqe Nationale.

12. Jurji, "The Alids of North Syria," 338–39. For a synopsis of the Philosophy of al-Ishraq, see M. Arkoun, "Ishrak," *The Encyclopedia of Islam* (Leiden and London: E. J. Brill, 1973), 4:119–20. See also, W. R. Inge, *The Philosophy of Plotinus* (London and New York: Longmam, Green, 1918), 113–12; and A. V. Williams Jackson, *Zoroastrian Studies: The Iranian Religion and Various Monographs* (New York: Columbia University Press, 1928), 174–75 and 187–93. Cf. Corbin, *Cyclical Time and Ismali Gnosis,* 98, 112, 131–33, and 136.

13. See "Ma'rifat al-Ta'liq," in Arab MS. 1450, fol. 160, Bibliothèque Nationale; and Dussaud, *Histoire et Religion des Nosairis,* 113–14.

14. De Sacy, *Exposé,* 2:578; and Dussaud, *Histoire et Religion des Nosairis,* 114.

15. See the names of these twelve in Dussaud, *Histoire et Religion des Nosairis,* 114–15.

16. Arab MS. 1450, fols. 160–67, Bibliothèque Nationale.

17. See this quotation in Lyde, *The Asian Mystery,* 258.

18. Arab MS. 1450, fols. 160–67, Bibliothèque Nationale; and Lyde, *The Asian Mystery,* 259.

19. Arab MS. 1450, Bibliothèque Nationale; and Lyde, *The Asian Mystery,* 261–62.

20. For this contract, see "al-Iqad" in Arab MS. 6182, fols. 36–37, Bibliothèque Nationale; and Lyde, *The Asian Mystery,* 256.

21. See al-Nashshabi, *Munazara,* Arab MS. 1450, fols. 16–167, Bibliothèque Na-

tionale. Cf. al-Hariri, *al-Alawiyyun al-Nusayriyyun,* 89–91; and Dussaud, *Histoire et Religion des Nosairis,* 115–19.

22. Al-Adani, *Kitab al-Bakura,* 2–3. I have followed closely the Arabic text giving a fresh translation in many places different from that of Salisbury.

23. Ibid., 3–4.

24. These suras constitute a part of *Kitab al-Majmu,* published in al-Adani, *Kitab al-Bakura,* 20–22, 25.

25. Al-Adani, *Kitab al-Bakura,* 4–7.

26. *Kitab Ta'lim al-Diyana al-Nusayriyya* in Arab MS. 6182, question 82, fols. 16–17, Bibliothèque Nationale.

27. Ibid., questions 88 and 92–93, fols. 18–19.

28. *Kitab al-Tawjih* in Arab MS. 6182, fol. 24; al-Adani, *Kitab al-Bakura,* 39–40; and *Kitab Majmu al-A'yad* ed. Strothmann, in *Der Islam,* 27:64, and 66, 183, 185, and 215.

29. Shihab al-Din Ibn Fadl Allah al-Umari, *al-Ta'rif bi al-Mustalah al-Sharif* (Cairo: Matbaat al-Asima, 1312/1894), quoted in Abu al-Abbas Ali Ahmad Ibn Ali al-Qalqashandi, *Subh al-A'sha fi Sina'at al-Insha,* (Cairo: al-Muassasa al-Misriyya al-Amma li al-Talif wa al-Nashr, 1964), 13:250–51.

30. *Kitab Ta'lim al-Diyana al-Nusayriyya,* Arab MS. 6182, fol. 15, Bibliothèque Nationale.

31. Ibid., fol. 16, questions 83 and 86; and Muhammad Ibn Ibrahim Ibn Said al-Ansari al-Akfani al-Sinjari, *Irshad al-Qasid ila Asna al-Maqasid,* ed. Abd al-Latif Muhammad al-Abd, (Cairo: Maktabat al-Anglo-Misriyya, 1978), 76–77; al-Umari, *al-Ta'rif bi al-Mustalah al-Sharif* in al-Qalqashandi, *Subh al-A'sha,* 13:249–50; and Badawi, *Madhahib al-Islamiyyin,* 2:442.

32. Wajdi, *Da'irat Ma'arif,* 250; and Badawi, *Madhahib al-Islamiyyin,* 2:440.

33. Langlois, "Religion et Doctrine des Noussaries," 435; and Lyde, *The Asian Mystery,* 160–61.

34—Nusayri Ceremonies: *Festivals*

1. Al-Tabarani, *Kitab Majmu al-A'yad,* ed. Strothmann.

2. Ibid., 27:4–5; and Catafago, "Notices Sur Les Anseriens," 149–68. The titles of these feasts are reproduced in Badawi, *Madhahib al-Islamiyyin,* 2:462, 470.

3. See the title page and the introduction of *Kitab al-Haft al-Sharif.*

4. Al-Tabarani, *Kitab Majmu al-A'yad,* ed. Srothmann, 10.

5. Al-Al, *Harakat al-Shi'a al-Mutatarrifin,* 8–33.

6. Saad Ibn Abd Allah al-Ashari, *al-Maqalat wa al-Firaq,* ed. Muhammad Jawad Mashkur (Tehran: Matbaat Haydari, 1963), 55.

7. Al-Nawbakhti, *Firaq al-Shi'a,* 81–82; al-Baghdadi, *al-Farq bayn al-Firaq,* 247; Abu al-Hasan Ali Ibn Ismail al-Ashari, *Kitab Maqalat,* 11; al-Sharastani, *Kitab al-Milal,* 2:17; Abu Hanifa al-Numan, *Da'a'im al-Islam* (Cairo: Dar al-Maarif, 1951), 62–63; al-Al, *Harakat al-Shi'a al-Mutatarrifin,* 74–75; and al-Shaibi, *al-Sila bayn al-Tasawwuf wa al-Tashayyu,* 136–40.

8. Al-Nawbakhti, *Firaq al-Shi'a,* 80.

9. Al-Tabarani, *Kitab Majmu al-A'yad,* ed. Strothmann, 20, 21, and 22; and *Kitab Ta'lim al-Diyana al-Nusayriyya,* question 101, Arab MS. 6182, fol. 38, Bibliothèque Nationale, where Muhammad is personified as a prayer.

10. Al-Adani, *Kitab al-Bakura,* 34.

11. See this festival listed among others in *Kitab Ta'lim al-Diyana al-Nusayriyya,* Arab MS. 6182, fol. 38, Bibliothèque Nationale.

12. Al-Kulayni, *al-Usal min al-Kafi,* 1:294–95; al-Razi, *Kitab al-Zina,* 256–57; Ibn Saad, *al-Tabaqat al-Kubra,* 3:14; and Ahmad Ibn Abi Yaqub Wadih al-Yaqubi, *Tarikh al-Ya'qubi* (al-Najaf: Matbaat al-Ghari, 1358/1939), 2:93.

13. See al-Tabarani, *Kitab Majmu al-A'yad,* ed. Strothmann, 55–59, which covers al-Khasibi's ode. I have tried only to give a translation of excerpts of this ode. The prayer and the sermon associated with this feast continue until p. 84 of the same.

14. Ibid., 55.

15. Ibid., 85–87.

16. Ibid., 97–102.

17. Ibn Khaldun, *al-Ibar wa Diwan al-Mubtada wa al-Khabar* (Beirut: Dar al-Qalam, 1956), 2:737–38; and Badawi, *Madhahib al-Islamiyyin,* 2:459. Cf. al-Hariri, *al-Alawiyyun al-Nusayriyyun,* 136.

18. Al-Tabarani, *Kitab Majmu al-A'yad,* ed. Strothmann, 104–6.

19. Ibid., 107.

20. Ibid., 107–10; and *Kitab al-Haft al-Sharif,* 116. For the commemoration of Ashura from the view point of the Twelver Shiites, see Ayoub, *Redemptive Suffering in Islam;* and Marcais, "Ashura," in *The Encyclopedia of Islam,* (Leiden and London: E. J. Brill, 1960), 1:705.

21. Al-Tabarani, *Kitab Majmu al-A'yad,* ed. Strothmann, 107–8. Cf. Ibn Babawayh (al-Qummi), *Ilal al-Shar'i* (al-Najaf:al-Matbaa al-Haydariyya, 1963), 1:227, where Ibn Babawayh condemns those who say that, like Christ, al-Husayn was not killed, but that he was thought to have been killed.

22. Ibid.

23. *Kitab al-Haft al-Sharif,* 116–20.

24. Ibid., 120.

25. Ibid., 121.

26. Ibid., 121–22.

27. Ibid., 123–26.

28. Ibid., 124–25.

29. Al-Nuri, *Nafas al-Rahman,* part 5, 53; and Massignon, *Salman Pàk et les Prémices Spirituelles de l'Islam iranien,* 48.

30. Al-Tabarani, *Kitab Majmu al-A'yad,* ed. Strothmann, 111–13.

31. Ibid., 124–25.

32. Ibid., 19–20.

33. Ibid., 154–55 and 163–74.

34. Al-Razi, *Kitab al-Zina,* 307; Abu al-Hasan Ali Ibn Isamil al-Ashari, *Kitab Maqalat,* 14; al-Baghdadi, *al-Farq bayn al-Firaq,* 251; and al-Shahrastani, *Kitab al-Milal,* 2:13.

35. Al-Tabarani, *Kitab Majmu al-A'yad,* ed. Strothmann, 188; Catafago, "Notices Sur Les Anseriens," 161–65; and Lyde, *The Asian Mystery,* 289–94, which is the English translation of Catafago's French translation of the original Arabic text.

36. Al-Tabarani, *Kitab Majmu al-A'yad,* 188–222.

37. Ibid., 223.

38. Ibid., 175–77; Catafago, "Notices Sur Les Anseriens," 154 and 158–59.

39. Al-Adani, *Kitab al-Bakura,* 34–35.

40. Lyde, *The Asian Mystery,* 177. Cf. Dussaud, *Histoire et Religion des Nosairis,* 149; al-Hariri, *al-Alawiyyun al-Nusayriyyun,* 140.

41. Lyde, *The Asian Mystery,* 177–78; and Dussaud, *Histoire et Religion des Nosairis,* 149.

42. Dussaud, *Histoire et Religion des Nosairis,* 150. For a very brief account of this and other Nusayri feasts, see Munir al-Sharif, *al-Alawiyyun Man Hum wa Ayna Hum,* 136–37. For Bast, see E. A. Wallis Budge, *The Book of the Dead* (New York: Bell Publishing Company, 1960), 187.

43. Al-Tabarani, *Kitab Majmu al-A'yad,* Ed. Strothmann, 175.

44. Badawi, *Madhahib al-Islamiyyin,* 2:466–69, especially 468.

45. Al-Tabarani, *Kitab Majmu al-A'yad,* ed. Strothmann, 175: Catafago, "Notices Sur Les Anseriens," 156–57 and Lyde, *The Asian Mystery,* 285–86, who gives a translation of the episode of the Christmas Eve.

46. Al-Tabarani, *Kitab Majmu al-A'yad,* ed. Strothmann, 175, 177; and Lyde, *The Asian Mystery,* 287.

47. Al-Tabarani, *Kitab Majmu al-A'yad,* ed. Strothmann, 177; and Lyde, *The Asian Mystery,* 187–88.

48. Al-Tabarani, *Kitab Majmu al-A'yad,* ed. Strothmann, 77; and Lyde, *The Asian Mystery,* 288.

49. Al-Tabarani, *Kitab Majmu al-A'yad,* ed. Strothmann, 178–79.

50. For an example, see White, "Saint Worship in Turkey," 8–18.

51. For these Ziyaras, see Lyde, *The Asian Mystery,* 167–75; and al-Sharif, *al-Alawiyyun Man Hum wa Ayna Hum,* 130–35.

52. Al-Sharif, *al-Alawiyyun Man Hum wa Ayna Hum,* 133. Cf. Lyde, *The Asian Mystery,* 168.

53. Al-Sharif, *al-Alawiyyun Man Hum wa Ayna Hum,* 134.

54. Ibid.

35—The Nusayri Mass

1. Lyde, *The Asian Mystery,* 158; al-Adani, *Kitab al-Bakura,* 36; and al-Hariri, al-*Alawiyyun al-Nusayriyyun,* 143.

2. Al-Adani, *Kitab al-Bakura,* 34.

3. Lyde, *The Asian Mystery,* 157.

4. Al-Adani, *Kitab al-Bakura,* 36.

5. Lyde, *The Asian Mystery,* 154–55.

6. Kitab Ta'lim al-Diyana al-Nusayriyya, Arab MS. 6182, fols. 17–26 especially fol. 24, Bibliothèque Nationale.

7. See chapter 28 of this book.

8. See *Kitab Ta'lim al-Diyana al-Nusayriyya,* Arab MS. 6182, question 97, fol. 18, Bibliothèque Nationale.

9. Al-Umari, *al-Ta'rif bi al-Mustalah al-Sharif* in al-Qalqashandi, *Subh al-A'sha,* 13:250.

10. *Kitab al-Mashyakha,* in Lyde, *The Asian Mystery,* 243–56.

11. Al-Adani, *Kitab al-Bakura,* 36–54.

12. Ibid., 36–37. Dussaud, who follows al-Adani's narrative, states that people assemble at daybreak at the house of Sahib al-Id to show that like the Harranians the Nusayris conduct their prayers before sunrise. While it is true that the Nusayris recognize

the sun and its rising, the celebration of the feast, as evident from al-Adani, is done in the evening, not at sunrise. See Dussaud, *Histoire et Religion des Nosaris,* 89–90. Furthermore, Dussaud, and also Salisbury, state that a vessel filled with wine of pressed grapes or figs is made ready. I found no mention of a juice of pressed figs in al-Adani's *Kitab al-Bakura.*

13. Al-Adani, *Kitab al-Bakura,* 37–38, 40–48, 53–54, 176–77, 198–99; and Dussaud, *Histoire et Religion des Nosairis,* 90–91. A French translation of the perfume mass is found in Langlois, "Religion et Doctrine des Noussaries," 436. The first English translation of the Perfume Mass was made by Rev. Samuel Lyde with the title Mass of the Ointment. See Lyde, *The Asian Mystery,* 246–48 and 298–99. For an explanation of the black turban, the thimble, and the two-edged knife, see al-Hariri, *al-Alawiyyun al-Nusayriyyun,* 147 n. 10, 156–58. See also *Kitab al-Mashyakha,* Arab MS. 6182, fols. 23–24, 28–30, Bibliothèque Nationale.

14. Lyde, *The Asian Mystery,* 155.

15. Lammens, "Les Nosairis Furent-Ils Chrétriens?" 33–50.

16. Dussaud, *Histoire et Religion des Nosairis,* 51–52, 64.

17. Ibid., 92.

18. Ibid., 48, 147, 201, 211, quoted by Lammens, "Les Nosairis Furent-Ils Chrétriens?" 47.

19. Lammens, "Les Nosairis Furent-Ils Chrétriens?" 33–39, 42, 44–49.

20. Al-Hariri, *al-Alawiyyun al-Nusayriyyun,* 186–87.

21. Badawi, *Madhahib al-Islamiyyin,* 2:466–69.

22. Lammens, "Les Nosairis Furent-Ils Chrétiens?" 48.

23. See above p. 260; Saad Ibn Abd Allah al-Ashari, *al-Maqalat wa al-Firaq,* 100–1; al-Nawbakhti, *Firaq al-Shi'a,* 102–3; Abu Jafar al-Tusi, *al-Ghayba,* 244; and Abu Mansur Ahmad Ibn Ali al-Tabarsi, *al-Ihtijaj,* 190–91.

24. Al-Tabarani, *Kitab Majmu al-A'yad,* ed. Strothmann, 19, and the discussion of the names of this sect in the previous chapter.

36—The Nusayris, Sunnites, and Twelver Shiites

1. Lyde, *The Asian Mystery,* 102–9; Burckhardt, *Travels in Syria and the Holy Land,* and Charles Williams Heckethorn, *The Secret Societies of All Ages and Countries,* (New York: New York University, 1966), 1:130.

2. Al-Adani, *Kitab al-Bakura,* 58–59, 93.

3. On the taqiyya, see Goldziher, "Das Prinzip des Takijja in Islam," *Zeitschrift der deutschen morgenländischen Gesellschaft* 60 (1906): 213–26; idem, *Vorlesungen über den Islam,* 215 and 246; Strothmann, "Takiya," *The Encyclopedia of Islam* (Leiden: E. J. Brill, 1934), 4:628–29, al-Sayyid Muhsin al-Amin, *al-Shi'a bayn al-Haqa'iq wa al-Awham* (Shaqra: al-Matbaa al-Amiliyya, 1975), 185–89; al-Shaibi, "al-Taqiyya: Usuluha wa Tatawwuruha," *Majallat Kuliyyat al-Adab,* 16 (1961–63): 233–67; al-Hariri, *al-Alawiyyun al-Nusayriyyun,* 123–30; and Muhammad al-Husayn al-Muzaffar, *al-Imam al-Sadiq* (Beirut: Dar al-Zahra, 1978), 1:83–93. Ihsan Ilahi Zahir, in *Al-Shi'a wa Ahl al-Bayt,* 4, contends that there is nothing to support the taqiyya in Islam.

4. Ibn Hazm, *Kitab al-Fisal,* 2:114–15. Cf. Muhammad Raghib Paha, *Safinat al-Raqhib wa Dafinat al-Talib* (Cairo: Bulaq, 1255/1839), 216, reprinted by Bulaq in 1282/1865.

5. Abd Allah Sallum al-Samarrai, *al-Shu'ubiyya Haraka Mudadda li al-Islam wa al-Umma al-Arabiyya* (Baghdad: al-Muassasa al-Iraqiyya li al-Diaya wa al-Tibaa, 1984).

6. Mahmud Ibn Umar al-Zamakhshari, *al-Kashshaf an Haqa'iq Ghawamid al-Tanzil* (Commentary on the Quran), (Cairo: Matbaat Mustafa Muhammad, 1354/1935), 4:112; Abu Nuaym al-Isfahani, *Hilyat al-Awliya,* 1, 140; al-Kulayni, *al-Usul min al-Kafi,* 2:219; Ibn Ibrahim, *Tafsir,* 236; and al-Shaibi, "al-Taqiyya: Usuluha wa Tatawwuruha," 235.

7. Al-Kulayni, *al-Usul min al-Kafi,* 2:219. In *Kitab al-Haft al-Sharif,* 54, this saying is ascribed to the Imam Jafar al-Sadiq.

8. *Kitab al-Haft al-Sharif,* 54 and *Kitab al-Hikam al-Ja'fariyya li al-Imam al-Sadq Ja'far Ibn Muhammad,* ed. Arif Tamir (Beirut: al-Matbaa al-Katholikiyya, 1957), 68–69. In his commentary on the Quran, Ibn Ibrahim states that the taqiyya is the "license of the believer." See Ibn Ibrahim, *Tafsir,* 54.

9. Al-Shaykh al-Mufid, *Kitab Sharh Aqa'id al-Saduq aw Tashih al-I'tiqad* (Tabriz: Matbaat Ridai, 1371/1951), 66. This book is printed together with al-Mufid's *Awa'il al-Maqalat;* Ibn Ibrahim, *Tafsir,* 55 and Tamir, *al-Hikam al-Jafariyya,* 68.

10. *Kitab al-Haft al-Sharif,* 54, 78, 198, and 201.

11. Al-Adani, *Kitab al-Bakura,* 82.

12. Al-Adani, *Kitab al-Bakura,* 25.

13. Heckethorn, *The Secret Societies of All Ages and Countries,* 1:130–31; and Bernard H. Springett, *Secret Sects of Syria and the Lebanon* (London: George Allen & Unwin, 1922), chapters 16–17, 140–65. Springett's account of the Nusayris is a rehash of the Rev. Lyde's *Asian Mystery* and Salisbury's translation of al-Adani's *Kitab al-Bakura.*

14. Springett, *Secret Sects of Syria and the Lebanon,* the introduction, 5–9.

15. F. Walpole, *The Ansayrii and the Assassins With Travels in the Further East in 1850–1851 including a Visit to Nineveh* (London: R. Bently, 1851), 3:354; and Lyde, *The Asian Mystery,* 162 who follows Walpole.

16. Langlois, "Religion et Doctrine des Noussairiès," 434 and Lyde, *The Asian Mystery,* 162.

17. Al-Adani, *Kitab al-Bakura,* 83–84; and Salisbury, "Notes on the Book of Sulaiman's First Ripe Fruit," 290, 296. Salisbury has misunderstood the meaning of these questions and answers.

18. See the fourth Sura in al-Adani, *Kitab al-Bakura,* 14–18; and Salisbury, "Notes on the Book of Sulaiman's First Ripe Fruit," 241–45.

19. Al-Adani, *Kitab al-Bakura,* 29–30; and Salisbury, "Notes on the Book of Sulaiman's First Ripe Fruit," 258–59.

20. Al-Adani, *Kitab al-Bakura,* 83; and Salisbury, "Notes on the Book of Sulaiman's First Ripe Fruit," 297.

21. Springett, *Secret Sects of Syria and the Lebanon,* 176, n.1.

22. Lyde, *The Asian Mystery,* 162.

23. Von Hammer-Purgstall, *The History of the Assassins,* 57 and Lyde, *The Asian Mystery,* 163.

24. Lyde, *The Asian Mystery,* 162.

25. Springett, *Secret Sects of Syria and the Lebanon,* 8 of the introduction.

26. For this Fatwa, see Guyard, "le Fatawa d'Ibn Taimiyyah," 167.

27. See al-Shaykh al-Saduq Abu Jafar Ibn Muhammad Ibn Babawayh (al-Qummi), *Ilal al-Shara'i* (al-Najaf: al-Matbaa al-Haydariyya, 138/1963), 1: 227. Cf. al-Shaykh al-Mufid, *Kitab Sharh Aqa'id al-Saduq aw Tashih al-I'tiqadx,* 63; Ibn Shahr Ashbub, *Manaqib Al Abi Talib,* 1: 226–27; Muhammad Ibn Ismail al-Hairi, *Muntaha al-Maqal* (Tehran: n.p. 1320/1902), 316; and Saad Ibn Abd Allah al-Ashari, *al-Maqalat wa al-Firaq,* 37.

28. Ibn Shahr Ahub, *Manaqib Al Abi Talib,* 1: 228.

29. Al-Askari, *al-Alawiyyun aw al-Nusayriyya,* 44.

30. See this fatwa in the newspaper *al-Sha'b,* 31 July 1936, reproduced in Munir al-Sharif, *Ai-Alawiyyun Man Hum wa Ayna Hum,* 59.

31. Munir al-Sharif, *al-Alawiyyun Man Hum wa Ayna Hum,* 59–60.

32. Shaykh Mahmud al-Salih, *al-Naba al-Yaqin an al-Alawiyyin.*

33. Muhammad Rida Shams al-Din, *Ma al-Alawiyyin fi Suriyya* (Beirut: Matbaat al-Insaf, 1956), 53–54.

34. Arif al-Sus, *Man Huwa al-Alawi,* in Uthman, *al-Alawiyyun,* 131.

35. Abd al-Rahman al-Khayyir, "Yaqzat al-Alawiyyin," reproduced in Uthman, *al-Alawiyyun,* 173–89, especially 179.

36. Ahmad Sulayman Ibrahim, "al-Alawiyyun bayn al-Muslimin wa al-Islam," reproduced in Uthman, *al-Alawiyyun* 190–91.

37. Shayk Muhammad Hasan Yasin, "al-Alawiyyun Shi'iyyun," reproduced in Uthman, *al-Alawiyyun,* 191–210.

38. See the anonymous *al-Alawiyyun Shi'at Ahl al-Bayt: Bayan Aqidat al-Alawiyyin,* (Beirut: n.p., 1392/1972), 8–10. Judging by the introduction, it is probable that this monograph has been compiled by the learned Shiite Hasan Mahdi al-Shirazi. This proclamation first appeared in the newspaper *al-Qabas,* 27 July 1937.

39. *Al-Alawiyyin Shi'at Ahl al-Bayt,* 10–32 and note 1 containing the signatories of the proclamation.

40. Maoz, "Syria under Hafiz al-Asad: New Domestic and Foreign Policies," *Jerusalem Papers on Peace Problems* 15 (1975): 10–11; and Gubser, "The Alawites of Syria," 44.

41. Kelidar, "Religion and State in Syria," 18; and Moshe Maoz, "The Emergence of Modern Syria," 30; and Hrair Dekmejian, *Islam in Revolution* (Syracuse, New York: Syracuse University Press, 1985), 114.

42. Gubser, "The Alawites of Syria," 43–44.

43. Ibid., 44.

44. Alisdare Drysdale, "The Assad Regime and its Troubles," *Middle East Research and Information Project Report* 110 (November–December 1982): 8 and al-Din, *al-Nusayriyya,* 190.

45. See the prayers of the Nusayris addressed to Sulayman al-Murshid and his sons Mujib and Saji as gods. These prayers consist of the following Suras: (1) Surat al-Sajda, (2) Surat al-Fath, (3) Surat al-Ma'rifa, (4) Surat al-Du'a, (5) Surat al-Iqtibas (6) Surat al-Itiraf and (7) Surat al-Iqrar, in Mujahid al-Amin, *al-Nusayriyya (al-Alawiyyun), 67–71.*

37—Pagan, Christian, and Islamic Elements in the Beliefs of the Ghulat

1. Al-Sarraf, *al-Shabak,* 118–121.

2. F. W. Hasluck, *Christianity and Islam,* 1:124–25.

3. Dunmore, report dated 24 October in *Missionary Herald* (1854): 56.

4. Herrick, report dated 16 November 1865, 68; and Grenard, "Une Secte Religieuse," 519.

5. Stead, "The Ali Ilahi Sect," 186–87; and Samuel Graham Wilson, *Persian Life and Customs,* 234–35.

6. J. G. Taylor, "Journal of a Tour," 297 and 320.

7. Grenard, "Une Secte Religieuse," 518–19.

8. White, "Survivals of Primitive Religions," 151–52. Cf. H. J. Van Lennep, *Travels*

in Little Known Parts of Asia Minor, 1:293 and 295; and David Marshall Lang, *The Armenians: A People in Exile* (London: George Allen and Unwin, 1981), 161.

9. Stead, "The Ali Ilahi Sect," 185–86. White associates the Devil's worship, which he calls "bondage through fear of evil spirits" with the "bondage through fear of the evil eye." See White, "Survivals of Primitive Religions," 158.

10. Samuel Graham Wilson, *Persian Life and Customs,* 240.

11. Al-Sarraf, *al-Shabak,* 116.

12. Samuel Graham Wilson, *Persian Life and Customs,* 240.

13. See *Kitab Ta'lim al-Diyana al-Nusayriyya,* Arab MS. 6182, question 1 and its answer, fol. 2, Bibliothèque Nationale, which affirms that Ali is the creator of mankind; and extracts from *Kitab al-Mashyakha,* in Lyde, *The Asian Mystery,* 111–16, 124, 233–42, and 271.

14. On all of these points, see Dunmore, report dated 24 October in *Missionary Herald* (1854): 55–56; Parson, ibid., 54 (1858): 23–24, Nutting, ibid., 56 (1860): 345–47, Herrick, ibid., 62 (1866): 68–69; M. F. Grenard, "Une Secte Religieuse," 512–19; Taylor, "Journal of a Tour in Armenia," 319–32; G. E. White, "The Shia Turks," *Faith and Thought, Journal of the Transaction of the Victoria Institute,* 42 (1980): 236; Horatio Southgate, *Narrative of a Tour Through Armenia, Kurdistan, Persia, and Mesopotamia,* (New York, 1844) 2:140–41; and F. W. Hasluck, *Christianity and Islam under the Sultans* (Oxford, 1929), 1:144–58.

15. See previous chapters of this book on the Ahl-i Haqq, and Charles Wilson, *Handbook for Travellers,* 68.

16. On all these points, consult the authorities cited above in footnote 14.

17. See Nutting, report dated 30 July 1860, 345–46.

18. White, "The Shia Turks," 230.

19. Ramsay, *Pauline and Other Studies in Early Christian History* (New York: A. C. Armstrong & Son, 1906), 180; and idem, "The Intermixture of Races in Asia Minor: Some of its Causes and Effects," *Proceedings of the British Academy* 7 (1917), 20.

20. Grenard, "Une Secte Religieuse," 513.

21. Trowbridge, "The Alevis, or Deifiers of Ali," 353.

22. Samuel Graham Wilson, *Persian Life and Customs,* 238, 240.

23. Stead, "The Ali Ilahi Sect," 189. Cf. Southgate, *Narrative of a Tour,* 2:140–42. Southgate considers the Ali Ilahis of Kerind as the remnants of ancient pagans in Assyria and Mesopotamia.

24. De Gobineau, *Trois ans en Asie,* 339.

25. White, "Survivals of Primitive Religions," 161.

26. For the spread of Christianity among the ancient Turks and Mongols, see Cheikho, "al-Nasraniyya bayn Qudama al-Turk wa al-Maghul" (Christianity Among the Ancient Turks and Mongols), *al-Mashriq* 26 (1913): 747–72; and Alphonse Mingana, *The Early Spread of Christianity in Central Asia and the Far East: A New Document* (Manchester: The University Press, 1925), printed with additions in the *Bulletin of the John Rylands Library* 9, no. 1 (July 1925); and Barthold, *Zur Geschichte des Christentums in Mittel-Asien bis zur mongolischen Eroberung,* trans. from the Russian into German by Rudolf Stübe (Tübingen und Leipzig: J. C. B. Mohr, 1901), 1–73.

27. Wittek, "Zur Geschichte Angoras im Mittelalter," 339.

28. Shaw, *History of the Ottoman Empire,* 1:121.

29. W. J. Hamilton, *Researches in Asia Minor, Pontus, and Armenia with Some account of their antiquities and geologies,* (London: J. Murray, 1842), 1:240.

30. Ramsay, *Impressions of Turkey,* 242.

31. Southgate, *Narrative of a Visit,* 32 n. 1

32. Cuinet, *La Turquie d'Asie,* 1:121.

33. Southgate, *Narrative of a Visit,* 31 n.1.

34. F. W. Hasluck, Christianity and Islam, 2:469–72.

35. Ibid., 1:8–97.

36. Jacob, "Die Baktaschijje," 15.

37. Von Hammer-Purgstall, *Histoire de l'Empire Ottoman,* 1:31.

38. Birge, *Bektashi Order,* 28.

39. F. Sarre, *Reise in Kleinasien—Sommer 1895. Forschungen zur Seldjukischen Kunst und Geographie des Landes* (Berlin: D. Reimer, 1896), 39–41; and Tamara Talbot Rice, *The Seljuks in Asia Minor* (New York: Frederick A. Praeger, 1961), 66.

40. Clement Huart, *Konia, la ville des Derviches Tourneurs, Souvenirs, d'une Voyage en Asie Mineure* (Paris: E. Leroux, 1897), 214–16.

41. Von Hammer-Purgstall, *Histoire de l'Empire Ottoman,* 1:45–47; E. Pears, *The Destruction of the Greek Empire and the Story of the Capture of Constantinople by the Turks* (London: Longman, green, 1903), 56; and Hasluck, *Christianity and Islam,* 2:370–71.

42. Yacoub Artin Pacha, *Contributions à l'Étude du Blazon en Orient* (London: B. Quaritch, 1902), 149.

43. Rice, *The Seljuks in Asia Minor,* 114.

44. Ibid., and Wittek, "Yazijioglu Ali on the Christian Turks of Dobruja," *Bulletin of the British School of Oriental and African Studies* 14, part 3 (1952): 639–68.

45. Rice, *The Seljuks in Asia Minor,* 114.

46. Birge, *Bektashi Order,* 28–33.

47. Al-Aflaki, *Manaqib al-Arifin,* 20–22, 44–45, and the preface by Idries Shah, 9; Ramsay, *The Revolution in Constantinople and Turkey: a diary* (London: Hodder and Stoughton, 1909), 202; Sir Charles Elliot, *Turkey in Europe* (London: E. Arnold, 1900), 185; and Hasluck, *Christianity and Islam,* 370–72.

48. G. Le Strange, *The Lands of the Eastern Caliphate* (London: Frank Cass, 1966), 146.

49. On Baba Ishaq, see chapter 2 of this book.

50. Herbert Adams Gibbons, *The Foundation of the Ottoman Empire* (London: Frank Cass, 1968), 29; and Shaw, *History of the Ottoman Empire,* 1:12–13.

51. For a more comprehensive treatment of the ruling and the subject classes in the Ottoman administration see Shaw, *History of the Ottoman Empire,* chapter 5, 1:112–67.

52. Ziya Gökalp, *Turkish Nationalism and Western Civilization,* trans. Niyazi Berkes (New York: Columbia University Press, 1959), 105.

53. Gibbons, *The Foundation of the Ottoman Empire,* 29 and 80–81.

54. Eli Smith and H. G. O. Dwight, *Missionary Researches in Armenia including a Journey Through Asia Minor and into Georgia and Persia with a visit to the Nestorian and Chaldean Christians of Oormiah and Salmas* (London: George Wightman, 1834), 83.

55. Gökalp, *Turkish Nationalism,* 105; Halide Edib, *Turkey Faces West* (New Haven: Yale University Press, 1930), 28–30; and Ramsay, *Impressions of Turkey,* 99.

56. Ramsay, "The Intermixture of Races in Asia Minor," 54.

57. Gökalp, *Turkish Nationalism,* 107; and Edib, *Turkey Faces West,* 37.

58. F. W. Hasluck, *Christianity and Islam,* 2:568.

59. Eugène Marie Melchior, Vicomte de Vogüe, *Histoires Orientales,* (Paris: Colmann-Levy, 1911), 198.

60. Von Hammer-Purgstall, *Histoire de l'Empire Ottoman,* 2:181–83; Hasluck, *Christianity and Islam,* 2:568; Inalcik, *Ottoman Empire,* 188–90; Brockelmann, *History of the Islamic*

People, 274; Babinger, "Schejch Bedr ed-Din," 1–106; and Köprülü, *Türk Edebiyatinda Ilk Mutesavviflar* (Istanbul: Matbaa-Yi Amire, 1918), 234.

61. Cuinet, *La Turquie de Asie,* 1:341; and F. W. Hasluck, *Christianity and Islam,* 1:83–84 and 2:571–72.

62. White, "The Shia Turks," 235.

63. Crowfoot, "Survival Among the Kappadokian Kizilbash," 305–15.

38—Armenian Elements in the Beliefs of the Kizilbash Kurds

1. Cuinet, *La Turquie d'Asie,* 1:855; F. Von Luschan and E. Peterson, *Reisen in Lykien* (Wien: Gerold, 1899), 2:198–213; and Hasluck, *Christianity and Islam,* 1:142.

2. Molyneux-Seel, "Journey in Derism," 66; White, "Alevi Turks," 690 ff; F. W. Hasluck, *Christianity and Islam,* 142–43; and Faruk Sumer, "Cepni," *The Encyclopedia of Islam* (Leiden and London: E. J. Brill, 1965), 2:0.

3. Dunmore, report dated 22 January 1857, 219–20; Ball, report dated 8 August 1857, 395–96; Nutting, report dated 30 July 1860, 345–46; Herrick, report dated 16 November 1865, 68–69; Livingston, report dated 30 March 1869, 59–246; Jewett, report dated 16 December 1857, 109; Winchester, report dated 28 November 1860, 71; Southgate, *Narrative of a Tour,* 1:170–71; and White, "The Shia Turks," 225–36. For the beliefs of Kizilbash who live between Sivas and Erzerum, see J. G. Taylor, "Journal of a Tour," 304.

4. Molyneux-Seel, "Journey in Derism," 44, 49.

5. Southgate, *Narrative of a Tour,* 2:140–42; and Stead, "The Ali Ilahi Sect," 184–89.

6. Charles Wilson, *Handbook for Travellers,* 62. Cf. Walpole, *The Ansayrii and the Assassins,* 3:226, where the author states that there is a tradition that the Kurds are Armenians who were converted to Muhammadanism.

7. Charles Wilson, "Notes on the Physical and Historical Geography of Asia Minor," *Royal Geographical Society* 6 (June 1884): 313.

8. J. G. Taylor, "Journals of a Tour," 318; idem, "Travels in Kurdistan, with Notices of the Sources of the Eastern and Western Tigris, and Ancient Ruins in their neighborhood," *Journal of the Royal Geographical Society* 35 (1865): 29–30; and Molyneux-Seel, "Journey in Derism," 44 and 67.

9. E. B. Soane, *Grammar of the Kurmanji or Kurdish Language* (London: Luzac, 1913), 5; and Ivanow, *Truth-Worshippers,* 9 n.1.

10. Moses Khorenantsi, *History of the Armenians,* trans. Robert W. Thomson (Cambridge, Mass: Harvard University Press, 1978), 79–80; and J. G. Taylor, "Journal of a Tour," 318.

11. Taylor, "Journal of a Tour," 319.

12. Elsworth Huntington, "Through the Great Canon," 186–87.

13. Yaqut al-Hamawi, *Mujam al-Buldan,* 1st. ed. (Cairo: Matbaat al-Saada, 1323/1905), 1:190.

14. See *The Travels of Ibn Battuta, 1325–1354,* trans. H. A. R. Gibb, (Cambridge: Cambridge University Press, 1962), 2:437.

15. E. Scott-Stevenson, *Our Ride Through Asia Minor* (London: Chapman and Hall limited, 1881), 218.

16. F. W. Hasluck, *Christianity and Islam,* 1:516.

17. Molyneux-Seel, "Journey in Derism," 67.

18. For example see Kannenburg, quoted in Jacob, *Die Baktaschijje,* 36.

19. White, "Alevi Turks," 697.

20. F. Macler, "Armenia (Christian)," *Encyclopedia of Religion and Ethics,* ed. James Hastings New York: Charles Scribner, 1908), 1:807; and Smith and Dwight, *Researches in Armenia,* 453 and 457.

21. Macler, "Armenia," 1:807.

22. Ivanow, *Truth-Worshippers,* 8–9.

23. Photius, *Adversus Manichaeos,* in *Patrologia Graecae 102,* ed. Paul Migne (1860):109; and Edward Gibbon, *The History of the Decline and Fall of the Roman Empire,* ed. J. B. Bury (New York: Fred De Fau & Company, 1905), 10:4.

24. Photius, *Adversus Manichaeos,* 109; John Lawrence Von Mosheim, *Institutes of Ecclesiastical History Ancient and Modern,* trans. James Murdock (New York: Harper & Brothers, 1844), 2:101, and notes 1 and 2; and Gibbon, *Decline and Fall,* 4 n. 5, 387–89.

25. Karapet Ter-Mekerttschian, *Die Paulikianer im byzantinischen Kaiserreich und verwandte ketzerische Erscheinungen in Armenien* (Leipzig: J. C. Hinrichs, 1893), 93.

26. Karapet, *Die Paulikianer,* 110; F. C. Conybeare, *The Key of Truth: A Manual of The Paulician Church of Armenia* (Oxford University Press, 1898), 142–47; Mosheim, *Ecclesiastical History,* 2:103; Gibbon, *Decline and Fall,* 5–6; N. Bonwetsch, "Paulicians," in *The New Schaff-Herzog Encyclopedia of Religious Knowledge,* ed. Samuel Macauley Jackson (New York: Funk and Wagnalls, 1910), 8:417; Adrian Fortesque, "Paulicians," in *The Catholic Encyclopedia,* ed. Charles G. Herbermann (New York: The Encyclopedia Press, 1913), 11:584; and C. A. Scott, "Paulicians," in *Encyclopedia of Religion and Ethics,* ed. James Hastings (New York: Charles Scribner's, 1917), 9:696.

27. Leon Arpee, *A History of Armenian Christianity from the Beginning to Our Own Time* (New York: The Armenian Missionary Association of America, 1946), 103.

28. See Gregory Magistros in Appendix 3, Conybeare, *The Key of Truth,* 148.

29. See the Statements of John the Philosopher, who became Catholicos of Armenia in A.D. 719, in Conybeare, *The Key of Truth,* 57–58. Although there were two former Catholicoi named Nerses one who died in 374 and the other (524–33), it is most likely that Nerses the Builder is intended here. See Arpee, *A History of Armenian Christianity,* 105.

30. Arpee, *A History of Armenian Christianity,* 105.

31. See the Statement of the Armenian Catholicos, John the Philosopher, in Conybeare, *The Key of Truth,* 57.

32. Conybeare, *The Key of Truth,* 59.

33. Peter Siculus, *Historia Manichaeorum,* in *Patrologia Graecae 104,* 1242–1303.

34. Photius, *Adversus Manichaeos,* 15–263; and Siculus, *Historia Manichaeorum,* 104, 1242–1303.

35. Photius, *Adversus Manichaeos,* 125; Siculus, *Historia Manichaeorum,* 104, 1242–1303, and George Cedrenus, *Compendium Historiarum* (Venice: B. Javarina, 1792), 2:480.

36. Siculus, *Historia Manichaeorum* in *Patrologia Graecae,* 104, 1242–1303; and vol. 4 of *The Cambridge Medieval History,* planned by J. B. Bury (New York: The MacMillan, 1936), 139.

37. See the letter written by Gregory of Nareg to the abbot of the Monastery of Kdjav in Appendix 1, Conybeare, *The Key of Truth,* 129, and the letter written by Gregory Magistros to the Catholicos of the Syrians in Appendix 3 of the same, 144 and 148. For a description and exact location of Thonrak see Conybeare, *The Key of Truth,* 59, 60, 76, and 129.

38. Conybeare, *The Key of Truth,* 60–63.

39. Arpee, *A History of Armenian Christianity,* 108.

40. Conybeare, *The Key of Truth,* 64.

41. Arpee, *A History of Armenian Christianity,* 108.

42. Conybeare, *The Key of Truth,* 64.

43. Ahmad Ibn Yahya al-Baladhuri, *Futuh al-Buldan,* ed. Salah al-Din al-Munajjid (Cairo: Maktabat al-Nahda al-Misriyya, 1956), 1:248. According to the Armenian Chronicler Vartan (d. 1270), Smbat was captured by the Turkish commander Bugha and sent to Baghdad, where he died a martyr's death, having refused to recant the Christian faith. See Conybeare, *The Key of Truth,* 65. Cf. M. Canard, "Arminiya," in *The Encyclopedia of Islam* (Leiden: E. J. Brill, 1960), 1:637.

44. Conybeare, *The Key of Truth,* 64–66, following relevant Armenian sources, especially Thomas Artsruni.

45. See Gregory Magistros in Appendix 3 of Conybeare, *The Key of Truth,* 145.

46. See the *History of Aristaces* by Vardapet of Lastivert in Appendix 2 of Conybeare, *The Key of Truth,* 134–36.

47. See Gregory Magistros, in Appendix 3 of Conybeare, *The Key of Truth,* 146–49.

48. Conybeare, *The Key of Truth,* 71.

49. Ibid., 111 and 139; R. Runciman, *The Medieval Manichee,* (Cambridge: Cambridge University Press, 1947), 122; Ivanow, *Truth-Worshippers,* 51; A. A. Vasiliev, *History of the Byzantine Empire 324–1453* (Madison: The University of Wisconsin Press, 1964), 2:383 and 473; and David Marshall Lang, *The Armenians a People in Exile.* (London and Boston, Allen and Unwin, 1981), 165.

50. The *Chronicle* of Paul W. Meherean is still preserved in manuscript form in the library of San Lazaro, Venice. Conybeare quotes page 120 of this manuscript. See Conybeare, *The Key of Truth,* 71 and 82.

51. Ibid., 22–28, 49, 82.

52. Ibid., 76.

53. Ghowkas Inchichian, *Storagrowt'iwn Hayastaneayts* (Description of Armenia) (Venice: Monastery of San Lazaro, 1822), 113.

54. Conybeare, *The Key of Truth,* 23, 27, 49, 77, 78, 86, 125, 162, 164, and Appendix 5, 155.

55. Ibid., 22, 26, 163, 173, and Ivanow, *Truth-Worshippers,* 54.

56. White, "The Shia Turks," 231.

57. Conybeare, *The Key of Truth,* 163.

58. Ibid.; and Adjarian, "Gyorans et Thoumaris," 302.

59. See Frédéric Macler's comment on Adjarian's article, printed with it, 305.

60. Al-Sarraf, *al-Shabak,* 120–21; Ivanow, *Truth-Worshippers,* 55; Grenard, "Une Secte Religieuse," 517–18; and Petrushevsky, *Islam in Iran,* 264.

61. Conybeare, *The Key of Truth,* 49.

62. Ibid., 36 and 124.

63. See Above chapter 8 of this book on religious hierarchy; Stead, "The Ali Ilahi Sect," 186–87 and Ivanow, *Truth-Worshippers,* 55.

64. See chapter 8 of this book on religious hierarchy.

65. Molyneux-Seel, "Journey in Derism," 64–65.

66. White, "Alevi Turks," 698.

67. See chapters 19–20 of this book.

68. See *Maqtal al-Husayn wa Masra Ahl Baytihi wa Ashabihi fi Karbala al-Mushtahir bi Maqtal Abi Mikhnaf* (the killing of al-Husayn and members of his household and companions at Karbala, known as the Episode of the Killing of al-Husayn related by Abu Mikhnaf), (al-Najaf: Matbaat al-Ghadir, n.d.), 107–8.

69. See chapter 9 of this book on the Twelve Imams; Ibn Kathir, *al-Bidaya wa al-*

Nihaya, 1:321–26 and 355–67; al-Majlisi, *Bihar al-Anwar,* 13:278–322; al-Maqdisi, *al-Bad wa al-Tarikh,* 77–78; W. C. Taylor, *History of Mohammedanism,* 31–33; LeStrange, *The Lands of the Eastern Caliphate,* 175; and F. W. Hasluck, *Christianity and Islam,* 2:319–36.

70. F. W. Hasluck, *Christianity and Islam,* 2:327. In Mosul he is called Khidr Elias and the people observe a feast in his honor and make certain sweets for the occasion, called the halawa of Khidr Elias. For more information see Wensinck, "al-Khadir," 2:861–65.

71. Molyneux-Seel, "Journey in Derism," 66; and Pietro Della Valle, *Viaggi di Pietro Della Valle il pelligrino.* (Rome: Apresso Dragondelli, 1658), 2: 258.

72. Molyneux-Seel, "Journey in Derism," 66.

73. Grenard, "Une Secte Religieuse," 518.

74. F. W. Hasluck, *Christianity and Islam,* 2:319–36; Dussaud, *Histoire et Religion des Nosairis,* 128–35.

75. Southgate, *Narrative of a Tour,* 1:196.

76. Molyneux-Seel, "Journey in Derism," 68.

77. Huntington, "Through the Great Canon," 188.

78. Von Luschen, "Early inhabitants of Western Asia," 241–44.

79. Dunmore, report, *Missionary Herald* 54 (April 1858): 113; and Parson, report dated 17 September 1857.

80. Michele Febure, *Théatre de la Turquie* (Paris: E. Couterot, 1682), 45–46.

81. J. G. Taylor, "Journal of a Tour," 323.

82. Von Luschan, "Early Inhabitants of Western Asia," 229.

83. Ibid., 241–44.

84. F. W. Hasluck, *Christianity and Islam,* 1:157–58.

85. Cuinet, *La Turquie d'Asie,* 1:121.

86. F. W. Hasluck, *Christianity and Islam,* 1:158.

Bibliography

Books: Eastern Sources

Abdin, Muhammad Amin Ibn Umar, known as Ibn. *Ijabat al-Ghawth bi Bayan Hal al-Nuqub wa al-Nujaba wa al-Abdal wa al-Awtad wa al-Ghawth.* In Ibn Abdin, *Rasa'il Ibn Abdin.* Vol. 2. Al-Asitana: Muhammad Hashim al-Kutubi, 1325/1907.

Adami, Muhammad Hasan al-. *Al-Haqa'iq al-Khafiyya an al-Shi'a al-Fatimiyya wa al-lthnay'ashariyya.* Cairo: al-Haya al-Misriyya li al-Tibaa wa al-Nashr, 1970.

Adami, Saad Ibrahim al-. *Al-Aqaliyyat al-Diniyya wa al-Qawmiyya wa Ta'thiruha ala al-Waqi al-Siyasi wa al-Ijtima'i fi Muhafazat Ninawa.* n.p:, 1982.

Adani, Sulayman al-. *Kitab al-Bakura al-Sulaymaniyya fi Kashf Asrar al-Diyana al-Nusayriyya,* Beirut: n.p. and n.d. For English translation of the same, see Salisbury, Edward, in the Articles section.

Adib, Muhammad al-Husayn al-, *Al-Mujmal fi al-Shi'a wa Mu'taqadatihim.* Al-Najaf: Matbaat al-Numan, 1381/1961.

Aflaki, Shams al-Din Ahmad al-. *Manaqib al-Arifin.* Edited by Tahsin Yazici. Ankara: Milli Egitim Basimevi, 1953–54. Partial English translation is found in *Acts of the Adepts (Manaqibu'l'Arifin),* translated by James W. Redhouse, London, n.p., 1881, reprinted with a preface by Idries Shah, London and Wheaton, Ill., Theosophical Publishing House, 1976.

Al, Muhammad Jabir Abd al-. *Harakat al-Shi'a al-Mutatarrifin wa Atharahum fi al-Hayat al-Ijtima'iyya wa al-Adabiyya li Mudun al-Iraq Ibban al-Asr al-Abbasi al-Awwal.* Cairo; Dar al-Maarif, 1954.

Al-Alawiyyun Shi'at Ahl al-Bayt. Beirut: n.p., 1391/1972. This contains the proclamations issued by Alawi (Nusayri) Shaykhs and dignitaries, indicating that the Nusayris are true Shiites.

Alami, Muhammad Sulayman al-. *Da'irat al-Ma'arif al-Musammat bi Muqtabis al-Athar wa Mujaddid ma Duthir.* Vol. 2. Qumm: Matbaat al-Hikma, 1375/1955.

Ali, Hamza Ibn. *Al-Risala al-Damiqha wa al-Radd ala al-Nusayri al-Fasiq.* Arab MSS. 1419 and 1449, Bibliothéque Nationale, Paris.

Ali, Muhammad Kurd. *Khitat al-Sham.* Vol. 6, Beirut: Dar al-Ilm li al-Malayin, 1971.

Allah, al-Husayni Abd. *Al-Judhur al-Tarikhiyya li al-Nusayriyya al-Alawiyya.* Dubai: Dar al-Itisam, 1980.

Amili, Muhammad Ibn al-Hasan al-Hurr al-. *Amal al-Amil fi Ulama Jabal Amil.* Transcribed by Fadl Ali al-Kashmiri on 10 Jumada al-Ula, n.p. 1306/1888. A printed copy of the same was made in Tehran, 1320/1902.

Amin, Mujahid al-. *Al-Nusayriyya (al-Alawiyyun), Aqa'iduhum, Tarikhuhum, Waqi'uhum.* Beirut, Dar al-Fikr: n.d.

Amin, al-Sayyid Muhsin al-. *Siyar al-A'imma.* Vol. 1. Beirut, Dar al-Taaruf, 1401/1980.

Amuli, Baha al-Din Haydar Ibn Ali al-Ubaydi al-. *Jami al-Asrar wa Manba al-Anwar.* Arberry MS. 1349, London. The India Office.

Arabi, Muhyi al-Din Ibn. *Al-Futuhat al-Makkiyya,* 4 vols. Cairo: Bulaq 1293/1876.

———. *Anqa Maghrib fi Khatm al-Awliya wa Shams al-Maghrib,* Damascus: Dar al-Yaqza al-Arabiyya, 1388/1968.

———. *Fusus al-Hikam.* Trans. into English by R. W. I. Austin. New York: Paulist Press, 1980.

Arabshah, Ahmad Ibn Muhammad Ibn Abd Allah al-Dimashqi, known as Ibn. *Aja'ib al-Maqdur fi Akhbar Timur.* Cairo: Bulaq, 1285/1868.

Asakir, Abu al-Qasim Ali Ibn al-Hasan Ibn. *Tahdhib Tarikh Ibn Asakir,* vol. 1. Edited by Abd al-Qadir Ahmad Badran. Damascus: Rawdat al-Sham, 1329/1911.

———. *Tarikh Dimashq,* Vol. 1. Edited by Salah al-Din al-Munajjid. Damascus: al-Majma al-Ilmi-Arabi, 1371/1951.

———. *Tajamat al-Imam Ali min Tarikh Dimashq li Ibn Asakir.* Edited by al-Shaykh Muhammad Baqir al-Mahmudi. Beirut: Massasat al-Mahmudi li al-Tibaa, 1980.

Ashari, Abu al-Hasan Ali Ibn Ismail al-. *Kitab Maqalat al-Islamiyyin wa Ikhtilaf al-Musallin.* Edited by Hellmut Ritter. Wiesbaden: Franz Steiner, 1980.

Ashari, Saad Ibn Abd Allah al-. *Al-Maqalat wa al-Firaq.* Edited by Muhammad Jawad Mashkur. Tehran: Matbaat Haydari, 1963.

Ashub, Muhammad Ibn Ali Ibn Shahr. *Manaqib Al Abi Talib,* 3 vols. Al-Najaf: al-Matbaa al-Haydariyya, 1376/1956.

Aşikpaşazade, *Tevarih-i Al-i Osman.* Istanbul: Matbaa Yi Amire, 1332/1913.

Askari, al-lmam al-Hasan al-. *Kitab Tafsir al-Imam Hasan al-Askari,* printed on the margin of *Kitab Tafsir Ali Ibn Ibrahim.* Tabriz: 1315/1897.

Askari, Abd al-Husayn Mahdi al-. *Al-Alawiyyun aw al-Nusayriyya.* n.p., 1980.

Askari, Murtada al-. *Abd Allah Ibn Saba wa Asatir Ukhra.* Beirut: Dar al-Kutub, 1968.

———. *Khamsun wa Mi'at Sahabi Mukhtalaq.* Beirut: Dar al-Kutub, 1968.

Asqalani, Shihab al-Din Abu al-Fadl Ahmad al-Kinani Ibn Hajar al-. *Lisan al-*

Mizan. 6 vols. Haydarabad: Matbaat Majlis Dairat al-Maarif al-Nizamiyya, 1329–31/1911–12.

Athir, Izz al-Din Ibn al-. *Al-Kamil fi al-Tarikh.* 12 vols. Leiden: E. J. Brill, 1851–1871.

Azzawi, Abbas al-. *Al-Kaka'iyya fi al-Tarikh.* Baghdad: Sharikat al-Tibaa wa al-Tijara al-Mahduda, 1949.

Baba, Ahmad Sirri Dede. *Al-Risala al-Ahmadiyya fi al-Tariqa al-Bektashiyya.* Cario: Matbaat Abduh wa Anwar Ahmad, 1959.

Babawayh (al-Shaykh al-Saduq) al-Qummi Abu Jafar Muhammad Ibn. *Ma'ani al-Akhbar.* Tehran: Matbaat al-Haydari, 1379/1959.

———. *Ilal al-Shara'i.* 2 vols. Al-Najaf: al-Matbaa al-Haydariyya, 1383/1963.

———. *Amali al-Saduq.* Al-Najaf: al-Matbaa al-Haydariyya, 1389/1969.

Badawi, Abd al-Rahman. *Shakhsiyyat Qaliqa fi al-Islam.* Cario: Dar al-Nahda al-Arabiyya, 1964.

———. *Madhahib al-Islamiyyin.* 2 vols. Beirut: Dar al-Ilm li al-Malayin, 1973.

———. *Al-Insan al-Kamil fi al-Islam.* Kuwayt: Wakalat al-Matbuaat, 1976.

Baghawi, Abu Muhammad al-Husayn Ibn Masud Ibn Muhammad al-Farra al-. *Mishkat al-Masabih.* 2 vols. Trans. into English by James Robson. Lahore: Muhammad Ashraf Press, 1975.

Baghdadi, Abd al-Qahir al-. *Al-Farq bayn al-Firaq.* Edited by Muhyi al-Din Abd al-Hamid. Matbaat al-Madani, n.d. For English translation, see *Moslem Schisms and Sects* by Kate Chambers Seelye, New York: Columbia University Press, 1920.

Bahrani, Hashim Ibn Sulayman al-. *Ghayat al-Maram wa Hujjat al-Khisam fi Ta'yin al-Imam min Tariq al-Khass wa al-Amm.* Lithographed Tehran: 1321/1903.

Baladhuri, Ahmad Ibn Yahya al-. *Futuh al-Buldan.* 3 vols. Edited by Salah al-Din al-Munajjid. Cario: Maktabat al-Nahda al-Misriyya, 1956.

Balaghi, Abd al-Hujja al-. *Maqalat al-Hunafa fi Maqamat Shams al-Urafa.* Tehran: Chap Khanah Mazahri, 1327/1948

Barqi, Abu Jafar Ibn Abi Abd Allah al-. *Al-Rijal.* Tehran: Chap Khana Daneshgah, 1342/1923.

Barthold, W. *Tarikh al-Turk fi Asiya al-Wusta.* Translated into Arabic from the original Turkish by Ahmad Said Sulayman. Cairo: Maktabat al-Anglo-Misriyya, 1958.

Battuta, Ibn. *The Travels of Ibn Battuta* A.D. 1325–1354. Translated by H. A. R. Gibb from the Arabic text edited by C. Defrémery and B. R. Sanguinetti. 2 vols. Cambridge: Cambridge University Press, 1958–1962.

Bazzaz, Tawakkuli Ismail Ibn. *Safwat al-Safa.* Lithographed Bombay, 1329/1911.

Benjamin of Tudela. *The Itinerary of Benjamin of Tudela.* Translated by Marcus Nathan Adler. New York: Philipp Feldheim, Inc., 1907.

Bibi, Nasir al-Din al-Husayn Yahya Ibn Muhammad Ibn Ali al-Jafari al-Raghdi knows as Ibn Bibi. *Al-Awamir al-Ala'iyya fi al-Umur al-Ala'iyya.* Edited by Adnan Sadiq Erzi, Ankara: Türk Tarih Kurumu Basimevi, 1956.

Biruni, Abu al-Rayhan al-. *Kitab al-Jamahir fi Ma'rifat al-Jawahir.* Haydarabad: Matbaat Dairat al-Maarif al-Uthmaniyya, 1355/1936.

———. *Al-Athar al-Baqiya an al-Qurun al-Khaliya.* Edited by Edward Sachau. Leipzig; O. Harrassowitz 1923.

Bukhari, Look under *Sahih al-Bukhari.*

Bursi, al-Hafiz Rajab al-. *Mashariq Anwar al-Yaqin fi Asrar Amir al-Mu'minin.* 10th ed. Beirut: Muassasat al-Alami, n.d.

Damiri, Kamal al-Din al-. *Hayat al-Hayawan al-Kubra.* 2 vols. Cairo: Matbaat al Istiqama, 1383/1963.

Dihlawi, Abd al-Aziz al-. *Mukhtasar al-Tuhfa al-Ithnay'ashariyya.* Edited by Mahmud Shukri al-Alusi. Cario: al-Matbaa al-Salafiyya, 1387/1967.

Din, Muhammad Rida Sham al-. *Ma al-Alawiyyin fi Suriyya.* Beirut: Matbaat al-Insaf, 1956.

Din, Taqi Sharaf al-. *Al-Nusayriyya: Dirasa Tahliliyya.* Beirut: n.p. 1983.

Erisen, Ihsan Mesut and Kemal Samancigil, *Haci Bektaş Veli: Bektaşilik ve Alevilik Tarihi.* Istanbul: Ay Yayinevi, 1966.

Eröz, Mehmet. *Türkiye De Alevilik-Bektaşilik.* Istanbul: n.p. 1977.

Evliya Efendi (Çelebi). *Siyahatnames.* Istanbul: Devlet Matbaasi, 1357/1938.

———. *Narrative of Travels in Europe, Asia, and Africa in the Seventeenth Century.* 3 Vols. Translated by Ritter Joseph von Hammer. London: Oriental Translation Fund Publications, 1846–50.

Fani, Shaykh Muhsin. *Dabistan al-Madhahib (School of Manners).* Translated into English by David Shea and Anthony Troyer. 3 vols. Paris: Allen & Co., 1843.

Farid, Abu Hafs Umar Ibn al-. *Diwan Ibn al-Farid.* Cairo: al-Maktaba al-Husayniyya, 1352/1933.

Fayyad, Abd Allah al-. *Tarikh al-Imamiyya wa Aslafihim min al-Shi'a.* Beirut: Muassasat al-Alami li al-Matbuat, 1975.

Fida, Imad al-Din Ismail Ibn Ali Abu al-. *Kitab al-Mukhtasar fi Tarikh al-Bashar,* Vol. 3. Beirut: Dar al-Fikr and Dar al-Bihar, 1959.

Futi, Kamal al-Din al-Fadl Abd al-Razzaq Ibn al-. *Al-Hawadith al-Jami'a wa al-Tajarib al-Nafi'a fi al-Mi'a al-Sabi'a.* Edited by Mustafa Jawad. Baghdad: al-Maktaba al-Arabiyya, 1351/1932.

Ghalib, Mustafa. *Al-Harakat al-Batiniyya fi al-Islam.* Beirut: Dar al-Andalus, 1982.

Ghiyathi, Abd Allah Ibn Fath Allah al-Baghdadi al-. *Al-Tarikh al-Ghiyathi.* Edited by Tariq Nafi al-Hamdani. Baghdad: Matbaat Asad, 1975.

Ghulami, Abd al-Munim al-. *Baqaya al-Firaq al-Batiniyya fi Liwa al-Mawsil.* Mosul: Matbaat al-Ittihad al-Jadida, 1950.

Hakim, Hasan al-. *Al-Watha'iq al-Tarikhiyya al-Muta'alliqa bi al-Qadiyya al-Suriyya.* Beirut: Dar Sadir, 1974.

Hakim, Sayyid Muhammad Taqi al-. *Sunnat Ahl al-Bayt wa Mawadi Ukhra.* Beirut: Dar al-Zahra, 1978.

Hakim, Yusuf al-. *Suriyya wa al-Ahd al-Faysali.* Beirut: al-Matbaa al-Katholikiyya, 1980.

Hallaj, Abu al-Mughith al-Husayn Ibn Mansur al-. *Kitab al-Tawasin.* Edited and translated into French by Louis Massignon. Paris: P. Geuthner, 1913.

Hamawi, Yaqut al-. *Mu'jam al-Buldan*. Cairo: Matbaat al-Saada, 1323/1909.

Hariri, Abu Musa al- (Rev. Yusuf al-Qazzi). *Al-Alawiyyun al-Nusayriyyun*. Beirut: n.p. 1980.

Harrani, Abu Abd Allah Muhammad Ibn Shuba al-. *Kitab al-Usayfir*. Arab MS. 1450, fols. 2–12, Bibliothèque Nationale, Paris.

Haythami, Abu al-Abbas Shihab al-Din Ahmad Ibn Hajar al-. *Al-Sawa'iq al-Muhriqa fi al-Radd ala Ahl al-Bida wa al-Zandaqa*. Edited by Abd al-Wahhab Abd al-Latif. Cairo: Sharikat al-Tibaa al-Muttahida, 1965.

Hazm, Abu Muhammad Ali Ibn. *Kitab al-Fisal fi al-Milal wa al-Ahwa wa al-Nihal*. 5 vols. Cairo: Muassasat al-Khanji, 1321/1903.

Hebraeus, Bar. See Ibri, Ibn al-.

Hilli, al-Hasan Ibn Yusuf Ibn al-Mutahhar al-. *Kashf al-Haqq wa Minhaj al-Sidq*. Arabic MS. 437, The Indian Office, Loth, London.

———. *Kitab Minhaj al-Karama fi Ma'rifat al-Imama,* printed together with Ibn Taymiyya's *Minhaj al-Sunna*. Look under Taymiyya.

———. *Al-Rijal*. Al-Najaf: al-Matbaa al-Haydariyya, 1381/1961.

Himyari, Abu Said Nashwan al-. *Al-Hur al-In*. Cairo: al-Khanji, 1368/1948.

Hisham, Ibn. *Al-Sira al-Nabawiyya*. Edited by Mustafa al-Saqqa, et al. 2 vols. Cairo: Mustafa al-Babi al-Halabi, 1375/1955.

History of Shah Isma'il. Browne Turkish MS., Add. 200, Cambridge, England.

Hujwiri, Abu al-Hasan Ali Ibn Uthman al-. *The Kashf al-Mahjub*. Translated into English by Reynold A. Nicholson. Leyden: E. J. Brill and London: Luzac, 1911. Reprinted Lahore: Islamic Book Foundation, 1976.

Husayn, Muhammad Kamil. *Fi Adab Misr al-Fatimiyya*. Cairo: Dar al-Fikr al-Arabi, 1970.

Husayn, Taha. *Ali wa Banuh*. Cairo: Dar al-Maarif, 1953.

———. *Al-Fitna al-Kubra*. Cairo: Dar al-Maarif, 1953.

Husayn, Yahya Ibn al-. *Kitab al-Ifada fi Tarikh al-A'imma al-Sada*. Arab MS. 1647, Leiden University, Leiden.

Husayni, Abu Talib al-. *Malfuzat Sahib Qiran*. Persian MS. 7575. British Museum, London.

Husayni, Sayyid Muhammad Ibn al-Sayyid Ahmad al-. *Rihlat al-Munshi al-Baghdadi*. Translated from Persian into Arabic by Abbas al-Azzawi. Baghdad: Sharikat al-Tijara wa al-Tibaa, 1367/1947.

Husri, Sati al-. *Al-Bilad al-Arabiyya wa al-Dawla al-Uthmaniyya*. Beirut: Dar al-Ilm li al-Malayin, 1970.

Ibrahim (al-Qummi), Abu al-Hasan Ali Ibn. *Kitab Tafsir Ali Ibn Ibrahim*. Lithographed, Tabriz: 1315/1897.

Ibri, Ibn al-(Bar Hebraeus). *The Chronology of Gregory Abu' L-Faraj Known as Bar Hebraeus*. Translated from the Syric by Ernest A. Wallis Budge. 2 vols. Oxford: Oxford University Press, 1932.

———. *Tarikh Mukhtasar al-Duwal*. Edited by Anton Salhani. Beirut: al-Matbaa al-Katholikiyya, 1958.

Imad, Abu al-Falah Abd al-Hayy Ibn al-. *Shadharat al-Dhahab fi Akhbar man Dhahab,* Vol. 4. Cairo: Maktabat al-Qudsi, 1350–51/1931–32.

Isfahani, Abu al-Faraj al-. *Maqatil al-Talibiyyin wa Akhbaruhum*. Cairo: Dar Ihya al-Kutub. 1357/1938.

———. *Kitab al-Aghani*. 20 vols. Cairo: Bulaq, 1285/1868. Reprinted Baghdad: Dar al-Fikr li al-Jami, 1970.

Isfahani, Abu Nuaym al-. *Hilyat al-Awliya*. Cairo: Maktabat al-Khanji, 1351/1932.

Isfahani, Imad al-Din Muhammad Ibn Hamid al-. *Kitab Tarikh Dawlat Al Seljuk*. Edited by Ali Ibn Muhammad al-Bandari. Cairo: Matbaat al-Mausuat, 1318/1900.

Isfarayini, Abu al-Muzaffar Tahir Ibn Muhammad al-. *Al-Tabsir fi al-Din wa Tamyiz al-Firqa al-Najiya an al-Firaq al-Halikin*. Cairo: Maktabat al-Khanji, 1359/1940.

Ishaq Efendi, *Kashif al-Asrar wa Dafi al-Ashrar.* See Georg Jacob, *Beiträge Zur Kenntnis des Derwisch-Ordens der Bektaschis,* Berlin: Mayer & Müller, 1908.

Iyas, Muhammad Ibn Ahmad Ibn. *Bada'i al-Zuhur fi Waqa'i al-Duhur.* Baghdad: Matbaat Hisam, 1983.

Jacob, Georg. *Beiträge zur Kenntnis des Derwisch-Ordens der Bektaschis*. Berlin: Mayer & Müller, 1908. See Ishaq Efendi

Jawzi, Abu al-Muzaffar Sibt Ibn al-. *Mir'at al-Zaman fi Tarikh al-A'yan*. Haydarabad India: Matbaat Dairat al-Maarif al-Uthmaniyya, 1950.

Jawzi, Bandali. *Min Tarikh al-Harakat al-Fikriyya fi al-Islam*. Beirut: Dar al-Rawai, n.d.

Jawzi, Jamal al-Din Abu al-Faraj Ibn al-. *Al-Muntazam fi Tarikh al-Muluk wa al-Umam*. Vol. 6. Haydarabad: Matbaat Dairat al-Maarif al-Uthmaniyya, 1357/1938.

———. *Talbis Iblis*. Beirut: Dar al-Kutub al-Ilmiyya, 1368/1948.

———. *Sifat al-Safwa*. 4 vols. Edited by Muhammad Fakhuri. Aleppo: Dar al-Wai 1389–93/1969–73.

Jili, Abd al-Karim Ibn Ibrahim al-. *Al-Insan al-Kamil fi Ma'rifat al-Awakhir wa al-Awa'il*. 4th ed. Beirut: Dar al-Fikr, 1975.

Jili, Abd al-Qadir Ibn Musa Ibn Abd Allah al-. *Al-Fath al-Rabbani wa al-Fayd al-Rahmani*. Cairo: Dar Sadir, 1380/1960.

———. *Kimya al-Sa'ada*. Arab MS. add. 422, Cambridge.

Jisri, Abu Muhammad Ali Ibn Isa al-. *Risalat al-Tawhid*. Arab MS. 1450, fols. 42–49, Bibliothèque Nationale, Paris.

Jufi, al-Mufaddal Ibn Umar al-. *Kitab al-Usus*. Arab MS. 1449, fols. 182–86, Bibliothèque Nationale, Paris.

Jumua, Saad. *Al-Mu'amara wa Ma'rakat al-Masir.* Beirut: Dar al-Katib al-Arabi, 1968.

Jundi, Sami al-. *Al-Ba'th*. Beirut: Dar al-Nahar, 1969.

Jurjani, Abu al-Hasan Muhammad Ibn al-Husayn Ibn Musa al-. *Al-Ta'rifat*. Cairo: al-Babi al-Halabi, 1357/1938.

Karmali, Anastase Marie al-. *Khulasat Tarikh Baghdad*. Basra: Matbaat al-Hukuma, 1919.

Kasrawi, Ahmad. *Al-Tashayyu wa al-Shi'a*. Tehran: Matbaat Peman, 1364/1944.

Kashif al-Ghita, Muhammad al-Husayn. *Asl al-Shi'a wa Usuluha*. 9th ed. Beirut: Muassasat al-Alami li al-Matbuat, 1956.

Kashif al-Ghita, al-Shaykh Ali. *Al-Nur al-Sati fi al-Fiqh al-Nafi*. 2 vols. Al-Najaf: Matbaat al-Adab, 1381/1961.

Kashshi, Abu Umar Ibn Abd al-Aziz al-. *Ma'rifat Akhbar al-Rijal*. Edited by Ahmad al-Husayni, Karbala: Muassasat al-Alami. n.d.

Kathir, Imad al-Din Abu al-Fida Ismail al-Qurashi al-Dimashqi, known as Ibn. *Al-Bidaya wa al-Nihaya*. 14 vols. Cairo: Matbaat al-Saada, 1351–8/1932–39.

———. *Qisas al-Anbiya*. Baghdad: Matbaat al-Wisam, 1983.

Kawtharani, Wajih. *Bilad al-Sham*. Beirut: Mahad al-Inma al-Arabi, 1980.

Kermani, Hamid al-Din Ahmad al-. *Rahat al-Aql*. Edited by Mustafa Ghalib. Beirut: Dar al-Andalus, 1967.

———. *Al-Masabih fi Ithbat al-Imama*. Edited by Mustafa Ghalib. Beirut: Manshurat Hamad, 1969.

Khaldun, Abd al-Rahman Ibn. *Al-Muqaddima*. Cairo: Matbaat Mustafa Muhammad, n.d.

Khartbart, Ahmad Ibn Elias al-Naqqash of. *Tuhfat al-Wasaya*. Arab MS. 2049, Hagia Sophia, Istanbul.

Khasibi, Abu Abd Allah al-Husayn Ibn Hamdan al-. *Kitab al-Hidaya al-Kubra,* appended to Hashim Uthman's *al-Alawiyyum bayn al-Ustura wa al Haqiqa,* 229–97.

Khunji, Fadl Allah Ibn Ruzbihan. *Tarikhi-i alam ara-yi Amini*. This has been Translated and abridged by V. Minorsky in *Persia in A. D. 1470–1490*. London: The Royal Asiatic Society of Great Britain, 1957.

Khwand Amir, Ghiyath al-Din. *Habib al-Siyar fi Akhbar Afrad al-Bashar*. 4 vols. Tehran: Intisharat Kitabkhane Khayyam, 1315/1897.

Khwansari, Muhammad Baqir al-. *Rawdat al-Jannat fi Ahwal al-Ulama wa al-Sadat*. Edited by Muhammad Ali Hauzati. Lithographed Tehran: 1367/1947.

Kitab al-Haft al-Sharif. Related by al-Mufaddal al-Jufi of the Imam Jafar al-Sadiq. Edited by Mustafa Ghalib, Beirut, Dar al-Andalus, 1964.

Kitab al-Hikam al-Ja'fariyya li al- lmam al-Sadiq Ja'far Ibn Muhammad. Edited by Arif Tamir. Beirut: al-Matbaa al-Katholikiyya, 1957.

Kitab al-Majmu. In Sulayman al-Adani's *Kitab al-Bakura al-Sulaymaniyya,* 7–34. For an English translation, see Salisbury, Edward, in the Articles section. The Arabic text of al-Adani was published with a French translation by René Dussaud in his *Histoire Et Religion Des Nosaris,* 161–98. Paris: Libraire Émile Bauillon, 1900.

Kitab al-Mashyakha. Arab MS. 6182, Bibliothèque Nationale Paris. For English translation of portions of this book, see Samuel Lyde, *The Asian Mystery,* 233–70. London: 1860.

Kitab Ta'lim al-Diyana al-Nusayriyya (catechism). Arab MS. 6182, Bibliothèque Nationale, Paris.

Köprülü, F. *Türk Edebiyatinda Ilk Mutasavviflar*. Istanbul: Matbaa-Yi Amire, 1918.

Kulayni, Abu Jafar Muhammad Ibn Yaqub Ibn Ishaq al-. *Al-Usul min al-Kafi*. 2

vols. 3rd edition by Ali Akbar al-Ghaffari. Tehran: Dar al-Kutub al-Islamiyya, 1388/1968.

Kuliyyat Shams-i Tabrizi: Diwan-i ghazaliyyat. Tehran: Amir Kabir, 1336–1957.

Maghribi, Ahmad Ibn Muhammad al-Siddiq al-. *Fath al-Malik al-Ali bi Sihhat Hadith Bab Madinat Ali*. Cairo: al-Matbaa al-Islamiyya, 1354/1935.

Maghribi, Abu Hanifa(al-Qadi)al-Nu'man Ibn Muhammad al-. *Da'a'im al-Islam wa Dhikr al-Halal wa al-Haram wa al-Qadaya wa al-Ahkam an Bayt Rasul Allah*. 2 vols. Edited by Asaf A. A. Fayzi. Cairo: Dar al-Maarif, 1951.

Majlisi, Muhammad Baqir al-. *Hayat al-Qulub*. Translated by James L. Merrick. Boston: Phillips, Sampson, 1850. Reprinted, San Antonio, Texas: Zahra Press, 1982.

———. *Bihar al-Anwar*. Vol. I, Tehran: Dar al-Kutub al-Ilmiyya, 1376/1956 and Vol. 13, 1378/1958.

Manaqib al-Awliya aw Buyruk. Turkoman MS. 1470/1, Iraqi Museum.

Manzur, Muhammad Abd al-Karim Ibn. *Lisan al-Arab*, Vol. 15. Beirut: Dar Sadir, 1955–56.

Maqalat Haji Bektash. Edward G. Browne Turkish MS. E 20, Cambridge.

Maqdisi, Mutahhar Ibn Tahir al-. *Al-Bad wa al-Tarikh*. 6 vols. Edited Clement Huart. Paris: E. Leroux, 1899–1919.

Maqrizi, Taqi al-Din Abu al-Abbas al-. *Itti'az al-Hunafa bi Akhbar al-A'imma al-Kulafa*. Edited by Jamal al-Din al-Shayyal: Cairo, Dar al-Fikr al-Arabi, 1367/1948.

Masudi, Abu al-Hasan al-. *Muruj al-Dhahab wa Ma'adin al-Jawhar*. 4 vols. Edited by Muhyi al-Din Abd al-Hamid. Cairo: Dar al-Raja, 1357/1938.

Masum Ali (al-Nimat Ilahi al-Shirazi), al-Hajj. *Tara'iq al-Haqa'iq*. 3 vols. Lithographed Tehran: 1319/1901.

Mathnawi of Jalalu 'ddin Rumi. Edited and translated into English by Reynold A. Nicholson. Cambridge: Cambridge University Press, 1926. Reprinted 1977.

Matlub, Ali Ahmad, et al. *Nahj Khomeini fi Mizan al-Fikr al-Islami*. Baghdad: Dar Ammar, 1985.

Mikhnaf, Abu. *Maqtal al-Husayn wa Masra Ahl Baytihi wa Ashabihi fi Karbala al-Mushtahir bi Maqtal Abi Mikhnaf*. Al-Najaf: Matbaat al-Ghadir, n.d.

Mokri, Hajj Nimat Allah Jayhun Abadi (Mujrim). *Shah Nama-ye Haqiqat*, vol. 1. Edited by Mohammad Mokri. Tehran: Departement D' Iranologie De L' Institute Franco-Iranien; Paris: Libraire D' Amerique et D' Orient Adrien-Maisonneuve, 1966.

Mufid, Abu Abd Allah Muhammad Ibn Muhammad Ibn al-Numan al-Baghdadi al-Ukbari, known as al-Shaykh al-. *Awa'il al-Maqalat fi al-Madhahib wa al-Mukhtarat*. Tabriz: Matbaat Ridai, 1371/1951.

———. *Sharh Aqa'id al-Saduq aw Tashih al-I'tiqad*. Tabriz: Matbaat Ridai, 1371/1951.

———. *Kitab al-Irshad Ila Fada'il al-Amjad*. Translated into English by I. K. A. Howard. New York: Tahrike Tarsile Quran, Inc., 1981.

Musawi, Abd al-Husayn Sharaf al-Din al-. *Al-Muraja'at*. Beirut: Muassasat al-Wafa, 1393/1973.

Muslim, Abu al-Husayn Ibn al-Hajjaj. *Sahih Muslim*. 8 vols. Cairo: Matbaat Muhammad Sabih wa Awladihi, 1334/1915.

Mustawfi (Qazvini), Hamd Allah. *Tarih-i Guzida*. Edited by Abd al-Husayn Hawai. Tehran: n.p. 1336–39/1957–60.

Muzaffar, Muhammad Rida al-. *Aqa'id al-Shi'a al-Imamiyya*. Matabi al-Numan, Al-Najaf: 1374/1954.

Nadim, Abu al-Faraj Muhammad Ibn Ishaq Ibn al-. *Kitab al-Fihrist*. 2 vols. Edited by Gustav Flügel. Halle: University of Halle, 1871–72. Reprinted. Beirut, Khayat, n.d..

Nahj al-Balagha, edited by Muhyi al-Din Abd al-Hamid with comments by Shaykh Muhammad Abduh, 3 vols. Cairo: Matbaat al-Istiqama, n.d.

Najjar, Mustafa Abd al-Qadir al-. *Al-Tarikh al-Siyasi li Imarat Arabistan al-Arabiyya*. Cairo: Dar al-Maarif, 1971.

Nashshabi, al-Shaykh Yusuf Ibn al-Ajuz al-Halabi known as al-. *Munazara*. Arab MS. 1450, fols. 68–155, Bibliothèque Nationale, Paris.

Nawbakhti, Abu Muhammad al-Hasan Ibn Musa al-. *Firaq al-Shi'a*. Al-Najaf: al-Matbaa al Haydariyya, 1389/1969.

Nisaburi, Muhammad Ibn al-Fattal al-. *Rawdat al-Wa'izin wa Basirat al-Mutta'izin*. 3 vols. Al-Najaf: al-Matbaa al-Haydariyya, 1386/1966.

Nisaburi, Nizam al-Din Hasan Ibn Muhammad Ibn Husayn al-Qummi al-. *Ghara'ib al-Qur'an wa Raqha'ib al-Furqan*. Printed on the margin of Abu Jafar Muhammad Ibn Jarir al-Tabari's, *Jami al-Bayan fi Tafsir al-Qur'an*. See Tabari, Abu Jafar.

Nuri, Husayn Ibn Muhammad Taqi al-Tabarsi al-. *Nafas al-Rahman fi Ahwal Salman*. Lithographed Tehran: 1285/1868.

———. *Kashf al-Sitar an Khabar al-Gha'ib an al-Absar.* Lithographed Tehran: 1318/1900.

Oruc Ibn Adil. *Tarih-i Al-i Osman*. Edited by Franz Babinger, *Die früosmanichen Jahrbücher des Urudsch*. Hanover: H. Lafaire, 1925.

Qalqashandi, Abu al-Abbas Ali Ahmad Ibn Ali al-. *Subh al-A'sha fi Sina'at al-Insha*. Vol. 13. Cairo: al-Mussasa al-Misriyya al-Amma li al-Tab wa al-Nashr, 1384/1964.

Qanun al-Uqubat al-Baghdadi. Edited by Kamil al-Samarra'i. Baghdad: Matbaat al-Maarif, 1957.

Qaramani, Abu al-Abbas Ahmad Ibn Yusuf al-Dimashqi al-. *Akhbar al-Duwal wa Athar al-Uwal*. Lithographed Baghdad, 1282/1865.

Qarqut, Dhuqan. *Tatawwur al-Haraka al-Wataniyya fi Suriyya*. Beirut: Dar al-Talia, 1975.

Qazwini, Muhammad Kazim al-. *Ali min al-Mahd ila al-Lahd,* 7th ed. Beirut: Dar al-Turath al-Arabi, n.d.

Qushayri, Abu al-Qasim Abd al-Karim Ibn Hawazin al-. *al-Risala al-Qushayriyya,* 2 vols. edited by Abd al-Halim Mahmud and Mahmud Ibn al-Sharif, Cairo: Dar al-Kutub al-Haditha, 1966.

Qutayba, Abu Abd Allah Ibn Muslim Ibn. *Ta'wil Mukhtalif al-Hadith*. Edited by Muhammad Zuhdi al-Najjar. Cairo: Maktabat al-Kuliyyat al-Azhariyya, 1966.

Raghib Pasha, Muhammad. *Safinat al-Raghib wa Dafinat al-Talib*. Cairo: Bulaq, 1255/1839. Reprinted 1282/1865.

Razi, Abu Hatim Ahmad Ibn Hamdan al-. *Kitab al-Zina fi al-Kalimat al-Islamiyya al-Arabiyya*. Appended to al-Samarra'i's *al-Ghuluw wa al-Firaq al-Ghaliya fi al-Hadara al-Islamiyya,* Part 3, 247–312. Baghdad and London: Dar Wasit li al-Nashr, 1982.

Razzaz, Munif al-. *Al-Tajriba al-Murra*. Beirut: Dar Ghandur, 1967.

Rida, Ali. *Qissat al-Kifah al-Watani fi Suriyya Askariyyan wa Siyasiyyan hatta al-Jala*. Aleppo: al-Matbaa al-Haditha 1979.

Risalat al-Bayan li Ahl al-Uqul wa al-Afham wa man Talaba al-Huda ila Ma'rifat al-Rahman. Arab MS. 1450, fols. 53–67. Bibliothèque Nationale, Paris.

Saad, Abu Abd Allah Muhammad al-Zahri Ibn. *Al-Tabaqat al-Kubra*. 9 vols. ed. by E. Sachau. Leiden: E. J. Brill, 1904–40.

Sabban, al-Shaykh Ahmad al-. *Is'af al-Raqhibin fi Sirat al-Mustafa wa Fada'il Ahl Baytihi al-Tahirin*. Printed on the margin of al-Shaykh Mumin al-Shabalanji's *Nur al-Absar*. See Shabalanji.

Sadr, Muhammad Baqir al-. *Bahth Hawl al-Mahdi*. Matbaat Offset al-Mina, Baghdad: 1978.

———. *Bahth Hawl al-Walaya*. 2nd ed. Beirut: Dar al-Tarıf bi al- Matbuat, 1978.

———. *Dawr al-A'imma fi al-Hayat al-Islamiyya*. Tehran: al-Maktaba al-Islamiyya al-Kubra, 1400/1979.

Sahih al-Bukkari. Translated by Muhammad Assad. Gibraltar: Dar al-Andalus, 1334/1915.

Saigh, Abu Abd Allah Ibn Harun al-. *Masa'il Abu Abd Allah Ibn Harun al- Sa'iqh an Shaykhihi Abd Allah Ibn Hamdan al-Khasibi*. Arab MS. 1450, fols. 49–53. Bibliothèque Nationale, Paris.

———. *Risala* (No full title is given) Arab MS. 1450, fols. 177–79, Bibliothèque Nationale, Paris.

Sakhawi, Shams al-Din Muhammad Ibn Abd al-Rahman al-. *Al-Dauw al-Lami li A'yan al-Qarn al-Tasi*. 5 vols. Cairo: Matbaat al-Quds, 1353–55/1934–36.

Salih, Shaykh Mahmud al-. *Al-Naba al-Yaqin an al-Alawiyyin*. n.p., 1961.

Samarqandi, Abd al-Razzaq al-. *Matla al-Sa'dayn*. Persian MS. Add. 185 (12), Cambridge.

Samarrai, Abd Allah Sallum al-. *Al-Ghuluw wa al-Firaq al-Ghaliya fi al-Hadara al-Islamiyya*. Baghdad and London: Dar Wasit li al-Nashr, 1982.

———. *Al-Shu'ubiyya Haraka Mudadda li al-Islam wa al-Umma al-Arabiyya*. Baghdad: al-Mussasa al-Iraqiyya li al-Diaya wa al-Tibaa, 1984.

Sarraf, Ahmad Hamid al-. *Al-Shabak*. Baghdad: Matbaat al-Maarif, 1954.

Shabalanji, al-Shaykh Mumin Ibn Hasan al-. *Nur al-Absar fi Manaqib Al Bayt al-Nabi al-Mukhtar,* Baghdad: Mabtabat al-Sharq al-Jadid, 1984.

Shabushti, Abu al-Hasan Ali Ibn Muhammad al-. *Al-Diyarat*. Edited by Gurguis Awwad. 2nd ed. Baghdad: Matbaat al-Maarif, 1386/1966.

Shadhan, Abu al-Fadl Sadid al-Din Ibn. *al-Fada'il.* Al-Najaf: al Matbaa al-Haydariyya, n.d.

Shahrastani, Abu al-Fath Abd al-Karim al-. *Kitab al-Milal wa al-Nihal.* Cairo: Muassasat al-Khanji, 1321/1903. Printed on the margin of Ibn Hazm's *Kitab al-Fisal.*

Shaibi, Kamil Mustafa al-. *Al-Fikr al-Shi'i wa al-Naza'at al-Sufiyya hatta Matla al-Qarn al-Thani Ashar al-Hijri.* Baghdad: Maktabat al-Nahda, 1966.

———. *Al-Tariqa al-Safawiyya wa Rawasibuha fi al-Iraq al-Mu'asir.* Baghdad: Maktabat al-Nahda, 1967.

———. *Al-Sila Bayn al-Tasawwuf wa al-Tashayyu.* Cairo: Dar al-Maarif, 1969.

Shaka Mustafa al-. *Islam bila Madhahib.* Beirut: al-Dar al-Misriyya li al-Tibaa wa al-Nashr, 1971.

Sharh al-Imam wa ma Yujab alayhi wa ma Yalzamuhu fi Mansibihi wa ma Yakun al-Imam Mutarattab Alayhi fi Kull Shay ma al-Nas wa ma Wasfuhu fi Hadhihi al-Riwaya. Arab MS 1450, fols. 155–67, Bibliothèque Nationale, Paris.

Sharh Nahj al-Balaqha, edited by Izz al-Din Abd al-Hamid Ibn Abi al-Hadid, 4 vols. Dar al-Fikr li al-Jami, 1388/1968.

Sharif, Munir al-. *Al-Alawiyyun: Man Hum wa Ayna Hum.* Damascus: al-Maktaba al-Kubra li al-Talif wa al-Nashr, 1946.

Shirvani, Haji Zayn al-Abidin. *Bustan al-Siyaha.* Tehran: Printed at the expense of Abd Allah Mustawfi, 1315/1897.

Shubbar, Jasim Hasan. *Tarikh ak-Musha'sha'iyyin wa Tarajim A'lamihim.* al-Najaf, Matbaat al-Adab, 1956.

Sinjari, Muhammad Ibn Ibrahim Ibn Said al-Ansari al-Akfani al-. *Irshad al-Qasid ila Asna al-Maqasid.* Edited by Abd al-Latif Muhammad al-Abd, Cairo: Maktabat al-Anglo-Misriyya, 1978.

Sirat al-Shaykh al-Ahsa'i, Edited by Husayn Mahfuz. Baghdad: Matbaat al-Maarif, 1957.

Subayti, Abd Allah al-. *Salman al-Farisi.* 2nd ed. Baghdad: Matbaat al-Azhar, 1969.

Sulayman, Muhammad Mahmud. *Al-Mujtama al-Alawi fi al-Qarn al-Ishrin.* Damascus: Kuiliyat al-Adab, 1956.

Suyuti, Jala al-Din al-. *Tarikh al-Khulafa.* Baghdad: Matbaat Munir, 1983. Reprinted from the Cairo edition 1371/1952.

———. *Al-Khabar al-Dall ala Wujud al-Qutb wa al-Awtad wa al-Nujaba wa al-Abdal.* In *al-Nashra al-Ilmiyya li al-Kuliyya al-Zaytuniyya li al-Shari'a wa Usul al-Din,* no. 5, ed. Miqdad Mansiyya, 319–91. Tunis: Tunisian University, 1979.

Tabarani, Abu Said Maymun Ibn al-Qasim al-. *Kitab Sabil Rahat al-Arwah wa Dalil al-Surur wa al-Afrah ila Faliq al-Isbah known as Majmu al-A'yad.* Edited by R. Strothmann in *Der Islam* 27 (1944): 1–160 and (1946): 101–273.

Tabari, Abu Jafar Ibn Jarir al-. *Tarikh al-Umam wa al-Muluk.* 8 vols. Cairo: Matbaat al-Istiqama 1357/1939.

———. *Jami al-Bayan fi Tafsir al-Qur'an.* 30 vols. Cairo: al-Matbaa al-Maymaniyya, 1322–30/1904–11.

Tabari, Abu Jafar Muhammad Ibn Abi al-Qasim al-. *Bisharat al-Mustafa li Shi'at al-Murtada*. Al-Najaf: al-Matbaa al-Haydariyya, 1383/1963.

Tabarsi, Abu Ali al-Fadl Ibn al-Hasan Ibn al-Fadl al-. *Majma al-Bayan fi Tafsir al-Qur'an*. Sayda: Matbaat al-Irfan, 1333/1914.

Tabarsi, Abu Mansur Ahmad Ibn Ali al-. *Al-Ihtijaj*. ed. by Muhammad Baqir al-Khirsan. Al-Najaf: Mabaat al-Numan, 1386/1966.

Tabbakh, Muhammad Raghib al-. *I'lam al-Nubala bi Tarikh Halab al-Shahba*. 5 vols. Halab (Aleppo): al-Matbaa al-Ilmiyya, 1926.

Taghri Birdi, Jamal al-Din Abu al-Mahasin Yusuf Ibn. *Al-Nujum al-Zahira fi Muluk Misr wa al-Qahira,* vol. 7 Cairo: Matbaat Dar al-Kutub al-Misriyya, 1938.

Tamir, Arif. *Khams Rasa'il Isma'iliyya*. Beirut: Dar al-Insaf, 1956.

———. *Al-Imama fi al-Islam*. Beirut: Dar al-Kitab al-Arabi, n.d.

Tankut, Hasan Rashid. *Al-Nusayriyyun wa al-Nusayriyya*. Ankara: Devlet Matbaasi, 1938.

Taşköprüzade, Isam al-Din Ahmad Ibn Mustafa. *Al-Shaqa'iq al-Nu'maniyya fi Ulama al-Dawla al-Uthmaniyya*. Printed on the margin of Ibn Khallikan, *Wafayyat al-A'yan*. Cairo: al-Matbaa al-Maymaniyya, 1310/1892.

Tawil, Muhammad Ghalib al-. *Tarikh al-Alawiyyin*. 4th ed. Beirut: Dar al-Andalus, 1981.

Taymiyya, Abu al-Abbas Taqi al-Din Ahmad Ibn Abd al-Halim Ibn. *Majmu'at al-Rasa'il wa al-Masa'il*. Edited by Muhammad Rashid Rida. 3 vols. Cairo: Matbaat al-Manar, 1341–49/1923–30.

———. *Minhaj al-Sunna al-Nabawiyya fi Naqd Kalam al-Shi'a wa al-Qadiriyya*. Edited by Muhammad Rashad Salim. Cairo: Mabtabat al-Madani, 1382/1962.

———. *Jami al-Rasa'il*. Edited by Muhammad Rashad Salim. Cairo: Matbaat al-Madani, 1389/1969.

———. *Majmu Fatawa Shaykh al-Islam Ahmad Ibn Taymiyya*. Beirut: Dar al-Arabiyya, 1398/1977.

Tiqtiqa, Muhammad Ibn Tabataba known as Ibn al-. *Al-Fakhri fi al-Adab al-Sultaniyya wa al-Duwal al-Islamiyya*. Cairo: al-Maktaba al-Tijariyya al-Kubra, 1351/1932.

Tirmidhi, Abu Abd Allah Muhammad Ibn Husayn al-Hakim al-. *Nawadir al-Usul fi Ma'rifat Akhbar al-Rasul*. Beirut: Dar Sadir, 1972.

Tusi, Abu Jafar Muhammad Ibn Hasan al- (Shaykh al-Taifa). *Rijal al-Tusi*. Edited by Muhammad Sadiq Al Bahr al-Ulum. Al-Najaf: 1381/1961.

———. *Talkhis al-Shafi fi al-Imama*. Al-Najaf: Maktabat al-Adab, 1383/1963.

———. *Kitab al-Ghayba*. Al-Najaf: Matbaat al-Numan, 1385/1965.

Tusi, Abu Nasr al-Sarraj al-. *Al-Luma*. Edited by R. A. Nicholson. Leyden: E. J. Brill, 1914.

Tustari, Nur Allah al-. *Majalis al-Mu'minin*. Tehran: Sayyid Hasan Tehrani, 1299/1881.

Umar, Abd al-Jabbar Mahmud al-. *Al-Khomeini bayn al-Din wa al-Dawla*. Baghdad: Dar Afaq Arabiyya, 1984.

Umari, Shihab al-Din Ibn Fadl Allah al-. *Al-Ta'rif bi al-Mustalah al-Sharif.* Cairo: Matbaat al-Asima, 1312/1894.

Umm al-Kitab. Edited by W. Ivanow in *Der Islam* 23 (1936): 16–107.

Uthman, Hashim. *Al-Alawiyyun bayn al-Uatura wa al-Haqiqa.* Beirut: Muassasat al-Alami, 1980.

Wahhab, Muhammad Ibn Abd al-. *Mukhtasar Sirat Rasul Allah.* Cairo: Maktabat al-Riyad al-Haditha, 1375/1956.

Wajdi, Muhammad Farid. *Da'irat Ma'arif al-Qarn al-Ishrin,* Vol. 10. Cairo: Matbaat Dairat al-Maarif 1925.

Wardi, Ali al-. *Wu'az al-Salatin.* Baghdad: n.p. 1954.

———. *Mahzalat al-Aql al-Bashari.* Baghdad: Matbaat al-Rabita, 1955.

———. *Dirasa fi Tabi'at al-Mujtama al-Iraqi.* Baghdad: Matbaat al-Ani, 1965.

———. *Lamahat Ijtima'iyya min Tarikh al-Iraq al-Hadith,* Vol. 2. Baghdad: Matbaat al-Irshad, 1971.

Yafii, Afif al-Din Abd Allah Ibn Asad al-. *Kifayat al-Mu'taqid fi Nikayat al-Muntaqid aw Nashr al-Mahasin al-Ghaliya fi Fadl Mashayikh al-Sufiyya.* Printed on the margin of al-Nabhani's *Jami Karamat al-Awliya.* Cairo: al-Matbaa al-Maymaniyya, 1329/1911.

Yaman, Jafar Abu Mansur al-. *Kitab al-Kashf.* Edited by R. Strothmann. Oxford: Oxford University Press, 1952.

Yamani, Tahir Ibn Ibrahim al-Harithi al-. *Al-Anwar al-Latifa.* In Muhammad Hasan al-A'dami's *al-Haqa'iq al-Khafiyya,* 67–182.

Yaqubi, Ahmad Ibn Wadih al-. *Tarikh al-Yaqubi.* 3 vols. Al-Najaf: Matbaat al-Ghari, 1358/1939.

Yunus, Abd al-Latif al-. *Thawrat al-Shaykh Salih al-Ali.* Damascus: Dar al-Yaqza al-Arabiyya, 1961.

Zahir, Ihsan Ilahi. *Al-Shi'a wa Ahl al-Bayt.* Lahore: Idarah Tarjuman al-Sunna, 1982.

Zahra, Muhammad Abu. *Tarikh al-Madhahib al-Islamiyya.* 2 vols. Cairo: Dar al-Fikr al-Arabi, n.d.

Zamakhshari, Mahmud Ibn Umar al-. *Al-Khashshaf an Haqa'iq Ghawamid al-Tanzil wa Uyun al-Aqawil fi Wujuh al-Ta'wil.* 4 vols. Cairo: Matbaat Mustafa Muhammad, 1354/1935.

Zirrikli, Khayr al-Din al-. *Qamus al-A'lam,* Vol. 3. Beirut: Dar al-Ilm li al-Malayin, 1979.

Zubaydi, Abu al-Fayd Muhammad al-Murtada al-. *Taj al-Arus min Sharh Jawahir al-Qamus.* 10 vols. Cairo: al-Matbaa al-Khayriyya, 1306–7/1888–89.

Books: Western Sources

Affifi, A. E. *The Mystical Philosophy of Muhyid Din-Ibnul Arabi.* Cambridge: Cambridge University Press, 1938. Reprinted Lahore: Ashraf Press, 1964.

Aga Khan III. *The Memoirs of Aga Khan.* London: Cassell, 1954.

Ainsworth, William Francis. *Travels and Researches in Asia Minor, Mesopotamia, Chaldea and Armenia*. 2 vols. London: John W. Parker, 1842.

Albèri, Eugenio. *Relazioni degli ambasciatori veneti al Senato,* Vol. 3. Firenze: Societa editrice fiorentina, 1839–63.

Allah, Umar F. Abd. *The Islamic Struggle in Syria*. Berkeley: Mizan Press, 1983.

A Narrative of Italian Travels in Persia in the Fifteenth and Sixteenth Centuries. Translated by Charley Grey. London: Hakluyt Society, 1873.

Andrae, Tor. *Die Person Muhammeds In Lehre Und Glauben Seiner Gemeinde*. Stockholm: Kngl-Boktryckeriet, P. A. Norstedtz Söner, 1918.

Archives du Ministère des Affaires Éstrangères. Vols. 419, 492, 493, 510. Levant, Syrie-Liban, Paris: 1930–40.

Arpee, Leon. *A History of Armenian Christianity from the Beginning to Our Own Time*. New York: The Armenian Missionary Association of America, 1946.

Artin Pacha, Yacoub. *Contributions a l'étude du blazon en Orient*. London: B. Quaritch 1902.

Ayoub, Mahmud. *Redemptive Suffering in Islam: A Study of the Devotional Aspects of Ashura in Twelver Shi'ism*. The Hague: Mouton publishers, 1978.

Barthold, W. *Zur Geschichte des Christentums in Mittel-Asien bis zur mongolischen Eroberung*. Translated from the Russian into German by Rudolf Stübe, Tübingen und Leipzig: J. C. B. Mohr (Paul Siebeck), 1901.

———. *Turkestan Down To The Mongol Invasion*. 3rd ed. Translated by T. Minorsky and edited by C. E. Bosworth. E. W. Gibb Memorial. London: 1968.

Barros, Ioao. *Daasiade Ioao De Barros Dos Feistos Que Ospar.* Decada Secunda. Lisboa: Impressa per Iorge Rodriguez, 1628.

Bell, Gertrude L. *Amurath to Amurath*. London: Macmillan, 1924.

Birge, John K. *The Bektashi Order of Dervishes*. London: Luzac, 1937.

Bode, Baron C. A. De. *Travels in Luristan and Arabistan*. 2 vols. London: J. Maddon and Co., 1845.

British Archive FO 225/226 (1944).

Brockelmann, Carl. *History of the Islamic People*. Translated by Joel Carmichael and Moshe Perlmann. New York: Capricorn, 1960.

Brown, John P. *The Darvishes or Oriental Spiritualism*. Edited by H. A. Rose. London: Frank Cass, 1968.

Browne, Edward G. *Persian Literature in Modern Times*. Cambridge: Cambridge University Press, 1924.

———. *A Literary History of Persia: 1500–1924*. Cambridge: Cambridge University Press, 1959.

———. *A History of Literature Under Tartar Dominion:* A.D. *1265–1502*. Cambridge: Cambridge University Press, 1960.

Burckhardt, John Lewis. *Travels in Syria and the Holy Land*. London: John Murray, 1822.

Caetani, Leone. *Annali del' Islam*. Vol. 8. Milano: U. Hoepli, 1918.

Cahen, Claude. *Pre-Ottoman Turkey*. Translated from the French by J. Jones Williams. New York: Taplinger Publishing Company, 1968.

Cherri, Muhammad Jawad. *The Brother of the Prophet Muhammad (The Imam Ali)*, Vol. 1. Detroit: Islamic Center, 1979.

Chwolsohn, Daniel. *Die Ssabier und der Ssabismus*. 2 vols. St. Petersburg: Buchdruckerei der Kaiserlichen Akademie der Wissenschaften, 1856.

Conybeare, Fred C. *The Key of Truth: A Manual of the Paulician Church of Armenia*. Oxford: Oxford University Press, 1898.

Corbin, Henry. *En Islam Iranien: Aspects spirituels et philosophiques*. 4 vols. London: Gallimard edition Kegan Paul International, 1978.

———. *The Man of Light in Iranian Sufism*. Boulder and London: Shambhala 1978.

———. *Cyclical Time and Ismaili Gnosis*. London, Kegan Paul International, 1983.

Creasy, Edward S. *History of the Ottoman Turks*. Beirut: Khayat, 1961.

Cuinet, Vital. *La Turquie d'Asie: géographie, administrative, statistique, descriptive, et raisonnée de chaque province de l'Asie Mineure*. 4 vols. Paris: E. Leroux, 1890–95.

Dam, Nikolaos van. *The Struggle for Power in Syria*. London: Croom Helm, 1979.

Dekmejian, H. Richard. *Islam in Revolution: Fundamentalism in the Arab World*. Syracuse: Syracuse University Press, 1985.

De Sacy, Antoine Isaac Silvestre. *Exposé de la Religion des Druzes*. 2 vols. Paris: L'Imperemeir Royald, 1838.

Devlin, John F. *The Ba'th Party: A History from Its Origin to 1966*. Stanford: Hoover Institute, 1976.

De Vogüe, Eugène Marie Melchior, Vicomte. *Histoires Orientales*. Paris: Colmann-Levy, 1911.

Donaldson, Dwight M. *The Shi'ite Religion a History of Islam in Persia and Irak*. London: Luzac, 1933.

Dussaud, René. *Histoire Et Religion Des Nosairis*. Paris: Libraire Émile Bouillon, 1900.

Edib, Halide. *Turkey Faces West*. New Haven, Yale University Press, 1930.

Elliot, Sir Charles (Odysseus). *Turkey in Europe*. London: E. Arnold, 1900.

Empson, R. H. *The Cult of the Peacock Angel*. London: H. F. Z. G. Witherby, 1928.

Febure, Michele. *Théatre de la Turquie*. Paris: E. Couterot, 1682.

Garnett, Lucy M. *Mysticism and Magic in Turkey*. New York: Charles Scribner's Sons, 1912.

Gibb, E. J. W. *A History of Ottoman Poetry*. 2 vols. London: Luzac, 1901.

Gibb, H. R. *The Arab Conquest of Central Asia*. London: The Royal Asiatic Society, 1923.

Gibbons, Herbert Adam. *The Foundation of the Ottoman Empire*. London: Frank Cass, 1968.

The Glory of the Shia World: The Tale of a Pilgrimage. Translated into English by P. M. Sykes. London: Macmillan, 1910. The author of this book is Nur Allah Khan, son of Muhammad Husayn Khan of Isfahan, but his name does not appear on the cover as the author.

Gobineau, Joseph Arthur Comte de. *Trois ans en Asie, 1855–1858.* Paris: Libraire de L. Hachetts, 1859.

———. *Les Religions et les Philosophie dans l'Asie Centrale.* Paris: Dedier, 1865.

Goeja, M. Jan De. *Memoire sur Les Carmathes du Bahrein.* Leiden: E. J. Brill, 1886.

Gökalp, Ziya. *Turkish Nationalism and Western Civilization.* Translated into English by Niyazi Berkes. New York: Columbia University Press, 1959.

Goldziher, Ignaz. *Vorlesungen über den Islam.* Heidelberg: C. Winter, 1910. Reprinted 1963.

Grothe, Hugo. *Meine Vorderasienexpedition: 1906 and 1907.* 2 vols. Leipzig: Hiersimann, 1911.

Grousset, René. *The Empire of the Steppes.* Translated by Naomi Walford. Rutgers: Rutgers University Press, 1970.

Haddad, George M. *Revolution and Military Rule in the Middle East: The Arab States.* 3 vols. New York: Robert Speller & Son, 1965–73.

Hamilton, W. J. *Researches in Asia Minor, Pontus, and Armenia.* London: John Murray, 1842.

Hammer-Purgstall, Joseph von. *The History of the Assassins.* Translated by Oswald Charles Wood. London: Smith & Elder Cornhill, 1840.

———. *Histoire de l'Empire Ottoman.* Translated by J. J. Hellert. 18 vols. Paris: Bellizard, Barthes, Dufour et Lowell, 1835–43.

Harnack, Adolph. *History fo Dogma.* 7 vols. New York: Dover, n.d.

Hasluck, F. W. *Christianity and Islam under the Sultans.* Edited by Margaret M. Hasluck. 2 vols. Oxford: Clarendon Press, 1929.

Heckethorn, Charles Williams. *The Secret Societies of All Ages and Countries.* 2 vols. New York: New York University, 1966.

Hitti, Phillip. *History of the Arabs.* 10th ed. New York: Macmillan, St. Martin's, 1970.

Hodgson, M. G. S. *The Order of Assassins: The Struggle of the Early Nizari Isma'ilis Against the Islamic World.* The Hague: Mouton 1955.

Hourani, Albert. *Syria and Lebanon: A Political Essay.* London: Oxford University Press, 1964.

Huart, Clement. *Konia, La ville des derviches tourneurs, souvenirs d' une voyage en Asie Mineure.* Paris: E. Leroux, 1897.

———. *Textes persons relatifs a la secte des Houroufis.* E. G. W. Gibb Memorial Series, Vol. 9, 1–41. Leyden, E. J. Brill, 1909.

Hudson, Michael. *Arab Politics.* Yale: Yale University Press, 1977.

Inalcik, Halil. *The Ottoman Empire: The Classical Age 1300–1600.* Translated by Norman Itzkowitz and Colin Imber. New York: Praeger, 1973.

Inchichian, Ghowkas. *Storagrowt'iwn Hayastaneayts.* Venice: San Lazaro, 1822.

Ivanow. W. *A Guide to Ismaili Literature.* London: Royal Asiatic Society 1933.

———. *Nasiri-i Khusraw and Ismailism.* Bombay: Ismaili Society, 1948.

———. *Brief Survey of the Evolution of Ismailism.* Leiden: E. J. Brill, 1952.

———. *The Truth-Worshippers of Kurdistan.* Leiden: E. J. Brill, 1953.

———. *Studies in Early Persian Ismailism.* Bombay: Ismaili Society, 1955.

Jacquot, Lieutenaut Colonel, Paul. *L'État des Alaoiutes, Terre d'art, de sourvenirs et de mystère*. Beirut: Emp. Catholique, 1929.

Joseph, Isya. *Devil Worship.* Boston: Richard G. Badger, 1919.

Keppel, G. *Personal Narrative of a Journey from India to England.* 2 vols. London: H. Colburn, 1817.

Khomeini, Imam. *Islam and Revolution: Writings and Declarations of Imam Khomeini.* Translated by Hamid Algar. Berkeley: Mizan Press, 1981.

Khorenantsi, Moses. *History of the Armenians.* Translated by Robert W. Thompson. Cambridge, Mass.: Harvard University Press, 1978.

Kinneir, J. MacDonald. *A Geographical Memoir of the Persian Empire.* London: John Murray, 1813.

Knolles, Richard. *The Turkish History.* 6th ed. with continuation by Sir Paul Ricaut. London: Charles Browne, 1687–1700.

Lammens, Henri. *Islam Beliefs and Institutions.* Translated by E. Denison Ross. New York: E. P. Dutton and Co., 1926.

Lane, Edward William. *An Account of the Manners and Customs of the Modern Egyptians.* London: A. Gardner, 1895.

Lang, David Marshall. *The Armenians a People in Exile.* London and Boston: Allen and Unwin, 1981.

Layard, A. *Discoveries in the Ruins of Nineveh and Babylon.* London: Harper & Brothers, 1853.

———. *Nineveh and Babylon.* London: John Murray, 1867.

Le Cabous-Name ou Livre de Cabous. Translated by A. Querry, Paris: E. Leroux, 1886.

Lennep, H. J. Van. *Travels in Little-Known Parts of Asia Minor.* 2 vols. London: John Murray, 1870.

Le Strange, G. *The Lands of the Eastern Caliphate.* London: Frank Cass, 1966.

Lewis, Bernard. *The Assassins: A Radical Sect in Islam.* New York: Weidenfeld & Nicholson, 1968.

Lockhart, Laurence. *The Fall of the Safawi Dynasty and the Afghan Occupation of Persia.* Cambridge: The University Press, 1958.

Loftus, William Kennett. *Travels and Researches in Chaldea and Susiana.* London: James Nisbet, 1857.

Longrigg, Stephen. *Syria and Lebanon.* New YorK: Octagon Books, 1972.

Lyde, Samuel. *The Ansyreeh and Ismaeleeh.* London: Hurst and Blackett, 1853.

———. *The Asian Mystery.* London: Longman Green, Longman and Roberts, 1860.

Macler, Frédéric. *Les Apocalypse Apochryphes de Daniel.* Paris: C. Noblet, 1895.

Makarem, Sami Naisb. *The Doctrine of the Isma'ilis.* Beirut: The Arab Institute for Research and Publishing, 1972.

Malcolm, Sir John. *The History of Persia from the Most Early Period to the Present Time.* 2 vols. London: John Murray, 1815.

Maoz, Moshe, and Yanir, Avner, eds. *Syria under Assad.* New York: St. Martin's, 1986.

Massignon, Louis. *Salman Pak et les Premices spirituelles de l' Islam iranien.* Translated into Arabic by Abd al-Rahman Badawi in his *Shakhsiyyat Qaliqa fi al-Islam.* Cairo: Dar al-Nahda al-Arabiyya, 1964, 3–58.

———. *Le Mubahala Étude sur la proposition d'ordalie faite par la Prophète Muhammad aux Chrétiens Balharith du Nejràn en l'an 10/631 à Médine.* Melun: 1944.

Mazzaoui, Michel. *The Origins of the Safawids: Shi'ism, Sufism and Gulat.* Wiesbaden: Franz Steiner, 1972. This is a published version of the author's "Shi'ism and the Rise of the Safavids." Unpublished dissertation, Princeton University, 1966.

Mez, Adam. *Die Renaissance des Islams.* Heidelberg: Carl Winter 1922. An English translation is by Salahuddin Khuda Bakhsh and D. S. Margoliouth, *The Renaissance of Islam,* London: Luzac: 1937. Reprinted New York: AMS Press. 1975. For an Arabic translation, see Muhammad Abd al-Hadi Abu Rida, *al-Hadara al-Islamiyya fi al-Qarn al-Rabi al-Hijri aw Asr al-Nahda fi al-Islam.* 2 vols. 3rd ed. Cairo: Dar al-Kutub al-Haditha, 1377/1975.

Minadoi, Giovanni Tommaso. *Historia della guerra fra Turchi et Persiana.* Venetia: Appresso Andraea Muschio & Barezzo Barezze 1594. For an English translation, see Abraham Hartwell, *The History of the Warres Between the Turks and the Persians.* London: John Wolfe, 1595.

Mingana, Alphonse. *The Early Spread of Christianity in Central Asia and the Far East: A New Document.* Manchester: Manchester University Press, 1952. Reprinted from *The Bulletin of the John Rylands Library* 9, no. 2 (July 1952).

Minorsky, Vladimir. *Notes sur la Secte des Ahlé-Haqq.* Paris: Ernest Leroux, 1921.

Mekerttschian, Karapet Ter. *Die Paulikianer im byzantinischen Kaiserreich und verwandte ketzerische Erscheinungen in Armenien.* Leipzig: J. C. Hirrichs, 1893.

Mosheim, John Lawrence von. *Institute of the Eccless iastical History Ancient and Modern.* Translated into English by James Murdock. 3 vols. New York: Harper and Brothers, 1844.

Muhy-UD-Din, Ata. *Ali the Superman.* Lahore: Muhammad Ashraf Press, 1980.

Musa, Munir Mushabih. *Étude Sociologique des Alaouites ou Nusairis.* Unpublished dissertation, Paris, 1958.

Mutahhari, Murtaza. *Master and Mastership.* Translated from the Persian by Mustajib A. Ansari. 2nd ed. Tehran: Foreign Foundation of Bethat, 1982.

Nanji, Azim. *The Nizari Isma'ili Tradition in the Indo-Pakistan Subcontinent.* New York: Delmar, 1978.

Nasr, Sayyid Hussein. *Ideals and Realities of Islam.* New York: F. Praeger, 1967.

Nicholson, R. A. *Studies in Islamic Mysticism.* Cambridge: Cambridge University Press, 1921.

———. *The Idea of Personality in Sufism,* Reprinted Lahore: M. Ashraf Press, 1973.

———. *The Mystics of Islam.* New York: Schocken Books, 1975.

Nöldeke, Theodor. *Sketches from Eastern History.* Translated by John Suntherland. Beirut: Khayat, 1963.

Nyrop, Richard F. editor. *Syria: A Country Study.* American University Foreign Area Studies, Washington, D.C.: 1979.

Palmer, E. H. *Oriental Mysticism.* London: F. Cass, 1867. Reprinted 1969.

Petermann, H. *Reisen im Orient.* 2 vols. Leipzig: Veit & Co., 1861.

Peterson, E. A. H. and F. von Luschan. *Reisen in Lykien.* Wien: Gerold, 1889.

Petran, Tabitha. *Syria a Modern History.* London: Ernest Ben, 1978.

Petrushevsky, I. P. *Islam in Iran.* Transalted by Hubert Evans. State University of New York: Albany, New York, 1985.

Polak, J. E. *Persien, das Land und seine Bewohner.* 2 vols. Leipzig, F. A. Brockhaus, 1865.

Purchas, Samuel. *Samuel Purchas His Pilgrimage.* London: Printed by W. Stansby for H. Fetherstone, 1617 and 1626.

Rabino, M. H. Louis. *Les Tribes du Louristan.* Paris: E. Leroux, 1916.

Rabinovich, Itamar. *Syria under the Ba'th 1963–1966.* Tel Aviv: Israel Universities Press, 1977.

Ramsay, William Mitchel. *Impressions of Turkey During Twelve Year's Wanderings.* New York: Putnam's Son, 1897.

———. *Pauline and other Studies in Early Christian History.* New York: Hodder and Stoughton, 1906.

———. *The Revolution in Constantinople and Turkey; a diary.* London: Hodder & Stoughton, 1909.

Rawlinson, C. *History of Herodotus.* 2 vols. New York: Appleton and Company, 1889.

Renan, Ernest. *Mission de Phénicie.* Paris: Impremerie Imperiale, 1864.

Rice, Tamara Talbot. *The Seljuks in Asia Minor.* New York: Praeger, 1961.

Rich, Claudius James. *Narrative of a Residence in Koordistan and on the Site of Ancient Nineveh.* 2 vols. London: J. Duncan, Paternoster Row, 1836.

R. Runciman. *The Medieval Manichee.* Cambridge: Cambridge University Press, 1947.

Sarre, Friedrich Paul; Theodor. *Reise in Kleinasien Sommer*-1895. *Forschungen zur seldjukischen Kunst und Geographie des Landes.* Berlin: D. Reimer, 1896.

Sarwar, Ghulam. *History of Shah Isma'il Safawi.* Aligarh: Muslim University, 1939. Reprinted New York: AMS Press, 1975.

Sell, Rev. Canon. *The Cult of Ali.* London, Madras, and Colombo: The Christian Society for India, 1910.

Shahid, Sadik. *Islam, Turkey and Armenia and How they Happened.* St. Louis: G. W. Woodward Company, 1898.

Shariati, Ali. *Fatima is Fatima.* Translated by Laleh Bakhtiar. Brooklyn, N.Y.: Muslim Students Council, n.d.

Shaw, Stanford. *History of the Ottoman Empire and Modern Turkey.* 2 vols. Cambridge: Cambridge University Press, 1976.

Smith, Eli and Dwight, H. G. O. *Missionary Researches in Armenia Including a Journey Through Asia Minor and into Georgia and Persia with a visit to the Nestorian and Chaldean of Oormiah and Salmas.* London: George Wightman, 1834.

Soane, E. B. *Grammar of the Kurmanji or Kurdish Language*. London: Luzac, 1913.

———. *To Mesopotamia and Kurdistan in Disguise*. London: John Murray, 1920.

Southgate, Horatio. *Narrative of a Tour Through Armenia, Kurdistan, Persia, and Mesopotamia*. 2 vols. London: Tilt and Bogue, 1840.

———. *Narrative of a Visit to the Syrian (Jacobite) Church*. New York: Appleton & Co., 1844.

Springett, Bernard H. *Secret Societies of Syria*. London: George Allen and Unwin, 1922.

Stern, S. M. *Studies in Early Isma'ilism*. Jerusalem: The Hebrew University, 1983.

Stevenson, Mary Esme Gwendoline Scott-. *Our Ride Through Asia Minor.* London: Chapman and Hall Ltd., 1881.

Tadhkira-i A'la, a version of the Ahl-i Haqq book called *Saranjam*. Translated by W. Ivanow and incorporated in his book *The Truth-Worshippers of Kurdistan*. Leiden: E. J. Brill, 1953.

Taylor, W. C. *The History of Muhammedanism and Its Sects.* London: John W. Parker, 1834.

Temple, Sir Richard Carnac. "A Commentary," appended to R. H. Empson, *The Cult of the Peacock Angel*. London: H. F. & G. Witherby, 1928.

Tozer, Henry F. *Turkish Armenia and Eastern Asia Minor.* London: Longmans, Green & Co., 1881.

Trimingham, G. Spencer. *The Sufi Orders of Islam*. Oxford: Oxford University Press, 1971.

Valle, Pietro Della. *Viaggi di Pietro Della Valle il Pelligrino*. vol. 2. Rome: Apresso Dragondelli, 1658.

Vámbéry, Arminius, *History of Bokhara*. London (1873). Reprinted, New York: Arno Press, 1973.

———. *Das Türkenvolk in seinen ethnologischen und ethnographischen Beziehungen geschildert*. Leipzig: F. A. Brockhaus, 1885.

Vasiliev, A. A. *History of the Byzantine Empire 324–1453*. 2 vols. Madison: University of Wisconsin Press, 1964.

Verneir, Bernard. *Armée et Politique an Moyen Orient*. Paris: Payot, 1966.

Vloten, Gerlof von. *Recherches sur la Domination arabe, et les Croyances Messianiques Sous le khalifat des Omayades*. Amsterdam: Johannes Müller, 1894.

Walpole, Lieu, the Hon. F. *The Ansayrii and the Assassins with Travels in the Further East, in 1850–51 Including a Visit to Nineveh*. 3 vols. London: R. Bently, 1851.

Watt, W. Montgomery. *Islam and the Integration of Society.* London: Routledge and Kegan Paul, 1961.

Wellhausen, Julius. *The Arab Kingdom and Its Fall*. Beirut: Khayat, 1963.

———. *The Religio-Political Factions in Early Islam*. Edited R. C. Ostle, translated by R. C. Ostle and S. M. Walzer: North Holland Publishing Company, 1975.

———. *Skizzen und Vorarbeiten*. Berlin: Georg Reimer, 1884–99.

Weulersse, Jacque. *Le Pays des Alaouites*. 2 vols. Tour: Arrault, 1940.

———. *Paysans de Syrie et du Proche-Orient*. Paris: Gallimard, 1946.

Wilson, Major General Sir Charles. *Handbook for Travellers in Asia Minor, Transcaucasia, Persia, . . .* London: John Murray, 1895.
Wilson, Samuel G. *Persian Life and Customs.* New York: Fleming H. Revell, 1900.
Woods, John E. *The AQ Qoyunlu Clan Confederates Empire.* Chicago: Bibliotheca Islamica, 1976.
Zinkeisen, J.W . *Geschichte des osmanischen Reiches in Europa,* vol. 3. Gotha: F. A. Perthes, 1840.

Articles

Adjarian, H. "Gyoran et Thoumaris." Translated into French by Frédéric Macler. *Revue de L'Histoire des Religion* 93, no. 3 (May–June 1926): 294–307.
Amkah [pseud.]. "al-Shabak." *al-Muqtataf* 59 (1920): 230–32.
Arjomand, Said Amir. "Religion, Political Action and Legitimate Domination in Shi'ite Iran: Fourteenth to Eighteenth Centuries." *European Journal of Sociology* 20 (1979): 59–109.
———. "Religious Extremism (Ghuluww), Sufism and Sunnism in Safavid Iran: 1500–1722." *Journal of Asian History* 15 (1981): 1–35.
Arkoun. "Ishrak." *The Encyclopedia of Islam,* 4 (1973): 119–120.
Arnaldez, R. A. "al-Insan al-Kamil," *The Encyclopedia of Islam,* 3 (1971): 1239–1241.
Babinger, Franz. "Scheych Bedr ed-din, der Sohn des Richters von Simaw." *Der Islam* (1921): 1–104.
———. "Der Islam in Kleinasien. Neue Wege der Islamforschung." *Zeitschrift der deutschen morgenländischen Gesellschaft* 76 (1922): 126–52.
Ball. Report dated 8 August 1857. *Missionary Herald* 53 (1857): 395–96.
Barnum. Report dated 22 July 1863. *Missionary Herald.* 59 (1863): 310–11.
Barthold, W. "Turgai." *The Encyclopedia of Islam,* 4 (1934), 894–95.
Basset, René. "Nusairis." *The Encyclopedia of Religion and Ethics* 9, 417–19.
Batatu, Hanna. "Some Observations on the Social Roots of Syria's Ruling Military Group and The Causes for Its Dominance." *The Middle East Journal* 30, no. 3 (Summer 1981): 331–44.
Ben-Tzur, Avraham. "The Neo Ba'th Party in Syria." *New Outlook* 12, no. 1 (January 1969):L 21–37.
Bent, Theodore. "Azerberijan." *The Scottish Geographical Magazine* (1890): 84–93.
———. "The Yourouks of Asia Minor." *Journal of the Royal Anthropological Institute of Great Britain and Ireland* 20 (1890–91): 269–76.
Blochet, E. "Études sur l" Historie Religieuse de l' Iran." *Revue de l' Histoire des Religion* 2 (1899): 1–25.
Bonwetsch, N. "Paulician," *The New Schaff-Herzog Encyclopedia of Religious Knowledge* 8 (1910): 417–18.
Boratav, P. N. "Khidr-Ilyas." *The Encyclopedia of Islam,* 5 (1979): 5.

Bosworth, C. E. "The Early Ghaznavids." *The Cambridge History of Iran,* 4 (1975): 162–197.

Brigham, Charles Henry. "The Asian Mystery." *North American Review* 93, no. 193 (October 1861): 342–66.

Browne, Edward G. "Some Notes on the Literature and Doctrines of the Hurufi Sect." *Journal of the Royal Asiatic Society* (1898): 61–94.

———. "Further Notes on the Literature of the Hurufis and Their Connection with the Bektashi Order of Dervishes." *Journal of the Royal Asiatic Society* (1907): 533–81.

———. "Notes on an Apparently Unique Manuscript History of the Safawi Dynasty of Persia." *Journal of the Royal Asiatic Society* (1921): 395–418. The history was written by Shaykh Husayn Zahidi. See Zahidi.

Cahen, Claude. "Baba'i." *The Encyclopedia of Islam,* 1 (1960): 843–44.

———. "Futuwwa." *The Encyclopedia of Islam,* 2 (1965): 961–69.

Canard, M. "Arṃiniya." *The Encyclopedia of Islam,* 1 (1960):634–50.

Canfield, Robert. "What They Do When The Lights are out: Myths and Social Order in Afghanistan." Paper presented to the joint committee on the Near Middle East American Council of Learned Societies Social Science Research Council: Conference on Symbols of Social Differentiation, Baltimore, 25–28 May 1978.

Caskel, W. "Ein Mahdi des 15. Jahrhunderts. Sajjid Muhammad Ibn Falah und seine Nachkommen." *Islamica* 4 (1929–30): 48–93.

Catafago, Joseph. "Drei Messen der Nosairier." *Zeitschrift der deutschen morgenländischen Gesellschaft* 2 (1848): 388–94.

———. "Notices Sur Les Anseriens." *Journal Asiatique* (February 1848): 149–68.

Carleton, Alfrod. "The Syrian Coups d'Etat of 1949." *The Middle East Journal* 4, no. 1 (January 1950): 1–11.

Cheikho, Rev. Louis. "Some Moslem Apocryphal Legends." Translated from the French by Josephine Spaeth. *The Moslem World* 2 (January 1912): 47–59.

———. "al-Nasraniyya bayn Qudama al-Atrak wa al-Maghul." *al-Mashriq* 16 (1913): 754–72.

Colebrooke, H. T. "On the Origin and Peculiar Tenets of Certain Muhammedan Sects." *Asiatic Researches* 7 (1807): 336–42.

Corbin, Henry. "Le Livre du Glorieux de Jabir Ibn Hayyan." *Eranos-Jahrbuch* 18 (1950): 47–114.

Crowfoot, J. W. "Survivals among the Kappadokian Kizilbash (Bektash)." *Journal of the Anthropological Institute of Great Britain and Ireland* 30 (1900): 305–20.

Driver, G. R. "Studies in Kurdish History." *Bulletin of the School of Oriental Studies* 2 (1921–23): 491–511.

———. "The Religion of the Kurds." *Bulletin of the School of Oriental Studies* 2 (1921–23): 196–213.

Drysdale, Alisdare. "The Assad Regime and Its Troubles." *Middle East Research and Information Project Report* no. 110 (November–December 1982): 3–11.

Dunmore. Report dated 24 October 1854. *Missionary Herald* 51 (1855): 55–56.

———. *Report dated 22 January 1857. Missionary Herald* 53 (1857): 219–20.

———. Report. *Missionary Herald* 54 (1858): 113.

Dusen, Michael H. Van. "Political Integration and Regionalism in Syria." *The Middle East Journal* 26 (Spring 1972): 123–36.

Einsler, Lydia. "Mar Elyas El-Chadr, und Mar Dschirjis." *Zeitschrift des deutschen Palästina-Vereins* 17 (1894): 42 ff.

Fortescue, Adrian. "Paulicians." *The Catholic Encyclopedia,* 11 (1913): 583–85.

Frey, R. N. "The Samanids." *The Cambridge History of Iran,* 4 (1975): 136–61.

Friedländer, Israel. "Abd Allah b. Saba, der Begründer der Schi'a und Sein Jüdischer Ursprung." *Zeitschrift für Assyriologie* 23 (1909): 296–327.

———. "The heterodoxies of the Shiites." *Journal of the American Oriental Society* 24 (1910): 1–46.

Gibb, H. A. R. "Constitutional Organization." In *Law in the Middle East,* vol. 1, edited by Majid Khadduri and Herbert J. Liebesny, 3–27. Washington, D.C.: The Middle East Institute, 1955.

Gilbert, T. "Notes sur les Sects dans le Kurdistan." *Journal Asiatique* 2, ser. 7 (July 1873): 393–94.

Goldziher, Ignaz. "The Influence Buddhism upon Islam." *Journal of the Royal Asiatic Society of Great Britain and Ireland* (January 1904): 125–41.

———. "Neu platonische und gnostische Elemente im Hadit, Zeitchrift für Assyriologie" 22 (1921): 317–44.

———. "Das Prinzip des Takijja in Islam." *Zeitschrift der deutschen morgenländischen Gesellschaft* 60 (1960): 213–26.

———. "Abdal." *The Encyclopedia of Islam,* 1 (1960): 94–95.

Golpinarli, Abdulbaki. "Bektasilik ve Haci Bektas." *Aylik Ansiklopedi* no. 41 (September 1947): 1194–95.

———. "Bektas Haci." Unpublished article written in the author's handwriting.

Gregory of Narek. "Letter to the Convent of Kdjay." In *The Key of Truth* by Fred C. Conybeare, Appendix I, 125–30. Oxford: Oxford University Press, 1898.

Grenard, M. F. "Une Secte Religieuse d'Asie Mineure: Les Kyzyl-Bachs." *Journal Asiatique* 3, ser. 10 (1904): 511–22.

Gubser, Peter. "Minorities in Power: The Alawites of Syria." In *The Political Role of Minority Groups in the Middle East,* edited by R. D. McLaurin, 17–48. Praeger, 1979.

Guyard, M. St. "Le Fetwa D'Ibn Taimiyyah sur les Nosariris." *Journal Asiatique* 18 (1871): 158–98.

Heard, W. B. "Notes on the Yezidis." *Royal Anthropological Institute of Great Britain and Ireland* 41 (1911): 200–19.

Herrick. Report dated 16 November 1865. *Missionary Herald* 62, no. 3 (March 1866): 68–69.

Hodgson, Marshall G. S. "How Did the Early Shi'a Become Sectarian?" *Journal of the American Oriental Society* 75 (January–March 1955): 1–13.

———. "Batiniyya." *The Encyclopedia of Islam,* I (1960): 1098–1100.

———. "Bayan b. Sam'an al-Tamimi." *The Encylopedia of Islam,* I (1960): 1116–17.

———. "Abd Allah b. Saba." *The Encyclopedia of Islam,* I (1960): 51–52.
———. "Ghulat." *The Encyclopedia of Islam,* 2 (1965): 1093–95.
Horovitz, Josef. "Salman al-Farisi." *Der Islam* 12 (1922): 178–83.
Houtsma, M. "Abd Allah b. Saba." *The Encyclopedia of Islam,* I (1913): 29.
Houtum-Schindler, A. "Shah Isma'il." *Journal of the Royal Asiatic Society of Great Britain and Ireland* (1897): 114–15.
Huart, Clement, "Ali Ilahi." *The Encyclopedia of Islam,* I(1913): 292–93.
———. "Kizil-Bash." *The Encyclopedia of Islam,* 2 (1927): 1653–54.
Huntington, Ellswroth. "Through the Great Canon of the Euphrates River." *The Geographical Journal* 20, no. 2 (August 1902): 175–200.
Ibrahim, Ahmad Sulayman. "al-Alawiyyun bayn al-Muslimin wa al-Islam." In *al-Alawiyyun bayn al-Ustura wa al-Haqiqa* by Hashim Uthmam, 189–91. Beirut: 1980. First published in *al-Nahda,* special issue, no. 8 (July 1938).
Ivanow, W. "Notes sur l' Ummu'l-Kitab." *Revue des Études Islamique* (1932): 419–82.
———. "An Ali Ilahi Fragment," *Collectanea* I (Leiden: E. J. Brill, published for the Ismaili Society, 1948), 147–84.
Jacob, Georg. "Die Bektaschijje in ihrem Verhältnis zu verwandten Erscheinungen." *Abhandlungen der philosophisch-philologischen Klasse der königlich bayerischen Akademie der Wissenschaften* 24, part 3 (1909): 1–53.
———. "Fortleben von Antiken Mysterien und Alt-Chrislichen im Islam." *Der Islam* 2 (1911): 232–34.
Jewett. report dated 16 December 1857.*Missionary Herald* 54, no. 4 (April 1857): 109.
Jurji, Edward., "The Alids of North Syria." *The Moslem World* 29, no. 4 (October 1939): 329–41.
Karam, Mirza. "The Sect of the Ali Ilahis or the Ahl-i Haqq." *The Moslem World* 29, no. 1 (January 1939): 73–78.
Karmali, Anastase Marie al-. "al-Yazidiyya." *al-Mashriq* 2 (1899): 32–37.
———. "Tafkihat al-Adhhan fi Ta'rif Thalathat Adyan." *al-Mashriq* 5 (1902): 576–77.
———. "Al-Dawuda aw al-Dawudiyyun." *al-Mashriq* 6 (1903): 60–67.
———. "Al-Abdal." *al-Mashriq* 12 (1909): 194–204.
———. "Laylat al-Hashush wa al-Mashush." *Lughat al-Arab* 8 (1930): 368–73.
Kasrawi, Ahmad. "Nijad wa-Tabari-i Safaviya." *Ayanda* 2 (1926–1928): 357 ff., 489 ff., 801 ff.
Kelidar, A. R. "Religion and State in Syria." *Asian Affairs, Journal of the Royal Central Asian Society* 61, n.s. 5 pt. 1 (February 1974): 16–22.
Khayyir, Abd al-Rahman al-. "Yaqzat al-Alawiyyin." In *al-Alawiyyun bay al-Ustura wa al-Haqiqa* by Hashim Uthman, 173–89. Beirut: 1980. First published in *al-Nahda* n. 3 (January 1937), no. 4 (February 1937), and no. 5 (March 1937).
Köprülü, M. F. "Anadoluda Islamiyet." in *Edebiyat Fakultesi Mecmuasi* no. 2 (1338/1919): 295 ff.

———. "Les Origines du Bektachisme." *Actes des Congrès Internationale d' Historie des Religions* 2 (1925): 391–411.

Lammens, Henri. "Au Pays Des Nosairis." *Revue de l'Orient Chrétien* 4 (1899): 572–90, and 5 (1900): 99–117, 303–18, 423–44.

———. "Les Nosairis Furent-Ils Chrétiens?" *Revue de l'Orient Chrétien* 6 (1901): 33–50.

Langlois, Victor. "Religion Et Doctrine Des Noussairiès," *Revue d'Oreint et d' l'Algerie et des Colonies,* in *Societe Orientale De France* 3 (June 1856): 431–37.

Levy, R. "The Account of the Isma'ili Doctrine in the Jami al-Tawarikh of Rashid al-Din Fadlallah." *Journal of the Royal Asiatic Society* (1930): 509–36.

Lidzbarski, Mark. "Ein Exposé der Jisiden." *Zeitschrift der deutschen morgenländischen Gesellschaft* 51 (1897): 592–604.

Livingstone. Report. *Missionary Herald* 65 (1869): 246.

Luschan, Felix von. "Die Tahtadji und andere Reste der alten Bevölkerung Lykiens." *Archive für Anthropologie* 19 p.d. (1891): 31–53.

———. "The Early Inhabitants of Western Asia." *Journal of the Royal Anthropologocial Institute* 41 (1911): 221–44.

Macdonald, D. B. "Al-Mahdi." *The Encyclopedia of Islam,* 3 (1971): 111–15.

Macler, Frédéric. "Armenia (Christian)." *Encyclopedia of Religion and Ethics,* I (1908): 803–7.

Madelung, Wilfred. "Bemerkungen zur imamitischen Firaq-Literatur." *Der Islam* 43 (1967): 37–52.

———. "Imama." *The Encyclopedia of Islam,* 3 (1971): 1163–69.

———. "The Minor Dynasties of Northern Iran." *The Cambridge History of Iran,* 4 (1975): 198–249.

Magistros, Gregory. "Letters." In *The Key of Truth* by Fred C. Conybeare, Appendix 3, 141–51. Oxford: 1898.

Maoz, Moshe. "Attempts at creating a Political Community in Modern Syria." *The Middle East Journal* 26, no. 4 (Autumn 1972): 383–404.

———. "The Emergence of Modern Syria." In *Syria Under Assad,* edited by Moshe Maoz and Avner Yaniv, 9–35. New York, St. Martin's 1986.

Marsais, Ph., "Ashura." *The Encyclopedia of Islam,* 1(1960): 705.

Massignon, Louis. "Nusairi." *The Encyclopedia of Islam,* 3(1936): 963–67.

———. "L'Homme Parfait en Islam et Son Originalité Eschalotogique." *Eranos-Jahrbuch* (1947): 287–314.

———. "Les Nusairis." *Opera Minora* 1(1960): 619–49.

Minorsky, Vladimir. "Shabak." *The Encyclopedia of Islam,* 4(1934): 238–239.

———. "Un traité de polémique Béhai-Ahle-Haqq." *Journal Asiatique* (1921): 165–67.

———. "Études sur les Ahl-i Haqq, i, 'Toumari'—Ahl-i Haqq." *Revue de l'Histoire des Religions* (1928): 90–105.

———. "The Guran." *Bulletin of the School of Oriental Studies* (1943): 75–193.

———. "Ahl-i Hakk." *The Encyclopedia of Islam,* 1(1960): 260–63.

Mittwoch, E. "Dhu l'Fakar." *The Encyclopedia of Islam,* 2(1965): 233.

Mokri, Mohammad. "l' ideé l' incarnation chez les Ahl-e Haqq." *Atken des Internationalen Orientalisten-Kongress* 24 (1959): 496–98.

———."Le symbole de la Perle dans le folklore persan et chez les Kurdes Fidèles Vérité (Ahl-e Haqq)." *Journal Asiatique* (1960): 463–81.

———. "Le Secret Indicible et la Pierre Noire en Perse dans la tradition des Kurdes et des Lurs Fidèles de Vérité (Ahl-e Haqq)." *Journal Asiatique* (1962): 369–433.

———. "Étude d'un titre de Propriété du début de XVI Siecle Provenant de Kurdistan." *Journal Asiatique* (1963): 229–56.

———. "La naissance du monde chez Kurdes Ahl-e Haqq." *Trudy Mezhdunarodonogo Kongressa Vostokovedov* (1963): 159–68.

Molyneux-Seel, Captain L. "A journey in Dersim." *Geographical Journal* 44, no. 1 (July 1914): 49–68.

Moosa, Matti. "Ahwaz: An Arab Territory." *The Future of the Arab Gulf and the Strategy of Joint Arab Action* 3(1983): 12–49.

Munajjid, Salah al-Din al-. "Mu'jam Musannafat Ibn Abi al-Dunya." *Majallat Majma ål-Lugha al-Arabiyya* 49(1974): 579–94.

Napier, G. S. F. "The Road from Baghdad to Baku." *The Geographical Journal* 52, no. 1 (January 1919): 1–19.

Nicholson, R. A. "Mysticism." *The Legacy of Islam* (1931): 210–38.

Nikitine, B. "Essay d'Analyse de Safvat us-Safa." *Journal Asiatique* (1957): 385–93. This is a French summary of *Safwat al-Safa* by Ibn Bazzaz.

Nöldeke, Theodor. "Haidar." *The Encyclopedia of Islam,* 2(1927), 218–19.

Nutting. Report dated 30 July 1860. *Missionary Herald* 56(November 1860): 345–47.

Parson. Report dated 17 September 1857. *Missionary Herald* 54 (1858): 23–24.

Perkins. Report. *Missionary Herald* 51 (1855): 279.

Photuis. *Adversus Manichaeos* in *Patrologia Graecae* 102 (1860): 15–263.

Pittman, Charles R. "The Final Word of Ahl-i Haqq." *The Moslem World* 37(1937): 147–63. This is another version of *Saranjam*.

Rabino, M. H. Louis. "Kermanchah." Revue de Monde Musulman 38 (March 1920): 1–40.

Ramsaur, E. E. "The Bektashi Dervishes and the Young Turks." *The Moslem World* 32(1942): 7–14.

Ramsay, William Mitchel. "The Intermixture of Races in Asia Minore Some of its Causes and Effects." *Proceedings of the British Academy* 7 (1917): 1–64.

Rawlinson, Major H. "Notes of a March from Zohab, at the foot of Zagros, along the Mountains to Khuzistan (Susiana), and from these through the province of Luristan to Kirmanshah in the year 1839." *Journal of the Royal Asiatic Society* 9 (1839): 26–166.

Rice, W. A. "Ali in Shi'ah Tradition." *The Moslem World* 4, no. 1 (January 1914): 27–44.

Richardson. Report dated 14 July 1856. *Missionary Herald* 52, no. 10 (October 1856): 298.

Rida, Ahmed. "al-Taqiyya." *al-Muqtataf* 40 (January 1912): 35–42, (February): 117–124 and (March): 226–230.

Ross, E. Denison, "The Early Years of Shah Isma'il." *Journal of the Asiatic Society of Great Britain and Ireland* (April 1896): 249–340.

Saeed Khan. "The Sect of Ahl-i Haqq (Ali Ilahis)." *The Moslem World* 17(1927): 31–42.

Sait, Baha. "Turkiyede Alevi Zumreleri." *Türk Yurdu* no. 22 (1926–27): 332–55.

Salisbury, Edward. "The Book of Sulyman's First Ripe Fruit Disclosing the Nosairian Religion." *Journal of the American Oriental Society* 8 (1864): 227–308. This is a translation of Sulayman al-Adani's *Kitab al-Bakura al-Sulaymaniyya.*

Savory, R. M. "Djunayd." The Encyclopedia of Islam, 2 (1965): 598.

———. "Haydar." *The Encyclopedia of Islam,* 3 (1971): 315.

Scott, C. A. "Paulicians." *Encyclopedia of Religion and Ethics,* 9 (1917), 695–98.

Shaibi, Kamil Mustafa al-. "al-Taqiyya: Usuluha wa Tatawwuruha." *Majallat Kuliyyat al-Adab* no. 16 (1962–63); 233–70.

———. "Kalimat Shi'a fi al-Lugha wa al-Tarikh." *Majallat Kuliyyat al-Tarbiya fi al-Jami'a al-Libiyya* no. 3 (1972): 171–204.

———. "al-Wahi lada al-Samiyyin wa al-Islamiyyin." *Bayn al-Nahrayn* 9, no. 36 (1982): 333–40 and 10, nos. 37–38 (1982) 27–50.

Siculi, Petri (Peter). *Historia Manichaeorum* in *Pastrologia Graecae* 104 (1860), 1242–1303.

———. *Adversus Manichaeos* in *Patrologia Graecae* 104 (1860), 1306–46.

Stead, F. M. "The Ali Ilahi Sect in Persia." *The Moslem World* 22, no. 2 (April 1932): 184–89.

Stern, S. M. "The Early Isma'ili Missionaries in North-West Persia and in Khurasan and Transoxiana." *Bulletin of the School of Oriental and African Studies* 23 (1960): 56–90.

Strothmann, R. "Takiya." *The Encyclopedia of Islam,* 4 (1934): 628–29.

———. "Die Nusairi im heutigen Syrien." *Nachrichten der Akademie der Wissenschaften* in Göttingen, I, *Philosophische-Historische Klasse* no. 4 (1950): 29–64.

———. "Seelenwanderung Bei Den Nusairi." *Oriens* 12 (1959): 89–114.

Suryani, al-Rahib (Monk) Behnam al-Mawsili al-. "Maqala fi al-Yazidiyya." *al-mashriq* 45 (1951): 533–48 and 46 (1952): 29–40. This is a plagiarism of Rev. Anstase al-Karmali's article, "al-Yazidiyya." See Karmali.

Suud, Shaykh Isa. "Ma Aghfalahu al-Tarikh: al-Alawiyyun aw al-Nusayriyya," In *al-Alawiyyun bayn al-Ustura wa al-Haqiqa* by Hashim Uthman, 156–73. Beirut: 1980. First published in *Majallat al-Amani* nos. 1–3 (October–December 1930) nos. 6–7 (March–April 1931), and no. 8 (May 1931).

Taeschner, F. "Akhi." *The Encyclopedia of Islam,* I (1960): 321–23.

Taylor, J. G. "Travels in Kurdistan, with Notices of the Sources of the Eastern and Western Tigris, and Ancient Ruins in their Neighborhood." *Journal of the Royal Geographical Society* 35 (1865): 21–58.

———. "Journal of a Tour in Armenia, Kurdistan and Upper Mesopotamia, with Notes of Researches in the Deyrsim Dagh, in 1866." *Journal of the Royal Asiatic Society* 38 (1868): 281–361.

Tisdall, St. Clair. "Shi'ah Additions to the Koran." *The Moslem World* 3, no. 3 (July 1913): 227–41.

Trowbridge, Stephen Van Rensselaer. "The Alevis, or Deifiers of Ali." *Harvard Theological Review* (1909): 340–53. Republished under the title, "The Alevis." *The Moslem World* 11, no. 3 (July 1921): 253–66.

Tschudi, R. "Bektashiyya." *The Encyclopedia of Islam,* I (1960): 1161–63.

Tyan, E. "Isma." *The Encyclopedia of Islam,* 4 (1973): 182–84.

Vaglieri, L. Veccia. "Fatima." *The Encyclopedia of Islam:* 2 (1965), 845–50.

Vinogradov (Rassam), Amal. "Ethnicity, Cultural Discontinuity and Power Brokers in Northern Iraq: The case of the Shabak." *American Ethnologist* (4 June 1973): 207–18.

Walsh, J. R. "Caldiran." *The Encyclopedia of Islam,* 2 (1965): 7–8.

Wensinck, A. J. "al-Khadir (al-Khidr)." *The Encyclopedia of Islam,* 2 (Leyden, 1927): 861–65.

White, George E. "Survivals of Primitive Religion, Among the People of Asia Minor." *Faith and Thought. Journal of the Transactions of the Victoria Institute* 39 (1907): 146–66.

———. "The Shia Turks." *Faith and Thought. Journal of the Transactions of the Victoria Institute* 43 (1908): 225–39.

———. "The Alevi Turks of Asia Minor." *The Contemporary Review Advertiser* 104 (November 1913): 690–98.

———. "Some Non-Conforming Turks." *The Moslem World* 8, no. 3 (July 1918): 242–48.

———. "Saint Worship in Turkey." *The Moslem World* 9 (1919): 8–18.

———. "Evil Spirits and the Evil Eye in Turkish Lore." *The Moslem World* 9, no. 2 (April 1919): 179–86.

Wilson, Charles and Rawlinson, H. C. "Kurdistan." *The Encyclopedia Britannica.* 11th ed. 15 (1911): 949–51.

Winchester. Report dated 28 November 1806. *Missionary Herald* 57 (March 1861): 70–73 and 273.

Wittek, Paul. "Zur Geschichte Angoras im Mittelalter." In *Festschrift Georg Jacob,* 329–54. (Leipzig: Harrassowitz, 1932).

———. "The Rise of the Ottoman Empire." *The Royal Asiatic Society of Great Britain and Ireland* 23 (1938) reprinted 1965): 1–54.

———. "Yazijioglu Ali on the Christian Turks of Dobruja." *Bulletin of the British School of Oriental and African Studies* 14, pt. 3 (1952); 639–68.

Wolff, "Auszüge aus dem Katechismus der Nosairier." *Zeitschrift der deutschen morgenländischen Gesellschaft* 3 (1849): 302–9.

Yalman, Nur. "Islamic Reform and the Mystic Tradition in Eastern Turkey." *Archives Européennes de Sociologie* 10 (1969): 41–60.

Yasin, al-Saykh Muhammad. "al-Alawiyyun Shi'iyyun." In *al-Alawiyyun bayn al-*

Ustura wa al-Haqiqa by Hashim Uthman, 191–210. Beirut: 1980. First published in *al-Nahda,* special issue, no. 8 (1938).

Yasui, Ignatius Abduh Khalifa al-. "al-Yazidiyya." *al-Mashriq* 47 (1953): 571–88.

Zahidi, Shaykh Husayn Ibn Shaykh Abdal. "Silsilat al-Nasab Safawiyya." Edward G. Browne, Persian MS. H. 12, Cambridge. Browne published an English summary of the same. See Browne, "Notes on an apparently unique Manuscript."

Zwemer, S. M. "A Moslem Aprocryphal Psalter." *The Moslem World* 5, no. 4 (October 1915): 399–410.

Index

EXTREMIST SHIITES
was composed in 10 on 12 Bembo on a Mergenthaler Linotron 202
by Coghill Book Typesetting Co.;
with initial capitals in Civilite provided by Job Litho Services;
printed by sheet-fed offset on 50-pound, acid-free P&S Smooth Offset,
and Smyth sewn and bound over binder's boards in Joanna Arrestox B,
by Maple-Vail Book Manufacturing Group, Inc.;
with dust jackets printed in 1 color by Niles & Phipps Lithographers;
and published by

SYRACUSE UNIVERSITY PRESS
SYRACUSE, NEW YORK 13244-5160